THE

Howe

DYNASTY

Langar Hall, 1792

THE
Howe
DYNASTY

THE UNTOLD STORY OF
A MILITARY FAMILY
AND THE WOMEN BEHIND
BRITAIN'S WARS FOR AMERICA

Julie Flavell

LIVERIGHT PUBLISHING CORPORATION
A Division of W. W. Norton & Company
Independent Publishers Since 1923

For information about permission to reproduce selections from this book,
write to Permissions, Liveright Publishing Corporation, a division of
W. W. Norton & Company, Inc., 500 Fifth Avenue, New York, NY 10110

For information about special discounts for bulk purchases,
please contact W. W. Norton Special Sales at
specialsales@wwnorton.com or 800-233-4830

Manufacturing by LSC Communications, Harrisonburg
Book design by Chris Welch
Production manager: Lauren Abbate

Library of Congress Cataloging-in-Publication Data

Names: Flavell, Julie, author.
Title: The Howe dynasty : the untold story of a military family and the women behind
Britain's wars for America / Julie Flavell.
Other titles: Untold story of a military family and the women
behind Britain's wars for America
Description: First edition. | New York, NY : Liveright Publishing Corporation, 2021. |
Includes bibliographical references and index.
Identifiers: LCCN 2021005099 | ISBN 9781631490613 (hardcover) |
ISBN 9781631490620 (epub)
Subjects: LCSH: Howe, Caroline, 1722–1814. | Howe family. | Great Britain—
Foreign relations—1760–1789. | United States—History—Revolution, 1775–1783—
British forces. | Great Britain. Army—Officers—Biography. |
Families of military personnel—Great Britain—Biography. | Brothers and sisters—
Great Britain—Biography. | Aristocracy (Social class)—Great Britain—Biography.
Classification: LCC DA512.H69 F53 2021 | DDC 973.3092/242—dc23
LC record available at https://lccn.loc.gov/2021005099

Liveright Publishing Corporation, 500 Fifth Avenue, New York, N.Y. 10110
www.wwnorton.com

W. W. Norton & Company Ltd., 15 Carlisle Street, London W1D 3BS

1 2 3 4 5 6 7 8 9 0

For Andy, who always finds a way

CONTENTS

LIST OF MAPS AND ILLUSTRATIONS

MAPS

ILLUSTRATIONS

Black-and-White Illustrations

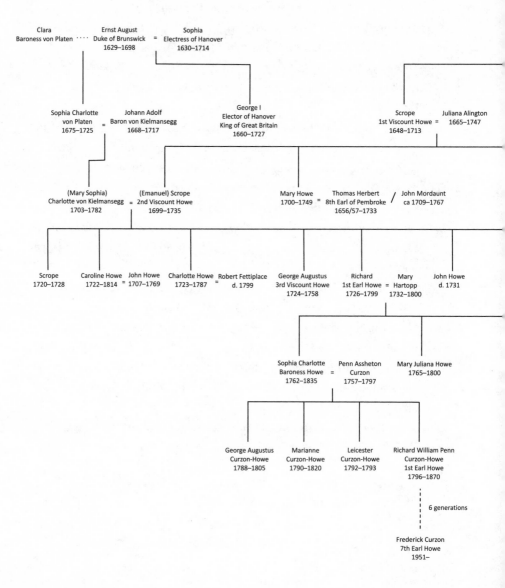

Howe Family Tree

Clara
Baroness von Platen · · · ·
Ernst August
Duke of Brunswick
1629–1698
=
Sophia
Electress of Hanover
1630–1714

Sophia Charlotte
von Platen
1675–1725
=
Johann Adolf
Baron von Kielmansegg
1668–1717

George I
Elector of Hanover
King of Great Britain
1660–1727

Scrope
1st Viscount Howe =
Juliana Alington
1665–1747

(Mary Sophia)
Charlotte von Kielmansegg
1703–1782
=
(Emanuel) Scrope
2nd Viscount Howe
1699–1735

Mary Howe
1700–1749
=
Thomas Herbert
8th Earl of Pembroke
1656/57–1733
/
John Mordaunt
ca 1709–1767

Scrope
1720–1728

Caroline Howe
1722–1814
=
John Howe
1707–1769

Charlotte Howe
1723–1787
=
Robert Fettiplace
d. 1799

George Augustus
3rd Viscount Howe
1724–1758

Richard
1st Earl Howe
1726–1799
=
Mary
Hartopp
1732–1800

John Howe
d. 1731

Sophia Charlotte
Baroness Howe
1762–1835
=
Penn Assheton
Curzon
1757–1797

Mary Juliana Howe
1765–1800

George Augustus
Curzon-Howe
1788–1805

Marianne
Curzon-Howe
1790–1820

Leicester
Curzon-Howe
1792–1793

Richard William Penn
Curzon-Howe
1st Earl Howe
1796–1870

6 generations

Frederick Curzon
7th Earl Howe
1951–

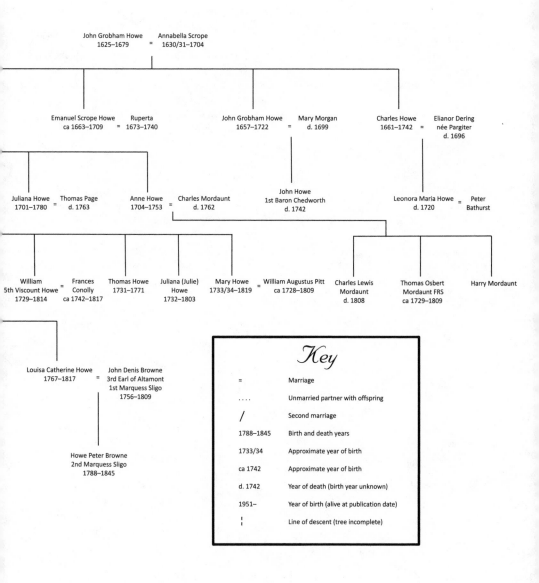

John Grobham Howe
1625–1679
= Annabella Scrope
1630/31–1704

Emanuel Scrope Howe
ca 1663–1709
= Ruperta
1673–1740

John Grobham Howe
1657–1722
= Mary Morgan
d. 1699

Charles Howe
1661–1742
= Elianor Dering
née Pargiter
d. 1696

Juliana Howe
1701–1780
= Thomas Page
d. 1763

Anne Howe
1704–1753
= Charles Mordaunt
d. 1762

John Howe
1st Baron Chedworth
d. 1742

Leonora Maria Howe
d. 1720
= Peter
Bathurst

William
5th Viscount Howe
1729–1814
= Frances
Conolly
ca 1742–1817

Thomas Howe
1731–1771

Juliana (Julie)
Howe
1732–1803

Mary Howe
1733/34–1819
= William Augustus Pitt
ca 1728–1809

Charles Lewis
Mordaunt
d. 1808

Thomas Osbert
Mordaunt FRS
ca 1729–1809

Harry Mordaunt

Louisa Catherine Howe
1767–1817
= John Denis Browne
3rd Earl of Altamont
1st Marquess Sligo
1756–1809

Howe Peter Browne
2nd Marquess Sligo
1788–1845

Key

=	Marriage
....	Unmarried partner with offspring
/	Second marriage
1788–1845	Birth and death years
1733/34	Approximate year of birth
ca 1742	Approximate year of birth
d. 1742	Year of death (birth year unknown)
1951–	Year of birth (alive at publication date)
¦	Line of descent (tree incomplete)

THE

Howe

DYNASTY

Dynastic Secrets

G rafton Street in early December 1774 was one of Georgian London's newest developments for the very rich. A terrace of handsome brick houses, the pale Tuscan columns of the doorways stood out through the gloom of an English winter afternoon. Eighteenth-century London remained one of the worst-lit capital cities in Europe, but candlelight shone from the windows of the street's prosperous dwellings. At Number 12, the Honorable Caroline Howe was writing, as usual, in her snug drawing room. Callers came and went at Number 12 on their way to or from the royal court, Parliament, a card party, or a club, all bearing news that was suitable or not for inclusion in whatever letter was in progress. Caroline did not write with a view to posterity and publication, like her contemporary, the famous memoirist and wit Horace Walpole. Her letters were spontaneous, purposeful, and altogether private.

On this particular afternoon, Caroline was composing a hurried note to her closest friend, Lady Georgiana Spencer. Just a few casual sentences evoke her daily life at the center of Georgian London's most fashionable set:

> I really shall have no writing time today, I have for the first time these ten days played half a dozen Games of Chess. It has been with Dr. Franklin. Lord Spencer came in, I was dressing yesterday when he was so good to call, he seems well & in spirits, & is to meet me at the Play to see Garrick in *Hamlet*.[1]

Lady Spencer's husband, handsome, moody John, 1st Earl Spencer, who would escort Caroline to the play, was one of the wealthiest men in Britain. He and Lady Spencer were the parents of Georgiana Cavendish, the celebrated Duchess of Devonshire, whose lifestyle of compulsive gambling and high fashion lent glamour to the Whig politics she espoused.

Caroline Howe's opponent at chess that day was an entirely different matter. Benjamin Franklin, premier spokesman in London for the American colonies, was notorious for supporting the colonial resistance to British rule that would break out into the American War of Independence in less than five months. He was not a man polite London expected to call, for he was under a cloud of suspicion for stirring up trouble in the colonies. But Lady Spencer required no explanation. She knew that the chess games were a front designed by Caroline to cover highly secret negotiations with the American in a last-minute quest for peace, negotiations that involved her brothers, Richard Admiral Lord Howe and General William Howe.

Benjamin Franklin's journal is the only surviving record that these talks ever took place. They are also the context for Caroline Howe's sole appearance, until now, in history books. Franklin would write of her, "I have never conceived a higher opinion of the discretion and excellent understanding of any woman on so short an acquaintance."[2] He was displaying his usual acumen, for Caroline was in reality more than a hostess; she was closely involved in her brothers' careers, and never more so than in their behind-the-scenes meetings with Franklin himself.

The Franklin talks marked the beginnings of an aura of mystery that would cling to Caroline's brothers throughout the years that they served together as British commanders in chief in the American Revolution between 1776 and 1778, and beyond. How had Britain suffered its only defeat in modern times to an army of unprofessional provincials? Richard and William Howe had both achieved hero status twelve years earlier in the Seven Years' War of 1756–1763, yet the nation's finest military and naval commanders seemed unable to outfight the rebel General George Washington, a tobacco planter from Virginia. The Howes were known to have pro-American sympathies; had they done less than their duty in suppressing the rebellion?

The suspicions, with their unmistakable insinuations of treason, began during the war and have persisted in the almost two and a half centuries since. Contemporary Britons saw the Howe family as intensely private, an iconic English military dynasty—stoical and self-contained. The "whole race" of Howes, as Horace Walpole put it, were "undaunted as a rock, and as silent."[3] The noted Howe trait of silence provided fertile ground for the conspiracy theories that proliferated as the nation reacted to the stain on British honor.

Historians have concurred with the stereotype, pronouncing the eighteenth-century generation of Howes to be inscrutable. The two major twentieth-century studies of the Howe brothers' joint American command have labeled them "difficult subjects," "reticent men who were involved in complex, covert transactions."[4] Recent biographers continue to strike the same note: Lord Howe's meetings with Franklin in 1774 at his sister's Grafton Street house were "the most mysterious episodes in the life of the admiral"; the admiral left nothing to reveal to us "what he thought about in his time ashore or around his family."[5] A history of William Howe's generalship named him "one of the most enigmatic figures" in the American War of Independence, lamenting that his inner thoughts remain concealed behind a "crippling lack of primary sources."[6] The destruction of the family papers in a house fire in the early nineteenth century seemingly set the seal on that verdict.

And yet the correspondence of their sister, the Honorable Caroline Howe, with Lady Georgiana Spencer forms one of the most extensive private collections of letters in the British Library. Past historians of the careers of Richard Admiral Lord Howe and General Sir William Howe have virtually ignored these manuscripts, only dipping into them to spotlight events in the lives of Caroline's brothers. After all, what relevance can letters between two women have for understanding the motives of military men?

In what has been called "the systematic privileging of masculine interests over feminine," it is too often assumed that the sphere of women and the drawing room is insignificant, while battlefields and high politics are important.[7] The result is that selective use has been made of Caroline's letters where they relate to the public business of the brothers, but she, the primary correspondent, has been presumed to be extraneous. The voice of the writer, so clear and so decisive and knowledgeable, is overlooked in the narrow quest for the political and military matters of men. It is an attitude that would not have been shared by Caroline or her brothers.

Historian Mary Beard has written powerfully that women's voices have been excluded from public spaces down the centuries.[8] But that does not mean that they have been excluded from private spaces. Within her family, Caroline's was a voice of authority. Consequently, her letters lead us directly into the conduct of the interests and affairs of the Howe dynasty, because Caroline herself was actively involved in its promotion and preservation.

The Howe women were a conspicuous example of that Georgian

phenomenon, the politically involved aristocratic woman. Caroline was born to a family whose women had a tradition of managing the dynastic fortunes. She grew up under the tutelage of her aunt, Mary Herbert Countess Pembroke, who served as a Lady of the Bedchamber to Queen Caroline between 1727 and 1737. It was the countess who launched the military careers of Caroline's brothers George, Richard, and William Howe, all of whom would achieve the status of national heroes while they were still young men, serving in America, France, Italy, and Flanders. Caroline watched her mother, Charlotte Viscountess Howe, play cards with the mistress of King George II, and politics with his prime minister, the Duke of Newcastle, promoting the careers of her sons in a world where determined women found a way to wield power in the service of their families. In her turn, Caroline, during the reign of prudish, awkward King George III, engaged in her own drawing-room politics, moving deftly between a straitlaced court and a London high life that was becoming scandalously amoral.

The Howe family was close-knit, with unusually egalitarian relations between its men and women. If the Howe men were known as epitomes of silent, daring English warriors, the women were by turns admired and caricatured for their unfeminine and forthright qualities. *The Howe Dynasty* tells the story of this celebrated and intrepid military family across four wars and spanning nearly a century, focusing on their crucial role—and their very personal odyssey—in the American Revolution.

As the first whole-family history of the Howes, it also breaks new ground on the history of Britain during the American War of Independence. In *First Family: Abigail and John Adams*, American historian Joseph Ellis has written of the power of family-based histories of the American Revolution to fuse personal emotional journeys with the "larger political narrative" of what was for America a transformative conflict.[9] The letters of elite American women such as Abigail Adams, and the papers of the Adamses, the Jeffersons, and the Washingtons, have been thoroughly interrogated in many fine works. But no historian has consulted the domestic papers of Britain's "first families," whose members were actively engaged in the conduct of the war. The result is that the home front of this tragic civil war has, until *The Howe Dynasty*, remained an American subject.

Biography is often dismissed as mere storytelling, but narrative history has the power to give a voice to the voiceless. As this book brings the silent

Howe brothers to life, the women, after two centuries of obscurity, also emerge unexpectedly and vividly into the light. Starting out with no ambition but to marry and have children, each of them in her own lifetime was compelled to manage the dynastic interests, and each proved equal to the challenge in her own highly individual way. By intervening in the careers of the famous brothers, the Howe women would influence the destiny of the British nation and the momentous events that led to American independence.

One

The Howe Women

"I saw the Duchess of Devonshire last night across the room at *The Messiah.* She and the Duke came alone. It was charming, my two sisters, Lady Howe and I sat upon an upper bench and the three Girls at our feet, the King and Queen seem'd to take great notice of such a collected Howery."[1]

Caroline Howe's playful vignette of a night at the concert in 1786 portrays her family as a well-known group in Georgian high society. Caroline's inner circle included some of the leading characters of the century: fashion diva the Duchess of Devonshire; gossip and eccentric Horace Walpole; the pleasure-seeking George, Prince of Wales; notorious adulteress the Duchess of Grafton; brave General James Wolfe, who had taken Quebec for the British empire in 1759.

Yet today little remains of Caroline's world. A fire destroyed the Howe family papers within twenty years of her death in 1814, and their dynastic seat of Langar Hall in Nottinghamshire was pulled down in the nineteenth century. The public careers of her brothers, George Augustus, 3rd Viscount Howe, Richard Admiral Lord Howe, and General Sir William Howe, are all that is remembered of this remarkable generation of eight siblings. The Howe women get barely a mention in the military biographies. Caroline, and the sisters and nieces who made up her fanciful "Howery" on that musical evening, have joined the legions of forgotten women who simply disappear from history.

It would be wrong, however, to imagine that the Howe women would care about being rescued from obscurity and restored to the pages of the history books. The feminist slogan "Well-behaved women seldom make history," coined two centuries after they flourished, would have had little meaning to them. These self-assured women did not crave posterity's validation, and they barely troubled to consider whether they were well behaved.

What they did care about was the welfare and reputation of their dynasty. Three notable Howe women, Charlotte Viscountess Howe, Mary Herbert Countess Pembroke, and the Honorable Caroline Howe, would have a decisive impact on the careers, fortunes, and characters of their more famous male relatives.

Caroline's mother, the Viscountess Howe, born Charlotte von Kielmansegg, was not yet sixteen when she married Scrope, 2nd Viscount Howe, in 1719. In her wedding portrait, she appears girlish, wearing a loose silk gown with her hair arranged around her shoulders and one hand fondly stroking her little spaniel.[2] For her, as for any woman of her day, marriage was the defining moment in her life. That one brief ceremony conferred on her as much formal authority as she would know in her lifetime, through the roles of wife, mother, and household manager. The bride in the portrait looks too young to take up the position of Viscountess Howe, presiding over the dynastic seat at Langar Hall in Nottinghamshire, managing a houseful of servants, establishing a proper footing with the tenants, and hosting balls and dinners for her aristocratic neighbors. But Charlotte von Kielmansegg was raised for the role of lady of the manor.

Charlotte was born in Hanover, Germany, in 1703, the daughter of Johann Adolf, Baron von Kielmansegg. Baron von Kielmansegg was Master of the Horse at the Hanoverian court, and Charlotte spent her early years moving between the royal residence of Herrenhausen Palace and the Kielmansegg family home of Faintasie, well known for its exquisite décor and *objets d'art*. The baron was well liked by the Hanoverian royal family, but it was Charlotte's mother, Sophia, who gave the Kielmanseggs their assured position as court favorites.

Sophia was the illegitimate half-sister of George Lewis, Prince-Elector of Hanover. She had been raised at court alongside her illustrious brother, and the two maintained a lifelong bond. Sophia was a vivacious, intelligent woman, but she could also be demanding and unstable. In the intense atmosphere of the royal family, she felt entitled to compete with George's mistresses and other family members for his attention. It was a dangerous game. The subjects of the absolutist Kingdom of Hanover did not have the rights and liberties of an eighteenth-century Briton. A cautionary tale was the fate of the Princess of Celle, who married George Lewis in 1682. Despite her royal blood, the princess was incarcerated for life when she was caught in adultery twelve years later. Her lover, a man of no great rank, was certainly murdered, although his body was never found. The sad fate of the young princess rippled throughout Europe, but it did not deter Sophia from courting the favor of her heartless and unscrupulous half-brother.

For anyone with ambitions, George Lewis had a great deal to give; not only was he Prince-Elector of Hanover, he also stood in line to become the king of Great Britain. In 1701, the British Parliament passed an act declaring the Protestant House of Hanover to be the successors should the House of Stuart fail to produce Protestant heirs. When the last Stuart monarch, Queen Anne, died childless in 1714, George Lewis ascended the throne of Britain, becoming King George I, the first of the Hanoverian Georgian monarchs.

The right of George Lewis to rule was quickly challenged by Anne's half-brother James, the Catholic Stuart claimant to the Crown. The Jacobite standard was raised at Braemar in Scotland the following year. The "Fifteen," as it was called—the Jacobite rising of 1715—was crushed, but the Jacobite threat to the British Crown would remain a fact of political life for many decades to come.

Yet King George I was securely on the throne, and young Charlotte von Kielmansegg, at the age of eleven, crossed the English Channel with her parents and four siblings to join his court. In London, the von Kielmansegg family took up residence in a suite of rooms at St. James's Palace, where Charlotte watched her mother carry on competing with the other leading ladies of the royal household. Sophia threw lively parties, inviting English wits and authors such as the poet Alexander Pope. Pope characteristically made fun of his pretentious hostess with her aristocratic German accent, calling her "Artemisia," who "talks, by Fits, Of Councils, Classicks, Fathers, Wits," but Sophia hardly cared, for she achieved her objective: The English courtiers preferred her salon to the dull society of her brother's mistress, Melusine von der Schulenburg, a German-speaking woman of noble blood who was nicknamed "the Maypole" for her tall, skinny figure. There was nonetheless a recklessness in such rivalry, arousing as it did resentment in powerful quarters, most ominously with Princess Caroline, wife of Sophia's nephew, the future George II.[3]

The parties at the palace came to an end with the death of Baron von Kielmansegg in 1717. His widow and five children moved to a house near Hanover Square. Sophia's popularity declined as rumors of affairs sullied her reputation. Her distress at being the subject of gossip was evident in court circles; she put on weight and earned the nickname "the Elephant," a caricature that has been preserved for posterity by English diarist Horace Walpole, whose childhood impression of her was of "two acres of cheeks spread with crimson, an ocean of neck." She was careless with money, and financial difficulties set in. The bestowal of two lifetime peerages— Countess of Leinster and of Darlington—by her indulgent brother the king did not make amends.[4] As a sign of her shifting fortunes, Sophia was obliged to appeal to Princess Caroline for assistance. Confessing herself to be "perpetually alone," she requested a small allowance from Her Royal Highness so that she could hire a companion. The request was denied.[5]

Charlotte had been in her early teens when she witnessed the rapid and humiliating decline of her mother's popularity. Perhaps it was partly to remove herself from such scenes that she accepted an offer of marriage to Scrope Lord Howe in 1719, when she was not yet sixteen. Charlotte's nature was very different from that of her gregarious mother: dignified rather than vivacious, cautious rather than impulsive. Her marriage to an Englishman showed an independent mind, for she was the only one of her Hanoverian siblings who made England her permanent home; her brothers and sister returned to Hanover after Sophia von Kielmansegg died lonely and unhappy in 1725.[6]

Through her marriage, Charlotte was entering a life away from the glamour of the court, in the world of Georgian England's rural aristocracy. Her bridegroom came from a family that had a precarious foothold in the ranks of titled nobility. Scrope Howe's title was Baron Glenawly and Viscount Howe, which sounds grand, but in fact his was only an Irish peerage. This meant that he did not have a seat in the British House of Lords, and if he wanted to enter Parliament, he would have to get himself elected to the House of Commons—a violent, vulgar process in eighteenth-century England, and an expensive one. Scrope's estate of ten thousand acres in Langar, Nottinghamshire, was modest by the standards of the aristocracy.[7]

Yet the Howes were an ambitious family from Gloucestershire. Since the mid-seventeenth century, using well-tried means, they had climbed steadily into the highest ranks of English society. Caroline's great-grandfather, John Grobham Howe, had projected himself into the exclusive county society of Nottinghamshire through his marriage to an illegitimate daughter of Emanuel Lord Scrope, Earl of Sunderland.[8] His eldest son, named Scrope in honor of the family's new blue-blood connections, sat in Parliament, married well, and in 1701 became Baron Glenawly and 1st Viscount Howe.[9] When he died in 1713, he had a great many debts and one son, fourteen-year-old Scrope, to carry on the family project of elevating the Howe dynasty. Young Scrope's marriage six years later to Charlotte von Kielmansegg gratified the family's ambition, for she brought both royal connections and much-needed income in the form of a royal pension.

What were the young Lady Howe's first thoughts when she stepped from her carriage before her new home of Langar Hall? She had lurched over a hundred miles of unpaved roads, from bustling, modern London to rural Nottinghamshire, whose rusticity was its chief claim to charm. Langar Hall was a fortified mansion house, glamorized locally as a castle, whose three centuries showed in its crumbling stonework. Scrope's grandfather had tried to improve it with the addition of a small park.[10] But this was nothing to a young woman who had grown up within the grounds of Hanover's spectacular Herrenhausen, famous throughout Europe for its orangeries, fountains and gardens, canals complete with gondolas, and avenues lined with hundreds of linden trees.[11] The castle court and pleasure gardens of Langar Hall covered a mere two acres; medieval moats had to serve in the place of fountains. The smell of a swineyard with well over a hundred hogs was offset by the scent of adjacent meadows full of wild grasses and native flowers, daisies, buttercups, campion, yarrow, clover, and meadowsweet.[12] Langar Hall, with its fields and farmsteads, belonged to the English countryside.

If Langar was different from what Charlotte had known, so was her new family. By the standards of the time, the Howe household was a young family, with unusually harmonious relationships between the sexes. The Howe patriarchs of the previous generation—the fathers and masters who were the conventional domestic authority figures—were gone. Two of Scrope's uncles were dead or dying by the time of his marriage.[13] The last surviving member of his father's generation was eccentric religious recluse Charles Howe, who occasionally passed through Langar when he was not composing spiritual literature.[14]

But Scrope had three sisters still at home, all single and in their teens. The oldest, Mary, would one day become Lady Pembroke, and would supplant her brother as manager of the dynastic fortunes. For now, however, she, Juliana, and Anne lived under the protection of Scrope, who was himself a very young head of household.[15] At Langar Hall they had only their widowed mother, Juliana Alington Howe, to act as a check on their youthful exuberance. Law and custom gave men the right to demand feminine submission within their households, but in practice family power structures were negotiated through the day-to-day interactions of the personalities in the home.[16] Scrope and his three sisters had a friendly, companionable relationship, illustrated by a rare surviving letter written while he was abroad: "I expect a Letter at Least writ 2 sides & all ye tittle tattle of ye Town in it," Scrope teased middle sister Juliana, saying her last had been too brief; "I know you are very full of yr. jokes." Scrope played the flute, and he and eldest sister Mary shared a love of music. He begged Mary to send him the overture to *Camilla*—probably the opera by Giovanni Bononcini, then popular in London.[17]

Charlotte's new home was a far cry from the atmosphere of a royal court. She found herself with a husband and three sisters-in-law who were close to her in age, close to one another, and fun-loving. The Howe sisters were preoccupied, as she had only recently been, with the business of finding husbands and the excitement of courtship.

Scrope and Charlotte's first duty as husband and wife was to be fruitful and multiply, but the fruit needed to be male. It was a condition of the dynastic title that only boys descended directly from Viscount Howe could inherit. Male cousins or nephews were disqualified. Scrope had no brothers, so he was the sole slender thread upon which his father's viscountcy hung.

But for the newlyweds, this fundamental duty proved easy. On September 20, 1720, just a year and a month after her marriage, seventeen-year-old Lady Howe gave birth to George Scrope. The baptism was a grand affair at St. James's Palace in London, with the Bishop of Bangor performing the sacrament. Lady Howe's royal half-uncle, King George I, was the godfather.[18] Splendor, rank, every high connection the proud parents could muster was assembled for this momentous christening.

A year and a half later, a second healthy child arrived, a daughter named Caroline. This time there was no grand celebration. Little Caroline was christened at the parish church of St. Martin-in-the-Fields in London.[19] As a girl, she could neither sustain the family title nor enter Parliament, nor take up lucrative posts at court or in the service of her country. Yet equally with her brother Scrope, Caroline was born into the most important role of her life, as eldest sister to a vital generation of Howes. While her brothers would travel the world in pursuit of their careers, Caroline's life would show that, in the service of an aristocratic family, a woman could be drawn deep into the world of male power.

Lady Howe was delivering babies approximately every year and a half. By the time Caroline reached the age of twelve, there were eight more: a second girl, Charlotte, in August 1723, was followed a year later by George Augustus, who would win fame in Britain and America for his military exploits. Richard, the future naval hero, was born in March 1726.[20] A son John who died in infancy most likely arrived between Richard and William, for there is a three-year gap in the record.[21] William—who would be commander-in-chief of the British army in America during the War of Independence—was born in August 1729.[22] Nineteen months later, the youngest of the brothers, Thomas, was baptized at Langar. Two sisters, Juliana and Mary, would follow within the next four years.[23]

In an age when the business of getting a family could be fraught with heartbreak at each stage, from conception and delivery through the tribulations of childhood illnesses, Lady Howe was a fortunate mother. But she could not have felt so when her firstborn, Scrope, destined to be the 3rd Viscount Howe, died at the age of eight.[24] The parents gave mute testimony to their fondness for the child by forgoing the rather heartless tradition of recycling the dynastic names of dead children, still common at this time.[25] The name of Scrope—a badge of honor in the family annals—disappeared from that generation.

Scrope's death transformed Caroline into the oldest in her sibling set. She would become the leader in play for her brothers and sisters alike. In a period when boys learned at a very early age to be dismissive of feminine authority, Caroline's brothers were content to follow their clever, tomboyish older sister.

As a very young child, Caroline had shadowed her all-important older brother Scrope, sensitive to the enhanced adult interest showered upon the next lord of the manor, and it was probably from him that she acquired her conspicuous liking for what were considered to be male activities. She was a keen rider of horses, an activity that as a child permitted her the freedom of wearing a riding habit—much less cumbersome than the women's clothes of the period—and she took part in the outdoor activities of the neighborhood, such as angling and blackberrying.[26] The love of competitive activities—chess, cards, and games—that distinguished her as an adult began with her early upbringing. All her life, by her own admission, she would blend a dose of rivalry with her affection for others.

Yet Caroline was the dominant personality with her sisters as much as her brothers. Juliana and Mary were more than ten years younger than Caroline, reinforcing her position as leader. Caroline's affinity for children as an adult, her knack with crying babies when not a mother herself, all suggest an active participation in the care of the youngest Howes when she was a girl. Alongside her sisters, she duly learned the rules of deportment that were a fixture of a genteel lady's education. She partook of purely feminine pursuits such as needlework and the trimming of gowns and hair. It seems certain that Caroline took over some of the mothering, as Lady Howe was so often pregnant or recovering from childbirth.

Caroline's generation of Howes was notable for its ability to mix with people of all levels and backgrounds and put them at ease. One likely reason for this was that Langar Hall, unlike the fashionable new establishments of the Georgian rich shut up in secluded parkland, was very close to the village.[27] The children had only to walk out of its gates, past the thirteenth-century parish church of St. Andrew's and its red brick vicarage, to find themselves on the main street of Langar, a tiny hamlet with a typical array of cottages, a public house, blacksmith's shop, wheelwright, and duck pond.[28]

The novelist Samuel Butler, one of Langar's famous sons, recalled a century later in his semiautobiographical novel, *The Way of All Flesh*, that there were few genteel families within easy visiting range. Yet the Howe family was popular in that rustic neighborhood.[29] Probably the Howe brood played with the children of the farmers and laborers from the village and the estate. Tenants' children and the children of the local lord would mix to make up teams for cricket matches, a sport played by all levels of English society during that century, and one which George was particularly keen on. The round of seasonal activities beloved of country children all formed a part of the upbringing of the children of Langar Hall.

Horses, of course, were an integral part of country life, but one that did not come cheap. Lord Howe kept a racehorse, Captain Frisky, that competed at the Nottingham Races, and then there was the gentleman's sport of foxhunting.[30] The Howes belonged to the Belvoir Hunt, whose enormous entourage of sportsmen, hounds, horses, whippers-in, and hunt-servants moved about throughout the hunting season of November to April.[31] The

Howe children grew up accustomed to the crowds, the mixed society, and the blare of horns, hounds, horses, and excited huntsmen that characterized the country sport. Eighteenth-century foxhunting enforced a rough-and-ready disdain for comfort, its followers rising at dawn and covering a wide territory in conditions that could be both dangerous and primitive.

Caroline, nevertheless, kept pace with her brothers. As a young woman, she was notable for riding a fox-chase, and her choice of sport shows her ease with male companionship. Girls of her class were routinely taught to ride, and sometimes to ride to hounds, but Caroline was a keener horsewoman than most. This did not mean that she loved blood sports; there is no evidence that Caroline could shoot, as some daring females did. A friend of her younger days, Mary Warde of Norfolk, who also rode with the hunt, observed that "a pack of Hounds" was just a pretense for socializing.[32]

Lady Howe, so often taken up with childbearing, could not join her daughter in such ferocious activity, but it would be a mistake to conclude that her influence was nonexistent. Mothers of the era were closely involved in the education of young children, and Caroline as an adult was conspicuous for her love of learning. Her lifelong uninhibited quest for knowledge reflects the legacy of her mother's early education at the court of Hanover, where aristocratic women engaged with ideas.[33] Once in London, Lady Howe's mother, Sophia von Kielmansegg, had entertained English intellectuals and authors at her popular salon; and the von Kielmansegg children were exposed to the cutting edge of the baroque music of the period in the compositions of George Frideric Handel, whose career had been cultivated by the von Kielmansegg family in Hanover and in Britain.[34]

Scrope Lord Howe also had been carefully educated by his ambitious parents. The fashion for aristocratic youths was to complete their education with a grand tour, and in 1716, while in his late teens, Scrope went to Paris with a cousin, William Howe, and William Capel, Earl of Essex. The French were regarded as having the most perfect manners in Europe, and urbane Paris was the place to go to acquire them. During a two-year stay, Lord Howe and his companions engaged dancing masters and French masters, ran up accounts for coffee and wine, and imbibed the polish of Parisian society. Scrope indulged his love of music—a family trait—with lessons on the flute.[35]

Caroline had parents who clearly valued learning. This was fortunate, for an eighteenth-century education began in the home. Typically, the

mother gave her children their first lessons in reading and writing. A
boy must next be instructed in Latin, arithmetic, history, the classics of
English literature, and attain at least a speaking knowledge of French.
At this stage, genteel families either engaged tutors or sent their boys to
school.[36] Scrope and George almost certainly attended boarding school
by the age of six, for their younger brothers Richard and William were to
do so.[37] The two oldest boys most likely were sent to Nottingham School,
an easy distance from Langar, where William would go in a few years'
time. Nottingham School educated a socially mixed set of boys from the
town and the sons of local gentry.[38] A stint at Eton was the ultimate goal
for the Howe boys as for other youths of their rank, a place where they
could supposedly acquire the air and refinement of a gentleman. But Eton
would come later, and under circumstances that compelled the family to
disperse to far corners of the empire.

The end result of the Howe brothers' education, as in every family,
appears to have been uneven. As a grown man, George Augustus, the
eldest son and heir, was considered the ideal of a British officer and a well-
rounded gentleman, intelligent and a man of action. William, at the height
of his military career, was privately described by a brother officer (no friend)
as "illiterate and indolent."[39]

Middle brother Richard, the steadiest of the lot, left school early to begin
his naval career. He certainly suffered from what today are known as speech
and language problems. Throughout his life, contemporaries described
him as confused or muddled in his writing and speech. A notable scholar
of the Howe brothers commented that even friends were sometimes so baffled by him that they doubted his intelligence. Those who knew him well
recognized that there was a disconnect between his intellect and his ability
to communicate. A brother officer recalled of him, "Lord Howe possessed
a very peculiar manner of explaining himself, both in correspondence and
conversation, but his mind was always clear, prompt, and willing to communicate with every person who consulted him, and who could get rid of
the apparent coldness of his manner."[40] It shall be seen that his actions
proved his intelligence and his shrewd grasp of the world in which he lived.

Caroline, on the other hand, could do it all. Without going to school,
she acquired Latin; she enjoyed mathematical problems, a quality that surprised Benjamin Franklin when he met her in London many years later.
She taught herself several modern languages. She was an avid reader

throughout her life, devouring the classics, histories, travel narratives, works of naturalists, novels, newspapers—anything but abstract philosophy. On hearing of a book that set out to prove the existence of the soul, she dismissed it, saying it might be better "not to look more closely into it, for what end could it answer?" Hers was a family of pragmatists. All her life she read for amusement; on a visit to her mother as an adult, she immersed herself in the "new idle books" she found in her mother's library. "[W]hy have not I writ to you between whiles?" she wrote exultantly to a friend on another occasion; "Why I have got a new book." By her own admission, she could neither draw nor sing, fatalistically shrugging that "whatever is, is right," because if she were endowed with either attribute she would be tempted to show off: "I for my part should never be content to hide my talent."[41] But like everyone in the family, she loved music.

Caroline's eclectic education tells us something about the dynamics between men and women inside the Howe household, for learning was widely considered to be unfeminine. There were plenty of fathers who disliked brainy women, and mothers who feared that too much education would make their daughters unattractive to men.[42] A girl's education in an aristocratic family normally concentrated on the graces required to entertain socially, together with the skills for managing a great house. Dancing, deportment, French, music, and enough arithmetic to keep household accounts were considered ample for one who would not occupy a position of public responsibility.[43]

Caroline's home was unusual, then, for there was clearly no message that learning was "unfeminine." Throughout her life, Caroline stood out to contemporaries as having a "masculine" intellect. Her mind, according to one, "possessed a power and firmness, that some would call masculine."[44] "[A] very clever woman, though very rough, and more like a man than a woman," ran another description.[45] In reality, Caroline was simply an educated female who had not been cautioned sufficiently by her mentors to hide her abilities. She may have shared her brothers' tutors; she most probably was also instructed by one or both of her parents, or—a pleasing notion—perhaps she learned from her brothers when they were home for the holidays. This fits with her lifelong practice of studying alongside her friend Lady Spencer, with whom over many decades she would keep up with the latest books and master ancient Greek and other languages.

Yet even at Langar Hall, marriage was the most important step of a woman's life. When Caroline was born in 1722, her aunts Mary, Juliana, and Anne, the younger sisters of Scrope, were spinsters. Over the next six years, they would each go on to acquire husbands, their separate experiences of courtship playing out the full spectrum of Georgian notions of matrimony: Mary, the practical eldest sister; Anne, the flighty youngest; and Juliana, the middle sister, in whom were blended the qualities of common sense and amiability.

Juliana—"an extremely pretty woman"—was first to approach the altar. She married Thomas Page, whose father, Sir Gregory Page, baronet and member of Parliament, had amassed a fantastic fortune as a director of the East India Company. The ceremony took place at the end of May in 1725. The bridegroom was "immensely rich," commented a contemporary, so much so that he allowed Juliana to give away her marriage portion of £3,000 to her youngest sister Anne.[46] The Page family owned several palatial estates and a notable private art collection. What they lacked was the noble lineage of the Howes, so the marriage united blue blood with a lordly income.[47] It was also a love match, and thus a perfect union according to Georgian notions of matrimony, blending money, pedigree, and affection—in that order.

The next month, older sister Mary made a very different sort of match. The most ambitious of the Howe girls, she had been appointed a maid of honor to the Princess Caroline in 1720, a post reserved for young unmarried women.[48] As we shall see, Mary was alert to the opportunities to find a suitable husband that service at court opened up to her. Yet Alexander Pope, who knew Mary, has left a picture of her that suggests that her planning and scheming was on behalf of family rather than self. Pope wrote of her that she did not love herself "so well as she does her Friends: For those she makes happy, but not Herself. There is an Air of sadness about her which grieves me."[49] It was Mary who would assume responsibility for the dynastic fortunes when disaster struck the Howe family more than ten years later.

Meanwhile she took up her post as maid of honor with the cautionary tale before her of her cousin, Sophia Howe, also in service to the Princess Caroline. Sophia's legendary reckless behavior began in 1719, when she fell hopelessly in love with Anthony Lowther, brother of Viscount Lonsdale. They consummated their love, but the villain had no intention of marrying her.[50] In an act of desperation, she disguised herself as a boy and slipped away from her home to her lover's house, where she loudly demanded admittance, attracting a large crowd. Lowther made his escape out the back door.[51] Now an outcast, Sophia turned to her mother, Ruperta Howe, and the newlywed Charlotte Lady Howe, hoping they could help her find another place. When that proved futile, she pleaded with Princess Caroline, complaining that she was being "treated as a mad woman" by her family.[52] Caroline relented and allowed her the stipend of a maid of honor for the next four years.[53] By 1726, Sophia was dead, and her public downfall was dramatic enough to be the subject of gossip for decades after her death. If Caroline Howe never heard the story as a girl, she could not fail to learn about it through the poems and novels based on her unfortunate cousin's tragedy that continued to appear during her lifetime.[54] Anthony Lowther was a real-life villain, like the libertines featured in the pages of contemporary novels; Sophia Howe served as a warning to young lady readers, a giddy girl who rejected the protection of her family. For cynics, the story underscored the emptiness of love—or lust, as they would have it—as a motive for marriage, a brief and unreliable passion that was sure to burn out long before more substantial advantages.[55]

Mary Howe was not going to make any such mistake when her turn came to serve Princess Caroline. In 1725, she married Thomas Herbert, 8th Earl of Pembroke, who was almost seventy years of age. The earl had already been married twice and had fathered thirteen children. The last wife to share the marital bed had been middle-aged when she died in 1721. In court circles, where no one was spared if any amusement was to be had, the usual jokes were made: The earl's heart surely could not hold out for long under the stimulation of a young bride. But the earl proved to be more robust than gossips predicted. He survived another eight years. Meanwhile, Mary was mistress of the magnificent Wilton House, its gardens and art collections. One wonders if it was worth it. She could not have married for love, and Lord Pembroke—whom some contemporaries thought a little mad—was an eccentric, controlling figure who insisted that she be home by ten every night (his "supper hour") and kept the household revolving around his whims.[56] But most disappointing was her failure, after maneuvering herself into the heart of an earldom, to conceive a child. She betrayed her mortification in court circles by fancying herself pregnant on several occasions.[57] Mary's best-laid plans had gone awry; above all, it was a woman's duty to produce offspring. And as their sister-in-law, Charlotte

Lady Howe, produced one baby after another, not only Mary but also Juliana remained childless. Juliana is known to have lost one infant; Mary
never conceived at all.[58] It was the fate of many women during that era, a
deficiency in the eyes of the world for which they had no recourse.

If she couldn't plan for every exigency, Mary Countess Pembroke was
nevertheless a commanding figure in the Howe family. She was an intelligent woman who enjoyed educated company. Her close friend at court
was the poet Judith Cowper, better known by her married name of Judith
Madan, who was a protégée of Alexander Pope.[59] She loved opera, her forthright personality coming out in an episode that took place in 1726, at the
height of a notorious dispute between two rival Italian sopranos, Francesca
Cuzzoni and Faustina Bordoni. When both singers appeared on stage, the
"Countess of Pembroke," it was reported, "headed the Cuzzoni party," rallying her supporters to boo and hiss Bordoni until neither performer could
be heard. She also had a down-to-earth sense of humor. "I hope the under-
butlers will toss him in a blanket," she once commented when a thrifty-
minded lord counted the bottles of wine the maids of honor had consumed
at dinner. She was a keen walker in all sorts of weather.[60] Above all, she
was an astute observer of developments at court, and as such she was part
of the Georgian phenomenon of politically involved aristocratic ladies. As
we shall see, she would teach both Lady Howe and her niece Caroline the
art of drawing-room influence. Lady Pembroke would be a mentor and role
model to Caroline, who grew up to be like her in many respects.

Anne, the youngest sister, was the last to marry. Several months after
Mary's marriage, a rumor circulated that Anne was betrothed to Charles
Seymour, 6th Duke of Somerset.[61] The hand of Mary could surely be
detected in this. The duke was another ancient widower, and Anne did
not want to have her future decided by her sister. She refused. It was a
wise choice, for the duke married another young lady of noble birth, who
spent the next twenty years nursing him through various ailments.[62] Three
years later, Anne eloped with Colonel Charles Mordaunt, not waiting for
the consent of her mother, the Dowager Lady Howe. "It is an extraordinary
good match for her," remarked a friend of the family, but the Dowager Lady
Howe disagreed, banishing her daughter from Langar for some time after
the wedding.[63]

The Mordaunts had wealth and rank, but they also had a reputation for
being eccentric.[64] The premier member of the family, Charles Mordaunt,

3rd Earl of Peterborough, had the dubious distinction of being the first peer ever known to marry a stage celebrity, the opera singer Anastasia Robinson.[65] Still more awkward was their status as an old Catholic family. The heads of the dynasty had converted to Anglicanism, but they remained embroiled with an English Catholic community in an undignified dispute that brought both sides into ill repute.[66] In any case, the Dowager Lady Howe's resentment did not last. Probably the marriage's fruitfulness helped, as Anne presented her mother with three grandsons.

For Caroline and her siblings, the first ten years of their childhood were halcyon days as happy, healthy, and privileged members of the aristocracy in the English countryside. Life revolved around sports and games, the almost annual arrival of a new infant, occasional trips to London—where, as MP for Nottinghamshire, Lord Howe stayed during the "season"—and the dilemmas and dramas of marriageable aunts. All of this informed Caroline's early knowledge of the world and would be reflected in the way she viewed life as an adult. If Lord Howe was the undisputed head of the household, the personalities of the women had a strong influence on its tone. If Caroline was not repressed, neither were her brothers, who grew into active, daring young men, fitted to the notions of masculinity that prevailed in Georgian society. The close, "horizontal" sibling attachments within the family fostered the qualities that made the brothers so admirably suited to lead fellow soldiers into combat. The family bonds were about to draw closer still, for disaster would bind the Howes into a tight-knit group that contemporaries remarked upon.

Two

Diaspora

I t was the male world of politics that demolished the idyll of life at Langar. The Langar estate belonged to Nottinghamshire, where the Howes ranked as one of the leading aristocratic families. By the thinking of the day, it was the due of the head of the Howe dynasty to sit in Parliament. The first Viscount Howe had been a member of Parliament, so it was natural that in 1722, when Scrope attained the age of majority, he should follow his father into the House of Commons.

Supporting him in the election was Thomas Pelham-Holles, the Duke of Newcastle, whose considerable holdings in Nottingham and its surrounds gave him a say in the outcome of any election. Newcastle was an eccentric man, a hypochondriac, an obsessive record-keeper, and a compulsive spender, but he was also one of the era's most powerful political figures, whose notable skill lay in ceaselessly electioneering on behalf of the Whig government. In the election of 1722, the duke aimed to defeat as many Tories as possible. In this, he and his fellow Whigs would succeed, giving them a decided majority in the House of Commons.[1] The Hanoverian succession and the failure of the Jacobite rebellion in 1715 had given the Whigs an excuse to smear Tories as supporters of the divine right of kings and the Catholic Stuart succession, and thus drive them from public office. The 1720s would usher in a long period of Whig dominance in British politics.

The Whigs had been born in the political turmoil of the previous century, when the Stuart monarch James II was driven from his throne in the "Glorious Revolution" of 1688 for being a lover of tyranny and Catholicism. By the middle of the eighteenth century, most politically active men described themselves as Whigs: They all supported the ousting of James in 1688 and the Hanoverian succession that followed the death of Queen Anne in 1714. Ideologically, all Whigs were committed to a constitutionally limited monarchy and the sovereignty of the king and Parliament. But although Whigs identified themselves as the defenders of revolution and popular liberty, the ensuing years had taken the luster off their zeal. By the 1720s, the aristocratic Whigs were less than enthusiastic about the notion of the right of the subject to resist tyranny. Government of course should protect the rights of all subjects and check the power of the king, but, after all, social inequalities were natural, and the lowest orders were unfit to dabble in politics. In this, Whigs and Tories—more alike than they cared to admit—shared common ground.[2]

The British Parliament was a representative body with its roots in the Middle Ages. The House of Commons was entirely elected, but the electoral districts had changed little over the centuries. By the eighteenth century, this resulted in such absurdities as Old Sarum, a deserted village that elected two MPs, handpicked by the local landowner. In sharp contrast, newly emerging large cities such as Birmingham and Manchester elected no MP at all. To add to the confusion, voting qualifications varied from one constituency to another. In most places, one needed to be a taxpayer or a property owner; in a few others, it was sufficient not to be on poor relief. The total electorate in Georgian England and Wales probably numbered about 20 percent of all adult males in those lands.[3]

Despite its eccentricities, the British were proud of their Parliament, unique in Europe and envied abroad. Its byzantine electoral process underscored that this was not a democracy by today's standards, yet the system was more inclusive than appeared at first sight. Contemporaries believed that elections were a fair indication of the national mood; popular resentment could certainly make itself felt during times of unrest. But it was a rough-and-ready means of collecting the sense of the nation, and it did not come cheap.

The eighteenth-century electoral system has been passed down to the present generation by its Victorian detractors as "Old Corruption," a system under which the aristocracy controlled elections through outright bribery and vulgar entertainments. It is true that wealthy individuals with a "parliamentary interest" in a constituency could influence the voting of their dependents; in the days before the secret ballot, tenants and working men could often be relied upon to vote as the local landlord or banker directed.

But this "interest," as it was called, was in many cases insufficient for overall control. In the counties and larger boroughs, there were enough floating votes to ensure that the result was not a foregone conclusion. This meant that other methods had to be used. To label these methods as brib- ery is to oversimplify how contemporaries understood them. Voters were aware of their own value and had to be courted. Very occasionally, out- right bribes were offered, but more often local goodwill was cultivated by spending a great deal of money. Charitable donations, provision of jobs, lavish treats and dinners, compensation for the expense and trouble of trav- eling to the polls—all were part of the business of getting a man elected to Parliament.4 Although electoral managers would have liked to have the power simply to designate candidates, this rarely happened in practice. In the election of 1722, by dint of hard work, the Duke of Newcastle was able to engineer the return of sixteen members to Parliament. But only in two "pocket boroughs," each controlled by a handful of electors, was he able to appoint his own personal choices as parliamentary candidates.5 Election- eering could be ruinously expensive, and so it would prove for Lord Howe.

The 1722 election proved to be a political turning point for Nottingham- shire. The Duke of Newcastle brought forward Scrope Lord Howe and Sir Robert Sutton as candidates for the county. Both seats had been seized by the Tories after Scrope's father had died in 1713, and Newcastle was deter- mined to regain them for the Whigs. He spent a small fortune visiting the area, holding open house twice weekly at his Nottingham Castle residence, and offering financial support to his candidates. "I have scarce been sober since I came," he complained. It was a hard-fought election, but in the end the Tories were so thoroughly ousted that they would not challenge the Whigs in Nottinghamshire again.6 Lord Howe was reelected unopposed in 1727. By now, however, he was so deeply in debt that it hardly mattered.

Scrope's debts were not just due to a contested election. Since his mar- riage in 1719, he and Lady Howe had lived well, mixing with the wealthiest figures in the county, improving the hall and pleasure gardens at Langar, joining in the Belvoir Hunt and keeping racehorses.7 The Howes were not as wealthy as their neighbor, the Duke of Rutland, but they strove to keep up with him. This has the look of vanity, but there was more to it. For gen- teel families like the Howes, a high profile at the royal court or in Parlia- ment offered the opportunity for lucrative offices or sinecures. This was seen as a wholly respectable and natural way of improving the family for- tunes.8 Young Lord Howe had a growing family and sisters who required dowries. In the quest for advancement, he needed to spend money in order to put himself where he was likely to receive an offer, and the House of Commons was such a place. Ironically, however, the post that was to repair Scrope's fortunes obliged him to resign his seat in Parliament. In 1732, on the recommendation of the Duke of Newcastle, he was appointed governor of Barbados, at a salary of £7,000 a year.[9]

Barbados! Surrounded by the Caribbean Sea, with a tropical climate and hurricanes, what could be more different from rural England? It was one of Britain's colonial American possessions, which extended in a vast arc from Newfoundland to the West Indies. The most profitable of these were the plantation colonies that produced such valuable crops as tobacco, rice, and sugar. The island of Barbados, less than a quarter the size of Nottinghamshire, was devoted to the cultivation of sugar. Like the other plantation colonies, it was dependent upon enslaved labor. Settled for more than a century, Barbados in the 1730s had a ratio of four blacks to every white. The grueling conditions of labor on the "sugar islands" were such that continuous imports of enslaved Africans were necessary to maintain the slave populations on the plantations.[10]

A passage to Barbados from England took up to six weeks by packet boat.[11] Lord Howe had heretofore only boarded a ship to cross the English Channel; now he would make a sea voyage of more than four thousand miles in an age when wooden vessels, at the mercy of the elements, sometimes never reached their destination. There were many preparations to be made. Scrope delayed his departure, remaining at Langar until the arrival of daughter Juliana in September; Lady Howe and the girls were going with him.

Caroline, Charlotte, and the baby, Julie, were bound for Barbados, but the Howe boys would remain in Britain. George and Richard were enrolled at Westminster School in London. George, who was eight, had probably already been boarded at Nottingham School for a year or so, but Richard was only six; this would be his first experience away from home.[12] While they were there, the two boys would be under the watchful eye of their aunt, Lady Pembroke, who lived on the outskirts of the metropolis. Three-year-old William and toddler Thomas would remain with their grandmother at Langar, although one of the two youngest, probably William, was brought to town to see the rest of his family off.[13]

Everything had to be done in style; Scrope Lord Howe was determined to look the part of the new governor of Barbados. He put on a lavish going-away banquet for the freeholders of Nottingham at Langar Hall, "an Ox and 3 Sheep being roasted whole, and ten Hogsheads of strong Beer."[14] His kinsman and neighbor, the Duke of Rutland, presented him with a new state coach.[15] He arranged transport of a large quantity of elegant furniture for his governor's mansion in Bridgetown, and he engaged English servants to accompany the family, although the enslaved service on the island would undoubtedly come cheaper.[16] An onlooker might be forgiven for not suspecting that his lordship was taking up his post in order to claw his way out of debt.

From the start, things went awry. First, the coach carrying the three girls to their port of embarkation overturned. Next, when the family finally boarded their ship at Portsmouth in late February, they were detained by contrary winds. When HMS *Rye* finally sailed very early on March 3, 1733, the entire party was beset by seasickness. To add to their distress, a messenger arrived, informing Lord Howe that the ship carrying his baggage and state coach had been lost off the coast of Ireland.[17] At least they were spared the news that one of their sons at Westminster had just fallen dangerously ill, an emergency Lady Pembroke was obliged to handle in her new role as surrogate parent.[18] All in all, it was an inauspicious beginning for a sea voyage in late winter. The reduced circle of the Howe family finally reached Bridgetown, Barbados, by mid-April.[19]

Numerous testimonies have survived to bear witness to Lord Howe's popularity as governor among the white planter population of Barbados, but one wonders what his wife and daughters thought of it. In many ways, colonial Barbados could be described as a vast slave compound punctuated by the homes of English planters who so desired normalcy that they ruined their health wearing London fashions in the sweltering heat, while their slaves went about clad in just a single garment.[20] The plants, the food, the climate, the African servants in house and in field, the landscape that ended relentlessly with the limitless blue of the Caribbean—all must have seemed alien to Caroline. Since her chief amusements in Langar had been outdoors, she was not well placed to ignore her new environment. And raised as she was in the English values of civil and political liberty, Caroline was now confronted by the hypocrisy of a British colony where human beings were treated as chattel and brutal punishments were routinely meted out for disobedience. She may have been screened from the whippings and beatings, but she must have been aware that white supremacy and the subjugation of the majority population of black slaves was sustained by force.[21]

Whatever she thought while there as a girl, she gave no sign of ever wanting to visit the West Indies again; almost fifty years later, when she heard
the news that a friend had just been appointed governor of Barbados, she
referred to it as a banishment from society.[22]

Barbados was a place where life expectancy for even the well-to-
do whites was low, with many not living past their forties.[23] Lady Howe
was pregnant again once they were ashore, and another daughter, Mary,
was born in the tropics. Ironically, despite his wife's condition, it was
Lord Howe who succumbed. On March 21, 1735, hardly two years after
his arrival, Scrope fell ill; six days later, at barely thirty-six, he was dead.
Onlookers recalled that he took leave of his family "in the most tender and
affectionate manner." For Scrope and Charlotte, it was the end of a love
affair. "More obliging Expressions never drop'd from the Mouth of a Bridegroom to his beloved Bride," wrote one observer feelingly. Yet the Howe
trait of stoicism was conspicuous throughout. Lord Howe appeared from
the first to know he was going to die, and he spoke of it "as of any other
common subject," trying to make all ready for the inevitable event.[24] He
arranged his funeral and appealed to the leading planters on the island to
assist his "prudent tender and most affectionate wife" in undertaking the
difficult return voyage to England.[25]

By June, Lady Howe was back in London with the new baby in her arms
and her three older daughters and servants in tow.[26] Such was her haste
to leave Barbados that her husband's body had to follow; not until October
was the 2nd Viscount Howe finally laid to rest in Langar.[27] His widow had
done what was necessary with determination and dispatch, but even she
had her limits. Within a few weeks of stepping ashore in England, Lady
Howe was dangerously ill. For a brief period, the children were in danger
of losing both parents in one year. But their mother survived, and when
she returned from convalescing in the countryside, the extended family
surveyed the damage done to the Howe fortunes.[28]

The West Indian adventure had worsened the tottering family finances,
and a donation from the colony of Barbados did little to mend the loss of
£7,000 a year. Lady Howe had brought pensions and annuities into her
marriage, the gifts of her uncle King George I, and royal generosity again
intervened to increase her income, but it never totaled more than £2,750—
at a time when £3,000 was deemed barely enough to sustain an aristocratic
lifestyle.[29] The Howes were faced with a minority, a period when the boys

were all under the age of twenty-one. For at least the next decade, the family would not be able to gain income from any of its male members. Following the Barbados disaster, the children would be scattered among their English relatives for the remainder of their growing-up years.

The Howe dynasty was in a precarious position. Although to modern eyes the charm of a title is that it ensures an unassailable social standing, in practice rank had to be sustained with money. Contemporaries expected it, and without conspicuous wealth, peerages could decline and disappear. A case in point is Henry Bromley, 1st Baron Montfort, who fell deeply into debt, in part through the expense of electioneering. His suicide in 1755 ushered in two generations of escalating ruin. His grandson, the 3rd Baron Montfort, ended up in a debtor's prison, where he married the warden's daughter.[30] The lesson was clear.

If the Howes wanted to retain their position near the top of the British hierarchy, they needed to make real changes. Retrenchment was immediate. George and Richard were withdrawn from Eton, where they had been placed only the previous year as a progression from Westminster. There would be no grand tour to finish their education, as their father before them had done. Further large savings could be achieved by closing down the family seat and maintaining only a skeleton staff. This appears to be what happened at Langar Hall. The hospitable "public days," which were expected of local aristocracy, were discontinued as an unnecessary extravagance.[31] Only elderly Lady Juliana Howe, Scrope's mother, remained in residence at the Hall, or at her nearby house in Epperstone. With her was her grandson William, who had lived with her since 1733, and Mary, born in Barbados, who was only two. Their grandmother assumed charge of their education.[32]

For Caroline, George, Charlotte, Thomas, and Julie, life shifted away from Nottinghamshire to the environs of London. Their new world was close to the fashionable life of the city and the court. The children had probably seen London before, but now its amusements—Vauxhall and Ranelagh Gardens, the opera, the theaters, royal parks and gardens, museums and bookshops—came to the foreground of their lives as Nottinghamshire receded. Lady Howe shared guardianship of the children with Thomas Page, the husband of her sister-in-law Juliana.[33] The Pages had a townhouse on Old Bond Street in London's West End and a roomy old mansion, Battlesden, forty miles from the city. This was the property of

Uncle Page's fantastically wealthy older brother, Sir Gregory Page, who had loaned it to his younger sibling for life.³⁴ Sir Gregory himself lived at Wricklemarsh in Blackheath near London, a magnificent Palladian mansion with an art collection that included works by Van Dyck and Rubens.³⁵ The Howe brood was filling a gap in the Page households, for, despite their wealth, neither of the Page brothers had children. In the years to come, Aunt Juliana would take a great interest in the lives of her nieces and nephews.

Lady Pembroke—their Aunt Mary—lived in Parsons Green, a London suburb.³⁶ In the heart of London's West End, on Gerrard Street, lived Aunt Anne, her husband Colonel Charles Mordaunt, and their sons, Charles Lewis, Osbert, and Harry.³⁷ The widowed Lady Howe made regular forays into the countryside with her older children, to visit William and Mary at Langar Hall or to stay at the country seat of the Mordaunts at Halsall Hall in Lancashire.³⁸ But her center of gravity was now the residences of her two sisters-in-law, Mary, Lady Pembroke, and Anne Mordaunt, in London.

For Richard, however, something very different was in store. In 1736, at the tender age of ten, the future "Black Dick" Howe began his career as a sailor, enlisting in the merchant service. His most distinguished biographer, David Syrett, casts doubt on this humble beginning to Lord Howe's notable naval career, for service on merchant vessels was incompatible with the status of a gentleman. "It is highly unlikely that Richard Howe owing to his family background, would be removed from school at the age of 10 and be sent to sea before the mast on a merchant ship," argues Syrett. Nevertheless, Richard's lieutenant's passing certificate states that he served for more than three years on "the merchant ship *Thames*, William Merchant, Master," and there is no reason not to believe it.³⁹ It has been estimated that more than one-fifth of young men who passed their lieutenant's exams had served in the merchant navy. Surely they were not all lying, as Syrett claims Richard did in order to strengthen his case for qualification for a lieutenant's commission. And another Howe, Richard's youngest brother, Thomas, would become captain of an East Indiaman ship, a commercial and ungentlemanly occupation perhaps, but at least a lucrative one.⁴⁰

The unvarnished truth was that the Howe boys needed to find gainful employment. Their previous biographers have presumed that they began their military careers from positions of privilege, based on wealth and advantageous connections. But this was not the case, particularly for Richard. The conventional choices for the sons of aristocracy—the army, the

church, the law—all required money, whether for an army officer's commission, a university education, or a stint at the Inns of Court. The navy
was cheap, and acceptable for a man from a good family. But a naval career
was far too risky for George, the eldest and heir to the Howe estate, so it was
second son Richard who was packed off to sea.

After three years' service as a merchant mariner, Richard entered the
Royal Navy in the rank of ordinary seaman on HMS *Pearl* in 1739. Here
again, the Howes' lack of influence in high places was evident, for the coveted entry point for a young gentleman joining a ship-of-war was on the
lowest rung of the officer class, as a midshipman, but competition for midshipman berths was strong.[41] A year later, on July 3, 1740, Richard was
finally made a midshipman aboard HMS *Severn*. He achieved that promotion on his own merits, for it would still be several years before his mother
acquired influence at court.

Midshipman Howe experienced the worst of life at sea aboard HMS
Severn during its disastrous attempt to round Cape Horn at the tip of South
America, resulting in the loss of more than four hundred men. Writing to
Lady Howe a few weeks after the *Severn* limped into Rio de Janeiro, in July
1741, fifteen-year-old Richard provided a graphic description of "the pretty
place your dear Dickie has seen": it was a chronicle of "sails splitting, the
supports to the masts breaking, men continually dying, the rest almost all
sick, and those that stood the deck and were left to take care of so large a
ship, were not above 30, and they left every man half eat up with the scurvy
and little water aboard."[42]

Yet Richard remained undeterred by the hardships he encountered. He
experienced battle before his brothers, who would not begin their army
careers until the mid-1740s. The year 1739 saw the outbreak of the War
of Jenkins' Ear against Spain, and in 1740 it widened into the War of the
Austrian Succession. As a midshipman in the 70-gun ship of the line HMS
Burford, Richard participated in a bloody British defeat off the coast of Ven-
ezuela in 1742. He passed his lieutenant's examination in English Har-
bour, Antigua, in May 1744. Two years later, he had his first command,
HM Sloop *Baltimore*. The Pages may have been able to help him with this
crucial promotion, for they had influence with the Duke of Bedford, then
First Lord of the Admiralty. Richard's first mission was to cruise the coast
of Scotland on the lookout for Jacobites. A blow to the head in a battle with
French privateers near the Sound of Arisaig left his companions convinced

he was dead, but he was soon restored to consciousness.[43] For more than twenty-five years, he was keen to serve in both wartime and peacetime, spending little time ashore between 1736 and the end of the Seven Years' War in 1763. By 1760, the newspapers reported that he had been involved in fifty-seven sea battles since joining the Royal Navy.[44]

It was a rough life that took Richard to far-flung parts of the world, and it was a very different life from that of his brothers George and William, who remained in England throughout most of their teenage years. The two soldier-brothers would not see action until late in the War of the Austrian Succession, and, in any case, an army life was less of a complete departure from home and hearth than a navy life. But Richard's lengthy duty at sea did nothing to dampen his attachment to his home. Of all his siblings, he was the one to return most often to Langar, with its childhood memories and country quiet.

Any account of the early years of this rising generation of Howes must give due recognition to the formidable Aunt Mary, Lady Pembroke. Her decisive role in shaping the careers of the three famous Howe brothers has gone unnoticed by historians, whose adherence to official correspondence and documents in reconstructing the careers of the men has overlooked the leading roles played by the women of the dynasty. Lady Pembroke did not simply offer emotional support and clean linen to her nephews. When her brother died, she became the virtual head of the family. Lady Pembroke worked for the rest of her life to ensure the survival of her brother's lineage, mentoring not only the boys but also the widowed Lady Howe and her daughter Caroline in the business of exercising influence at court and in the country. Both Caroline and her mother became apt pupils of their capable kinswoman.

By the time of her brother Scrope's death in Barbados, Lady Pembroke herself was widowed, the aged Lord Pembroke having died in 1733.[45] She retained the courtesy title of Dowager Countess Pembroke until her death. Perhaps she was relieved to be free of her eccentric husband. She had certainly not cultivated domesticity during her married life, for she had become a Lady of the Bedchamber to Queen Caroline when her husband King George II ascended the throne of Britain in 1727.[46] In 1735, Lady Pembroke wedded again, this time to Jack Mordaunt, a grandson of the 3rd Earl of Peterborough. Seven years earlier, her sister Anne had married a Mordaunt, and the union had been fruitful.[47]

If Lady Pembroke hoped for children with Jack Mordaunt, who was at least eight years her junior, she was disappointed. It remained her fate to be mother to her numerous fatherless nieces and nephews. Her house at Parsons Green became home not only to Lady Howe and her daughters, but also to the daughter of her cousin William. William Howe had been a student in Paris with Scrope when the two were teenagers, chalking up bills in the cafés and acquiring a veneer of French manners. By 1733, William had married, been widowed, and had died, leaving a daughter, Mary, who was slightly younger than Caroline.[48] Mary became part of the Howe brood in Lady Pembroke's Parsons Green household, where she joined her cousins Caroline, Charlotte, and Julie.[49]

Lady Pembroke's creative networking skills now came into play in the service of her brother's family. Income was necessary; the widowed Lady Howe must have a place at court, the only paid position open to one of her rank. A few months after her brother's funeral in 1735, Lady Pembroke began to lobby to have her sister-in-law named as a lady-in-waiting to the Princess Augusta, wife of Frederick, Prince of Wales, a post that brought an annual salary of £400.[50] However, it would not be until May 1743 that Lady Charlotte Howe took up a position in the princess's household.

One wonders about Charlotte's thoughts on this turn of events. Many years earlier, she had made her escape from the sinuous, incestuous politics of court life. Now necessity compelled her to return; the royal family was no less dysfunctional, but it was a new generation. Heir to the throne Prince Frederick and his father, George II, detested one another. Frederick's sisters and his brother, the Duke of Cumberland, were split into factions, the result of an upbringing riven with family politics.[51] But Lady Howe could remain outside the tumult of this latest generation of royals. The old hatreds and rivalries of her mother, the insecure Sophia von Kielmansegg, had been consigned to dust. Even Queen Caroline was dead. Lady Howe—refined, correct, brought up to understand the court etiquettes of Hanoverians as well as Britons, and able to speak German in a court where many of the great still stumbled over their English—was admirably adapted for her new role in life. In an echo of the old days, Prince Frederick was heard to call her "aunt," an acknowledgment of a distant cousinship.[52]

As soon as Lady Howe became a lady-in-waiting, with its associated increase of income and influence, the Howe family fortunes began to revive. George was made an ensign in the First Regiment of Foot Guards in 1745. At the age of twenty, he finally had a job. Within two years, he was a captain as well as aide-de-camp to the British army's captain general, William Augustus, Duke of Cumberland.[53]

William, who had been a toddler when his father died and the household at Langar broke up, had lagged behind George in his education. In 1742, at the comparatively advanced age of thirteen, he had been sent to Eton for a year, together with his younger brother Thomas.[54] Lady Howe now finished her third son's education by obtaining a post for him as page of honor to George II in 1744.[55] This position, with an annual salary of £200, was sometimes given to youths like William Howe from impoverished genteel families. Limited attendance on the king was expected, but royal pages were also taught horsemanship in the Crown stables and were prepared for entry into the army. William, like many pages, was commissioned after a few years.[56] He followed his brother into the army in 1746, at age seventeen, becoming a cornet in the 15th Dragoons; within a year, he was a lieutenant.[57]

William and George both saw action in Flanders before the War of the Austrian Succession ended in 1748. The conflict was part of more than a century of Anglo-French rivalry between 1689 and 1815. During this war, Prussia emerged as a leading power in Europe, and Anglo-French rivalry was extended to include colonial possessions in America and India. By the time the two brothers had enlisted, Britain and France were the main combatants. Both Howes gained repeated promotions; no doubt they were as conspicuously brave in this early stage of their respective careers as they would prove to be ever after, but the fact that their mother now had access to the royal ear can only have helped their advancement. Richard's comparatively gradual ascent up the naval ladder provides an instructive contrast.

But as far as Lady Pembroke was concerned, finding careers for her nephews was not enough to ensure the future of the Howe dynasty. Since 1673, the men of her family—her father, followed by her brother Scrope—had represented the county of Nottinghamshire as Whig MPs. She was determined that George should follow in their footsteps. In 1739, while George was still too young to enter Parliament, Lady Pembroke installed her obliging young husband, Jack Mordaunt, in one of the two parliamentary seats for Nottinghamshire. The understanding was that he was doing so to protect "the Howe interest" and would step aside when George came

of age. Staking a claim to a seat on behalf of a minor was not unprecedented, and the Howes felt entitled to the honor. Lady Pembroke, however,
did this over the loud protests of some of the established political figures in
Nottinghamshire, drumming up enough support to override them.[58]

It was not until 1747 that George was finally of an age to stand as a candidate; by then, however, he was serving in Flanders. Lady Pembroke was
left with a battle on her hands to secure her nephew's seat in Parliament,
for the county of Nottinghamshire put up such resistance to his candidacy
that she was obliged to transfer her sights to the town of Nottingham itself.
There, however, she discovered that the Duke of Newcastle was blocking
George in favor of one of her distant relatives, John Plumptre, who had represented the town for more than thirty years.[59] If the duke was not going
to lift his hand to help young Lord Howe, Lady Pembroke had another
idea that involved pushing Mr. Plumptre out of the race. Once again, she
resorted to matrimony to secure advantages for the family.

Abel Smith was a prominent Nottingham banker whose family had
emerged from obscurity just a generation or two earlier. They had money,
but the air of the countinghouse still clung to them. The Smiths had a great
deal of influence in the Nottingham elections, for Abel had loaned money
to half the businessmen and grandees in town, including the Howes, and
the two families had known each other for years.[60] Now each had something the other wanted: Abel Smith wished to climb into the ranks of the
gentry, and Lady Pembroke needed a seat in Parliament for her nephew. On
August 14, 1747, George Smith, eldest son of Abel, was married to Mary
Howe, Lady Pembroke's ward. Mary was not just a Howe; she boasted royal
blood, for her grandmother was Ruperta Howe, natural daughter of Prince
Rupert of the Rhine, who had Stuart blood and was the uncle of George I
to boot.[61] The wedding took place less than two months after George Howe
had been elected a member for the town of Nottingham.

The newspapers proclaimed that George had been elected "without
Opposition," but there had been plenty of it behind the scenes, for the Duke
of Newcastle's favorite, Mr. Plumptre, had been obliged to drop out of the
race once he realized he had lost the support of the ambitious Abel Smith.[62]
The unhappy Mr. Plumptre complained to the duke of "the ungentlemanlike and the ungrateful behaviour of that family," the Howes.[63] The Duke
of Newcastle was upset at the flap—he wailed that he was "accused by the
Howe family of endeavouring to drive them out of the county and town."[64]

If Mr. Plumptre found the family "ungentlemanlike," perhaps it was because it was a Howe lady who was directing affairs. Since George was overseas and could not make a public appearance in Nottingham, Lady Pembroke did it for him.[65] She did it with great panache, Mr. Plumptre reported grudgingly: "Lady Pembroke made her Entry here today with a great Appearance of People to meet her & great Acclamations on her Arrival."[66] One trusts she greeted the voters from the safety of her coach, since the army—the only effective police force of the day—was not allowed by law within two miles of a place of election until the polling was over, to preserve the boasted independence of the British electorate. The result was a frightening carnival atmosphere in which drunks, hecklers, stone-throwers, and obscene remarks were common, with the occasional eruption of serious violence.[67]

Other heads of the Howe clan—Lady Howe and Mr. and Mrs. Page— came along to give their determined sister moral support.[68] George Howe would not be denied his birthright if his family could help it. Determined to leave nothing to chance, Lady Pembroke wrote to her influential friend at court, Lady Yarmouth, mistress of King George II, advising her that certain members of the rival political camp had Jacobite tendencies. Lady Howe no doubt joined her sister-in-law in the campaign of character assassination, for Newcastle's political agent wrote that "the women of the Howe family are perpetually teasing Lady Yarmouth to intermeddle in [George's] Favor."[69]

All this striving and conniving was worth it in the end, because not only did George became MP for Nottingham, but the Smiths also were satisfied with their bargain. George Smith was given the trappings of gentrification by his rich father, including a handsome income, a townhouse in Nottingham and a country seat at East Stoke.[70] Nor was George Smith's spouse, cousin Mary Howe, forgotten. Lady Howe influenced the Duke of Newcastle to make George Smith a baronet in 1757.[71] After all, it was only right that Mary should end up as "Lady Smith."

Lady Pembroke was entirely a pragmatist in matters of matrimony, so it is not surprising that she also made plans for her niece Caroline, who came of age while under her ladyship's wing. Caroline made her first appearance in the rumor mill when her name became romantically linked with Edward Walpole, brother of Horace and son of Robert, the all-powerful prime minister, who was still in office when an engagement was mooted.

In November 1741, Horace wrote to a friend that his brother Edward "had agreed to take [Caroline] with no fortune, she him with his four children." Edward had hard work obtaining his father's consent, probably because the bride was poor. Finally he prevailed, and then, in a tragicomic episode, instantly "repented; and instead of flying on the wings of love to notify it, He went to his Fair one, owned his Father had mollified, but hoped she would be so good as to excuse Him!"[72]

Edward Walpole was a truly awful character. In London, he mixed with a set who drank and gambled; in Ireland, where he held a minor government post, he was associated with the Dublin Hellfire Club, whose members set fire to cats and added violent brawls to the usual indoor vices. By the time he was in his thirties, he had fathered four illegitimate children by a beautiful milliner's apprentice who died in 1738. His one saving grace was his acknowledgment of his children, whom he raised in his household, to the disapproval of polite society.[73] He was a well-educated man, and Caroline was the only woman he ever seriously considered marrying, perhaps because she was an intelligent young woman.[74]

It may be that the engagement was never as solid as Horace Walpole believed, because just a few months later Caroline was engaged to John Howe of Stokes Manor, Hanslope, in Buckinghamshire, and they would marry in 1742. Despite his name, John was no relation. He was a friend of the Pages and part of their circle of regular visitors.[75] Like them, he came from a family of religious dissenters. His paternal grandfather had served as chaplain to Oliver Cromwell, the Puritan soldier who toppled Charles I, and his maternal grandfather had fought alongside Cromwell during the Civil War.[76] Since then, the family had settled down and acquired property, following the prescribed English path to upward social mobility.[77]

If John Howe's family history was unconventional, he himself was not. Throwing off his dissenter heritage, he moved in rarefied circles that included Frederick, Prince of Wales.[78] He shared with the Howes their love of the country life—riding, the hunt, chess, and visiting. Also, like Caroline and her brothers, he was fascinated by the world opening up to science in the eighteenth-century age of exploration. Caroline's attractiveness for educated men was a constant note in her adult relationships. She was the first of her sisters to marry, and the only one who married while still only twenty years of age, despite having no dowry. In choosing John

John Howe's Member Portrait for the Society of Dilettanti, painted in 1741, the year before his marriage. The members posed in fancy dress; Howe pours wine from a vessel in the shape of a globe.

Howe, Caroline reaffirmed her ties to the life she had known as a girl in Nottinghamshire.

Lady Pembroke died in 1749. Her will contained a heartfelt note that belied her persona of a hardheaded matriarch: "I wish you my Sisters and all my Friends all manner of Worldly Happiness and that we may all meet Joyfull in that blessed place." To her, family was everything. Her brother Scrope had died in his prime, but there was still the next generation and the future of the dynasty to work for. This she had done to the utmost of her ability. "If it will not be too much Expense," was her final wish, "I would like to have my Remains Interred at Langar near those of my Dearest Brother."[79] She rests today in Langar Church.

Lady Pembroke left an abiding impression on her eldest niece, Caroline. Her shrewd understanding of the politics of the private and public worlds through which she moved, her lack of inhibition about entering spheres that were usually reserved for men, and above all her loyalty and her sense of family destiny—these qualities would later show themselves in Caroline.

During the early years of Caroline's marriage, when the War of the Austrian Succession scattered her brothers far and wide into danger, she first learned to watch which way the wind blew as she waited for news of them from abroad. "North East & nothing but North East so no news"; "The Wind fair, but it is very uncertain when we shall have news"; "The wind has lately been easterly, so I fear we must wait still longer for intelligence."[80] It would become a lifetime habit. The Howe siblings would be separated often by war, but the close bonds of childhood would prevail.

Three

The Brothers

On a late spring morning in 1755, in the cold waters off Newfoundland, Captain Richard Howe, commanding HMS *Dunkirk*, ended a prolonged game of hide-and-seek in the fog with three French men-of-war by firing a broadside into the 64-gun *Alcide*. Although war between Britain and France would not be officially declared for another year, Captain Howe's action on June 8 began the Seven Years' War at sea. The *Dunkirk* had sailed from Plymouth six weeks earlier as one of a squadron of twelve warships under the command of Vice Admiral the Honorable Edward Boscawen. Their mission was to intercept French ships carrying reinforcements to Canada.[1]

Britain's prime minister, the Duke of Newcastle, did not want war, but rivalry with France over colonial possessions in America was forcing him down that road. The peace that concluded the War of the Austrian Succession in 1748 was little more than a temporary truce. Within five years, France began a project of aggressive fort-building to the west of the British seaboard colonies in America, with the objective of uniting its own colonies in Canada and Louisiana, encircling the British settlements, and obstructing further British westward expansion.

When the French began construction of Fort Duquesne on the banks of the Allegheny and Monongahela Rivers in 1753, the British colony of Virginia was provoked to respond. The following year, young Colonel George Washington was sent off with a Virginia provincial regiment, and a series of inconclusive frontier clashes ensued. This was the first time that a war between Britain and France would begin in the colonies and then spread to Europe. America's importance was clearly beginning to be felt. But the question by 1755 was, Could the British protect their American colonies without starting a war in Europe? Early that year, the government shipped two regiments of redcoat regulars under General Edward Braddock to the colonies to seize French forts in the Ohio Valley. The French, who also hoped hostilities could be confined to America, responded by shipping troop reinforcements to Quebec.[2] It was this flotilla that Admiral Boscawen was ordered to intercept.

The mission posed an interesting problem for Boscawen. What was he to do when he intercepted the French that would not provoke outright war? This was why the account of Richard's clash with the *Alcide* would be pored over in the press. The public wanted to know who had fired the first shot, as they would twenty years later with the Battle of Lexington and Concord. It would not be the first—or the last—time that Richard found his acumen as well as his physical courage put to the test in an extreme situation.

The British squadron had first sighted four warships on June 2, but the French managed to evade their pursuers westward in dense fog, which persisted throughout the entire operation. Five days later, Richard sighted three French ships heading toward Quebec. He chased them until he realized these were merchantmen, not fighting ships. This was not yet war, and he could not interfere with the enemy's trading vessels. The next morning, June 8, the four French adversaries were sighted again. It was the eager Richard who overtook the *Alcide*, the hindmost warship in the little fleet. There was a brief exchange of words, during which the French commander, Houquart, demanded to know "whether it were peace or war?" It was a question Richard could only answer by insisting that the *Alcide* shorten her sails, which Houquart quite reasonably refused to do. The parley was cut short when Richard received a signal from Boscawen's flagship and opened fire into the French vessel, which surrendered in just fifteen minutes. A second French man-of-war, the *Lays*, was captured a few hours later by HMS *Defiance* and HMS *Farqueur*.[3]

The British had made only a token effort to negotiate with the French forces, and the newspapers back in Britain tried to give a veneer of legitimacy to the incident. One reported that before firing, Richard called a genteel warning to the French officers on the *Alcide*; others asserted that the French had fired first.[4] But British opinion didn't really care. The public was proud of Richard's aggressive daring against the nation's chief enemy. Different versions of his action against the *Alcide* rapidly proliferated, giving free rein to the imaginations of jingoistic journalists. The *Leeds Intelligencer*, in what was probably a pure flight of fancy, claimed gleefully that the French sailors were so terrified by the intensity of the British fire that they deserted their posts, and that poor Monsieur Houquart, upon boarding the *Dunkirk* as a prisoner, "told the brave Capt. Howe *that it was cruel to engage so very close.*"[5]

The episode brought Richard to public notice for the first time.[6] Dark-complexioned like all the Howes (within the service, his nickname was "Black Dick"), at age twenty-nine he had the rugged good looks associated with a man of action. He was enthusiastically hailed as a hero. A decisive blow had been struck by a son of Britain against a creeping French threat.[7] And yet the mission overall was a failure. The French reinforcements reached their goal; Boscawen's warships searched for them fruitlessly for weeks in the Grand Banks and the Gulf of St. Lawrence. Richard spent the summer blockading the French fortress at Louisbourg and hunting for enemy ships with their warlike cargoes.

Only at the end of August 1755 did the Admiralty issue explicit orders for taking all French vessels encountered on the high seas. Even this did not quite constitute a declaration of war. "The absurdity is inconceivable," commented one frustrated courtier, and indeed it was.[8] As usual in such cases, no one was satisfied. Despite Newcastle's prevarications, Britain was seen within Europe as the aggressor in the action off Newfoundland, while the British public chafed under the indignity of what it saw as British submission to French arrogance.[9] The very next month, news reached London of the bloody defeat by Indians and French soldiers of the British expedition under General Braddock, sent to capture Fort Duquesne. National humiliation was complete. The "weakness and worthlessness" of the Duke of Newcastle while the country drifted into war became the talk of the town.[10]

While Richard was winning laurels for heroics at sea, his elder brother George appeared perversely to be damaging the standing of the Howe family in Parliament. On November 13, 1755, during a debate in the House of Commons that lasted "til near five in the morning," William Pitt, best known to posterity as Pitt the Elder, blasted the feeble foreign policy of the Newcastle administration. "[I]ncoherent, *un-British measures,*" shouted Pitt, famous for his stirring oratory. The young George Lord Howe was one of just a handful of Whig MPs who put their heads above the parapet that night to vote with Pitt against the government.[11]

Newcastle's policy involved paying expensive subsidies to Russia and the German state of Hesse-Cassel in return for the pledge of their military assistance should Britain go to war on the European continent. Newcastle hoped this tactic would prevent war altogether, but it was unpopular within the British nation at large. There was widespread suspicion that its real purpose was to protect George II's beloved native Hanover at the expense of the rest of the nation.

Pitt lost the vote on October 13, but George Lord Howe won the lasting admiration of his constituents in Nottingham for taking a bold stance against Newcastle's government, even though it seemed certain to hurt his prospects for advancement. Twenty years later, on the eve of the American War of Independence, the voters of Nottingham still recalled how George had cast his vote against the unpopular subsidy treaties at that all-night session in the House of Commons. Young Lord Howe had "dared to act *in opposition to a Court*, when his judgment informed him his opposition was right."[12]

George dared because he saw himself as obliged to no one in the government for his seat in the House of Commons, least of all the Duke of Newcastle. The Howe family had not forgotten that Newcastle had tried to block George's candidacy in Nottingham in the election of 1747. Back then, it had required all of Lady Pembroke's skillful management to secure a victory for her nephew while he was abroad serving his country in Flanders.

Lady Pembroke was dead by the time of the next general election in 1754, but George had been an able pupil of her methods of political management. He duly visited the Duke of Newcastle, asking the duke to support him as the candidate for the borough of Nottingham. The duke was charmed, and within a couple of weeks of their meeting, he agreed to back the young Lord Howe. In doing so, he brushed aside John Plumptre—son of the John Plumptre who had been outmaneuvered by Lady Pembroke in 1747.[13]

In the same vein as his father, the younger Plumptre was furious, refusing to give way a second time to the scheming clan of Howes. But George, beneath his charming exterior, had an iron resolve and a strong work ethic and canvassed far and wide in his quest for votes.[14] He had already contributed £500 to a lawsuit by the Nottingham municipal corporation against the town's burgesses, a sweetener to gain the support of the politically important corporation. When the burgesses reacted with hostility, he appeased them with a round of feasting at Langar Hall that reputedly was so excessive that it resulted in several fatalities. Threats of stoning from his opponents could not stop the veteran soldier from walking the town of Nottingham, and he took up a staff and led a mob during the final balloting. George won the election, alongside the Tory candidate Sir Willoughby

Aston.[15] The following year, George installed a "magnificent mansion" in Castle Gate, right in the shadow of the duke's seat of Nottingham Castle. The new residence made it clear that George intended to represent Nottingham for keeps if he could.[16]

From the age of four, George had been groomed to be the heir to the dynasty, and he had learned the role well. Since his father's death when he was barely eleven, he had been in training to revive the Howe family's shattered fortunes. Oldest sons and heirs normally did not risk going to war, but George, like all the Howe boys, had to work for his living. It was during the War of the Austrian Succession that he embarked on an army career, joining the First Regiment of Foot Guards as an ensign in March 1745, at the age of twenty. Just six months later, he would make a name for himself in the British press in a most unexpected quarter, fighting alongside the Sardinian army at the Battle of Bassignano in Northern Italy against French and Spanish forces. Britain's chief theater of operations in the war was the Low Countries (present-day Netherlands and Belgium); its involvement in Italy was restricted to financial and naval support for its Sardinian-Austrian allies. Not so for the ambitious Lord Howe, however.

A letter from George to his mother, dated September 30, 1745, and newly discovered among the Hardwicke Papers in the British Library, recounts his adventures at the Battle of Bassignano. George was almost certainly there in the role of a gentleman volunteer, probably as an aide-de-camp to Count Johann Matthias von der Schulenberg.[17] At Bassignano, Britain's Sardinian allies were defeated by the combined Bourbon armies of France and Spain. But for George, it was a great chance to distinguish himself, and he did. The London newspapers concluded their account of the battle with "My Lord Howe, an English Nobleman, who was present at the Whole, behaved with such Spirit and Courage, as has done him much Honour, and acquir'd him a very great Character in this whole Army." Impervious to danger, always in the thick of the fight, George singlehandedly took two prisoners, receiving only "a slight Cut on the Thumb."[18] George sent a lengthy account of the battle to his mother, assuring her he had bandaged his thumbnail, "which is half cutt off." It was a small price to pay for his first appearance on the national stage as a hero. "I am dear Madam yr most Dutiful Son Howe," he finished happily, then scribbled at the bottom, as an afterthought to his brother, "pray my service to Dick I wrote to him a piece of a letter but had not time to finish it."[19]

George rose quickly after his Italian exploits. Two years later, he was off to campaign in Flanders with the British service. There he served as aide-de-camp to the Duke of Cumberland. By 1749, a year into the peace, he was a lieutenant colonel in the Guards.[20]

In the years between the War of the Austrian Succession and the Seven Years' War, 1748–56, George spent much of his time in London, where his military duties often placed him.[21] Members of his regiment were house-hold troops, at the service of the sovereign. As such, they were stationed in Westminster or Windsor, leaving the officers with plenty of time to enjoy the metropolis. So George had a chance to shine, not only in politics and the military but also among the fashionable society of the capital. The Guards officers were seen in London's clubs, coffeehouses, ballrooms, brothels, and assemblies more often than on the parade ground.[22] In an age when there was no formal education for officers, and the upbringing of a gentleman was deemed sufficient preparation for an army command, Lord Howe stood out as officer material, intelligent and brave.

He soon caught the eye of one of London high society's most desirable women, Elizabeth Chudleigh. The child of an impoverished gentry family, Elizabeth grew up determined to live as a woman of fashion. Her face proved to be her fortune; acknowledged by society as a beauty, she was somebody's mistress by the age of fifteen. She had joined the royal household of Princess Augusta in 1743, the same year as Lady Howe, becoming a maid of honor through the influence of her "protector."

It was not until after the war—by which time Elizabeth and George had undergone many separate adventures—that their affair began. While George had been in Europe building his military reputation, Elizabeth had secretly married a young naval officer, the Honorable Augustus John Hervey. Maids of honor were supposed to *be* maidens, and once married, Elizabeth would lose her post and £200 per annum. As a result, she kept her marriage such a close secret that when Hervey went to sea shortly afterward, she was rather openly unfaithful to him. His return in 1746 led to a painful reconciliation; a son was born and then died a year later. In 1749, they parted. Unable to terminate their union during a period when divorce was almost nonexistent, they agreed never to reveal the marriage. Mr. and Mrs. Hervey would be obliged to revisit their mistake much later in their lives, but at this point, Elizabeth reveled in her position as one of the most attractive young women at court, while baffling society gossips as she refused marriage offers from such eligible figures as the Dukes of Hamilton and Ancaster.

In May 1749, probably celebrating the departure of the husband she despised, Elizabeth Chudleigh committed the escapade for which she was to be best remembered. At a masquerade in Ranelagh, a famous pleasure garden, she appeared virtually naked in the presence of George II and the Duke of Cumberland, in a costume designed to represent Iphigenia, the tragic Greek princess. Supposedly ready to receive the sacrificial knife, she exposed a controversial amount of flesh, described by some as nothing more than transparent gauze and a strategically placed garland of leaves. The descriptions vary, but the outfit was enough to cause the scandalized Princess Augusta to throw her cloak over her maid of honor. George II and the Duke of Cumberland were dazzled; the story goes that the king asked to touch her breasts and rumors abounded afterward that she would become a royal mistress.[23] She did not, but the notoriety occasioned by her audacity caused her to be bombarded by suitors and would-be lovers. George Howe, by now home from war, was among them. "[E]very butterfly of fashion" hovered around her, wrote one biographer, but Lord Howe "was the only person whom she did not repel." According to rumor, George received "the last favour" from Miss Chudleigh, a coy reference to an affair.[24]

The affair with George Lord Howe has been omitted from Chudleigh's most recent biography, but it bears the hallmarks of truth. The Howes knew the secret of Elizabeth's marriage; years later, one of the Howe sisters testified to it in court.[25] The newly liberated Mistress Chudleigh, however, wanted a lover, not a husband. This would have been no discouragement to George, who, at this stage of his life, with his fortune still to earn, certainly did not want to be encumbered with a wife. The two had little money between them and both were risk-takers. For as long as Elizabeth posed as a single woman, she and George could enjoy an intimate liaison with no ties and no commitments.

By the middle of 1752, Elizabeth Chudleigh was the acknowledged mistress of Evelyn Pierrepont, 2nd Duke of Kingston.[26] This relationship would continue until the duke's death in 1773. Older and much richer than George, he provided the security she sought. And as he was a neighbor of the Howes in Nottinghamshire, perhaps she did not have to entirely dispense with her intimate friendship with the rising young hero of the Guards.

Outwardly, George possessed the charismatic traits of a young English aristocrat: an easy self-assurance, a love of fun, a good-natured charm. But he had been destined from an early age to lift the burden of head of the family from his mother. Like many growing up under the weight of responsibility, there was something driven about him, and this sat poorly with his aristocratic exterior. During a summer game of cricket at Moulsey Hurst, in Surrey, where he played on the Duke of Cumberland's side, his charm slipped. A spectator described his "brutal ill temper," even to Cumberland, who as team captain was not aggressive enough for George. "I fancy he rather prefers the profit of a Woburn match [on which bets were placed] . . . to the honour he gains" playing for the duke, added the onlooker in disgust.[27] Perhaps George's display of temper was indeed directed at his royal captain, or perhaps he was simply frustrated at having the game called off because of rain. The spectator did not mistake George's ungentlemanly urge to win. On the afternoon of the rematch a week later, after a victory for Cumberland's side, George scheduled another game, this time as captain of his own team against the Earl of Sandwich. He won again.[28]

Eighteenth-century cricket matches were often played for high stakes, adding to the pressure and excitement. This was clearly to George's taste. A total of £20,000 had been at stake in a match that took place in 1751 between Eton and "the Rest of England," at which George had played for his old school. Over the summer, his Eton team played subsequent matches at Woburn and elsewhere, always for money.[29] In autumn of the same year, he threw himself into the hunting season and was injured in a fall from his horse that kept him confined until December.[30] The young war veteran was making a reputation for himself as one who was determined to succeed at whatever he did. George was bred to be an aristocrat, but the urge to excel that was born of his childhood circumstances was not characteristic of his class. It was, however, a key element of his personality, and one that would affect his destiny.

George had decisively entered into his legacy as the 3rd Viscount Howe, but his mother, the Dowager Lady Howe, continued actively to support him. Since becoming a Lady of the Bedchamber to the Princess Augusta in 1743, Charlotte Howe had cultivated powerful connections at court, which was crucial for her sons, since the king controlled promotion in the armed forces. Charlotte, skillful as always at negotiating court life, was able to maintain good relations with both branches of a royal family that was deeply riven by conflict.

The Princess Augusta was the widow of Frederick, Prince of Wales, and the mother of the future George III. Her marriage had aligned her with the political opposition; in the tradition of the Hanoverian royal family, Crown Prince Frederick and his father, George II, had hated one another. Frederick's royal household of Leicester House became a rival court for those who opposed his father's government.[31]

Frederick's death in 1751 did nothing to change his widow's dislike of the king and his policies. Although a German princess, Augusta was not a Hanoverian. She was born in the principality of Saxe-Gotha. In 1755, she saw Newcastle's attempt to postpone war with France as a contemptible display of weakness that would come back to haunt her son when he at last ascended the throne.[32] Augusta had influence in Parliament, and William Pitt had visited Leicester House on a quest for support while preparing for his attack on Newcastle in the House of Commons on October 13.[33] Pitt was a familiar figure in the household of the princess, having served earlier as a Groom of the Bedchamber to Prince Frederick. So Lady Howe and her son George were well acquainted with the man who made himself a thorn in the side of the administration.

But Lady Howe also had ties to a powerful woman in the opposite camp. The strong friendship between Lady Howe and Amalie von Wallmoden, Countess of Yarmouth, has been overlooked by court biographers. Lady Yarmouth had arrived in London from Hanover in 1738, to be installed as the mistress of George II after the death of Queen Caroline. It is not surprising that Lady Yarmouth was drawn to the company of Charlotte Howe, for the two women had much in common. Close in age, both were German-speaking Hanoverians. Each was accustomed to life at court, and each had grandmothers who had been mistresses to the royal heads of the House of Hanover.[34] Their friendship would remain strong even after the death of George II in 1760, when Lady Yarmouth became Charlotte Howe's neighbor in Albemarle Street, and the two women dined together frequently.[35] When she returned to Hanover in 1763, Lady Yarmouth would choose Lady Howe to be her sole traveling companion.

Lady Yarmouth lacked the political acumen of Queen Caroline, but she was an effective conduit to the king, sought after by politicians on all sides, including William Pitt. She proved to be adept at persuading the stubborn King George to change his mind.[36] In sharp contrast to the late Queen Caroline, who had detested her own son Frederick, Lady Yarmouth urged conciliation with Leicester House.[37] This made her doubly useful, as one who could influence the king and act as an intermediary between royal households that had become uncomfortably polarized.

Lady Howe's foothold in the king's Court of St. James's went beyond her friendship with the royal mistress, for she had two sons in service to George II. In his military capacity, George Howe served the king's favorite son—a man intensely disliked by Princess Augusta—Prince William Augustus, Duke of Cumberland, known to posterity as "Butcher Cumberland" for his part in the brutal repression of Scotland's 1745 Jacobite rising. William Howe served as a page of honor to the king for more than two years, until he began his army career in 1746. With service at the Court of St. James's and at Leicester House, the Howes risked alienating both branches of the dysfunctional royal family. But at the age of fifty-one, Lady Howe had learned her life lessons well. Unlike her neurotic mother, she managed to negotiate her way through the sinuous royal relationships with great aplomb. Her friendships in both camps of the divided court allowed her to have influence without the disadvantage of being compelled to take sides.

She would need to be discreet, of course, for her service at Leicester House placed her constantly in the company of others and within earshot of gossip and intrigue. A lady of the bedchamber was in attendance throughout the day, assisting her queen or princess when dressing and dining, accompanying her when she went out of doors, and performing formal introductions at court events. In essence, she was a species of high-ranking servant whose task was to see that her mistress wanted for nothing, was treated with proper ceremony always and everywhere, and looked every inch her rank. While at Leicester House, Lady Howe was engaged in a continuous round of cardplaying and dinners, walks in the royal gardens followed by supper and polite conversation with whomever the princess cared to invite, outings to shows and entertainments of Augusta's choosing. She had to understand without being told when to keep quiet and when to withdraw from earshot during the frequent discussions of politics at the "young court" (as Leicester House was called).[38]

During the eighteenth century, there was a trend for the duties attached to these coveted posts to become merely ceremonial. Ladies of the bedchamber were supposed to oversee the emptying of the royal chamber pot; in practice, they merely observed while a bedchamber woman carried out the unpleasant task. A lady-in-waiting, when she assisted at the *toilette* of her royal mistress, typically did nothing more than hand over an article of clothing or two and a fan, while humble bedchamber women and personal maids dressed the royal hair and pulled on the ponderous items of clothing that were a feature of the era.[39] In theory, more could be required; Queen Caroline, it was said, out of spite requested her husband's mistress, Lady Suffolk, to kneel before her with a basin of water while Her Majesty washed.[40]

Charlotte's pay was £400 a year, much of which went toward purchase of the formal court attire that was required of the position. Royal birthdays, drawing rooms, and other special court occasions required prescribed dress. Members of the aristocracy were expected to shine at these public displays. The cost of just the fabric for a gown—silk or velvet with gold or silver embroidery—could amount to hundreds of pounds, and the elaborate trimmings of buttons, lace, buckles, along with shoes, stockings, wigs, and jewelry, meant that a lady of the bedchamber could easily spend her entire annual salary on dress.[41] The real value of the position was that it gave one the much-sought-after influence that was the key ingredient in the aristocratic jockeying for places and positions.

In her early years of service, Lady Howe lived at Leicester House when she was attending on the princess. She was in the royal bedchamber throughout the night that the infant Prince Frederick was born in 1750.[42] But however easy or onerous the service—and the burden was largely determined by the character of the royal personage in question—ladies of the bedchamber served in turns, their schedules allowing a week or more off duty at a time.[43] It was a life that called for tact, forbearance, and a substantial loss of privacy. In the diary of a courtier at Leicester House, Lady Howe comes across as reticent and courteous, in a setting where many were outspoken about their political views.[44]

Intriguingly, though, Lady Howe's behavior while in service at Leicester House may not always have been impeccable. Her name is linked with the one scandal in the life of her employer, the famously upright Dowager Princess of Wales. In the late summer of 1755, while the threat of war rumbled across the land, rumors began circulating of an improper relationship between Augusta and John Stuart, 3rd Earl of Bute, tutor and adviser to her son, the Prince of Wales—and a married man. There is no doubt that Bute was a confidant of the princess, and a father figure to her son George. But the stories that there was something more between the princess and her favorite took root, even outliving both of them. Georgian society relished a scandal, but it also dreaded political conspiracy, and the idea grew that Augusta and her adulterous lover might seek to control the prince and, in due course, the throne. This adultery-and-conspiracy narrative was so successfully promulgated by that most literate gossip Horace Walpole that it survived into the twentieth century, when most historians finally dismissed it.[45]

A curious and little-known version of the story has it that Bute was first the lover of Lady Howe, who was for a time his "protectress" in the princess's household and passed him over to her mistress unwillingly.[46] We could dismiss this as mere nonsense, but it is the sole instance of Lady Howe's name being linked with gossip, let alone scandal. If it was a fabrication, Lady Howe was a strange choice as its subject, for Augusta was known to be closest to another of her ladies-in-waiting, Lady Middlesex, whose name was already linked with an adulterous affair.[47]

What is certain is that in the late summer of 1755, while Richard Howe chased French men-of-war in the North Atlantic and George fretted over the subsidy treaties, Lady Yarmouth was endorsing the rumor about the princess and Bute in high circles. Her source, however, has never been identified. Historians and contemporaries alike have presumed it was servants' gossip, a suggestion that fits with the idea that the accusation was spurious.[48] But the surviving kernel of gossip associating Lady Howe with this highly private business hints at a more credible authority. Perhaps it was she who first whispered it to Lady Yarmouth, and over time her connection with the rumor ensnared Lady Howe in the guilt.

If her source was Lady Howe, Lady Yarmouth had good reason to take the story seriously, and to be sure to make use of it. Gossip was valuable political currency in court circles, where outward behavior was closely watched. At any rate, it was a curious episode, a damaging smear on Augusta's reputation that she must have found humiliating, and one that followed her to the grave. A recent historian has pointed out that she could have easily extinguished it by simply dismissing Bute from her household, ending with the ambiguous conclusion, "No one but Augusta and Bute will ever know the true nature of their friendship."[49] Perhaps the widowed dowager princess did have a brief affair. And in the same vein, perhaps Lady Howe allowed herself a fling in middle age; she was by now too old to bear children, a fact of life that, in an era without effective birth control, was often seen as an opportunity to enjoy a fuller sex life. Bute was ten years her junior, well educated, good-looking, and, though reserved in public, very engaging in private.[50]

The rumors about Bute coincided with Lady Howe's release from the strictures of Scrope Lord Howe's will, which stipulated that she would lose custody of her children if she remarried or returned to Hanover before the youngest had reached the age of majority. It was not uncommon for such a condition, designed to prevent a second marriage, to be included in wills of the period.[51] Since Lady Howe's youngest child, Mary, had turned twenty-one in 1755, the mother of eight may have finally felt entitled to indulge her own inclinations in this most private sphere of her life. In any case, Lady Howe, after almost a decade of service under the Princess Augusta, was probably looking forward to scaling down her role as matriarch of the Howe dynasty. By the age of fifty, she was no longer residing at Leicester House, and her duties had been reduced to a token presence at court.[52]

THE HOWE MEN, by now in the midst of their careers, spent much of their time in exclusively male environments: the navy, the army, or the merchant marine; clubs and taverns; the House of Commons and the hurly-burly of electioneering. But this by no means severed their ties with the women of the family. None of the Howe men could afford to maintain independent establishments of their own. When the brothers were on leave from their professions, it was to a mother, an aunt, or a sister that they went. Lady Howe's residence in Albemarle Street, Aunt Juliana Page's country place at Battlesden, and Caroline's Buckinghamshire manor at Hanslope were places to go to rest and relax, but they were also locales that replicated much of the same social and political maneuvering that the brothers were engaged in elsewhere.

At a time when dedicated government buildings were almost nonexistent—when the House of Commons met in a cramped, uncomfortable chamber that had once served as a chapel in the ancient Palace of Westminster, and politicking necessarily spilled out into London's all-male clubs and coffeehouses—a great deal of public business was also transacted in private settings: dinners, house parties, afternoon visits. This gave women many informal levers of influence. Society gatherings, so frequently the

venues for political networking and political business, were largely organized by women; high-profile hostesses were important connections for
aspirational men during the Georgian era. Yet the "social politics" that
took place under the auspices of private hospitality defies precise historical
assessment or quantification.[53]

Reconstructing the private places and spaces occupied by the extended
Howe family, both male and female, restores to the women the significant
roles they played in the family fortunes. It also re-creates the world that
the brothers actually lived in and knew, removing them from the narrow
context of military camps and parliamentary politics that has served as a
backdrop for their appearances in every previous history.

As we have seen, throughout the Seven Years' War, Lady Howe remained
the head of the dynasty for the purposes of exerting influence where it mattered and managing her sons' careers. In training to replace her mother
was eldest daughter Caroline. Although she lived in the country, Caroline was ideally situated to keep a finger on the pulse of political trends.
Her husband John Howe's seat of Stokes Manor was a small estate in
Hanslope, Buckinghamshire, the house itself more than two centuries old.
Stokes Manor was rather small and probably past its best days.[54] "[F]right-
ful Hanslop," Caroline once called it.[55] But it was a comfortable life. John
and Caroline joined in all the diversions of the neighborhood—assemblies,
card parties, hunt balls, the excitement of races at Newport Pagnell.[56] As at
Langar, the society in the neighborhood of Hanslope was mixed, cutting
across the ranks of the middle and upper classes. The Howes lived near
enough to the Pages at Battlesden to visit regularly. Hanslope was also close
to the magnificent Stowe House, where Pitt the Elder called upon his politically powerful in-laws, and Caroline was able to report on his comings and
goings to her friends in town.[57]

It was not only over a tea table that Caroline kept pace with men's news
and men's gossip; thirteen years into her marriage, she was still indulging
her love of riding. Out of more than seventy riders of the Belvoir Hunt
listed in 1758, she was the only woman. "Her Husband was a great sports-
man," a contemporary recalled of her at this period in her life, "& Hunted
much with the Old Marquiss of Granby, & at the time she wd. follow him
in the field & afterwards would enjoy the social parties at the table with the
gentlemen." The Belvoir Hunt included two dukes and two marquesses,
clergymen, army officers and county gentry.[58] Caroline and John Howe

followed the life of the rural gentry and nobility, staying for long periods at Grantham, the estate of John Manners, the Marquess of Granby, or at the elegant country seats of the Duke of Grafton or Lord Spencer, all of whom were keen hunters. At any of these places, discussion of sport, cards, and society doings would be interspersed with a strong dose of politics, for these foxhunting noblemen were all leading Whig politicians.

But John Howe's interests also took him where Caroline could not follow. He was a founding member of the famous Society of Dilettanti, a dining club created in the 1730s by young gentlemen who had taken the grand tour to Italy. The society's nominal objective was to promote appreciation of classical art in Britain. They had a great deal of fun while doing it, the members deliberately courting the image of privileged men who defied conventional morality. Club accessories were laden with rather juvenile pornographic jests. Horace Walpole sneered that the real club activity was "being drunk." The Dilettanti, however, did transform the study of archaeology during the eighteenth century, funding research expeditions to Italy and Greece.[59] The notorious Francis Dashwood—best remembered for hosting the Monks of Medmenham Abbey, a club that reputedly staged orgies against a backdrop of obscene art and satanism—designed the apt motto of the Dilettanti, *Seria Ludo* (Serious Play). They drank as much as Horace Walpole thought they did, and the society included well-known womanizers, chief among them Dashwood, the Earl of Sandwich, and Lord Middlesex, who was known to have misused the funds of an opera company to pay for the "secret services" of his Italian mistress.[60]

Caroline had a reasonable idea of what went on at the Dilettanti proceedings, despite the "men-only" rule. Her life connected with that of the members in many ways. Her friend the Marquess of Granby was a Dilettanti, and the wife of the philandering Lord Middlesex served at court alongside Lady Howe. While John Howe met such men at the exclusive society meetings, Caroline's correspondence reveals that she met their wives in drawing rooms and across card tables.[61] In such a tight-knit set, the inevitable pillow-talk between husbands and wives did the rest, and the ladies could pool information on the secret activities of their Dilettanti spouses. Caroline was probably not shocked. Contemporary remarks make it clear that she was not one who affected ladylike delicacy.

Caroline Howe at Hanslope—whether in the field following the hunt or mixing with the Dilettanti members and their wives—was always certain to be in a position to be well informed. She became renowned as a letter-writer and a reliable purveyor of the latest social and political news, a reputation that gave her a purchase in the circles of the politically active. When her brothers George, Richard, William, or Thomas arrived to visit Caroline, they could easily blend in with the country society of Buckinghamshire.

It was while staying at his sister's home that Captain Richard Howe experienced what was probably his first courtship, a hurried affair conducted as the nation moved toward war. The young lady who caught his eye was Elizabeth Raper, the niece of Matthew Raper, an astronomer and a Fellow of the Royal Society. Matthew Raper was a relative of the Pages, and a close friend of John Howe, who shared his interest in the latest scientific discoveries.[62] The Raper house, Thorley Hall in Hertfordshire, where Caroline and her husband often stayed, was a showcase for intensive European exploration, a household full of curios, books, coins, and rare objects. The hall itself was topped by an astronomical observatory.[63]

Richard met Elizabeth Raper while on leave at Hanslope in early 1756. He barely had time to court her, for he was ashore only a few months before the *Dunkirk* sailed from Plymouth in March under Vice Admiral Hawke's command, cruising the western approaches to the English Channel and the Bay of Biscay for French ships. By May, Richard was back for refurbishment, and by the time the *Dunkirk* left Portsmouth on June 16, war had been declared with France. For the next four months, he would be at sea protecting the Channel Islands and blockading the coasts of Brittany and Normandy.[64]

Despite their brief encounters, Richard had clearly made an impression on Elizabeth Raper; by the autumn of that year, she confessed to her "dearest friend"—his sister Caroline—that she was in love with him. "Mrs Howe got the grand secret from me," she confided to her diary. "Cried and was pitied." A few days later, Caroline and John Howe accompanied Elizabeth on a visit to the Pages at Battlesden, where she nurtured her infatuation by going over Richard's customary walk alone by moonlight. "[I]t was a favorite walk of Captain Howe's," she had been told, and "the last time he was there he used to walk for hours in the wood every night."

Caroline, well informed as always on the movements of her brothers, was able to give notice to her young friend when Richard came ashore at Plymouth to refit for four days in October, but if they met, the diary is silent. In fact, it seemed that Richard had forgotten all about her. When next the *Dunkirk* put in at Portsmouth Dockyard, in early 1757, he did not even make an appearance. "Damned mad in my mind, and do not care 3 straws if I never see him again;—damn all the sex!" exclaimed Elizabeth to her diary at the end of March. She did not mean it, of course, but their courtship fizzled out. Like many servicemen on the eve of war, Richard may have resolved to get married. His flirtation with Elizabeth Raper was hot on the heels of his celebrity as the captor of the *Alcide*. Judging by the other *affaires de coeur* recorded in her diary, it was encouraged by a great deal of "kissing and squeezing," favors she granted other gentlemen even while she still had hopes for Richard. But whatever went on in early 1756, Elizabeth Raper clearly expected him to make a formal declaration.[65] Richard, however, as will be seen, would manage to get enough shore leave during the war to find a woman more to his liking.

What of Caroline's other brothers? Thomas, the other mariner in the Howe family, was just twenty-five when war was declared. He had probably been serving on merchant vessels since leaving Eton in 1743. Thomas's first command was as captain of the East Indiaman the *Winchelsea*.[66] By sailing eastward, he was not, of course, sailing away from war, for Anglo-French rivalry extended to India. The notorious episode of the Black Hole of Calcutta in 1756 would be one of several national catastrophes for Britain at the outset of the conflict. But service in the East India Company was not likely to earn glory at home, and Thomas was the only Howe brother who did not emerge from the Seven Years' War as a national hero.

At the start of the war, William Howe was with the 20th Regiment of Foot, commanded by Lieutenant Colonel James Wolfe, who would one day achieve fame as the general who captured Quebec from the French. He and William had been stationed together in Scotland in 1750, effectively in an army of occupation following the Jacobite rebellions. By the winter of 1755–56, the 20th Foot was on the Kent coast, seventy miles from London, preparing for a French invasion, for there was ominous activity across the channel at Dunkirk. Wolfe was just two years older than his junior officer Captain William Howe, and the two had sharply contrasting personalities: Wolfe, the only surviving son of an army officer, was hypercritical, moody, and intolerant of others; William, the younger brother in a large family, was easygoing, fun-loving, and affable—"the sweet William," as Caroline called him.[67]

Wolfe drilled his men hard, and he and William must have found their relative proximity to London a welcome diversion. The two officers must have gone to the capital whenever they could. There they would have met with other Howe family members. No correspondence survives between Wolfe and George Lord Howe, but their friendship has been presumed by historians because of the close-knit nature of the British officer corps, and Wolfe's unstinting admiration of George expressed in his letters to others.[68] A 1755 letter from Wolfe to his mother, discussing what to do with his unmanageable pack of nine dogs, provides a glimpse of a relationship that was on a familiar footing; he begged her to keep two puppies, promising that "Sancho" would go to Lord Howe.[69]

Looking beyond the handful of surviving letters, the shared family and social connections of the two men reveal far more about their relationship. They must have known one another well, for their personal lives intermingled in many ways. Wolfe and his parents knew wealthy Sir Gregory Page, and Aunt Juliana and Uncle Thomas Page of Battlesden.[70] And General Sir John Mordaunt, a patron and friend of Wolfe, was connected to the Howe circle through the marriage of their Aunt Anne to Colonel Charles Mordaunt.[71] The Howe women would have met the young Wolfe frequently in Mordaunt's London drawing room, for in 1747 Wolfe fell in love with the general's niece, Elizabeth Lawson, who was also a maid of honor serving alongside Lady Howe at Leicester House. Wolfe pined for Miss Lawson for several years, and Lady Howe, Caroline, William, and George must have listened to his recitals of her many perfections.[72]

By the time war broke out in 1756, Wolfe was over Elizabeth Lawson. The attention of Wolfe and the Howe brothers during these momentous days was wholly directed toward the conflict with France. As they gathered together in the London homes of the Pages or Lady Howe, the conversation must have been exciting and intense—and frightening—as the young officers exchanged opinions on developments around the globe, the talk at court, and the concerns of senior officers such as the Duke of Cumberland, who as captain-general of the army had a leading role in defense planning. Cumberland had been concerned since the 1755 massacre of Braddock's Road with the problem of waging war in the wilds of America. The vast forested terrain and indigenous methods of warfare, so successfully adapted by the French, presented new challenges to British troops. Some hoped that British colonists steeped in Indian methods could be put to use, but Cumberland believed that regular British troops must ultimately master wilderness skills in order to achieve victory over France in America.[73]

Caroline would have frequently been present, for she and her husband stayed with Lady Howe in Albemarle Street when they were in London. No doubt she listened closely; her subsequent correspondence shows that she paid careful attention to her brothers' military business. For Londoners like Caroline and her mother and sisters, fighting on the colonial frontier was a vivid and bloody drama. In this conflict, America, not Flanders, was to be the new theater of war, and the savages of the New World supposedly practiced warfare with a ferocity unparalleled in the history of Europe.[74] If the Howe brothers avoided the gory details of combat in America as they talked in the drawing rooms of family members, the British press did not. Newspapers gave grisly details of actual combat, the facts of which would have been known to British servicemen, who could not contradict them. Accounts proliferated of attacks on Indian settlements with no quarter given, dwellings burned with the inhabitants inside, and scalps taken; and Indian murders of settler women and children on the colonial frontier. Scalpings became the gruesome emblem of Britain's latest foe in the minds of Britons on the home front. A military family whose conversation always readily turned to the growing war could never entirely avert a visceral consciousness of such horrors.[75]

The Howe women must have heard from their brothers and their circle of friends in the armed forces that Prime Minister Newcastle and his cabinet were getting it badly wrong as the nation moved toward global war. William Pitt jeered that the ministers "shift and shuffle." He had been shouting for months that the real objective of the French was not Kent, where William and his regiment under Wolfe were preparing to oppose invasion, but the island of Minorca. And this proved to be true; the French soldiers encamped across the English Channel served as a ruse to divert attention from their true target. In fact, on April 18, 1756, the French landed unopposed on Minorca. Just in case the island should be attacked, Admiral John Byng had been sent there with an ill-conditioned squadron of ten ships, and they were unable to prevent its fall. Byng was arrested as soon as he returned home and was tried for failing to do his utmost to assist the garrison. The ill-fated admiral's controversial execution on the quarterdeck of his own flagship in Portsmouth Harbor on March 14, 1757, did nothing to quiet the national outrage at seeing the French everywhere victorious.[76] Pitt as usual expressed the mood of the nation, pronouncing, "In every quarter of the world we are inferior to France."[77]

By the time the news of the fall of Minorca reached London in June 1756, war had already been declared. The nation was soon reeling from more bad news from America. The French had swooped down on Fort Oswego, a western outpost in the colony of New York, capturing it in August. On the continent, the upshot of all the labyrinthine maneuverings after subsidy treaties had resulted in only one British ally, Prussia. Its ruler, Frederick the Great, chose to forestall attacks from his enemies in Russia and Austria by invading Saxony at the end of August 1756, and Britain was now committed to a war on the Continent whether it liked it or not.[78]

The nation seemed rudderless in its hour of need. Newcastle resigned in November, and a new ministry headed by William Pitt and Whig leader William Cavendish, 4th Duke of Devonshire, began the next month. Three months later, George Howe was bound for America, a colonel in command of the 3rd battalion in the newly created Royal American Regiment.[79] The Royal Americans, raised in the wake of General Edward Braddock's defeat, were designed to meld the discipline of the British regular with the wilderness qualities of woodland scouts. The regiment was the brainchild of the British-serving Swiss officer Colonel Henry Bouquet, a friend of the Duke of Cumberland.[80]

George Howe was almost certainly handpicked by the duke to join the Royal Americans. Evidently Cumberland had forgiven the young Lord Howe for voting with Pitt (whom the duke detested) over the subsidy treaty, and for losing his temper at His Grace over a cricket match. As the newly promoted young colonel readied himself to depart for America in late March 1757, Cumberland placed in his hands a letter for the commander in chief in America, John Campbell, 4th Earl of Loudoun: "You will receive this Letter, by the Hands of Lord Howe, whom the King has been pleased to appoint to one of the American Batt[alion]s in the Room of Colonel *Jefferays*. I need not recommend him to you as you know him already. You will find him an intelligent, capable & willing officer, & can not help hoping that it will come to his Lot, to command one of the *Batt[alion]s*, that will be employ'd upon Servi[c]es."[81]

There can be no doubt that George was fully aware of the ideas being exchanged between Cumberland and his deputy in America on the army's urgent need to acquire fighting skills suited to the wildernesses of the New World. George would prove to be a credit to the duke's sagacity—the perfect choice to enter the kaleidoscope of cultures and peoples that were now assembling to wage a war against the French in America.

Four

World War

The Seven Years' War was Britain's first true world war. Three of the Howe brothers—George, Richard, and William—would emerge from the conflict as household names in Britain and America, with reputations as daring men of action and epitomes of English heroism. The Howe family itself would come to be seen as the personification of a stoical British military dynasty. Notably, George Lord Howe's exploits would make him "the most liked and admired British soldier ever to serve alongside Americans."[1] The dangers and privations experienced by the Howes as they ascended to hero status are largely forgotten today, and they deserve to be revisited. The immense risks and grueling suffering they underwent would be glossed over during the American Revolutionary War by pro-American propagandists.

The war brought military actions in North America, the West Indies, Africa, India, and the Philippines, but Britain would confront its greatest challenges on land in the American theater of operations. Collisions between alien cultures in the hothouse atmosphere of war presented special problems. The British war effort in North America during the Seven Years' War pulled together a mix of diverse peoples, many of whom had lived in the vicinity of one another with varying degrees of friction and now had to unite against a common foe. These included Native Americans, indispensable to the European armies for their skills in the exotic terrain of the American backwoods; colonial soldiers with their own local notions of military discipline, and their social divergences from the regular British rank and file; backwoods irregulars called rangers, who were another species of colonial fighting man; kilted Highland regiments, relocated from the relatively recent war in the glens of Scotland; and, finally, the British army itself, with its aristocratic officer ranks and redcoat enlisted men, some of whom had signed up to escape a level of poverty almost inconceivable for free whites in the colonies, and who originated not only in the British Isles but also in Europe.[2]

Britain sent to America about twenty-two thousand army regulars, the largest force it had ever dispatched to those shores.[3] Never before had so many been sent to war so far from Britain, and the logistical obstacles were immense. Close cooperation between army and navy—never an easy business—was critical. But for the army and its officers, the greatest problem was adaptation to the conditions of warfare in the American wilderness. The sheer effort of getting armies out into the American wilderness to fight each other was staggering.

A conventional British army moving through hostile territory in Flanders, where George Lord Howe had served during the War of the Austrian Succession, encountered relatively familiar countryside on level roads, with small towns and villages and the possibility of provisions nearby. In stark contrast, the virgin wilderness of frontier America reduced armies to a slow crawl through almost impenetrable forest, involving backbreaking toil, hauling artillery and all of its own food supplies, and sometimes, as in the case of Braddock's ill-fated expedition, cutting its own road as it went.

Flankers and advance guards were needed by any army no matter where it fought, to protect its peripheries from surprise and harassment, and scouting parties would gather intelligence and harass the enemy in turn. In Europe during the last war, conventional armies had employed native irregular fighters such as the Croatian Pandours—recruited to serve Maria Theresa of Austria—or mastered their techniques, like the French Arquebusiers de Grassin, or the skirmishing Miquelets at Bassignano, both of which George would have seen in action on the Continent.[4]

But the American wilderness was a challenge on an entirely new scale for the British army. Without any established system of roads, the British invasion of French Canada had to be confined to the two major waterways of the St. Lawrence River, or the Lake George–Lake Champlain–Richelieu River corridor. The latter route necessitated transport by water as well as overland. On the rivers and lakes, whaleboats and bateaux carried the entire army, its stores, and its wagons and artillery. On reaching land, the boats had to be unpacked, all the stores had to be repacked into wagons, and the empty boats themselves were then manhandled through the forest. At the next waterway, the whole process had to be reversed. And throughout it all, each army was dependent on scouts versed in woodlore to guard its flanks and sometimes even to tell it where it was. Armies on both sides got lost in the woods.

In addition, the North American climate posed a major problem for the British army, as standard uniforms proved unsuited to the extremes of heat and cold and the swampy, muddy, and rocky terrain. Soldiers donned Native American moccasins and snowshoes in turn to cope with dramatic seasonal fluctuations, or they stripped to their waistcoats to bear the heat of summer.[5]

The best guides in such conditions were Native Americans, but the French had always been better than the British at winning and keeping Indian allies. "[R]eally in Effect we have no *Indians*," lamented Loudoun to Cumberland in late 1756. Loudoun sought to make up the deficiency with a company of colonial American rangers, for "it is impossible for any Army to Act in this Country," without one or the other.[6] A few months later, Cumberland sent him a young officer whose enthusiasm would lead the way in introducing new fighting techniques to the British army in America: George Lord Howe.

GEORGE REACHED HALIFAX, Nova Scotia, in July 1757 with a Royal Navy squadron sent to reinforce Lord Loudoun, who was planning a strike against Louisbourg, the nearby French fortress and naval support base on the coast of Cape Breton Island. The campaign had to be abandoned, however, because delays and fog had allowed the French to reinforce their position. By August, Loudoun had returned to New York, leaving most of his army to winter in Halifax. George left, too, disembarking at Boston in early August, where the newspapers reported that he was bound inland for "the forts at Lake George." He probably went directly to Fort Edward on the frontier of New York province, because on September 28 he was made a colonel in the 55th Regiment of Foot stationed there.[7]

It would be an exciting posting for George. Just a few weeks earlier, Captain Robert Rogers, head of the famed Rogers' Rangers, had officially launched a company of volunteers, based at Fort Edward, whose remit was to teach British regular soldiers ranging techniques. George had already met Rogers in Halifax, where he and his colonial rangers were serving alongside the British army. They had probably discussed Rogers's plan to launch an innovative seven-week course to train fifty-five "gentleman" volunteers

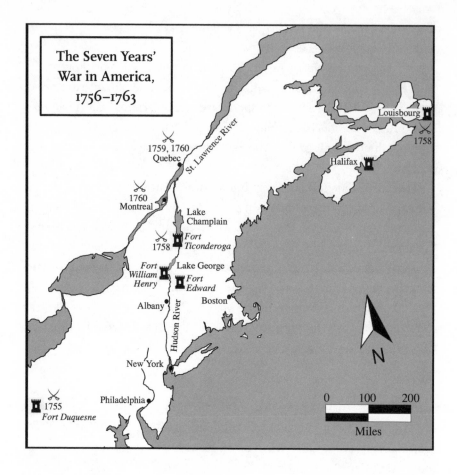

The Seven Years'
War in America,
1756–1763

Louisbourg

1758

1759, 1760
Quebec

St. Lawrence River

Halifax

1760
Montreal

Lake
Champlain

1758 Fort
Ticonderoga

Fort   Lake George
William   Fort
Henry   Edward

Albany   Boston

Hudson River

New York

Philadelphia

1755
Fort Duquesne

N

0   100   200

Miles

from the British regiments in wilderness fighting skills. George was too senior to volunteer, but that did not prevent him from diving in; as winter approached, the rangers were on duty patrolling the woods between Fort Edward and the French-held Fort Ticonderoga. "In one of these parties," wrote Captain Rogers, "My Lord Howe did us the honour to accompany us, being fond, as he expressed himself, to learn our method of marching, ambushing, retreating, &c. and, upon our return, expressed his good opinion of us very generously."[8]

Now George began to apply what he was learning from Rogers to his own regiment, the 55th Foot, turning it in effect into a light infantry regiment. The changes were designed to enable the soldiers to move quickly and effectively through the woods. Hat brims were trimmed; hair was cropped short, a practice that aroused derision in a period when gentlemen wore their hair long. Coats were cut to the waist, heavy braid and sashes were discarded, buckskin and protective leggings replaced army-issue breeches and gaiters. Even muskets were cut down to make them lighter, and the metal barrels were blackened to keep them from flashing in sunlight. Soldiers learned to march, shoot, and ambush in small parties in heavily forested terrain. George was not the only British officer interested in developing light infantry, but he was unparalleled in inspiring a tradition-bound army to adopt the reforms. He was charismatic, beloved by his own soldiers and the provincial Americans alike, and he enforced the changes without respect to rank. The reforms in dress and living arrangements lessened the distinction between officers and men. "You could not distinguish us from common plough men," wrote one officer.[9] When confronted with officers who refused to obey, George had them arrested "for setting a bad example to the army."[10]

At home in England, George's mother, aunt, and sisters waited with great impatience and anxiety for news of their prodigy's daring activities. The few surviving private letters of George Howe suggest that he was a poor correspondent. In a letter from Albany to his Aunt Juliana Page in March 1758, he began, "You are very good to take any notice of me, for I really do not deserve to be remembered at Battlesden." He must have known that he was rarely out of their thoughts, but he went on in the same disingenuous vein, saying that he had "deferred writing" in hopes of having a letter to send that was "worth reading." "I have been cruelly disappointed," he said, and ended his letter of just four sentences with his respects.[11] Juliana must have been cruelly disappointed by the brief contents. George's own disappointment had been caused by the cancellation of the winter campaign against Fort Ticonderoga that he and Loudoun had been planning.[12] A stone fortification constructed by the French at the southern end of Lake Champlain, Ticonderoga was a wilderness outpost of crucial strategic significance in the fight to control the rear of the British colonies.

At least the family at home had the newspapers for information about their beloved George, for he was becoming something of a celebrity. The papers had been predicting a "Campaign in the Snow, under my Lord Howe, and Capt. Rogers, a famous Partisan." Lord Howe, the papers said, "has, ever since his Arrival in America, gained the Affections of the People here more than any other Military Gentleman that ever came from Europe;

Fatigue to him is trifling; and a Bear's Skin and the soft side of a Board is as agreeable to him as a Bed of Down."[13]

Did his family guess his hardships when they read that, under his command, even the officers slept in tents and ate the king's plain provisions, their clothing limited to a change of shirts and stockings, liquor prohibited, and the women camp-followers excluded? George set the example by washing his own shirts in nearby waterways and baking crude cakes of flour and water over a fire; word of this even reached the ears of an enemy Frenchman, who, impressed, described George as "strong-willed and highly admired."[14]

One wonders whether Caroline laughed to picture her brother, always surrounded by admiring women at home, scrubbing his own linen and trying to learn the art of making drop scones on heated rocks. But, interspersed with these colorful stories, there were reminders of the real and present danger: attacks by a hidden enemy, scalpings, ambushes. The notorious massacre at Fort William Henry of English prisoners by Indian allies of the French had shocked Britain and its colonies in the summer of 1757 and heightened anti-French feeling. The *Derby Mercury*, reporting on the example set by George in camp, concluded with an account of recent scalpings and murders by Indians who had been believed to be "our Friends."[15]

By the time George wrote to Aunt Juliana in March 1758, he had become a brigadier general, and Lord Loudoun had been recalled to England. William Pitt was now secretary of state in a new administration that he shared with his old foe the Duke of Newcastle—a surprising political alliance that would last until Britain won the war. The recall of Loudoun was somewhat unfair, for he had established the groundwork for much of the future success of the campaigns in America, but Pitt was impatient—the next campaign had to be a success—and Loudoun had a hostile relationship with the American colonies that were supposed to provide him essential aid and assistance. Frustrated by what he saw as their parochial attitudes toward the common cause, Loudoun acted out the stereotype of the haughty British officer, his tactlessness hindering the war effort.

Pitt moved quickly to get past the problems hindering Anglo-American cooperation, offering subsidies to the colonial governments in return for troops. He also removed the humiliating condition of colonial military service stipulating that all colonial officers of whatever rank were beneath the rank of a British regular captain.[16] Pitt wanted active, ambitious command-ers who would get the job done, and Lieutenant General John Ligonier, who had recently replaced the Duke of Cumberland as commander in chief of the army, agreed with him. An obstacle to this positive strategy was the conventional King George II, who valued long-serving, experienced officers over youth and panache.[17]

Lady Yarmouth's close friendship with Lady Howe explains the path by which the young Lord Howe, despite the king's misgivings, came to be appointed as the guiding light for the forthcoming 1758 campaign against Ticonderoga. For it was Lady Yarmouth who persuaded her royal lover to give Howe the position of second-in-command, with the older and unimag-inative Major General James Abercromby only nominally in charge. Else-where, in keeping with Pitt's wishes, the same arrangement was used when the dynamic James Wolfe was promoted to brigadier general under Major General Jeffery Amherst for the 1758 Louisbourg campaign.[18]

A well-known description of George on campaign in the summer of 1758 comes from the journal of a young provincial soldier from Connecti-cut whose regiment formed part of the force sent to Ticonderoga. George, he wrote, was "the idol of the army":

> From the few days I had to observe his manner of conducting, it is not extravagant to suppose that every soldier in the army had a per-sonal attachment to him. He frequently came among the carpenters, and his manner was so easy and familiar that you lost all that con-straint or diffidence we feel when addressed by our superiors, whose manners are forbidding.[19]

That was the thing: George had a talent for meeting people at their own level. His social versatility made him admirably suited to promote inno-vations that blurred the distinction between officers and men. No wonder Abercromby's army, assembling at Albany, New York, in June 1758, gravi-tated to him as their natural leader. They numbered seventeen thousand all told—British regular and light infantry, Highland regiments, companies of rangers and Stockbridge Indians, provincial troops from New York and New England—all coming together for the business of making war against the French.[20] As one historian put it, George "fully understood that if he gave provincial soldiers what they expected from their leaders, they would follow willingly."[21] The force of his personality inspired his multicultural army to work well together.

In Albany, civilians also were charmed. George befriended Madame Margarita Schuyler, matriarch of one of the town's leading families. She adored him—his gentle manners, his fine hair, his sense of justice, his willingness to share the hardships of his men in contrast to some of the other officers—and he was not too proud to accept advice and counsel from those best qualified to know, including Madame Schuyler herself. To her delight, he called her "Aunt Schuyler," not realizing that George came from a world where aunts were the authority figures.

On the night before the army was to move from Albany, Madame Schuyler had a serious conversation with the young brigadier general, cautioning him about the dangers of his expedition. George knew the dangers just as well as she possibly could, but he evidently listened with the utmost politeness. The next morning, she presented him with a full breakfast ("he smiled and said he would not disappoint her, as it was hard to say when he might again breakfast with a lady"), and, having accepted her farewell tears and embraces, he was off.[22] Yet it was not so much the upcoming hazards that George needed to bear in mind, but rather his own inborn impetuosity.

By July 5, Abercromby's army was encamped at Lake George, a thirty-two-mile-long lake in northeastern New York that drains into the much larger Lake Champlain. In a carefully planned and executed operation, hundreds of boats, forming a mile-wide flotilla, were ready to transport the troops over water. Twenty-five miles up the lake, the army disembarked and set up camp, pitched tents, lit fires, and appeared to settle down for the night.

Captain John Stark of Rogers' Rangers later recalled that night. Lord Howe lay on a bearskin "(his Lordship's camp bed)" discussing the tactics for the next day.[23] But the English lord and the New England scout could not have conferred for long, for their encampment was a ruse. The entire army reembarked under cover of darkness, while the fires still burned, and slipped past the watching French scouts. At dawn on July 6, Abercromby's waterborne army was spotted by French advance posts at the north end of Lake George. Abercromby and Howe were delighted to find that the French had retreated before them, burning their entrenched camps as they went. Everything was going according to plan.[24]

Once the army was ashore, just two miles from Fort Ticonderoga,

George lost no time. Rogers' Rangers, together with British skirmishers of the 80th regiment, had gone ahead to secure the area. George formed the main army into three columns, putting himself at the head of a fourth, made up of American provincial rangers and soldiers. It was two in the afternoon by the time all was ready. The objective was to trap the French on the peninsula where Ticonderoga stood. As the columns moved independently through the woods, a disoriented 350-strong French scouting party, deserted by its Indian guides who chose not to wait for the English juggernaut sailing up Lake George, collided with the American rangers. It was four in the afternoon.

A fierce firefight ensued. Hearing the shots, George, at the head of his column, rushed to the scene. He reached the crest of a hill within sight of the engagement. At that instant, a shot went through his lungs and heart, shattering his backbone. He sprawled on his back, one hand quivered, and George was dead.[25]

When George Augustus Lord Howe died, it was said that the campaign died with him; "the soul of General Abercrombie's army seemed to expire," as one put it.[26] "[M]e Lord was cilled," a foot soldier from Massachusetts wrote simply in his journal, his use of the shortened nomenclature reflecting the affection in the ranks for the aristocratic leader.[27] The campaign had been substantially George's inspiration.

General Abercromby vacillated for a day or two, uncertain of how to proceed without his dynamic young brigadier general. Then, with the poor judgment that so often adds to the horror of war, he decided to launch a frontal assault on an incomplete fortification spotted by his advisers. The result was "the heaviest loss of life that His Majesty's forces sustained during the whole American war," as British and American soldiers were mowed down "like a field of corn." In a series of futile charges on the fort, they found themselves trapped between a murderous wooden abatis of sharpened tree trunks and the incessant fire of the enemy. The British artillery sent by water to provide cover for the assault had been unable to land, neutralized by enemy fire. By the end of that bloody day, more than five hundred American and British soldiers had died, and well over a thousand were wounded. Although they still outnumbered their enemy, the Anglo-American army withdrew to lick its wounds, leaving the French in possession of Ticonderoga, to the joy and astonishment of their commander, the Marquis de Montcalm.[28]

George Lord Howe was only thirty-three when he died. His tragic end perhaps vindicated the reluctance of King George II to appoint young and less experienced officers to high command. Tradition has held that Lord Howe's own impetuosity exposed him to fatal danger. As second in command, he should not have been at the head of any march, but he had insisted and Abercromby had given way—"a stupid mistake" in the verdict of one historian. A week after the disaster, an eyewitness recalled briefly that "Lord Howe was at the head of the Rangers, notwithstanding all the remonstrances made him."[29] American ranger Major Israel Putnam was with George at the moment when they heard the noise of the firefight between the French scouting party and the American advance force. According to Putnam's biographer, the ranger urged Lord Howe to remain behind while he investigated. But "your life is as dear to you as mine is to me. I am determined to go," declared Howe, forging ahead to his death.[30] The story of George's final moments no doubt became embellished over the years, but the implication of rashness has clung to it. Two hundred years later, it was still asserted that George had placed personal bravery ahead of "his responsibility to keep alive" as he pushed into the action.[31] The internal pressure that was an integral part of his character, whether labeled courage or recklessness, had played a part in his death.

By early August, rumors of George's death were reaching the Howe family through the newspapers.[32] Yet rumors were not always credible— back in 1755, the newspapers had even peddled rumors that Richard had been killed when he took the *Alcide*.[33] The family could only sit and wait. Official confirmation reached the government in the third week of August, and word spread quickly. Lady Howe and her daughters were sent a detailed account of George's last moments, written by eyewitness Captain Alexander Moneypenny of the 55th. It was Moneypenny who took charge of the remains; George was to have rested in the family vault at Langar, but the intense heat of that New England summer meant that he was buried at St. Peter's Church in Albany, New York. Only his personal effects went home with his servant Thomas.[34]

William Pitt was distraught. "The loss of Lord Howe afflicts me with more than a public sorrow," he wrote to his brother-in-law George Grenville, who was later to play a leading role in Britain's attempts to tax her American colonies. "He was, by the universal voice of army and people, a character of ancient times: a complete model of military virtue in all its branches. I have the sad task of imparting this cruel event to a brother that loves him most tenderly, because he has himself all the same virtues."[35] Richard, now Commodore Howe, the brother in question, was conducting raids along the French coast and did not hear of George's fate until his flagship, HMS *Essex*, anchored in Portland Roads in Dorset on August 25.[36]

Richard had scant time to grieve for his lost brother. The Duke of Newcastle, as usual full of political intrigue, lost no time in pressuring the new Lord Howe to take George's parliamentary seat at Nottingham. He was "extreamly concern'd" at the death of George Lord Howe, wrote the duke, before hurrying on to his point. Would Richard be willing to vacate his seat at Dartmouth and undergo a by-election for the Nottingham seat left absent by the death of George? Newcastle could not promise success, but he would do his utmost.[37] Even in the face of family tragedy, he could not stop his compulsive politicking.

Richard had been elected MP for the seaport town of Dartmouth the previous year, while he was cruising the Western Approaches of the English Channel. It had been the new administration of Pitt and the Duke of Devonshire, formed on the heels of Newcastle's resignation in 1756, that had recommended him to the borough. It made no difference that Richard was at sea fighting for his country at the time, for he was elected unopposed.[38] Now, a year later, Newcastle was back in office, and, with the news of George's death, he saw a chance to finally help his faithful friend John Plumptre gain a seat in Parliament. Plumptre could have Dartmouth, he reasoned, and Richard could replace his deceased brother in Nottingham. That would make "every thing easy," thought the duke happily.[39]

Even in the midst of her bereavement, Lady Charlotte Howe was too quick for Newcastle. The corporation of Nottingham had turned to the grieving mother rather than the duke to name George's successor, and she had chosen William. She informed Newcastle of her preference, politely hoping it would have "yr Grace's Countenance." Then, in a tactic that did credit to her mentor, Lady Pembroke, she gave the duke a mere week to respond before publishing her own choice in the newspaper, claiming she was obliged to succumb to pressure from the "unanimous, requests I have received from Nottingham, to declare my Son." She flattered herself that she had his grace's approbation. She did not have it, of course—Newcastle thought himself "extremely ill-used" by the town of Nottingham, and he thought the Howes aimed for "too much, to bring in a younger Brother for such a town as Nottingham."[40]

Lady Howe's tactic of using the media to outmaneuver her political opponent was so unusual a step for a Georgian lady that it received widespread notice. Indeed, her one brief foray into the public eye is what she is best remembered for today. Her letter to the voters of Nottingham was succinct, but with a personal touch:

> As Lord Howe is now absent upon the public service, and Lt.-Col. Howe is with his regiment at Louisburg, it rests upon me to beg the favour of your votes and interests, that Lt.-Col. Howe may supply the place of his late brother as your representative in parliament.
>
> Permit me, therefore, to implore the protection of every one of you, as the mother of him whose life has been lost in the service of his country.
>
> Charlotte Howe[41]

As usual, Horace Walpole waxed sarcastic over the affair: "I was really touched with my Lady Howe's advertisement, though I own at first it made me laugh, for seeing an address to the voters for Nottingham signed *Charlotte Howe*, I concluded (they are so manly a family), that Mrs Howe, who rides a fox chase and dines at the *table d'hote* at Grantham, intended to stand for member of parliament."[42] The "Mrs Howe" meant by Walpole was Caroline, a manly enough female, in his opinion, to pass for the opposite sex. Lady Howe's action was unfeminine in his eyes, and he took the opportunity to include Caroline in his sneer at this family of women whose forthright dispositions he found unattractive.

Walpole's witticism is sometimes quoted in the history books alongside Lady Howe's announcement, but in 1758 his feelings did not jibe with those of the rest of the nation at war. Charlotte Howe's appeal was greeted in the newspapers as the natural and becoming act of an afflicted mother; her grief caught the imagination of the public, and inspired poets. In the *Scots Magazine*, the town of Nottingham was exhorted to "Comfort a mother weeping o'er her son" by selecting William as their representative; "She cannot ask a boon and be deny'd."[43] Another writer set in verse an imaginary family tableau in which all the Howes were gathered round the body of George, laid upon a bier. First Lady Howe indicates "the purple stream" that issues from his wound, reminding her children,

> My sons! Your brother dy'd in Honour's cause,
> Obey'd its dictates, and fulfill'd its laws—

She next falls in a faint and the brothers grasp their swords, intent on revenge. The sisters approach George and "Press his cold lips, and kiss his icy hand." Finally the poet reassures his readers:

> Yet boast not, France, of this successful day,
> Brave Richard's acts his brother's debt shall pay.[44]

Lady Howe's assertive foray into a so-called man's world might have been expected to provoke more criticism like Walpole's, because the defeats that marked Britain's first years of the Seven Years' War had aroused national self-scrutiny and widespread indictments of the nation's degeneration in heavily gendered terms. Britain was becoming effeminate, emasculated, "a Nation which *resembles Women*," and therefore doomed to decline. One symptom of this worrying trend was the intrusion of women into such masculine spheres as politics. But the eighteenth century was also a period when domesticity was becoming celebrated as an English trait; in wartime, mothers, wives, and sisters were privileged to assume a special and almost sacred role on the home front.[45] "[W]orthy of a Roman matron, in the virtuous times of the republic," proclaimed one publication approving Lady Howe's advertisement.[46]

In the months following George's death, the Howes were portrayed in the press as an iconic English family. The public was aware of this band of soldier-brothers, their sisters, and their inspired mother, and their sufferings struck a chord with a country that was in the midst of a fiercely contested war. One unusually extensive elegy reflected the celebrity George had attained during his brief military career:

> Albion with secret pride her son beheld,
> Form'd for the senate, or the hostile field;
> Youthful in action, but in prudence old;
> In counsel steady, and in danger bold;

Next followed a romanticized account of George's career in America, where he drilled his men on "the ambush-fight" before tragically falling on the battlefield. Finally, the reader is assured that the family will close ranks and avenge him. All three surviving brothers are mentioned by name:

> 'Tis done! Brave *Richard* to the fight returns,
> The Gauls affrighted fly; their navy burns.
> *William* again shall scour the hostile plain,
> And foes shall fly his youthful ire in vain.
> *Thomas* enrag'd shall draw th'avenging steel,
> Til Gallia's sons their triple fury feel.
> That these survive imperious Lewis know,
> Who bear the terrors, with the name of HOWE.[47]

It was characteristic of the press to be melodramatic, but the harsh reality for the Howe family was that the savior of the dynasty was dead. Almost no letters from the distaff side of the family survive. Lady Howe, even as she was tilting with Newcastle over the Nottingham seat, wrote briefly to William Pitt: "[T]he ill state of my health has, till now, deprived me of the power of returning you my most gratefull acknowledgements for the obliging part you have taken in my affliction." She went on to thank him for "all the marks of friendship" she and her family had so often received from him.[48] Her drooping words to Pitt were written the day after she penned her disingenuous letter to Newcastle explaining that William would be chosen for Nottingham.

It would be wrong to assume that Lady Howe's ability to play politics with Newcastle at such a time proceeded from anything more than the conviction that the welfare of her family absolutely required it. During her lifetime, her distress when her sons were in danger was evident in court circles. Unfortunately, her note to Pitt is the only surviving communication from her during this period.

It was not his mother who wrote to console William. In 1758, William, like George, was in America, serving under James Wolfe in an amphibious attack on the French fortress at Louisbourg. After receiving the devastating news about his brother from his sister Caroline and aunt Juliana in late July, he was unable to eat for several days. "I thought he would have been starved," wrote Wolfe. Lieutenant-Colonel Howe "could not bear to have anyone near him, even of his most intimate friends." For Wolfe himself, the news was a disaster. "[T]he best soldier in the army," he wrote of George. "Heavens! What a loss to the country! the bravest, worthiest, and most intelligent man among us!" Thinking of the family at home, Wolfe added, "Poor Mrs Page will die of grief."[49] William came close to doing just that at a stopover at Castle William in Boston, where he almost succumbed to a "severe and dangerous illness."[50]

By November, back in Halifax, William finally poured out his feelings in a rare personal letter to his brother Richard:

> What a loss we have sustained! If it is a weakness I acknowledge to you the stroke was such to me as I had not firmness to bear. I must wish that yr. Calmness has not felt quite so much. Live & be a Comfort to us all___Remember how much our dependence is on you. If we lose yr. only support left to us we shall fall never to rise again. Excuse me & think of a Family whose only hope now is yr safety.

The letter is most unusual, revealing as it is of William's sense of vulnerability at this critical moment for the family. It is likely that William barely remembered his father, who left for Barbados when he was a toddler, and he regarded his oldest brother George as the head of the family. But feelings of loss on George's behalf were mixed in equal parts with alarm over the danger sustained to the family cause. It is striking that twenty-nine-year-old William did not consider himself the equal of his elder brothers; they were the leaders, and he and the rest of the family looked to them.

It was probably Caroline who told William of his mother's political stratagem at Nottingham. She had written to him twice, he told Richard, two "most excellent letters." William was not altogether pleased to find himself honored, unasked, with a seat in Parliament while on service abroad, although the same fate had befallen George and Richard in their turns. "Why chuse me for Nottingham?" he wrote. "It cannot be of any service to either of us. They would chuse you instantly without ye. least hesitation. It cannot be a similar case wth. me."[51] But, of course, he bowed to Lady Howe's wishes.

Now Richard was Lord Howe and head of the family, although he had already established himself in his own right. In September 1757, the year before George's death, he had performed one of his most celebrated exploits, when he and the helmsman stood alone on the quarterdeck of his ship, the *Magnanime*. While the rest of the crew lay on the deck, and with the enemy firing shot and shells around him, Richard coolly piloted his vessel to within forty yards of the French fort on the Île d'Aix before bringing up "with a spring on his cable" and commencing such a heavy bombardment that the fort surrendered in half an hour.[52] The waters around the fort were supposed to be impossible for navigating large ships, making it out of range of the guns of the *Magnanime*. But Richard had the assistance of an expert French Huguenot pilot, and he shrewdly calculated that the enemy would offer only minimal resistance. His fellow officers thought him foolhardy, but the capture of the fort at Île d'Aix would become one of his most famous deeds.[53]

The episode was a single moment of triumph in yet another expedition that had gone very wrong. The objective was an amphibious attack on the French port of Rochefort in the Bay of Biscay. Sir John Mordaunt was in command of the land forces, which included Wolfe's 20th Regiment of Foot. The naval squadron, under the command of Admiral Sir Edward Hawke, consisted of sixteen ships of the line plus transports. Yet Richard Howe's destruction of the fortifications on the Île d'Aix was the sole accomplishment of this mighty force. After several councils of war, the assembled officers decided not even to attempt the principal objective; some thought the fort at Rochefort was too well defended, others felt a landing would be too difficult.

The reaction at home to the Rochefort expedition was one of shock and despondency. And the press peddled a conspiracy theory that would have resonance for the Howe brothers years later, in another war. The inaction of Sir John Mordaunt, the newspapers hinted, had been deliberate, an attempt to discredit the administration through the failure of an expedition that was the brainchild of Pitt in particular.[54] Such notions were not taken seriously in government circles, but the virtual failure of a venture that had cost a million pounds could not go unquestioned. An inquiry and a court-martial followed. Sir John Mordaunt was luckier than Admiral John Byng because his instructions had given him wide discretionary powers and he was acquitted.[55] Nevertheless, he lost his favor at court and only his protégé, James Wolfe, and his kinsman, Richard Howe, emerged from the episode with their reputations enhanced.[56]

History would record 1757 as a year of failures for Britain. Lord Loudoun's summer campaign against the French naval base at Louisbourg—George Howe's first posting in America—had been abandoned in July because of delays in the arrival of British reinforcements; the massacre of English prisoners at the surrender of Fort William Henry in August had horrified the nation. The war, many felt, was over for Britain; the nation looked trifling to its European allies and enemies alike.

But for Richard, his triumph at Rochefort was shortly capped by the happiness of courtship and marriage. Mary Hartopp, daughter of the governor of Plymouth, became his wife during a three-month leave ashore. Richard seized the opportunity for a wedding when a shortage of provisions had forced him to halt his pursuit of French ships in the Bay of Biscay, and he put in at Plymouth on January 18, 1758.[57] When he and the *Magnanime* put to sea again on April 16, he was a married man.

This was not necessarily a whirlwind romance. Richard and his bride had known each other all their lives. Mary's father, Chiverton Hartopp, was from Welby, Leicestershire, not far from Langar. The Hartopps and the Howes moved in the same circles. Mr. Hartopp had supported George in his parliamentary campaign in Nottingham a few years earlier, walking the streets of the town with him.[58] William, writing to Richard from Halifax in his letter of November 1758, congratulated him in terms that showed that he already knew and liked Mary Hartopp. Richard's flirtation with Elizabeth Raper at Hanslope a couple of years earlier indicated that he was intent on finding a wife. With so little time ashore, the young ladies among his sisters' acquaintance—the Miss Rapers and Miss Hartopps—were the most likely candidates. At any rate, it was Caroline who had to break the news to Elizabeth Raper. "Heard from [Mrs. Howe] that Dick was married to a Miss Hartop, thought I should have died, cried heartily, damned him as heartily," Elizabeth confided to her diary.[59] But her regrets were for herself alone. Mary Hartopp would fit in easily with the Howe clan; within a year, Caroline had christened her "Dickess," and a comfortable, sisterly rapport had been established.[60]

There was, however, no time for a honeymoon, for 1758 was the year that Richard was singled out by William Pitt for his project of coastal expeditions against France. The objective was to harass the French coast as a diversion for Britain's continental allies, Frederick the Great of Prussia and Prince Ferdinand of Brunswick, who now led the defense of Hanover.

Predictably, once in office, Pitt moved away from his extreme—and simplistic—views on Britain's engagement in Europe. Under Pitt's parliamentary leadership, the armies of Britain's allies continued to receive subsidies. The necessity of sending British troops as well became evident by the spring of 1758.[61] But even as Pitt bowed to the reality of British participation in the

Portrait of Richard Howe by Thomas Gainsborough, thought to have been painted in 1758. It may have been a gift to his bride, Mary Hartopp.

continental war, he adhered to his dictum that the nation's greatness resided in her naval power. Raids on the French coast were taken up by Pitt as "his most distinctive contribution to the war." The Rochefort affair, he believed, had failed in part because the several commanders had been allowed to shelve individual responsibility in long-drawn-out and inconclusive councils of war.[62] This would not happen again—Pitt would take charge on a more personal level. In a novel command arrangement, the secretary of state assumed overall direction of the military and naval forces that would carry out the 1758 coastal raids. The naval officer he chose to conduct these operations was none other than Richard Howe, who was promoted to commodore. For Richard to be directly under the control of the minister was sufficiently unusual to cause temporary misunderstanding and affront to Admiral Hawke, who at first believed that Pitt had passed him over for a junior officer.

It has been suggested by Richard Howe's biographer that he was selected to command these missions because of his experience along the coastline around Normandy and Saint-Malo.[63] But Richard was also a good political choice in a year when Pitt found that his loyalty to the "young court" at Leicester House was becoming a headache. The Prince of Wales—the future George III—and his mentor Lord Bute persisted in their opposition to sending British troops to a ground war in Germany, pushing coastal raids as an acceptable alternative. As Pitt in office became increasingly aware that this would not be enough to win the continental war, he found himself walking a tightrope between Leicester House and opponents who thought coastal raids were a waste of money—or, worse, a dangerous leaching of resources from the main theater of war in Europe.[64] Richard Howe must have seemed the ideal man for a strategy that needed to find favor with both courts: a skillful and experienced officer whose influential mother was connected closely with both Princess Augusta and Lady Yarmouth.

On June 1, 1758, while George's army was assembling at Albany, New York, for the Ticonderoga expedition, Richard's flagship, the 64-gun HMS *Essex*, sailed from Spithead. The *Essex* was smaller than the *Magnanime* and better adapted to coastal raiding. The squadron Richard commanded included another three ships of the line, plus several frigates and transports.[65] At the head of the army was Charles Spencer, 3rd Duke of Marlborough, grandson of the illustrious first duke. His second-in-command was Major General Lord George Sackville, a Leicester House favorite, although Sackville and Richard would become firm enemies during the course of the expedition.[66]

The first objective, an amphibious raid on Saint-Malo, was a partial success when a well-executed British landing failed to take the fort but succeeded in destroying considerable enemy shipping. The next objective was the French port of Cherbourg, where, in a sequence of events reminiscent of Rochefort, the army commanders had ordered their troops into the landing craft before calling off the operation at the last minute, citing bad weather and shortages of water and provisions. Richard's conduct of the naval side of the amphibious operations went "almost without a fault," but the carping Lord George Sackville, despite knowing little of naval matters, wrote home, criticizing even Richard's ability to gauge and make use of a fair wind.[67]

Walpole recorded the story of their falling-out after the return of the expedition. "Lord George Sackville was not among the first to court danger: and Howe, who never made friendship but at the mouth of a cannon, had conceived and expressed a strong aversion to him." Things came to a head eventually: "They agreed so ill, that one day Lord George putting several questions to Howe, and receiving no answer, said, 'Mr. Howe, don't you hear me? I have asked you several questions.' Howe replied, 'I don't love questions.' "[68] As far as London society was aware, the two men did not speak again for almost twenty years.

When Marlborough and Sackville returned to Portsmouth, dissatisfied with their portion of glory from what Sackville called "buccaneering," they learned that British troops were finally going to Germany. They then used their influence to place themselves in command of what appeared to offer surer laurels. Leicester House, angry, let down, and determined to shore up the prestige of the coastal raids favored by its royal household, decided on a gesture that would land Richard with an unwelcome level of responsibility. Prince Edward Augustus, Duke of York, younger brother of the Prince of Wales, would join the navy under Richard's command.[69]

It was a prestigious honor to have the young prince aboard, and one that Richard surely owed to his mother's influence, for Princess Augusta was directly involved in the decision.[70] But it was expensive; Richard had been subsisting on his officer's pay, and he found that the prince had been dispatched without a full complement of bedding, linens, and uniforms, which had to be made up out of Richard's pocket. The debt was never repaid, a circumstance the underpaid and newlywed naval officer never forgot. Worse, though, was the extreme danger of the subsequent coastal expeditions, during which the prince insisted on being by Richard's side, as cannon fire came down all around them.[71]

In early August 1758, Richard, commanding twenty-three warships, together with Lieutenant General Thomas Bligh at the head of more than ten thousand troops, launched a second amphibious attack on Cherbourg. It was a success. Everything of value—ships, warehouses, even stone bastions and jetties—was destroyed. On September 3, the expedition reached its next objective: Saint-Malo again. Historians have speculated over this choice, but it was the result of Leicester House intrigue. Lord Bute had proposed it behind Pitt's back to Richard Howe and the expedition's quartermaster-general, Clark, one of Bute's favorites.[72] If Richard disliked receiving confidences from both Pitt and Bute, who were now increasingly at odds, he remained characteristically silent.

Saint-Malo did not prove to be a happy choice. The troops landed without opposition several miles west of the town, but bad weather and other obstacles obliged Richard to move his anchorage nine miles westward to the Bay of St. Cast. When the attack was ultimately abandoned, the troops began a poorly directed march to the fleet's anchorage at St. Cast, under pressure from the approaching enemy. On the morning of September 11, reembarkation at St. Cast began under heavy French fire directed at the remaining troops on the beach and the flat-bottomed boats that had conveyed them. Seeing the oarsmen hesitate as shot and shells poured around them, Richard jumped into his launch and stood, fully exposed to the fire, directing the embarkation of the remaining soldiers, some of whom waded or swam into the sea toward the boats.

It was a bloody day, with between five and seven hundred officers and men of the army killed, and all four naval captains responsible for supervising the embarkation were taken prisoner. The army was blamed for the disaster, as General Bligh had delayed marching the troops to St. Cast. Richard, however—by now the new Lord Howe to the public—came out of the business with an enhanced reputation as a daring commander.[73] When the Duke of Newcastle criticized Richard for exposing Prince Edward to danger, the king asked how else the boy could become a proper fighting sailor.[74]

But the Howes suffered a personal loss in the calamity of St. Cast, for among the dead was youngest sister Mary's fiancé, Sir John Armytage. A wealthy baronet and a member of Parliament, Sir John was close in age to Mary, who probably met him through her brothers. Armytage had served as a volunteer under the Duke of Marlborough in the amphibious expeditions of June.[75] That may have been his undoing, for by the end of August, when Richard was about to embark once more on his coastal raids, Armytage was planning his nuptials to Mary Howe and did not intend to serve this time. Happening to go to court on the day when officers and volunteers were taking leave of the king—so the story goes—the young baronet was caught off guard when His Majesty, assuming he would be volunteering again, asked him "when he meant to set out." "Tomorrow," was Sir John's instant response, for a hint from a king was almost a command. He never returned. For the rest of her life, Mary wore a black collar around her neck that concealed "a splendid brilliant necklace" Sir John had presented to her as a wedding gift.[76] More than a year after St. Cast, Horace Walpole noted that "Molly Howe has not done pining for Sir Armitage."[77]

The St. Cast affair marked the end of Pitt's enthusiasm for coastal raids. Inevitably, his relationship with Leicester House broke down.[78] In view of the fiasco that had ensued at Saint-Malo, one wonders whether Richard also was tired of his Leicester House entanglements. But despite the complex connections he and his family had in the competing royal households,

Richard did not make enemies in court circles, and he remained a firm friend of William Pitt, who demonstrated repeatedly his reliance on Richard's discretion. Richard's involvement in Pitt's project of coastal raids was an apprenticeship in the sinuous interplay between politics and military strategy. Lord Bute, too, felt he could confide in the young commodore. Richard Howe was not a politician or a courtier at heart, but he was someone who could keep a secret.

THE YEAR 1759 at last saw an upturn in fortunes for the British, with a string of victories on land and at sea. Richard returned to his favorite ship, the *Magnanime*, and joined the Channel Fleet under Admiral Hawke. For some months, the British maintained a close blockade of the French fleet at Brest, waiting for the enemy to emerge and give battle. Finally, in the Battle of Quiberon Bay on November 20, Hawke gained a victory so decisive that

The Battle of Quiberon Bay. In 1759, Admiral Hawke's Channel Fleet prevented a French fleet from escaping the British blockade of Brest in this daring sea battle that was fought dangerously close to shore among the rocks and reefs of Quiberon Bay.

the French offered no serious challenge to British control of the sea for the rest of the war.[79]

As usual, Richard was in the fore, pursuing and attacking the enemy. The *Magnanime* lost almost eighty men dead or wounded after a fierce battle among the shoals and rocks of Quiberon Bay. His men revered him for his boldness. A junior officer recalled that there was "an appearance of the greatest joy" on every face when the admiral gave the signal to give chase, and the *Magnanime*, "one of the fastest ships in the Royal Navy," put itself at the head of the British squadron.[80] "Perhaps there was an element of vengeance in his conduct, an intention to pay the French back for his brother's death at Ticonderoga," wrote one historian. *Magnanime* sank the 80-gun *Thésée* and left the *Formidable* a wreck.[81] When another enemy ship, the *Heros*, struck its flag to Howe, then disappeared in the confusion of the battle and the growing darkness, Richard was visibly chagrined. His prize had escaped; he "wrung his hands, and said, 'We have lost the honour of the day.'" His crew members were all sympathy.[82] Richard had begun the Seven Years' War as an able but little-known captain; he finished as a famous commodore with a reputation for daring that made him beloved of British seamen and the British public alike.

Quiberon Bay brought with it the first hint that the war might soon come to an end. When Richard went ashore after the battle to arrange an exchange of prisoners, the governor of Brittany, the Duc d'Aiguillon, suggested that France might be prepared to begin peace negotiations and that Lord Howe would be a proper person to take his proposal to Pitt. So Richard went home aboard the *Magnanime*, reaching Spithead on Boxing Day in 1759.[83]

At last, Richard had the opportunity for a holiday with family members. "[W]e staid in Town to see my Brother," wrote Caroline happily early in the new year; "he came to us vastly well after great fatigue, for he was a Month in his Passage from Sr. Ed. Hawke which is commonly done in 5 or 6 days & he very near lost his ship off the Isle of Wight, it was 5 hours upon a rock."[84] But he was home. And there was more reason to celebrate, for during 1760, Richard's wife, the young Lady Howe, was pregnant. Perhaps this was why Richard took an unprecedented break from active duty, not returning to sea until the autumn of that year.[85] But danger and sadness remained for the family. When the child did not survive, Richard resumed his endless cruises off the coast of France, and William fought on in America.

"What a glorious year this has been!" Caroline had written exultantly in December 1759.[86] The triumph at Quiberon Bay was accompanied by other successes around the world: in India, on the Continent, in America. British forces had captured strategically vital Quebec City on the St. Lawrence River in September, in a campaign commanded by Wolfe, now a general. But victory came at a cost; Wolfe was killed on the Plains of Abraham as British redcoats routed the French troops defending Quebec in one of the most famous battle scenes in colonial American history.

For William, Quebec was his hour of conspicuous heroism. He led a small band of light infantry volunteers spearheading the British landing, scrambling in the dark up a steep, rocky cliff above a cove called the Anse-au-Foulon. William and his twenty-four volunteer "forlorn hopes"—he had warned them that this could be a suicide mission—dislodged the hundred-strong guard at the summit and stormed ahead, scattering the remaining defenders and opening the Foulon road for the oncoming British troops. Howe and his men then shouted a spirited "Huzza!" to signal their success to the troops waiting below. William Howe's ascent of Foulon has been called "one of the most celebrated military achievements in British imperial history," and it is rightly mentioned in every account of his life.[87]

By the time William scrambled up the cliff at Quebec, he had seen four years of active service in the war. Like his brothers, he had been involved from the start of hostilities, preparing for a French invasion of the Kentish coast that never occurred back in the winter of 1755–56. Then he had been under the command of his friend James Wolfe, and the two men would finish the war together, for Wolfe at least, at Quebec. In the interim years, their paths diverged and recrossed. William left Wolfe's 20th Foot sometime in 1756 to join Lieutenant General Robert Anstruther's new 58th Foot, which had been raised the previous winter. William was promoted to major when he joined the 58th, and he played a leading part in recruiting its first complement of men. By Christmas 1756, he was its lieutenant colonel, a great step forward in his military career. He may not have thought much of his duty, however, for in the year when the war officially got started, he was posted back to the homeland, guarding French prisoners and discouraging an uprising of discontented Cornish tin miners ("tinners") in the West Country.[88]

In the spring of 1758, when George was planning his expedition to Ticonderoga and Richard was readying his squadron to raid the French coast, William's regiment was heading to America to take a second crack at Louisbourg, in Nova Scotia. This campaign had all the wearying aspects of an amphibious expedition fought in an inhospitable environment, a combination that would become all too familiar to William during his career. The troops slowly converged on Halifax from New York, Boston, and Ireland, coping with the typical delays of an Atlantic crossing in early spring. The commander of the campaign, General Jeffrey Amherst, arrived last, in late May, by which time the campaign was two months behind schedule. Then came the difficult business of landing the army on Cape Breton Island, complete with artillery pieces and equipment, under the obstacles of enemy bombardment and a swelling sea.

Once the British forces were established on land, the fall of Louisbourg could be presumed eventually, but the French were not going to give up without a fight. Thus followed a grueling six weeks of neutralizing French outlying posts, suffering sudden enemy counterattacks, and hauling artillery into position to fire at the French men-of-war defending the fort. When Louisbourg surrendered on July 27, one triumphant British onlooker commented, "We had taken the strongest garrison in North America, and opened the road to Canada."[89] The French defenders had fought while knowing their defeat would be a prelude to further British aggression.

After weeks of what was effectively a nasty form of guerrilla warfare, hostility ran high against the French, and they were wise to surrender unconditionally.[90] By this time, "civilized" warfare had already been badly compromised; New England rangers serving at Louisbourg scalped French soldiers and Indians in one encounter, and Wolfe noted approvingly that no quarter was given to the Native American combatants who fought with the French—"We cut them to pieces whenever we found them, in return for a thousand acts of cruelty and barbarity."[91]

It was after the Louisbourg campaign that Wolfe wrote fulsomely of William that "His Majesty has not a better soldier in those parts—modest, diligent, and valiant," noting that William led "the best trained battalion in all America."[92] But one wonders what William's thoughts were in the month after Louisbourg fell, when his regiment was part of an unpleasant operation to destroy the fishing industry in the Bay of Gaspé. The assignment involved systematically putting to the torch the homes and livelihoods of the French fishing families. The military rationale was that they were destroying food supplies bound for Quebec. Wolfe was at pains not to kill the defenseless inhabitants, but it was hardly an inspirational mission.[93]

THE CAPTURE OF QUEBEC a year after Louisbourg was a highlight of the American campaign, but little attention has been paid to the fate of the victorious British soldiers who remained there over the winter, William's 58th Foot among them. The army was not prepared for a six-month stay in Canada during the coldest, darkest months of the year. Shelter was basic; food was of such poor quality that scurvy set in. Sentries froze to death, and parties sent out on snowshoes to gather firewood were ambushed by Native Americans. Hundreds died, and the ground was too frozen to bury them. At Christmastime 1759, when Richard was ensconced in the comforts of London society with his family after the dangers of Quiberon, William and his depleted regiment were making the best of the season on starvation rations in Quebec.[94] The British navy could not bring any relief, for the St. Lawrence estuary was frozen until spring.

April 1760 saw an army of seven thousand French, marching overland and intent on recapturing the city. The Battle of St. Foy, bizarrely, reenacted the battle of the previous September, but with the armies reversed. The sick and starving British troops were forced back into the walled city, and casualties were higher than on the day of Wolfe's victory. Now the French besieged Quebec and the British hung on, waiting to see which flag would be flying on the first man-of-war to enter the St. Lawrence with the spring thaw. On May 9, 1760, HMS *Lowestoft*, flying the Union Jack, came into view. Six days later, the sight of two more British ships convinced the French commander to end his siege.[95] It was the victory at Quiberon Bay the previous November that had ultimately saved Quebec for the British, by ending the French challenge at sea. In the end, it was the supply lines that determined victory or defeat in far-flung America, a lesson that would not be lost on William.

The 58th regiment stayed in America after the relief of Quebec, and William was present when the French surrendered Montreal in September 1760. He must have embarked for home soon afterward, for newspapers announced on October 17 that he had "arrived at the House of Lady Howe, his Mother, in Albemarle-Street, from North-America."[96]

Perhaps 1760 marked the first Howe family Christmas gathering in several years, for that autumn saw all seven surviving Howe children in England for the first time since George had departed for America three years earlier. At the end of September, the youngest brother, Captain Thomas Howe, commanding his East Indiaman the *Winchelsea,* had reached home in a Royal Navy convoy from China.[97] And Richard, who had been cruising the western approaches of the English Channel, may also have had leave over the holiday season, because he was injured in late November while observing the demonstration of a new secret weapon.

The circumstance was a test at Woolwich of the newly invented "Smoke-Balls." One of the balls burst its shell, breaking the arm of an officer, the sword of a lord, the calf of a baronet, and involving the Duke of York in a near-escape as he backed away from the gushing cloud of smoke. But it was Richard rather than his royal protégé the duke who was singled out in the press report. Splinters lodged in the side of Lord Howe, fortunately inflicting only minor injury. His loss would have been "irreparable," gushed the newspaper.[98] For Richard, the accident may have provided a welcome chance for rest and recuperation while his brothers were in town.

None of the brothers chose to stay off duty for long while there was a war on. By the end of March 1761, William was part of an expedition departing England for Belle-Île, an island dominating the Bay of Biscay. The war on the Continent was dragging on; expenses were mounting up. Pleased with the recent naval victories, William Pitt returned to his old scheme of coastal raids. He thought that the seizure of Belle-Île, and the establishment of a British naval base, would divert the French from the fighting in Germany. And as tentative peace negotiations with the French had now begun, it could prove a useful bargaining chip—as indeed it did, in the final treaty.

But the Peace of Paris frustratingly remained two years away.[99] George II had died in October 1760, collapsing of a stroke at Kensington Palace. His mourners appeared to be more curious than grief-stricken, for the old king had been uncharismatic and too Germanic for the tastes of many of his British subjects.[100] His young grandson George III came to the throne amid a general feeling of national goodwill. But Pitt's own days as a member of the new king's government were numbered. His break with Leicester House years earlier was not forgotten or forgiven by George III, and in other quarters he was seen as irresponsibly prolonging an expensive war. Still, for now the expedition to Belle-Île went ahead.

The accession of the new king appeared to do no harm to Lieutenant Colonel William Howe's prospects for promotion in the army, for he became Brigadier General Howe for the Belle-Île campaign, just as his brother George had been at Ticonderoga. The campaign had all the usual difficulties of an amphibious operation—the countless obstacles to the troops' landing, the shifting of heavy artillery and equipment, followed by a protracted six-week siege. The fortress fell on June 8, 1761. William had not been in the vanguard this time, for he had been wounded a few days before the final capitulation, his first such mishap.[101] The British newspapers were able to publish the worrying news within weeks; Belle-Île was much closer to home than America.

Caroline quickly received letters of reassurance from her younger brother, the first arriving "the day after we heard of his being wounded"; he sent good accounts of himself, "tho' he was still confined" in early July. By August, she wrote to a friend, "except some remains of lameness, he was perfectly well by his last letters, I cannot learn when we may expect him from Belleisle."[102] It was like Caroline to sound casual about a subject that was so near to her heart. The news of William's safety was sandwiched in among tidbits about the impending coronation of George III, which was to take place on September 22, 1761. In October, William Pitt, the aggressive wartime leader, would resign from the cabinet in protest over the conduct of the final stages of the war.

But if the nation was in the mood to relax and celebrate, the war seemed to hang on intractably. William was offered the governorship of Belle-Île, perhaps because he had been wounded there. Here was a chance for a less dangerous service, but William declined, "as he preferred to serve in the field as long as the war lasted." It is not too much to assume that he sought—as the newspaper poets had so colorfully suggested back in 1758—to avenge his brother's death. His Hanoverian cousin Friedrich von Kielmansegg, whose visit to England had been timed so he could attend the coronation (an event that attracted throngs of tourists), described a gathering of the Howe family in London—the lady mother and her seven surviving children—in January 1762: "[A] very rare occurrence, which is not likely to last long, as all three sons will soon be dispersed in different parts of the world. My Lord Howe will shortly take command of the fleet on the French coast; the second son will probably go with the expedition to the West Indies; and the youngest will sail in February with his ship to East India."[103]

The "expedition to the West Indies," soon to be undertaken by William, was an attack on Havana, Cuba, in 1762. In the eleventh hour before the peace, Spain had entered the war against Britain, hoping to gain Minorca and other advantages from a war-weary British nation, and giving new heart to the French. The Spanish aggression thus seemed to justify a British attack on Cuba.[104] In fact, Britain had had its eye on Havana since the days of Queen Elizabeth I, seeing it as a foothold into the rich opportunities for trade and expansion in Spanish America. Havana was a fortress and a shipyard, but also a flourishing center of trade—an entrepôt for slaves, sugar, foodstuffs, logging, and tobacco, and a sophisticated seaport where a vast service sector looked after the needs of the sailors and traders who came and went. In Spanish Havana, wealthy Cuban merchants and planters mixed with British merchants, for the British had since 1713 been permitted by treaty to engage in the immensely profitable trade of enslaved Africans to Spanish America.[105]

Now Britain would move to seize this rich prize from the Bourbon monarchs of Spain. Pitt was gone from office; a new ministry headed by Lord Bute, the favorite of the new king, directed the expedition of more than twenty-eight thousand men. Ten thousand were sailors; the army, like the forces under George Lord Howe at Ticonderoga, was a multicultural assemblage of British regulars; five hundred free black militiamen from Jamaica; American mainland provincial troops recruited from New York, New Jersey, Rhode Island, Connecticut, and South Carolina; and more than two thousand enslaved Africans raised from the plantation labor force of Jamaica. The Jamaican planters, reluctant to risk their human property despite official promises of compensation, preferred to send sick or intractable slaves and insisted that they be used for hard labor rather than being taught the dangerous skill of handling firearms. It was this disparate force that converged on Spanish Cuba.[106]

When the British fleet arrived off Havana on June 6, it caught the enemy entirely by surprise, a tribute to British maritime skill. The main British force had approached Havana through the poorly charted and dangerous Old Bahama Channel, rather than the usual route from the west by way of the Gulf of Mexico. Dispatches alerting Havana that Spain was now at war with Britain had been intercepted by the British, so Cuba's Spanish governor thought the fleet was just passing through when it was first sighted. The illusion did not last long, of course; the usual arduous struggle to land

the troops ensued, with nasty piecemeal skirmishes for control of the surrounding countryside; the fortress would not fall until August 14.

Just as the frigid climate was a force to be contended with in Canada,
the tropical Caribbean was notorious as a graveyard for British soldiers
because of disease. William's regiment, the 58th, reached Havana from
New York in August, much later than he did, along with a contingent of
colonial troops. By then, Lieutenant General the Earl of Albemarle, commanding the land forces, was desperate for healthy troops to replace the
sick and dying. By the campaign's end, the 58th regiment lost 40 percent
of its men, most from disease.[107]

William, however, was spared, and led a diversionary expedition of eight
hundred marines and two thousand light infantry, landing at the mouth
of the Chorrera River in an effort to draw Spanish troops away from the
defense of their El Morro fortress. Two days later, he was reinforced by a
company of "free Negroes and mulattoes." From his camp, he organized
transportation of water to the men digging in for the siege, who were almost
dying of thirst while building fortifications and hauling artillery. William's
force also undertook dangerous reconnoitering expeditions, repelled enemy
attacks, kept their supply lines open, and relentlessly struck at the Spanish
in a series of sorties. On July 30, an eyewitness described William's unit as
prepared to assist in the reduction of the city, despite the fact that by now,
"Colonel Howe, whose numbers had proportionally decreased with the rest
of the army, had only been able to hem in the town, to keep his own position, and to cover the watering of the navy in the Chorera [sic] River."[108]

Yet even while operating in a burning maelstrom, William found time
to perform acts of kindness for the men who served under him. Francis
Browne, a young officer in his regiment who was dangerously ill, recalled
that Howe, "hearing that the Captain Lieutenancy of our Regiment was to
be sold, purchas'd it for me for £300 and the first thing he did on my going
to him after my recovery, was to present me with my commission, telling
me at the same time I was appointed Captain Lieutenant." "Such an act of
friendship as this," asserted the newly made Captain Browne, "in advancing so much mony [sic] without being ask'd, or without letting me know
any thing of the matter 'till he gave me my new Commission, is rarely to
be met with."[109]

The siege at Havana was one of the closing campaigns of the war. The
Peace of Paris was signed in February 1763. France effectively gave up her

pretensions to establish a rival New France in America, and Great Britain emerged as a world power, with vast acquisitions in North America, including Canada, Florida, and the disputed hinterland east of the Mississippi. Britain retained conquests in the Caribbean and Africa and also became the dominant European colonial presence on the subcontinent of India. National pride was mollified with the restoration of Minorca. If Pitt and his friends in the City of London thought the treaty conceded too much to France, others, including Bute and the king, were insistent on achieving peace. Eighteenth-century diplomacy ruled that it was bad policy to have an overly successful victory, maintaining that it would result in humiliated enemies who would inevitably seek revenge.

And the nation was war-weary. It had been a long struggle, and those at home had not been immune to the hardships. There were shortages, high taxes, and invasion scares.[110] The fighting men destined to face the enemy had been highly visible on English soil, as the regiments of the regular army performed exercises on Salisbury Plain and the heaths near London; county militias drilled; and the presence of unpopular Hanoverian soldiers aroused controversy. As the war came to an end, bands of demobilized soldiers—ragged, tired, maimed, or wounded—became common sights around the metropolis.[111] The veteran foot soldiers came from the laboring classes, but the aristocracy, too, had visibly thinned its ranks in support of the cause.

The Howe family provides a cameo of the impact of Britain's first world war on its wealthy families, the sacrifices it extorted reminiscent of the world wars of the twentieth century. George had given his life, as had Mary's fiancé, Sir John Armytage. With one exception—that of Caroline's husband, John, the most senior among them—every male member of the Howe family served in the war effort. In addition to the four brothers, sister Charlotte Howe's husband, Robert Fettiplace, enlisted. Charlotte had married Robert Fettiplace, from a landed gentry family in Oxfordshire, in 1752.[112] Although he preferred to spend his time hunting or betting on racehorses, during the Seven Years' War he became a lieutenant in the Marquess of Granby's Royal Foresters.[113]

And even at home, nothing escaped being touched by the conflict; John Howe's favorite club, the Society of Dilettanti, shut down because so many of its members were in military service. In January 1763, nine Dilettanti members were present for the first meeting in years, "an intimate but celebratory affair."[114]

Despite the hardships, the victorious British nation was swept up in a surge of patriotism. Popular nationalism and pride swelled, grounded in the novel sensation that the emergent British empire was saving the world from French tyranny. National self-belief was restored, as not only the French but also the Spanish had been driven back from their aggressions. This "populist, conservative patriotism," aroused by the war, would be embellished by even greater future conflicts—notably the struggle thirty years later against revolutionary France and dictator Napoleon Bonaparte.[115] The British nation was finding its modern identity as a major military power.

The Howe men entered the pantheon of British war heroes in 1762 with the installation in Westminster Abbey of a monument to George. Paid for by the grateful and admiring General Assembly of Massachusetts, it was unveiled in July. Richard oversaw the work; it included the Howe coat of arms and the figure of a graceful woman in mourning, intended to represent the colony of Massachusetts. "He lived respected and beloved," read the inscription, "the publick regretted his loss; to his family it is irreparable."[116] Indeed it was. The monument must stand duty in place of a grave, for George's body never returned home. Feelings ran deep, and the Howes were to sustain a sense of attachment to Massachusetts and America that would have important consequences in a little more than a decade.

The Howes, like their nation, came out of the war with a distinct identity. The brothers came to represent a new generation of British heroes, men of action rather than speech, "strong, silent types" who got on with their duty. To contemporaries, they looked the part; the surviving portraits of the brothers suggest rugged good looks and the dark complexion that characterized the whole family.[117] Shortly after George's death in 1758, Horace Walpole, the self-appointed pen portraitist of his generation, spoke of "the hot-headed and cool-tongued Lords Howe."[118] Both George and Richard were comprehended in the tribute. Walpole, who had known the Howes all his life, always described them thus: "those brave and silent brothers," courageous, daring, but of little speech. Richard was "undaunted as a rock, and as silent: the characteristics of his whole race."[119] Even Thomas was known for his "coolness of Temper." The successful clash of his armed East Indiaman the *Winchelsea* with a French frigate off Bengal in the final days of the war was pronounced hardly an extraordinary event for a Howe.[120] And the acclaim was extended to the women. The widowed Lady Howe was

This engraving shows the monument to Viscount Howe where it was originally installed, in the south nave aisle of Westminster Abbey. Above the white marble inscription and mourning female figure was placed an obelisk embellished with the Howe coat of arms and crest, featuring three wolves' heads. Behind the obelisk were military trophies and flags. Today the monument stands in the northwest tower chapel in the nave of the abbey. The obelisk and trophies have been removed.

compared to a Roman matron. Caroline all her life was said to have had the stoical nature suited to a sister of warriors—a "Virago," as Horace Walpole once called her.[121]

Richard and William, much like their brother George, earned reputations not only as brave commanders but also as considerate and popular officers. It was during these years that Richard earned his well-known sobriquet, "the sailor's friend." He showed active concern for the living conditions of his crew, personally visiting the wounded below decks after each battle and contributing to their comfort with delicacies from his personal stores. In a day when sailors were rigorously confined aboard while in port to prevent desertion, Richard won the gratitude of the crew of the *Magnanime* by trusting them to take shore leave. It was said that he never lost a man thereby.[122]

But behind the stereotype of fortitude, the Howes had strong feelings. Not only George, but also Caroline, William, and Richard had hot tempers. Although so often described as reserved, they could also be engaging. Caroline was a popular figure in high society. George had also possessed a notable social charm. William resembled him in this respect, but without the ingrained sense of responsibility. Of all of them, it was middle brother Richard who most aptly fit the family image, appearing unapproachable or cold to those who did not know him well.

Yet all of them had one thing in common: They did not share their inner intentions and motives readily with anyone outside of the family circle. "It's the Howe fashion to be silent," as a longtime friend put it. Even Aunt Juliana was closemouthed about family matters.[123] This was no doubt an attribute born of their early hardship, when the loss of their father had bonded them together. By 1763, after service in two wars, the Howes had lived through great adversity and suffered grievous losses. These were things that they did not mention. "She covers up the wound from the sight of others," wrote Caroline with insight of a young kinswoman who, many years later, seemed in good spirits after suffering a bereavement.[124] The public image of the Howes was a caricature, but they did know how to keep their secrets. And this would become a recurring motif in the history of the dynasty.

For now, though, the war was over; the nation was in the mood to celebrate, and so were the Howes. Stopping by the London home of Lord Howe near Whitehall Stairs on a visit in April 1763, Caroline was surprised by the proposal of a party to Ranelagh Gardens. Ranelagh was one of London's famous pleasure gardens—a place where, for a small entrance fee, visitors could stroll the acres of avenues lined with verdure, enjoying refreshments, music, fireworks, and other entertainments. This was a public space that drew Londoners of all ranks together to celebrate the peace. Spring was coming, troubles were at bay, and young Lady Howe sent a spontaneous invitation to Mary and Julie. "We all dined together," wrote Caroline happily, and at nine o'clock in the evening Richard and his wife, William, Caroline, and her two youngest sisters "rushed into the Ranelagh Mob."[125]

Five

The Peaceful Years

T he end of the war in 1763 was greeted with a sigh of relief by a nation eager to return to normalcy. London leapt over its old boundaries as postwar prosperity brought in a phase of intensive building for the middling and wealthy ranks of society, now seeking to enjoy the fashionable lifestyle of the metropolis. Restrictions on travel were lifted and British tourists flocked to Paris, Italy, and other celebrated attractions on the Continent.[1] An ambition to cultivate the arts, spurred by national pride, led to the foundation of the Royal Academy of Arts in 1768. The capital saw its first-ever purpose-built exhibition rooms, and the English public discovered a new taste for viewing art galleries.

Peacetime brought an unaccustomed and welcome domestic focus to the lives of the Howe siblings. Richard became a parent. He was at sea when his daughter Sophia Charlotte was born in February 1762. By early June, he was back ashore to see his long-awaited offspring, calling on his mother and sisters Julie and Mary at Richmond to show her off. "She is grown a great Girl, & will be 16 weeks old next Friday," wrote the Dowager Lady Howe proudly of her first grandchild.[2] If Richard was absent for the birth, he was around when his daughter took her first steps in the London home where he and the young Lady Mary Howe had settled a few months after the conclusion of the peace. "My Brother & Lady Howe are much pleased with their new Habitation, they have got little Charlotte with them who trots about all day long," wrote Caroline, happy in her role as aunt.[3]

Richard's days as an impecunious naval officer were a thing of the past. The title and income of the Langar estate, although heavily encumbered, was his to make use of since the death of George. Also, less than a year later, in 1759, Lady Mary's father, Chiverton Hartopp, died, leaving his considerable wealth to his two daughters.[4] Richard could afford to take his family to Bath, the famous spa town, by then at its height as a fashionable resort where the aristocracy mixed with England's burgeoning middle classes. Assemblies, balls, promenades, and concerts were put on for the wealthy clientele, who came on the pretext of poor health and stayed to be entertained. Richard's complaint, however, was genuine—gout that would afflict him for the rest of his life.

It was in Bath just after the war that Richard and his wife sat for their famous portraits by Thomas Gainsborough. One of the preeminent British portrait painters of the century, Gainsborough had moved to Bath during the war.[5] The sittings for Lord and Lady Howe began in July 1763, at a time when Caroline Howe and her husband John were also staying in the spa town. The separate full-length portraits of the couple capture the spirit of these first months of peace, when prosperity, romance, and success were emerging from the preceding years of tragedy, danger, and hardship. Richard poses in the everyday uniform, or "undress," of a commodore.[6] After the dare-devilry of bombarding the fortifications on the Île d'Aix and the risk-taking at Quiberon Bay, he has an insouciant air that befits an English hero. Barely forty, he has the strong features suggested by Horace Walpole's well-known characterization, "undaunted as a rock."

Richard's wife, Lady Mary Howe, looks both beautiful and contented. After all, her celebrated husband has survived the war, she has a new child, and she is a wealthy titled lady, charmingly attired and mixing in the highest circles. Her unusual, forthright stance, seemingly about to step forward from the canvas, achieves a sense of movement, creating the feel "of a breezy summer day whipping forward her skirts." Countess Howe is among the most inspired of Gainsborough's portraits of English ladies. Her pink taffeta dress and luminous pearl necklace and earrings bring out her delicate English complexion.[7] But she does not look delicate; she is a Howe woman, and Gainsborough has taken her measure.

The couple's portraits were intended to hang together, but there is a separateness about them that is emphasized by their contrasting backgrounds. Richard is positioned against a dark, rather stormy scene, "almost abstract" in its inclusion of unadorned barren rocks and a remote expanse of water. Absent are the ships or stirring battle scenes that so often appear in the portraits of naval officers. Instead, Gainsborough chose to lavish detail on the surroundings of the hero's wife: the park that represents aristocratic pride of ownership, the path that suggests forward motion, and the breeze that the artist has, curiously, chosen to ruffle the dress of the lady on a country walk, rather than the naval hero on his quarterdeck.

The lack of integration between the two portraits was almost certainly intentional, and not, as has been suggested, the accidental result of sittings done months apart.[8] Victory in war for Richard was not a matter of unmixed glory and happiness. The conflict had made him a national hero and a viscount, but it also had cost him his beloved brother. It is appropriate that the picture reveals a tinge of sadness. This was an age well aware of the unattractive sibling competition fomented by patrilineage, whereby a younger brother might be suspected of rejoicing at the death of the eldest son and heir.[9] If Richard looks every inch the warrior-aristocrat as he looks out on us, behind him lies a shadow that any contemporary gazing at the portrait would understand. In a reversal of the usual roles, happy triumph was reserved for the Lady Howe, not her victorious husband, and it is her portrait that is most redolent of the couple's future prospects.

The end of the war ushered in new prospects of happiness for yet another Howe, youngest sister Mary, who became engaged to Colonel William Augustus Pitt. The young colonel was a distant relation of the great William Pitt, but Mary almost certainly met him through her kinsman Sir John Mordaunt, in whose regiment Colonel Pitt had served since before the war.[10] Caroline wrote of him, "[H]is Character is a very good one, his Constancy very particular indeed, I wish his Fortune was equal to either of them, but such as it is, they both make no doubt of their living happily & comfortably upon it."[11]

Caroline's reference to "Constancy" suggests that Colonel Pitt had been in love with Mary for some time. He was wounded and taken prisoner in October 1760 at the Battle of Kloster Kamp in Germany, but he was home before Christmas.[12] Perhaps a wounded officer who was in need of her care and attention gave Mary something to distract her from the death of Sir John Armytage, whose loss she had been visibly mourning for some time. In any case, she and Colonel Pitt came to an understanding almost as soon as the war was over; they were married on June 21, 1763, only seven weeks after Caroline had first learned of their engagement.[13] "Mary & her William seem perfectly content & happy," reported Caroline five months later.[14] The third of the Howe sisters, Julie, who had always been close to Mary, added a note of worry. "My Dear Mary is very happy with *her* Husband, but very poor!, that misfortune was in our family."[15]

In sharp contrast to the happiness of the newlywed Pitts were the burgeoning marital problems of second sister Charlotte. Robert Fettiplace had looked like a good match when Charlotte married him eleven years earlier. His family were descended from baronets; he boasted an income of £7,000 a year.[16] When Charlotte wed, she was twenty-nine, an age considered to be rather advanced in an era when women were expected to marry young. Perhaps that is why Horace Walpole, critical as usual, suggested that "three bottles of burgundy" were necessary to get Fettiplace to the altar.[17] Others thought that it was the bride who had made the greatest sacrifice. "[H]e is a simpleton," pronounced one lady, suggesting that Charlotte and her mother, the Dowager Lady Howe, should take charge of him, for "it is not every body that is fit to be trusted to themselves."[18] Fettiplace had the usual vices of the age—gambling and philandering. His great weakness was owning racehorses, and he was unlucky. "I pitty Charlotte excessively to be joined to such a wretch!" pronounced her mother, after Fettiplace absconded to the Continent to escape creditors in 1762.[19] He was back a few years later, and he and his horses were once again scattered across the sheets of the newspapers.[20]

The Dowager Lady Howe certainly did not remain an onlooker while postwar Britain came back to life. Now almost sixty, Charlotte Howe joined the surge of tourism to the Continent, taking the opportunity to return to Hanover for the first time since her girlhood. The occasion was the decision of the Countess of Yarmouth to retire to her native country following the death of George II, and Lady Howe was her sole traveling companion. The two set out in April 1763.[21]

Caroline reported excitedly that her mother and Lady Yarmouth saw Frederick the Great when he and his entourage made a stopover in Hanover. Frederick—lauded in the mid-eighteenth century as a military genius who had unleashed Prussia as a major power in Europe, a self-styled "enlightened despot" who played the flute and entertained Voltaire at his palace of Sanssouci, and famously shouted to his hesitating troops, "Dogs! Do you want to live forever?"—was not a figure who played to the crowds.[22] But at Hanover he was coaxed out of his coach by the news that Lady Yarmouth was among the spectators. Caroline recounted:

We had a fine account of my mother of the King of Prussia's person, & his passing through Hanover, . . . the Guards all drawn up, & men women & Children collected together to have a sight of this extraordinary man, he excused his alighting on account of great hurry, but when he heard that Lady Yarmouth stood in the Street, he immediately opened the Door, threw himself out, & made her a very pretty compliment, he staid talking about a quarter of an hour whilst his Horses were changed, & then with many bows went off.[23]

Frederick had been Britain's most important ally on the Continent during the war. His army was heavily subsidized by Parliament and his victories made him a hero among the British public. As the war drew to a close, however, the cabinet of George III saw fit to end the unpopular subsidies to Prussia, and many, including Frederick himself, felt he had been abandoned by "perfidious Albion." Lady Yarmouth nevertheless remained his faithful ally throughout, a fact he was no doubt aware of when he leapt from his carriage to pay his respects.[24]

By July, Charlotte had taken her leave of Lady Yarmouth and was in the Ardennes at the famous resort of Spa, the leading continental health resort for British tourists. Like Bath, Spa always had a community of fashionable English travelers who maintained a lively social scene.[25] Renowned for its healing waters since the fourteenth century, it was a difficult place to get to by coach, a small town lying in hilly, heavily wooded countryside. Life there was pleasant and genteel, yet with an atmosphere more unconventional than in Bath. Outlawed Scottish exiles of the "Forty-five" Jacobite rebellion could be found there, as well as loyal supporters of Britain's Hanoverian dynasty, impoverished continental aristocrats, and convalescing officers of the Austrian and French armies.[26] Viscountess Charlotte Howe was probably more in her element at Spa than in rural Langar. At any rate, the change seemed to be good for her. She was back in London by November, "perfectly well & with good looks."[27]

William Howe came back from the war determined to enjoy himself. As MP for Nottingham, his official residence was at Epperstone Manor, not far from Langar.[28] But he was often busy elsewhere, visiting and participating in country sports and games, and his presence weaves in and out of his eldest sister's letters during these years. He went to Ranelagh Gardens with Richard and Caroline; he was a frequent guest at Hanslope, where the family played games of bowls on the summer lawn; he went to Wakefield Lodge with Caroline, where the Duke of Grafton laid on foxhunts, and then on to the Nottingham Races.[29] He ice-skated in London's Kensington Gardens; he resumed his beloved pastime of angling, prompting his mother to boast to her fashionable court friends that "Son William out does you all at fishing."[30] He brought back partridges from the campaign at Havana as a gift for a family friend, leaving them in the care of his obliging oldest sister Caroline while he set off on excursions of pleasure.[31] His playful nature was what Caroline liked.

William had a striking family nickname, "the Savage." The earliest known reference to it is in Caroline's letters in 1761, the year after he had returned from the American campaign. Its origin is unknown, but historians have offered various theories. Historian Ira Gruber has speculated that it could have been "a tribute to his long service in America or his primitive behavior at home."[32] David Hackett Fischer refers to a legend that William returned from his American service during the Seven Years' War wearing buckskins and Indian moccasins, but no source is given.[33] This ties in with another longstanding Howe family tradition regarding William—that he is a figure dressed in buckskins and a dark-green ranger's coat in Benjamin West's famous painting *The Death of General Wolfe*.[34]

Art historians have challenged the identification of West's ranger as William Howe, pointing out that he was not a ranger and there is no direct proof that he modeled for West. And the ranger in the painting is wearing a powder horn inscribed "S(r). W(m) Johnson." Sir William Johnson, 1st Baronet, was a superintendent of Indian affairs in the colonies and an able military commander who led Native American forces. But just as William was not a ranger, Johnson was not in Quebec in 1759.[35]

Johnson may not have been in Quebec, but he did meet George Lord Howe in America.[36] He may well have gifted the powder horn to his prestigious brother-in-arms. Exchanging and gifting of accessories and weapons between Native American warriors and British officers was widespread. Sir William Johnson made a regular practice of it.[37] George Howe's personal effects were returned to England after his death.[38] It is entirely possible that the powder horn belonged to George, and that when asked to pose for the artist Benjamin West, William assembled the outfit of a ranger from his own personal American souvenirs and those of his brother. This would explain why West, who sought out authentic artifacts for his history paintings, would include a powder horn inscribed with the name of someone who was well known in London military circles not to have been present at Quebec. If the figure leaning toward the dying Wolfe, pointing to the victory of British arms in the distant field, is indeed William Howe, it is the only substantiated surviving image of him.

William remained in the army in the years following the peace. He was a lieutenant colonel of the 58th Foot until November 1764, then became a full colonel in the 46th Regiment of Foot.[39] This meant Ireland. The 58th had been stationed there after the peace, and the 46th was also in Ireland by 1764.[40] It is clear from Caroline's letters that William was traveling back and forth between Ireland and England during this period. In peacetime, he was not always required to stay with his regiment. His freedom no doubt suited him very well, for the woman he was to marry, Frances "Fanny" Conolly, belonged to a wealthy Anglo-Irish family with aristocratic English connections, and she also moved between England and her brother's estate of Castletown in County Kildare.

Fanny Conolly was not a typical Howe woman. Barely twenty when William met her, she was timid, with a "little meek way" of speaking that aroused a protective response in some, and irritation in others.[41] A comical, wild-looking girl was how one lady described her.[42] But she clearly caught the eye of William Howe. He probably courted her in Ireland, because Caroline knew nothing of the chosen bride of her favorite brother. "The Savage is going to be married to Miss Conolly," she wrote to a friend in May 1765. "I fancy it is no secret, but if you do not hear of it from other people do not mention it from me, I am not at all acquainted with her, those that are commend her, & her appearance & manner deserve it."[43]

They were married less than a month later. If Caroline ever discovered what William saw in Fanny, she did not say. The sisterly camaraderie that comes through clearly in her relationship with Richard's wife Mary—"Dickess"—never developed between Caroline and Fanny. Perhaps Caroline saw that Fanny was not cut out to be a military wife, but the young lady did love William dearly. If she seemed to lack backbone, her mother made up for it. Lady Anne Conolly was the eldest daughter of Thomas Wentworth, Earl of Strafford. She had very strong notions of the rights of daughters to inheritance, even disputing bitterly with her own son in her pursuit of equitable portions for her six daughters. She has been described (perhaps unfairly) as "a strong-willed, volatile, meddlesome, domineering woman."[44] Still, she, like her daughter, adored William; through his marriage, "the Savage" extended his circle of admiring kinswomen.

William's new family had strong English ties. Lady Anne, who was widowed, lived mainly in London or at the family seat of Stretton Hall, Staffordshire. Fanny's brother Tom Conolly was "the richest commoner in Ireland," having inherited a fortune while still in his teens. He was an MP in both the British and the Irish Houses of Commons and had townhouses in London and Dublin.[45] Tom, almost ten years younger than his new brother-in-law, William, was most happy while gaming and chasing foxes.[46] Fun-loving and good-humored, he was described variously by contemporaries as empty-headed or merely immature. But there was nothing imprudent about his marriage in 1758 to Louisa Augusta Lennox, sister of Charles Lennox, 3rd Duke of Richmond.[47] The Duke of Richmond— wealthy, Whiggish, and a race enthusiast with a celebrated horse-racing track at his estate of Goodwood—was a life-long friend of William Howe, who had served alongside him in the 20th Foot.[48] The ties between the Howes and Richmond were strengthened by William's marriage into the Conolly family.

The youngest of the Howe brothers, the elusive Thomas, returned home shortly after the end of the war. It was not the close of hostilities that brought about his return, however, but rather a pilot's blunder guiding his vessel, the *Winchelsea*, out of the Bengal River. His men were saved, but the cargo was lost. The accident brought Thomas home in 1764, "near two year sooner than he would have done," reported Caroline, giving an idea of the stretches of time he spent seafaring far from home and family.[49]

Thomas Howe is the least known of the brothers. His biography in *The History of Parliament* is four sentences long, gives the wrong year of birth, and provides no information about his life other than the fact of his seat in Parliament.[50] We have seen that Thomas likely joined the merchant marine when he left Eton, at age twelve or thirteen. He was twenty-six when he became captain of the 499-ton East Indiaman, the *Winchelsea*, in 1757.[51] Over the next ten years, he traveled farther and saw more of the world than any of his brothers. During the Seven Years' War, the *Winchelsea* was part of a convoy arriving at Madras (now Chennai) that ended the French siege of Fort St. George in 1759. From Madras, Thomas and the *Winchelsea* proceeded to China, reaching the coast by July 1759. On May 12, 1760, by then off the coast of Natal, South Africa, the *Winchelsea* encountered a Portuguese ship, and Thomas learned of the victories involving his brothers at Quebec and Quiberon Bay. By June, the *Winchelsea* had arrived at the island of St. Helena in the South Atlantic.[52] Thomas was back in England in September 1760, shortly before his brother William returned from America. He had been away for almost two years.

Like all the Howe men, Thomas had physical courage and was known for his "coolness of Temper."[53] He also had the charm of George and William. A friend of Caroline's described him as "remarkably pleasing," intelligent, knowledgeable, and "a very extraordinary young man."[54] He also knew how to fight, according to Caroline, who described his encounter with a French frigate near the end of the war. Thomas "contrived to kill him[self] a number of men & to drive [the Frenchmen] off with the loss of only 3 of his men, we are told he has gained great honour," reported his sister, always eager to laud the feats of her brothers.[55]

Being remote from his mother country did not mean Thomas was disengaged from it. As a sailor on the far-flung margins of Britain's overseas empire, he was very aware of the French aggressions against British possessions in North America and the Caribbean, and the British East India Company's factories at Calcutta (now Kolkata) and Madras. Like all the Howes, he was interested in imperial matters, and he contributed valuable information to the proliferating maps and charts of the outermost edges of British navigation. Thomas Howe's charts were used by Sir William Draper when he attacked the Spanish stronghold of Manila in 1762. Draper had left Madras on the *Winchelsea* in 1759, and the idea of the expedition against the Spanish walled city in the Philippines had been hatched during the long voyage home.[56]

But despite his patriotic credentials, Thomas showed himself capable of flagrantly self-serving behavior in pursuit of personal wealth. In March 1766, a year and a half after the accident off Bengal, he went to sea once again, this time in command of the East Indiaman *Nottingham*, bound for Mumbai.[57] When he reached his destination, he found himself the subject of a rather unpleasant inquiry at Calcutta. Howe and the commanders of three other East Indiamen had been detected smuggling on a very large scale. In May 1766, all four were dismissed from their commands. This was really just a suspension, for the East India Company needed skilled commanders, and smuggling was an acknowledged fact of life; reinstatement in a few years was usually taken for granted. Thomas, however, was obliged to apply by letter to be forgiven and restored to his command, for his offenses were initially considered too flagrant to be pardoned. This probably means he was smuggling military stores—cannon and small arms. Even so, he was permitted to return to the service in 1770.[58]

By then, however, this fourth Howe brother had found himself more honorable if less profitable employment in Parliament. In 1768, he ran as MP for the borough of Northampton. Once again, it was the hand of a Howe woman that set this youngest brother's political career in motion, for Caroline was on an intimate footing with the wife of John Spencer, 1st Earl Spencer. Lord Spencer provided the funds and the political influence needed for Thomas's campaign. In 1768, the Spencers wanted to wrest control of the borough of Northampton from two fellow peers, Lords Halifax and Northampton, who for many years had controlled the local elections without serious opposition. The resulting election was so hotly contested that it became known as "the contest of the three earls." Levels of corruption were legendary. Election officials looked the other way as voters neglected to take the oath against bribery. The wool-combers, weavers, and shoemakers who constituted much of the electorate feasted and drank as Lords Halifax, Northampton, and Spencer all held open houses. In support of their respective candidates, they drained their cellars of the best port and claret. The lucky electorate numbered only about a thousand souls, who knew their value and gathered as much as they could in kind and cash.

After fourteen days of voting, Thomas Howe came last, mainly because the polling officer, in the pay of another earl, found excuses for rejecting 110 of the votes cast for Thomas. His mother anticipated the outcome. A society gossip, who met Lady Charlotte Howe playing at quadrille, reported: "She told me her Son wou'd certainly lose the Election at Northampton, but there had been such unfair practices that Ld Spencer intended he shou'd petition."[59] Just as Lady Howe predicted, the weary business of petitioning Parliament against the results came next. The expense was monstrous, as the three earls now shifted their focus away from the Northampton electorate to try their arts of persuasion on members of Parliament. Thomas Howe, however, ultimately prevailed, becoming the fourth Howe brother to take a seat in the House of Commons.[60]

For now, the Howes had three of their men simultaneously in Parliament, enough to fulfill a family ambition to create a recognizable Howe "interest." In the years to come, they would also be able to call upon the votes and support of a handful of other MPs who owed their positions to the Howes. This was quite an accomplishment for a dynasty that did not boast great wealth or the control of any seat or borough. And it was wholly respectable in an age of aristocratic supremacy in politics.

In what was possibly the only example of all three Howe brothers acting together in the House of Commons, they would show their interest in imperial affairs. In early 1771, Thomas, William, and Richard opposed a bill to allow the East India Company to maintain a regiment in Britain for the defense of its possessions in India.[61] One of their objections was purely practical: that an East India regiment in Britain would compete with the regular British army for recruits. But there was a more important ideological objection as well. The Howes feared that the East India army would become a threat, in its own right, to British liberties. The old connection with Pitt the Elder was in evidence, as he approved of the stance taken by the Howes.[62] The brothers were not political theorists or ideologues, but they and Pitt shared many of the same political instincts with respect to managing an empire. This is noteworthy, because, as will be seen, in the political conflict between Britain and her colonies that would dominate the decade after the Seven Years' War, William Pitt was seen by the American colonists as the greatest champion of their rights.

The rising generation of Howes well understood that interest must be cultivated at court as well as in Parliament. Toward that end, the Dowager Lady Charlotte Howe would remain Lady of the Bedchamber to Princess Augusta until Augusta's death in 1772, and she was now supported in royal circles by her son Richard and daughter Caroline. In 1760, Richard Lord Howe joined her in court service when he was appointed Lord of the Bedchamber to the Duke of York, Prince Edward Augustus. The duke was loyal to the man who had commanded him during the dangerous missions off the coast of France in 1758.[63] And the appointment was almost certainly welcomed by the duke's brother, George III, for he liked and admired Richard throughout his life, even acknowledging the blood tie by referring to him as his "Trusty and well Beloved Cousin."[64]

But it is unlikely that Richard's service was more than ceremonial; he and Prince Edward were too dissimilar to become close companions. One was a family man and the other a notorious rake. Prince Edward had led an unsettled existence since his early buccaneering days off the coast of

France with Richard Howe. Despite seeing little more service at sea, he was a rear admiral by the end of the war. Formerly close to his staid brother George III, the Duke of York had become a man-about-town, with a coterie of rakish aristocratic friends and prostitutes. The king disapproved of his behavior, fearing he would tarnish the luster of the royal family.[65] Edward's premature death in 1767, aged only twenty-eight, meant that Richard's court service would in any case be short-lived.

A more secure court connection was Caroline Howe's association with Princess Amelia, aunt of George III. Caroline was never formally in the service of the princess; theirs was a genuine friendship of long standing. Amelia, like the Dowager Lady Howe, had been born in Hanover. Caroline, eleven years younger than the princess, had probably known her since girlhood. There was a sibling quality to the dynamic between the two women, reflected in Caroline's reference to "the old sisterly jokes" she shared during a visit to the princess.[66]

Amelia had never married. She was a rambunctious, un-regal woman who loved riding, hunting, and cardplaying. Loud and sometimes tactless, she drew conflicting reactions from those around her. Horace Walpole found her unfeminine and unattractively self-assured, writing that on one occasion she attended chapel "in riding clothes with a dog under her arm."[67] Yet a lady wrote of her that she was "one of the oddest princesses, that ever was known; she has her ears shut to flattery, and her heart open to honesty. She has honour, justice, good-nature, sense, wit, resolution, and more good qualities than I have time to tell you."[68]

It is not surprising that Caroline, also noted for her plain speaking, cardplaying, and love of the chase, was a regular attendee at Amelia's levees and parties. Walpole, who also attended them, noted jealously that the princess, "one evening, when I was present, gave [Mrs. Howe] a ring with a small portrait of George I. with a crown of diamonds." Walpole took this as an acknowledgment of kinship on the part of the princess; he believed that the Dowager Lady Howe was the illegitimate daughter of George I.[69]

Walpole could be as jealous as he liked in private. Amelia was a royal princess whose opinions exacted outward deference. If the stories were true, her unmarried state did not prevent her from finding love. She was reckoned when young to be the prettiest of the daughters of George II; she was said to have had affairs with the Duke of Newcastle and with the 2nd Duke of Grafton. The last rumor was probably true—on one occasion, she went out riding alone with Grafton for almost an entire night.[70] Horace Walpole suspected that she had borne a daughter by Admiral Lord Rodney.[71] She was also whispered to have been the mother of the composer Samuel Arnold, which would have meant an affair with an obscure commoner.[72] She was unlikely to have had all these affairs and children, but the point is that she was a royal who provoked gossipy speculation. One thing that does seem certain is that she enjoyed the company of the down-to-earth Caroline Howe, a regular figure in her exclusive circles.

For Caroline, the greatest change wrought by the end of the war was the resumption of regular family life as her brothers came home. The year after the peace saw Caroline and her husband, John, looking for a house in London. Hitherto, they had stayed with the Dowager Lady Howe in Albemarle Street when they came to town. The Howes, however, did not have a palatial town residence on the scale of the wealthiest aristocracy. Lady Charlotte Howe's house was small enough that Caroline had to sleep in a camp bed in her younger sister Julie's room when the family got together—"brim full," as she described it, "generally 8 or 9 at breakfast." In the summer of 1764, she and her husband were looking for a property large enough to include a spare room for her brother William.[73] This was before Caroline knew of William's marriage plans. The house in Bolton Row that she and John would rent in 1765 would be their London residence for the next six years.

Nonetheless, the couple remained rooted in the country. They were part of an aristocratic set that moved continuously throughout the year, from London and its wintertime "season" to the provinces in June. Their itinerary over a four-month period in 1759 was typical: Beginning in August at Bristol, Somersetshire, where John Howe was recovering from a bout of illness, the couple moved on to Harleyford Manor, a modern elegant country house in Buckinghamshire and the home of Caroline's friend Mary Clayton and Sir William Clayton 1st Baronet and MP. From there, the Howes were the guests of Sir Francis Dashwood at West Wycombe House, also in Buckinghamshire. Caroline was amused by the marble columns and statues, temples and lake, all inspired by Sir Francis's exotic experiences on the Continent. There were also the Hell-Fire Caves, carved out on the estate as a venue for the notorious club of the same name.[74] Next up was "the Race Week," most probably at Newmarket, which had a regular meeting in October. After a brief stopover at their home in Hanslope, the Howes at the end of October joined the Althorp Hunt in Northamptonshire. By December, Caroline was back in Hanslope, preparing for more travels. They would shortly leave for Battlesden to visit Aunt and Uncle Page, then four or five days in London, then Grantham in Lincolnshire and the Belvoir Hunt with their friend Lord Granby.[75]

Life at these country estates followed a similar rhythm, though each great seat was stamped with the personality of its aristocratic host. If there was foxhunting, it began very early and might go on for the entire day. On other days, breakfast was typically served at nine or ten, followed by riding or shooting for the men and walking and visiting for the women. A guest at Wimpole Hall in Cambridgeshire recalled that breakfast finished at eleven and guests could please themselves until after three, when dinner was served. Outdoor activities normally came to a close by 2 p.m. to allow an hour to dress for what was the most important meal of the day. After dinner, the ladies withdrew and left the gentlemen to drink and talk sports and politics. The custom of separating the sexes in this way was English, and unknown on the Continent. Its origins are obscure, but it was well established by the mid-eighteenth century. Evenings brought the men and women together again and included games, billiards, music, and cardplaying. One aristocratic household might retire to bed by 10 or 11 p.m., while another might carry on into the early hours of the morning. A guest at Chatsworth House in Derbyshire recalled that the night's revelries ended "as the Housemaids begin to twirl their mops and open the shutters to the sunshine."[76]

It appeared to be a life of continual enjoyment, but Caroline may have felt trapped in what was an unvarying pattern with limited opportunities for change or self-expression. John Howe did not always include her in his excursions. He regularly went away from her for long periods, hunting or visiting. "I believe I shall be of the Party as he does me the honour to admit me," she wrote with good-humored sarcasm of an impending visit to Althorp to hunt with Lord Spencer in November 1762. John Howe passed Christmastide 1763, when Caroline was forty-one, hunting with friends, leaving her with her mother in Albemarle Street. On another occasion, she wrote in a playful note, "Mr Howe runs away again from me." This time he was off to "conjure" with learned astronomer Matthew Raper. Caroline was often excluded from these visits, despite the fact that her interest in the latest scientific discoveries of the Royal Society equaled that of her husband.[77]

The reality was that, as a wife in Georgian Britain, she was under the direction of her husband. John Howe—to all appearances a worthy but rather dull character—could limit her engagement with the wider world merely by instructing her to remain at home.

Being childless no doubt added to the predicament. Her mother, the Dowager Lady Howe, had given birth to ten children, and eight had reached adulthood, but this luck changed with the next generation, when both Caroline and her sister Charlotte failed to produce offspring. The two sisters had plenty of company; a fifth of aristocratic marriages during the century were barren, at a time when producing a male heir was the chief duty of a lady in a dynastic marriage. "All property," writes one historian without exaggeration, "depended on the chastity of women"; and aristocratic property inherited through the male line was all-dependent on the birth of a legitimate son.[78] Unsurprisingly, with this sort of pressure no married woman could escape scrutiny. Typical was the attitude of a society gossip at a social event in the autumn of 1774, who inspected the fashionable newlywed young ladies and pronounced it "extraordinary" that only one appeared to be pregnant.[79] The pressure was intense and relentless.

Caroline herself routinely reported on pregnancies and childbirths in her letters. She was blunt about the fact that boys were the longed-for outcome. "I am sorry the boy has turned into a girl," she wrote of a false report that a friend had delivered a son. Upon the arrival elsewhere of a baby girl, "[Y]ou will be sorry to hear Lady Weymouth has a fourth daughter."[80] Although she had grown up in the midst of her mother's fecundity, she had also witnessed the childless marriages of her two aunts, Lady Pembroke and Juliana Page. At the age of forty-one, after more than twenty years of marriage, she found herself in the same unhappy situation.

It was common to blame the woman in such cases, although scientific opinion of the era was divided. A woman's barrenness could never absolutely be proven, so a wife who had intercourse with her husband but failed to conceive gave him no grounds for an annulment. Childless marriages could be dissolved, but only if it was proven that the man was impotent.[81] The main thing was to keep trying, for anecdotal evidence suggested that there was hope in even the most desperate case. Caroline wrote to an acquaintance about a friend who gave birth at age forty-six. And another, Mrs. Edward Morant, "is going to lye in after having been married many years without any prospect of the kind."[82]

Georgian Britons, even the most refined, were very technical about these matters. A young wife who was not conceiving was criticized if she took herself away from her husband's bed, even for a short visit. A married couple who disliked one another and lived apart might still make arrangements to have regular intercourse in the interest of producing an heir.[83] Caroline's conspicuous love of riding and foxhunting would certainly have opened her to criticism, because it was widely assumed that excessive physical activity could lead to miscarriage. It would not be surprising if John Howe blamed his younger wife for contributing to their childless state.

One circumstance suggests that Caroline may have experienced a miscarriage. When the wife of Thomas Villiers, Lord Hyde, miscarried in 1763, the unhappy couple turned to John and Caroline Howe for sympathy. "Mr Howe has given up a few days hunting to make Ld. Hyde a visit, who wrote word *she* had miscarried & that they wished much to see us, talked of charity &c."[84] It was an unusual request in a period when child mortality was high and miscarriages consequently counted for less. Villiers was an old friend of John Howe, a fellow founding member of the Society of Dilettanti. His wife was Caroline's age.[85] The two women had probably known each other all their lives, for their fathers had been together on the grand tour to Paris in their teenage years. Caroline was reluctant to go. "[W]e could not well excuse ourselves," she confided to a friend, as the Howes were already engaged to visit Lord and Lady Hyde on some undetermined future date, and were about to set out to hunt at Althorp and Wakefield, "and they might not understand the difference." Perhaps Lady Hyde was eager to pour out her feelings to a fellow sufferer, although Caroline was not one to enjoy this sort of thing. In any case, sincere sympathy might well have been difficult for Caroline, since Lady Hyde had four healthy children, though she would have no more.[86]

The notable life changes that came to siblings William, Mary, Richard, and Thomas in peacetime—marriage for the first two, the start of a family for Richard, shifts in Thomas's career, both voluntary and involuntary—passed by Caroline, the oldest of them all, now in her early forties. But one significant new change did occur, for it was at this time that she began one of the most important relationships of her life, her friendship with Lady Georgiana Spencer.

Six

Caroline and Company

Caroline Howe's correspondence with Lady Georgiana Spencer begins with a score or so of letters written during the Seven Years' War. Over the ensuing fifty years of friendship, it swells to tens of thousands, only ending with the deaths of the two women just months apart in 1814. Today the correspondence between Caroline Howe and Lady Spencer, as she was known, is believed to be the largest single private collection of letters in the British Library.[1]

It is a striking illustration of the challenge of re-creating the lives of eighteenth-century women—even conspicuously privileged women who left behind significant archival material—that Caroline is barely mentioned in biographies of the two famous daughters of Lady Spencer: Georgiana Cavendish, Duchess of Devonshire, and Harriet Ponsonby, Countess of Bessborough.[2] She was a familiar figure in their lives from infancy onward, a fact that comes through in her correspondence with their mother. Caroline took great delight in her friend's children, particularly the girls. She had an acronym for them—"the dear GAH" (George/Georgiana And Harriet). When Lord and Lady Spencer went on an eighteen-month tour of the Continent in 1763, taking their eldest daughter with them, Caroline checked in on the two youngest and sent Lady Spencer regular reports. "George looked charmingly[,] read to me almost as well as his dear Mamma can do, & showed me his writing," she wrote after one of her visits. "[Harriet] is vastly grown, & after the first shyness came & took me by the hand of her own accord & chattered away all the time I staid."[3] Both Spencer girls were fond of Caroline and called her by her nickname of "Howey," a mark of familiarity in a period when formal titles were often used even among family members. "Georgiana screamed out 'it is Howey' before I had time to see what it was," reported Lady Spencer, amused, when a letter from Caroline arrived.[4] Caroline Howe remained a part of their everyday lives into adulthood and marriage, a virtual aunt who visited and supported them and was included in their circles.

Lady Georgiana Spencer, born Georgiana Poyntz in 1737, was Caroline Howe's half-cousin. Her mother, Anna Maria Mordaunt, had been a celebrated beauty at court, where she served as a maid of honor to Princess Caroline. In 1733, she married Stephen Poyntz, a steward to the household of the Duke of Cumberland.[5] Georgiana was the fourth child of their fruitful marriage. She must have met Caroline through her mother's half-brother, Colonel Charles Mordaunt, who had married Caroline's Aunt Anne.[6] When the teenage Howe sisters visited their cousins Lewis, Osbert, and Harry Mordaunt in London, Georgiana Poyntz was probably often present as well. With fifteen years' difference in age, however, it is unlikely that the two girls were childhood friends.

When she was just eighteen, Georgiana was transformed into a leading figure in high society when she married wealthy, handsome John Spencer in 1758. One of the richest men in the kingdom, Spencer had inherited the estate of his great-grandmother, Sarah Churchill, Duchess of Marlborough. Worth £750,000, the inheritance corresponded roughly to £160 million in today's currency. John's family was taken aback at his choice, surmising that teenage Georgiana had ensnared him: "[S]ome accident has occasioned a familiar acquaintance with the girl, and that is sufficient to make a conquest of a boy of his age," insinuated a relative.[7] No wonder the bride's luck occasioned jealousy, for with no great wealth or connections to boast of, she became mistress of four huge stately houses and the possessor of the fabulous Marlborough diamonds (said to be worth £100,000).[8]

But John Spencer had married for love. In an age when marriage was too often a financial transaction, John was wealthy enough to please himself in choosing a wife. Georgiana Poyntz had auburn hair, dark brown eyes, and a sweet manner. In many respects, she embodied the era's ideal of femininity. When newly married, she captured society's heart by shedding tears over a begging letter from an indigent stranger while standing in the midst of her enormous trousseau—a pink, blue, and gold heap of lace negligees and satin gowns.[9] For Georgiana had sensibility, a gift that was even more highly admired than the musical skills, drawing, and dancing usually displayed by young ladies. In a society that rarely allowed women to be superior to men, the quality of responding with feeling to the world around one was conceded to be a feminine attribute. Women were admitted to be more caring than men.[10]

High society's appetite for romance was filled to overflowing by the circumstances of the wedding itself. John's family refused to give him permission to marry Georgiana until he was of age, so the day after he became twenty-one, he took his betrothed aside at a ball at Althorp, showed her the license, and "he smilingly asked me if I would marry him now," recalled Georgiana Spencer. "I told him with all my heart," and the two were privately married in a bedchamber of the vast palace on December 20, 1755. They rejoined the dance immediately afterward, none of the guests suspecting a thing.[11]

London society competed to pay its respects to Georgiana. Her aristocratic status was confirmed when John Spencer became a viscount in 1761, making her Lady Spencer; when he was elevated to the rank of earl four years later, Georgiana became a countess. If Caroline had overlooked her little cousin back in their childhood days, she now must have seen her in an entirely different light.

The friendship that developed between the two women was an attraction of opposites. In contrast to Caroline's forthright personality, it was said that Georgiana Spencer had the womanly art of "seducing people into right ways."[12] Her emotional empathy may have been a bit of a pose; her desire to help the unfortunate was genuine, but so was her urge to show off. The incongruous mixture was not lost on Caroline, who once observed to her friend: "I have often wonder'd that you who cast so much light, & who do not appear to me quite to dislike that others should observe the bright shine, have more than once expressed sentiments expressive of liking the ___secretum iter, et fallentis semita vitae [the untrodden paths of life]."[13]

The Spencers were pronounced one of the happiest married couples of their day. They had wealth, rank, youth, and, within a few years of their marriage, three children. The eldest, Georgiana, born in 1757—"my Dear little Gee," Lady Spencer called her—was to become the famous Duchess of Devonshire, a fashion leader, gambler, and politician. A year later, in 1758, Lady Spencer produced the all-important male heir, George, followed by younger daughter Harriet in 1761.[14]

Though outwardly their marriage must have looked like a fairy tale, John Spencer was a difficult person, often moody and withdrawn in company and subject throughout his life to bouts of ill health. Acquaintances complained of his penchant for "fretting," and looking on the worst side of things. Six years into the marriage, Caroline was reassuring her friend that she was "not half so afraid of [Lord Spencer's] grave looks as I used to be."[15] Spencer's one significant display of emotional intelligence was his marriage to an affectionate, communicative woman whose warmth had the capacity to open him up. But if Georgiana listened sympathetically to the introverted John, he did not listen to her in turn. Rather, Caroline would become an emotional mainstay to her over many years, a friend to whom she could confide her worst fears. Caroline understood Georgiana's need to unburden herself and encouraged her, counseling, "whenever you have these black ideas hovering round in your mind, . . . I wish you, if you cannot at once drive them away, that you'll sit down & write to me, I am certain it would be useful to let them out that way, & I shall always receive such communications as the greatest mark of confidence & friendship you can give me."[16] Her friendship with Lady Spencer would in many respects reprise Caroline's greatest role in life, that of eldest sister.

Caroline often came across as direct and unfeminine in her interactions with others, but, like all the Howes, she only talked about her deepest feelings with reluctance. "I well know," she wrote, quoting from contemporary poet William Mason's *Caractacus*, that " 'The Heart that bleeds from any stroak of Fate, or human wrongs, loves to disclose itself, that listning Pity may drop a healing Tear upon the wound,' yet I fear such indulgence is sometimes detrimental, & the Nerves afterwards the worse for it."

Emotional venting was not always wholesome, she thought. Even in the midst of a Howe family crisis, she apologized to Lady Spencer for "unburthen[ing] my mind"; "I am afraid of probing myself too deep when I am with you lest I should hurt you." Yet she was unstinting in expressing affection. "[M]y dearest best beloved friend," she wrote to Lady Spencer, "I will not attempt to tell you how happy I shall be to see you again." And on other occasions she wrote artlessly, "do love me," and "I do most heartily wish you to love me," and "I have only to repeat that I for ever think of you, & am always wishing for a letter."[17]

Their shared love of gambling brought into relief the contrasting personalities of the two friends. Both women enjoyed competitive games. Lady Spencer played billiards, becoming so adept at the tabletop game that her friend confessed to feeling jealous. Caroline's consolation was her superior skill at chess. "[A]ll my hopes are you never will find time for it," she warned Georgiana, as she could not endure being beaten.[18] But their chief love was the card games played for money that were ubiquitous to high society, such as quinze, whist, faro, loo, and macau.

During the century, betting as a means of adding zest to any activity was endemic to every social rank of the nation. The proverbial story is often told of the London club where, when a member fainted, his fellows immediately laid bets on whether he was dead or alive. For aristocratic women gamesters such as Caroline and Lady Spencer, gambling was a chance to test their courage in the roll of dice or a play of cards.[19] Caroline was a risk-taker, like her brother George, and she was naturally attracted to "high play" (betting large sums). But if Caroline sometimes liked to coax her fellow players to place ever-higher bets, she kept her own gambling under control.

Lady Spencer, on the other hand, came from a family of compulsive gamblers.[20] Over many years of friendship with Caroline, she confessed her attempts to overcome her addiction. Once, when she had failed in a resolution to put a time limit on her cardplaying, Caroline counseled her that it was much easier not to begin to play in the first place. Trying to quit midplay, "when spirits & hopes of winning back, eggs one on," was almost sure to fail. It was not the money, she warned, but "a desire to win," that kept one at the table. Lady Spencer admitted, "I am an Idiot about play, & make what amends I can for that Vice—by being something of a Lady Bountiful to the poor. I believe these two qualities hang by some whimsical Connection together," acknowledging that her celebrated charity was at least in part driven by a guilty urge to compensate for her gambling.[21]

For both Caroline and Lady Spencer, love of cards brought them into another crucial social space where aristocratic women were able to engage in the men's world of politics. Women played alongside men in private settings rather than clubs, but that did not inhibit them from throwing themselves into the same excesses as the male gamblers, presiding at the table in the role of dealer or banker, running up fantastic debts, and staying up until dawn in pursuit of winnings.[22] The relationships established around the gaming table segued naturally into the social politics that was never far below the surface of eighteenth-century aristocratic gatherings.

Like other politically involved aristocratic women of their time, Caroline and Georgiana always operated in private and informal spheres. As long as they did so, they were recognized and accepted by their contemporaries. In sharp contrast, the women who occasionally crossed boundaries—for example, by excessive public involvement in political campaigning—could find themselves barraged with criticism. In such cases, the so-called sexual slander in the press could be extremely hostile, depicting them as unfeminine and power-hungry.[23]

Women like Caroline Howe and Lady Spencer were not feminists. Their political engagement was accepted by them and by the world only insofar as it was clearly for the sake of family, not of self. "It was a society," writes historian Elaine Chalus, "that accepted women as political actors as long as their participation did not threaten the fiction of a male polity on the one hand or that of female inferiority and natural subordination on the other."[24] An example of this was Dowager Lady Howe's successful newspaper appeal to the Nottingham constituents in 1758 without drawing criticism upon herself.

Caroline Howe and Lady Georgiana Spencer gathered and purveyed political intelligence, acted as go-betweens in requests for political favors, and protected the images and reputations of the men in their families. Lady Spencer was uniquely situated in this respect. The eccentric Duchess of Marlborough, John Spencer's great-grandmother, had stipulated in her will that he must take no active part in Parliament. Spencer was confined to managing elections for others, something his great wealth made possible. Even after his elevation to the peerage placed him in the House of Lords, he continued to sponsor candidates for the House of Commons, as he did for Thomas Howe for Northampton in 1768.[25] Because of the vicarious nature of his involvement in parliamentary politics, and also because of his poor health, John Spencer relied heavily on his wife as a political collaborator. This put husband and wife on the same level in many respects as they both pulled strings from a distance.[26]

Caroline, for her part, had been raised in a family whose women regularly exerted whatever influence they possessed on behalf of their men. She had served an apprenticeship under the indomitable Lady Pembroke, and, after twenty years of marriage, she continued to act on behalf of her brothers—although, curiously, never her husband. John Howe was sometimes assumed to be one of the famous "brothers," in the newspapers, but he had no aspirations to enter Parliament, nor did he have extended kin who might gain advantage from his wife's court and political connections.[27] In fact, John was somewhat in the shadow of his wife's more eminent family. In an era when wives were firmly subordinate to their husbands, advocating for her younger brothers instead allowed Caroline an unusual degree of latitude. As we shall see, it was the sister and the brothers acting together that brought the Howe dynasty into the American War of Independence.

CONFLICT WITH THE American colonies was one of the most divisive issues in British politics after 1763. The Seven Years' War had generated an immense national debt that led to a series of attempts to tax the American colonies. The most famous of these—the Sugar Act of 1764, the Stamp Act of 1765, the Townshend Duties Acts of 1767, the enforcement of duty on tea that led to the Boston Tea Party in December of 1773—gave the hitherto-disunited thirteen mainland American colonies a focus around which they moved toward nationhood.

But American nationalism was still in the future. At the outset of the colonial protests against British taxation, the Americans were loyal Britons. There was not yet any idea of an American nation. On the contrary, Americans felt that they had just helped their mother country to vanquish a hated French threat to British liberties in America. They were sincere in their admiration of British military heroes—to some, martyrs—like General James Wolfe and George Augustus Lord Howe. This sparked all the more outrage at what they believed were unconstitutional taxes imposed on them in the decade after 1763. They naturally looked for a champion in the metropolis for their cause, and they found it in Richard Howe's patron, William Pitt, who would earn the admiration and gratitude of many American colonists for his forthright speech against the Stamp Act, enacted just a few years after the peace.

In 1763, George Grenville became prime minister with a determination to enforce taxation of the American colonies. It was under his administration that the Stamp Act was passed, placing duties on a range of everyday items from playing cards and dice to newspapers, legal forms, and shipping documents. This sparked protests on an unprecedented scale in America. The Stamp Act Congress that met in New York in October 1765 announced the mantra "No taxation without representation." Merchants in the major American seaports canceled their orders from London, adopting a boycott of British goods as a means of forcing a repeal. Meanwhile, a wave of riots throughout the colonies successfully prevented peaceful distribution of the stamps. In Boston, in particular, fierce riots had raged for days in August, culminating in the notorious destruction of the home of Lieutenant Governor Thomas Hutchinson, who saw his fine house with its woodwork wainscoting vandalized, his garden torn up, his family's money, clothes, and library destroyed. In practice, royal authority was nullified by the crowd actions.

In January 1766, American colonists eagerly hailed Pitt as their savior when he was reported to have declared in Parliament that Britain had no right to impose taxes on the colonies. Pitt was already a hero on both sides of the Atlantic for leading the nation to victory in the Seven Years' War. Now he declaimed that American rights were as dear to him as the rights of Englishmen, as he championed American resistance. There were very few British politicians, if any, who would agree that Parliament had no right of taxation over its American colonies. It has remained a moot point whether in fact Pitt actually said it or was misreported.[28] Pitt himself would subsequently distance himself from such a huge concession of Parliament's sovereignty, but he certainly thought that assertion of full British authority over the colonies was impolitic and an error. He was a high-profile figure who might naturally have stepped forward to resolve Anglo-American differences, yet he was also a mercurial—perhaps manic-depressive—and unpredictable individual who did not work well with others. His health would break down repeatedly after 1763, until his death fifteen years later.

George Grenville had no chance to respond to the colonial unrest, because George III, who had a personal antipathy toward him, had removed him from office by July 1765. His replacement was the Marquis of Rockingham, whose government would repeal the Stamp Act in 1766, but with the mitigating declaration that Parliament had the right to legislate for the American colonies "in all cases whatsoever."[29] If leading American patriots understood this to be a mere sword of state—words to appease members of Parliament but never to be put into practice—they would find themselves disabused of that idea in the years to come.

William Pitt's mental imbalance was only one contribution to the instability of the nation's politics during the crucial decade when a resolution of Anglo-American tensions was needed. Another was the determination of its new king, George III, to assert what he saw as his proper position as a "patriot" prince. George—remembered as the monarch who endured lengthy bouts of insanity in the final half of his almost-sixty-year reign—had come to the throne as a young man in 1760 with rigid ideas about his role.

The previous two Georges had been strongly attached to their Kingdom of Hanover, a bias that aroused anti-Hanoverian feeling within the British nation. George III was determined to show that he was a true Englishman, famously asserting in his accession speech, "I glory in the name of Britain." But if he loved Britain, he was unhappy with the mainstream Whig party politics that had prevailed since the time of his great-grandfather George I. As we have seen, leading politicians like the Duke of Newcastle had for decades presided over a political system that managed elections and distributed places and pensions to MPs in order to control Parliament. In practice, the Whig political machine never entirely controlled the House of Commons, but it constituted a monolith that prevented effective opposition.

The Whig argument that the rival Tory party constituted a threat to liberty and the Protestant Hanoverian succession was wearing thin. In the first half of the eighteenth century, Tories had been tarred as disloyal Jacobites who sought the restoration of the absolutist Catholic Stuarts to the throne. The stereotype—never really accurate in any case—was badly outdated. In fact, the Tories shrank as an organized movement to the point where almost everyone in British mainstream politics called himself a Whig. Instead of rival parties, it was Whig factions—headed by people such as the maverick William Pitt or the mainstream Duke of Newcastle—who clashed with each other for power.[30]

By the middle of the century, the Whig party appeared to some as a bloated political system that was improperly diminishing the power of the Crown rather than saving the kingdom from a Tory threat. Ministers such as the Duke of Newcastle, who had headed the Whig government party since 1754, purportedly undertook to manage the House of Commons in the service of the king. In practice, George II had been obliged at times to give way to his powerful prime ministers. Nevertheless, leading Whigs could defend their methods with the argument that their political machine ensured a functioning and responsible Parliament that checked the power of the monarch, secured stability against faction and mob rule, and safeguarded British liberty—a system that was in marked contrast to the absolute monarchies on the European Continent.[31]

But George III had a different view of the matter. He saw the powerful Whig magnates as unconstitutionally curbing his royal authority and obstructing good government. He believed their "corrupt politics of place and pension" served the few at the expense of the nation's welfare. The young king was determined to act independently for the good of his realm, breaking the rigid party pattern by employing good men, whether Whig or Tory, and creating a "non-party government."[32]

George III's ideas were not unique; the notion that party politics got in the way of the public good was a commonplace one. But George, a stubborn young man who did not easily accept points of view that were not his own, accelerated the process of dismantling the old Whig system. His first actions in office triggered a lengthy period of political instability as long-standing political alliances fell apart. From 1763 until the 1770 appointment of Frederick North, 2nd Earl of Guilford, whose administration would oversee the start of the American Revolution five years later, George III had no fewer than five prime ministers.

The Howe brothers, who would play a leading role in the only effort to bring a peaceful resolution to the conflict between Britain and her colonies in 1776, have left scant evidence of their attitude toward the burgeoning American controversy during the decade leading to war. They were not political thinkers, but rather men of action. The brothers, unsurprisingly, were not given to great speeches in Parliament. In the twelve years between the end of the Seven Years' War and the start of the American Revolution, there is almost no record of William having spoken before the House of Commons.[33] Richard did better, speaking on at least a score of occasions, but contemporaries complained that his delivery was confused.[34] It has been said of Richard that "his primary allegiance was to himself," because he appeared to accept government office without regard to people or principles.[35] But viewing Richard's career moves through the prism of his sister's letters during a decade of political turmoil reveals a different story.

When Richard Howe became a junior Lord of the Admiralty under Prime Minister George Grenville in 1763, his first "land job" in more than twenty years, it was a natural move for him. Richard was an MP and a landed gentleman; as head of a growing family, he was needed at home to support and strengthen the position of the Howe dynasty. But the move did raise some eyebrows, for Grenville, once a friend and ally of William Pitt, had become permanently estranged from Richard's mentor. Caroline, always vigilant to protect her brother's image, betrayed some defensiveness on the subject when she wrote to Lady Spencer in April 1763: "I had a line from Lady Howe, to say I should be surprised to hear that my Brother was that day to kiss hands for the Admiralty, that his motives &c must be kept, till we meet, but that she believed we should when we learnt them, see, that his acceptance was unavoidable."[36]

Caroline, however, did not need to fear that her brother would become isolated from his political friends by accepting a place in the Grenville administration. William Pitt, always a rather enigmatic figure, proved to be strangely unwilling to assume leadership at this tumultuous time. The opposition was in disarray, incoherent, barely led by an aging Duke of Newcastle. Within the immediate social circles of the Howes, John Manners, Marquess of Granby, whose hunt Caroline regularly joined, would also take up office under Grenville in 1763.[37] Richard's political associates could not have been all that astonished to see him accept a place under the man who, as it transpired, would two years later introduce the Stamp Act and set the American colonies ablaze.

Richard's other close political ally was the Duke of Grafton. Augustus Henry FitzRoy, 3rd Duke of Grafton, was a lifelong admirer of Pitt. Almost a generation younger than Richard and Caroline Howe—born in 1735— Grafton loved country pursuits, hunting, husbandry, and the racetrack, dividing his time between Euston Hall in Suffolk and his Northamptonshire seat of Wakefield Lodge. Caroline and John Howe formed a regular part of the duke's circle. In a letter written near the end of the Seven Years' War, Caroline captured the casual footing of her stay at Wakefield in just a few lines to Lady Spencer: "The Duke of Grafton went yesterday to Newmarket [races], Mr Howe had a very pretty fox chase with him on Friday with Mr Selby's Hounds, they two fight at Chess the Wakefield evenings, the rest at Loo [a card game] don't be frightened my dearest Ly. Spencer, I am not gone mad; it is only [betting] 5 half crowns."[38]

Outside of his personal coterie, however, the duke had a reputation for being unapproachable and a self-indulgent aristocrat who—as Walpole put it in his usual unsparing terms—thought "the world should be postponed to a whore and a horse race."[39] This is undoubtedly too harsh, but the fact is that until Anthony Eden became prime minister in 1955, Grafton had the distinction of being the only British prime minister ever to be divorced at all, and, until Boris Johnson's arrival in Downing Street in 2019, he was the only PM to be divorced while in office. This made him the focus of intense criticism, as there was a growing public perception that divorce and immorality were on the rise within the ranks of the aristocracy, with supposedly grave implications for public morality. The press played a role, zealously reporting scandals such as the Grafton divorce and trumpeting the modern notion that the public had a right to know about those in positions of public trust. Those who deplored both the immoral actions themselves and the publicity they garnered believed that the social order was under threat.[40] The Grafton divorce looked particularly bad because it involved a lord who occupied a high office; it was not finalized until 1769, a year after Grafton became prime minister. The marriage, however, had broken down several years earlier. And Caroline's inside knowledge of the events leading to the split reveals that she was on an intimate footing with the Graftons, far closer to them, in fact, than her less sociable brother Richard.

In 1756, the Duke of Grafton had married heiress Anne Liddell, the only child of Sir Henry Liddell, an old friend of Caroline's husband and a fellow founding member of the Society of Dilettanti. Sir Henry, the wealthy owner of northern coal mines, became Baron Ravensworth in 1747.[41] His daughter's marriage to a duke united new money with blue blood, but Anne Liddell always declared that it was a love match.

And therein, perhaps, lay the problem. The notion that marriage was for love or companionship, and not solely for the advancement of the family, was on the rise during the century.[42] Expectations were changing. But Georgian society had by no means accepted the principle that a wife could kick against the married state merely because she disliked her spouse. By the standards of the day, Anne seems to have had very high expectations for her marriage that were unfulfilled, for the acrimony between the duke and his duchess was obvious after five years of marriage and three children. To preserve a shred of privacy, they argued in French in front of their servants, but everyone knew that she resented his nights out on the town, and he disapproved of her noisy card parties, too often still in full swing when he arrived home from his club. In 1761, the ducal couple took an extended trip to the Continent, partly, so whispered gossip Horace Walpole, in hopes of a reconciliation.[43]

It was on their return the next year that Caroline formed an intimate relationship with the Duchess of Grafton. Lady Spencer was abroad; no doubt Anne FitzRoy filled a gap. Caroline toured Oxford with the duchess in the summer of 1763 while the duke was in London. The two ladies were "escorted by a Soldier & a Sailor two very good sort of men, I believe you know neither of them," a coy reference to her brothers, Richard and William. The autumn of that year found Caroline constantly at Wakefield

Lodge. When she spent Christmas at Euston Hall, Lady Spencer was jealous, writing from Naples: "[W]hen did you ever pass so much time in one year with me, as you have this last year with the Dss of Grafton," her tone reproachful. "I think her clever & sensible enough, to make you find me Monstrously insipid when I come back. . . ." She can't have been reassured to hear that Caroline had been presented with a ring set with the duchess's own hair.[44]

As Caroline's friendship with the duchess blossomed, the rift between the ducal couple only deepened, for not long after they returned from the Continent, the duke met Nancy Parsons, a notorious high-class prostitute who had once performed at the opera. She had a long list of former lovers and boasted that she once earned "100 guineas in a single week, charging clients a guinea a time."[45] None of this seemed to deter the unhappy Grafton from falling in love with her. Miss Parsons could be both cultured and charming. Clearly he felt that his wife did not understand him and he longed for sympathy.

In the summer of 1764, when the duchess was heavily pregnant with their fourth child, she received an anonymous letter informing her of the duke's affair. This was hardly necessary, for even before the baby arrived in July, Grafton was seen openly with Nancy Parsons at the Ascot races.[46] There could be no keeping it a secret at that rate, and he did not try to, scandalizing a world in which outward appearances mattered by showing himself frequently in public with his mistress on his arm. The duke spent handsomely on Nancy Parsons; the duchess decamped to London with the children.[47]

Caroline tried to protect her friend, glossing over the break-up in a letter to Lady Spencer with a story that Anne FitzRoy was visiting family. "With regard to the report you mention," she wrote, "be it with or without foundation it is a most disagreeable one," but it was groundless. The duke was at Wakefield Lodge as usual, and the duchess had gone on a visit to her parents. They write to one another constantly, she assured Lady Spencer, and she was confident that the ugly rumor of a split would die of its own accord once the duchess returned to Wakefield Lodge.[48] Caroline was being disingenuous. Although she knew the real reason the pair had separated, she was attempting to limit the damage in order to smooth the way for a reconciliation.

But a permanent break between the Graftons was inevitable. In 1764, they agreed to a legal separation. The duchess maintained her own residence in London on an allowance of £3,000 per annum.[49] Caroline was sympathetic, visiting the duchess before the separation, and she wrote to Lady Spencer, "She seems the most miserable of human beings; indeed I do not wonder at that."[50]

It was not until the duchess began an illicit affair with John Fitzpatrick, 2nd Earl of Upper Ossory, in late 1767 that the Duke of Grafton saw an opportunity to obtain a divorce. It was the scandal of the decade, if not the century, because by this time Grafton was prime minister. The fact that Grafton was cohabiting with Nancy Parsons was public knowledge, and both he and his errant wife were tarred as dissolute in the eyes of the nation. They obtained their divorce, and she married Lord Ossory weeks later, in March 1769; the duke discarded Miss Parsons with a pension and married a new duchess in June. Anne, now Countess of Upper Ossory—a step down from a duchess in rank—lived chiefly in the country and was parted from her children by the duke, although she was to have others in her second marriage.[51] Some years later, the enterprising Nancy Parsons married Charles Maynard, 2nd Viscount Maynard, and finally became a titled lady.[52]

Caroline duly befriended the new Duchess of Grafton, but the close intimacy she had had with the first duchess was not replicated the second time around. Elizabeth Wrottesley was ten years younger than the duke, and at twenty-four was half Caroline's age. Perhaps the duke was relieved, because Caroline Howe was almost certainly one of the ladies who had kept his first wife playing cards well into the night.

If Caroline was an accomplice as Anne FitzRoy flouted her husband's injunctions against late-night parties, she nevertheless was no more a feminist than she was a political reformer. She did not seek to extend women's rights. She behaved and spoke throughout her life as one who felt herself to be empowered because a combination of circumstances—her personality, the dynamics of her family, and her rank in society—meant that she was, in essence, in control of her own happiness. She did not speak out against the blatant double standard that prevailed during the eighteenth century, under which men were allowed or even rewarded for sexual adventures, and women were ruined by them. Nevertheless, a sense of equity and fair play ran through her reactions to the marital problems of the women she knew. When her friend Lady Cork was brought to court by her husband on a trumped-up charge of adultery, Caroline was indignant—"quite wild," she exclaimed, in wanting to see Lord Cork punished. She appeared in court on her friend's behalf. Lord Cork dropped the charges and paid the costs.[53] When her sister Mary's brother-in-law, George Pitt (later to become Baron Rivers of Strathfieldsaye), abused his wife until she left him, Caroline sympathized with the wife, Penelope Pitt, and maintained a correspondence with the beleaguered lady when she moved to Europe, tactfully representing her perambulations around Europe as necessary for the sake of her health.[54] By Caroline's code of behavior, Mrs. Pitt was to be pitied and supported in her navigation through an impossible marriage.

It is unsurprising, then, that after the Graftons separated in 1764, Caroline remained a friend to the duchess, only dropping her acquaintance (at least to all appearances) after Anne began the affair with Lord Ossory.[55] We may even speculate that Caroline did in fact keep in touch with the former Duchess of Grafton, for she had many opportunities to do so discreetly. Lord Ossory played cards in Caroline's London set, and called at Battlesden, where Aunt Page supported his successful candidacy as MP for Bedfordshire in 1767.[56] And Caroline's personal maid, Mrs. Read, had a niece in Lady Ossory's service for many years after the divorce, ensuring a very private conduit for news of her old friend.[57]

Thus, Richard Howe always had impeccable sources regarding the political intentions of the Duke of Grafton and others via the Howe social network. This means that during a period when William Pitt held himself aloof from his associates, Richard was able to follow closely the plans of this statesman whom he so admired.

In a single set of letters written over a four-month period in 1763, Caroline has left a vivid cameo of how she kept her finger on the pulse of political trends. Shortly after Richard entered the Board of Admiralty, Caroline reported to Lady Spencer that the Duke of Grafton was dining with Pitt and Lord Temple. A few weeks later, she informed her friend, "the Duke of Grafton & Ld. Villiers set out for Chatsworth & afterwards they go on to Ld. Rockingham's, they meet the Duke of Cumberland at both places," including in one sentence most of the leading old Whigs trying to regroup into an effective opposition. Her contacts in this instance were not only Grafton but also the Duke of Cumberland, the favorite brother of Caroline's friend the Princess Amelia.

And what was the upshot of these political consultations? Caroline did not commit that to paper, for letters were frequently opened by the post office during that century, and political letters were sometimes stopped. To avert this, Caroline sometimes wrote in cipher, another precaution taken by those in the know. She patiently tried to explain the system to Lady Spencer, but her less technically minded friend found decoding a challenge. Using cipher was not foolproof in any case; Caroline was convinced that the post office stopped one of her letters when the clerks found they could not decipher her code. "I am satisfied the post people, angry they cannot make out our Cypher, are determined it shall be of no use to us; I am vastly vexed."[58]

But there was no need to interpret the sight, quickly reported to Caroline in early September 1763, of William Pitt's chair going into Buckingham House, the royal residence. Pitt's meeting with the king was intended to be "a profound secret," wrote Caroline, but it did not stay one for long. A colonel in the guard saw Pitt go in, hurried to his club, and reported to "Ld. Sandwich Mr. Thynne Mr. Calcraft & Mr Jenkinson." Thus, the political grapevine that was part of Caroline's life was set in motion, spreading the word that the king had sent for Pitt to discuss asking him to join the cabinet. Pitt spent three hours with the king, according to the willing spies watching outside, and five hours the next day with the Duke of Newcastle, whom Pitt left "in very high spirits." On Monday, Pitt returned to Buckingham House to find that he was not to be offered a place after all.[59] The young king showed his inexperience by this spontaneous and too-public consultation. The episode only increased the sense of instability of the Whigs in opposition.

This minor political drama illustrates the world Caroline knew. Watching events, collecting political information, disseminating it to her friends, was second nature to her, for she and her mother had done it all their lives. She was a close, careful observer, as her letters show, and whatever she knew, Richard knew. The two eldest Howe siblings were constantly in each other's company—traveling together, visiting one another's homes, eventually living almost next door to one another.

Richard occupied a succession of government posts after 1763 that trace his continued loyalty to William Pitt. In July 1765, he resigned from the Board of Admiralty in anticipation of a new administration; Grenville's days as prime minister were known to be numbered. A week later, Richard was treasurer of the navy in the newly formed administration of Charles Watson-Wentworth, 2nd Marquess of Rockingham, which would preside over repeal of the Stamp Act. Joining the Rockingham government may have given Richard the appearance of abandoning Pitt, but this was not so. He would have known that Pitt would have been most welcome in the new administration, for he had been courted by the Duke of Cumberland but had steadfastly refused to join. Richard would also have been aware that his friend the Duke of Grafton had also been prevailed upon to take up office with the Rockinghams, on the condition that Pitt could still change his mind and come into the government whenever he chose.[60]

In 1766, at the height of the Stamp Act Crisis, Richard Howe showed that he shared William Pitt's sympathetic attitude toward colonial protests when he favored admitting the petition of the American Stamp Act Congress to the House of Commons. His stance was a bold one, because the Congress was an extralegal organization widely seen as a threat in Britain, even by politicians with American sympathies.[61]

Shortly after the repeal that same year, the Rockingham administration collapsed and Richard resigned as treasurer of the navy, only to be reappointed in a new government, this time one headed by the Duke of Grafton himself, and William Pitt. Pitt accepted a peerage on the occasion, becoming the Earl of Chatham. But Chatham's health was poor, and he never really directed the administration that was named for his title. Richard remained in office when Grafton became official head of the ministry in 1768 and resigned with him in early 1770. In that same year, Richard was promoted to the rank of rear admiral of the blue and was sent to command the Mediterranean squadron during a short-lived international crisis when war threatened with Spain.[62]

In a period when, as we have seen, no fewer than five prime ministers had been appointed in seven years, leading to a constant reshuffling of political alliances, Caroline's letters show that Richard had been able to remain loyal to Chatham throughout. He had accepted offices under other prime ministers only when doing so did not go against the interests of his patron. Caroline's excellent contacts, coupled with those of other senior members of the family—the Dowager Lady Howe, and Richard himself—meant that they were able to follow Chatham's lead. It was characteristic of the Howes that they did not explain their motives to anyone outside their immediate circle. This inscrutability opened them up to accusations of self-interest by cynics such as Horace Walpole. But the period between the Seven Years' War and the American War of Independence was a decade of unusual instability, which posed challenges to many in Britain's political class.

William Pitt's admiration of the brothers George and Richard Howe, born of their exploits in the Seven Years' War, suffered no diminution. In 1770, writing of Richard, Chatham said that "no man living [has] more zeal for the service of his country." A few years later, in 1773, he applauded Richard's forthright parliamentary petition requesting a much-deserved increase in the half-pay of junior navy officers. Richard was going against government, for the proposal was opposed by Prime Minister Lord North, but he prevailed, and the petition was approved by a large majority of MPs. Caroline gave Lady Spencer the whole story:

> [H]e has been at a great deal of trouble & for some time, & I believe had not great hopes of succeeding, I was as you would be certain of, quite wild with joy, when I heard he had carried his point, the division was 154 to 45, all the minority of course were with us, we had also the Duke of Grafton's interest, . . .

"I am happy that the captains of the navy have triumphed over the *misère* of Downing Street," wrote Lord Chatham approvingly when he heard the news.[63] Like all the Howes, Richard was a political pragmatist, but one who was willing to take a stand when he knew the cause to be a just one. His care of those subordinate to him in rank in the naval service was a conspicuous attribute, and one that made him a popular officer. Richard's maintenance of independence in the political arena, without being a radical or an agitator, was a significant factor in the role he was to play in the American crisis that was just a few years away.

In late August 1769, Caroline Howe, just forty-seven, suffered a seismic change in her life when John Howe died suddenly at their London home in Bolton Row.[64] He was barely sixty. No letters on Caroline's side survive, but Lady Spencer's concerned replies give an idea of their tone—open, straightforward, and honest, conveying a natural sense of her loss of a husband and a married life that had been one of quiet companionability. "Your letter my Dear Howey conveys every sentiment a heart like yours must feel, in the most natural & consequently the most affecting manner, I flatter myself the writing of it was some relief to you, & I assure you the reading it was to me." Howey, she urged, must write again soon: "I shall be impatient to hear from you toward the latter end of the Week, when I trust you will be much Calmer." Caroline could be relied upon not to make a fuss. "I depend upon your own fortitude & resolution to support you," wrote Lady Spencer hopefully, for she was unable to pay an immediate visit to her friend, "& I have the Comfort of being sure you will exert it to the utmost."[65]

Fourteen years later, when Lady Spencer in turn lost her husband, she would react very differently, churning out an emotional diary and a voluminous cache of letters addressed to Caroline that minutely documented her feelings as the events surrounding the death of Lord Spencer played out.[66] The need to vent to a sympathetic listener seemed to be a Spencer family trait; Lady Spencer's famous daughter the Duchess of Devonshire regularly poured her heart out to her bosom companion, Lady Elizabeth Foster. Caroline, meantime, spent the month following the death of her husband recuperating in the countryside. In October 1769, back in London, she told an inquiring friend that she was well, with only "some degree of nervous complaints."[67] After that, life seemed to go back into the usual grooves.

But of course, something very important had changed for Caroline. She was now an independent widow in her late forties, with more personal freedom than at any other time in her life. No longer did she need to frame her plans to Lady Spencer with "Mr Howe discourages it," or "he leaves me quite at liberty to determine for myself."[68] The most striking difference was that her life became more centered on London. John Howe's favorite hunting grounds at Wakefield, Euston, and Grantham receded into the background. Hanslope, too, became a thing of the past, although Caroline would not finally sell Stokes Manor until 1774.[69]

In 1771, Caroline moved into a townhouse at Number 12 Grafton Street in the Mayfair district of London. This would be her home for most of the rest of her life. The house was part of a new development on land held by the Duke of Grafton. Richard moved at the same time, into Number 3. The two houses were just around the corner from their mother Charlotte's house in Albemarle Street. Richard's new residence, larger than Caroline's, was part of "the grandest section of the whole scheme," and perhaps this is why Number 3 still stands today. Caroline's house was an ordinary gentrified dwelling of the time in its dimensions, but all of the new houses were unique and incorporated the elegant features characteristic of Georgian London's luxury premises, such as vaulted entrance halls, ornate plasterwork, and classical columns in both the exterior doorways and the blind arcades of interior walls.

Photographs survive of the north terrace of Grafton Street before its

Number 12 Grafton Street, viewed from Albemarle Street, London. The bay
windows of Caroline's house are visible. The house was redressed with a
terracotta façade in the nineteenth century; originally its facing resembled that
of Number 11, barely visible here on its left. When this photograph was taken
in 1964, Number 12 was the premises for Sawyer Booksellers. It has since been
demolished.

demolition, with the striking canted bay windows of Number 12 in evidence. Caroline also acquired the adjacent house at Number 11. MP John
Crawfurd—"Fish" Crawfurd, as he was known—lived at Number 10
and was one of the many regular callers on Caroline in her new, stylish
townhouse.[70]

At Grafton Street, Caroline Howe was not a political hostess in the style of
her friend, Lady Spencer. The influential aristocratic hostesses of the period
required wealthy husbands and correspondingly palatial London residences

The first-floor landing of Admiral Howe's residence at 3 Grafton Street. Located on the west terrace, it forms part of the grandest section of dwellings on the street. The exterior of Number 3 is plain, apart from handsome columned door frames, but the interiors boast marble staircases and magnificent plasterwork.

that could accommodate large formal dinners and balls. Widows of the period were unlikely to have the requisite domestic space, and, in any case, Caroline lacked the income for extravagant entertainment.[71] Nevertheless, as we will see, the politically active found their way with regularity to her Grafton Street drawing room. The widowed Mrs. Howe kept abreast of the doings of London society—its political battles, domestic conflicts, heartbreaks, and aspirations—by drawing people to her fireside. She could not enter the exclusively male domains of her brother Richard, but her wit, her warmth, and a deck of cards often brought the denizens of that world to her.

Once she settled into her new home, Caroline's drawing room became a gathering place for a select group of friends, relatives, and political gossips. The Howes, the Spencers, the Devonshires, and many others came and went. She left a lively description of a typical afternoon. Sitting down to her household accounts at noontime, "before I cd. get thro' that, Col Mordaunt came, & soon after Sir Fran[ci]s Molyneux. As he rose to go in walked Ld Fred: [Cavendish] who greeted me with a how do you." No sooner was Lord Frederick dispatched when "Mrs Heywood came. After all were gone" (by this time it was 3 p.m.) "I finished my money matter, have writ thus far, must now read my newspapers, then dress my head for the opera."[72]

Much of the cast of characters on this particular occasion were relatives of one sort or another. Cousin Mordaunt, one of Aunt Anne's sons, was also a regular part of the Spencer set and a member of the Althorp Hunt.[73] The Molyneux family were distant kin and neighbors from Caroline's juvenile years in Nottinghamshire. "Mrs Heywood" was Catherine Heywood, née Hartopp, the sister of Lady Howe. Lord Frederick Cavendish was an army officer and an old comrade of Richard's from the amphibious raids on France. One of the aristocratic and politically influential Cavendish family, he remained for life a handsome bachelor and called frequently at Number 12.[74]

Caroline liked male company, sometimes telling her servants not to admit ladies: "[Y]ou understand the diff[erence] of letting in men only," she explained to Lady Spencer,

> one picks up news, one can say go, one likes their chat in general better than what one has with the other sex, still I mean in general, reasons sufficient I think. Sad paper this;—well! I read a note, set about answering it, in walks [my brother] William, we talked whilst he franked [a letter], then another dear man came; it was [George Spencer] Ld. Althorp, he went away a minute before William, . . .

and Caroline resumed her note until she heard once again upon her front door "a rap; up they brought Ly Irwin, very pleasant and agreeable, a sensible companion is she, we talked & talked" until joined by Lady Waldegrave and Miss Lloyd. And so the day flew by.[75] It is no wonder that Horace Walpole called Caroline well informed.[76]

In the privacy of her home, Caroline could indulge her lifelong love of learning, purchasing the latest publications in science, exploration, and fiction. Her letters over many decades throw up a serendipitous picture of her literary tastes, which were profoundly eclectic: Smollett's *Humphry Clinker*, Miss Burney's *Evelina*, *The Female Quixote* by Charlotte Lennox, all testify to her avowed love of novels ("idle books," she called them). She admired the plays of Colley Cibber, and scolded Lady Spencer: "What never read before *The Careless Husband?* I believe it is reckoned the best of Cibbers, & has been much admired. You do come out sometimes with some pretty ignorancies." She consented to read Hugh Blair's immensely popular *Sermons*, much commended by Lady Spencer, but remarked, "I do not expect he will cause me to submit more quietly than I already am disposed to do, & which all people in their senses should do, to any evil, that is absolutely unavoidable." She read Shakespeare and Pope, Swift and Addison, Cumberland and Voltaire. Benjamin Franklin would find that she followed keenly the most recent scientific discoveries in the publications of the Royal Society. At the age of forty, she was commenting to Lady Spencer that it was horrid weather for everything "but reading Hooke," hardly an enthusiastic endorsement for what was probably *The Posthumous Works of Robert Hooke*, the natural philosopher. She read the classics—the names of Virgil, Plutarch, Homer, Aeschylus, Horace, and Thucydides all appear.

She enjoyed studying languages. She could read fluently in French, and also, with a little effort, in Italian. From her youth, she could read and write in Latin, and, at the end of the American War of Independence, she and Lady Spencer began to study ancient Greek together. She was struggling with a Greek translation on Christmas Day in 1783, and the joint labors of the two friends would continue over many years, as usual with a vein of competition on Caroline's part. "You are got so forward & so far beyond me [with ancient languages], that I will not read a word of either Greek or Latin whilst I am on my next visit to you, & expect you will answer to this, *Vanity, envy & Jealousy*—may be so, but so it must be."[77] Book catalogs kept Caroline up to date with the latest publications, and she purchased the most intriguing titles just as soon as they came out—for example, Lord Chesterfield's *Letters to His Son* in 1774, and, three years later, Robert Watson's *The History of the Reign of Philip the Second, King of Spain*, the first authoritative book in English on the subject. Living as she did in an age of exploration, travel books abounded, and Caroline, who had never been abroad since she was a girl in Barbados, loved them. She read Joseph Banks's *Letters on Iceland* and Eyles Irwin's *A Series of Adventures in the Course of a Voyage up the Red-Sea* in 1780, the year both titles appeared. She was lucky enough to have access to the manuscript version of an early account of New South Wales, *An Historical Journal of the Transactions at Port Jackson and Norfolk Island*, published in 1793 by naval officer John Hunter, who was serving on HMS *Queen Charlotte* under Lord Howe at the time. Australia had captured her imagination since its earliest British settlement, and in 1802 she snapped up the second volume of David Collins's *An Account of the English Colony in New South Wales.*[78]

This was the heyday of the famous Bluestocking circle, a network of intellectuals and lovers of learning whose meetings were hosted at the homes of a set of wealthy women. Inspired by the French salons of the eighteenth century, the Bluestocking assemblies aimed to be enjoyable as well as intellectually stimulating, but they eschewed the cardplaying and political gossip that was endemic at fashionable West End parties. In this respect, they were not the natural environment of Caroline Howe. Nevertheless, she counted the eminent Bluestocking hostesses Elizabeth Montagu and Elizabeth Vesey among her friends, writing to Lady Spencer, "I was very much amused at a blue stockings at Mrs. Vezey's & staid till betwixt 11 & 12 without being in the least tired."[79] Elizabeth Montagu left a brief tribute to Caroline shortly after the death of George Augustus Lord Howe in the Seven Years' War, writing to a friend, "I am very glad you are acquainted with Mrs. Howe, and do not wonder you are charmed with her. There is an inexpressible magnanimity about her without any thing fierce or masculine."[80] Men described Caroline as masculine; Bluestocking hostesses did not.

WHEN SHE WALKED OUT of her front door onto Grafton Street, a wide world of choice confronted Caroline, for a well-to-do middle-aged widow could visit many places in Georgian London without a male escort. Like her Aunt Pembroke, she loved the opera. By the time Caroline had moved into Grafton Street, King's Theatre in Haymarket was one of the leading European venues for Italian opera, which, with its exotic settings and continental performers, had electrified London aristocracy since the days of George I. It remained both expensive and exclusive throughout the century, but it also made attendance at other musical performances both fashionable and popular. Concert halls of many flavors were proliferating, but Caroline

remained devoted to the opera.[81] It was not just the music. The irrepress-
ible tendency of Georgian London to turn every venue into a club meant
that King's Theatre was a center for court intrigue, gossip, and flirtations
by the wealthy.[82]

In the same year that Caroline moved into Grafton Street, the Ladies'
Coterie opened at Almack's Club in Pall Mall. This was the first mixed-sex
club for gambling and sociability. Despite its name, both men and women
were admitted. It was the brainchild of a set of leading society ladies.[83]
No records of the club's activities survive, but Caroline—who called it the
Ladies' Club, and attended regularly—mentioned cardplaying and dining.
Members had to be admitted by ballot.[84] Caroline's brother Thomas, and
her sister Charlotte and husband Robert Fettiplace, were among the earliest
members, as well as a host of other members of her West End circle.[85]

However elevated its membership, the Ladies' Coterie came under fire
in the newspapers as another instance of the deplorable trend toward female
independence that ill-became the high-ranking women who joined.[86] The
Bath Chronicle published a satirical account of "a brilliant meeting of the
members of the Coterie," supposedly attended by a list of well-known adul-
teresses, including the former Duchess of Grafton, Lady Ossory.[87] Attacks
of this sort had no effect on Caroline, who described the club a year later as
"very flourishing."[88]

With her expenses as a widow now entirely under her own control,
Caroline was free to indulge her liking for betting at cards. She referred
good-naturedly to "me, & my gambling," tacitly admitting the risky recreation as part of who she was. She played weekly at the residence of Princess
Amelia—"My princess day," as she called it to Lady Spencer.[89] It was five
years after the death of John Howe that Lady Mary Coke, another regular attendee in Amelia's circle, wrote of being ushered into the drawing
room of the princess, "where I found the usual party, but a change in the
playing that I extremely disapprove." Caroline Howe had raised the stakes
significantly, "for which I think her much to blame," and Lady Mary told
her so.[90] Caroline made a practice of ignoring the fastidious Lady Mary, of
whom more later. Over the years, she won and lost, but she had too much
good sense to risk the financial ruin that befell so many of her aristocratic
contemporaries.

When Caroline ventured outside of London as a widow, she typically visited the Spencers at Althorp, her brothers, and her sister Mary Pitt. William

Howe became lieutenant governor of the Isle of Wight in 1768.[91] He and Fanny stayed at Somerley in West Sussex. In 1772, Richard purchased a country seat at Porter's Lodge in Hertfordshire, which became his principal residence for the rest of his life.[92] Sister Mary and her husband, William Augustus Pitt, still serving in the army, lived at Heckfield Park in Hampshire.[93] And Battlesden, where Aunt Page had lived alone since becoming a widow in 1763, continued to be frequented by Caroline and her siblings, just as they had done in childhood.

Caroline also visited her husband's old friend Matthew Raper at his home in Thorley, Hertfordshire. No longer did she sit apart while the men "conjured" on scientific questions of the day and the activities of British explorers. Caroline was interested in these things in her own right, and she was a favorite with confirmed bachelor Mr. Raper. Despite the fact that he was old enough to be Caroline's father, her sister Julie disapproved of the unchaperoned stays at Thorley Hall. She confided to Lady Spencer, "Howey is at Battlesden, she goes from thence next Saturday for a week to Mr Rapers, which I don't approve of at all for her."[94] Yet Matthew Raper was an old friend whose discretion Caroline could count on; she would rely on him soon, in the crisis over the American colonies that followed the Boston Tea Party.

Other changes were in the wind for Caroline. In 1771, Thomas, who was living with his sister Julie and his mother, the Dowager Lady Howe, fell seriously ill. It began in August. Julie described pain and swelling in his legs, sickness, and weakness, calling it "very bad rheumatism." At the time, "rheumatism" could encompass a wide range of disorders. The illness dragged on for weeks. Thomas made the most of it as long as he could, getting up for meals and speaking of when he would be well again. Caroline visited the invalid, but she felt she could do no good. "Tom lived entirely by himself whilst I was last at Richmond wd. not let us read to him or sit with him," she wrote unhappily.

Concerned for her brother, Caroline wanted to cancel visits to her sister Mary at Heckfield and brother William in Somerley in order to stay close, but her mother would not hear of it. Caroline must visit William, the Dowager Lady Howe insisted. Caroline gave way to her mother, writing to Lady Spencer, "[S]he could not imagine why we all wanted so much to have me with her just now, that we cd not persist." But the truth was that elderly Lady Howe was herself unwell, with symptoms suggestive of heart disease.[95] No one dared tell her, so Caroline went on her round of family visits while Richard took charge at home. He moved both Tom and Lady Howe to his more spacious house in Grafton Street, where the doctors could be at hand. He kept distant siblings informed and stood ready to summon them if either of the patients became critically ill, while trying not to panic his mother and sister Julie.

It did Caroline no good to be exiled to Somerley, where she could not be useful. As soon as she arrived, William showed her a letter from Richard, reporting that Tom was much worse. Isolated and deeply unhappy, her self-possession slipped. Imagining that Lady Spencer had transferred her affections to a recent new acquaintance, she wrote what was perhaps the most insecure letter of her life:

> I can no longer flatter myself in being the first in your affection, after Lord Spencer, [Lady Spencer's mother] Mrs Poyntz, and the dear GAH [George, Georgiana, and Harriet], as I used to tell you I was. Do not think I reproach you, indeed I do not mean it, far from it, friendship[,] affection is no more in one's power than love is. . . . Do not be angry this one time I will never write so again.[96]

Lady Spencer's reply has not survived, but she could hardly have had the heart to be angry toward the forlorn Caroline. Tom died a month later, in November 1771.

The loss of another brother must have given the Howe siblings a brutal reminder of the passage of time. Caroline was approaching fifty. They were a vigorous generation, but, despite five marriages among them, only Richard had children and none were boys who could carry on the family title. It is striking that children of such fertile parents were unproductive, but it was not unusual. Only in the case of Charlotte could marital discord have been the cause—hers was an unhappy marriage.

And thence came the next family crisis. Charlotte's husband, Robert Fettiplace, had learned nothing from the disaster that befell him in 1762, when he had been obliged to flee across the English Channel to the Continent to escape debts incurred while gambling on horses. In August 1772, he was arrested and sent to debtors' prison. Richard, as head of the family, had to deal with his bickering creditors. When Fettiplace was released, he left the country again. "Mr Fettiplace has somehow or other contrived to get at liberty," wrote the exasperated Caroline, "& is gone abroad but we hope it will not prevent the agreement going on with the creditors, who at last have all consented to the propositions made them in the summer," the result of Richard's frustrating negotiations. It would be many years before he returned, and Charlotte meanwhile was forced to board with her brother-in-law or stay from time to time with her mother and sisters.[97]

But Caroline, now ensconced in Grafton Street and an established figure in London society, began a new phase of her life with zest. Most unexpectedly, she would soon make her mark on history by taking the first step that drew her brothers into the American War of Independence.

Seven

A Game of Chess

The full story of the involvement of the Howes in the American War of Independence began months before the outbreak of hostilities in Lexington and Concord in April 1775. And it began not on any battlefield, but in Caroline Howe's Grafton Street drawing room. In December 1774, Benjamin Franklin, in London as agent for several American colonies, found himself being drawn into a series of highly secret talks with two private individuals, David Barclay and John Fothergill. Both men, by profession a banker and a physician respectively, claimed to have unofficial links to the British cabinet. Their objective was to find a way of stopping the slide toward armed conflict.

These talks were so secret that Franklin's "Journal of Negotiations in London," written on his homeward journey in March 1775, remains the only evidence that they ever took place. Franklin never fully understood who Barclay and Fothergill were working for, or how close they were to government policymakers. But his bemusement deepened when, weeks after the first talks began, he was approached by Richard Howe, seeking to undertake what appeared to be a separate and parallel negotiation. By what route had Lord Howe become involved? How closely associated was he with the two original negotiators and their shadowy government contacts? Franklin never found out, and historians have proclaimed it "an enigma." But within Caroline's letters are clues revealing that she was the one who was working behind the scenes, facilitating her brother's activities in this last-ditch and secret government peace initiative.

Benjamin Franklin, the self-made polymath from Pennsylvania who began his career as a printer and rose to become a renowned scientist, inventor, politician and author, did not move in the aristocratic circles of the Howes during his years in London. Yet from the start of 1774, his name was to be heard in every fashionable drawing room. "The American business at present engrosses the whole talk of the town," noted one of the Cavendish brothers on January 29, 1774. It was on that day that Franklin, as agent for the colony of Massachusetts, appeared before His Majesty's Privy Council in Whitehall with a petition requesting the removal of the colony's unpopular governor, Thomas Hutchinson.[1]

Just nine days earlier, the metropolis had been shocked by the news of the so-called Boston Tea Party of December 1773: a riot in Massachusetts, in which colonial activists, opposing British taxes on tea, had dumped a shipload of the beverage into Boston Harbor to prevent it from being unloaded. When the news reached London, it brought rebellious Massachusetts into the limelight. Franklin's imminent meeting with the Privy Council was transformed into a showcase for metropolitan outrage at the Bostonians, who, ever since the Stamp Act, had distinguished themselves for violent protest.

On January 29, the gallery was crowded with members of the public, eager to witness the dressing-down of the irritating Doctor Franklin, that too-vocal champion of American rights. In a tirade lasting an hour, the government's solicitor general, Alexander Wedderburn, publicly demolished Franklin's character. Wedderburn roared that the American was "malignant," a man without honor, an incendiary who inflamed the innocent people of Massachusetts against British rule. Onlookers laughed as the agent was humiliated.[2] West End card parties buzzed with "the American business" for a week, but it would be many months before the full implications of Franklin's ordeal before the Privy Council would become clear. A serious crisis with America was indeed brewing, and the most influential colonial spokesman ever to serve in London had been discredited at the outset.[3]

Franklin, for his part, considered going home to Philadelphia. He had been in London on colony business for ten years, and his wife, Deborah, was ill and wanted to see him again. But his private travails were quickly engulfed by the response in London to the Boston Tea Party. Most MPs were outraged at the wanton destruction of the tea by the Massachusetts protesters, so there was little opposition on March 14 to the Port Act, which proposed closing the port of Boston until the town paid for the tea.[4] This was the first of the four so-called Coercive Acts—introduced over a period of three months and all passed by large majorities—which would lead directly to the War of Independence. Together with the Quebec Act, they were known in America as the Intolerable Acts.

But war was very far from the expectations of the British government in the spring of 1774. The intention was simply to isolate and punish Boston, long seen as the instigator of colonial defiance, a troublemaking locality whose restraint surely would restore imperial harmony. This plan backfired spectacularly across the Atlantic, where many leading patriots from the other colonies, who had initially been disgusted by the Boston Tea Party, swung around in support of beleaguered Massachusetts when they learned of the British government's heavy-handed punitive measures.[5] Twelve of the thirteen colonies that would become the United States endorsed a proposal to hold a Continental Congress, scheduled to meet in Philadelphia in September.

As the crisis deepened, Franklin found that there were some who wished him to remain in London. Over the summer of 1774, there were rumors on both sides of the Atlantic that the First Continental Congress would send a panel of delegates to England to represent colonial grievances. An optimistic few hoped that a "constitutional line" could be negotiated that would ensure the rights of the colonies and put an end to a decade of Anglo-American discord.[6] If such talks took place, Benjamin Franklin would have an important role to play in the proceedings. Despite the debacle at the Privy Council, he was still seen in British government circles as the foremost spokesman for the colonies in London, and the best informed.[7] John Pownall, a government undersecretary in the American Department—the ministerial department responsible for the American colonies—quietly consulted with Franklin in August about what to expect from the Congress, because, as he put it to a colleague, the delegates in Philadelphia "will probably do what [Dr. Franklin] bids them to do."[8]

Pownall's interest in Franklin was purely professional, but old friends also urged him to overlook his poor treatment and stay. One of these was Jonathan Shipley, the Bishop of St. Asaph, a close friend whom Franklin often visited in the Shipley family home in Twyford, Hampshire.[9] The Shipley family shared his love of books and chess—and the bishop shared his American friend's support for colonial rights. In his sermons, he described the colonists as "the only great nursery of freemen left on the face of the earth"; in the House of Lords, Shipley voted against coercive measures.[10] The unfailing hospitality of the Shipleys in rural Hampshire would be a refuge for Franklin while he hung on in Britain.

Another was Dr. John Fothergill, like Franklin a Fellow of the Royal

Society, and also a member of Franklin's favorite London club, the Club of Honest Whigs. Fothergill was an eminent Quaker physician whose clientele included the aristocracy. He was a distinctive figure in his characteristic broad-brimmed hat, which, according to Quaker practice, he did not remove in the presence of ladies. "An old prig," one fashionable woman called him, but Fothergill was a kindly, intense man with strong principles. He hoped that the Continental Congress would be a vehicle for peacefully settling the question of American rights, and he thought Franklin should remain in Britain in case talks took place.[11]

It would be Fothergill and another long-term Quaker associate of Franklin's, banker and merchant David Barclay, who initiated Franklin's secret negotiations in London. They began in earnest early in December 1774, when the two Quakers approached Franklin with a request that he set out on paper a list of terms—"Hints," as they came to be called—that might be acceptable to the American Congress.[12] Fothergill and Barclay undertook to convey Franklin's paper to moderate British ministers, who wanted to avoid war, without revealing its author. All three agreed that Franklin's involvement should remain a "dead Secret," as he was persona non grata with the ministry since his public dressing-down in January.

Who in the government would wish to read the "Hints"? David Barclay suggested Thomas Villiers, Lord Hyde, a member of the Privy Council who had influence in the cabinet of Prime Minister Lord North. Another whose name was mentioned was American Secretary of State William Legge, Earl of Dartmouth. Fothergill volunteered that he had daily access to Dartmouth in his role as the family's physician.[13]

But Franklin, looking back months later, realized that the first contact made by the band of peacemakers had actually taken place earlier, in what seemed to be a totally unrelated event. In early November 1774, Franklin was attending a Royal Society dinner when he was approached by fellow member Matthew Raper. "[T]here was a certain Lady," Mr. Raper told him, "who had a Desire of Playing with me at Chess, fancying she could beat me." Mr. Raper thought Franklin would be flattered when he found out the identity of this lady—no less than Mrs. Caroline Howe, the sister of Lord Howe. If Dr. Franklin accepted the challenge, he was instructed to wait upon her at her house in Grafton Street as soon as possible, and "without farther Introduction." Franklin agreed, but he found the whole business "a little awkward," and put it off.[14] The timing of that first, inconclusive contact with Mrs. Howe, weeks before his meeting with Barclay and Fothergill, never made sense to Franklin. He knew nothing of the lady and, even if he had known her, it would have given him no inkling of what was to come.

For it was the unlikely conjuncture of a ladies' charity, a newborn baby, and a childhood illness that was the route by which Caroline—and, through her, the Howe brothers—became involved in the American crisis. The episode is a case study in how the overlap of public and private spheres enabled aristocratic women to become deeply engaged with politics.

IN THE SPRING OF 1774, while the Coercive Acts were coming before Parliament, Caroline Howe was generally avoiding politics in her letters. Only Lord Spencer's vote against the Massachusetts Government Act on May 11 found its way into her news to Lady Spencer. "They sat till eleven," Caroline reported, and Lord Spencer found himself "in the minority 20 to 70 odd," after which he sought consolation at the fashionable Almack's Club "& played at Quinze and won."[15]

Instead of politics, Caroline's letters were full of a unique business that was almost entirely undertaken by women: The Ladies' Charitable Society. The brainchild of Lady Spencer, the society was a response to the steady stream of begging letters that were delivered to her door.[16] In Lady Spencer were united two qualities that made her irresistible to beggars: a reputation for benevolence, and a husband who was one of the richest men in England. Not only was she genuinely moved by Georgian England's widespread poverty, she also was a sincerely religious woman in an age when religion was unfashionable among the aristocracy.

But a compassionate heart was not enough to relieve the sufferings of the Georgian poor. The era saw the proliferation of private charitable institutions, and with them, inevitably, arose new controversies over the impact of charity on public morality. Especially in London, that Babylon of the modern world, philanthropists quickly found their good intentions mired in controversy.[17] Two of the best-known charities of the century—the Foundling Hospital, established in 1739, which took in abandoned, poor, and illegitimate children, and the Lock Hospital, established in 1746, which treated venereal disease—found themselves under fire for promoting vice.

Despite the protests of the governors of the Lock Hospital that some of their patients were under the age of ten, theirs remained a relatively unpopular cause. The Foundling Hospital, which attracted a great deal of public support, also took its share of criticism. Abandoned infants and children were appallingly commonplace in Georgian London, but there seemed to be no alternative—no effective birth control existed, and a large number of parents lived in poverty, unable to support their families.[18] Critics predicted that such organizations would encourage sex outside of wedlock and irresponsible sensuality in the lower orders, who would no longer need to worry about ridding themselves of unwanted offspring.

More novel to modern ears was the view that orphanages would encourage laziness in poor married couples, who would seize the opportunity to cast off their legitimate progeny and "lead lives of idle abandon." This was a public concern that affected patterns of fundraising; wealthy ladies in particular carefully avoided the association of their names with any cause that could be construed as encouraging immorality.[19]

Lady Spencer's new society addressed a different moral dilemma: how to separate the deserving from the undeserving in the mountain of appeal letters arriving at her door. Begging letters were a part of everyday life for Georgian London's wealthy, some of whom instructed their servants to discard them unopened. Lady Spencer, however, who received more than her share, took them all seriously.

Unfortunately, it was both easy and profitable for the dishonest to send fake hardship letters to the wealthy. Lady Spencer was no fool, and she sometimes employed agents to weed out fraudulent or undeserving cases. But she also refused simply to lapse into cynicism. By 1773, Lady Spencer had decided to organize The Ladies' Charitable Society, one of the first philanthropic organizations that tested the means and characters of applicants to determine their eligibility for charitable assistance.[20]

However enthusiastic Lady Spencer was about her new project, in 1774 she was obliged to curtail her involvement. Her eldest daughter Georgiana was about to be married. By mid-March, the London papers were carrying the rumor that "a treaty of marriage is on foot" between "his Grace the Duke of Devonshire, and Lady Georgiana Spencer, eldest daughter of Earl Spencer."[21] Georgiana was only sixteen. Lady Spencer had once declared that she feared her little Gee would be "snatched" from her while still a child, but she and Lord Spencer could not resist when their daughter caught the eye of the Duke of Devonshire, probably the most eligible bachelor in the kingdom. Immensely rich and powerful, he was also undemonstrative and aloof; friends argued that he had hidden depths, but others suspected he was simply dull and self-absorbed.

Lord and Lady Spencer would never consciously subject their daughter to an arranged marriage. It was supposedly a love match, but Georgiana barely knew the duke and was probably more in love with the idea of a marriage. In any case, the wedding date was set for June 1774, by which time Georgiana would be seventeen. Lady Spencer collected a trousseau for her daughter that cost more than a thousand pounds (around a quarter of a million pounds today), a foreshadowing of the future duchess's role as a paragon of fashion.[22]

The bustle surrounding the wedding was not made easier by Lady Spencer's slow recovery from a miscarriage suffered the previous November. Since giving birth to Harriet in 1761, she had lost two other infant daughters, and was apparently unable to carry a pregnancy past the first trimester.[23] Now in her mid-thirties, each miscarriage took its toll, the painful event itself followed by the characteristic hormone-induced depression, "my usual Miserable lowness & Sleepless nights," as she described it to Caroline.[24] In April 1774, while she was in Bath recovering from a recent miscarriage, Caroline took charge of the Ladies' Charitable Society in her absence.[25]

By August, Caroline was handed the reins of the society; Lady Spencer wrote that she was miscarrying yet again, this time while visiting her newly married daughter at Chatsworth, the magnificent Derbyshire estate of the Duke of Devonshire. Ten days later, she admitted that she seldom passed a day without "Violent fits of crying." Caroline tried to comfort her friend: "if this *was* to happen, & I believe we none of us had much hopes that it would not, it is better it should be thus early, than later." And yet she cautioned Lady Spencer about having had two miscarriages within ten months. Take a cure at Bath, she enjoined her, or whatever the physicians advise, if it would restore "to your constitution what your frequent miscarriages take from it."[26]

Taking charge of the Ladies' Charitable Society meant that Caroline was assuming a public role for the first time in her life. She was required to hire new staff, manage conflicts among the little team of caseworkers, oversee the budget, smooth the ruffled feathers of aristocratic patrons who felt their contributions were underappreciated, and solve trivial issues of places and spaces for record storage and society meetings. Lady Spencer thought it was all to the good; Caroline's trait of "active benevolence," she wrote, had been kept hidden from the world.[27]

Inevitably, Caroline was pressured to do more. Lady Spencer hinted that the organization required "a Dictator to be chosen to settle every thing—I am delighted to see that you are at present *that* in effect tho' not in name." By no means, replied Caroline, backing away from the hint: "[I]ndeed I am forced to lead much more than I like or would do, but if I meddle at all I cannot help doing it in earnest," for, like her brothers, she was by nature systematic and thorough.[28]

During a Howe family gathering at her mother's house in Albemarle Street, Caroline was obliged to compose a long letter on charity business to Lady Spencer. Writing in the midst of them all—the Dowager Lady Howe and Julie, brothers William and Richard with their wives Fanny and Mary, and sister Mary with her husband General Pitt—Caroline remarked longingly that when Lady Spencer returned to town, "I shall feel again, what it is to be at Liberty." But a few weeks later, she was still busy, working out a filing system that would enable efficient retrieval of the society's growing archive of letters.[29]

In a world where private charities were organized and directed by men, the Ladies' Society was conspicuous for its almost entirely female management. More than thirty ladies sat on the two committees, and the membership list was sprinkled with titles. Of the five "Lady Presidents" selected to direct the committees in early December, three were ladies by right as well as by nature: Lady Mayne, Lady Dartmouth, and Lady Caroline Egerton.[30]

We have seen that this was a period when aristocratic women were being blamed for a growing moral decline, with figures like the Duchess of Grafton held up as cases in point. But the women who dedicated their time to the Ladies' Society were more typical of their era and their class. After a Sunday evening meeting, one wrote, "I could not help reflecting with how much more real pleasure [we] retired to [our] pillows after a Sunday evening spent in this manner, than if it had been passed amidst the gay tumult of the world."[31]

The privileged lifestyles of the society members were underpinned by numerous domestic servants, but this did not mean that they felt free of family responsibilities. Lady Charlotte Finch, for example, widowed with two children, was also royal governess to the young Princesses Charlotte, Augusta, and Elizabeth, the daughters of George III. In attendance at the royal nursery morning and evening, she was nevertheless keen to contribute to the Ladies' Society whenever she could. Caroline explained that she was restricted to times when she was satisfied that "her *Children* will be properly taken care of & etc. so that she can be at her ease." Lady Spencer still had two children at home, and a duty to try to produce more. Lord Spencer did not want her to overexert herself attending committee meetings, and she would not deny him—he was, of course, her "lord," as she always called him. Caroline was understanding: "If Lord Spencer objects to your coming to our committee we must submit, tho' the common doing there, is no very great Fatigue."[32]

The most heroic mother of the group was Frances Legge, Lady Dartmouth. Indefatigable in her role as Lady President of the Society, she was religious, unpretentious, cheerful, and kind. Both she and her husband, Lord Dartmouth, the American Secretary of State, stood out as a devoted couple in a world of matrimonial cynicism.[33] Although Frances and Caroline had long known one another from a distance, it was the Ladies' Charitable Society that brought them together. In early autumn of 1774, the two met continually between committee meetings, sometimes for hours at a time.[34] Lady Dartmouth was heavily pregnant, and on October 5, 1774, she gave birth to her ninth child.[35]

HISTORIANS HAVE LONG PUZZLED over how Admiral Howe became involved in the secret negotiations of Benjamin Franklin's "Journal." His most recent biographer, David Syrett, declared the whole business to be "shrouded in veils of mystery created by a lack of information." He has concluded that the reason Howe became involved, and at whose instigation, "can only be guessed at."[36] The obvious assumption has been that he was somehow approached by Lord Dartmouth. But as one Franklin scholar admitted, "[W]e have found no direct link between the Admiral and Dartmouth."[37] The direct link was not, however, to be found in the papers of politicians but rather by triangulating seemingly domestic and private events in Caroline's letters with the other known facts of the timeline of Franklin's negotiations with Richard Howe.

On November 1, 1774, Caroline wrote to Lady Spencer: "Ly. Dartmouth's little Girl has been dying since you went of something like St Ant:[hony's] fire, & the [christen]ing put off."[38] Lady Spencer had been in town the previous week. Since her departure, the Dartmouth baby had fallen seriously ill, probably with scarlet fever. The christening, scheduled for October 28, was to be a grand affair in which Queen Charlotte and the Countess of Strafford were to stand as godparents. Instead, on that day little Charlotte Legge was fighting for her life, and the family physician, Dr. John Fothergill, was in constant attendance. The crisis had come on suddenly; just the day before, Lord Dartmouth had been at court, publicizing his happiness at the arrival of his first and only daughter.[39]

As if by some unlucky conjunction of the stars, news of the Suffolk County Resolves in America reached London on the very day of the canceled christening. Suffolk County in Massachusetts had seized the initiative in opposing the Coercive Acts, ratifying a set of local resolves that declared the British acts illegal and unconstitutional, and threatening armed resistance. When the patriot courier Paul Revere delivered the resolves to the Continental Congress in Philadelphia in September, the Congress endorsed them as a show of solidarity with Massachusetts. But the endorsement of the extreme document was a disaster for watching politicians in London, who had hoped the Continental Congress would be a moderating influence on American opinion. A visitor to the American Department in Whitehall described the beleaguered Lord Dartmouth as "thunderstruck," carrying on his duties despite the crisis at home. "[T]hey have declared war against us: they will not suffer any sort of treaty," cried Dartmouth as he reeled from the shock.[40]

As the American secretary, Lord Dartmouth was the cabinet member who most favored conciliation. In the spring of 1774, he had wanted to soften the Coercive Acts with the repeal of the tea duty that had caused all the trouble.[41] Over the summer, he had been receiving disturbing reports from the colonies that the Coercive Acts had not had their desired effect.[42] Rather than restoring order to the Massachusetts Bay Colony, the legislation was spreading disaffection and rallying the other colonies to its cause. The Continental Congress was seen by most British statesmen as a dangerous development, an illegal organization that would lead to unreasonable assertions of American autonomy. But the peaceable Dartmouth saw it as a possible way of negotiating a solution to the crisis. In his well-meaning, diffident manner, he wrote:

> I am not without hopes that some good may arise out of it [the Congress], and illegal as it is, if it should chalk out any reasonable line of accommodation, or make any moderate or temperate proposal, I should in my own private opinion think it wise in government to overlook the irregularity of the proceeding, and catch at the opportunity of putting our unhappy differences into some mode of discussion.[43]

Dartmouth had penned these hopeful lines at the end of August. Now, at the end of October, the Continental Congress looked set to disappoint him by its endorsement of the Suffolk County Resolves. Of course, the Congress had not yet sent the outcome of its own deliberations—it might yet offer a more moderate position—but there was no time to lose. Dartmouth urgently needed a formula for conciliation that he could press in cabinet meetings, one that stood a credible chance of appealing to the broad body of opinion in the colonies. The obvious person to turn to was Benjamin Franklin.

As we have seen, Dartmouth had already sent his undersecretary John Pownall to sound out Franklin in August. But approaching him openly was impossible. Franklin was known to be a key figure in the crisis, and his comings and goings attracted public notice. Dartmouth's predicament was illustrated in the chain of events that ensued when radical Bostonian patriot Josiah Quincy arrived in London in late November. Quincy insinuated himself into the offices of Lords North and Dartmouth for just an hour or so, but that was enough to create trouble. The newspapers blew it out of proportion, reporting that Quincy had had "a long Conference with the Secretaries of State," sparking rumors of a government climbdown.[44] This made it even more impossible for Dartmouth, as a cabinet member, to be seen consulting with Franklin. In addition, Dartmouth probably did not want his hawkish cabinet associates to be aware that he was exploring terms with the notorious American.

An unexpected opportunity, then, was created by the timing of his baby's illness—for, as Caroline's letters reveal, it discreetly drew into the beleaguered Dartmouth's home two people who could assist his project of peacemaking: Caroline and Dr. Fothergill. Fothergill shared Dartmouth's enthusiasm both for the American Continental Congress as a vehicle for peace, and for Benjamin Franklin as someone who could facilitate it. Now the physician found the ideal opportunity to become a discreet go-between for the American secretary and Franklin, for the Dartmouth baby would require medical attention for many weeks to come.[45]

Caroline was an excellent companion in a sickroom. No doubt she listened sympathetically in the Dartmouth nursery as the worried mother weighed up the relative merits of camphor or boiling vinegar as a means of containing the infection.[46] But as a Howe woman, she was naturally also drawn into the urgent discussions in the drawing room between Dartmouth and Fothergill over the recent bad news from America.

Dr. Fothergill would wait another month from the start of the baby's illness to approach his friend Franklin on Dartmouth's behalf. Franklin's "Journal" reveals that Caroline acted immediately, contriving unsuccessfully to set up a game of chess with him in early November, in the midst of the medical crisis in the Dartmouth home, for motives that would remain unclear for many weeks.

Little Charlotte had recovered enough for the christening to go ahead on November 8, but she was still under the watchful care of Dr. Fothergill in early December when he and David Barclay asked Franklin to draw up his "Hints."[47] At the same time, Franklin found himself once again importuned by Mr. Raper to call upon Mrs. Howe, this time in a manner not to be refused. Meeting at another Royal Society event, Mr. Raper "put me in Mind of my Promise [to play chess with Mrs. Howe]," recalled Franklin, "and that I had not kept it, and would have me name a Day when he said he would call for me and conduct me." This time, he was not left to find his own way; Mr. Raper personally escorted him to Caroline's residence. "I had not the least Apprehension that any political Business could have any Connection with this new Acquaintance," recalled the bemused Dr. Franklin when he knocked on the door of Number 12 Grafton Street on December 2, 1774.[48]

Benjamin Franklin might have guessed that "political Business" was afoot had he realized the connections between Mrs. Howe and the other parties urging him to join the peace process. He did not know, any more than his biographers did, that Caroline Howe visited regularly with Lord and Lady Dartmouth. He did not know that Thomas Villiers—the government contact to whom David Barclay proposed to convey his "Hints"—was an old and intimate friend of Caroline Howe and her husband, John. Mr. Raper of the Royal Society was another long-standing friend of the entire Howe family. Even the figures circling Franklin over the summer led back to the Howes. John Pownall, Dartmouth's undersecretary, who consulted Franklin back in August, was a member of the mixed-sex Ladies' Club that met at Almack's.[49] Jonathan Shipley and his family, who had provided a refuge for Franklin in their Twyford home after his ordeal at the Cockpit, were relatives of the Howes and Lady Spencer.[50]

The Shipley ladies visited regularly at Grafton Street. Their connection was most significant, for they would have conveyed to Caroline the hopes of pro-Americans in London that the Continental Congress would open a door to talks. In a London awash with rumors of conciliation, as well as schemes of armed repression, Caroline was well versed in the political trends, and when fate brought her together with Lord Dartmouth and Dr. Fothergill in the home of a sick baby in early November, she was primed to become involved.

The timing of Caroline's involvement with the peace initiative clears up another longstanding conundrum: a promise made, and then broken, by William Howe to his Nottingham constituents. In the first half of October 1774, William was in the midst of running for reelection to Parliament in Nottingham. There were many voters in his constituency who were sympathetic to the colonial cause. General Howe publicly condemned the Coercive Acts as unnecessarily harsh and assured the voters of Nottingham that he would not serve in America.[51]

There was understandable rage in Nottingham when, just months later, he went back on his word. On February 10, the day that William was officially appointed to his military post in Boston, an angry Nottingham grocer named Samuel Kirk wrote him an embarrassing letter reminding him of his election promise. Brushing aside William's excuse that he was commanded by King George and could not refuse, Kirk recalled the stance taken by the late George Augustus Lord Howe in the House of Commons against the subsidy treaties twenty years earlier. The then-Lord Howe had "dared to act *in opposition to a Court*," wrote Mr. Kirk bluntly, adding that William fell short of the standards of his heroic brother.[52] Ever since, the episode has remained as a blot on William's reputation.

If William wasn't exactly lying in Nottingham, argues a major biographer of the Howe brothers, he was at least deliberately altering his views to suit his audience. In January 1775, he let Lords North and Dartmouth know privately that he was willing, after all, to serve in America, while continuing publicly to assert that he would not. This has been seen as a shrewd, if somewhat disingenuous, move by a man who hoped to advance his career despite his ambiguous feelings about the conflict. It has been assumed that William's January bid to serve in America was made independently of his brother Richard, and perhaps with the salve to his conscience that the American crisis might be patched up without bloodshed.[53]

Yet William had made his promise to the Nottingham voters weeks before his sister had been drawn into the secret consultations at the Dartmouth home. There is no reason to doubt his sincerity when he spoke the words. While the elections were in full sway, in mid-October, Caroline was regretting that Richard had been unable to accompany William to Nottingham, because the admiral was obliged to appear at his own constituency of Dartmouth.[54] Ideally, the family had hoped that Richard could have been present to give his support to William's campaign. The family had planned for the brothers to act in solidarity at Nottingham. It is unbelievable, then, that William would have made such a forthright statement on the American crisis at Nottingham—one with major implications for his career and that of his brother—if it were not in accord with the views of the Howe family members at the time.

William's private communication to members of government in January did not come out of the blue, as past historians have assumed, and it fits with the chronology of Caroline's involvement in Franklin's secret negotiations. By mid-October, Dartmouth's American Department was pushing the notion of replacing General Thomas Gage, in command of British regiments in Boston, who was blamed for mismanaging the rebellious colony of Massachusetts. General Amherst, who had served with great success in America during the last war and was a popular figure in the colonies, was proposed as his replacement. Along with Amherst, the cabinet considered sending two major generals. The notes of the cabinet meeting mention no names, but William Howe was an obvious candidate.[55] Everyone remembered George Howe's popularity, which still lent charisma to the Howe name in the colonies.

It is entirely possible that when Lord Dartmouth met Mrs. Howe and Dr. Fothergill in his home at the end of October 1774, the three would discuss not only the chances of a negotiated solution to the crisis but also the role that the military leaders on the ground might play in the proceedings, issues that were then uppermost in the mind of the American secretary. Within days, Caroline took steps to draw Benjamin Franklin to her door. Her views on a military posting for her brothers in the conflicted colonies were already beginning to change.

Franklin's journal of his secret negotiations shows that he was aware that William was being considered for the American command before the end of 1774. This has puzzled historians, who have argued that there is no evidence surviving in government correspondence to indicate that General Howe's name had been put forward at this stage.[56] In fact, Franklin's source was the London newspapers, which since November had been publishing rumors that William would be appointed commander in chief in place of Gage, who was to be recalled "on account of his *Tameness*."[57] Well before January 1775, someone was at pains to publicize the notion that a Howe would, after all, be serving in America.

But on Benjamin Franklin's first visit to Grafton Street, on December 2, 1774, politics did not intrude. He had been invited to play chess. Almost seventy years old, Franklin had by now grown into the image best remembered by posterity, that of a balding, genial figure with shoulder-length hair and plain clothing. The woman he found pitted against him across the game board was sixteen years his junior, also no follower of fashion, dark-complexioned, of forthright manners, yet unmistakably aristocratic. Franklin recalled that he "play'd a few Games with the Lady, whom I found of very sensible Conversation and pleasing Behaviour, which induc'd me to agree most readily to an Appointment for another Meeting a few Days after."

The two rapidly became friends; Franklin succumbed to Caroline's charm offensive, and for the next three months they met regularly to compete over the chess board. His calls at Number 12 became a familiar sight to her neighbors. In a tribute to Caroline, Franklin wrote, "I had never conceiv'd a higher Opinion of the Discretion and excellent Understanding of any Woman on so short an Acquaintance."

Franklin was a man who liked the company of lively, intelligent women, and in Caroline he found one whose interests matched his own. She shared his love of chess and mathematics. Her aptitude in the latter was, in Franklin's experience, "a little unusual in Ladies." They talked about the transactions of the Royal Society, which would have delighted Caroline, recalling to her the visits she and John Howe made to Matthew Raper at Thorley Hall years earlier, when they had discussed recent scientific discoveries. Franklin gave Caroline a copy of his *Experiments and Observations on Electricity*, which she found "great entertainment"—and which gave her an excuse to invite him once again to play chess.[58]

Although Caroline had an ulterior motive, one suspects that she was keen to meet the famous American for reasons of her own. She must have heard all about him from the Shipley ladies. The philosopher was gregarious, amusing, and a lover of games, especially chess. Caroline also prided herself on her skill at the game; she had played it for years with her husband, with friends, and with relatives.[59] Now she would challenge the great Dr. Franklin.

It is a tragedy that neither of the antagonists left a record of their results during three months of matches. They were players with very different styles. Franklin saw chess as a metaphor for life; in his famous "Morals of Chess," he asserted that "[L]ife is a kind of chess," that chess inculcated virtues such as foresight and circumspection, and that the game had the civilizing effect of requiring one to show the utmost consideration to one's fellow player. One should never cheapen the game, cautioned Franklin, by resorting to tricks such as hurrying or distracting one's opponent, or feigning a bad move to put him off guard. And one should not, of course, crow at a victory or "show too much pleasure; but endeavour to console your adversary."[60]

Caroline, by contrast, played to win, and she was not above crowing when she did win. She let Lady Spencer know when she played "two games at Chess with General Conway, and what is more have won them both." Nor did she hide her triumph when she defeated Lady Spencer's brother: "I have just won a Guinea of him at Chess, giving him a Knight."[61]

Yet perhaps Caroline was simply more honest than her American adversary. His contemporaries painted a rather different picture of his behavior over the chessboard to that suggested in his "Morals of Chess." He was known as an impatient player, and as determined to win as Caroline. He was reputed to drum his fingers on the table to distract his opponent, sometimes even moving pieces when a back was turned.[62]

And so the two battled it out—the aristocratic Englishwoman and the Pennsylvania philosopher. One thing seems certain: If Franklin had not found a challenge in Caroline Howe, he would not have visited so often.

Franklin's friendly chess games with fashionable French ladies while he was in Paris during the War of Independence are famous. Caroline Howe was their English counterpart.

The chess parties at 12 Grafton Street, interwoven as they were with the business for the Ladies' Society, provided a mechanism for indirect communication among the Howes, Benjamin Franklin, and Lord Dartmouth without attracting attention. The matches with the American were scheduled close to Caroline's meetings with Lady Dartmouth, enabling the discreet exchange of information. On December 2, for example, she mentioned Franklin's first visit to Lady Spencer: "I really shall have no writing time today, I have for the first time these 10 days played ½ a dozen Games of Chess. It has been with Dr. Franklin." She had also attended two meetings about Ladies' Society business the day before, she reported, one of them "a long confab with Ly Dartmouth." Now she had society correspondence to complete (in between receiving the usual callers), and by six o'clock she was to meet Lord Spencer at the theater to see David Garrick in *Hamlet*.[63] Two days later, when she played her second match with Dr. Franklin, she scheduled a four-hour visit with Lady Dartmouth.[64]

At first, Franklin saw nothing beneath the surface of his games with the charming Mrs. Howe. At their second meeting, on the fourth of December, they briefly discussed the American crisis, in terms that could be described as flirtatious. When they had finished with their game, Franklin recalled, "[W]e fell into a little Chat."

"And what is to be done with this Dispute between Britain and the Colonies?" his hostess asked him. "I hope we are not to have a Civil War."

'They should kiss and [be] Friends," he replied. "[W]hat can they do better?"

Here Caroline inserted a little flattery: "I have often said, says she, that I wish'd Government would employ you to settle the Dispute for 'em. I am sure no body could do it so well. Don't you think the thing is practicable?"

Franklin demurred. The British Government would not employ *him* on such a mission; "they chuse rather to abuse me. Ay, says She, they have behav'd shamefully to you. And indeed some of them are now asham'd of it themselves."

Caroline's quick sympathy no doubt moved Franklin to wax optimistic. If Britain and America wanted peace, he told her, it was eminently practicable, for they had "no clashing Interest to differ about. It is rather a matter

of Punctilio, which Two or three reasonable People might settle in half an
Hour." The American did not want to spoil the atmosphere of a pleasant
afternoon. That very evening, he met with Dr. Fothergill and Mr. Barclay
and agreed to draw up a list of "Hints" upon which to base a plan of conciliation. At the time, he recalled, he still saw no connection between his
meeting with the two emissaries and his "accidental Conversation" with
Mrs. Howe that afternoon.[65]

It was not until Christmas Day that Franklin began to see things in a
new light. No sooner had he arrived in Grafton Street when his hostess
asked whether he would like to meet her brother, Lord Howe. "[S]he was
sure we should like each other," he recalled. Within minutes, Richard Lord
Howe was in the room, expressing "some extreamly polite Compliments"
on the honor of meeting the American. But Lord Howe quickly made it
clear that this was no social visit. The situation in America was alarming,
he said, and he and others in his circle believed that Dr. Franklin was the
man best placed to reconcile the two sides. Richard stressed that he was
acting as an independent member of Parliament who was concerned for
the good of the empire, but that he was well assured that certain ministers
sought a formula for peace.

In what must have struck Franklin as a repetition of his dealings with
Dr. Fothergill and David Barclay a few weeks earlier, Lord Howe requested
the American to draw up a set of terms that would be acceptable to the colonies, promising to act as a go-between and convey them to the ministers.
But why ask for terms from me, wondered Franklin, when the petition of
the Continental Congress to the king was now at hand? He read aloud some
of its ringing phrases, which called in dutiful terms "for peace, liberty, and
safety" and professed loyalty to King George. The words "seem'd to affect
both the Brother and Sister," he recalled. But Richard returned to the point:
In case the petition seemed to ask too much, could Franklin put together a
realistic alternative set of terms? Franklin agreed; they would meet again
in three days at Caroline's house, where Franklin now called so frequently
that his appearance would raise no curiosity.[66]

At their next meeting, on December 28, Lord Howe made his role in
the secret negotiations much clearer. He admitted to Franklin that he had
already seen the "Hints" that Dr. Fothergill had promised were to be kept
under wraps; he named Prime Minister Lord North and American Secretary Lord Dartmouth as the ministers who were interested in finding a

peaceful accommodation; and he asked what Franklin thought of the idea of sending a commissioner to the colonies to "enquire into the Grievances of America upon the Spot."[67] With these words, Richard revealed that he was involved in the only unequivocal conciliatory proposal being considered in the British cabinet by the end of 1774.[68]

It was Lord Dartmouth, of course, who was proposing a commissioner in the cabinet, but the idea had a much longer pedigree. Dr. Fothergill had suggested it to Dartmouth during the crisis that ensued after the enactment of the 1765 Stamp Act. Benjamin Franklin's friend Thomas Pownall, sometime governor of Massachusetts and brother of John Pownall, was pushing the idea a few years later.[69] He had written to Dartmouth in 1773, seeking to be employed as a special commissioner for conciliation. The subsequent Boston Tea Party, however, closed the ears of ministers to such moderate measures.[70]

Now, at the end of 1774, a little band of peacemakers—the Quakers Barclay and Fothergill, Lords Dartmouth and Hyde, the Howes and Franklin—were looking for a solution to a confrontation that was framed in terms of abstract questions of principle and seemed irreconcilable. Perhaps the uncompromising issues could be sidestepped—"blurred," so to speak—so that everyone would be satisfied. What was needed was a formula that resolved some of the immediate grievances, defusing the atmosphere of crisis without requiring Parliament to renounce explicitly its right to tax, or the colonies to acknowledge that it had that right.[71] If everything could only be slowed down, negotiations could replace the move toward armed conflict.

Since early December 1774, Fothergill and Barclay had been actively working with Benjamin Franklin to achieve this, going over his list of "Hints" in several intense meetings. Franklin's original "Hints" were not a blueprint for imperial governance but rather a list of specific suggestions designed to resolve the collective conflicts of the previous decade. On the point of taxation, for example, he proposed that all duties laid on the colonies for the regulation of trade be paid into their respective colonial coffers; that in wartime, the colonies might be requisitioned to contribute to the cost of imperial defense, but only with the consent of Parliament and in a fixed proportion to the amount raised in Britain. The authority of the British government over the empire was to be conceded by the reenactment of the Navigation Acts—legislation that restricted much of colonial trade to the mother country—in all the colonial assemblies. By this mode of acquiescence, the colonies would be consenting to, rather than submitting to, the Navigation Acts. Parliament was to disclaim the right to legislate for the colonies on internal domestic matters.[72]

At the core of the conflict was the issue of the sovereignty of Parliament. The story is usually told as one of an overweening central authority claiming power over nascent local governments. However, it is more accurate to say that Parliament had problems of its own that made it impossible to accommodate the demands of its colonies. In the eighteenth century, Britons still feared that the power of the Crown could increase to become an absolute monarchy of the sort that had existed under the Stuarts. It was the British Parliament that stood in the way of this happening. Because of this, the ministers who were dealing with the crisis in 1774 would never succeed in pushing legislation through Parliament that diminished its authority.[73]

Ironically, George III, the supposed tyrant, was just as committed to a constitutional monarchy as were his ministers. Putting thirteen colonial assemblies on an equal footing with the British Parliament, all under the Crown, threatened to subvert British liberty and enhance the power of the Crown. In the nineteenth century, when the monarch was more clearly a figurehead, such an arrangement became feasible; in the 1770s, it was not. As one British lord—who sympathized with American grievances—put it to Lord Dartmouth, the idea of an American and an English parliament united under the authority of one crown "would add exceedingly to the weight of the Crown & at home, to which I can't say at present that I think *any Increase* at all necessary."[74] The delicate balance between the Crown and its eighteenth-century Parliament was not to be disturbed.

The big question in 1774, then, was this: Could both sides agree to a set of compromises that would back away from armed confrontation, and at the same time avoid thrashing out abstract questions of the rights of British versus colonial legislatures? In addition, there were important practical points of substance that needed to be addressed. Most British MPs were eager to find a way to get the colonies to contribute to the cost of imperial defense. They also wanted reassurance that the Navigation Acts—essential to protect Britain from predatory enemies in a world of global trade—would be obeyed by colonists. Franklin tried to address both these issues in his "Hints."

In the present crisis, the government also needed a face-saving offer from the colonies that would allow Britain to climb down from its uncompromising response to the Boston Tea Party. Ministers had hoped that Boston would offer to pay for the ruined tea, paving the way for reconciliation, but the Boston town meeting voted overwhelmingly against this measure in the summer of 1774.[75] Hopes that the First Continental Congress would offer to pay were dashed when its disappointingly extreme resolves reached London.[76] As the colonies continued to refuse to back down, a military "solution" loomed ever closer.

The peace proposals circulating during this critical period are liable to be misunderstood if they are seen as attempts at final answers to the constitutional impasse. There were leading figures on both sides who did not want war and believed it unnecessary to agree upon a final settlement of the constitutional relationship between Britain and the colonies—at least, not right then. Some British statesmen privately thought it preferable to watch the American colonies gradually free themselves from the bonds of empire. The presumption was that they would naturally become larger and wealthier over time, thus moving peacefully toward a virtual independence and obviating the need for a bloody conflict that might destroy the prosperity of both Britain and America.[77]

Richard's political patron William Pitt, Lord Chatham, offered a plan for conciliation to the House of Lords in two stages in early 1775. Although it was rejected, its contents are worth examining as a demonstration of what British legislators were prepared to concede at this stage of the conflict. Chatham's conciliatory proposal did not address all of the issues raised by the First Continental Congress, but it clearly opened the door to some kind of resolution. He proposed that the British troops in Boston should be withdrawn as a goodwill gesture; that Parliament's authority outside of Britain should be limited to matters that solely affected the empire, such as the regulation of trade; and that Parliament would not tax a colony without the consent of its legislature. Chatham was careful not to open himself up to the charge of denying parliamentary sovereignty, as he had done during the Stamp Act Crisis. Parliament would agree not to tax the American colonies as a concession, not as an admission of the colonies' right to tax themselves. Congress would be declared legal on a temporary basis in order to consider the bill and consent to Parliament's authority as defined in it. Congress would also be asked to consider contributing a permanent revenue to the king, to be granted by the colonial assemblies.[78]

When Parliament rejected Chatham's proposals, the Virginia

Assembly declared, "Lord Chatham's bill, on the one hand, and the terms of the congress, on the other, would have formed a basis for negotiation, which a spirit of accommodation on both sides, might perhaps have reconciled."[79] The defining word here is *might*, for by 1775, not all the American leaders would have agreed to talk, even on the basis of the terms set out by Lord Chatham.

The Howes and their associates working behind the scenes were better informed on opinion in the cabinet than was the maverick Earl of Chatham. They were also closer to the mood in Parliament. In both places, the upstart Continental Congress was abhorred; the idea of opening talks with the illegal body was met with incredulity. An undersecretary recalled the reaction in the cabinet when John Pownall tried to convince ministers to appoint commissioners "to meet deputies from the Colonies to discuss & settle all claims & Parliament to confirm if approved." At first, the cabinet was receptive to the idea. A bill appointing the commissioners could perhaps be brought into Parliament. But, on second thought, the prospect of the Continental Congress elevated to a legal footing "carried so much the appearance of an American Parliament that the whole Cabinet revolted against it."[80]

On the eve of the American War of Independence, the British government neither wished nor saw the need to tear up its constitutional arrangements in order to pacify recalcitrant colonists. It is not surprising, then, that when Benjamin Franklin met Lord Howe, he found that the admiral was less interested in hammering out precise terms than in finding a face-saving opening for the British government to make concessions. Over the next two and a half months, Richard revisited time and again the issue of reparations from Boston as an overture for a peaceful initiative from the British government. A military man like Richard would understand the problem of how Britain, a leading world power since 1763, could retreat from a confrontation with its colonies without appearing weak. Lord Barrington, the Secretary at War, had written to Lord Dartmouth along the same lines on Christmas Eve, putting forward his doubts over the practicability of coercion. He insisted that armed enforcement of colonial taxation was out of the question, and that Britain should look for a way to make concessions "with dignity." He also suggested that withdrawal of the army from flashpoints like Boston should proceed immediately, coupled with a blockade of troublesome New England and possibly a repeal of the tea duty for colonies to the south that had not associated with the Continental Congress.[81] New York, given its sympathetic loyalist population, was the colony that stood out in such a scheme. Its Assembly had decided by early 1775 to break with the Continental Congress and send a separate address to London, appealing for conciliatory measures.[82]

Caroline was still at the center of the behind-the-scenes negotiations. Dr. Franklin remained a constant guest during the holiday season. The upshot of his first two meetings with Richard in Grafton Street, on December 25 and 28, was a request by the admiral for a new set of conciliatory proposals. Within days, Franklin conveyed these to Caroline. In order to conceal Franklin's handwriting and protect his anonymity, Caroline transcribed them herself before passing them on to her brother. She invited the American to visit her again on New Year's Eve and assured him that Richard had received the proposals. Things now moved quickly. Richard did not think Franklin's specific suggestions were very promising. But a week later, Caroline put into the American's hands a letter from her brother, which he was instructed to read and return to her on the spot. It asked whether Franklin would engage to pay for the tea on behalf of the colony of Massachusetts as a preliminary to concessions from the British government. Franklin wrote back immediately that he was certain that Massachusetts would not pay for the tea unless the British government had first repealed the Coercive Acts. Massachusetts would not blink first. While he waited, Caroline transcribed his letter for her brother and returned the original.[83]

Although her role was nominally that of a go-between, Caroline was present at every meeting with Lord Howe. At the first of these, she made a gesture of "offering to withdraw" from what was clearly men's business, but Franklin "begg'd she might stay, as I should have no Secret in a Business of this Nature that I could not freely confide to her Prudence."[84] After that, she made no further pretense; she must have been in on every subsequent development.

The chess matches continued, as Caroline and her Grafton Street drawing room remained at the heart of Franklin's secret negotiations. In February, Richard divulged that he was being considered as peace commissioner; his hope was that Franklin would accompany him "as a Friend, an Assistant or Secretary." Franklin discovered that the idea of sending a commissioner now also formed part of the thinking of his friends Dr. Fothergill and David Barclay, who continued their parallel negotiations with him.

Again, though, the issue of the ruined tea cargo intruded. The two Quakers asked whether Franklin, along with the other colony agents in London, would engage to pay for the tea on behalf of Massachusetts, to pave the way for the government to appoint a commissioner. Franklin did not budge from his position that the Coercive Acts would have to be repealed if the tea were to be paid for. But he did think that the idea of sending a commissioner was a promising one, "as it might be a Means of suspending military Operations, and bring on a Treaty."[85]

Lord Howe was a good choice as a peace commissioner. As a naval commander, he had been handed the role of negotiator before, in remote outposts of the empire and in preliminaries with the French at the end of the last war.[86] His well-known ability to meet people at their own level had impressed Franklin, who "lik'd much his Manner, and found my self disposed to place great Confidence in him."[87] And, of course, the Howe dynasty was popular in America; George's hero status was such that it would outlive even the War of Independence. The Howes could expect to be accepted as friends of the colonies, as they had fought for them. And, as independent members of the House of Commons, they were conveniently neutral—part of neither Lord North's administration nor the opposition.

Richard and William took care to maintain their neutrality in what became the countdown to war. When the newly elected House of Commons held a significant debate on armed repression of America, on December 5, the two brothers quietly left the chamber. They made their way to their mother's house in Albemarle Street, where they met Caroline, writing as usual to Lady Spencer. Commenting on the debate, she remarked briefly, "[M]y brothers stole from the House of Commons," leaving her friend—obviously in the know about the Howe family's secret project—to deduce the reason.[88]

By February, when the British public began to react to the prospect of war, the Howe brothers choreographed a double act in the Commons as they presented two conflicting petitions from William's own constituency of Nottingham—one for coercion and one against it. Nottingham was divided over the subject of America, but it had a core of local leaders who opposed armed repression of the colonies. Each brother presented a petition, taking care between the two of them to appear evenhanded.[89]

Meanwhile, the growing tension in Massachusetts brought General John Burgoyne to Whitehall to sound out his chances of a posting in

America. Best remembered as the man who surrendered a British army to the Americans at Saratoga in 1777, Burgoyne was a handsome, pleasure-loving individual who is often recalled today by his apt nickname—"Gentleman Johnny"—a sobriquet coined by George Bernard Shaw in his 1897 play, *The Devil's Disciple*.[90] Burgoyne wanted to be assigned to the regular garrison at New York because he had heard a rumor that it would involve a negotiation with the colonial leaders—a political role that the showy Burgoyne thought would lend glamour to his career. At Boston, he thought, his duties would be entirely routine. When he approached the ministers in hopes of the New York assignment, he discovered to his intense irritation that William Howe had gotten there ahead of him.

Although several members of the cabinet strongly preferred Burgoyne in the event of any negotiations, Lord Dartmouth and his undersecretary, John Pownall, adhered to Howe. They were vague about their reasons. Finally, Burgoyne appealed to Lord North, who admitted that a promise had already been made to General Howe regarding New York. Not wishing to go behind the back of a brother officer, Burgoyne approached William about the matter. William was friendly but evasive, saying only that he wished to avoid going to Boston if possible. "I knew the reason given publicly by all his friends for that wish was the obligation his family owed to the Bostonians, who had raised a monument to the late Lord Howe." But "General Howe's friends were, nevertheless, indefatigably at work," Burgoyne noted drily. He believed that the real reason William wanted the New York posting was because he did not want to serve under the lackluster General Gage in Boston. "I knew that General Howe was using every engine of interest for the preference," Burgoyne complained.[91] But he did not know—as few did, even in the cabinet—that Richard Lord Howe himself was secretly working to be appointed a commissioner, and that any negotiations in New York would, within this scheme of things, be undertaken by him rather than by his less-experienced brother William. William, of course, would not tell Burgoyne this, and Dartmouth and his undersecretary were not to be budged from their inexplicable preference for General Howe.[92]

The Howes and their fellow peacemakers were swimming against the tide. As we have seen, even before Richard's first meeting with Franklin at Christmas, the prospects for a peace commission were poor. When Lord Dartmouth pitched the idea to the cabinet in early December, it became obvious that he was out of step with most of the other members, and even the king himself. The idea of sending commissioners, the king confided to Lord North, "looks so like the Mother Country being more afraid of the continuance of the dispute than the Colonies and I cannot think it likely to make them reasonable, I do not want to drive them to despair but to submission which nothing but feeling the inconvenience of their situation can bring their pride to submit to."[93] The inconvenience mentioned by the king involved British stoppage of American trade, or, in the worst case, armed repression of a local uprising in New England.

Over the previous ten years, there had been a growing conviction in British political circles that colonial protests had been encouraged by concessions from the mother country, and that the government should put its foot down this time around. The most extreme Americans were making demands that Britain could never concede to, even had there been the will to do so. The petition from the Continental Congress directly challenged the position of the British government as the sovereign legislature within the empire.

From the point of view of the majority of British MPs and statesmen, Parliament, a pillar of British liberty and a counterweight to the monarchy, was under threat from the pretensions of colonial legislatures. In some circles, there was a sense of relief that complicated and perplexing theoretical questions of right could be resolved by a contest of strength (which, of course the colonies would lose). Now came the hour to confront a troublemaking colonial minority, enforce Britain's authority over its empire, preserve the sovereignty of Parliament, and thus protect the nation's liberties at home and its standing abroad as a major power.

The petition of the Continental Congress reached London just before Christmas in 1774; whatever Franklin thought, it was seen as an uncompromising list of American constitutional claims, and it was a great disappointment to Lord Dartmouth. Nevertheless, on Christmas Eve he informed all the colonial agents, including Franklin, that the petition had been received graciously by His Majesty and would be laid before the Houses of Parliament in January. This sent out a false signal to the colonies: Once in Parliament, the petition lay buried in a mass of papers.

Dartmouth was undoubtedly hoping that, despite the petition, something acceptable could be worked out with Franklin over the Christmas season. He and the Howes persisted with their behind-the-scenes maneuvers. Caroline and Lady Dartmouth met on Ladies' Charitable Society business on

December 21, the day Franklin and his fellow agents handed the petition to Lord Dartmouth; and, as we have seen, Richard met Franklin on December 25 and proceeded to explore the potential for a commissioner.[94] Franklin would discover that both Richard Howe and Lord Hyde believed erroneously that he was empowered to make concessions that would water down congressional demands.

On February 20, 1775, Lord North laid before the House of Commons the sole proposal for conciliation to be offered by the British government during the final months before war. North proposed that when any colony assembly raised revenues to pay for its own civil government and defense, Parliament would desist from taxing it, but the sum raised would be subject to parliamentary approval. Franklin thought he detected the influence of his backstage negotiations, but the prime minister's offer did not address most of the issues raised by the Continental Congress.[95] Franklin dismissed North's concession as British taxation by another route. Still worse, the meager olive branch was sandwiched between further warlike measures—Massachusetts would be declared in rebellion, and the trade and fisheries of New England were to be restrained. Everyone knew that more regiments were to be sent to Boston.[96]

North's proposal was passed by Parliament, but government hardliners still thought it offered too much, while the opposition thought it offered too little. North had attempted to please both sides and met with the usual success. The tide continued in the direction of war.[97]

Meanwhile, Richard quietly continued to try to win support for a peace commission. On March 7, 1775, he and Caroline met Benjamin Franklin for the last time at Number 12 Grafton Street. Assuring the American that his intentions had been good, Richard regretted the failure to establish a commission. But, he concluded, things "might yet take a more favourable Turn; and as he understood I was going soon to America, if he should chance to be sent thither on that important Business, he hop'd he might still expect my Assistance." And so, concluded Franklin, "ended the Negociation with Lord Howe."[98]

William, however, was going to America, and he was going without his brother. By the middle of February, all of London knew that Generals Howe, Burgoyne, and Henry Clinton were to go to Boston with additional regiments to provide much-needed backbone for General Gage's flagging command.[99]

In London, William's appointment was popular. Lord George Germain, the hawkish MP who would soon replace the pacific Dartmouth as American secretary, was delighted. General Howe's expertise in wilderness fighting would perfectly qualify him to lead a command in America. George III also was gratified. He had been impressed by a demonstration of William's light infantry in Richmond in the summer of 1774.[100]

According to Horace Walpole, the king had turned to William in January as a sympathetic shoulder to cry on when news reached him about the high desertion rates of British soldiers posted in Boston.[101] Walpole himself, while dismissing the abilities of Burgoyne and Clinton, opined that William "was one of those brave and silent brothers, and was reckoned sensible, though so silent that nobody knew whether he was or not." In the House of Lords, the Duke of Richmond spoke up for his friend, complaining of "the cruelty of sending Howe to command against Boston," a province that had raised a monument to his brother George Lord Howe.[102] Even Arthur Lee, a Virginian who was about to become a secret agent for the American cause in London, spoke of General Howe as "an honorable man, respected in the Army, & trained in the late American war. He goes reluctantly."[103] William retained his popularity, at least for now.

On March 6, Richard rose to speak in the House of Commons during the debate on the New England Trade and Fisheries Act, which would block the seafaring industry of the New England colonies. The proposal sounded draconian, but at least it offered a means of coercing the colonies without resorting to bloodshed. Richard supported it as the only "moderate Means of bringing the disobedient Provinces to a Sense of their Duty, without involving the Empire in all the Horrors of a Civil War." He spoke "so very low and indistinct, that it was extremely difficult to collect what he said." One newspaper suspected that, with his brother going to Boston, he might appear to have a personal motive for wishing to avoid a fight.[104]

After fifteen years, William was returning to America, and his family knew from previous losses that he might never return. Caroline had seen her father die in Barbados, and her brother George had been slain in New York. She could not have been indifferent to the prospect of her "dear William" crossing the Atlantic yet again, especially knowing that there was likely to be fighting in America. "My heart aches for the Howe family," wrote one member of the Ladies' Charitable Society shortly after William's departure.[105]

One Howe did not trouble to hide her emotion. Fanny had married William during peacetime and had no notion of what it meant to be a soldier's wife. Timid by nature and at least a dozen years younger than her husband, Fanny's distress was obvious to her friends. A few days after William's appointment, one wrote, "I am very sorry for Mrs Howe, who I believe would most willingly have gone with her husband had it been possible."[106]

After William departed on April 15, 1775, Fanny returned to her family home in Ireland, where her brother Tom and his wife, Lady Louisa Conolly, still lived. Lady Louisa tried to divert her favorite sister-in-law, whose "weak little frame and nerves" were not robust enough for stoicism. Horseback riding and picnics in the early summer verdure of Ireland were of little avail. Louisa wrote to her sister, the Duchess of Leinster, "Poor Mrs Howe is really one of the most moving objects I ever saw, for she suffers as much as it is possible for anyone to do; but so patiently, so meekly and with so little fuss, that her distress quite goes to one's heart." And the worst of it, confided Lady Louisa, writing on June 25, was that she had "but too just grounds for her fears." Hostilities had begun in Massachusetts while William was crossing the Atlantic. And Fanny was not the only one who feared for the charming Savage: "I love General Howe so much," Lady Louisa told her sister, "that if Mrs Howe was out of the question, I must be very anxious."[107]

What Louisa did not know as she wrote her letter—what no one in Britain knew yet—was that seven days earlier, William had stood on Breed's Hill, across the bay from Boston, facing some of the hottest fire he had ever experienced in a lifetime of soldiering. The Howes were plunged into their third war, and it would be their sternest test yet.

Eight

American Destiny

T he Battle of Bunker Hill on June 17, 1775, was one of the bloodiest battles of the American War of Independence. Almost half of the British combatants were killed or wounded, including an appallingly high number of officers, deliberately picked off by rebel marksmen. More than one-eighth of the British officers to fall during the eight-year war died here.[1] For the British, it was a technical victory; the rebels were driven from their hastily erected fortifications overlooking Boston Harbor. But the battle was a game changer, and news of it sent shock waves through the British nation. Cabinet ministers suddenly realized they faced a prolonged struggle in the colonies, not an easy pushover, as predicted by some. In command of British troops on that fateful day was General William Howe.

The first shots of the war had famously been fired two months earlier at Lexington and Concord, on April 19, when British troops, on a mission to seize military stores in the Massachusetts countryside, had been chased back to Boston by American militia. But on that spring day, the Americans were pursuing a small enemy detachment in retreat. Bunker Hill, by contrast, was a major battle in which citizen-soldiers proved they had the courage to face and inflict grievous damage upon a large force of highly trained professional soldiers.

The story of Bunker Hill has been told and retold so often that it has assumed mythic proportions. Legend has it that arrogant redcoat officers led their men in a criminally incompetent frontal assault upon a well-fortified position, expecting the colonials to melt away in the face of a British charge. William Howe, of course, has a starring role in every account, and Bunker Hill is where the indictments of him as commander of the British war effort during the American Revolution always begin.[2] "Light-Horse Harry" Lee, an American veteran of the War of Independence, was the first to suggest that William was so traumatized by his Bunker Hill experience that it sowed the seeds for British failure in the war. According to Light-Horse Harry, Howe ordered a mindless advance against the American entrenchments, and when he saw his men slaughtered around him, the horrific experience "sunk deep into the mind of Sir William Howe; and it seems to have had its influence, on all his subsequent operations, with decisive control." For the rest of his service in America, William supposedly did not dare to attack the Americans head-on, fatally compromising his ability to defeat General Washington.[3]

This story has become part of the folklore of the American Revolution. But it is not taken seriously by military historians. William's original plan was to bypass the American main defenses, break through the enemy's left flank, and attack the American rear, while other British forces mounted a frontal assault against the fortification itself. Instead, the light infantry and grenadiers led by William were driven back by a murderous round of fire from the reinforced rail fences that stood in front of and to the left of the advancing British soldiers. William's troops crashed into each other in the smoke and confusion, and he had to abandon the flank attack, turning it into a feint and concentrating on the frontal assault. Two more charges ensued against the American ramparts—and Breed's Hill was theirs at last, a peak so insignificant that the battle became named after the more conspicuous Bunker Hill just behind it.[4]

More than thirty years after the war, Light-Horse Harry Lee would claim that William Howe emerged from the battle with what would now be termed post-traumatic stress disorder. It was rather late in William's career, however, for him to succumb to combat fatigue. He was a veteran of two wars, with a reputation for carelessness where his personal safety was concerned; he had famously led the "forlorn hopes" up the cliffs to the Plains of Abraham in the battle for Quebec in 1759. At Bunker Hill, he had stood entirely alone for almost a minute in front of the rail fence after the blast of fire had mown down his staff around him, his breeches spattered with the blood of his men. Several times, he allowed himself to be a clear target for rebel marksmen as he turned his back on them and returned to his troops, before leading the charge again. Miraculously, he sustained only a slight injury on one foot. His "gallant behavior" on that day, reported one officer, charmed his men.[5] Historians who relate his command decisions during the War of Independence to his supposed trauma at Bunker

Hill would do better to explore fully his lengthy military career, which is typically consigned to a paragraph, or at most a few pages, in books on the Howe brothers in the War of Independence.[6] As we will see, it was William's earlier experience of amphibious and irregular warfare in America during the Seven Years' War, and his personal impressions of the fighting skills of colonial Americans, that informed his subsequent conduct of the campaign against the rebellion.

Ironically, William's own words have been quoted against him to support the notion that he was scarred psychologically at Bunker Hill. In his report on the battle to the adjutant general, writing of the incident at the rail fence when his troops were torn apart by American fire, William wrote, "[T]here was *a Moment that I never felt before.*" If he had foreseen how often this line would be used by his critics and by posterity to depict him as a victim of nerves, he undoubtedly would have scored it out.[7] It has been interpreted as a conviction that he was about to die, but what he actually felt was that he was about to lose control over his men, who might refuse to continue their advance. He completed his sentence with the words "[B]ut by the gallantry of the Officers it was all recover'd and the Attack carried." General Henry Clinton, also present at the action, made a similar report: "[O]fficers told me they could not command their men and I never saw so great a [want] of order."[8]

Clinton, in fact, is the source of an additional sustained criticism of William's generalship on that grueling day. At the planning stage of the battle, Clinton had reasoned that since Breed's Hill was on the Charlestown Peninsula, why not land troops on the narrow isthmus connecting it to the mainland, thus neatly cutting off the rebel retreat while also pinning them down from the front? Clinton claimed in his surviving papers that he had suggested this, but he was ignored.[9] It has been cited by historians as more evidence of the complacency and lack of imagination in British strategic planning that resulted in disaster.

Superficially, this strategy sounds strong, but historian Thomas Fleming, in a highly detailed account of the battle, showed that William lacked the specialized flat-bottomed boats, with raised sides to protect troops from enemy fire, that would be needed for amphibious operations in the shallow tidal waters around the isthmus. Howe had indeed noticed the shortage within a few weeks of landing in Boston, writing three separate letters about it to alert his brother Richard and his superiors at home.[10]

On the day that William wrote the first of these letters, General Gage, still commander in chief in Boston, wrote a dispatch reporting the same problem.[11] Newly arrived Major General Howe had evidently drawn Gage's attention to the deficiency, but it was too late. Just five days later, the Battle of Bunker Hill suddenly confronted the British. Without flat-bottomed boats, the army would have to ferry the roughly 2,400 soldiers in navy rowboats, which would leave them unprotected from enemy fire while crossing. William therefore landed them at Morton's Point, as far out of range as possible from the American troops. The choice of Morton's Point was a good alternative; it took the Americans on Breed's Hill by surprise, and their cannons were facing in the wrong direction.[12]

General Clinton claimed that his advice about the isthmus was ignored because his fellow generals thought him ignorant of warfare in America.[13] But what the general lacked was experience with amphibious warfare. Most of his military service had been in Germany during the Seven Years' War. He could not match the expertise of William Howe (or his naval brother) in amphibious operations, which played a role in eighteenth-century American warfare that was equally as significant as the more glamorous wilderness fighting pioneered by George Howe and others. This is important to remember, because Henry Clinton has become a highly influential reference for the performances of the Howe brothers in the War of Independence. In 1778, he became commander in chief of the British forces in America. After he retired, he composed an extensive apologia defending his conduct of the war, which only became accessible to historians in 1925.[14]

Clinton's lengthy self-exculpations, which contrast sharply with the reticence of the Howes, make him an irresistible source in assessing British failures, but one that must be used with great caution. He was hardly a disinterested witness. During the war, Clinton was busy broadcasting his own version of events in letters to London, seeking to promote his career and managing his image with those who mattered. In his many letters home, he complained, excused himself, and sometimes sought to chip away at the reputations of his fellow generals. His boosterism would have ramifications far beyond the offices at Whitehall. As we shall see, private gossip about the war conveyed in the letters of British officers serving in America was regular fare over the card tables of London's aristocracy. It became part of the "talk of the town" and was integral to Caroline's experience of the home front as she managed the images of her brothers commanding the army and navy overseas.

William did not try to evade criticism of the Battle of Bunker Hill, admitting that it was a pyrrhic victory for the British. In his official report of the battle to the adjutant general of the army, he spoke of "the fatal Consequences of this action—92 Officers killed & wounded—a most dreadfull Account—," adding, "I freely confess to you, when I look to the consequences of it, in the loss of so many brave Officers, I do it with horror—The Success is too dearly bought__"[15]

WORD OF THE BATTLE was greeted with alarm by the Howe women. Fanny "dropt down as dead, on hearing of the engagement, before she cd. know whether [William] was safe or not," wrote Caroline.[16] At the time, Fanny was still in Ireland at Castletown, the estate of her brother Tom Conolly and his wife Lady Louisa. Also at Castletown was Louisa's sister, the scandalous Lady Sarah Bunbury. She was waiting for her divorce to be granted—the denouement of her well-publicized extramarital affair that had resulted in the birth of her illegitimate daughter. Although Lady Sarah knew and liked William Howe, she was more strong-minded than Fanny on receiving the news of the battle. She recalled, "[P]oor little Mrs Howe fainted away with only the shock of the word *action*, and could not for a long time believe her husband was alive till luckily his letter came."[17] Lady Louisa described the gloomy family scene in early August: "[A]ll our spirits are depressed with the bloody action in America, where, thank God, our friends have escaped; but so desperate an engagement as they have had is really a public calamity."[18]

Lady Louisa Conolly's letter also gives us a glimpse of another Howe woman on the home front, William's sister Mary, who was at Castletown that summer with her husband, General Pitt. More than twelve years earlier, during the previous war, Mary had only recovered very slowly from the death of her then-fiancé, Sir John Armytage. Now her nerves were once again stretched to their limit at the thought of a beloved brother standing alone on a hillside she had never heard of, facing a barrage of fire.

The aftermath of Bunker Hill raises the curtain on the reality behind the media-constructed image of the Howes, promulgated in the Seven Years' War, as a stoic British military family. Julie Howe, third of the four sisters, was the most vulnerable of the siblings. She had always lived with her mother, Lady Charlotte Howe. Contemporary letters reveal her as emotionally dependent on her family to an unusual degree. When her brother Thomas died in 1771, a friend wrote, "I have not heard in what manner Miss Howe supports this stroke, her affection for him used to hurt her health extremely, upon every absence. How will it stand this last separation!"[19] Thomas had lived with Julie and their mother whenever he was home from seafaring, and after his death, Julie's health suffered in what was probably an emotional breakdown. A year later, Caroline described her younger sister as "continuing in much in the same state of head." Julie came to stay at Grafton Street over Christmastide 1772 with her "head & nerves as bad as ever," but Caroline trusted that she would settle down "when the first flurry" of her arrival was over. The new year came and went with Julie no better, "her nerves still dreadfully weak," Caroline confided to her friend.[20]

It is not surprising, then, that two and a half years later, the news of Bunker Hill hit Julie hard. She "has at times suffered as much as has poor Mrs [Fanny] Howe," wrote Caroline to Lady Spencer at the end of the summer of 1775. An indistinct portrait of Julie comes through in Caroline's letters: her "gentle Tone of voice," which made it a pleasure to hear her sing (if only she could be persuaded to perform), her strong attachments to old friends and family, the messages of love and admiration to Lord and Lady Spencer that she conveyed so frequently in her elder sister's letter closings that Caroline sometimes lost patience.[21]

Older and steadier, Caroline was protective of this sister who did not seem born to endure the rigors of a military family. It was probably to get her away from news of the war that Julie was dispatched in 1776 to Scotland, where Dr. Samuel Johnson's biographer, James Boswell, met her walking in the woods around Douglas Castle.[22] Sitting in London waiting to hear news could become oppressive, as Caroline knew from long experience.

Caroline was staying with her Aunt Juliana Page at Battlesden, where her intelligence about Bunker Hill arrived in suspenseful fits and starts. On July 20, she wrote to Lady Spencer about a report in an Irish newspaper of a battle at Boston. "It is supposed, my dear Lady Spencer, that there is no truth, in the paragraph."[23] But just days later, General Gage's report of the battle surfaced in the *London Gazette*.[24] On the evening of July 26, the Duchess of Bedford descended upon Caroline from nearby Woburn Abbey, bursting to discuss the bloody engagement, despite having "no particulars only a General account just arrived, that we had 70 officers killed; sad sad work indeed!" The next day, newspapers had reached the neighborhood of Battlesden, and, more important, an express message arrived from Richard containing only the terse assurance that William had written to say he was safe and well. Lady Howe sent Caroline a slightly fuller account of William's letter: "The attack was a very severe one, for the Americans were very strong by position & numbers, they being well entrenched." "He has lost Sherwin his Aid de Camp," added Caroline unhappily, "who was a very useful & trusty officer."[25]

A week later, Richard himself arrived at Battlesden with the full contents of William's letter, describing how he and his small corps of regulars had been assigned the unpleasant duty of clearing up the aftermath of the battle, gathering up the wounded, and burying the dead.[26] William was "just beyond the entrenchments from whence he had drove the provincials," noted Caroline, where he and "his little army not 2000 men" had remained since the battle seven days earlier. Caroline wrote to Lady Spencer, "What horrid work it all is! & how much more of it may we not expect. [D]id you observe that 12 officers attending upon William were either killed or wounded[?]; We every instant suppose fresh accounts may come, but nothing can be satisfactory unless proposals for an accommodation." Yet she ended the letter on a note of reassurance, writing, "[D]o not be uneasy about me, you know I always hope the best, I mean with regard to William's safety, for as I said before, as to the general matter nothing except peace can be good."[27]

Caroline continued unflinchingly to reassure others as the gory details omitted in William's own dispatches came out in the newspapers. "I hope you did not long suffer for us," she wrote to Lady Spencer, "sensible as I am to your goodness & feeling for us all, you may depend ever upon the earliest intelligence I can give you." In the same letter, she expressed her gratified pride that William had just been appointed commander in chief in America, replacing General Gage. "Everything said of William's behaviour & conduct is more flattering than you can imagine, & with regard to him (if he escapes) we have nothing to wish but that he may be the means of a satisfactory peace being made, I fear that cannot be immediately."[28]

Caroline cleverly used William's promotion to reassure Fanny, who returned to London in late August with Mary Pitt. "I wish to encourage

[her] in the hope his situation is a safer one from his having the Chief command," she confided to Lady Spencer.[29] Fanny thought his elevation would preserve him from exposure to the dreaded *"bush fighting,"* the wilderness-style warfare that had filled the newspapers during the Seven Years' War.[30] Caroline, of course, knew that William was by no means safe; George had been a brigadier general when he was shot down at Ticonderoga.

THE BATTLE OF BUNKER HILL took place almost twenty years to the day after Richard Howe's heroic capture of the *Alcide* in the fog off Newfoundland at the start of the last war. But on that hot afternoon in Massachusetts, British soldiers were not up against France, their ancestral enemy. Men who had served side by side in the last war were now pitted against one another in what was a civil conflict. John Stark and Israel Putnam, commanding on the American side at Bunker Hill, had served with Rogers' Rangers in the Seven Years' War, and Putnam, like William Howe, had been at Havana in 1762. Both Americans had been with George Howe when he died at Ticonderoga.

On June 17, 1775, almost seventeen years since he and George Lord Howe had planned the attack on Ticonderoga as they lay on a bearskin looking at the stars, John Stark was shouting orders to colonial volunteers on the opposite side of the murderous rail fence.[31] A story trickled back to the women of the Howe clan that the Americans had deliberately spared William as he stood alone before the barricade. "I don't know if their avoiding him is true or not, but it's very moving if it is," pronounced Lady Sarah Bunbury, who was horrified at the thought of a bloody conflict "among one's own people almost." She reflected the view of many when she called it so "vile & fruitless a service, where [General Howe] may be killed & cannot get any honour."[32]

Caroline knew that in this war against ramshackle British colonists, William's hero status could not be taken for granted. She wrote in a self-conscious vein to Lady Spencer of General Howe's persisting popularity, "tho[ugh] employed in a service so odious."[33] In the coming years, Caroline would be sure to broadcast in influential social spheres whatever news or intelligence enhanced her brother's reputation. As his sister, it was her duty.

From the start of 1775, when news from America made it clear that the leaders in the Continental Congress were not backing down, the British public had become uneasy at the looming conflict. In the ensuing months, there was a flurry of petitions on both sides of the issue—loyal addresses supporting the government, and appeals for conciliation—that revealed the divisions within the nation.[34] Many who had no sympathy for American constitutional claims nevertheless hoped that a full war could be avoided. There was widespread concern that fighting in America would disrupt the British economy; still worse, it might expose the nation to attack from its traditional French enemy. The newspapers spoke of the "Butchery of a Civil War" as distinguished from a war against foreign enemies.[35] Within Parliament, Thomas Howard, Earl of Effingham, created a buzz in May 1775 when he announced in the House of Lords that he would not serve in America. He refused to partake of "the guilt of enslaving my country, and embruing my hands in the blood of her sons."[36] Even Lord Chatham withdrew his son, John Pitt, from the army in early 1776. Beyond Parliament, others wrote and spoke in favor of the colonial cause, including naval officer John Cartwright, who had served under Richard Howe in the Seven Years' War but would refuse to serve in the new war.

Nevertheless, the majority of Britons wanted the American challenge to British authority to be suppressed, quickly and with as little bloodshed as possible. Everywhere in London, heated debates over the American question could be heard—in the coffeehouses, taverns, clubs, and even in the parlors of the growing middle class. In May 1775, the *London Chronicle* ran a fictitious vignette called "The City Patriot: A Breakfast Scene," in which a fashionable husband and wife, teacups in hand, argued over the crisis. The husband championed the plight of the oppressed colonists, while the strong-minded wife was the "rational" supporter of Lord North's administration.[37] The debate raged everywhere across the great city.

Caroline, of course, was ready to wade in, cleverly negotiating her way through groups on all sides of the issue. In late August 1775, while her brother William was in Boston directing the government's policy of armed coercion, she arrived at Park Place in Berkshire, the country seat of Henry Seymour Conway, a prominent member of Lord Rockingham's parliamentary opposition. Conway was a military officer who had served with the Howe brothers. Like all the Rockinghams, he opposed the use of force in America. He would soon condemn the war before the House of Commons as "cruel, unnecessary, and unnatural; called it a butchery of his fellow subjects."[38] Also at Park Place was another supporter of Lord Rockingham,

Charles Lennox, Duke of Richmond, brother of Lady Sarah Bunbury and Lady Louisa Conolly and a longtime friend of William Howe.

The Rockingham Whigs were the main parliamentary opposition group at the start of the American War of Independence. They were the foremost champions of the conspiracy theory swirling around George III since his accession to the throne, claiming that the king aimed to increase the power of the Crown by unconstitutional means. This had no basis in reality, and their opposition most probably was motivated more by resentment at being pushed out of power. But the Rockinghams sincerely believed they had a mission to protect English liberties from the overweening ambitions of the Crown. What is novel to modern ears is that they sought to curb royal power without increasing popular democracy.

One of their number, Lord George Cavendish, famously declared that "he liked an aristocracy, and thought it right that great families with great connexions should govern." To their aristocratic way of thinking, what mattered was getting the "right men" into power—men who understood the malign influences surrounding the throne and who would undertake reforms to decrease the king's corrupt influence in Parliament. These men, naturally, were the members of the Rockingham group. The fact that they did not wish to share power with other parliamentary groups was an unusual stance at the time, but it has since emerged as the model for modern political parties held together by shared principles and policies.[39]

The leading spokesman for the Rockinghams was Edmund Burke, the famous political theorist and author. As colonial agent for New York, Burke had worked with Benjamin Franklin in lobbying for American interests in London and had spoken publicly about conciliation with America. While not abandoning the concept of parliamentary sovereignty, Burke showed a willingness to compromise and an open-minded approach to conducting talks with leading Americans. In what was his second proposal for conciliation, rejected by Parliament in November 1775, he allowed a limited role for the upstart American Continental Congress in negotiations, a move that the Rockinghams recognized as crucial in maintaining the trust of patriot leaders.[40]

It was inevitable that a house party at Conway's country seat in late summer 1775 would lead to animated discussion of the American crisis, but as always, Caroline was discreet in her report of the activities. "This is a pleasant house to be in," she wrote to Lady Spencer, praising "the delightful near

& distant views" of its extensive grounds, where General Conway had made lavish improvements. She said nothing of America to her friend, other than to assure her that there had been no more news from William. And she noted in closing that Lady Spencer's daughter, the Duchess of Devonshire, had called at Grafton Street while Caroline was in Berkshire.[41]

There was nothing politically neutral about the duchess, eighteen-year-old Georgiana Cavendish, young as she was. Her husband William Cavendish, Duke of Devonshire, and his uncles were powerful Whigs who supported the Rockinghams.[42] Despite an age difference of more than thirty years between the duchess and Caroline Howe, they moved in the same social circles, where the American crisis was a constant topic.

But in late 1775, Lady Spencer was far more worried about her daughter's marital problems than about politics. The duke and duchess had been married for more than a year, and Georgiana was discovering by this time that the duke was rather uninterested in having a wife, whom he expected only to produce children and sustain the dynastic social position. He had his mistress and his West End gentlemen's club. His duchess was therefore finding consolation in a very public manner, by becoming a fashion diva and a doyen of the gaming table. While on the Continent in 1775, she had developed a friendship with Marie Antoinette, the ill-fated queen of France. Both ladies suffered under the cloud of childlessness. Georgiana had already miscarried at least once by the time the Devonshires and the Spencers set out for Spa together.[43] When she returned to England ahead of her parents in September, she miscarried again.

Georgiana's travails were the main topic of conversation at a dinner party in early October that included Caroline Howe and Lord Frederick Cavendish. "[S]o the Duchess of Devonshire has miscarried, but how is it possible she can ever go on her time if she will not be a little more quiet. Lord Frederick says she cannot walk into a room she must come in with a hop & a jump, she seems to have unfortunate good spirits & tho' I believe she is perfectly good humour'd & innocent I don't believe she will ever be a day older," wrote Lady Mary Coke, one of the dinner guests and a rare critic of the popular duchess.[44]

Lady Mary was herself a well-known figure in high society, an unusual—even eccentric—woman who combined willfulness and an egotistical self-assurance with a slavish devotion to monarchy and rank. Beginning in 1766, she kept an extensive and detailed diary, a mixture of gossip, politics, and news, in the form of letters addressed to her sister Anne. She maintained the diary for twenty-five years, leaving behind a fascinating account of Georgian aristocratic life.[45] In it can be found the full spectrum of opinion on Britain's war with its colonies within the social circles of the Howe women between 1775 and 1783.

Contemporaries were aware of Lady Mary's dedicated journal-keeping, which preserved in writing much of the ephemeral gossip circulating in drawing rooms. In the spring of 1767, Lady Spencer and Caroline each took turns pressuring Lady Mary to allow them a read. First Lady Spencer urged that she "wou'd be contented with a Single page." When that tactic failed, it was Caroline's turn to try. "Mrs Howe talk'd of my journal, & said She wish'd much to read it. I assured her I could not comply with her request." Caroline and Lady Spencer would never have their curiosity gratified.[46]

Lady Mary Coke was the youngest daughter of John Campbell, 2nd Duke of Argyll. She was considered a beauty by some, and a professional virgin by all, because in 1747 she had refused to consummate her marriage to Edward Viscount Coke, the heir of the Earl of Leicester. Following the ceremony, the feckless heir—perhaps irritated by a courtship in which the bride-to-be relentlessly played hard to get—shunned the marriage bed for a night of revelry with his friends. Twenty-year-old Mary in turn denied her husband what, by the thinking of the day, were his marital rights. Edward's father, the distraught Earl of Leicester, whose only thought was to maintain the family line, railed at both of the young people. When that got no results, he resorted to locking Lady Mary in her quarters at the family seat of Holkham, a lengthy virtual imprisonment that today would undoubtedly be considered abuse, if not kidnapping.

Mary reveled in the role of victim, entertaining guests in her room and refusing to give in to the demands of the Cokes. Eventually, in 1750, Leicester agreed to a legal settlement by which Mary was allowed to live with her mother. Luckily for the virgin bride, her husband died in 1753 and Lady Mary Coke, as she was known ever after, became an independent widow at the age of just twenty-six.

The Howes knew Lady Mary via two separate connections. Her sister Anne was related to the Conollys through her marriage to the Earl of Strafford. In addition, Lady Mary was also a conspicuous figure at court, famously harboring a crush on the king's brother, Prince Edward Augustus, while

Lady Mary Coke wearing an ermine-trimmed red cloak, painted by Joshua
Reynolds.

Richard Lord Howe was serving as the duke's Lord of the Bedchamber. The
prince died in 1767, and with him Lady Mary's hopes of becoming royalty.[47]

Unsurprisingly, Lady Mary Coke was a strong opponent of the rebellion
in America, but there were plenty in her set who disagreed. On a visit in
October to William Ponsonby, 2nd Earl of Bessborough, a supporter of the
pro-American Rockingham group, Lady Mary mentioned the American
rebels, "upon which he look'd at me and answer'd in a most complaining
voice do you call them all rebels?" A few weeks later, Lady Mary called upon
the ailing and elderly Lady Blandford, who gave forth quite an opposite
opinion: "'[I]f the Stamp Act had not been repeal'd,'" she pronounced to
the startled Lady Mary, "'all wou'd have gone well,' & that she wish'd Lord
Rockingham & all those who had any hand in it were hanged." "This you'll
allow was being pretty warm," thought Lady Mary privately.

By December 1775, Lady Mary was seated at a loo table where the players were discussing "a rumour of bad news from America." Horace Walpole, always outspoken in his support for the Americans, was present. "I
expressed my concern that any of our people shou'd fall into the hands of

those cruel Americans," she recorded, "upon which Mr Walpole laugh'd in my face & told me I had many sorrows that he had not." "This is the person who pretends to humanity," the indignant Lady Mary confided to her journal.[48] That same day, Walpole had written gleefully to a friend with the news that American General Richard Montgomery had captured Fort St. John in Canada from the British. By now, the Americans had shown enough spirit to convince him that it would be a long war; and "the commissioners for treating of peace, who are still talked of, will not find their [American] minds in good temper, when provoked on one hand, and victorious on the other."[49]

As Walpole's words show, the prospect of a peace commissioner persisted eight months after the start of hostilities. Richard and his associates had continued to keep the idea alive over the summer of 1775. Less than a fortnight after William had embarked for America on April 20, Richard was in Bath for his gout, a condition that would worsen with the years. But he was back in London by June. In the midst of dining at Lord Dartmouth's, an officer arrived bearing word that Benjamin Franklin had reached Philadelphia and been appointed a delegate to the Second Continental Congress.[50] Now it would be seen whether the talks with Franklin the previous winter, when the American philosopher had endorsed the notion of a peace commissioner, would bear fruit.

But Richard and his associates did not wait for news from the Congress. In late July 1775, after word of the Battle of Bunker Hill reached London, Lord Dartmouth introduced "several American Gentlemen" to the king at a reception at St James's Palace. Among the Americans was probably the wealthy South Carolina planter Ralph Izard, a friend of the Rockinghams who also had contacts in the Continental Congress. Hoping to help broker talks between the British government and American leaders, the South Carolinian lingered in London.[51] Izard was among those who advised Lord Dartmouth and other members of government that moderates in the Congress were making a last-ditch effort to send a petition to the British government pleading for reconciliation.[52]

Benjamin Franklin, meanwhile, arrived in Philadelphia on May 5, almost two months after his final meeting with the Howes in Grafton Street. There he discovered that, just as in London, all eyes were turned on him as the individual most qualified to act as a middleman between the colonies and Britain. The day after his return, he was appointed a delegate to the Congress. Four days later, on May 10, 1775, the Second Continental Congress opened in crisis. Fighting had started, and from all along the Atlantic seaboard, requests for instructions, aid, and leadership poured into Philadelphia. The Congress was a de facto government for the rebelling colonies, yet the members could not even fully agree on what to do next. Hopes were high that Franklin would know. A Philadelphia merchant wrote, "The Doctor has yet said but little, and People seem much disappointed," for they had expected him to have a plan drawn up by Lord Chatham, "but Nothing of the Sort has yet appeared."[53]

Franklin was immediately co-opted onto the committee drafting a petition to the king. This was an obvious assignment for a man who surely knew more than anyone in Philadelphia about the mood in London and the inner intentions of the ministers. The ghost of his talks with the Howes and others can just be discerned in the scattered records of that turbulent session. Franklin sketched out proposals for the committee that reflected some of the ideas he had pitched in London—namely, that the colonies should offer Britain an annual revenue, in return for which they would be allowed to trade freely with the rest of the world. This would have been a significant concession in the eyes of British legislators. Surprisingly, members of the Congress seem to have thought the proposals worth considering.[54] But things were moving too fast now to allow for in-depth and divisive deliberations.

Franklin's committee instead drafted what would be the final petition of the Continental Congress. The "Olive Branch Petition," as it would be known, was associated from its inception with the hopes that a royal commission would be sent to the colonies. The first (discarded) draft made an outright request for the king to "commission some good and great Men to enquire into the Grievances of [England's] faithful subjects." Such words, had they been retained, would have given support to the case for a peace commission being pushed by Richard Howe and others at that very moment in London. In the end, however, the committee members opted for vagueness; they merely requested that King George "direct some mode" for a permanent reconciliation.[55]

Nevertheless, it was plain that the petition called for negotiations. This was enough to sway that great friend of Caroline and Richard, the Duke of Grafton. When the Olive Branch Petition reached London in August 1775, he believed that the government should call a temporary halt to military preparations and give colonial delegates a chance to be heard. Recalled Grafton years later, "[I]t was . . . well known, that a compromise had taken place [in the Congress] in order to render the petition unanimous, by a promise of a declaration of Independency from the majority, in case of the rejection of this final application."[56] Grafton firmly believed that the Americans would be propelled down the road to declaring independence if the British government ignored this final appeal.[57]

A few days after the Olive Branch Petition reached London, on August 23, Lord North's administration issued the proclamation of rebellion. Grafton was appalled, and by November he had resigned from the cabinet. No doubt Caroline and Richard listened to the evolution of his ideas that summer and autumn as he moved toward his decision to quit the government.

With William in America, Richard took up the role of maneuvering in the corridors of power on behalf of his brother. This was the first war in which a Howe male remained in England while one of his brothers served abroad. During the previous war, it had been the Dowager Lady Howe who oversaw the interests of her sons at court. Unluckily, the man Richard had to deal with in 1775 was his old nemesis from the Cherbourg expedition in 1758, Lord George Sackville. It was well known in fashionable circles at the start of the War of Independence that Lord Howe and Lord Sackville had not been on speaking terms since Cherbourg. William also knew Lord George, having served under him in the 20th Foot before the Seven Years' War.[58] He probably shared his brother's animosity, for he was not likely to warm to a man who made Richard his enemy, and in any case the Howes moved in circles where Lord George was detested.[59] It was not a promising start to what was, professionally, an important relationship for the Howes.

Gifted with his tongue, circumspect when in danger, Lord George Sackville was as unlike the Howe brothers as it was possible to be. The year after Cherbourg, he made a dismal reputation for himself by misunderstanding three separate orders to advance at the Battle of Minden in 1759. At the subsequent court-martial, he was "adjudged to be unfit to serve his Majesty in any military capacity whatever." There followed a period of social ostracism, but the tenacious Sackville somehow clung to his seat in Parliament and steadily built up his political career. In 1770, he inherited a fortune, taking the surname Germain, according to the terms of the bequest.[60]

Lord George Germain, as he was known thenceforth, may not have been a coward, but in a period when physical bravery was an indispensable element of masculinity, he managed to cast doubt. When he fought a duel in 1770, he appeared to hesitate over the business, drawing a comment from the king himself that the delay in issuing his challenge did "not give much of an idea of his resolution."[61] Yet Germain was a skilled orator in the House of Commons—so much so that, by 1775, Lord North sought his support as an able spokesman for government policy, and the king approved of his hard-line attitude toward the colonial crisis.[62]

By the time word of the Bunker Hill debacle arrived, in July 1775, Lord George Germain had already been making himself conspicuous as a man in quest of a government post, and he was tipped to get one. Thus, it was to Lord George that Richard sent extracts of William's letter of June 12, remarking, "I thought some passages of sufficient moment to merit the notice of Government."[63] A letter from William describing the battle followed shortly. Copied by Richard, it was shorn of the emotive language that William had used in his report to the adjutant general. A third letter to Germain in early August reviewed the military requirements for the garrison at Boston, at the same time expressing Richard's gratification on the occasion of his brother's promotion to commander in chief in America.[64]

In September, however, Richard conveyed to Germain a very different message, which must have caused surprise in government circles: William Howe himself was less than overjoyed about his promotion. In a letter that has not survived, William admitted as much to his elder brother, and Richard was delegated to speak in London on his behalf. Richard paraphrased William's words in his communication with Lord George. Writing that General Howe calculated that he would need between twenty and twenty-four thousand additional troops next year to conquer New England, he added that the general's plan "on the enlarged Scale he now deems the State of that Country requires, he professes to be of much greater Compass than he feels himself able to direct. And . . . [he judges] it proper that a Chief Officer vested with unlimitted Powers in the Character of a Viceroy should be chosen for the occasion."[65]

It probably took some effort for William to admit that the command being offered him in 1775 was of "greater Compass than he feels himself able to direct." We do not have his own words, only those chosen on his behalf by Richard. As Germain's biographer noted, "The Howes were as proud in their way as Lord George was in his, and both brothers must have suffered in making this confession, particularly to a man they disliked."[66]

But William was not alone in identifying the need for a director general of operations in America. General Burgoyne, who was with him at Boston, made the same proposal of a viceroy to Germain, writing: "There is no possibility of carrying on a war so complicated as this will be, at the distance we are from the fountain head, without these full powers being at hand."[67]

It is easy to see why the two British generals wanted a supreme commander on the spot to take overall responsibility. The logistics of coordinating a land war in the American colonies would be immense, and the perils of awaiting decisions made at a distance of thousands of miles were obvious. During the Seven Years' War, William had experienced firsthand the innumerable pitfalls of conducting a war an ocean away from Britain in an age of very slow and uncertain communications. British forces in America had ultimately prevailed against France only after several alarming false starts; they had been facing a European adversary with logistical problems identical to their own, but with an inferior fleet to protect its communications and transport.

The warning from two serving generals in America just months into the war appears to have been ignored in London. With the benefit of hindsight, this was a mistake in a conflict in which poor communications are always cited as a significant factor in Britain's defeat. But the reservations expressed by William may have produced results, for one historian has suggested that the idea of appointing Admiral Richard Howe as joint commander was partly intended to give General Howe the support he felt he lacked. Certainly it was around this time that Germain began to wish the other Howe "to have the Command of the Fleet" in America.[68] After all, "two brothers certainly have a more thorough knowledge of each other, & consequently a confidence that they cannot have in anyone else."

These enthusiastic words were Caroline's. She had written them back in 1762, when she learned that George Keppel, in command of the land forces on the Havana expedition, would not be able to have his brother Augustus alongside him as commander in chief of the navy. "I am amazed the higher powers did not contrive it so, as being the likeliest way to ensure the success of the undertaking," she pronounced.[69] Now, thirteen years later, she would see her strong ideas on the virtues of sibling solidarity put into practice. What could be more natural?

There is every reason to believe that Caroline used her own influence to install Richard as joint commander in chief and peace commissioner with William. Her social connections put her close to the men who were involved in the decision-making. In early September 1775, she visited Phyllis Court in Oxfordshire, where she remained for the rest of the month. This was the family seat of Lord Hyde, who had been privy to the secret negotiations in Grafton Street. While she was there, Richard kept Caroline abreast of the latest news from William.[70] She would have talked openly to her friends about William's ideas, including his proposal of a viceroy. In the same month, Lord Hyde began to push the idea that Richard should go to America in the dual role of peace commissioner and naval commander in chief.[71]

Caroline could also exert her personal influence on Germain, for she had a better footing in the Germain household than her brother the admiral had. Although the Howe men openly disliked Lord George, Caroline regularly played cards with Lady Diana Germain.[72] A pleasant, popular woman, Lady Germain had no great fortune, and she was not known as a beauty. But she was a good match for her husband, offsetting his social shortcomings and drawing polite society into her orbit with kindly manners and good breeding. Lady Germain had played a key role in rehabilitating Germain in social circles after his disgrace at Minden, and she was a significant conduit to her rather unapproachable husband.[73] Thus, Caroline could venture into the home where her brothers could not.

But in September 1775, Richard's appointment in America was still only an idea. The great business of government was prosecuting the war. Bunker Hill had exposed the unpleasant reality that Britain faced more than just the suppression of a local uprising. Lord North wrote to the king that "the war is now grown to such a height, that it must be treated as a foreign war, and that every expedient which would be used in the latter case should be applied to the former." George III did not flinch in his reply, saying, "I am clear as to one point, that we must persist and not be dismayed by any difficulties that may arise on either side of the Atlantic."[74]

Ministers intended to have a twenty-thousand-man army in America by the spring of 1776. As in the Seven Years' War, Britain would hire foreign troops to augment its armed forces. To that end, negotiations were opened with the German states of Brunswick and Hesse-Cassel.[75] The Prohibitory Act in November 1775 established a general blockade of all thirteen rebellious colonies, thereby cutting off all trade between Britain and America. It was to be war, both by land and by sea.

Yet in the midst of these hawkish measures, the King's Speech opening the new session of Parliament on October 26, 1775, asserted that authority would be given to designated persons to grant pardons and restore peace in the colonies. This led to some confusion and speculation. Perhaps the ministers, daunted by the prospect of full-scale war in America, "began to be alarmed, and wished to treat." Hopeful opposition MPs speculated that the ministers were finally considering negotiating directly with the Congress.[76]

The government was considering no such thing. Lord North may have been trying discreetly to reach out to moderates in the American Continental Congress, but, by the opening of the new session of Parliament in October, he believed that the foremost leaders of the rebellion in America were aiming for total independence, whatever they pretended. They would therefore have to be convinced through the grim medium of the sword that they were unable to shake off British rule before talks could be productive. He wrote privately, "Till the provinces have made some submission, it will be vain to hope that they will come into any reasonable terms."[77] Yet he also realized that hostilities would have to come to an end eventually and a lasting solution to the Anglo-American conflict hammered out. A commissioner would be required for the highly sensitive task, one who could be trusted not to compromise the rights and sovereignty of Parliament while still reassuring colonials that their liberties would be safeguarded.

Lord George Germain was seen as the most trusted man for the job, but in early October he declined going to America.[78] Instead, on November 11, 1775, he became American Secretary of State, the post formerly held by Lord Dartmouth. It was around this time that Richard was finally appointed as peace commissioner. Lords Hyde and Dartmouth had been pushing for it behind the scenes throughout the early autumn.[79] Although the news would not become official until May 1776, rumors quickly leaked out in the small, aristocratic circles of Caroline and her friends. At the same time, news of the earlier meetings with Benjamin Franklin, so carefully concealed, were becoming an open secret, and "Mrs. Howe's Interest with Dr. Franklin" was spoken of.[80]

In late 1775, Howe prestige was in no way diminished by the family's involvement in the controversial American war. Caroline was enjoying herself. She triumphed over Horace Walpole when she played cards at the home of Lady Hertford. "Mr Walpole lost forty guineas & Mrs Howe won them," recorded Lady Mary Coke. "Mr Walpole was of the party aiming at wit all the night but in my opinion never succeeding. He is certainly less entertaining than he was, others think so as well as myself."[81] The Howe star was rising, whether Walpole liked it or not. Caroline was engaged in a round of seasonal parties.[82] She spent the Christmas holiday at Althorp, where the entire Spencer family, including the Duke and Duchess of Devonshire, had gathered in the majestic Spencer country palace; the usual indoor diversions of eating, drinking, cards, billiards, and music spilled over onto the extensive grounds with skating, foxhunting, and riding.[83]

The Earl of Huntingdon, a friend of the Howes, described the mood in London as "very gay, and not in the least concerned about what is passing on the other side the Atlantic." The nation had confidence in the North administration's handling of the American crisis, he reported. "Whilst my Christmas party was with me," he added, the army at Boston and General Howe "were commemorated in the first glass after dinner." Caroline must have been gratified to hear William pronounced "in fashion" that winter.[84]

IN THE BELEAGUERED TOWN of Boston, William was facing a very different Christmas. On December 14, he wrote to London, advising that his army had only enough fuel for three weeks; when that ran out, he was planning to start hacking up the wharves. Provisions were growing scarce, and the capture by the rebels of a ship laden with military stores a few weeks earlier had alarmed him. The threat of being cut off by sea was serious, he wrote, more serious than the siege of the town from landward.

Five days later, the anticipated provision ships finally arrived, but the livestock had suffered badly during the voyage. Salted food supplies were depleted, so William sent an armed transport to St. Eustatia, a Caribbean island, where the markets were rumored to be "glutted with provision." Two transports, convoyed by a man-of-war and two armed schooners, had been ordered to Georgia for a cargo of rice. For good measure, the captain of the man-of-war had orders to seize any rice cargoes he might intercept during the voyage.[85]

Boston had been fortified with earthen walls, floating batteries, and sharp wood abatis, but as the cold set in, and ice began forming, the rebels could attack across the marshes and mudflats. And they did, launching a fiery raid on the houses left standing on the Charlestown Peninsula and leaving them in ruins, no longer useful for firewood or shelter for the British soldiers stationed on Bunker Hill.[86]

William had been stationed on that hill before his promotion in late September moved him into headquarters in Boston. Over the summer, his little outpost had engaged in sporadic fighting with the rebel Americans who sought to nibble away at the British encampment.[87] Now he found himself and his army hemmed in on the Boston Peninsula. The plight in December 1775 was reminiscent of the winter William spent in Quebec sixteen years earlier, when the garrison of victorious but subsequently besieged British soldiers stacked their frozen dead, surviving on starvation rations and waiting for spring and the sight of a British ship on the St. Lawrence.

William was also aware of another conflict from still earlier in the century: Scotland's 1745 rebellion, when Scottish clans rose in support of Bonnie Prince Charlie. William knew all about both its violent suppression by "Butcher Cumberland" and the lasting damage done to the Duke of Cumberland's reputation in its wake. Now he was faced with direct orders from London to deal with yet another uprising on the peripheries of the empire. The Proclamation of Rebellion on August 23, 1775, had laid the entire thirteen colonies open to military repression "by fire & Sword." William, however, did not relish the prospect of becoming "Butcher Howe."

But Admiral Samuel Graves, still in command of the fleet at Boston, embraced the new British government policy on October 18, when he directed the bombardment and burning of Falmouth (now Portland, Maine), leaving two-thirds of it in ruins. The utter destruction of more than four hundred houses, a church, and customs buildings was followed by three days of driving rain, leaving entire families exposed to the elements. Graves was following the directive to get tough with the rebellion, but the shock in Britain at news of what was widely regarded as a barbaric act led to his recall—and provoked the Americans to authorize a privateer navy that would harass British shipping.[88]

Twice over Christmastide, William confided to General Clinton his uneasiness over this act of aggression, worrying "he shoud be blamed about Falmouth." "[T]o which I did not answer a word," recalled Clinton, then reassured his commander in chief with the helpful rejoinder, "[I]f he was blamed for burning he woud be blamed for C[harles] Town," the town set ablaze during the Battle of Bunker Hill. But "we all had our little share in it," Clinton quickly added.[89] Both men knew, however (and Clinton took care to stress), that it had been done under William Howe's orders.

Henry Clinton would be happy to look good at William's expense. Competition was rife in the British army's officer class. Clinton was one of a clique of army men who had served in Europe during the last war, and who prided themselves on having training and experience superior to that of officers like William, whose service had been in America. Only the fighting in Germany had "made men" in the last war, ran the thinking; an officer friend of Clinton's dismissed William Howe's soldiering abilities as "great Bravery without a ray of conduct__a *Soldier*__no officer__."[90] This sort of verbal attack would accelerate as the war continued.

But Clinton would soon find himself mired in the same sort of trans-atlantic verbal squabbling. When he finally got a crack at an amphibious expedition in South Carolina in June 1776, it was a disaster. The Royal Navy was bombarding a fort on Sullivan's Island, guarding the entrance to Charleston. Clinton, directed to support the naval operation, landed his troops on nearby Long Island, intending to wade across the inlet separating them. It turned out to be seven feet deep, and he could only watch while the naval bombardment was repulsed. Clinton would spend several years explaining away this instance of ineptitude to his critics at home.

THAT CHRISTMAS, while Caroline gambled at Althorp and William scoured British America for provisions, Richard was embroiled in a row with Admiral Sir Hugh Palliser over a lucrative position that had just become available. It quickly escalated into a grab for posts and positions that ultimately involved four admirals.

It began in December with the newly vacated sinecure of lieutenant general of the marines. Embarrassed ministers discovered that it had been inadvertently promised to both Richard Lord Howe and Sir Hugh Palliser. Attempts by Lord North to keep everyone happy only spread the problem, as two more admirals were drawn into the dispute and refused to give way to one another in the round of prizes and honors proffered by nervous ministers. The predicament was resolved for Richard with his formal appointment on February 5, 1776, as commander in chief of the squadron in America. Vice Admiral Keppel was promised command of the Channel Fleet if the French entered the war.

Walpole told the story of the quarrel among the admirals as evidence that Richard's appointment had been pure chance, the result of ministerial incompetence and mismanagement.[91] But Walpole was not as much in the know as he thought—Lord Howe had been in the sights of ministers for the American station for some months.

Unfortunately, Admiral Molyneux Shuldham had just been installed as commander in chief on the coast of North America on September 29, 1775. Barely in his post before he was superseded by Richard, Shuldham was consoled with an Irish peerage.[92] The awkwardness of the situation was deepened by the fact that Shuldham had been the choice of John Montagu, Earl of Sandwich and First Lord of the Admiralty.

Sandwich is best known to posterity as the father of the handheld repast of the same name, for he liked to eat while working or gambling. In public, he was a dedicated professional; in private, he was a famous libertine. His marriage of twenty years having disintegrated under the strain of his wife's mental illness, starting in 1761 he lived openly with his mistress, Martha Ray, a milliner's apprentice who was twenty-six years his junior and shared his love of music.[93]

Sandwich of course knew the Howes. He had played cricket with George; he knew Caroline as well through her husband's membership in the Society of Dilettanti. But he disliked Richard Howe, and the feeling was mutual. Sandwich believed that a partnership of siblings directing the naval and land wars across the Atlantic was a bad idea: "[W]ho does not know that when two Brothers are partners in deep play as whist they are not an over match for two rustics who have never played any at Games beyond Putt or Loo." In plain terms, he was apprehensive that the brothers would prove to be too clever by half, as the old saying goes, in dealing with the malcontent colonists. Perhaps his rather cryptic comment was informed by his impression of the notable insularity and secretiveness of the Howe family.

A contemporary remarked, "Lord Sandwich did not chuse to give [Howe] the Command of the Fleet but all the other Ministers having set upon him he at last give way." Lord Howe was taking a risk serving under a hostile first lord.[94] Military operations needed to run smoothly, and internecine strife within the service could be disastrous.

The sinuous process by which Richard was appointed both commander in chief of the navy in America and peace commissioner reveals the striking lack of consensus among cabinet ministers over their precise objectives as they embarked on a war against their colonies. In sharp contrast to his fellow cabinet member Lord Sandwich, Lord George Germain was happy to appoint Richard as naval commander in chief, but he mistrusted him as a peace commissioner. Germain tried to appoint a crony of his own as a fellow commissioner to keep tabs on Richard, in order to prevent him from making unacceptable concessions to the rebellious colonists. Richard resisted, pointing out that he "had been promised to go alone." In the end, it was agreed that General Howe would act as the second peace commissioner. Richard affirmed his willingness to adhere closely to his instructions. Now there only remained the matter of hammering out those instructions, which, recalled an undersecretary in a classic understatement, "[I]t was foreseen would be very difficult to settle."[95]

During March 1776, Richard struggled with Lord George over the exact conditions under which he could open talks with the rebellious colonists. Germain was highly optimistic about what the British army could accomplish, and he insisted that talks could not even begin until the vanquished colonists had submitted and acknowledged Parliament's supreme power in the colonies. Lord North, as always trying to adhere to the middle of the road, agreed that acknowledgment of Britain's supremacy should be made in due course, but that step need not precede the restoration of peace and the start of negotiations. Lord Dartmouth did not want any American acknowledgment of parliamentary sovereignty to be required. The argument among the three cabinet members over this abstract point became so severe that Lord Dartmouth threatened to go public with his opposition to Lord George's plan.[96] The peaceable-minded Dartmouth had remained in the cabinet as Lord Privy Seal, despite the war he so deplored, to act as Richard's ally.

The fight over the terms of the peace commission ended with a compromise. As a concession to Dartmouth, the commissioners did not have to demand colonial submission before opening negotiations, but they did have to wait for each colony to request a pardon.[97] Richard was being put in a very tight box by Germain, who feared that if the fighting stopped before an acknowledgment of parliamentary sovereignty from the colonists, Britain would never muster the forces to coerce America again. It was now or never. For Germain, this was also a second chance to shine in the public sphere. "The truth was, Lord George," recalled an undersecretary, "having now collected a vast Force, and having a fair prospect of subduing the Colonies, he wished to subdue them before he treated at all."[98]

For his part, Richard would adhere to the letter of his instructions. In the weeks before he embarked for America, he thrashed out certain details in the clauses of his commission with Germain and his secretaries.[99] He had no intention of incurring blame on such a momentous undertaking because of vague or imprecise wording. Every military man was aware of the danger of a situation of that kind, where London authorities left themselves the means of evading responsibility for the outcome of a mission through ambiguously worded orders. There had been plenty of examples in the previous war.

George III was keenly aware that Richard chafed under the terms of his instructions as peace commissioner. The king's affection toward Richard and trust in his integrity are reflected in a curious story. During the convoluted and tense exchanges over the terms of the peace commission, Sir Charles Thompson, one of His Majesty's Grooms of the Bedchamber, was traveling with Richard and one other companion from Bath to London. They stopped to eat at a pub, and conversation turned to the American crisis. Lord Howe became very angry and declared loudly that he thought Lord North deserved impeachment for his handling of the situation. Then, to the consternation of all present, he added, "[T]here was something infinitely worse, and that was the persevering and invincible obstinacy of the King."

When next at court, Sir Charles was summoned by the king and grilled on what occurred at the inn. To the horror of the courtier, His Royal Highness was able to quote what was said almost word for word. While Sir Charles, dismayed, stood at respectful attention, the king suddenly laughed. "Well, well," pronounced George, "every man has a right to his own opinion in public affairs; but I have too high an esteem for Lord Howe not to advise him, through you, at any future time, before he brings his Minister to the scaffold, and inveighs against my 'persevering and invincible obstinacy,' to take the precaution of sending the common waiters of an inn out of the room first!"[100] Richard had been a favorite with George III since his own brother, the Duke of York, had served aboard the *Essex* in the last war. The Howes all had a temper, the king knew, but he also knew he could rely on Richard. The king's final instructions to him as peace commissioner opened with "Our Right Trusty and well Beloved Cousin."[101]

It is no wonder that Richard was irritable. He had no room to maneuver.

The peace commissioners were empowered to pardon colonies, districts, towns, and individuals, but not before an almost impossible raft of preliminaries were met. These included the cessation of armed struggle, disbandment of rebel armies and all illegal congresses and committees, and assurances of future good behavior. When this was all accomplished, the peace commissioners could call an election for a new legislature, which in turn could apply for relief from the Prohibitory Act. The rehabilitated colonies could confer with the commissioners on agreeing to a form of taxation on easy terms (as Lord North expressed it), based on the formula set out in his conciliatory motion of February 1775.[102]

John Pownall, Lord Dartmouth's accomplice in the secret talks with Franklin the previous winter, declared that the commission was "wholly repugnant to all Ideas of conciliation."[103] He was not alone. The Continental Congress had already objected to holding talks under warlike conditions, "with the Bayonet at their Breast," as they put it. South Carolinian Ralph Izard, hearing the terms in London, pronounced it absurd to send a commission to pardon people before they were conquered. If the British backed up negotiations with an army, he warned, they were more likely to irritate than to pacify.[104]

But Richard was still willing to try. As one of Germain's undersecretaries put it, someone had to be commissioner, and, by April 1776 Lord Howe was the only person in the running.[105] In the House of Commons, eleven days after Richard's departure for America, Lord North parried questions about exactly what the peace commission would accomplish by saying the commissioners went *not to treat, but to confer, and to sound, for grounds of peace.* He assured testy MPs that all would be referred to Parliament for its approval.[106] The government was aggressively preparing for armed repression, but its prime minister was indulging in a thread of hope for a short war and a lasting peace. Not all in the cabinet felt as hawkish as Germain.

MEMBERS OF THE HOWE FAMILY found themselves simultaneously getting involved in the war effort in America and forming an initiative at home to replace fighting with talks. Their peace-promoting activities made themselves felt in society in a pattern suggestive of Caroline's influence—in many cases, it was the wife who persuaded the husband to change his politics.

Lady Mary Coke noticed in November 1775 that parliamentary followers of the Duke of Bedford, who took a hardline stance on the colonies, were experiencing internal divisions. Lord Ossory, she wrote, had deserted the Bedfordites for the opposition, and it was rumored that the Duchess of Bedford herself had acquired American sympathies. "[W]ho has converted her I can't tell you," added Lady Mary.[107] But both the duchess and Lord Ossory led back to Caroline: The Duchess of Bedford was a frequent caller at Battlesden; Lord Ossory was the husband of Caroline's old friend, the former Duchess of Grafton. When Lord Ossory was finally wooed away from supporting the North administration's American policy in the autumn of 1775, rumor had it that his wife was to blame.[108]

Horace Walpole heard that another Bedfordite, Lord Gower, was also questioning the wisdom of coercion, at the urging of his wife.[109] Caroline and Lady Gower had been close friends for years, and both ladies came from families whose women were schooled in drawing-room politics. The two women shared political intelligence and kept in close touch.[110] In the end, Lord Gower would remain a supporter of government, but the story reflects Caroline's careful politicking among the wives.

As the nation hovered on the brink of full-scale war, doubts proliferated in many quarters, and men were willing to listen to other ideas. Was the best way to lasting peace to send diplomatic feelers to American leaders, even as outright rebellion was being suppressed? Or would that only serve to signal weakness to the rebellious colonists?

The political give-and-take in the private spheres of drawing rooms and card tables made itself felt in Parliament. In early March 1776, Lord Sandwich made a curious accusation against the Duke of Richmond in the House of Lords. Richmond, he asserted, claimed that some men who served the government, and who publicly supported its American policy, "secretly disapprove" and express their disapproval "in private company." "I do not pretend to say what company the noble Duke keeps, who so confidentially impart their opinions to him," concluded Sandwich angrily.[111] But Sandwich probably could guess. Richmond kept company with the Howe siblings and their friends, including government members Dartmouth and Hyde.

There can be no doubt that Caroline played a role in the political maneuvering that went on over the winter of 1775–76. Once her brothers were overseas, government contacts treated her as the head of the Howe dynasty, despite the fact that nominally she was nothing more than the widowed sister of the brothers. This was the same role that her mother, Charlotte, now living retired at her residence in Albemarle Street, had occupied during the Seven Years' War. Lord and Lady Germain issued Caroline an open invitation to their London home: "It is very pleasant to me to be so near Ld. G. Germain I have a general invitation from him & her to dine there every day if I like it, & without sending which is very agreeable, & he promises the instant he hears anything I shall know it," she declared with satisfaction.[112]

Caroline suddenly had patronage at her command; she arranged for her relative by marriage, John Collett, to become the British consul in Genoa, writing to Lord Weymouth with the request in the morning and receiving word the same day that "his majesty had graciously consented."[113] Mothers wrote to her, asking her to advance the careers of their sons in the army or navy, as they once did to Charlotte.[114] And her old friend Lady Hyde, who had cried on Caroline's shoulder thirteen years earlier after suffering a miscarriage, was to see a long-standing ambition come to fruition.

In June 1776, Lord Hyde became Earl of Clarendon. His wife Charlotte's grandfather had been Earl of Clarendon, but the title had gone extinct with his death. For more than twenty years, Lady Hyde had worked indefatigably to make her husband an earl and herself a countess.[115] Caroline must have heard all about it many times. Finally, the honor was forthcoming. The Hydes had been part of the team who had worked to send Lord Howe to America, and they apparently earned their reward.

In April, while Richard was making preparations to depart for America, a very private part of the Howe family story resurfaced in a wave of scandal. George's former lover, Elizabeth Chudleigh, electrified London society by taking center stage in a bigamy trial. In 1769, she had colluded with her legal husband, Augustus John Hervey, to have their reckless secret marriage of twenty-five years earlier declared void.[116] She then speedily married her longtime lover, the Duke of Kingston.

Elizabeth had achieved her goal of becoming a duchess, but the title would not stick. When the duke died four years later, in 1773, his relatives disputed his will and charged Elizabeth with bigamy. The ponderous legal process, dragged out over several years, finally reached court in April 1776. Charlotte Fettiplace was obliged to testify, for she had been "in a summerhouse in a garden" in Hampshire, when Chudleigh, still a maid of honor, confessed the secret of her marriage. Charlotte was "exceedingly agitated" on the witness stand, the newspapers reported; her brother Lord Howe accompanied her to the courtroom.[117] Richard could hardly avoid supporting his sister, although at the time he was readying his flagship HMS *Eagle* for departure. He was, after all, head of the family. It was probably something he would rather not have been dragged into, but the trial of the Duchess of Kingston came to overshadow the American crisis.[118] The duchess was found guilty, but, ever resourceful, she escaped in a boat to Calais before she could be prevented from leaving the country. She traveled throughout Europe and Russia, a wealthy but increasingly difficult middle-aged woman, until her death more than ten years later.[119]

With the fleet finally in readiness, Richard would embark at Spithead on May 11, 1776. It has been argued that he landed the contradictory roles of peace commissioner and naval commander in chief in America by systematically concealing from all but a few moderate cabinet members his misgivings about the government's policy of armed repression. From the start of hostilities in early 1775, he supposedly decided that the only means of being sent to America in order to fulfill his personal project of saving the empire was to consent to go in a military capacity.[120] This thesis has been put forward as a significant reason for Britain's defeat in the war: The Howe game plan supposedly weakened the impact of the British war machine on the untried rebel army in the critical year of 1776. The time would come when Britain faced defeat in America—its only military defeat in modern times—and this story would take root as the nation searched for a reason.

BUT THE HOWES' QUEST for a middle way at the start of the American Revolution was shared by many in the political establishment. Richard's opinions, as we have seen, were no secret, and he and his brother had been appointed by the king and Parliament to resolve the conflict one way or the other. When Richard was assigned his dual role, America had not yet declared independence, attitudes toward war-versus-peace were fluctuating even in the highest circles, and many Britons, whatever their political persuasion, hesitated, uncertain, on the brink of embarking on a full-scale war against their fellow subjects. It still seemed the course of wisdom to adopt a flexible posture towards replacing fighting with talks, to carry a sword in one hand and an olive branch in the other, as Lord Hyde expressed it to Lord North.[121]

Richard departed amid a mixture of hope and censure from his political associates. Few thought his peace commission would yield quick results; most were pinning their hopes on military action to check the rebellious spirit in America. In contrast, Edmund Burke, who was opposed to using force against the colonists, concluded cynically that the government intended the Howes to conquer New York, set up a puppet assembly, and then effectively force it to adopt Lord North's conciliatory proposal.[122] Opposition spokesman Charles James Fox believed that Lord George Germain had deliberately prolonged the dispute over the terms of the peace commission in March because he calculated that, by the time Lord Howe reached America, the Congress would have declared independence, scuppering any chance of what Germain took to be fruitless talks.[123]

The Howe brothers, then, were undertaking a complex mission that stood a significant chance of disappointing expectations on both sides of the conflict. They had never shied away from public service in the past, but this time there was also a private motive. They had lost their eldest brother, George, the dynastic head, in the wilderness of Ticonderoga, fighting to protect Britain's American empire. The Howe family felt a personal stake in the future of America; now they would set out to ensure that George's sacrifice had not been in vain.

Nine

Home Front

With the departure of Lord Richard Howe and his fleet, the eyes of the entire nation turned toward America. Even those who neither understood nor cared about arguments over colonial rights could see all around them evidence of the conflict wrought by such seemingly abstract ideas. That spring, royal guardsmen paraded with great pageantry in London's parks before embarking for service in the colonies. Three redcoat regiments encamped on Wimbledon Common, near the country house of Lord and Lady Spencer, awaiting a royal review before shipping off to the war.[1]

From May 1776 onward, there would be a lengthy hiatus in military intelligence arriving from America. The epicenter of the war was far-off New York, and news took a month with a favorable wind; going in the other direction, the norm was at least two months. It was common for military communiqués to reach the commanders in the field three or four months after they were dispatched, and some never arrived at all.[2] The campaign against New York did not begin until late August, and it concluded in mid-December. Not until the end of 1777 would its full outcome be known in London.

Private mail suffered even greater disruption. The regular post office packet boats that sailed between England and New York or Charleston, South Carolina, were discontinued after October 1775. Only a less reliable wartime service from Halifax, operating under the constant threat of enemy privateers, struggled on. Yet people who were determined to get their letters across the Atlantic found other means of doing so, and private letters from America often arrived in Britain ahead of the official dispatches.[3] People improvised in many ways; ship captains and crews who manned the vessels crossing and recrossing the Atlantic as part of the British war effort could be prevailed upon to carry mail. Servicemen coming from and going to the front in America carried not only letters but also word-of-mouth news. Junior officers sometimes called upon Caroline in Grafton Street to give her the latest intelligence about her brothers.

The American War of Independence was the third war in which the Howe women saw the brothers go overseas to fight, but it was the first war that has left us a wealth of personal letters that reveal their home-front experiences. Caroline's own surviving correspondence is enriched by the hitherto-neglected letters of Jane Strachey, whose husband Henry crossed the Atlantic with Richard Lord Howe. The Stracheys and the Howes had moved in separate circles during peacetime, but, as we shall see, the women of the two families would draw close as they shared the anxious wait for word from loved ones.

The prospect of news of her brothers meant that Caroline was reluctant to leave Grafton Street after Parliament broke up for the summer recess on May 23, 1776. British politicians dispersed to their summer estates, but information from America would reach London first, by means of rapid post riders from ships putting in at Falmouth in the west of England or Portsmouth on the south coast. In early June, Caroline begged off paying a day visit to the Spencers, probably at their villa in Wimbledon, explaining that she was expecting her sister-in-law Lady Howe for the day.[4] She was still in town in mid-July, attending an evening of dinner and cards hosted by Princess Amelia at her fine Palladian house at Gunnersbury.

In Princess Amelia's verdant garden estate, the little party of a dozen or so genteel guests included Lady Mary Coke, Lord and Lady Spencer, and Horace Walpole. The summer fruits at Gunnersbury had ripened prodigiously, and the guests exclaimed at the luscious fare. But the talk around the table gave the lie to this apparent idyll. There was discussion of Lady Charlotte Finch, the royal governess, who had recently learned that her son George had gone to America as a volunteer under General Howe. George, only in his midtwenties, had inherited his deceased father's title of Earl of Winchilsea. At the end of June, he secretly took ship at Portsmouth, leaving his friends and his widowed mother in the dark as to his destination. Lady Mary Coke had called on Lady Finch just before the party, and she described to the guests the anguish of the mother, who at first had been unable to control her distress. Lady Finch clung to the belief that the war would be short and Lord Winchilsea would be home by November—an idea that Lady Coke did not wish to discourage.[5]

In Parliament, men could argue that the fighting would quickly be over, but the wives and mothers, watching their menfolk depart, knew that they were heading into real danger. Since William had left in 1775, Fanny Howe had never been entirely able to hide her anxiety.[6] Now Richard's wife, Lady Mary Howe, was in the same unhappy situation. Although Mary was an experienced navy wife, Caroline described her spirits as only "so so" at best when she parted with her husband in May. Caroline as usual made no mention of her own feelings. Instead, she became preoccupied with the direction of the wind—a west wind was needed to bring news from America. Years later, she confessed to Lady Spencer the sensation of "a little heart ache in the middle of the night listening to a high wind" when loved ones were far away.[7]

For Caroline, there was a new edge to the tension, as it would be the command decisions of her own brothers that would expose the husbands and sons of friends like Lady Charlotte Finch to potential injury or death. Before long, she would be assessing the accounts of battles in America with apprehension, sending confidences to Lady Spencer that expressed a doleful sense of relief when the list of the dead did not include the names of any officers they knew.[8]

The Howe women took up their usual wartime posts of overseeing the interests of the brothers in political and court circles. Since the Dowager Lady Howe's retirement, there was no family member serving at court, but regular ties persisted. Caroline played cards with Princess Amelia, who remained close to her great-nephew George III and entertained his children with skittles and outdoor games at Gunnersbury. One of George III's sons would later recall that the Howes were "a sort of connexion with the family."[9] Caroline's regular presence in court circles could only benefit her brothers, and she also had an active ally in her sister-in-law Lady Mary Howe, who attended the drawing rooms and passed on all the news to Caroline.

Drawing rooms were receptions for presentation to the monarch that were attended weekly by both sexes, in contrast to the more formal levees, which were exclusive to men and restricted to high-ranking ministers and nobles. The numbers at the drawing rooms varied, but sometimes they were so crowded that the ladies, in their expensive finery, found themselves crushed ruthlessly against their neighbors. "Oh! Oh! Oh! My hips! My feet! My head!" cried one of the Spencer women after enduring the

throng. Even when thinly attended, the drawing rooms were not comfortable for women, who stood in stiff court dresses, managing fans and
trains while curtseying. When it was over, a seemingly interminable
wait ensued, as coaches queued up outside to carry home the exhausted
ladies and gentlemen, who often collapsed as soon as the footman closed
the door. But it was all worthwhile, because drawing rooms were venues
where the latest news—whether political, foreign, or simply town gossip—
was circulated.[10]

Lady Mary Howe's visits to the drawing rooms must have been gratifying to her family in the months after her husband's departure. Throughout
1776, the Howe influence was at its height. Caroline had an open invitation
to dine with the Germains, and she could wield patronage on behalf of
family friends. One of these, Charles Brett, ran successfully as a member
of Parliament for Sandwich in a November by-election because the Howes
were "high in Government favour."[11]

Christopher D'Oyly, an attorney and the son of an attorney, also benefited from his Howe connection when in May he was appointed an undersecretary in the Whitehall office of American Secretary of State Lord
George Germain. Although he had been an MP since 1774, D'Oyly did not
stand as high in the world as the Spencers or the Cavendishes. Yet he and
his wife, Sarah, had for years been on a familiar footing with the Howes.
The families were related, a D'Oyly having married one of the ubiquitous
Mordaunts, cousins of the Howes.[12] "I am to pass the evening & sup with
a very private party; chiefly Howes, at Mr. D'Oyleys," wrote Caroline to
Lady Spencer in 1767, in words that summed up the informal nature of
the friendship.[13]

Outside of Germain's office, the D'Oylys supported the British war
effort in a quite domestic fashion. Warmhearted, and without children of
their own, the D'Oylys were at the center of a circle of families that drew
together as their men went overseas. Among them were Fanny and Mary
Howe, the wives of the commanders in chief, but aristocratic rank was
not a prerequisite for inclusion. Another solitary wife who would often call
upon the D'Oylys for the proverbial tea and sympathy was Jane Strachey,
whose husband Henry, as Lord Howe's secretary, had departed for America in May. Jane was left with three young children under her care. She
was quickly invited to dine *en famille* with the D'Oylys at their residence
in Hampton Court. Whenever Mr. D'Oyly was called away to his office in

Whitehall, Mrs. D'Oyly virtually moved into the Strachey house in Greenwich to assist with the children.[14]

Jane Strachey's letters to Henry in America, long overlooked, are unparalleled as a glimpse into the thoughts and feelings of an Englishwoman on the home front during the American War of Independence. As the private letters of a wife, they are buried within the collection of Strachey family papers in the Somerset Archives. Yet they are the English equivalent of Abigail Adams's wartime correspondence, written an ocean away, to her own husband, John, a future president of the United States. A gifted letter-writer, Jane wrote in poignant terms of the British families at home, waiting for news of the war. The feelings of the women and children who stayed behind come alive in lifelike and emotive detail.

In 1776, as the nation waited for news of the outcome of the New York campaign, Jane's words reflected the feeling of incredulity that the Americans were going to war over seemingly abstract questions of rights:

> I say to myself that one of the greatest Evils arising from the ambitious and restless spirit of the Americans, is the interruption they have occasioned in the Domestick Tranquillity of many happy familys in this country, how much more will you say they have hurt themselves?

With characteristic gentleness, she added, "I am not malicious, I only wish them peace, and that my dear Harry may soon appear with the glad Tidings." For Henry was not in America as a military man, but as part of Lord Howe's peace mission.[15]

Henry Strachey was bound for America as secretary to Richard and William Howe in their capacities as peace commissioners. Although Henry credited his friend Christopher D'Oyly with bringing him to the notice of Admiral Howe, he was employed not so much because of who he knew, but rather for his known abilities as an intelligent administrator with an understanding of imperial problems. He was one of a rising category of men from the middling ranks of society, what would come to be called the middle class. A modern civil service did not yet exist, but the needs of government were growing. Government departments had for long offered "do-nothing" positions for impecunious young gentry-folk. Now these were joined by a new breed of earnest men like Strachey who took their work seriously.[16]

In 1764, Henry Strachey had become private secretary to the dashing and notorious Robert Clive, better known as Clive of India. For the next three years, Henry was in Bengal with his ambitious employer, acquiring a sustained reputation for hard work, intelligence, and industry. Clive's military conquests and aggressive consolidation of East India Company control in Bengal had left him enormously wealthy but mistrusted at home. In contrast, Strachey survived a high-profile parliamentary inquiry with an unsullied reputation.[17] Clive was exonerated, but he died soon afterward from an overdose of laudanum. Accident or suicide? The verdict was never in. Caroline suspected the latter, as she wrote to Lady Spencer: "I find there is some foundation for the report that Ld. Clive destroyed himself, Ld. Piggot who is in town & enquires after you & yours, is vastly sorry for him, gives him the greatest of characters."[18]

This was in late 1774, when Caroline was busy secretly wooing Benjamin Franklin over a chessboard. The conscientious Henry Strachey now found himself without a steady income, while needing to support a wife and three young children, the expense of a seat in Parliament, and a risky investment in a Florida plantation.[19] The chance to join Lord Howe's staff could not have been better timed.

Jane said good-bye to her husband on May 8, 1776; six days later, she was composing the first of her many long letters.[20] Her method was to write continuously over several days, heading each entry with the day's date. She did not write in the typical stoical tone of a military wife or sister. She spoke with an open heart of "this long cruel separation" from one whom she loved "above every other being." "I shall never forget it, I saw your concern at leaving me and your poor little ones," she recollected feelingly of the day, less than a week earlier, when he bade her farewell.[21]

Jane's letters bring to life the emotional cost of a long separation in an age when transportation was slow and communication even slower. She confessed that she never got used to her husband's absence. Opening each letter from America created a moment of unbearable suspense: "[W]ith what a trembling hand do I break the seals that lock up the intelligence on which all my tranquillity depends." She dreamt that she had joined her husband in New York, only to find that he was then ordered on a mission that took him hundreds of miles away from her. "This mortification occasioned such distress that it awakened me." When a well-meaning friend lectured her that Mr. Strachey might be absent for more than a year, she rounded upon him with the retort that, "if ever he threw out such a thing again I would disclaim his acquaintance."

Their extended separation meant that husband and wife would not look upon one another's faces for at least a year. This triggered insecurities; nine months after they had parted, on almost the same date, both wrote letters warning of the advancing signs of age. Reminding Henry that she was almost forty, Jane added bluntly, "I am growing old, as you will not want a pair of spectacles to discover this on your return, I may as well drop the subject."[22] A week later, in far-off New York, her husband was beset by the same worry: "I desire you will not be surprised if I appear somewhat older than when I left you," wrote Henry, though he advanced the possibility that youthfulness would be replaced by rugged good looks: "I flatter myself that a more healthy Look will apologize for the Wrinkles of Age."[23]

Jane's children registered their awareness of their father's absence according to their own childish perceptions. Interestingly, even the youngest realized the nature of Henry's business in America. "Little Edward," reported Jane, "who is louder and stouter than either his Brother or Sister goes upon his [hobby] horse as he tells us several times a day to 'Make peace in America.'" The peaceable Edward was only three. Five-year-old Harry, taken to a military review in Hyde Park, was so shocked by the noise of the artillery that he comforted himself with the fiction that they were not real— "[H]e said he knew the smoke was nothing more than Tobacco," wrote his bemused mother, but Harry then recalled with fright that his poor papa was in America, where genuine cannon would "make more noise."[24]

Jane Strachey did not go to court or attend fashionable card parties, but she understood that etiquette required her to pay a courtesy call upon her husband's employer. Less than a week after Henry's departure, she duly visited Lady Mary Howe and was "received with great kindness."[25] This first visit to the admiral's residence in Grafton Street was described as "paying her respects," but over the next twelve months, the two women would draw much closer, as Jane became part of a circle of army wives.

LADY HOWE WON Jane's admiration because she belied the stereotype widely held in the eighteenth century of an aristocratic woman who neglected her family for fashionable living. "[E]xclusive of [Lady Howe's] civilities to me," Jane wrote to Henry, "it is impossible for me not to admire her for her uncommon affection, and devotion to her absent Lord, as well as for her extreme attention and regard to her Children. Such Characters," continued Jane, expressing the prevalent attitude, "are very rare in high Life."[26]

Eventually Jane would meet all of the Howe women. She was introduced to Caroline one afternoon at the admiral's house in Grafton Street. At the D'Oylys', she met Fanny, the general's wife—"pretty and agreeable" and very polite. On yet another occasion at the D'Oylys', the Dowager Lady Charlotte Howe made an appearance, together with her daughter Julie. As a former lady-in-waiting to Princess Augusta, the elderly woman was an object of great respect. Jane wrote to her husband of her gratified pride when the Dowager Lady Howe and Julie visited her soon afterward at her Park Street address.[27] Struck by the close Howe family dynamics, she was moved to say, "How very amiable are strong family attachments, and how exceedingly do I respect the Howe family for their Love to each other."[28]

Just as the crucible of war brought the Howe men easily into close quarters with fellow soldiers from lower social ranks, so the Howe women welcomed Jane into their circle of those who had to stay behind. Nevertheless, a vestige of self-consciousness remained, for Jane betrayed a feeling of defensiveness when she wrote to Henry of including the Howes in a musical party hosted in her home. Among the guests were the wives of Admiral and General Howe, and also Mary, youngest of the Howe siblings, and her husband, General Pitt. "You will not I hope suppose that I have been guilty of any impropriety in pushing myself to be introduced to Lord Howes family," she protested. The D'Oylys had encouraged it, and had been present themselves. The Howes loved this sort of informal musical evening. The gentlemen sang popular tunes, there was fiddling, and the young ladies provided musical performances. General Pitt was delighted to discover that he had attended the same academy as some of the other gentlemen guests, and the sparkling occasion finished up with a simple supper of cold chicken.[29]

In October 1776, William Howe's aide-de-camp, Captain Nisbet Balfour, arrived in London on a mission to deliver military dispatches, and he quickly became a regular in the private circles of the Howes and their friends. Balfour had first drawn William's notice in June 1775 at Bunker Hill, where he led a light company and bravely fought on at the bloody rail fence after being wounded. Since then, William had been sure to make use of Captain Balfour. A large, powerful figure of a man, still only in his early thirties, he was charming, gregarious, and popular with men and women alike. As the son of an impoverished Scottish laird, he never married.³⁰ But he was a man of warm feeling. In his will, he remembered a woman who had once been his mistress. She had married elsewhere by the time of his death many years later, but Nisbet bequeathed a generous legacy to their natural daughter, Euphemia.³¹ Balfour's friendship with the Howe family was also strong, and we shall see that it would entangle him in the byzantine story of the mismanaged campaign of 1777.

Jane Strachey met Balfour almost as soon as he arrived in town, at an evening party at the D'Oylys' that included Lady Howe and Caroline. He was "just what you describe," Jane wrote to her husband, "communicative, good-natured and Chatty." She observed with gratitude that the captain spoke as much of Henry Strachey as he did of the two "worthy" Howe brothers, carefully answering all of Jane's many questions while the Howe women listened with kindness. That evening, she pressed Balfour to dine with her family on whatever day suited him; the children would be overjoyed to have a guest who could give them news of their father, and she promised him a "Scotch song into the bargain" from her young brood, who would prepare a list of questions in advance of the exciting visit.³²

But Jane soon discovered that Major Balfour (he was quickly promoted once in London) would be in great demand that autumn. While the Strachey household waited in vain for him to call, he dined in Grafton Street with Caroline and was presented at court by Lord George Germain.³³ A week later, Jane confessed that "the young ones and myself staid at home the whole day in expectation of seeing him," but he did not appear. "I imagine he has much upon his hands," Jane concluded generously. But it was difficult to explain this to six-year-old Charlotte, who had been wearing her best cap for three days running in hopes of seeing the captain. The children "have a string of questions to ask him concerning their [Papa]." Jane was chagrined to discover that when she finally ventured out to the park with the children, Balfour had stopped by in their absence. Five-year-old Henry's expectations had been raised so high that he asked a strange officer in the park "if he was not Captn. Balfour."³⁴

Eventually the major did come, and more than once. Part of his charm lay in an obliging disposition and an easygoing willingness to mix with all levels of people. He joined the Strachey family on a night out at the theater; he was present at the musical party hosted by Jane in January for the Howes; he took Fanny Howe to Portsmouth to view the shipping.³⁵ While on leave in London in late 1776, William's aide-de-camp functioned as a sort of proxy for the absent male family members.

Jane Strachey did not begrudge the fact that the good-natured Balfour's first duty was to the Howes; the titled wives of the commanders in chief took precedence, and Jane in turn received due consideration. But her patience had limits. On a morning visit to Lady Howe, while the two women were shedding tears together for their absent husbands, Lord Shuldham visited—the same Admiral Molyneux Shuldham who had had to surrender his new American command to Richard Howe. His lordship arrived to reassure Lady Howe that worrying rumors concerning the health of Richard—whom he had seen recently in New York—were exaggerated. This seemed to complete the purpose of his visit. "Lord Shuldham spoke with great civility to Lady Howe," noted Jane angrily, "but when she was so kind to say who I was he had not the complaisance to say even that you was well." Thank goodness *she* did not need to rely on Lord Shuldham for news of Henry, she asserted. Reassuring her husband that she had taken care to conceal her dudgeon, she concluded with uncharacteristic ill humor, "[H]ow can a Lord, and such a Lord, think of the Secretary's wife?"

Jane would also find that letters from America routed via the office of Lord George Germain were delivered to Lady Howe as the admiral's wife at least a day before they reached her. Even Lady Howe's servants received letters sooner than she, sent as they were, "under his Lordships cover." But Lady Howe herself corrected this injustice. She arranged a mutually supportive system whereby Lord Howe was requested to report on the health of Henry in all his letters, and Henry was requested, in turn, to make mention of Richard's health whenever he wrote to Jane.[36] Thus, the two wives could console one another with news from America.

Sharing news was an important component of the support offered within the little community of home-front families. Early in the new year of 1777, Jane generously conveyed to Lady Mary Howe several pages of a letter written to her by her husband Henry. She hoped thereby to give her ladyship some peace of mind, for Richard had been seriously ill in New York over Christmas.[37] William had tried to downplay the danger in his most recent letter, but he met with the usual lack of success. Lady Howe was convinced he was hiding something. "[H]er Ladyships fears suspected more," wrote Jane, "and carried her to the greatest degree of apprehension." When Henry Strachey sent his wife a franker account of the illness, together with

Wedding Portrait
of Charlotte von
Kielmansegg, 1719.

Sophia Charlotte
von Kielmansegg,
Countess of
Darlington
(1675–1725).

Aunt Juliana Page dressed as the goddess Diana, probably for a masquerade. She is seen here in her midthirties. Masquerades were highly popular in the eighteenth century.

Wedding Portrait of Mary Howe, 1725. The ceremony made her Countess Pembroke. In her left hand is a peer's coronet.

Young George Augustus Howe dressed as Cupid, probably for a masquerade ball.

Portrait of George Augustus, 3rd Viscount Howe (half-length), wearing the uniform of the 1st Guards (oil on canvas).

Thomas Gainsborough's
famous portrait of Mary
Countess Howe, painted
in the year following the
Peace of 1763.

Commodore Viscount
Howe (1726–99).

The Death of General Wolfe (1727–59), ca 1771 (oil on panel).

Lady Spencer with her oldest daughter, Georgiana, ca 1760, her "Dear Little Gee."

Mezzotint of "The Honble. Sr. Wm. Howe." The lettering reads "Knight of the Bath, & Commander in Chief of his Majesty's Forces in America." This print was created in London in 1777, while William was in America. It is probably a copy of an earlier portrait by another artist. The star and shoulder sash of the Order of the Bath would have been added by the creator of the image to bring it up to date.

Lord Howe and the Comte d'Estaing off Rhode Island, 9th August 1778. The two fleets had arrived off Newport, Rhode Island, by August 9, 1778, but it was not until several days later, after a severe storm, that the battle commenced.

Sophia Charlotte, eldest daughter of Admiral Howe. The similar backgrounds and costumes of the two sitters in this and the portrait below, of Lady Mary Howe, suggest that these portraits were painted at the same time, probably on the occasion of the marriages of two of the Howe daughters in 1787.

Portrait of Lady Mary Juliana Howe, middle daughter of Admiral Howe.

The Battle of June 1, 1794. The *Queen Charlotte*, in the center, is engaging with the *Montagne*, at right. In the foreground, crew of the wrecked *Vengeur* cling to its spars.

Caroline Howe in 1812.

an assurance that his lordship was on the mend, she hurried to the D'Oylys' with the relevant pages.

Mr. D'Oyly was out, and, feeling it was important, Jane pursued him to the homes of Lord George Germain and General Edward Harvey before giving up and leaving the extracts with Mrs. D'Oyly. That evening, Jane met Major Balfour, who was able to tell her that her letter had finally been put into the hands of Lady Howe, "and this it seems has been the greatest comfort she has rec[eive]d. I know myself what I should feel in her circumstances, and therefore sincerely sympathize with her." Jane's good nature, however, was severely taxed when Mr. D'Oyly refused to return the letter.[38] It was probably passed around in a cabinet meeting. Richard's physical state was now a matter of national security.

ADMIRAL HOWE'S WIFE, Lady Mary, was not born into the high aristocracy. When she married Richard in early 1758, he was merely a naval officer in midcareer. She was a very private person, about whom there is little record. But Jane Strachey has left a unique portrait of Mary's life during the War of Independence, for she was invited several times to stay at the Howe country home, Porter's Lodge. To the wife of Lord Howe's secretary, this was unlooked-for kindness, and she was grateful. Writing on a visit to Porter's Lodge with her daughter Charlotte in April 1777, she wrote of her hostess:

> I must say something of Lady Howe and her three amiable Daughters. In high Life I never met with a Character so truly calculated for Domestick happiness, with the most tender and affectionate attachment to her Dear Absent Lord she secludes herself from the world and spends almost her whole time at this retired place with no other company but her three Children, and her time is totally taken up in the most watchful attention to their improvement.

The girls were deeply attached to their mother, she reported, venerated their father, and were devoid of pretension.[39] The three Howe children fussed over six-year-old Charlotte Strachey, to the younger girl's delight. They took her in the family coach and gave her a heart-shaped locket to wear around her neck "in which they told her she must put some of her Papas hair—and you may easily suppose how happy and vain this made her."[40]

The departure of many male members of British households to wage war in America meant that the women left behind had to assume responsibility for household finances, farm and business management, and other traditionally male tasks. Historians have written about their counterparts in America, but little attention has been given to the experiences of British women during the eight-year conflict.[41] Jane Strachey's correspondence reveals that she herself took full control of the family income once Henry had departed. She oversaw Henry's rather complex finances, directed repairs on the house in Greenwich, paid taxes, and received and transmitted reports on the struggling Strachey plantation in Florida.[42]

And Jane left a similar picture of Lady Mary Howe, who managed the farm at Porter's Lodge and supervised laborers on the estate. "I never met with any Woman that appeared to me so fit to govern a large family," she wrote, revealing her unstinting admiration. Lady Howe was in charge of both indoor and outdoor servants and workmen on her "very large farm," "which appears to me to be conducted with the utmost order and regularity, and which affords the most wholesome delicious provisions for the family."[43] Although Lady Mary was not born a Howe, she had the Howe attributes of personal dignity, self-reliance, and a capacity for management. If she was more domestic than her sister-in-law Caroline, she was also much more worldly-wise than Jane Strachey realized.

William Howe has been described in history books as a deplorably poor letter-writer whose infrequent communications would eventually be cited by his chief, Lord George Germain, as having serious consequences for the direction of the war.[44] Whatever the truth of Lord George's charge, it bore no relation to William's qualities as a private correspondent. He wrote such long and frequent letters to his wife that it drew comments from Jane, who at one point noted enviously that Fanny had received a letter of twenty pages from the general; "[H]ow happy it must make her."[45]

Henry Strachey confessed to being intimidated by the active devotion of his superior. He accused General Howe of putting himself and Lord Howe to shame in the eyes of their wives. He went on, "I understand he writes a scrap now & then at his leisure & throws it by, and when a packet [ship] goes, huddles them together."[46] William and Fanny persisted in their devotion to one another, despite the fact that wartime private correspondence was often intercepted and opened. At Christmastime 1776, Fanny was mortified to learn that the Continental Congress in Philadelphia "had the Delicacy to peruse publicly a Letter from Mrs. Howe to the General, her Husband," probably a message captured from a packet ship.[47]

Caroline made frequent mention of letters from William and Richard to their wives, sometimes conveying the contents to Lady Spencer.[48] Yet although she wrote constantly to her brothers in America, none of this has survived; her comments to Lady Spencer provide an idea of just how much has been lost. "This is my 6th letter of today besides three or four notes," she wrote during the tense autumn of 1776, and again, "I've been obliged to send letters & notes in abundance." Her close relationship to the commanders in chief meant that anyone seeking news of America looked to her as a natural source, and she accepted the role of family representative with her customary enthusiasm. But her chief epistolary efforts were on behalf of William and Richard: "I have been making up my American packets & writing almost the whole day, & have hardly head or eyes left," she explained on one occasion to Lady Spencer, excusing herself for dashing off a letter.[49]

While the brothers conveyed firsthand news of the war to their families, Caroline could reply with gossip about their reputations at home. For military men overseas, their individual reputations required constant vigilance from watchful family and friends. An instructive example comes from General Henry Clinton, who attempted to minimize the damage to his reputation at home after the fiasco of the South Carolina expedition in June 1776. Both Clinton and the naval commander, Sir Peter Parker, had been made to look ridiculous by the affair, and their chief had not spared them. Germain published a piece in the *Gazette* exposing Clinton's disastrous decision-making. Clinton, thin-skinned and unable to ignore criticism, sent his secretary, Richard Reeve, back to England to promote an alternative and more flattering version of events. Reeve called on the people who mattered, including General Harvey, the adjutant general (who was soon "broadcasting to quiet critical tongues"), and Clinton's illustrious kinsman Henry, 2nd Duke of Newcastle, on whose influence Clinton relied. (The old duke, who had locked horns so often with the Howe women, had died in 1768.)[50]

Eventually Clinton's cause would be taken up by his supporters in the House of Commons. But so pervasive was the gossip mill that first it filtered down to the drawing-room chatter of the West End. Clinton had plenty of friends who were willing to publicize his innocence in social circles. Caroline would certainly have heard the whole story more than a few times in a succession of card parties. But she had a more direct source of intelligence: her friend and relative Christopher D'Oyly. Richard Reeve's first port of call when he arrived back in London was Germain's office. The American Secretary of State was in the countryside, but his undersecretary, Mr. D'Oyly, opened and read Clinton's dispatch while Reeve waited. Two days later, when Reeve was finally ushered into Germain's presence, Mr. D'Oyly entered the room during their interview.[51] D'Oyly effectively knew everything that went on in Germain's office, including the opinions of the American secretary regarding the campaigns and commanders. And what he knew, the Howe women knew, a fact that in time would come to cause his lordship much disquiet.

BUT SUCH UNEASINESS still remained in the future. In 1776, the British nation expected the rebellion to be repressed in a single campaign. At the end of July, word of the army's progress finally began to reach Germain's office. General Howe, together with an enormous contingent of nine thousand men, had set sail from Halifax, Nova Scotia, on June 10, bound for New York. William landed at Staten Island on June 25, and Richard joined him on July 12.[52] In the face of the impressive British show of force off rebel-held New York, the leaders in the Continental Congress did not hesitate. On the Fourth of July, the American Declaration of Independence was signed in Philadelphia.

Londoners learned of American independence in mid-August. The reception was anticlimactic; newspapers published it with little comment. People had been anticipating such a move from the Congress for many months; it only underscored what everyone had expected, that fighting would be necessary to bring the Americans to reason. Germain thought the news would silence the parliamentary opposition, who were so keen to depict the colonists as victims seeking only restoration of their historic rights.[53]

Within London's fashionable circles, the tension mounted. Despite the presumption that the enemy was an ill-trained provincial force, there was no sense of complacency. Germain confessed that he waited "with great impatience for an account of Genl. Howes operations."[54] He probably did not enjoy being importuned for American news by his persistent neighbor, Lady Mary Coke.[55]

September of 1776 was the worst month. Fanny Howe's unease was evident at a tea party at the D'Oylys'. "Mrs Howe discovers great anxiety, which is not to be wondered at," commented a guest.[56] At the same time, across the Irish Sea at Castletown, Fanny's sister-in-law, Lady Louisa Conolly, wrote, "How very impatient one does grow! It seems such a critical time for one's friends there!" She confessed her fears for General Howe. Less than a week later, still with a sense of foreboding, her sympathies were transferred to Fanny: "[S]he is in such a miserable state of anxiety that I tremble for her continually. 'Tis so terrible to think of a person suffering what she would do if anything happens to General Howe."[57] Lady Sarah Bunbury chimed in with her sister on her anxiety for William Howe, who had always been a favorite: "I suppose you are as anxious as everybody must be to hear news from America. I own I feel most excessively so." Reflecting her American sympathies, she added, "[I]t gives one some comfort to think that so *vile* a war is at least as well conducted as it is in the General's power to do."[58]

During that most critical month, Lady Mary Coke confided to her journal that those she knew with sons, husbands, or brothers in America were suffering under the suspense, adding, "tho' the news which is hourly expected may be very happy for this Country to individuals it may be terrible."[59] Almost to the day, Caroline reported to Lady Spencer that Richard's wife was finding the stress unbearable. "I think Lady Howe's anxietys & fears are the worst, most black of any of us." She added briefly that her mother, the Dowager Lady Howe, who had raised three sons to serve their country, was "pretty well." But the sharp-eyed Lady Mary Coke discerned the elderly woman's anxiety for news at a polite card party.[60]

Caroline refused to budge from London throughout September. "I should have been happy to have gone to Chatsworth could I have flown back," she wrote in reply to an invitation to Derbyshire from Lady Spencer, but she could not rid herself of the feeling that she had to remain within reach. Two weeks later, she was with her mother at Richmond, declining another tempting invitation from her friend; if she were to receive good news from America soon, it might be possible, but, "as the wind is I shall hardly hear soon enough to give me an option." Fanny had just called, having received a letter from William dated July 30, she added. Admiral Howe had reached New York on July 12 and was in good health, and more troops were due within hours. News of a military action could be expected to follow. On the last day of September, Caroline sent Lady Spencer the latest:

"Lady Howe & Mrs. Howe had letters from my brothers yesterday, of the 15th of Aug[u]st." There was still no decisive news; "[W]e must patiently as may be, wait for the next dispatches, which will probably be very interesting, & may be expected every hour."[61]

As she wrote this, Caroline could not know that William had already made his move against the rebel forces on Long Island. In late August, while she was staying at Battlesden with her sister Charlotte and her Aunt Juliana Page—"a heap of women," as she put it—William began the campaign for New York.[62] It would be the defining episode of his career, and one that would weave an aura of mystery around the entire Howe dynasty.

Ten

New York, 1776

At 2 a.m. on August 27, 1776, General William Howe was standing at the bar of Howard's Half-Way House, a plain wooden tavern at the foot of the Jamaica Pass on Long Island. A rough tweed cloak covered his uniform and he held a drink in his hand. Since 9 p.m. the previous evening, he had led a column of ten thousand men through the dark, quietly and cautiously, toward the village of Bedford, behind the American lines.

Like George Howe's nighttime advance on Ticonderoga almost twenty years earlier, the British had left campfires burning to deceive enemy look-outs. The advance guard was on the alert to apprehend any stray traveler who might warn the enemy. The slow progress of the two-mile-long redcoat column through unfamiliar countryside was a dangerous move. Obstacles in the road had to be removed quietly, and anyone found still out and about was detained for the night. The British allowed themselves twelve hours to cover the eight miles to their destination, expecting every moment that they would be checked by an American ambush.[1] This was the sort of thing William had done before. Now, standing at the bar of Howard's Half-Way House, he called for a drink before ordering the tavernkeeper, William Howard, to act as a guide through the Rockaway footpath that would lead the redcoats behind the American defenses.

Years later, Howard's young son recalled the incident. His father had replied to the British commander, "We belong to the other side, General, and can't serve you against our duty." Howe replied, "That is alright—stick to your country, or stick to your principles, but, Howard, you are my prisoner, and must guide my men over the hill." When his father continued to object, he was silenced by the general, who said, "You have no alternative. If you refuse, I shall have you shot through the head."[2]

William meant business. Five months earlier, he and his army had shipped out of Boston Harbor, their departure inevitable. All the military men agreed that Boston was a poor base for the forthcoming military campaign. What was essentially a tactical retreat had been hastened by the appearance of rebel cannon and artillery on nearby Dorchester Heights in early March. American Colonel Henry Knox, who had been running a bookshop in Boston just a year earlier, had accomplished the heroic feat of dragging the guns from Fort Ticonderoga through the snowy wastes of New England in December 1775. The British would never return, and March 17 would become known as Evacuation Day in Massachusetts.

The previous September, Richard had chivied Lord George Germain on William's behalf, warning that he needed transports right away if the army were to evacuate Boston before winter. In the same letter, he had shared William's opinion that the theater of war should be moved to New York.[3] Instead, the British army had been obliged to decamp to Halifax, Nova Scotia, more than four hundred miles northeast of Boston, because it needed to evacuate more than a thousand loyalist civilians to safety, reload, reprovision, and drill discipline into the troops that had faltered at Bunker Hill.[4]

William, writing to Germain, was unhappy that the British evacuation of Boston would raise rebel morale.[5] But in the midst of his frustration, he saw the possibility that this might make the rebels overconfident, and thus tempt them into a false move. William wanted to use psychology in his strategic planning. Inexperienced, naïve soldiers were too likely to make much of inconsequential victories. To turn this to his advantage, however, he required speed. He wrote from Halifax in April that the rebel leaders, "flushed with the idea of superiority, may be the readier brought to a decisive action"—the quickest way, he added, to end "this expensive war." But he warned that if his army could not move quickly against the enemy at New York, the rebels were likely to dig in and assume a defensive posture, thus prolonging the conflict.[6]

A challenge for any general is calculating how to get his enemy to do what he desires. General George Washington continually hoped to entice William to "obligingly assault his entrenchments, taking losses [Howe] couldn't afford." Washington would acquire a reputation for avoiding direct confrontation, for preferring instead to wear down the enemy slowly with constant small attacks. Such tactics had been used two millennia earlier by the Roman commander Fabius during the Punic Wars against Hannibal's invading army; by 1777, British newspapers were dubbing Washington "the American Fabius."[7]

For his part, William sought to lure the enemy into a confrontation on equal, open ground, with sufficient British reserves to follow up on any victory. That would require luck, strategy, and a large force. If we try to get away with less, William warned prophetically in early June 1775, "I apprehend this war may be spun out, untill England Shall be heartily Sick of it."[8]

William wrote this evaluation of the challenge confronting the British army more than a week before George Washington, in far-off Philadelphia, was appointed commander in chief by the Congress. William's assessment was based on his experience of warfare in outlying regions of the Atlantic world, such as Scotland, Canada, and New England—all of which, in the eighteenth century, were considered to be less developed than the mother country. Writing days before the Battle of Bunker Hill, he described the mode of fighting used by American irregulars, who would fire from an entrenched position, reload, and renew the attack, falling back all the while, drawing the redcoats after them and then picking them off. This, he informed the government, was not unique to New England; rather, it was what "all other Inhabitants of a Strong Country" would do.[9] Experienced British officers like William Howe regarded New England as the most militarized region in colonial America, precisely because it was a rustic province whose menfolk were trained to bear arms. In fact, it was frequently compared to Scotland, with its highland warriors.[10]

William's shrewd appraisal contrasted sharply with loud declarations in Parliament that the Americans were "raw, undisciplined, cowardly men" who "would never dare to face an English army."[11] He understood that the rebel army in New England included "all or most of the young men of spirit in the country who are exceedingly diligent and attentive to their military profession."[12] The Massachusetts countryside that was bristling with militia before the Battle of Bunker Hill would evolve into the Continental Army led by famous Virginian George Washington, but the fundamental challenge for the British would remain the same: to bring the enemy to a confrontation on a level playing field.

William's hopes of descending upon New York early in 1776, before Washington's army had entrenched itself in fortifications, evaporated. He could not leave Halifax until June 10, and he and his army didn't reach Staten Island, off New York, until June 25.[13] By that time, Washington had been in New York since April, and his deputy, Major General Charles Lee, had been fortifying the city since February. William's most sensible move now was to wait until he had his full quota of troops, which began to arrive from Britain in July. On July 27, he received a letter from Lord George Germain, concurring with his opinion and ordering him to delay until he had all his reinforcements.[14] Now William would have to wait until mid-August before his army finally took to the field. But his suspense was partly relieved by the arrival, on July 12, of his brother, Admiral Howe.

That summer of waiting has become part of a legend that has clung to the Howe brothers—that in the critical first year of war, when the British stood the best chance of victory, they compromised British military operations by pushing their peace commission beyond its official remit. The chief responsibility for this error of judgment has been placed on Richard, who supposedly arrived in New York full of ambition to save the empire. Reasoning that less force would improve the prospects for a genuine reconciliation, he persuaded his brother to relinquish the quest for a decisive battle, which had been his goal while back in Halifax. The story goes that, throughout the New York campaign, the brothers sought only limited victories, each of which was followed up with renewed peace overtures.[15] Richard, for his part, has been portrayed as a man motivated by hubris, stubbornly persisting with attempts to open talks because he privately disagreed with the government's policy of coercion.[16] Such long-standing suspicions about the brothers carry an implication of conspiracy—even treason—that is only rarely acknowledged by historians of their American command.

But we will see that the Howes did not wait a moment longer than was necessary to begin their campaign against New York. And historians assessing the brothers' motives for pushing the peace commission have overlooked their anxiety to satisfy opinion in Britain, where—as they and the Howe women at home understood—some sort of peacemaking gesture was expected to precede the launch of military operations.

The arrival of Richard Howe on Staten Island in July precipitated a confrontation that has survived as an American founding legend. Within days, Richard sent a letter to General Washington, suggesting they meet aboard a British frigate off New York to discuss conciliation. It was a letter between gentlemen; Richard presumed Washington would accept his word for the promise of "the perfect Safety of your Person, & free liberty to return on shore at your Pleasure."[17] His emissary returned with the letter undelivered.

It had been addressed to "George Washington, Esquire," and Washington's aide-de-camp denied the existence of any such person in the army. Washington was adamant that official correspondence had to acknowledge his rank. A week later, Washington declined to receive communications from the Howes regarding the exchange of prisoners. This, of course, was a crucial issue in any war, but prisoner exchange would defy formalization throughout the American Revolution, in part because British negotiators could not officially recognize the United States.

To negotiate this impasse, the Howes sent their adjutant general to confer with Washington. The British adjutant was welcomed with great pomp into the rebel stronghold in New York City, where he met Washington, who was dazzling in his most elegant attire. The adjutant was happy to sprinkle "Your Excellency" throughout his conversation, but the British military still could not acknowledge in writing Washington's rank as commander in chief of a United States army. Washington declined the proposal of peace negotiations, saying he lacked the authority.[18] Thus concluded the Howes' peace overture to General Washington.

In the popular version of the story, the British commanders are characterized as baffled, exasperated, and thwarted by Washington's bold insistence that the Howes bow to diplomatic protocol and acknowledge him as leader of the American army. But, seen from the point of view of the Howes, this can be dismissed as a folkloric caricature.

Although a picture of outraged redcoat officialdom makes a good story, it came as no surprise at British headquarters when Washington rejected the letter. The same obstructive give-and-take over official titles had taken place in communications between General Gage and George Washington in Boston in 1775. William had seen it all back then.[19] Before Richard sent his letter to Washington in July 1776, his brother the general predicted the American commander's response. Washington would not agree to any meeting "except in the highest Style," William warned, with an equal number of officers on each side, and there would be meticulous scrutiny of any venue the Howes might suggest. William also predicted that the American general would refer Lord Howe to the Continental Congress as the power under which he served.[20] When Richard showed William his public declaration of the Howe peace commission, the general pointed out that the Congress had declared independence just days earlier, and would listen to no commissioners. Knowing all this, Richard nevertheless proceeded to circulate the declaration to the Congress, and he persisted in attempting to open talks for weeks after reaching New York.

Throughout the month of July, the Howes were open to anyone inclined to talk of peace. Americans found they could come and go aboard Lord Howe's flagship, HMS *Eagle*, where they were treated with respect and Washington was carefully referred to as "General Washington."[21]

The brothers had sound reasons that summer for extending the hand of peace. The Declaration of Independence notwithstanding, there were still members of the Continental Congress who hoped war could be avoided. The result was that some Americans thought the Howes should at least be heard, and even some members of Congress wavered. What harm could it do to listen and talk? Washington had an answer to that, as enlistments into his young army slowed down with rumors that peace might be at hand. Furthermore, any discussion of peace talks in Congress delayed war preparations, to the intense frustration of its most extreme members.[22]

Much ink has been expended by historians criticizing William's delay between arriving on Staten Island and the start of his offensive almost two months later, but, compared to other amphibious operations in America during the Seven Years' War, it is unremarkable. William confessed that he was mortified that the army was "still upon this island" in mid-August, but he could hardly have been surprised.[23] He had witnessed a similar delay at Louisbourg in 1758, when the slow convergence of troops and commanders from Ireland, New York, Boston, and England delayed the campaign by two months. When he was at Havana, British warships required six weeks to assemble from their far-flung ports of origin: New York, the British Isles, the Antilles, and Jamaica.[24] He also would have recalled the experience of his brother George in 1757, when the strike against Louisbourg had to be canceled because British ships were delayed so long that French reinforcements forestalled them. Such were amphibious operations in the age of sail.

As soon as the transports had been sighted at sea on August 11, the brothers began wrapping up the business of the peace commission and getting on with making war. With the fleet still expected hourly, Richard and William signed letters to Lord George Germain, stating that they had seen "no disposition to reconciliation" among the American leaders. They had duly circulated the declaration of the peace commission to the colonial governors, the Congress had seen it, and the Howes had approached George Washington—all to no avail.[25]

The last contingent of William's American army arrived the next day, on August 12. He now had a force of around twenty-four thousand under his command, with four hundred transports and thirty men-of-war.[26] It was even greater than the force the British had brought to bear against the French in America in the Seven Years' War. He began landing troops on Long Island immediately.

On the same day that the transports had been sighted, Richard requested Henry Strachey to write to Germain's office, setting out the thinking of the brothers on the eve of military action. Strachey's letter has barely been used by historians of the Howe peace commission, who either do not refer to it or attribute the opinions it contains to Strachey himself.[27] It reveals how the brothers expected their dual remits as soldiers and commissioners to play out in that final summer before the fighting resumed.

On the eve of the campaign for New York, the Howes understood that the Americans would not listen to any proposals until they had been soundly beaten; only force could move them from their claim of independence. "The present Situation of Affairs here, is simply this," Strachey explained. "Every sort of Communication that might possibly produce an Opening to Peace Treaty, or even Discussion, is industriously Avoided by the American leaders." The Americans had made it clear that they would not negotiate except "on the footing of free independent States." "As things now are," he went on, "the whole seems to depend upon Military and Naval Operations." The ensuing campaign would be decisive; if the British army was victorious, the Americans would listen to proposals for an accommodation. "But," he warned, such were "the infatuated Expectations" of the "present Rulers of America" that it was difficult to predict the effect of "even the completest Victory." Strachey's letter shows that, far from believing a limited use of force would incline the Americans toward reconciliation, the Howes believed they needed an overwhelming victory to end the rebellion.

Strachey's letter also reveals that to fully understand the thinking of the brothers regarding the peace commission, we must look beyond the localized give-and-take between the Howes and the rebel leadership in America. Both brothers were mindful not only of opinion in America but also of opinion back home, where British sensibilities preferred that there be a gesture of peace before proceeding to war against a kindred people. At his first meeting with Richard on July 12, William had been in favor of offering peace talks in order to "prevent any Clamor at home that might arise if some such Overture were not made before the prosecution of the War."[28] Henry Strachey made the same point in his letter written a month later on behalf of the admiral: The peace commission was useful as a vehicle for putting the enemy in the wrong. If the American leaders continued to prefer to fight, they would be abandoned by every ally they had in the House of Commons.[29] The British statesmen who were sympathetic to American resistance—men such as the Duke of Grafton, Henry Seymour Conway, and Lord Chatham—were well known to the Howe family. The brothers were determined to publicize back in Britain that they had made every effort to open talks, but now they had to proceed to battle.

In the summer of 1776, the peace commission seemed a natural component of an admittedly complex mission. The fact was that some kind of conciliatory overture was inevitable at this stage of the American War of Independence, and it was anticipated at home. Even before Lord Howe arrived with his commission, other serving generals had considered engaging in negotiations with rebel groups. General Burgoyne, for instance, explored negotiating with Congress while he was in Boston during the summer of 1775.[30] General Clinton wanted powers to negotiate with the southern colonies at the outset of his ill-fated expedition to South Carolina in early 1776.[31]

The Howe women understood this as they managed the images of the brothers in the metropolis and took care to publicize their kinsmen's efforts to open talks. During July, William was still writing to Fanny of the "liklyhood of treating," but on August 15, days after the arrival of Commodore William Hotham and the fleet, both Richard and William wrote to their wives that the next dispatches would probably bring news of an action. These letters were in the hands of Mary and Fanny by September 30, and any prospect of peace negotiations ceased.[32] Fanny's letter was reported in the newspapers. "General Howe's Lady," the public was told, "has received a letter from the General," informing her that he and Lord Howe "had done their utmost endeavour with the Congress to bring about a reconciliation, but in vain; and therefore they were preparing to take New York, which they had no doubt of doing in a day or two."[33] Like the Dowager Lady Howe's letter to the voters of Nottingham almost twenty years earlier, the letter to Fanny was evidently placed in the papers by one of the women of the family. It was important to broadcast the brothers' disposition to peace, and to demonstrate that their hand was forced by an obstinate rebel leadership.

In late September and early October, the British newspapers sounded the refrain that "all hopes of Accomodation are now at an end."[34]

It was not only through the newspapers that the Howe version of events was spread during these two critical weeks. The Howe women were perfectly positioned to publicize the brothers' rejected peace overtures within London's fashionable circles, and, predictably, word traveled fast. Lady Mary Coke picked up the chatter at a royal drawing room on October 3: "I find there is no hopes of an accommodation till the Americans are well beat."[35] Within days, across the Irish Sea, Lady Louisa Conolly wrote angrily, "How one does hate those American ringleaders that would not listen to the terms Lord Howe had to offer, but determined at once to try the fate of battle!" She had clearly received the latest report, whether from Fanny or from William himself, with whom she corresponded during the war.[36]

A mood of uneasy suspense hung over London. For several months, the British press had been predicting more butchery of His Majesty's troops in New York, like the bloody action at Bunker Hill. The rebel entrenchments around New York were said to be so strong that the like were "never seen in an Enemy's country."[37] In late July, false rumors circulated around London of a New York engagement that inflicted such losses on the British that "one regiment had not 5 men left."[38] Memories of the last war in America, with its wilderness massacres, added to the sense of dread caused by the Battle of Bunker Hill. The British people braced themselves for reports of mass slaughter as they waited for news of William's strike against the rebellion.

And William, in the early hours of August 27, was at Howard's Half-Way House, explaining to the hapless tavernkeeper that he must guide the redcoat column, whether it suited his principles or not. At about the same time, less than seven miles away, on the far right of the American position, Major General James Grant and two brigades of British troops were drawing the attention of the rebel defensive line at the Shore Road–Martense Lane Pass, in what was effectively a diversionary attack. The sound of their artillery could be heard across the water in New York City. Lieutenant General Philip von Heister, commander of the Hessian troops hired to assist the British, would contribute to this feint by shelling rebel defenders of the American center at Flatbush Pass. The battle appeared to the Americans to be going well when suddenly, at about 8:30 a.m., two cannon shots were heard—the signal that General Clinton was in the village of Bedford,

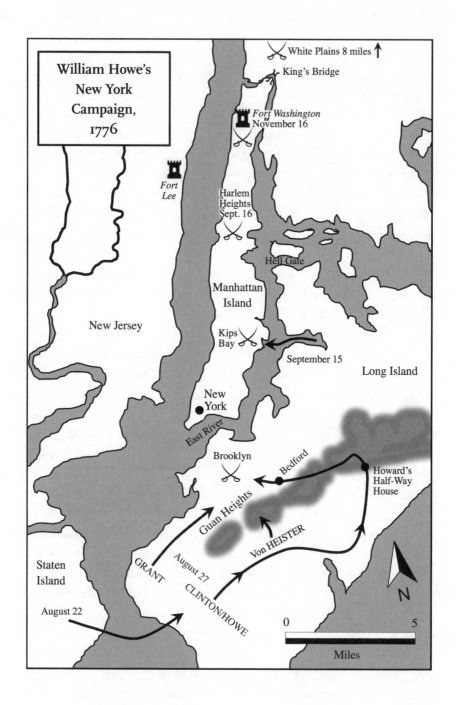

William Howe's
New York
Campaign,
1776

White Plains 8 miles ↑

King's Bridge

Fort Washington
November 16

*Fort
Lee*

Harlem
Heights
Sept. 16

Hell Gate

Manhattan
Island

New Jersey

Kips
Bay

September 15

Long Island

New
York

East River

Brooklyn

Bedford

Howard's
Half-Way
House

Guan Heights

Von HEISTER

Staten
Island

GRANT

August 27

CLINTON/HOWE

August 22

N

0   5

Miles

behind the American defenses. He and William Howe, with ten thousand men, had slowly and successfully worked their way around to the back of the Americans.

To their astonishment, the British force met with no opposition. General Washington had posted no defenders, and the Americans were taken completely by surprise. Despite putting up some resistance, the rebels had been badly outmaneuvered and were obliged to run from the battle, as Clinton put it, "reduced to a *sauve qui peut*; over bays, marshes, creeks &c." By midday, they had retreated to their main defenses at Brooklyn.[39]

Then, in what would become the most controversial decision of his career, William ordered his men to halt, declining a frontal assault on the American entrenchments and instead beginning the safer, much slower process of opening regular siege works. The rebel position was also vulnerable to being cut off by water, as British warships could enter the East River and block an evacuation to New York City. Nobody knew it at the time, but this would be the best chance William would ever have of destroying the American army. The opportunity was soon lost. On the night of August 29, Washington and his troops managed to slip away, under cover of heavy rain, to the island of Manhattan.

Following Washington's withdrawal, the reigning mood in the British ranks was one of triumph. British officers were jubilant, predicting that the rebellion would collapse. "[T]his business is pretty near over," wrote General Hugh Lord Percy to Lord George Germain. Morale within the British army soared. George III conferred the Order of the Bath on William for his victory at Long Island, making him Sir William Howe.[40]

Nonetheless, William would live to regret the report he sent to Germain days after the Battle of Brooklyn. Describing the moment when his troops halted their pursuit, William wrote that the grenadiers and the 33rd regiment pushed ahead toward the enemy's lines, "with such eagerness to attack it by storm that it required repeated orders to prevail upon them to desist from the attempt." The next words were used against him many times in the years to come:

> Had they been permitted to go on, it is my opinion they would have carried the redoubt, but as it was apparent the lines must have been ours at a very cheap rate by regular approaches I would not risk the loss that might have been sustained in the assault. . . .

William then ordered his men back out of the reach of the American gunshot.[41] His assertion that they most probably would have succeeded, if permitted to carry on, has since been singled out for criticism in numerous assessments of the battle. "[V]ictorious soldiers were stopped in full cry," as one historian put it.[42]

This command decision has been debated for more than two hundred years. Did General Howe overestimate the strength of the enemy lines? Did he have poor intelligence? Alternatively, did he have good intelligence, and were his detractors the ones who underestimated the rebels' ability to repel a British charge?[43] Some historians think Howe's caution was reasonable or understandable and requires no special explanation.[44] The issue has never been entirely laid to rest. And it was the Battle of Brooklyn that inspired Light-Horse Harry Lee to suggest that Bunker Hill had permanently shaken William's nerve.

Yet William Howe was celebrated throughout his military career for conspicuous bravery that was careless of his personal safety. He was not a man to falter at Brooklyn. Years later, referring to the controversial lines in his report to Lord George Germain, he explained, "To this I am free to own, the Paragraph was written in the fullness of my Heart, exulting on the approved Bravery of the Troops on that Day." These words were part of a draft of a speech he prepared in 1779 to be delivered before the House of Commons. He omitted them in the final version, and they are not included in published accounts of the speech.[45]

Certainly Germain himself saw nothing to criticize at the time, writing to William that it was "the first Military Operation with which no fault could be found." And the British public was overjoyed. The carnage that everyone had predicted at Brooklyn had not occurred. The newspapers extolled "the extreme judgment, the cool bravery, the recollection, and the humanity of those gallant brothers."[46] In Britain, there was no criticism of a commander who had taken his objective without severe loss of life; there was only national relief.

It is more likely that William's caution that day was on behalf of his troops. Bunker Hill was still a pervasive worry in his mind—would they balk in the face of enemy fire? Historian David Smith argues that William stopped the assault on the entrenchments at Brooklyn because he saw his troops pushing forward without orders, carried by a wave of enthusiasm— to his mind, a near-lapse of battlefield discipline. Smith has observed that throughout the New York campaign, General Howe was worried that British troops would "misbehave" again as they had at Boston, boosting enemy morale in the process and resulting in losses that couldn't be afforded. He makes a convincing case that William Howe saw instances of risky and impetuous behavior in three separate actions: Bunker Hill, Brooklyn, and a minor scuffle a few weeks later on September 16, the day after the British landed on Manhattan Island. Known as the Battle of Harlem Heights, British light infantry troops pursued and taunted retreating Americans with shouts of "View halloo!" as if on a foxhunt. The redcoats were then met with such determined resistance from the infuriated rebels that they were obliged to beat a hasty retreat.[47]

Unfortunately for William, after the Battle of Brooklyn General Washington would never again risk a pitched battle with the British. Washington had been obliged to learn fast from the near-disaster. On August 28, the day after the surprise attack by the British, and while still besieged by the redcoats, he had come close to making his own "potentially huge mistake."[48] He called for further reinforcements from across the river in Manhattan, still hoping to maneuver the British into making a bloody frontal assault. He did not intend it, but by thus concentrating his forces, he would be acting exactly as General Howe could wish. It was only the next morning, when the British siege works could be seen to have advanced to within only 600 yards from the American lines, that the American commander changed his mind. There would be no rerun of Bunker Hill. It was time to get out of there. Indeed, there was no time to lose; one more day would bring the Americans within range of British fire.

Washington's about-face in the space of just twenty-four hours revealed his inexperience. However, luck was with him, as unfavorable winds stopped Lord Howe's ships from cutting him off in the East River, and a summer storm provided cover as the desperate Americans made the crossing from Brooklyn to Manhattan in the dark. The evacuation on the night of August 29 was a dangerous exploit that has been called "the American Dunkirk." At the time, though, it was seen not as an iconic event but rather a show of weakness that badly affected American morale.[49] A few weeks later, the American commander famously wrote, "We should on all occasions avoid a general action, or put anything to the risk, unless compelled by a necessity into which we ought never to be drawn."[50]

Brooklyn, viewed retrospectively, offers the tantalizing "what if" of a single action by which Britain might have ended the rebellion. It was also destined to become a cornerstone of an argument that William was "soft" on the rebel army throughout the New York campaign, always hoping that hostilities would melt away and be replaced by the peace talks sought by Richard Howe. Not only did William fail to push forward when the enemy appeared to be in the palm of his hand—or so the argument goes—but he repeated the same pattern for the rest of his campaigns in America.[51] In battle after battle, William's army emerged victorious, yet the rebellion remained unsuppressed. Was General Howe actually avoiding the destruction of the American army?

At the time, however, the New York campaign opened with a clear victory for the British, and this success continued. Two weeks later, on September 15, the British landed at Kips Bay, on the east side of Manhattan. William had chosen it as the best point for invading the island. His second-in-command, Clinton, had strongly demurred; by now, Clinton's criticisms of his chief were becoming noticeable to his brother officers, and word was getting back to William.[52] Clinton had urged William to land British forces farther up Manhattan, at King's Bridge, which connected the famous island to the mainland, thereby trapping the Continental Army. Looking at a map, it seems an obvious idea. Clinton thought that Howe ignored his advice because the commander in chief was more interested in securing the city of New York as a base for the winter than in confronting the Continental Army. Other historians have followed Clinton's reasoning, seeing it as evidence that General Howe preferred "safe plans for recovering territory to more hazardous schemes that promised to destroy the Continental army."[53]

But, as with so much of the campaign, the evidence is also open to an entirely different interpretation. The action at Kips Bay has been described by some military scholars as a brilliant success that demoralized the Americans.[54] The British correctly believed that, after the Battle of Brooklyn, the Americans had begun evacuating Manhattan, so the opportunity to trap the rebel army was melting away. Clinton's plan would have involved an extensive amphibious landing in the turbulent waters around Hell Gate. In those waters, the navy would probably move more slowly than Washington's men could retreat.[55] The lightly equipped rebel soldiers might well have had time to evacuate Manhattan before the British fleet and army could reach King's Bridge.

And there is evidence that William hoped that, at Kips Bay, the rebels would stand and fight at last. There were two conditions in place that he believed were necessary to coax them into a confrontation: fortifications, and open country at their backs.[56] This was what had given inexperienced rebel troops such confidence at Bunker Hill. If this was William's careful calculation, it came to naught; the American soldiers fled under the bombardment of the Royal Navy, and Washington visibly raged at the sight.[57]

The day after the Kips Bay landing, the British army entered New York City. In advance of the fighting, a third of the population had departed, but a joyful loyalist crowd welcomed the redcoats as they marched down Broadway. The army then settled down to an occupation that would last until the war's end: Officers took up residence in the best of the homes vacated by fleeing rebels, other buildings were converted into barracks, and loyalist militia patrolled the streets, where, as one loyal clergyman recorded, "Joy and gladness" appeared on all faces. In this complex civil war, however, no success remained secure for long.

By capturing Manhattan, General Howe had now established a base for his army, but this was no time to relax. Just six days later, a fire swept through the city, destroying hundreds of homes. Washington had threatened to burn the city as he departed, seeing it as a nest of Tory traitors, but the fire probably was an accident. Nevertheless, the harassed General Howe was not the only one who believed it was arson, and two people were hanged.[58] The rebel army still lurked in the vicinity of New York, and the campaign would go on until December.

It has been said that, throughout the New York campaign, William was a "victim of his own success," driving his enemy to make desperate bids to avoid an engagement on the British general's terms, and thereby increasing William's frustration as the campaign wore on.[59] This is probably true; two engagements toward the close of the campaign—at White Plains and Fort Washington—show that William, far from avoiding frontal assaults, was in fact exasperated at being unable to draw out his enemy, and he was willing to mount an offensive in order to incite a decisive battle.

On October 12, the British army was on the move again, landing first at Throg's Neck, a narrow peninsula where the East River meets Long Island Sound, then four days later arriving at the superior landing place of Pell's Point. The Americans were maneuvered off of the island of Manhattan, and by October 21 they had taken up a position on a line of hills to the rear of the village of White Plains. There, on the night of October 27–28, British and American forces clashed. The outcome was indecisive, and the British lost at least two hundred men during an uphill charge that met with heavy fire from rebel defenders. In the ensuing several days, William prepared for a second frontal assault on the enemy, ordering reinforcements from New York. By the time they arrived, however, extreme weather had set in, the terrain had turned to mud, and the Americans had shifted their position to a much stronger second line. Nevertheless, it required strenuous arguments from General Clinton, supported by the Hessian General von Heister, to persuade William to call off the attack on October 31.[60]

Two weeks later, on November 16, the British stormed and captured Fort Washington, on Manhattan Island. The Americans had believed it was "impregnable," but William's redcoats took the fort in a neatly executed action that went against his determination to use slower siege tactics against well-prepared defensive positions. It has been suggested by one astute historian that William, frustrated in his intention to mount a frontal attack on the enemy at White Plains, reacted by overturning his own rule at Fort Washington, in what has been described as a "dashing and ruthless action."[61] This is characteristic of the William who emerges from his military record and the pages of his sister's letters: a careful, skillful commander, but also a man with a tendency toward reckless courage and temper.

Fort Lee, just across the Hudson River from Fort Washington, capitulated four days later; the rebel garrison fled, in their haste abandoning vital military supplies that were quickly captured by the British. By early December, Washington and his dwindling army had been chased southward across the Raritan River into New Jersey; Newport, Rhode Island, had surrendered without resistance, providing a safe winter haven for Lord Howe's shipping. The rebellion looked as if it was in its last gasp. Even the Continental Congress, unnerved by the thought of British troops just sixty miles from Philadelphia, decamped to Baltimore. And yet—the rebel army, small as it was, kept going. Britain seemed to have sent its great army and warships to America to play a cat-and-mouse game that thus far had resulted in no definite outcome.

It is no wonder that debate continues to this day over the motives, skill, and luck of William Howe in his first-ever campaign as a commander in chief. The competing assessments of his generalship during 1776 persist: that for unacknowledged reasons he was actually avoiding the destruction of Washington's army; or that he was a conventional and overcautious general who let the enemy slip through his fingers; or that he was an able commander who had bad luck. Like all military operations, the New York campaign can never be replayed. In addition to the complex of facts mustered by historians, it involved a multitude of circumstances that by now are irretrievable—for example, details relating to terrain, tide and weather, and morale. The surviving testimonies of combatants are colored by personal tensions, partial intelligence, and the self-justifications of those who bore responsibility for the outcome. Even the opinions of the ever-voluble General Clinton tend to distort as much as they enlighten, particularly when they are juxtaposed against the taciturnity of the Howes. William Howe, in fact, did not always explain his plans to his officers—they often did not have the benefit of his thinking as they pondered his decisions.

But one thing is certain: William understood that to forgo knowingly an opportunity to destroy Washington's army would be to place at risk the lives of British soldiers and the security of the British nation. That such behavior would amount to a "flirtation with treason" is a point made by surprisingly few historians, but it is one General Howe would have been well aware of.[62] With each passing month, the conflict in America threatened to provoke the intervention of the French. The notion that William and Richard Howe attempted some form of "soft" warfare using those bluntest of instruments—eighteenth-century amphibious tactics and weaponry—is simply not believable.

The Howes were loyal Britons; they shared bonds of blood and friendship with English aristocratic dynasties and leading military figures; they had close ties to the royal family—ties that did not diminish after the War of Independence. Waiting for them at home were wives, sisters, and a mother who moved in the highest circles, where personal reputation and family honor were palpable qualities that mattered.

William and Richard Howe knew well that the command decisions they made in America would be narrowly scrutinized by their fellow officers and a critical audience in the metropolis. There had been plenty of courts-martial in the last war, most notoriously the case of Admiral Byng, executed on his own quarterdeck for failing to pursue his enemy to the fullest degree. Their own kinsman Sir John Mordaunt had been court-martialed and acquitted after the failed expedition to Rochefort in 1757.

It has been suggested that the illegitimate bond between the Howe family and the king protected them from the hostile scrutiny endured by other British commanders. This cannot be so; in the Seven Years' War, even full royal status had not been enough to save the Duke of Cumberland, the favorite son of George II, who was removed from his military post in disgrace by his father when he surrendered to the French at Hastenbeck in 1757. George told his son "that he had ruined his country and his army."[63]

Finally, one does not need to be a military expert to realize that every military commander fights to win. No general would allow the escape of an enemy who lay in the palm of his hand. The Howes knew they needed to strike hard to end the rebellion. Before the battle, Henry Strachey had written that the Howes believed that "even the completest Victory" might not be sufficient to bring the Americans to the table.

Against the backdrop of General Howe's offensive against New York, Admiral Lord Howe finally had his conference with delegates from the Continental Congress. What ended up being the "last official meeting between England and her American colonies" took place on September 11, 1776.[64] Congress sent delegates to meet with Lord Howe to explore what his peace commission had to offer.

The meeting had been broached by American Major General John Sullivan, who had been taken prisoner at the Battle of Brooklyn. Subsequently, he was wined and dined by Admiral Howe, and then released. New Englander John Adams—short, stocky, irascible, and the foremost champion of independence in the Congress—was his usual blunt self on the subject of this latest invitation from the Howes. He would have preferred to see Sullivan shot through the head on the battlefield, he said, rather than carrying another insidious proposal of talks to Philadelphia. Yet Congress did not wish to appear to be unwilling to explore an avenue for reconciliation.[65]

The proposal was for a conference "with some of the members in their private capacity," since the British commissioners could not negotiate with the illegal Continental Congress. The invitation should have been treated as a private matter, but somehow word got around in Philadelphia, perhaps through Richard himself, and the resulting publicity put pressure on Congress to agree.[66] For his part, Richard was disappointed to learn, on September 9, that the congressional delegation was restricted to the role of a fact-finding mission: ". . . [T]he object of this deputation apparently was

Billopp House on Staten Island, New York. Today it is part of historic Conference House Park.

to interrogate rather than to confer." Everyone was being circumspect. The brothers, after considering, decided to receive the delegates.[67]

With William preparing for the operation at Kips Bay, it was left to Richard to set the stage for the conference. Benjamin Franklin proposed as a location the royal governor's mansion in Perth Amboy, New Jersey, or else Staten Island. The Howes chose Staten Island. There, just across the river from Perth Amboy, stood the Billopp House, a comfortable old stone manor house owned by wealthy loyalist Christopher Billopp.[68] By this time, however, a Hessian officer, Colonel Ludwig von Wurmb, had made it his headquarters.[69] It had gone the way of most homes ceded to the military—It was "as dirty as a stable," recollected John Adams—but Lord Howe had ordered it beautified for his guests. Moss carpeted the floor, and military ingenuity had resorted to the classical manner of adorning the meeting room, using shrubs and foliage from the island, making it "not only wholesome, but romantically elegant." A cold repast was served: "good claret, good bread, cold ham, tongues, and mutton."

The entire episode was marked by careful good manners on both sides. The American delegates declined the admiral's offer of leaving a British hostage behind on the New Jersey shore to ensure their safe return. John Adams noted that Lord Howe in turn treated the delegates "with the utmost politeness."[70] Henry Strachey, who was present for the meal and the conference afterward, recorded that an exchange of conventional pleasantries began as soon as the delegates stepped ashore, "A general and immaterial Conversation from the Beach to the House. . . ."[71] The delegates were at the Billopp House for three hours, two of which apparently involved small talk, for the conference itself only lasted an hour.[72]

No record remains of the conversation that took place among these ill-assorted dinner guests. As well as Lord Howe and Henry Strachey, Colonel von Wurmb was present for the meal. Franklin's fellow delegates included John Adams, whose opposition to conciliatory measures in Congress had already been published in London newspapers by September 1775. Adams recalled later that, after one of his own heated remarks, Lord Howe commented to the others, "Mr. Adams is a decided character." Even before they began, Richard knew that the delegate from Massachusetts would not budge on independence.[73]

Adams rendered his personal opinion of his host in a letter to his wife, Abigail, written a few days later: "His [Lordship] is about fifty Years of Age. He is a well bred Man, but his Address is not so irresistable, as it has been represented. I could name you many Americans, in your own Neighbourhood, whose Art, Address, and Abilities are greatly superiour. His head is rather confused, I think."[74] Adams, like many others from his native New England, had seen little of the Anglo-Atlantic world from which to judge Richard's manner. We have seen that Richard, unlike his brother George, often appeared standoffish and remote to those outside of his private circle. One wonders who had briefed Adams on Lord Howe's "irresistable" address. Perhaps it was Ben Franklin, who had seen Richard at his most engaging at his sister's house in Grafton Street, where Franklin, too, had felt at home. It is not surprising that Richard's "confused" demeanor was evident that day, for the admiral had been unwell, and Lady Howe was concerned.

South Carolinian planter Edward Rutledge, who had studied law at the Inns of Court in London, probably felt more at ease than the Yankee Adams. Rutledge's support for independence had been slow to come, and many in his native colony had harbored doubts.[75] Lord Howe's secretary afterward reported a rumor from a well-connected loyalist that Congress had voted for Rutledge's inclusion in the delegation because "they could be sure to come at the *Truth* from *him*, which they could *not* from the other *two*."[76]

The third and most eminent delegate, Benjamin Franklin, had changed since his games of chess in Grafton Street more than a year and a half earlier. After returning to America, he turned his back on the prospect of reconciliation with Britain. For months, he had kept his fellow delegates in Congress guessing—some hoping he had a plan of conciliation, others suspecting he was a British spy. But by July 1775, despite giving his support to the Olive Branch Petition, he believed that America and Britain needed to part ways. "Words and arguments are now of no use," he wrote to an old friend in London. "All tends to a separation."[77] Franklin had made his position clear in a terse exchange of letters with Admiral Howe during the summer of 1776. Henry Strachey, dispatching the correspondence to Lord Germain's office, summed it up briefly: "[N]o accommodating Measures are yet likely to be countenanced by the Congress, if it be true that the Doctor is One of the greatest Influence among them."[78]

At the outset, the inevitable discussion of protocol arose, and Franklin finally agreed that they could speak on the footing of private gentlemen: ". . . the Conversation might be held as amongst friends." But the American delegates nonetheless insisted that any formal negotiation would have to take place between Britain and the "free and independent states" of America. This was more than mere posturing. Edward Rutledge pushed the notion that Britain could gain greater advantages from alliance with an independent America than a colony. The former mother country would continue to have the lion's share of American commerce, the benefit of its raw materials, and its alliance in protecting the valuable West Indian sugar islands and the Newfoundland fisheries. Britain, he urged, should seize this opportunity "before anything is settled with other foreign Powers"—a pointed allusion to France.

It was an incredible long shot, but the delegates were taking it in earnest. Franklin hinted that Lord Howe might apply to the ministers back home for authority to confer on this basis, calculating that it would require three months to hear back, by which time the constituents of Congress would be able to give their own reactions to such a proposal.[79] In fact, Franklin had been secretly mulling over the possibility of returning to London to promote a peace treaty with an independent America. That, of course, required that Congress first be put on a legitimate footing. He probably was feeling around at the conference for reactions to such a move. However, within two weeks of the conference, Franklin would instead accept a mission to represent the fledgling United States in Paris.[80] Richard seemed aware that this was in the offing, for John Adams recalled that the admiral blundered a little, saying to Franklin, "I suppose you will endeavor to give us employment in Europe"—an indirect allusion to France. The delegates maintained a rigid silence.[81] After an hour of discussion to no purpose, there was nothing more to say and the conference came to a close.

Each of the men sitting around the table had had his own agenda. Franklin wanted to return to Europe to negotiate somewhere; uncharitable onlookers in London thought he wanted to leave America before the rebellion collapsed entirely.[82] Edward Rutledge was anxious to avoid the necessity of an alliance with the French—no less the traditional enemy of British America than of Britain itself—and was the most sincere of the American delegates in hoping for some constructive outcome. He was said to have quarreled with John Adams after the conference, "declaring that Adams has greatly misrepresented the Substance of the Conversation" with Lord Howe.[83] John Adams wanted to extinguish once and for all the illusion of a reconciliation with Britain.

For his part, Richard wished to explore the potential for talks held out in the Olive Branch Petition of the previous year. In his opening remarks to the delegates, he said so explicitly, and he regretted that he had arrived after the Congress had declared independence. John Adams recalled years later that Lord Howe also briefly struck a personal note, mentioning George Lord Howe, his brother who had died at Ticonderoga in 1758. The admiral remarked that if America fell, "I should feel and lament it like the loss of a brother."[84]

Richard's official account of the Billopp House conference, however, written on September 20, was brief and unsentimental. It was in the hands of Lord George Germain by November 3, 1776. He reported that he had informed the delegates that he could not enter into any treaty with an independent United States. The delegates, in return, attempted to persuade him that it was in the interests of Britain to do so. "Their arguments not meriting a serious attention, the conversation ended and the gentlemen returned to Amboy."[85]

In the government offices of Whitehall, there was vexation at the outcome of the Staten Island meeting. A memorandum in the Germain

Papers concluded that the American leaders, learning that the British government had appointed peace commissioners, rushed the Declaration of Independence "before Lord Howe's Arrival," in order to forestall the negotiations proposed by the Congress itself the previous year in its Olive Branch Petition.[86] There was certainly anger; an apocryphal story was circulated in London that Admiral Howe's parting words to the delegates had been "To let the Blood that should be shed in consequence [of their refusal to negotiate] lye at their door."[87] The congressional leaders had proved to be obstinate. There remained only the thin consolation that the bluff had been called; they aimed at independence.

For the British public, the news of the Billopp House conference gave the impression that Britain had tried to find a way toward peace. The reported obduracy of the rebels served to dilute the impression of a British Goliath crushing the American David. One British newspaper reported the "very unreasonable Demands" made by the Americans, which ended the conference. There were stories that General Washington had lied to his troops, warning them that the British commanders had refused to listen to any terms of accommodation, so the Americans must perforce fight for their very lives.[88] As an exercise in public relations, the meeting was an antidote to the earlier news that Washington had spurned communication with the Howes until they recognized his rightful rank. That had made the rounds in British newspapers in September, evoking widespread admiration for the "spirited" rebel general.[89] Now the Howes were the heroes of the hour.

As the Howes had predicted, the American rejection of the peace commission put the rebel leaders "still more in the wrong" (as Henry Strachey put it) at home. The King's Speech of autumn 1776, marking the opening of Parliament (just as it does today), asserted that the American leaders "have rejected, with circumstances of Indignity and Insult, the Means of Conciliation held out to them under the Authority of our Commission; and have presumed to set up their rebellious Confederacies for Independent States." The American appeal to talks had been exposed as insincere, but this at least would lead to "Unanimity at Home, founded in the general Conviction of the Justice and Necessity of our Measures." There must be another campaign, said His Majesty; the rebellious colonies had enjoyed great happiness and increased wealth by land and by sea under a mild government. Now, British dominion must be reasserted. The cause of the

British nation was as benevolent as it was just. John Stuart, Lord Mount-stuart, rose to support the speech and spoke "vastly well," noted Caroline with approval.[90]

Word of the Battle of Brooklyn reached London at 4 a.m. on October 10. Lady Mary Coke, hurrying to Grafton Street, found Caroline in an ele-vated state of happiness. A few days later, Horace Walpole, whose Ameri-can sympathies Lady Mary abhorred, failed to appear at the usual game of cards at Lady Blandford's. ". . . [H]e said he had the gout in his knee but I suspect he did not care to come where everybody was pleased with our last good news," she wrote shrewdly. She believed that he particularly wanted to avoid the Dowager Lady Howe, for "it w[oul]d have been brutal not to have expressed satisfaction at her Son's success & as we all know he wish'd him beat. I imagine the pain in his knee came to his aid."[91]

Caroline was satisfied with all that her brothers had accomplished, both on the battlefield and at the conference table. For her, the most momentous news was the military victory at Brooklyn, not the Staten Island talks. Jubi-lant, she began a letter to Lady Spencer: "No indeed my dear Lady Spencer I have not suffered from anxiety, & if I had, it would have been amply made up, by the great & good news we have received, & by the hopes I now have of the possibility of a proper & lasting peace being the end of the pres-ent unnatural contentions." Caroline was convinced that Brooklyn was the turning point for the discord in America. "[W]ild I was with Joy," she told her friend, "& unable to do anything quietly." She felt as if *feriam sidera vertice*," she was elevated to the stars. "I have been writing without ceasing for hours," she concluded, a joyous bearer of the news to London's aristo-cratic world.

Four days later, Caroline sent Lady Spencer news of the other Howe women: "I am but just come from Fanny, who arrived in town this morn-ing late, she is in delightful spirits, had not been well for two or three days before the arrival of the dispatches, but is now perfectly so, & says she never shall be ill again." Fanny, the Dowager Lady Howe, and Caroline were to dine at "Dickess's," her reversion to the old childish nickname another indicator of Caroline's high spirits.[92] Fanny was now a titled lady; shortly after arriving in town, she was presented for the first time at court as "Lady Howe." On the same day, William became Sir William Howe, when the red ribbon conferring the Order of the Bath was presented to his aide-de-camp at a royal drawing room. The British army was carrying all before it, the

war would be short, bonfires were lit, and church bells were rung in celebration. The "honour, the interest, and consequence of the British empire"
had been at stake and had been upheld by the Howes.[93]

This was not the first time the Howe dynasty had been on the front line
in defending the nation's honor, and the venerable Dowager Lady Charlotte
Howe was honored with a private royal audience. Within a week of Fanny's
appearance at court, William's proud mother was received by King George
III and Queen Charlotte at the Queen's Palace of Buckingham House. "This
worthy Lady has had the singular Happiness of seeing three of her Sons head
the British Armaments against the common Enemy," reported the press.
Touching upon the death of her son George, the report went on to reprint
Lady Howe's famous letter to the voters of Nottingham in 1758, asking them
to return William as their MP. Once again, she was compared in the press
to a Roman matron.[94] For Lady Howe, the Howe dynasty had reemerged as
an iconic military family, just as it had in the Seven Years' War.

It was a final moment of glory for the elderly woman. Writing to her
Kielmansegg relatives in Hanover, she boasted happily, "General Amherst
has spoken publicly of the great qualities of Sir Wm Howe, your nephew."
Quoting Amherst's praise of the action at Brooklyn, in which he referred
to the "magnamity and Judgement" of "the brave Howes," she concluded
proudly, "The King himself said 'these are the only people I could have
made choice of on this occasion.' "[95] She was probably repeating his private
remarks to her at Buckingham House.

Others were just as happy and relieved. Adjutant General Edward
Harvey, who had prophesied the previous year that the army would be
"destroyed by damned driblets" in a mainland war in America, was overjoyed at the commander in chief's conduct of the campaign. "We may build
on the solid Prudence of Howe's Conduct," he wrote to the Duke of Newcastle. With reasoning that reflected William's, he added, "We must not be
Impatient. In this war, men must not be wantonly sported away. Difficult
to Replace them."[96] William's cautious tactics were applauded in the face of
his success.

At the end of November, the Howes issued a proclamation commanding
the rebel fighting bodies to disperse and calling on Congress to renounce
the authority it had assumed. This was the second of their proclamations
to the American public. The first, published a week after the conference on
Staten Island on September 19, was a predictable outcome of the conjunction

of the victory in the Battle of Brooklyn and the stalemate on Staten Island. It went over the heads of the members of Congress to invite "well-affected subjects" to negotiate directly with the Howes. On the surface, the brief document seemed to promise much, undertaking to review legislation that "may be construed" to restrain the freedom of the colonial legislatures, or "may" cause Americans to "think themselves aggrieved." Patriot pamphleteers quickly exposed its flimsy wording, but they could not suppress the false rumors of conferences with Lord Howe that proliferated over the next weeks and months, threatening to undermine congressional leadership. In London on November 2, Caroline received a copy of the document from Lady Mary Howe, and she publicized its contents as far as possible, sending it to the wives of Whig opposition leaders and broadcasting it at social gatherings. It was soon in the metropolitan newspapers. To Caroline, it was a natural component of her brothers' campaign to end the rebellion; in her letters, the successes of the army were the main news.[97]

The second proclamation of November 30 was a more down-to-earth document. Full pardon was offered to any individual who appeared within sixty days before a British official and took an oath of loyalty. It was issued toward the conclusion of the campaign, when the Howes seemed tantalizingly close to ending the rebellion. By mid-December, the rank and file of the Continental Army was fading away as short-term enlistments expired, and the search for new recruits, even in zealous New England, went badly. Many deserted as the advancing British army sapped morale. The response from the American public to the November proclamation was striking. Nearly five thousand colonists claimed pardon during December.[98]

Henry Strachey, administering the pardons, wrote cheerfully to his wife: "Affairs wear a better Aspect than they have hitherto done. The Proclamation of the 30th of last Month has reformed a Croud of Culprits, and I cannot deliver out the King's Pardons so fast as they are claimed." In high good humor, he continued: "One of the Delinquents who came to me the other day for the Pardon, asked me what was the Expence? I answered, 'You have nothing to pay; this is the King's free Pardon for all offences committed against His Majesty, down to the present time: it is given, not sold. Go, and sin no more.' "[99]

Let us leave the Howes happy and triumphant as 1776 draws to a close. While a few pointed out that Washington had still not been decisively defeated, and his army had been allowed to escape to New Jersey, instead of remaining bottled up in freezing New England, New York was nevertheless safely in British hands and the rebels were in retreat.[100]

Caroline ended December with a stream of welcome news of her brothers' successes. She had been ill a few days before Christmas, but she could not resist going to a dinner at the home of her old friends the D'Oylys, where she could dress informally and be comfortable. There, surrounded by a crowd of guests, she wrote to Lady Spencer that letters had reached the Howe women from the admiral, and the brothers were taking everything before them. William had landed in Connecticut, and, "on his first Landing, part of his army was engaged, as usual with success," she could not help boasting.

Eleven days after her evening at the D'Oylys', Caroline received word of the capture of Fort Washington: "[T]wo thousand prisoners," she exclaimed, "with very little loss on our side." She could now name her brother "Sr. Wm. Howe," and she was about to set out for an evening at Princess Amelia's, where there were prospects of more delightful news of her heroic brothers.[101] During December 1776, wherever Caroline went, she would only hear good of her beloved Richard and William.

Eleven

The Tide Turns in America

The year 1777 would be an *annus horribilis* for the Howe dynasty, surpassed only by the tragedy of George's death in America in 1758. The Howes saw their status as a military family disintegrate in the third year of the American War of Independence, when the tide turned against Britain. Character assassination by the British press would ultimately play a part in the brothers' decisions to give up their commands. The chief target was William Howe, though he would never lose a major battle. While William's star fell, that of his nemesis, General George Washington, steadily ascended on both sides of the Atlantic. The media-driven conspiracy theories that would soon be swirling around the brothers continue to this day to haunt the legacy of the Howe command in America.

As the year opened, the Howe women maintained their customary wartime roles of managing the reputations of their men in influential circles. But all control over the narrative of the brothers' command would be wrested from the hands of Caroline and her kinswomen by the overwhelmingly negative newspaper coverage that gained traction in mid-1777, feeding the hunger for news in a national readership that was larger than that of any previous war of the century.

Early January, however, saw Caroline still basking in her brothers' successes. She was in Oxfordshire at Phyllis Court, the Villiers family residence, where an extravagant Gala Week was planned. Lord Villiers and his friends had put together an amateur production of *The Provoked Husband*, a sentimental comedy by popular playwright Colley Cibber. What was originally intended as a private family entertainment swelled to three separate performances and drew in the surrounding neighborhood. A renowned French actor was engaged to follow up the play with a rendition of Ovid's "Pygmalion."[1] A detailed and vivid account of the Gala Week has survived in a lady's journal. It makes no mention at all of the war an ocean away.

Caroline Howe took an active part in the proceedings, assisting as a prompter. Private theatricals were all the rage during the period, giving upper-class women in particular an opportunity to assume a public role without the stigma associated with the commercial stage.[2] On this occasion, a debutante played the part of the irresistible statue in "Pygmalion."[3] Her costume was an unlikely one for a marble monument: a gown of pink satin and gauze finished with £12,000 worth of the Villiers family diamonds (nearly £2 million today).

The weeklong gala included musical performances, dancing, and cards. Sisters Charlotte and Mary, and Mary's husband General Pitt, were there along with Caroline's political friends. These included members of the Villiers family, of course, who had been involved in Lord Howe's peace commission, as well as Lord Frederick Cavendish and General Conway.[4] The happy atmosphere reflected a national conviction that all was well; the Howe brothers had put an end to the unnatural conflict. In the City of London, they were being toasted as *"par nobile fratrum,"* a pair of noble brothers.[5]

Yet even during the holiday season of 1776–77, there was a trickle of criticism. A guest at the Villiers gala whispered a rumor that General Clinton was on his way back to London, discontented with his commander in chief.[6] And sandwiched among the praises sung by the British press were carping remarks that the brothers had failed to defeat Washington decisively. In late January, the *London Evening Post* accused the North administration of exaggerating British successes in America, giving a "false varnish" to their victories. The reality, declared the paper, was that General Howe's army could not venture very far outside of the city of New York.[7]

At this stage, such accusations circulated mainly through the medium of gossip rather than print. But transatlantic gossip traveled quickly—so efficiently, in fact, that it even posed problems for military security.[8] Private letters from serving officers were sometimes published or read aloud in coffeehouses. Even mere talk could be reported; the gist of a conversation between Nisbet Balfour and an unnamed gentleman in London ended up in the *Boston Gazette* just a few months later. The press often shadowed what was being said in clubs, eateries, and fashionable salons.[9]

In early 1777, a few discontented army personnel were muttering that the Howes had deliberately allowed General Washington to escape because the brothers had Whig sympathies. There were also whispers in New York that the Howes were in no hurry to wind up the war because they were making money from it.[10] The suspicions were fed by a conviction that the Howes could have easily suppressed the rebellion in 1776, when they were commanders of the largest army Britain had ever assembled in America.

Remarks such as these were being made even within the private circles of the Howe women. In December, Richard Fitzpatrick, a captain in the Foot Guards with close family and social connections to the Howes, was told by an officer just returned from America that General Howe's latest victory over the rebels had had no important consequences. Fitzpatrick himself thought the New York campaign would end without having dispersed the American army, leaving the outcome of the war uncertain. He concluded: "I Believe Ministers, are not over and above satisfied with the conclusion of this successful campaign."[11]

Fitzpatrick's belief was well-founded. In private, Lord George Germain was irritated with the Howe brothers. William's dispatch reporting the capture of Fort Washington, which reached London on December 29, displeased him. Major Nisbet Balfour, who had been in Germain's Whitehall office, had the impression that the American secretary thought William had not slaughtered enough of the defeated rebels. And that was so; Germain saw unnecessary compassion on the part of the commander in chief. In what was a conventional prelude to taking a fort, General Howe had called upon the garrison to surrender, saying he would take no prisoners if the rebels put up a resistance. The rebels did, of course, resist, and William did not execute his threat.[12]

Germain thought the Howes were too soft. Their joint report as peace commissioners, which arrived at the same time as the dispatch on the capture of Fort Washington, only served to deepen his impression. The brothers sent a copy of their proclamation of November 30, offering pardons to all individuals who would take an oath of loyalty within sixty days. Germain confided to an undersecretary that this latest proclamation would have a bad effect on loyal Americans, who would see the rebels "without distinction put upon the same footing with themselves." He feared that what he termed "this sentimental manner of making war" would not extinguish the rebellion.[13] The American secretary then wrote to both Howes, admonishing them that such liberal terms had to end when the proclamation expired; criminals and rebels must be duly punished.[14]

By mid-March 1777, Richard, still in New York, was perfectly aware of Germain's opinion that he and William were using their roles as peace commissioners to let the rebels off lightly. Richard responded to this in full, directly addressing the suspicion that he had pro-American sympathies—"my supposed prejudices," as he called them. In a patient tone, he explained that he was not inclined to excuse the guilty: "I am of opinion, that Compassion & Forgiveness, ornaments in private Life, if not tempered with justice & Policy, may become Defects in a public Character." The proclamation of November 30, he asserted, had helped to create a favorable disposition toward the British government within the general American population. Since the rebel leaders in Congress—the chief targets of Germain's hostility—had already rebuffed several clear calls to negotiate, they would hardly be likely to accept its less favorable terms.[15] That was the important point—the proclamation was intended to gain the sympathies of the American populace.

By attempting to win the hearts and minds of Americans, the Howe brothers hoped to deny Washington recruits, and the congressional leaders their power base in the civilian population. In the new year, William began recruiting loyalists to augment his own forces. New York was a fertile province for loyalist soldiers; by early January of 1777, William had two thousand provincials serving in the area. That winter, he offered pardons and bounties to rebel soldiers who would come over to the British lines and serve in a provincial corps.[16] During 1777, more than three thousand loyalist soldiers were recruited; in 1778, when the British campaign had shifted to Pennsylvania, the total more than doubled, to more than seven thousand—a significant number of Americans fighting for the king. When Washington fought Howe at the Battle of Brandywine, thirty-five miles from Philadelphia, the American general had roughly twice as many men under his command, but it must be recalled that the recruiting area for the Americans in rebellion was always many times larger than that of the British.[17] The competition for resources and men in America would be fierce, and would last as long as the war itself.

THE AMERICAN WAR of Independence was a civil war in which two regimes contended for authority in America—one under the control of the British army and the other under the new United States. The rebellion received active support from roughly forty to forty-five percent of the white population; the number of active loyalists probably ranged between fifteen and twenty percent. A substantial percentage of Americans of European origin—perhaps as many as half overall during the course of the war—simply tried to avoid getting involved.

African Americans, who made up about a fifth of the total population of the thirteen colonies that would become the United States, were drawn into the conflict, but the sides they chose followed a pattern that was inverse to that of white colonists. As many as five thousand Black men are believed to have served in the American armed forces, both volunteers and escaped slaves, but a far greater number of Black colonial Americans thought their best interests lay with the British. It is estimated that fifty-five thousand slaves absconded during the American Revolution. Perhaps a third of them were women. Many of these took up arms in the service of the Crown, joining the British army as fighting men and servants; others followed the British army to perform valuable unskilled labor—cooking, laundering, and nursing.[18]

The British nation would not take up the abolition of slavery as a popular cause until several years after the American War of Independence, and the British army never had a consistent policy toward the recruiting and arming of slaves. During the war, both sides were apprehensive of alienating their white supporters by adopting a policy of enlisting Black soldiers. Throughout the conflict, however, British officers proposed, and sometimes tried out, plans for including Black Americans in their war effort.[19] There was informal cooperation with slaves by the British army throughout the war, and there were instances of officers assisting former slaves to secure their freedom.[20] The experience of commanding mixed-race rank-and-file soldiers was familiar to any British officer, like William Howe, who had served in the Caribbean during the Seven Years' War.

At the start of the American Revolution, in November 1775, eight hundred slaves fled their masters and enlisted in the cause of the king in response to a royal proclamation offering them their freedom. Issued by John Murray, Lord Dunmore, the governor of Virginia, the proclamation offered freedom only to slaves who were the property of rebels, and only to able-bodied men who would serve with the British army. Nevertheless, enslaved Americans were quick to seize an opportunity to escape from servitude, and many of those who joined Dunmore were women and children. The Howe proclamation of November 1776, so deplored by Germain, also resulted in many Black Americans seeking protection behind British lines in New York. Several thousand took refuge in the city.[21]

Loyalists came from every rank and walk of life in American society; they were not confined to the wealthy and privileged. In London, where loyalist refugees escaping the war arrived in growing numbers, there were artisans, skilled laborers, and tradesmen, as well as ousted royal officials, professionals, and planters.[22] The refugees pleaded their cause to the British government and lobbied for continued support for a conflict in which their homes and livelihoods were at stake. The Howe proclamation of November 30 was resented by some loyalists in New York, who thought it too lenient to rebels and criminals, and they complained in writing to Germain.[23] In early 1777, their complaints dovetailed with Germain's own ideas of what was wrong with the Howes' command.

THE HOWE WOMEN were certainly aware of the buzz of negativity emanating from the office of the American secretary. Anything said by Germain would be readily conveyed to them from a number of sources. Germain's secretary, Christopher D'Oyly, was their confidential friend. David Garrick, the celebrated actor and playwright, who was part of Lady Spencer's social set, heard firsthand Germain's criticism of the brothers, writing that the Howe proclamation "extending Mercy to all without exception has given much offence to L'd: G[eorge] G[ermain]—I speak not from hearsay, but certainty."

Germain's innate unsociability in a world that functioned on gossip and networking was taking its toll. Nisbet Balfour was exposed to his irritation when he visited Whitehall: "[T]he ministry were very angry at the last Proclamation," he confided over a dinner in mid-January.[24] Balfour's personal loyalty to the Howes was public knowledge; as we have seen, the young aide-de-camp was constantly in the company of the Howe women over the winter of 1776–77. Yet Germain spoke his mind freely before the Scots officer. The case of Christopher D'Oyly was similar. It was more than a year after he took up his post in Germain's office that his close relationship to the Howe family drew comment: "Lady Howe and Mrs D'Oyly always together."[25] That should have been obvious from the start.

Competition among generals serving on the same side is an uninspiring fact of life in most wars. In the Seven Years' War, the Dowager Lady Howe had looked on at court as Secretary of State William Pitt and King George II made the decision to oust Lord Loudoun as commander in chief in America and replace him with dynamic young generals—including George Lord Howe and General Wolfe. Loudoun, far from the scene of decision-making in London, was unable to defend himself when he was apportioned an unfair share of blame for the string of defeats in 1757. The American War of Independence would see the same inevitable jockeying for command in London, a competition for glory that was played out in the corridors of Whitehall as much as on the battlefields of America.

If Germain was impatient with the Howes, his spleen was also directed toward Sir Guy Carleton, governor of Quebec. Carleton had successfully defended Quebec against an American attack over the winter of 1775–76, but in the ensuing campaign, he had not managed to retake Fort Ticonderoga from the rebels, despite successes on Lake Champlain. The ambitious General Burgoyne had been second-in-command on the expedition; by December 1776, he was back in London, quite willing to cast blame on Carleton as he sought an independent command for himself. In Germain, Burgoyne would find a sympathetic ear. Germain had never liked Carleton, who many years earlier had not supported him over the humiliating court-martial that followed his inaction at the Battle of Minden.[26]

It quickly became the talk of the town that Burgoyne was at odds with his superior in Canada. "Burgoyne is not very communicative, it is easy to perceive that he & Carleton are far from friends. Ld. G[eorge] G[ermain]'s people rail at Sr. Guy most furiously," observed Captain Richard Fitzpatrick.[27] Rivalries and jealousies over the management of the war were food for genteel gossip. Lady Mary Coke, hearing about it at a West End soirée, wrote, "General Carleton did not take the fort at Ticonderoga which all agree might easily have been done." Now, "they will have the same work to do over again next year," recorded Lady Mary waspishly, for Carleton had decided to withdraw from the lakes and go into winter quarters in Montreal.[28] Drawing-room generals consulted maps of America over their billiard tables, confirming their notions of the vulnerability of the wilderness fortress.

At this time, in New York, William was not thinking about the buzz in Germain's office. He was deciding on his strategy for the next year. Between the end of November 1776 and mid-January 1777, he wrote home in three substantial letters, reflecting his ideas about the forthcoming campaign. These letters were to become a major strand in the sinuous tale of British mismanagement of the American War of Independence.

The starting point of William's strategy outlined in his first letter was the notion that New England was the core of the rebellion, and a decisive victory there would guarantee victory in the war. Since the start of the conflict in April 1775, there had been a plan to invade the rear of New England, using both the Lake Champlain waterway, extending down from Canada, and the Hudson River, thrusting upward from New York, that connected with it. An attack from both sides would sever the region's links to the other colonies, which were thought to be less committed to the rebellion.

At the end of November 1776, flush with his successes around New York, William proposed that ten thousand men should push up the Hudson to Albany, meeting the army under Carleton that would march southward from Quebec. A further ten thousand would march against Boston from Rhode Island, five thousand would defend New York City, and eight thousand would be stationed in New Jersey, keeping Washington in fear for the safety of Philadelphia.[29]

The problem with this plan was that it required a reinforcement of fifteen thousand men, which William proposed could "be secured from Russia or Germany." William did not realize how very unwelcome this appeal for reinforcements was to Germain, who the previous year had sent William more men than he had requested for the New York campaign. But, as we have seen, the extra troops sent in 1776 had arrived too late for William to attack the city before the rebels could get dug in.[30] And it was the recollection of this delay that was behind the change of strategy in William's next letter.

By December 20, the situation around New York had shifted again. Lord Cornwallis had chased Washington's dwindling army across New Jersey and the Delaware River into Pennsylvania. This looked very well, but the expectation had been that Washington would retreat north into New England, where he retained the strongest civilian support. Instead, he had gone south, spreading the war. Before William had received a reply to his November letter, he sent a replacement plan in which he proposed to assemble ten thousand men and follow General Washington to Philadelphia, "where the enemy's chief strength will certainly be collected." Boston could wait. Leaving smaller holding forces to defend New York, Rhode Island, and the Hudson, William would now need only nineteen thousand men to start the campaign. He still expected reinforcements, but they, and any additional campaigning, could come later in the season. "By this change," he wrote to Germain, "the offensive plan towards Boston must be deferred, until the proposed reinforcements arrive from Europe."[31]

William was considering advancing on Philadelphia as early as possible, perhaps as soon as the Delaware River froze over. But on December 26, just days after William had dispatched his second plan, Washington struck back. In what has been called one of the iconic moments of the Revolutionary War, the American commander and his troops recrossed the Delaware in extreme winter conditions of ice, sleet, and snow and captured a garrison of Hessian troops in Trenton. Their commander, Colonel Johann Rall, was probably not drunk from Christmas revelries as the legends claim, but he was certainly taken by surprise and lost his life in the attack. The British were forced to draw in their forces, retreating from most of New Jersey.[32] A second successful American attack on a British garrison in Princeton followed swiftly.

In letters dated December 31 and January 20, William grimly related these setbacks to Germain: "The rebels have taken fresh courage upon this event," he wrote, adding ominously, "I hear French officers flock to them fast." But he concluded on an optimistic note, urging that if the reinforcements he requested arrived by spring, the rebellion could still be stopped—provided the Americans still saw no sign of any real assistance from France.[33]

The pains William had taken to appear as an irresistible force were being eroded, and his future successes were starting to rely upon that dangerous word *if.* The British army would be on the defensive for the remainder of the winter, constantly harassed by the enemy. In a foretaste of what was to come, William reported that on January 18 a body of rebel militia moved within cannon shot of a British force at King's Bridge and had the "presumption" to demand the surrender of the British troops stationed there. This was mere showmanship, and the adversaries stared at each other from a distance in the freezing January weather until the Americans, lacking cover, were driven off by the cold.[34]

William was facing the identical dilemma that had confronted him at the start of the war: How would he get irregular troops to stand and fight? "Philadelphia being now the principal object," in the same letter he suggested mounting an attack by land and sea on that city. The main body of the British army would march overland through New Jersey to Pennsylvania, and another would go by sea, reaching Philadelphia via the Delaware

River. By this pincer movement, he hoped to force Washington to fight. The double offensive, writes one historian, "might well have caught the American army between its jaws."[35]

As the war spread south, William's gaze was turning away from New England. By the end of 1776, he was surely thinking—for it also occurred to the ministers in London—that if the Canadian army were going to join with his own, it might just as well go by sea from the St. Lawrence River. There was no point in undertaking the arduous business of capturing the Lake Champlain corridor unless it were a prelude to invading New England, and that looked less and less likely. It seemed to make sense on the map, for the forts dispersed along that waterway were the only inland strongholds of any military significance in the American colonies. But operations in New England, guarded by its militarized inhabitants and protected by hilly terrain, posed great problems for the British forces. These problems were obvious enough that one of Washington's aides-de-camp, trying to guess British strategy in April 1777, reached the same conclusion as William regarding the feasibility of a linkup overland between the two British armies, commenting, "[I]t would require a chain of posts and such a number of men at each as would never be practicable or maintainable but to an immense army."[36] Yet, as William knew, it was not likely that any immense army would readily be forthcoming.

From the very start of the war, William Howe had always sought to concentrate all the British forces posted in America. He had advised against the ill-fated expedition of General Henry Clinton and Sir Peter Parker to South Carolina. He had tried to argue in early 1776 that the greatest share of reinforcements should go to New York rather than to Quebec. Quebec, he knew, could in any case not be held for long by the rebels, even if they should capture it, because they could not keep it without a substantial naval force. William well understood its vulnerability from his own experience there in the winter of 1759–60. But the ministry did not take the advice of its own commander in chief.[37]

Years later, preparing his testimony for a parliamentary inquiry into the war, William wrote, then deleted, a passage pointing out that it would have been simpler and more effective if General Burgoyne and his army had gone by sea to New York in 1777. But he had drawn back from proposing the idea to Germain, wary of appearing to seek the command of the entire British armed forces in America for himself: "A scruple of Delicacy which I confess had weight with me at the time."[38] Sitting at his desk in New York, William Howe was unable to tell Germain what was really on his mind. Canada was, after all, a separate command. It was not for him to dispose of the army there.

The problem that had been raised at the start of the war was coming back to haunt the British. In 1775, Generals Howe and Burgoyne had called for a viceroy to be appointed in America. A centralized command, on the spot, was the only realistic way to coordinate troop movements on the continental scale, far remote from the mother country. These warnings had been ignored, and the men now commanding the major British forces in America were the ones who stood to lose the most from this error of judgment.

Back in London before Christmas, Burgoyne found his way into Germain's office the very day after he arrived. His thinly concealed ambition was to displace Governor Carleton and command the northern army in Canada. On Christmas Day of 1776, Burgoyne famously placed a fifty-guinea bet at the fashionable Brooks's Club in the West End, wagering that in a year's time he would return victorious from America. He had a weakness for high-stakes gambling; he was also not a man to be modest. His swashbuckling manner ingratiated him with Germain, who by now was disappointed with Howe and Carleton for failing to deliver a decisive victory in America. The king also thought that Carleton, despite his merits, was not sufficiently resourceful. Burgoyne spoke of the necessity for bold strokes.[39] This was the sort of language that Germain wanted to hear, and by March Burgoyne had the command he coveted. The lackluster Carleton was to put his army at Burgoyne's disposal and remain behind to defend Canada. Carleton naturally took this as a signal to offer his resignation.[40]

The fifty-three-year-old John Burgoyne was a handsome, elegant man. His portrait by Joshua Reynolds, painted ten years earlier, shows him in his regimentals and clasping his sword, his chin lifted to give him a dashing air. He could hardly have been more different from the Howes. An amateur playwright who loved an audience, he occasionally trod the boards himself. He enjoyed self-dramatization and moved in the sparkling company of the Duchess of Devonshire's circle.[41] As a young man, he had eloped with Lady Charlotte Stanley, daughter of the Earl of Derby.

Lady Charlotte Burgoyne was part of Caroline Howe's circle. She was of a type with the Howe women, managing her husband's military reputation and circulating extracts of his letters when he was on campaign. She was an intelligent woman who, like Caroline, followed the political and social scene and maintained an extensive correspondence. Charlotte Burgoyne did not, however, always approve of her husband, who promoted a flamboyant image of himself and deliberately courted publicity. But she was unable to restrain him in this latest war in America, because she was ill when he left for Boston in 1775. By the time he returned to London more than a year later, she was dead.[42]

The plan Burgoyne pitched in London for his campaign of 1777 was to lead a force down the Lake Champlain route, but with one significant change from the previous expedition—he intended to force his way to Albany. He would not turn back, as the timorous Carleton had done. Burgoyne had already loudly criticized Carleton in 1776 for being overly cautious. He promoted himself as a bold officer who would do things differently. What he would do once he reached Albany was less certain. He might form a "junction" with Howe's army from New York, if that was to be Howe's primary objective, or he might provide a diversion if the commander in chief went south. He even optimistically suggested that Albany could be a jumping-off point for invading New England.

It is revealing that Burgoyne also briefly considered abandoning the whole "line of the Hudson" plan and simply joining Howe's army in New York by sea, obvious idea that it was. Yet he dismissed that without offering any real explanation, merely asserting, "I do not conceive any expedition from the sea can be so formidable to the enemy or so effectual to close the war as an invasion from Canada by Ticonderoga."[43] The fact was that Burgoyne wanted an independent command, and as both he and William Howe knew, sailing straight to New York would have placed him under the orders of the commander in chief. Operating overland would give General Burgoyne the chance to show his mettle.

Certainly Burgoyne's style, once he began his southward advance through New England in mid-June 1777, was more in keeping with Germain's ideas. Not for him were the offers of pardon and forgiveness proclaimed by the Howes. Instead, he loftily demanded that the inhabitants come forth and beg for mercy, warning that he had only "to give stretch to the Indian forces under my command" to unleash "Devastation, famine and every concomitant Horror."[44] When his proclamation was reprinted in London, it was "universally ridiculed," as Jane Strachey reported to her husband. Horace Walpole was quick to point out that Burgoyne would be a laughingstock if he failed, and he compared him unfavorably to the Howe brothers: "Have you read General Burgoyne's rodomontade [boasting], in which he almost promises to cross America in a hop, step and a jump? I thought we were cured of hyperboles. . . . I own I prefer General Howe's taciturnity, who at least if he does nothing does not break his word."[45] We shall see the impact that Burgoyne's arrogant decrees had on backwoods New Englanders.

General Henry Clinton also returned home in early 1777, reaching London at the end of February. Even before he arrived, it was known in Caroline's circles that he was dissatisfied with his commander in chief. His indiscreet criticisms of General Howe during the New York campaign had been repeated to William himself.

Henry Clinton's character contrasted sharply with that of the confident Burgoyne, who was his senior by six years. Always ready to disparage the command decisions of the Howes in private, Clinton himself was highly sensitive to criticism and had a prickly, aloof nature. Once he replaced William as commander in chief in 1778, he discovered that planning bold campaigns from the sidelines was much easier than actually carrying them out, as he himself proved to be a circumspect and cautious military leader.

In early 1777, Clinton, like Burgoyne, sought an independent command, but his meetings with Germain proved less satisfactory. Clinton's natural diffidence prevented him from pushing hard enough to oust his more assertive rival, who had already worked his way into Germain's favor. Instead, Germain promised Clinton in early April that if he would return to America as second-in-command to Howe, he would be made a Knight of the Bath—the "red ribbon," as it was called.[46]

In a sample of Lord George Germain's managerial style, he made sure that Clinton felt grateful to him alone for the knighthood. He privately insinuated to Clinton that General Howe would be jealous, but "Mr. H[owe] had no right to monopolize all the red ribbons or anything else."[47] Lord George clearly perceived Clinton's resentment of his commander in chief, and he understood how to manipulate it. Germain knew well that William Howe did not feel remotely possessive of the red ribbon. He had received a letter from Howe, stating frankly that he did not want the knighthood.[48] Even before the arrival of that letter, Major Balfour was blunt over dinners in London about his general's attitude, saying, "Sr. Willm. Howe will be rather displeased wth. the red ribband than otherwise, as he always express'd great contempt for it."[49] Clinton never suspected; he was mollified, believing he had been offered the red ribbon over the implied objections of the unappreciative William Howe, giving it even greater value in his eyes.[50]

Clinton's gratification at being installed as a Knight of the Bath exposed him as something of an outsider. The Order of the Bath was not highly prized by those in the know. Horace Walpole, on hearing the news, observed cattily: "a paltry way of [Clinton] retrieving his honour, which he had come so far to vindicate."[51] General Burgoyne had already refused one while he was in London planning his expedition to Albany. To make sure it was not foisted on him in his absence, Burgoyne left instructions with his relatives in England that if it were offered again, it should be politely declined.[52] Lady Louisa Conolly, upon hearing of the news of William's knighthood, spoke for the Howe women when she wrote that the king had accompanied the honor with a personal letter of congratulations, which, she wrote grudgingly, "makes it *something*, or else I am provoked at his having it." She trusted that something more would be done for General Howe in due course.[53]

The Howe women knew how to guard the backs of their men in society. The Clinton women did not; they belonged to a lower social level, and the effect of this on Clinton's career provides a telling example of the difference well-connected kinswomen like Caroline could make to a man's ambitions in Georgian England.

Henry Clinton boasted only a single great connection, the 2nd Duke of Newcastle. But the duke was merely a cousin by marriage. His own marriage should have been the means of consolidating his rise into the highest ranks, but Clinton had chosen a wife without money or connections. Harriet Carter, whose family members were minor gentry, died in 1772 after five years of marriage and as many children. Harriet's sisters moved in to keep house for the widower.[54]

One of the sisters, Elizabeth Carter, kept a diary that revealed the style of the Clinton household. The Carter women lived the life of prosperous, genteel landowning farmers—tea drinking, haymaking, and other country pursuits were the reigning concerns of each day. The domestic diary registered the war an ocean away only through periodic entries of "dreadful news" and "cruel reports"—tales of warfare and violence that intruded on the peace of the little household. The Carter ladies did not go to court or participate in high society; they did not pick up drawing-room gossip or political trends. Instead, Aunt Elizabeth dutifully recorded the forays made by Clinton—her "dearest general"—into the world of the fashionable while he was home on leave in 1777: to royal levees, to Lord Germain's office at Whitehall, and to the dinner tables of the great.

Only occasionally did Clinton's set overlap with that of the Howes: a dinner with General Conway, a single evening at the D'Oylys'. At the end of April 1777, Clinton took his leave amid the sighs of "his miserable Family" and returned to America, taking with him his red ribbon, the prospect of a promotion, and a much better idea of what was expected of the army in the next campaign than William could possibly have.[55]

But no British commander in America in 1777 could claim to have a clear understanding of the overarching plan of that campaign. While William's evolving strategy was turning him toward the south and Philadelphia, Burgoyne was seated face-to-face with Germain, hatching a plan that presumed his army and the army in New York would be acting together in some undefined way in the wildernesses of the upper Hudson River. Germain knew both plans, yet, inexplicably, he did not reveal to Burgoyne what William was thinking. Burgoyne reached Canada in early May 1777, expecting that some sort of coordination between his army and William's would occur, although he was never sure what form this would take. British grand strategy lacked the precision needed for success.[56]

The 1777 British campaign operated across an area that was far greater by hundreds of miles than the European theaters in the War of the Austrian Succession and the Seven Years' War. The armed forces were obliged to deploy over vast tracts of wilderness, to police intricate coastlines, and to maintain communications with a government that was on the other side of the Atlantic Ocean, rather than just across the English Channel. The resources committed were enormous; the New York campaign had involved a "logistical effort on the oceans" not to be equaled by Britain until 1944.[57] The British experience of the Seven Years' War in America meant that they understood the challenges facing any military operation there, and that experience should have taught caution in the planning of complex strategies such as the one Germain was now pitching to Howe and Burgoyne.

Twenty years earlier, multipronged attacks against the French enemy in America had been planned in London, and some, of course, had gone awry. A tragic example was the failed mission against Ticonderoga, where George

Lord Howe had been killed. Significantly, however, London strategists had made allowance for potential individual failures in the Seven Years' War. No single American expedition was entirely dependent on the outcome of the others, so if one failed, the others might still succeed.[58]

As a veteran of the last war, Germain should have known all this. It is sometimes suggested that he intentionally gave his generals leeway to use their own initiative in a war conducted so far from the metropolis. But we have seen that both his generals had declared in 1775 that they did not want such latitude—they desired an overall commander to be on the spot in America.

Yet neither general foresaw what lay ahead for the northern army at Saratoga. Significantly, both William Howe and John Burgoyne assumed that the Americans could only put one large army in the field, and all the strategies under consideration revolved around that critical and mistaken assumption. William also presumed that Burgoyne's army would be capable of standing on its own feet if need be. That chimed in with what he understood to be the modus operandi of the previous war.[59]

As William planned his campaign for 1777, slow and inadequate communications remained an issue. But just as bad in William's mind was Germain's unwillingness to give "clear, explicit orders." Instead, he was frustrated by what he called the "[a]mbiguous messages, hints, whispers across the Atlantick" that emanated from the American secretary's office. Nevertheless, William continued to look for feedback from London as he sent his different plan variants. In late 1776, he requested Germain's own ideas of how the ensuing campaign should unfold, particularly with respect to the arrival of reinforcements from home, its timing, and its impact on strategy. This was no token request, and William felt aggrieved when it went unanswered. In a draft speech written several years later, he confessed, "[I]t hurt me, that a Solicitation, which appeared to me so dutiful and reasonable, was never thought proper to be complied with."[60] But William deleted this sentence from the final version offered for public consumption. Instead, he faulted Germain for couching his instructions in the form of suggestions that would leave him room to shift the blame onto his commanders in the field if things went wrong.[61] It was one thing to give his generals discretion in carrying out their orders; it was quite another to inject ambiguity to evade responsibility for the outcome of those orders.

When William did hear back from Germain on March 9, he must have been shocked at the contents; he was certainly angry. The king, wrote Germain, was still considering his strategy, and in due course would send Major Balfour to New York with a response. This was in a war where geography meant that anything sent in May at the very latest could have no realistic prospect of affecting events in America. And Howe's request for fifteen thousand reinforcements was declined. Germain reckoned that Howe had twenty-seven thousand men currently under him—a number that the minister arrived at by including all the sick and the wounded—so he should need fewer than eight thousand after all. Ultimately, William received just three thousand extra men.[62]

William had spent the winter in New York, awaiting further word from London, while his army—on the defensive since the rebel victories at Trenton and Princeton—found itself harassed almost daily by an elusive enemy that could not inflict defeat but could deny his troops their comfortable winter quarters and sap morale. He could not have avoided feeling frustrated and restless. Meanwhile, there were determined efforts to enjoy winter quarters. The Queen's Birthday, for example, was marked in January with fireworks and a ball; there were dinners, receptions, and assemblies of "the Beaus & Belles" of New York City. Officers staged amateur theatricals for their own amusement and for the benefit of servicemen's widows.[63]

But the American victories at Trenton and Princeton forced the British army to draw in its outposts: Food and forage were difficult to find, prices rose, and every detachment sent in search of hay was sure to be drawn into a nasty skirmish. One did not have to venture very far from the city to witness the devastation wrought by the war. Deserted dwellings in a desolate landscape could be seen along the New Jersey shore; the bodies of unburied rebel soldiers were visible in the Long Island countryside. In the vacated New York City homes of wealthy rebels, now claimed by British officers, living quarters were cramped and junior officers complained of having to share a floor with their comrades-in-arms.[64] Civilians faced high prices and hardship, and the poorest, many of them Black loyalists, crowded into improvised hovels in a district called "Canvas Town."[65] Henry Strachey sent his wife a description of a winter cooped up in the city—unable to ride because of impassable roads, on constant lookout for a ship from England bearing news.[66]

Both William and Richard, as commanders in chief, were nevertheless expected to lay on entertainments for their own officers, their troops, and the local citizenry. That winter, the contrasting personalities of the two brothers began to be noted—the admiral was dignified and reserved, the younger general appeared irresponsible and loved a good time. In fact, William garnered severe censure from New York loyalists for his libertine lifestyle. Their stories, which were conveyed to London in private letters, depicted a general who surrounded himself with "scenes of dissipation and gaming," gambling for high stakes and losing his temper over his losses, and corrupting his junior officers by his example. "What can the nation expect from a luxurious and licentious army," raged one angry New Yorker, "and an indolent and dissipated general?"[67] In addition, a rumor began to make the rounds of his scandalous affair with a Boston woman named Elizabeth Loring. The story gained wide circulation, with what accuracy we shall see. One junior officer, writing privately about his commander in chief in March 1777, called him a "R__h_ll" (rakehell), a word that would translate today as "hellraiser." The letter was written just nine days after William received Germain's letter denying his request for reinforcements.[68] It would be almost two more months before William received a decisive official response to his proposals for the next campaign.

The response finally arrived on May 8, when Major Nisbet Balfour reached New York with a dispatch from Germain that gave William the go-ahead for the action against Philadelphia. This was the point where Germain should have communicated Burgoyne's plans, but there was no mention of the Canadian army. By now, William himself had already informed General Carleton in Quebec that he could offer little help to Burgoyne. He had also resolved to go to Philadelphia by sea.[69]

By traveling entirely by water, William could avoid being harassed by the Continental Army that constantly skulked on his flank, and his communications and supply lines would be secure. He would now have another chance to destroy Washington's army, because the rebels had to defend Philadelphia. If the mission were a success, the British army would gain control of Pennsylvania's plentiful granaries, and thus deny them to Washington. And taking Pennsylvania—whose population included pacifist Quakers and neutral German communities of Amish and Mennonites, and where there was reputedly only a mixed commitment to the rebellion— would divide rebellious New England from its strongest ally in the south, Virginia.[70] Even though William had not received everything he'd asked for, he was determined to go ahead with his plan.

Historians have sometimes wondered how William Howe came up with a strategy that deviated so sharply from the "line of the Hudson" idea that had been the centerpiece of British strategic thinking almost from the start of the war. But the idea of dividing and conquering the colonies by invading the Chesapeake Bay instead of New York and the Hudson had been bruited about in London since 1775.[71] By 1777, the war was clearly no longer confined to New England, as strategists had initially envisioned, so encircling that intransigent province made little sense militarily. Amphibious warfare was an advantage the British would do well to exploit in their war against the rebellious seaboard colonies.

Meanwhile, Germain was getting worried. His last letter to William, written on May 18, which the general received weeks after he had already embarked from New York with his army, approved the expedition to Philadelphia but added the hope that whatever General Howe undertook, "it will be executed in time for you to cooperate" with Burgoyne in the north.[72] By this time, it was far too late for William to be ordered to go up the Hudson to meet up with the army heading south from Canada.

Germain's May 18 letter has the ring of a last-minute attempt by the American secretary to evade responsibility should the campaign go wrong.[73] And in this it had some effect. In late 1778, after William had resigned and gone home, the letter would be published in New York by partisans of Germain, purporting to be proof that General Howe had disobeyed direct orders to support Burgoyne's expedition. The faithful Nisbet Balfour, still serving in America at the time, rushed in a rage to the printer's office, declaring, "I am Sir W[illiam] H[owe]'s friend and *I shall allow it to go no further.*"[74] He got no satisfaction, but perhaps it relieved his angry feelings.

Curiously, in Britain, the false rumor that William Howe had been ordered to go up the Hudson to meet Burgoyne was already spreading by the summer of 1777, even before William and his army had embarked for Philadelphia. In July, British newspapers carried a story that General Howe had received explicit instructions for a rendezvous with General Burgoyne and a conquest of New England *before* going to Pennsylvania.[75] Newspapers published all sorts of nonsense and outright falsehoods, but the articles can be seen as the harbingers of a narrative that never entirely died down: that William had ignored direct orders to meet Burgoyne in Albany.

The inadequate communication between Germain's office and the commander in chief that dogged the entire campaign of 1777 was so stark that

William wondered aloud two years later in the House of Commons whether a letter from Germain had gone missing that spring.[76] Conspiracy theories sprang up to explain the glaring deficiency. An apocryphal story circulated that Christopher D'Oyly had failed to transmit critical orders to William from his chief, Lord George Germain.[77] Nisbet Balfour also came under suspicion, for he was known to be Germain's messenger in early 1777, carrying royal instructions with him when he reached New York from London in May. A story made the rounds that Balfour had also conveyed separate, verbal orders from Germain to William regarding Burgoyne and the Canada expedition, orders that General Howe allegedly ignored.[78]

In reality, Balfour's sole verbal message from Germain was a reproof for General Howe's too-infrequent communications, a source of immense frustration to the American secretary.[79] The written dispatches carried by Balfour approved of the campaign to the south, but they also urged the brothers to conduct raids on the New England coast.[80] No doubt Nisbet went beyond his remit and gave Sir William an earful of what was being said about him in the offices of Lord George. The brothers wrote back, coolly declining to undertake the New England coastal raids, stating that they lacked the resources.

Germain would later claim that the raids on the New England coast were intended as a diversion for Burgoyne, although the dispatches themselves contained no such suggestion.[81] There is no doubt that Germain was becoming worried about where the blame would lie if the campaign miscarried. The crucial weakness in the planning was Germain's failure to issue explicit orders to William to meet up with Burgoyne's army on the Hudson—or not. Was Burgoyne's offensive supposed to be a diversion for Howe, or a decisive move to divide the rebellious colonies, or what?

THE SIMMERING DISCONTENT between Germain and his commander in chief had its parallel within the British nation at large, as the public became aware that the victories hailed at Christmastime had not ended the rebellion. In February, news of the reverses in Trenton and Princeton began to be known around London, and a picture of a faltering British war effort began to take shape: George Washington's numbers swelling, an emboldened rebel army harassing British troops. Armchair critics in London "began to abuse General Howe in all the coffee houses." Germain attempted to rally morale in Parliament with a speech outlining his great hopes for the next campaign, but two weeks later, on May 30, Lord Chatham rose in the House of Lords and called for an end to the war. All we have now in America, declaimed the aging Pitt, is "a military station." After two years of fighting, not one American province had been restored to royal rule. Chatham was supported by the Duke of Grafton, the longstanding friend of Caroline and her brothers.[82]

On the night of Lord Chatham's speech, Caroline happened to be playing cards and winning money at Princess Amelia's summer residence in Gunnersbury. "Mrs Howe won the rest all lost," recalled Lady Mary.[83] The talk around the card table was of Chatham's outspoken opposition to the war, but there was no reason for Caroline to be off her game. It was the government, not her brothers, that was under attack. If Chatham thundered that the conquest of the colonies was a chimerical idea, he also said much that echoed the opinions of the Howes themselves: The civil conflict in America threatened to squander the achievements of the Seven Years' War; the colonists should have their most substantial grievances redressed, their trade and wealth should be retained for Britain, and the danger of an attack from France lurked in the wings and should be averted. Chatham's motion for peace was easily defeated, but there was a growing concern that "we shall have a French war," as Walpole confided ominously in a private letter.[84]

Caroline could not ignore the fact that admiration for her brothers was turning into hostility at an alarming rate. "[T]he Howes are not in fashion," wrote Walpole succinctly in June. At the same time, the pro-government *Morning Post* ran a series of articles calling for the recall of the brothers. "The Howes have received positive orders from Administration to *make their play* the present campaign," the *Post* cried, adding bitingly that they were "not to let the grass grow under their feet," as they had for the previous two years.[85] As the nation registered its powerlessness to quell the colonial uprising, William's 1776 seizure of New York was downplayed by newspaper scribblers.

It was Caroline's job to support her brothers at aristocratic gatherings, where parliamentary business spilled over into the social politics that was the lifeblood of Georgian society. That month, her self-control slipped in a crowded room when she reacted to news of a slight on Admiral Howe. The lucrative post of treasurership of the navy had just fallen vacant; Lord

Howe was considered by everyone to be a likely candidate, and yet—Lord North conferred it elsewhere. Horace Walpole described Caroline's obvious vexation in the midst of the party of polite tea-drinkers: "I tell you, this is irreconcilable," she exclaimed, in such heated tones that it set her apart from the rest of the company. In the competitive milieu of high politics, the oversight seemed to point to the decline of the Howe influence.[86] "[T]he rest of ye world as well as the Howe family are struck with the injustice," wrote Jane Strachey. The fear was that Lord Howe would resign.[87]

Jane's loyalty could be taken for granted, but Caroline was not going to rely on goodwill alone. She tried to control the narrative as the story took shape in the mouths of society gossips, coaching her friend Lady Spencer on what to say if the subject were to be brought up in her presence: "[I]f any body talks to you concerning the Treasurer of the Navy matter," she instructed, "be so good to say, that it was not solicited by my Brother, that he did not refuse it, & that it was not offered him, but that Ld. North knew it would have been accepted by him." After thinking it over, Caroline hinted at the close of the letter that her friend might as well bring it up herself as wait for it to be raised in conversation: "I had rather every body should know than not what I have said to you."[88]

That was in June. The very next month, General Howe sent home a report of a late start to the campaign, once again giving the impression of a failure to take head-on an army of homespun soldiers. Inaccurate reports circulated in England that when Howe did finally march out to engage the enemy, he found Washington so strongly entrenched that he did not dare to attack, and he lamely retreated back to New York. In reality, William had tried twice to lure Washington from his strongholds in New Jersey, and he had very nearly succeeded on his second attempt when Washington spotted the trap just in time to withdraw.[89] Nisbet Balfour wrote dejectedly, "[W]e could only see [Washington] getting up the Hills before us at a Distance. Had he been a few miles further from his stronghold, he would never have got there again."[90] But Balfour's frustration did not even register at home, where the newspapers reflected national exasperation as they carried the attacks on the brothers to a level that was well beyond the management of a sister.

The pages of Britain's newspapers were an important arena in the apportioning of blame or praise for wartime events. A growing readership and a rising middle class meant that in the 1770s there were more than 140 newspapers, magazines, and periodicals in circulation. Available in public houses, clubs, and coffeehouses, they reached a far wider audience than their print runs indicated. Although newspapers of the period had loose political affiliations, they were for the most part independent. In pursuit of the widest possible readership, they expressed a variety of opinions, but they played a distinctive role in purveying metropolitan political trends and opinions to the rest of the nation.[91] During the War of Independence, the British press would engage a wide cross section of British society in the debate that raged in Parliament and at court over the government's handling of the war.

The implications for the Howe brothers would be significant. Beginning in mid-1777, a derogatory public image of the two commanders in chief emerged in the newspapers, reaching such a level that the brothers would be unable to ignore it. Significantly, the negative stereotypes originated in London, rather than in the English provinces.[92] The mudslinging undoubtedly had its origins in the metropolis, in the small, intense, aristocratic society of the West End, but also in the bustling merchants' and tradesmen's clubs and coffeehouses in the business district of the city, which were hothouses for news, gossip, and speculation. Reputations— in a world in which reputation mattered—could be at the mercy of evolving opinion in such volatile arenas. As we will see, a stereotype quickly emerged of the performance of the brothers in America that drew upon anti-aristocratic tropes that had begun circulating in the early years of the previous war.

'[W]e have another instance of Howe's declining a general engagement with Washington," bellowed the *Stanford Mercury* in July. "Advices from America so late as July 6th, and nothing effective done or attempted.—Our grand army retreating under the supposition of a feint!" wailed the *London Evening Post*. The attacks were so prolific that they degenerated into cruel satire. A spoof advertisement appeared for "A Collection of Capital Paintings" to be exhibited to the public, including "A picture of an army advancing backwards—By General H—." The war, it was charged, was being dragged out so that Howe and other elite officers could obtain promotion and pay.[93]

To William Howe were attributed the traits of a self-indulgent aristocrat whose love of recreation trumped his commitment to his duty. "Considerable betts have been laid at a certain coffee-house in the West end of the town, that General Howe would not relinquish the *pleasures* of New York, for the *toils* of the field, before the first of August," read one newspaper. An anonymous writer declared that the American war was merely an opportunity to extract money from the public to enrich the wealthy and powerful.[94]

The Howe brothers—all three—had been lionized in the Seven Years' War as the epitomes of active, daring, silent Englishmen. Now the dynasty found itself on the receiving end of the same media-generated personal attacks that had been deployed twenty years earlier against the nation's unsuccessful commanders. In a century when, to the derision of ordinary Britons, the upper classes adopted many of the fashions and manners of France, failed military leaders were often pilloried as cultural traitors. The outstanding example was the unfortunate Admiral Byng, executed in 1757 for his failure to relieve Minorca from the French. Byng was popularly depicted as a Frenchified fop, a man whose supposedly un-English style of living, modeled on French decadence and effeminacy, lay at the root of his inadequacy as a naval commander. Conspiracy theorists went further, conjecturing that behind Byng's failure was a treacherous plot by aristocratic British ministers to undermine the empire. Public hostility reached such a pitch that it played a part in the decision to deny the admiral a reprieve from execution.[95]

Closer to home for the Howe dynasty than the fate of Byng were the experiences of their kinsman Sir John Mordaunt—the army commander for the notorious Rochefort expedition in 1757. Mordaunt was abused, ridiculed in the press, called a coward, and heaped with contempt. The ministry succeeded in shifting much of the blame onto him in the tribunal of public opinion, despite his acquittal in a court-martial. Conspiratorial rumors suggested that the Rochefort expedition had miscarried because of suspicious orders whose contents had been concealed from the public.[96] In 1777, as we have seen, similar tales would emerge regarding allegedly suppressed orders to General Howe from Lord Germain.

But the attacks on the Howes had an entirely new dimension as well, for the American War of Independence was the most atypical war of the century.

The narrative that carried Britain into war in 1775 was strikingly different from that of any previous war against a European foe. The string of failures confronting the nation at the start of the Seven Years' War twenty years earlier—Braddock's Road, Rochefort, Fort William Henry, to name

but a few—provoked a national outcry, but they also fit into a British tradition that regarded unpreparedness for war as the characteristic of a free
people. Britons were proud of the fact that they did not maintain the repres-
sive standing armies of absolute monarchies, even if one consequence was
a slow start to wars against major continental military powers like France.
The reaction in the Seven Years' War had been a bout of national despair
and soul-searching, which was succeeded by a return to the struggle with
renewed vigor.

In 1775, the situation was very different. This was essentially a civil war,
and there was nothing inherently noble in it. Instead, armed repression
was a necessary evil needed to bring the Americans to their senses and
restore imperial harmony. William Howe was expected to win, and win
quickly. Success alone would vindicate the use of force. A large number of
Britons did not support American constitutional claims but nevertheless
did not like the war. They saw it as a threat to British national security, and
they were uncomfortable with their nation's unaccustomed role of a Goliath pitted against the colonial Davids.

This no doubt was an important factor in the extraordinary circumstance that, during the American War of Independence, the British public
was reluctant to assign hero status to its own military leaders. Instead,
it handed acclaim readily to the rebel commander, George Washington,
who was popular in the British press throughout the conflict. William
Howe never lost a major battle, and George Washington lost more than
he won, yet it was the American who was portrayed as the model military
commander and citizen, the "Flower of American Chivalry," as one newspaper put it.[97]

Even in the social circles of the Howes, Washington had his open
admirers. Lady Mary Coke angrily recorded a spat over cards in which Lady
Sarah Napier—the former Sarah Bunbury, now remarried—declared she
"adored Mr Washington." "[S]o do I said the silly Old Dowager [Lady Albe-
marle]," who was also present and had taken too much champagne. Lady
Mary retorted that she hated the rebel general, to which Lady Albemarle
tried to set her down with "I don't believe Mr Washington cares what you
or I think of him."[98] Tea-table tiffs of this kind were going on while William
was being subjected to bitter abuse.

George Washington is known to have cultivated his image carefully to
suit the part he was to play on the world's stage. In one sense, he was in

new territory, as the commander in chief of a self-declared republic that consciously rejected the titles and aristocracy of its former mother country. He strove to live up to the image of a republican military leader, a citizen-soldier who, like the Roman hero Cincinnatus, reluctantly left the comforts of private life to fulfill his duty to his country. And yet he also appropriated the contemporary ideal of an English fighting man. Like popular British figures of the Seven Years' War, such as George Lord Howe, he spurned grand living quarters and shared in the hardships of his men. The British press responded by embracing Washington as a man who embodied an "antique of self-sacrifice" that the British people had now lost. Even the circumstance that Washington was a slaveholder was dwelt upon lightly if at all, despite the fact that American hypocrisy on this score was a favorite trope of British pro-government writers. It was widely reported that, from the start of the war, Washington accepted no pay for his services. The contrast between the American leader and their own supposedly greedy and self-serving commanders was not lost on the British public.[99]

If the public had been unaware of the Howe family's relative poverty at the beginning of the American war, it was public knowledge now, and it lent credibility to the accusation that they were profiting from their posts. A satirical cartoon appeared in Fleet Street entitled "The Conference Between the Brothers How to Get rich." The Devil, seated between them, counsels, "How, How, continue the war."[100] In July 1777, when the press was losing all restraint, one newspaper announced that the Howes were making "100,000 per annum each, by the present American war." "[T]hey will at least no longer be distinguished by the epithet of the *poor* Howes," snickered the newspaper, "whatever other appellation their conduct may merit from their countrymen on their return to England."[101] The same slanderous stories were circulating in America, where John Adams recounted them to Abigail: "These two Howes were very poor, and they have spent the little Fortunes they had in bribery at Elections, and having obtained Seats in Parliament, and having some Reputation as brave Men, they had nothing to do but to carry their Votes and their Valour to Markett, and it is very true, they have sold them at an high Price." Adams pronounced, "I would not be an Howe, for all the Empires of the Earth, and all the Riches, and Glories thereof."[102]

Curiously, as the British public lost patience with its own commanders, the Americans in rebellion continued to revere the English heroes of the

The Conference between the Brothers HOW to get Rich.

This cartoon, published in October 1777, shows Admiral Howe and General Howe discussing how they can enrich themselves. "How, how, continue the war," advises the Devil.

previous war, George Lord Howe and General James Wolfe. General Wolfe was depicted by patriot newspaper scribblers as the embodiment of the vanishing type of a noble and virtuous British officer, and one who, had he lived, would undoubtedly have sided with the American cause.[103] When General William Howe's army was a week away from landing on Staten Island, in June 1776, the New York provincial Congress actually toasted his brother, "the late noble [George] Lord Howe," at a dinner for General Washington.[104]

Perhaps this is why Thomas Paine, the foremost propagandist for the American cause, was at pains to extinguish William and Richard's prestige, which had been sustained for too long by the memory of George. English-born, Paine was the author of *Common Sense*, the single most influential publication to champion American independence. He took up his pen in January 1777 to discredit British military leaders in general, and the Howes in particular. He drew a deliberate and stark comparison between the supposedly venal middle-aged commanders in chief that William and Richard had become, and their brother George, who died young and was known for his rugged irregular soldiering and his willingness to accept hardships in the service of his country. In an open letter "To Lord Howe," he wrote,

> America, for your deceased brother's sake, would gladly have shown you respect and it is a new aggravation to her feelings, that Howe should be forgetful, and raise his sword against those, who at their own charge raised a monument to his brother. But your master has commanded, and you have not enough of nature left to refuse. Surely there must be something strangely degenerating in the love of monarchy, that can so completely wear a man down to an ingrate, and make him proud to lick the dust that kings have trod upon.

With the passage of years, sneered Paine, the Howe brothers had supposedly sacrificed their characters, adopting the effete refinements and easy virtue of courtiers. Once valiant men of action, they now served a tyrant and a debauched court.[105] A year later, the indefatigable defender of republicanism would transfer his attacks to William, calling him indolent, incompetent, and "the hero of little villainies and unfinished adventures." Sir William Howe, pronounced Paine dramatically, had made his "exit from the moral world."[106] All of this would quickly be republished in Britain.

Caroline Howe's peace of mind was eroding under the barrage of media assaults on her brothers in the summer of 1777. Lady Mary Coke, who saw her at Lady Spencer's villa in Wimbledon in July, noticed that Caroline appeared subdued. It was a delightful day, wrote Lady Mary; the young Duchess of Devonshire was there, and the Spencers had a menagerie of exotic pet birds on view to amuse their guests, but Mrs. Howe was not herself.

Lady Mary, a staunch supporter of the king and of the government, was disturbed by reports that Britain would soon find itself at war with France. "[S]ome say it is unavoidable," she wrote with concern. She expressed the view of many in English society when she accused the French of playing "a treacherous part" from the beginning of the conflict, professing peaceful intentions to British diplomats while secretly sending arms and French military advisers to America.

Caroline's mother, the Dowager Lady Howe, was also visibly failing under the pressure. Now seventy-three, Charlotte had seen her sons go away to war three times, one never to return. Maintaining a stoic front did not get easier with advancing years. Lady Mary, encountering her at a party, noted that "[s]he droops very much & if we have not some good news from America to revive her, I question whether she will hold out long." Her eyesight was impaired, and she was unable to play cards.[107]

It was Caroline who now had to act as dynastic head. A few weeks after the Wimbledon party, Lady Mary met her again and found her in better spirits. She rallied to Lady Mary Coke's comments on the "many disagreeable reports in the papers" about British military operations in America. "[N]one of them are to be believed," Mrs. Howe had assured her in convincing terms; it was simply too early in the campaign for any reliable news to reach the metropolis. Two days later, Lady Mary heard a rumor that General Burgoyne had captured Fort Ticonderoga. "Everybody grows impatient to hear from Sir William Howe," she added.[108]

Burgoyne had indeed taken Ticonderoga, something General Carleton had failed to do in 1776. Confirmation reached England in late August. Although it was greeted as good news, it did not relieve the pressure on the Howe women. Instead, gossips were incited to make unfavorable comparisons between William Howe and Burgoyne. A mutual friend of the Stracheys and the D'Oylys contrasted Burgoyne's "spirited conduct" with the puzzling maneuvers of General Howe.[109] At a high-society party, Lady Greenwich whispered to Lady Mary Coke and several others that the Dowager Lady Howe and her daughter Julie were jealous of Burgoyne's victory. "[B]ut I cannot say I observed it," wrote Lady Mary. She saw in the anxious mother only a wish for the success of all British arms in America.[110] By this time, Lady Howe found herself living in a goldfish bowl, her very expressions and moods observed by critical onlookers. Her uneasiness could only have been magnified by the fact that she, along with everyone else, wondered where, exactly, William Howe and his army were bound.

When William had embarked from New York with his army, he had ensured that his destination was kept a secret; the enemy would of course find out in time, but meanwhile it could only be advantageous to keep Washington guessing. The aura of mystery heightened the demand for news in England. Caroline, at Battlesden in August with her Aunt Page and her sisters, found herself pursued there by letters imploring for intelligence of her brothers. She had no idea whether the army's destination was Philadelphia or Boston. Responding to her friend Lady Susanna Leveson-Gower, she wrote that the last letters received from the brothers had been dated mid-June. The army was to embark from New York in the first week of July, and whatever her brothers undertook, whether in New England or Pennsylvania, "will be a stroke of consequence," she asserted stoutly.[111] She dropped the confident veneer with Lady Spencer, simply lamenting, "No news yet from America, horrid lies in this days papers."[112]

Speculation about the whereabouts of General Howe and his army was laced with frustration and ill will. "No news of Sir William Howe," recorded Lady Mary Coke, who had remained in London for the summer. In the absence of concrete intelligence, she lamented, "ill-natured reports" about the commander in chief were rife. Lord and Lady Hertford, both of whom played cards with Caroline, thought General Howe was being unduly influenced by his brother the admiral, who was "an excellent Sea Officer" but did not understand military operations.[113] Lady Mary was not reading newspaper chatter but instead listening to critical remarks between individuals who knew the Howes personally.

As their numbers shrank, Caroline's supporters closed ranks against the malice of high-society gossip. Lady Spencer wrote to Caroline from Spa, where Lord Spencer was taking his cure, "& now my Dear Howey let me beg you to give me all the intelligence you possibly can about America. I hate the Newspapers more than ever because they abuse your Brothers—I never will read them—nor believe any thing but what I hear from you upon that Subject."[114]

When Lady Spencer wrote this, she had probably already received a letter from Lord Jersey that illustrated her friend's growing isolation. Lord Jersey had been at the Christmastime theatricals at Phyllis Court in January, but a great deal had changed since that happy time. After discussing the widespread despondency over the course of the war, he concluded his letter with a damning summary of what was being said about the Howes:

> The Blame is entirely upon the two Brothers, a general condemnation of their conduct; everything almost is laid at their charge; Want of Spirit & quickness last year. . . , delay now, want of generalship in the one, & want of management in the other in not defending the coast & letting the Boston Fleet get out. In short the fault must be laid somewhere to account for the miscarriage of an undertaking which has been given out as impossible to fail.

Lord Howe had been much criticized when a rebel squadron escaped from Boston in late May 1777. By August, the American ships were harassing the coast of Britain, snatching up provision-laden merchantmen and even boldly threatening the shipping lanes in the English Channel.[115] The war was being brought home; its depredations impinged upon Caroline's own set, as aristocrats bound for a tour on the Continent were constrained to be careful. At the end of August, Lord Jersey again cautioned Lady Spencer that he was hearing malicious talk against the Howes. "I trust you will not suffer those Friends [the Howes] to be run down," he enjoined her. "If you have read the Paper you will know what I mean."[116]

The lack of faith infiltrated even family circles. William had always been a favorite with his mother-in-law, Lady Anne Conolly, who was now "a good deal hurt to find people dissatisfied with Sir William."[117] These people included her own brother, William Wentworth, Earl of Strafford. Wentworth was tactless enough to go to MP George Byng, a brother-in-law of Fanny Howe, to ask whether it were true that Sir William was using his command for personal profit. The Wentworths must have experienced considerable family tension, for some strongly suspected that the Howes had dodged the opportunity to end the war in New York in 1776 in order to push their peace commission, and that they had thereafter strung out the war to make money.[118]

In September, when, unbeknownst to the people of Britain, General Howe and his army were confronting George Washington in the fight for Philadelphia, and when Burgoyne's troops were fast approaching Saratoga, Caroline left Battlesden to stay at her mother's home in Richmond. "No news yet," she reported to Lady Spencer, "nor is any body at all certain where my brothers have gone; as usual the newspapers will know more, than I thank God they possibly can." Charlotte was in tolerable health, although her eyesight continued to trouble her. Julie and Fanny, the least resilient of the Howe women, had gone for a stay in the countryside. Caroline coined a new word to describe her own mood: *humgrumcious*. She managed, however, to fill four sheets of paper with society news. She was not staying at home; she and Lady Mary Howe were the public faces of the family. Lady Mary attended the royal drawing rooms and conversed with their majesties, monitoring the tone in that all-important sphere. Caroline's task was to stick close to her enemy. "I am often with Lady George Germain," she wrote to Lady Spencer.[119]

Caroline by now had reason to see Lady Germain's husband, the American secretary, in the light of an enemy, for it was widely reported that he was behind the newspaper attacks on her brothers. By July 1777, the *London Evening Post* was publishing accusations that Germain's "creatures" were the authors of the abuse aimed at General Howe.[120] The accusations were plausible, since it was normal practice for government staff to hire writers to argue their cases before the public. Ministers had been known to contend with generals indirectly via the press over responsibility for failed military operations.[121] Certainly if Germain was not behind the media attacks, he did nothing to discourage them.

Conspicuous among the government writers in the American War of Independence was Israel Mauduit, a London cloth merchant, religious dissenter, and lobbyist who had risen to prominence as a pamphleteer during the Seven Years' War. Mauduit would become one of William Howe's most virulent critics, and his pamphlet attacks would be passed down to posterity. Historians have agreed that he most likely was writing at the instigation of Germain.[122] The Howe family and the rest of the world needed no proof; they assumed that Germain was using the press to discredit his disappointing and vexing commander in chief.[123] Meanwhile, Caroline exchanged pleasantries with Germain in his home and played cards with his wife.

For the Howe brothers, the one sure way to silence censure was to win the war. In July, while Caroline was parrying criticism at polite gatherings in London, William was still in New York, impatient to get his army aboard ship and begin his campaign in the south. It required several weeks to load the transport ships. Seeking to galvanize his men, he ordered them to carry only a minimum of baggage, in the manner of the light infantry pioneered by George Lord Howe twenty years earlier. Company commanders were told to sell their mounts, as only a limited number of riding horses would be accommodated.[124] For William, the hectic preparations were unpleasantly interrupted by the arrival of General Clinton from England. The two generals, who never saw eye-to-eye, engaged in bouts of arguing over the campaign plan. Clinton didn't like it. He was worried that once William and his army were at sea, Washington might turn back to New York and pounce on Clinton's garrison forces, or decide to attack Burgoyne in the north, rather than defend Philadelphia. He urged William to consider moving up the Hudson at the start of the campaign and leaving Philadelphia to the last.

Clinton's arguments, which he carefully recorded, have added to the impression that William's move on Philadelphia was counter to the

intentions of the British government. But William's plan had been approved
by Germain, and Clinton knew it. Nor were Clinton's protests a premoni-
tion of what was to happen at Saratoga. Both generals assumed that the
Americans could put only one large army in the field. William would never
have acted the part of a willing bystander in the face of such a disaster
for British arms in America.[125] William waited until he received the news
that Burgoyne had captured Fort Ticonderoga, which reached New York by
express messenger on July 17. That very day, he boarded his brother's flagship, HMS *Eagle*.[126] The Howe brothers embarked for Philadelphia on July
23 with a fleet of almost three hundred warships, transporting fourteen
thousand troops.

A month later, the armada of British warships entered the Chesapeake Bay in Maryland. The sea journey had been delayed by storms,
and by a pause at the Delaware River, where General Howe had investigated the possibility of landing. He had also used it as an opportunity to touch base with developments inland, in order to ensure that
Washington was still after him, and not headed north toward Burgoyne.
After receiving faulty intelligence that Washington had already crossed
the Delaware River and had made "uncommon preparations" to oppose a
British landing, William proceeded to his first choice of disembarkation,
the Chesapeake Bay. This turned out to be a serious mistake, delaying
his campaign and lessening the chance of his having time to go north
to help Burgoyne. At the end of August, he wrote to Germain, warning
him that he would not be able to fulfill his objectives in time to cooperate
with the northern army.[127]

British troops landed at Head of Elk on Maryland's Eastern Shore on
August 25, 1777. Nine days later, light infantry and Hessian soldiers moving north toward Philadelphia clashed with a rebel advance guard at Cooch's
Bridge. Morale within the British forces was high, and only the swampy
terrain that bordered the Christina River prevented the light infantry from
crossing the waterway and attacking the Americans from the rear.[128]

William was in a confident mood. Traversing the extensive Christina River watershed with his army, he knew that Washington would
try to stop him again at Brandywine Creek, a natural defensive barrier
blocking the route to Philadelphia. In fact, Washington had concentrated
his troops at Chadds Ford, where the main road to the city crossed the
Brandywine. What Washington didn't know, and what local loyalists had

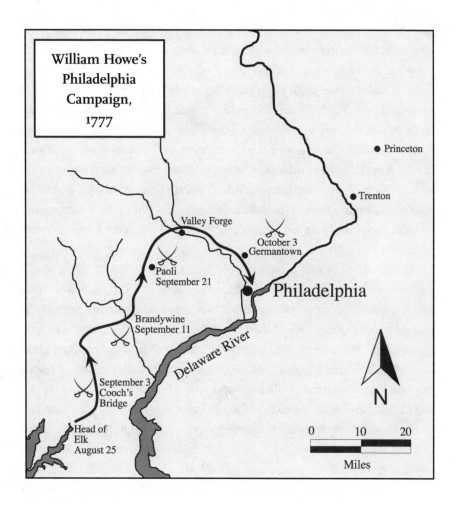

William Howe's Philadelphia Campaign, 1777

Princeton

Trenton

Valley Forge

October 3
Germantown

Paoli
September 21

Philadelphia

Brandywine
September 11

Delaware River

September 3
Cooch's
Bridge

Head of
Elk
August 25

N

0   10   20
Miles

volunteered to General Howe, was that there were other fords beyond the far right of Washington's line. As at Brooklyn, William planned a flanking attack.

The action began at midmorning on September 11, 1777, with a feint at Chadds Ford that appeared to the Americans to be the main British offensive. While the Americans were distracted by the Hessians under Lieutenant General Wilhelm von Knyphausen, eight thousand men under General Cornwallis, accompanied by General Howe, began a long flanking march. Washington, receiving mixed intelligence reports during the day, ignored the danger on his flank; he was convinced that the Hessian combatants at Chadds Ford were the real threat. It would be an eighteen-mile march in the heat for William and his men before they stopped at 3 p.m. at a hill that hid them from the view of the enemy.

While Howe, Cornwallis, and several officers of the light Hessian Jaeger Corps climbed the hill to survey the Americans fighting in the midst of noise and dust, the British troops had a moment to rest and eat before the battle to come. Their commander in chief descended from the lookout and joined them, and an officer left a description of William Howe sitting on the grass with his light infantry officers, his composure charming the men around him: "Everyone that remembers the anxious moments before an engagement may conceive how animating is the sight of the Commander-in-chief in whose looks nothing but serenity and confidence in his troops is painted."[129]

The Battle of Brandywine has been called Howe's finest battle, and it was assuredly a victory. It demonstrated his skill as a tactician. Washington was taken by surprise, and after two hours of fierce fighting—with the Hessians pushing across Chadds Ford and an intense American firefight gradually forced to give way to the enemy that had materialized on the right—Washington conceded defeat and withdrew, having lost at least a thousand men wounded, killed, or captured. It was in some ways a reprise of Brooklyn, and yet it was not. The Americans, more experienced now, had retreated in orderly fashion; their morale remained high. A lack of cavalry and the fatigue of his troops meant that Howe was unable to harass the retreating Americans. Even the so-called Paoli Massacre ten days later—in which British Major General Sir Charles Grey made a surprise attack on sleeping continental soldiers in Paoli, Pennsylvania, killing or wounding three hundred of them—did not deter Washington's fighting men from their cause.[130] As many British observers had predicted in 1775, the lengthening conflict had given the Americans time to form themselves into a professional army.

William and his army marched into Philadelphia on September 26, two weeks after Brandywine. In advance of his arrival, the Continental Congress and hundreds of prominent patriots had fled the city. Hundreds more, unable to escape in time, were arrested when they were identified by local loyalists, who were happy to provide the British army with good intelligence. Philadelphia merchants, many of them Quakers, who always had had mixed feelings about the rebellion, welcomed the prospect of a return to stability. Young men signed up for newly formed loyalist army units. As in New York, there were many fine houses vacated by rebels for the British officers to occupy, and wealthy Philadelphians entertained the redcoat heroes with dinners and dances.[131] Philadelphia would become the winter quarters for the British army.

William found greater favor with the citizens of Philadelphia than those of New York. His conduct in Pennsylvania, in the opinion of many, was "very proper, except in one or two instances."[132] During the nine months that his army occupied the area, recreations that had been suppressed by the Continental Congress were revived. Cockfights and horse races were put on, and a theater troupe called "Howe's Strolling Players" was organized, with British officers taking to the boards. Henry Strachey wrote to Jane of seeing performances of *The Minor* and *The Deuce Is in Him*, in company with General Howe. It was as good as the London theaters, he enthused. All the roles performed by officers of the army and navy were excellent, and only the actresses, most of whom were officers' mistresses, were "insufferable."[133] A casino was established at Philadelphia's City Tavern, described as the center of a social whirl. William hosted concerts and dances, and at least two balls were held at his headquarters. He was very popular. When he left, a Pennsylvania loyalist wrote with affection, "The civilities and attention of the noble Brothers to many of us at Philad'a. ought never to be forgot."[134]

But, as with everything in this complicated war, it was not to be an unmitigated triumph. On the night of October 3, just a week after the British army marched into Philadelphia, Washington unexpectedly led a counterattack at nearby Germantown. He was repelled by redcoat forces, but only after great confusion, and he had shown that he could strike back. When news of the attack reached William, he was said to have exclaimed, "That cannot be!" Washington and his army were growing in experience and confidence.[135] Now the British army was confined to Philadelphia and cut off from supplies in the surrounding countryside.

It was not until November, after protracted, exhausting fighting, that William's army and Richard's navy managed to open the sea route to Philadelphia via the Delaware River. By this time, news of disaster in the north had reached them. Burgoyne's early victory at Ticonderoga in July diverted him from his planned route in order to chase the fleeing American garrison. A few days later, he and his men scattered the retreating rebels but found themselves in thickly forested territory, running short of supplies and hiking overland toward their next target, Fort Edward.

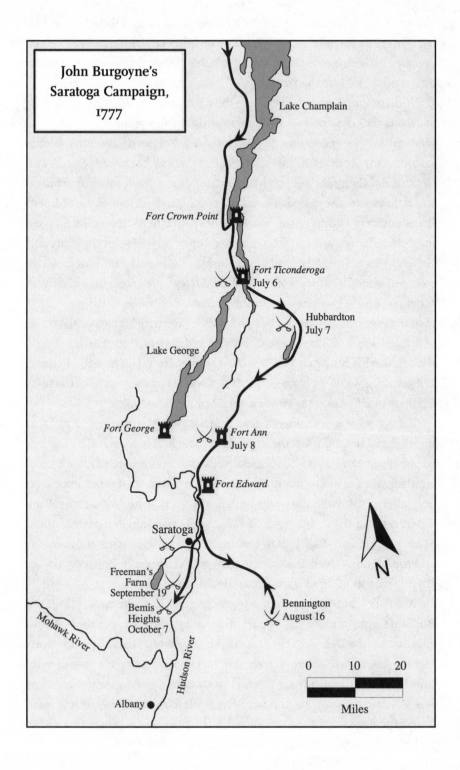

John Burgoyne's
Saratoga Campaign,
1777

Lake Champlain

Fort Crown Point

Fort Ticonderoga
July 6

Hubbardton
July 7

Lake George

Fort George

Fort Ann
July 8

Fort Edward

Saratoga

Freeman's
Farm
September 19

Bemis
Heights
October 7

Bennington
August 16

Mohawk River

Hudson River

Albany

N

0   10   20

Miles

Twenty years earlier, George Howe had trained with Robert Rogers and his rangers in these woods. One of those rangers, John Stark, who had been with George when he fell at Ticonderoga, led a successful attack on one of Burgoyne's detachments, sent on August 16 to secure supplies at Bennington.[136] This marked the beginning of a reversal of Burgoyne's good fortune. He began to sprinkle his letters to Germain with excuses for not withdrawing to the safety of Fort Edward or Fort Ticonderoga, pointing to Germain's positive orders not to turn back as a pretext for forging ahead.

Burgoyne crossed the Hudson River on September 14, a disastrous decision that severed his 200-mile-long supply line from Montreal. He only had sufficient provisions for thirteen days. Several major historians of the war have delivered unsparing verdicts on this ill-fated move, with Piers Mackesy putting it most succinctly: "The choice of Burgoyne was the worst ministerial error of the campaign."[137] It may be that Mackesy's opinion of the flamboyant general was shared by the inner circle of the Howe brothers, for Henry Strachey, always close to the two commanders in chief, declared rather enigmatically to an associate a full year before the catastrophe at Saratoga that Burgoyne was a man "under whose orders no consideration on Earth shall ever induce me to serve."[138] Henry did not consign his reasons to paper.

Led by General Horatio Gates, the rebel troops waiting to meet Burgoyne had been reinforced steadily as New England militiamen poured in. The backwoods inhabitants had been inflamed by Burgoyne's June proclamation, which had threatened to unleash Native American warriors against all who opposed him. Even in Britain, there was an outcry against Burgoyne's enlistment of indigenous allies. All recalled that during the Seven Years' War, Native American fighting techniques had become a byword for barbarity. Burgoyne's army of more than seven thousand men included, in addition to regular soldiers, Native American scouts, German auxiliaries, and French Canadians, giving it the appearance of a foreign invasion in the eyes of the New Englanders.[139]

For the Native American nations themselves, the civil war within the English-speaking colonies imposed a choice between the upstart entity of the United States, and Great Britain. Long-standing and essential trade ties with the latter, as well as the fact that encroachments on Native American lands were typically made by colonists, while protection against those encroachments was typically provided by British authorities, meant that the vast majority of Native fighting men during the war—approximately thirteen thousand in total—fought for the British.[140]

Nevertheless, when Burgoyne crossed the Hudson on September 14, most of his Indian scouts deserted him, leaving his army uncertain of enemy movements in an unfamiliar landscape. The series of conflicts that culminated in Burgoyne's surrender at Saratoga began five days later, after a British foraging party collided with an American patrol. The ensuing Battle of Freeman's Farm, and the Battle of Bemis Heights several weeks later (also called the first and second Battles of Saratoga), convinced Burgoyne of the perilousness of his situation. General Clinton recalled that it was not until the end of September that he received notification from Burgoyne that he required help; even then, his letter did not project a real sense of urgency.[141] Yet Burgoyne's army was outnumbered and hungry, with more than a third of his men unfit for action.

General Gates had nearly twice as many troops as his opponent. At Saratoga on October 12, after grueling intermittent fighting and heavy losses, Burgoyne opened negotiations with Gates. He obtained liberal terms for his surrender, because Gates mistakenly thought reinforcements from General Clinton were coming up the Hudson and were not far away. In fact, they had been blocked from reaching their goal. The melancholy ceremony of surrender took place on October 17. Defeated British troops piled up their weapons as the Americans played "Yankee Doodle."[142] Burgoyne's poor judgment would bring France into the war, transforming it into a worldwide conflict.

Rumors that Burgoyne's army was in danger began arriving in London by late October 1777, and confirmation of the surrender at Saratoga appeared in the press by December 2. A newspaper described the astonishment and gloom on the faces of MPs when Lord George Germain was obliged to report the disaster in the House of Commons.[143] Lady Mary Coke was in town the very next day and recalled hearing "terrible news from Burgoyne." "[T]his is a terrible blow," she wrote without exaggeration, "& has sunk the spirits of the friends to Government."[144]

William's victory at Brandywine was officially announced in London just ten days after the news of Saratoga, but of course it was overshadowed by the disaster of Burgoyne's defeat. Lady Mary bemoaned a rumor that the French had signed a treaty with the Americans.[145] In fact, they had not done so yet, but treaties between France and its new ally, the United States, would be concluded by February 1778. That April, a dozen French warships departed from the French naval base of Toulon for New York, bent upon capturing that city from the British.

With the news of Saratoga in December, the British press went to work apportioning blame among Burgoyne, Germain, and General Howe. Burgoyne was ridiculed for overconfidence and poor judgment and Germain was blamed for incompetence, poor planning, and failure to ensure that the necessary reinforcements reached Burgoyne. For William, the falsehood that had been peddled during the summer—that he had ignored direct orders to join with Burgoyne on the upper Hudson River—resurfaced. Those who did not accuse him of this grave charge nevertheless blamed him for leaving Burgoyne's army in the lurch by being too dilatory during his southern campaign.[146]

The criticism was not confined to the newspapers. Hans Stanley, an MP who, as a relative of the D'Oylys and a friend of Lord and Lady Spencer, moved in the same social circles as the Howe women, wrote an unusually candid letter to a naval officer in America, repeating exactly what people in the metropolis were saying about the commanders in chief in January 1778. There was general agreement, he wrote, that the campaign was poorly planned in London and poorly executed in the field. Burgoyne's backwoods expedition only made sense if the objective was to invade New England; that not being the case, the Canadian army should have simply gone to New York by sea. Instead, Burgoyne undertook a hazardous trek through wilderness and refused to turn back while he still had the chance, foolishly crossing the Hudson to the ruin of his army. The Howes also came in for criticism. It was agreed that Sir William Howe wasted time at the start of the summer trying to tempt General Washington into battle, and that he began his Philadelphia campaign much too late. He lost more time by proceeding with his army to the Chesapeake, instead of landing at the Delaware River.

But what was most damning in Stanley's letter was the widely held belief that William Howe had left New York in July 1777 with the full knowledge that Burgoyne was in trouble and needed help. Stanley regretfully accepted this serious indictment of William's command. "I am sorry to find People are but ill satisfied with the general Superintending of Sir Wm Howe," concluded this friend of the Howes.[147] Falling for the false narrative that William headed south knowing Burgoyne needed assistance, it is no wonder that even some of the Howes' friends felt unable to support the brothers under the weight of the public attacks.

The Howe women had a duty to try to maintain a confident front, but Fanny was visibly affected. When the war began in 1775, she took up the role of the wife of the commander in chief as best she could. After William left for America, she hosted breakfasts for loyalists in London. She sent gifts to William's staff officers.[148] Now, however, she was called upon to play a part that life had not prepared her for. The London mob was notorious for acting out its resentment on military figures who did not deliver victory. Fanny's coach, which sported the Howe coat of arms, was easily recognized. By early January 1778, she only dared to venture out in the mornings, and Lady Mary Coke reported that she "does not go into publick places poor Woman."[149] She was not like Caroline, who had been known to open her window and harangue a crowd that gathered in Grafton Street to abuse Admiral Howe; "[S]he stilled the waves, and they dispersed quietly."[150] It was an unhappy time for Sir William Howe's wife. "Fanny plays [cards] now & then but in a very quiet way," wrote Caroline to Lady Spencer.[151]

As the clouds gathered in January 1778, Caroline strove to keep up appearances. She was busy as usual, attending a party hosted by the Princess Amelia, occupied with the Ladies' Charitable Society, sending news when she could to anxious women with husbands or sons in the service. She was, however, having an ominous run of bad luck at cards. She was off her game. "My bad run seems not inclined to stop yet," she told Lady Spencer. "If I win a little one night I lose double the sum the next." On a visit to Lady Mary Howe in Grafton Street, her poise slipped as three nieces frolicked about her. "I am writing at Lady Howe's, the Brats are turning my Brains, dancing, singing & romping," wrote the normally affectionate aunt.[152]

Perhaps it had been unwise during that month, when feelings in the Howe family were running high, for Caroline to take her mother to the Germain household. But the hospitable Lady Germain had contracted a bad case of the measles, and both the Howe women wished to pay her a bedside visit. When, however, the two of them arrived at the elegant Germain residence in Pall Mall, the sight of Lord George Germain in his own home was too much for the Dowager Lady Howe. She openly accused him of being behind the torrent of media abuse of her sons. The story was relayed with glee in the newspapers, where Lady Howe was reported to have rounded upon Germain, saying that "the abuse originated from his Office; that he must take the consequences when her sons came home; and that upon this occasion, her Ladyship added, that she wished *she* was a man"—a clear allusion to a duel from this German matriarch.[153] Charlotte von Kielmansegg, raised among royalty, had the self-assurance to dispense with etiquette when it suited her. For the last time, she was roused to defend her cubs. There were probably other guests present, and they were the most likely means by which the whole episode entered the rumor mill, and then the newspapers. It is highly unlikely that Caroline would have courted any publicity; her mother was troubled by a heart condition and needed to be sheltered. Tragically, Lady Germain took a turn for the worse and died soon afterward. The Howe women would not be darkening Lord George's door again.

In the last war, the Howe dynasty had been celebrated in the press. Now, however, the newspapers were the destroyers of all peace of mind for the entire family—not only the women at home but also the brothers in America. The media-driven attacks were a major motive behind William's request to return home. On October 22, 1777, he wrote to Lord George Germain from Philadelphia, asking for permission to be relieved of his command. The letter might have referred to the many ways in which the southern campaign had not accomplished what William had hoped; Washington still eluded defeat, the population around Philadelphia was not as active in support of the Crown as he had been led to expect, and opening up the Delaware for British shipping was proving a far more difficult, tedious, and messy task than had been anticipated.[154] It did not mention any of this. Instead, it was a direct response to a letter from Germain dated August 4 and marked "Private." Germain's original letter has not survived among the official correspondence deposited in the Public Record Office in London, and that is perhaps why it is so often assumed that William's request was prompted by rumors of Burgoyne's surrender.[155] Rumors of that disaster were indeed arriving in Philadelphia, but William did not believe them. He thought Burgoyne might have retreated to one of the forts to his rear.[156] That is what he or General Clinton would have done.

A copy of Germain's August 4 letter to William is in the George Sackville Germain Papers at the University of Michigan. It is not very long, just a little over three pages. It opened with platitudes assuring General Howe of his fullest support. The next paragraphs evinced just the opposite, taking a swipe at both brothers for failing to bottle up American privateers. Germain then descended into his notable sarcasm, writing that while General Howe undoubtedly knew best how to wage war, "as the People in this Country cannot all judge of well concerted Military Operations, they are looking for bold & enterprising Measures, & I should be happy in seeing you meet with the Applause & Admiration of the Ignorant, as well as the abler judges of Military Merit."[157] The reference to "the ignorant" who withheld their applause was a snide allusion to the copious gibes against the brothers in the popular press. William could send all the refined excuses he wanted for his inconclusive campaigning, Germain insinuated, but Britain as a whole was looking for clear-cut boldness and enterprise. The American secretary closed with the expectation of imminent good news from the favored Burgoyne.

William was certainly angry when he replied to this letter, reminding Germain that since April he had sent clear warnings that he would be unable materially to assist Burgoyne, and in addition telling him the unwelcome truth that the war would require yet another year's campaigning. But when he went on to request that he be relieved "from this very painful service," he gave as his reasons the fact that, from the start of his command, his advice had been ignored, and his "superiors"—Germain himself—had shown no confidence in his judgment.

For William, in Philadelphia in October 1777, nothing was going as planned. He had not been given the troops he had needed, Pennsylvania had turned from an opportunity to trap Washington into a trap for him and his men, and the news from the upper Hudson was extremely worrying. William knew that if Burgoyne had failed as badly as rumor had it, every commander in America would come under public scrutiny. But the immediate provocation for William's request to be replaced was Germain's sarcastic letter, because by now the brothers were deeply angry about their negative public image, which was spread all over the London news sheets and probably fed by Germain.[158] This was hard to bear, and impossible to combat from a distance, so it was time to go home.

William Howe's first and only service as a British commander in chief ended with a loud demonstration of love and loyalty from his army. This was the famous Mischianza, which was organized by a score of army officers on May 18, 1778, a week before he embarked for Britain. The word *Mischianza* comes from the Italian for "medley," and so it was—a celebration that involved a kaleidoscope of entertainments. The original inspiration for this gala was a fête at Lord Derby's estate of "The Oaks" in Surrey, England, in 1774. The daylong event for Howe involved a regatta along the Delaware River, a medieval joust, musical bands, a ball, and fireworks. Costumes were designed, sets were created, and young ladies from Philadelphia's first families attended, wearing gauze turbans and Turkish outfits. Richard was also present, obliged to pass through a triumphal Doric arch that one might suspect was not much to his taste. The Mischianza was a gesture of loyalty to General Howe that was inspired in reaction to the virulent public attacks on his character and his command. Major John André, the chief organizer, took care that a full account of the event was published in the press at home.[159]

In histories of the American Revolution, the Mischianza has assumed an importance far out of proportion to what it had at the time, because it became a favorite subject in nineteenth-century American fiction and antiquarian histories of the war. Fifty years after independence, the "romantic grandeur" of the British empire could be safely enjoyed in escapist literature written by Americans who had no contemporary memory of the conflict itself. Just as nineteenth-century American tourists in England often looked past the state-of-the-art factories and railroads to see the quaint castles and thatched cottages, so American readers of the same period ignored the fact that both nations were rising powers, each well-established on their own trajectories to full modernization and engaged in a complex competition over the implications of industrialization and economic expansion for manners, lifestyles, and social values.[160] The story of Sir William Howe's Mischianza, an extravaganza that supposedly epitomized the bygone traits of the old mother country, was popular.

In fact, it was customary for departing generals to be treated to a round of farewell parties. The Mischianza was just one example of these, although it was assuredly the grandest.[161] William himself may have had a few qualms about its excesses, for he suppressed the reading of two lengthy tributes to him as general.[162] Although a few in Britain were persuaded that the elaborate send-off reflected well on a general who returned with no overall victory to show, for most it only served to confirm the impression that the army was not doing enough to win the war and was given over to pleasure and amusement.[163] Overall, the British nation was far more preoccupied with the realities of the ongoing conflict.

When the parties were over, William spent several days aboard his brother's flagship, the *Eagle*, taking his leave—for Richard would stay to serve in American waters—and no doubt speculating on the sort of reception he could expect at home.[164] William embarked for England on May 24, 1778. It was said that some of his officers wept as they said their farewells at dockside. A week later, in London—where by now his return was widely anticipated—Lady Mary Coke was a witness to Princess Amelia's fury that the war was going so badly. Such dissatisfaction in royal circles boded ill for Sir William's reception; "Tis a terrible thing to be employ'd in these times," Lady Mary wrote of William Howe with sympathetic understatement.[165]

And at roughly the same time that William was crossing the Atlantic, another whose name is forever linked with his own in the story of his failed command also boarded ship for the mother country. Mrs. Elizabeth Loring must have felt a trepidation that was almost equal to that of General Howe himself at the prospect of what awaited her in England.

Twelve

About Mrs. Loring

William Howe's rakish exploits during his American command are short on detail, with one exception: his relationship with Elizabeth Lloyd Loring. As it is usually told, the story of his affair with Mrs. Loring, a Bostonian whom he met in 1775, showcases the character deficiencies that led, inexorably, to General Howe's failure to end the rebellion. She kept him too busy with her irresistible company to pursue his military duties; she gambled and drank to excess, and she and her husband—for she, like William, was married—were conspicuous for profiting from the gravy train that was supposedly the Howe command in America.

So persistent is the story of General Howe's dalliance with Mrs. Loring that it is mentioned in most accounts of his command, although military historians dismiss the accusation that she had any effect on his conduct of the war. Those who are more inclined to romanticize the American Revolution do not; in Kenneth Roberts's novel *Oliver Wiswell*, published in 1940, she is the reason he underestimated the enemy on Bunker Hill and charged his troops into the murderous rebel fire. Roberts renders her as a mincing flirt who purred at General Howe, "[S]o masterful! There's no resisting you, I vow!" Other, more fantastic works of fiction have carried her influence to unintentionally humorous extremes, suggesting that she was a clandestine agent working for General Washington, a Mata Hari figure who deliberately distracted Howe from his duties, to the destruction of the British war effort.[1] Mrs. Loring's ultra-vamp persona has survived into the twenty-first century, where she emerges vividly in Lora Innes's historical fantasy graphic novel series, *The Dreamer*, as a self-serving adulteress intent on profit and pleasure while her native country bleeds.

Elizabeth is, in fact, the central figure in the transformation of William Howe's identity by his critics and enemies during the War of Independence.

Yet everything she is accused of comes from the pens of men who hated William Howe. She has no genuine voice of her own; not a single letter written by her as an adult has survived. There is an unmistakable element of misogyny in the portrayals of her as a "squeak-voiced, turnip-headed female," a passive object to be handled by men, or a "handsome wife" handed over to William Howe by a husband seeking office. "He fingered the cash, the General enjoyed madam," in the words of one contemporary.[2] Elizabeth Loring surely deserves a closer look in a personal biography of the man reputed to have been Antony to her Cleopatra.

MRS. LORING WAS BORN Elizabeth Lloyd, in October 1752, to a gentrified family that owned a manor house on Long Island. Known today as the Joseph Lloyd Manor, the house still stands in the town of Huntington, and it includes slave quarters behind its main bedrooms on the second floor. Being so close to New York City—one of the largest slave markets in the thirteen colonies—Long Island had a number of affluent slave-owning families like the Lloyds, who are now largely forgotten. When Betsey, as she was known, was eight years old, one of her family's slaves, Jupiter Hammon, achieved the distinction of being the first published black poet in America.

Young Betsey no doubt received the polite education of a girl from a wealthy home. Her sole surviving letter, written at the age of nine to her grandfather Lloyd, asks him to write often to encourage her in her "learning."[3] By then, she was living in the home of her stepfather, Nathaniel Hatch, in Dorchester, Massachusetts. Her own father, Nathaniel Lloyd, drowned when she was an infant.

Almost nothing is known of Betsey Lloyd as a young girl. She was barely seventeen when she married Joshua Loring in 1769. She has been passed down to posterity as a flashing blonde with blue eyes, but somewhere along the way the storytellers ignored her sole portrait, which shows a pleasant-looking woman with brown hair and eyes of uncertain color. Joshua, eight years her senior, had joined the British army as an ensign in 1761, while he was still a teenager, and had served in the Seven Years' War. By the time of his marriage, he had left the army and was a businessman who held several public positions, including as a British customs officer and as surveyor of the King's Woods in New Hampshire. In marrying Elizabeth, he acquired her inheritance, since she was her father's sole child. In 1771, when he served as Comptroller to the Port of Philadelphia, Joshua took his wife with him; other business later took him to New York, New Hampshire, and Canada.[4] Mr. and Mrs. Loring were not provincial yokels who would be overawed by a British official with an aristocratic air.

Elizabeth's father-in-law, Commodore Joshua Loring, had commanded a flotilla on the North American lakes during the Seven Years' War.[5] The Lorings were prosperous, owning a townhouse in Boston and a country seat in nearby Roxbury. And they had standing in the community; in early 1775, Elizabeth's husband was appointed sheriff of Suffolk County, Massachusetts. There were both patriots and loyalists in the extended Loring family, but Elizabeth's father-in-law and her husband sided with the Crown when the fighting started in April 1775.[6]

Elizabeth was in her early twenties when she and her husband took refuge in besieged Boston after the Battle of Lexington and Concord. William Howe arrived in Massachusetts a month later. In both history books and fiction, their affair is presumed to have begun in Boston, but it could not have started before the Battle of Bunker Hill on June 17, as the stories have claimed. When General Howe first entered the city on May 25, Mrs. Loring was four months pregnant with her third child, and hardly in a position to lure him from his duties. And there must have been still more delays before the consummation of their lust, for William was posted on Bunker Hill until September, and Elizabeth did not deliver baby John Wentworth Loring until October 13.[7] How soon after childbirth the mother would be tempted to commit adultery must be left to the reader's imagination. If their affair were to have begun in Boston, as has always been claimed, they had a window of just five months between the arrival of the baby and the British evacuation of the city.

Like many loyalists, Elizabeth and Joshua had to abandon their home and possessions with the outbreak of hostilities. But Joshua had found new opportunities as a refugee in Boston when General Gage appointed him sole auctioneer for the city.[8] In addition, his business, Loring & Company, sold spirits to the British officers and troops. The Lorings then followed the British army from Boston to Halifax in March 1776; in June, they were with the fleet when it departed for New York.

In New York, William appointed Joshua Loring commissary of prisoners, an office that paid twenty shillings a day plus a house and rations. It was an attractive post, particularly during wartime, and it was there that rumors of an affair began. In letters written by the same disgruntled loyalists who had complained of William's gambling and hell-raising, the gossip was quickly conveyed across the ocean to London. Allegedly, Loring's position as commissary was payment for William's access to his wife.

By the spring of 1777, word of the affair with Mrs. Loring began making the rounds as transatlantic gossip. An anonymous letter reported, "[O]ur Commander has been enjoying his pleasures while every thing has been going to wreck in the Jerseys," gambling alongside his "favourite sultana," the "Boston Lady" who three years earlier was penniless but now lost at cards at the rate of three hundred guineas a night with the utmost complacency. Her husband, the letter-writer added, had also grown rich and "looks fat and contented."[9] Two months later, the *Pennsylvania Evening Post* waxed poetic about the image of Sir William with his mistress on his arm, viewing his troops on parade:

> Without wit, without wisdom, half stupid and drunk,
> And rolling along arm in arm with his punk,
> The gallant Sir William, who fights all by proxy,
> Thus spoke to his soldiers, held up by his doxy. . . .[10]

Even without the newspapers, the Howe women knew the story during that worrying spring, when news from America was first beginning to go against the brothers. Jane Strachey learned of it at the home of her cousin Lady Clive in Berkeley Square, where a vociferous guest called across the crowded drawing room to tell her of an "affair of gallantry of a certain married man now in America." Jane tried to look unconcerned, replying before all the listening company that, with his wife an ocean away, General Howe was "much in the right to console himself." In an age of double standards, she tried to cast Sir William's indiscretion in a sympathetic light. But she sent her husband a warning: "[A]s all Wives are not liberal in their sentiments on these subjects it is not amiss to tell you that such stories as these do not lose by the distance that they are carried."[11]

That year, as the gossip intensified, Mrs. Loring became an oft-cited reason for the sluggish start to General Howe's campaign. An English newspaper jibed:

Awake, arouse, Sir Billy,
There's forage in the plain.
Ah, leave your little filly
And open the campaign.[12]

The story began gaining traction. In July 1777, William's troops supposedly sweltered aboard ship for two weeks before departing for Philadelphia because Sir William was dallying in New York with the captivating
Bostonian. It was even said that his controversial decision to go to Pennsylvania by sea was for the convenience of his mistress, who was pregnant
and required "the benefit of sea-air." By the end of the war, the mushroom-
ing scandal had retrospectively placed Mrs. Loring in bed with William in
March 1776, when the American cannon on Dorchester Heights forced the
British evacuation of Boston.[13]

The catch in all this is that the story of the Loring affair was probably
not true. A few historians have noted that there is a dearth of evidence for
an intimate relationship.[14] What makes it still more implausible is that Elizabeth Loring was the niece of a man William Howe regarded as a personal
friend. When he arrived in Boston in May 1775, it was not Betsey's blue eyes
that drew him to her; he already knew the Lloyds and the Lorings.

Elizabeth Loring's uncle, James Lloyd, had saved William Howe's life
seventeen years earlier. Lloyd, an eminent Massachusetts physician who had
trained in London hospitals, was a surgeon at the garrison of Castle William
in Boston in 1758. When William's regiment arrived there after the grueling siege at Louisbourg, William, still reeling from the death of his brother
George Lord Howe, fell dangerously ill. In later years, he always felt a debt of
gratitude toward Dr. Lloyd, to whose care he believed he owed his recovery.
At the siege of Havana in 1762, William met and befriended Joshua Loring
Jr., whose family was connected to the Massachusetts Lloyds. It was natural, then, that thirteen years later, in 1775, William Howe sought out his old
friends Dr. Lloyd and Joshua Loring as soon as he reached Boston.[15] This
was the means by which he was introduced to twenty-two-year-old Betsey.

Set against the unlikely proposition that General Howe would choose as
his mistress the wife of his former comrade-in-arms, and the niece of the
doctor who saved his life, is the alternative narrative, held out by purvey-
ors of gossip since 1777. The story has always gone that the arrangement

between General Howe and the Lorings followed the stereotype of an officer of high rank awarding a post of profit to a compliant husband. There
were other examples of this during the war. General Clinton took Mary
Baddeley as a mistress while he was in America. Mrs. Baddeley was the
daughter of an Irish country gentleman who had married a lowly carpenter and was consequently rejected by her family. The carpenter became a
foot soldier, then worked his way up to sergeant major, stationed at Boston.
There he was demoted, rumor had it, because he would not allow his commanding officer to make free with Mary. Clinton took an interest in the
man's misfortune, and Mary became Clinton's housekeeper. In time, she
became his mistress, and her husband benefited.[16] General Burgoyne also
took with him a mistress, the wife of a subordinate officer, on his ill-fated
march to Saratoga. Throughout the campaign, the nature of their relationship was plain for all to see. Just before Saratoga, Burgoyne was described
by a critical onlooker as making merry with his mistress, eating and drinking.[17] The tale of William Howe and Mrs. Loring, then, seemed to fit easily
into the established cliché.

But the Lorings occupied a higher social sphere than the mistresses of
Burgoyne and Clinton. Joshua Loring was a logical choice for William to
appoint as commissary of prisoners in New York, a man of business who
had held other public positions before the war. And whatever their relationship, Elizabeth Loring certainly did not live openly with William Howe, as
did the mistresses of Burgoyne and Clinton. William's household in New
York included no women at all, not even among the servants.[18] While William resided in New York, the Lorings lived in a house near Harlem. They
were not poor or needy: Joshua's few surviving letters indicate that the family retained the services of enslaved servants during the British occupation.
His letters to his wife are caring and affectionate, referring to her virtues
as a mother and giving no idea of a disturbance in their relationship. Nor is
there any evidence that Elizabeth Loring went to Philadelphia with General
Howe. Malicious contemporary gossip was contradictory, claiming simultaneously that she followed her military lover to Pennsylvania and that she
was left behind in New York while William found himself a new mistress
(or even two) in Philadelphia.[19]

There is yet another reason why William Howe would have been throwing caution to the winds by taking up with Mrs. Loring: She had a connection, albeit a slender one, with his wife's social circle at home in London.

His prewar post in New Hampshire had placed Joshua Loring in the service of Governor John Wentworth, who had formerly lived in England and knew Fanny Howe's uncle, the Earl of Strafford. Wentworth and his wife Frances arrived in Boston in August 1775, escaping from patriot activists in New Hampshire. While in the besieged town, they would certainly have mixed socially with both William Howe and the Lorings. Joshua and Elizabeth would shortly name their newborn son John Wentworth Loring, after Joshua's honorable patron, the New Hampshire governor. The governor's wife, Mrs. Wentworth, was in London by 1776, where she associated with Fanny Howe.[20] The Lorings, then, stood a real chance of being introduced to Fanny and other members of the Howe family if they had taken refuge in London. If they were not aristocrats, they occupied a social rank similar to that of the Stracheys.

Elizabeth Loring left for England as a loyalist refugee in 1778, the same year that Sir William Howe returned home. She settled with her children in the English countryside in Reading, Berkshire. Joshua continued as commissary of prisoners for the remainder of the war. After the peace, he was reunited with his wife in Berkshire, where they had three more children. When Joshua died in 1789, Elizabeth received a government pension until her death in 1835.

There is no evidence that Elizabeth and William had any contact with each other after they returned to Britain. Her four sons went on to serve in the army and the navy, and in one case the church. Notable was John Wentworth Loring, who gained a knighthood and became an admiral.[21] It may be that the Howe patronage can be detected in the successful careers of the Loring boys, but nothing particularly suggestive can be read into that, even should it be true. In later years, there was no evidence that Elizabeth was treated like a woman of notoriety. Wealthy young New Yorker John Aspinwall, great-grandfather of Franklin Delano Roosevelt and a relative of the Lorings, seemed to think it no indiscretion to meet his cousin, Mrs. Loring's daughter, during a tour of England in the 1790s, merely commenting that she "Plays very well on the Grand Piano fort." After Elizabeth's death, a "Sacred to the Memory" plaque enumerated her virtues as an affectionate wife and mother.[22]

But false reports can take wings even with an ocean to cross. The story that Sir William Howe was too busy in bed with Elizabeth Loring to fight the enemy reached its peak in the British press in early 1778. "We hear that a great General's first *Sultana*," announced the *Public Advertiser*, "is an American Lady, whom he *bought of her Husband* for a *Contract.*—Alas! poor Old England, how thou art reduced! who must not only pay the *Piper*, but pay for *pimping!*"[23]

Two months later, in March, a letter purporting to be from a gentleman in New York to a private correspondent was printed and distributed as a handbill to members of Parliament. It pointed the finger at General Howe's alleged illicit affair as a cause of his dereliction of duty.[24] The scandal as peddled in the newspapers was eagerly consumed by the reading public, but the handbill itself seems to have made no impression on the august assembly that it targeted. The charge was absurd: Taking a mistress was prevalent in the army, and it had never before been cited as an impediment to valor in the field. In any case, the Mrs. Loring story was not much of a scandal to members of a political elite that included the Duke of Grafton and the husband of Lady Sarah Bunbury. General Howe was married, unlike widowers Burgoyne and Clinton, but even so, the notion that a man should find consolation elsewhere (as Jane Strachey expressed it) while separated from his wife by an ocean was not likely to shock England's Georgian aristocracy.

The Howe women showed no sign of believing the story. Fanny welcomed William home with tender solicitude, and the Conollys showed no lessening of loyalty. The Stracheys, who can be regarded as a barometer of the mood in the Howe family during the war years, also did not believe it. After her embarrassing exposure to the rumor in her cousin's drawing room, Jane Strachey appeared to dismiss the whole business, writing indignantly to Henry that "I cannot express to you how much I am provoked at such repeated illiberal low attempts to soil a great Character." Henry himself directly contradicted the reports. "The News Papers . . . as unjustly accuse [Lord Howe] of Avarice, as I trust they do his Brother of criminal Gallantries." Writing of the hospitality that the two commanders in chief were obliged to lay on during the winter of 1777–78, Henry said that both the brothers had hosted balls and parties, but that with respect to Sir William, "I never have seen even the smallest Symptom of that sort of Gallantry which your scandalous News Papers attribute to him."[25]

The tale of General Howe and Mrs. Loring appears to have been a middle-class preoccupation. It probably was an invention of New York loyalists angry at a war that was supposed to have ended in 1776 but was bungled and mismanaged, so they believed, by the same class of self-serving and decadent aristocrats who had almost lost the last war in the botched campaigns of 1757 and 1758. American loyalists, while not republicans, shared the anxiety of the middling ranks in eighteenth-century Britain and America that the aristocracy were questionable trustees of a nation's interests. As we have seen, this same concern had become conspicuous early in the Seven Years' War, when the war effort seemed to founder. And the longer the American War of Independence dragged on, the more such issues grated on the sensibilities of unhappy civilians. The story of Sir William Howe and Mrs. Loring was an important element in the transformation of William from an active and daring young officer to the stereotypical wealthy, decadent court aristocrat with a penchant for ease and luxury. The fatal flaw in the hero who had scaled the heights of Abraham for General Wolfe twenty years earlier was not cowardice—it was lasciviousness. Such a person could not win Britain's wars for her.

As in the last war, indictments of the commander in chief's character were made in heavily gendered terms. He was emasculated by the intrusion of the voluptuous Mrs. Loring into his camp and his bed. Her malign influence was frequently couched in terms of drink, indolence, and sleep, making William Howe a Samson who lost his virility to his American Delilah.

Elizabeth Loring, who never uttered a word on her own behalf, became the focus as angry critics of William Howe attacked him in terms that reflected ingrained misogynistic attitudes. One of the most frequently quoted sources on the alleged affair remains the *History of New York during the Revolutionary War*, written by Judge Thomas Jones, an embittered loyalist. Jones left New York as a refugee in 1781, never to return, and died in England in 1792. His colorful and highly partisan narrative of the American Revolution, in which he seeks to allocate blame for a military defeat that blighted his life, was written during his exile. The manuscript remained in the family until it was published in 1879. Judge Jones's descendants explained, understandably, that they did not wish to make it available to the public until all persons connected with the narrative and their immediate descendants were dead.[26] Its publication ensured that the story of Mrs. Loring and General Howe would live on.

Yet if the Loring affair was pure fantasy, what are we to make of William Howe's remark to the famous diarist James Boswell at a party in London in May 1779, less than a year after he returned from America? "We talked of Married Men," recalled the Scotsman. "The General said he thought a husband quite constant must be a cold companion not worth having, and the best is one who, after being away a while, likes his Wife better than any other woman."[27] William's suggestion—that a happily married virile man will naturally find alternative companionship while separated from his wife—was in keeping with the double standards of the day. The fact that he volunteered such a remark to Boswell at a time when he was aware of what people were saying about him smacks of a guilty conscience.

If William's remark did betray a consciousness of genuine guilt, it was not on behalf of Elizabeth Loring. There is another, more intriguing possibility: a story, little known at the time and almost forgotten now, concerning Judith Verplanck, the wife of a prominent patriot, whose Wall Street mansion was a salon for redcoats during the British occupation of New York. The Dutch Verplanck family arrived in America in the seventeenth century, when New York was still New Amsterdam, and became prosperous merchants and landowners. The historic family homestead, Mount Gulian, in the Hudson Valley, remains open to visitors. The family's in-town residence at 3 Wall Street no longer exists, but New York's Metropolitan Museum of Art has the Verplanck Room, an installation that re-creates a pre-Revolutionary New York City drawing room. Here are assembled the furnishings and many of the objects that once graced the elegant parlor of the Verplanck townhouse. William must have known well the mahogany Chippendale card table, the rococo silver tea set from London, and the high-backed sofa, for the residence was a favorite gathering place for British officers.[28]

Judith Verplanck was a loyal supporter of King George, but her husband, Samuel Verplanck, supported the rebellion. Throughout the war, he resided at their country estate in Fishkill, far up the Hudson River. The Verplancks, like many well-to-do Americans, did not want to lose their property, whichever side won, and it has been suggested that the husband and wife split up at the start of hostilities to ensure a foothold in both camps. But there was more to it than this, for Judith and Samuel continued to live separate lives after the peace. Judith remained in the Wall Street house until her death in 1803. Perhaps Samuel was not pleased that his wife went well beyond the minimal requirements of neutrality, offering liberal hospitality to high-ranking redcoat officers, notably Sir William Howe.[29]

Like all the Howe men, William enjoyed the company of clever women, and he would find much to attract him in the company of Judith Verplanck. Born Judith Crommelin in Amsterdam, the daughter of a wealthy banker, she was well educated, urbane, and celebrated for her brilliant conversation. Like Caroline Howe, she was also well-read and versed in several languages. Judith had taken the tour of Europe after marrying her cousin Samuel Verplanck, a New York merchant and banker, and by 1763, she had settled down with him in New York.

When Judith and William Howe met, she was in her mid-thirties. No portrait survives, but she was described even in old age as "a lively little lady, often seen walking up Wall Street, dressed in pink satin and in dainty high heeled shoes, with a quaint jewelled watch swinging from her waist." She sounds rather like Lady Mary Howe as Gainsborough painted her. Judith's grandson recalled that, when dressed for formal occasions, she powdered her hair and wore diamond earrings, and she was both formidable and comforting, teaching him to declaim in Latin while rewarding him with hot pound cake.[30] If we imagine Judith in her silk gown seated among the tea things and the pretty, polished Queen Anne–style furniture in the Metropolitan Museum of Art's Verplanck Room, the light of the candles bringing out the warmth of the damask chair coverings and the gilt-framed mirror, it is easy to see why William Howe should have chosen to visit the house on Wall Street so often that he is always described as her particular friend.

And, in a quiet way, the rumor that there was something more between them has also persisted. No contemporary newspaper ever took up the story, no scandalous gossip was ever committed to letter. William Howe would be discreet when a lady's reputation was at stake. She would have been no mistress, but his lover. After he returned to England, though, he was moved to send her gifts that some might have thought entailed a certain risk of exposure. In the museum's reconstructed Verplanck parlor, a single teacup survives from an elegant French porcelain service decorated with blue cornflowers and gold bands—a present from William. But more striking are two paintings in the style of the artist Angelica Kauffmann. *The Temptation of Eros* depicts a mischievous Cupid urging his suit on a rosy young lady. *The Victory of Eros* shows the young lady, disheveled, grasping after the departing Cupid, who leaves with a knowing smirk. These telltale pictures still reside in the heart of Judith Verplanck's drawing room, yet she has virtually disappeared from the drama of William's personal War of Independence, while the story of Mrs. Loring goes on and on.

The Temptation of Eros and *The Victory of Eros*. Gifts of William Howe to Judith Verplanck.

By the end of 1777, a fully developed narrative of William Howe's career as commander in chief in America had emerged, and its basic features have persisted to this day. William lied to his constituents in Nottingham in the election of 1774, promising not to serve in America and then, within a few months, breaking that promise. His ponderous conduct of the war reflected at the least profound character and professional flaws, and, at the worst, a conspiratorial ambition to promote the Howes and their quest to save the empire. He held back from delivering a decisive blow to Washington's army at Brooklyn. He chose not to attack

Washington at White Plains. Despite having superior forces by land and sea, he dragged the war out over two campaigns, inflicting relatively little damage on the Americans and leaving General Burgoyne in the lurch.[31] His alleged affair with Mrs. Loring testified to his corruption, his indolence, his incompetence, or all three.

When we contrast the real man with the distorted image of him created during the conflict, it is not too much to say that the American War of Independence robbed William Howe of his identity. The picture of a decadent English aristocrat who was wedded to hidebound military tactics and underestimated Yankee wilderness warcraft would become prevalent in popular narratives of the American Revolution. It was by means of such a caricature that General Howe, commander in chief of the British war effort, would be transformed into a foreigner in the eyes of Americans.

That is the paradox: William Howe, like his brother George Lord Howe, was the type of an eighteenth-century Anglo-American fighting man. In his knowledge and experience of wilderness warfare, his leadership abilities, and his willingness to accept hardship with his men, he had much in common with his adversary, General Washington. In fact, the two are often compared in histories of the war. Both were tall, of a similar age, and both had polished manners and pleasant bearings. Both men served with distinction in the Seven Years' War—both were known to be fearless in the face of enemy fire—and historians, unaware that William took a bullet at Belle-Île, have asserted that both got through their military service without so much as a scratch.[32]

Besides outward traits, there were other similarities. William, like Washington, was a foxhunting country gentleman, a product of the rural aristocracy and gentry rather than the court and the West End. Both he and Washington had only a limited formal education. They were pragmatic men, rather than speculative thinkers. Both had quick tempers. Both had endured grueling hardships in the Seven Years' War. And in 1775, neither had had experience as a commander in chief. On this last count, each had experienced a degree of self-doubt at the start of the war.[33] After the war, a Philadelphia woman recalled: "Sir William Howe was a fine figure, full six feet high, and well proportioned—in appearance not unlike his antagonist, General Washington. His manners were graceful and dignified, and he was much beloved by his officers, for his generosity and affability."[34]

Ironically, William was actually more egalitarian in manner with his men than was Washington, who was transformed into almost a regal figure as the rebellious Americans discarded their king. This fits with the William who had grown up in a large, boisterous family in the English countryside, down-to-earth and careless of personal comfort, self-contained and convivial by turns. He had fought for king and country to the best of his ability, his fighting spirit quickened by the loss of his brother—in sum, he was the eighteenth-century ideal of an English army officer.

Thirteen

Survival

The Howe brothers returned to England determined to counter the chorus of criticism that had sprung up during their absence, but they would face a maddening mixture of gossip, anonymous press scribblings, and political maneuvering. They needed actions, not words, to redeem themselves. Within a year of their return, they would demand, and receive, a parliamentary inquiry into their command, but it was Richard Howe's naval exploits that would restore the luster of the Howe name.

William was back in England by the summer of 1778. Lady Mary Coke got word of his return on July 2, the day he reached London. "Sir William Howe . . . has been with his Majesty & I hope graciously received for I cannot believe he has been to blame," she wrote.[1] Unfortunately, Lady Mary's opinion was not shared by the majority. Nisbet Balfour, back in London later that year, lamented that his former commander in chief's enemies "have so far succeeded, as to make the world lay it down as a first principle of their faith that he is guilty of something."[2] Friends were rallying to his defense, but the British nation was not accustomed to failure, and William Howe could not escape from this debacle with his reputation intact.

William met with Lord George Germain at his Pall Mall residence soon after his return. The visit was a matter of form, which neither man could possibly have relished. On the same day William appeared at court, and afterward had a private audience with the king. George III sent Lord North a brief account of what had occurred between them. General Howe, he said, had given assurances that neither he nor his brother the admiral would join the political opposition, but since Germain and his secretaries had vilified him, "he must therefore be allowed some means of justifying himself."

At the same meeting, William strongly disapproved of the government's plan for a military expedition to the French possession of St. Lucia in the Caribbean. General Clinton, now commander in chief in America, had been ordered to detach five thousand men for the attack on the island. Since France had entered the war in February 1778, Britain was concentrating her forces on the old enemy, and the war in mainland America must take second place. Clinton had also received orders to withdraw from Philadelphia to New York. So determined were ministers to focus on the new theater of war in the Caribbean that they instructed Clinton that he could even abandon New York and retreat to Halifax if he thought it safer.[3] William could not be silent as he saw his army put to such a purpose. "[T]here is not so fine an army in the world as the troops in America," he told the king, adding that the expedition to St. Lucia would succeed, "but end in the destruction of the troops."[4]

The attack on St. Lucia was Germain's idea; perhaps that was what he and William had discussed—or, rather, argued about—when they had met earlier that day. Tragically, William's prediction that it would end badly for the soldiers who had once served under him was vindicated. The British army would indeed capture St. Lucia by the end of 1778. But the mortality rates for troops serving in the fever-ridden Caribbean—as William knew from personal experience—were so great that about half the men he had commanded in Pennsylvania in 1777–78 were destined to perish within eighteen months of their arrival on the island.[5]

William, however, was no longer commander in chief. The only task before him now was defending his own honor. A government undersecretary observed that the Howes did not seek to receive thanks so much as to have their names cleared.[6] To do this, William required some sort of public gesture. Lord Clarendon, who had worked to obtain Richard's appointment as peace commissioner in 1776, once again intervened on behalf of the brothers. He wrote to Lord North just ten days after William's interview with the king, suggesting that since the Howe brothers were both going to withdraw from the war, a tangible mark of royal favor would be appropriate—a peerage, a pension, a peacetime post of some kind.[7] Such recognition was routine upon retirement, and it could be taken as evidence that, in the circles where it mattered, the service of the brothers in America was approved.

That summer of 1778, William dutifully showed his face. He attended military camps, he appeared at a royal drawing room at St. James's Palace, he was at the Nottingham Races and added a silver cup to the annual sweepstakes.[8] He wrote to brother-in-law Tom Conolly from Marble Hill

House outside of London, where he and Fanny were staying. "I am in an odd state here," he said, "most graciously received by ye K___& still censured in ye Ministerial Paper, or Morning Post." There was a kind of forced heartiness in the letter; William must have been quite worn out. He congratulated Tom on his recent winnings at Almack's, the exclusive gambling club in Pall Mall, and asked about his horses and hounds, adding, "I find Fanny in charming health."⁹

Fanny was delighted to have her William home again. "It is pleasant to think of her, poor soul," wrote Louisa Conolly that summer. "I do, continually, because I saw her in all her distress" while William was overseas.¹⁰ Yet Fanny was destined to have her nerves wracked a little longer. No sooner was William restored to his family than he was ill with an abscess in his back. In the days before antibiotics, such infections could be fatal.

Caroline had been spending the month of August as usual with Aunt Juliana Page at Battlesden when she learned that her brother was unwell. "[P]oor William," she wrote to Lady Spencer, "we heard yesterday has been very bad indeed." The abscess would have to be opened. Caroline decamped to Marble Hill the very next day, when William was scheduled to go under the surgeon's knife. Adopting a matter-of-fact tone, she pronounced her brother out of danger forty-eight hours later.¹¹ Despite her protestations that the crisis was over, her handwriting was a nervous scrawl, a testimony to an uncharacteristically overwrought state of mind.

William, however, was in a great deal of pain, confined to a couch while the wound healed. Caroline used this as an excuse to remain at Marble Hill, helping to amuse her younger brother. "At present I am wanted here as a nurse, as I am constantly with him now he's so well," she explained. Soon, their mother Charlotte arrived to contribute her own forthright brand of maternal solicitude for "the *dear Savage*," as Fanny called him.¹² For two weeks, the former commander in chief's world narrowed down to feather beds, familiar faces, and a comfortable room or two. Marble Hill House, with its trim lawns, fine trees, and spacious classical interiors, was a perfect place to convalesce. Given the circumstances, perhaps illness was a welcome relief.

The Howes concealed William's ill health from the outside world. Lady Mary Coke seemed entirely unaware of it when she saw five of them, including William, at a party in the home of Lady Blandford in early September. She declared, "'Tis the first time I've seen Sir William Howe, I think he looks well, he told me we might expect to hear from his Brother Ld. Howe every day."[13] William's disappearance from the public sphere, however, was quickly noticed by his detractors in the press. General Howe was passing his time resting and relaxing near Richmond, as *"unknowing* and *unknown"* to the fashionable and political world as if he had been sent to America to bring home "a Cargo of Yankee *Potatoes,* instead of *British Laurels,"* jeered one.[14] William, it seemed, was continually caught idling. Even when he was quietly ill, he could not escape negative publicity.

What of the war? The British now faced their global enemy, France, allied with the American colonies in a war likely to spread to the Caribbean, Africa, and Asia. At Christmastime in 1777, the North administration had made strenuous efforts to avert a Franco-American alliance. Lord North had sent feelers to Benjamin Franklin in Paris to see whether there might be some way to achieve an immediate peace with America that still preserved a connection with Britain. But it was too late for that; the rebellion's leaders had independence firmly in their sights.

Now North moved to offer the terms that Richard had sought when he had agreed to act as peace commissioner in 1776. On February 17, 1778, North presented a shocked House of Commons with a bill for a new peace commission, which would be empowered to negotiate directly with the Continental Congress and suspend hostilities. Parliament would renounce its right to tax the colonies for revenue, retaining only the power to impose taxes to regulate trade. The principle of parliamentary sovereignty would be relaxed, and the colonies would be assured greater autonomy in the conduct of their internal affairs. With these concessions, Britain in effect would choose regulation of America's trade over taxation—an idea mooted by Franklin and others at the start of the conflict but rejected by British statesmen in 1775.[15]

Upon hearing the details of this spectacular U-turn, the House of Commons was stunned. MPs listened attentively, but "[a] dull melancholy silence for sometime succeeded to this speech." To the astonished assembly, Lord North declared that "the sentiments he expressed that day, had been those which he had always entertained." When pro-government MPs spluttered that the bill reversed everything the nation had been fighting for over the previous three years, they were informed that the war had been not for revenue but rather to crush the spirit of independence.[16]

North's new legislation passed nevertheless. War with France was popular in a way that the conflict in America had never been. The newspapers screamed that defeating the French in Europe and the West Indies was now the route to ending the American insurgency. A few months later, in June, Lady Mary Coke gleefully reported the first Anglo-French engagement in the English Channel. The French had been bested in the brief exchange. "[W]e are all rejoiced at the news," she wrote stoutly, trusting that the treacherous French now would be made to repent for their "insolent conduct."[17]

The new peace commission, called the Carlisle Commission for its head, Frederick Howard, 5th Earl of Carlisle, left England in mid-April and reached Philadelphia by June 6. Unbeknownst to them, however, Lord North had very quickly lost interest in his peace project. His communications with Benjamin Franklin had convinced him that it was almost certain to fail.[18] Upon their arrival, the commissioners were both shocked and angry to learn that the British army, adopting a defensive stance in America, was evacuating Philadelphia. Their peace mission had been fatally undermined while they were en route to America.

Both Howe brothers were named to the commission, but William had departed for England two weeks before Carlisle and his delegates had even arrived. And it was understood that Richard also wished to return home. Indeed, Lady Howe had already written on his behalf to Lord Sandwich, citing concerns over his health. It was no surprise, then, when the admiral declined to serve with the new peace delegation. Richard's leave was granted, pending the arrival of his replacement, Vice Admiral John Byron.[19]

Meanwhile, however, Richard remained on active duty in America. Philadelphia was evacuated in June, with military equipment and loyalists going by sea while the British army returned to New York overland. The redcoat army, marching in the heat with wagons, artillery, and loyalist refugees, was harassed constantly by a skulking enemy, a campaign of attrition that reached a head on June 28 in an inconclusive clash known as the Battle of Monmouth Courthouse. If Clinton had done well to retreat overland without losing any military baggage, his troops were of a different mind. When they reached their point of embarkation for New York at the end of their arduous march, they sighted Admiral Lord Howe's ships off the coast of New Jersey. The weary soldiers gave a spontaneous cry of "a Howe! a Howe!—we see one of the Howes again!" a vote of confidence in the brothers that was hardly music to Clinton's ears.[20]

On June 29, while his fleet was off the New Jersey coast, Richard met a packet ship carrying the news that a squadron of seventeen ships under the command of the French Vice Admiral Charles-Hector, Count D'Estaing, was expected imminently. The packet commander had sighted the fleet at sea and been chased for three days before losing his pursuers.

Up to this point, the British had fought the war in America without fear of danger from the sea. Yankee privateers were an annoyance, but not a serious threat. Now all was changed. The strange new alliance of revolutionary America and despotic France, adversaries in the last war, would try to trap the British army by attacking simultaneously from land and sea. The war would effectively end with the British surrender at Yorktown, in 1781, as a result of the successful execution of this strategy.

Now, in the summer of 1778, British commanders feared for the safety of their position in New York. Reinforcements from home under Vice Admiral Byron were expected, but they had not yet arrived when Richard and General Clinton began making defensive preparations. Rear Admiral James Gambier, sent out by Lord Sandwich, was considered to be incompetent, so he was appointed port captain in New York in order to remove him quietly from operations. Richard was needed.

Between July 8 and 10, it became apparent that D'Estaing's objective was the British base at Newport, Rhode Island. Units of the Continental Army were also marshaling for a land-based attack on that garrison.[21] D'Estaing kept Howe and Clinton guessing for several more weeks, as he appeared to switch among objectives. Now it was New York; now it seemed to be Newport again; now he headed out to sea, destined for who knew where? At the end of July, word reached Richard that Admiral Byron and the crucial reinforcements had been held up by bad weather.[22] The situation was looking desperate; the French had superior firepower, and Admiral Howe needed Byron's ships.

In mid-September, a captain carrying official dispatches for Lord Howe called on Caroline in Grafton Street with news of D'Estaing's maneuvers. The detailed intelligence that she passed on to Lady Spencer shows how closely the Howe women followed the military operations of their men. D'Estaing had left his station off Sandy Hook in New York on July 22, Caroline wrote; three days later, he was sighted off the Delaware River. Meanwhile, four warships from Byron's scattered fleet had reached New York, and the captain informed her that he had learned of six more warships during his Atlantic crossing. Caroline rejoiced that D'Estaing had abandoned his station at Sandy Hook, leaving the way open for the delayed warships to "get safe to Lord Howe," and "if they do arrive safe, they will make my Brother strong enough to face D'Estaing if he dare return."[23]

On July 29, D'Estaing's squadron dared to return, appearing off Newport. Ten days later, several thousand American troops began to surround the British positions. The redcoat garrison prepared for a siege. Meanwhile, Richard faced adverse winds that prevented him from quickly reaching Rhode Island from New York. Howe's squadron finally arrived off Newport on August 9. D'Estaing put to sea and prepared to confront the enemy.

In this age of wooden ships, it was not until August 12 that the opposing fleets managed to form their battle lines. Then, at four in the morning, a series of severe thunderstorms hit the fleets. Hours later, after the storms cleared, the damage was revealed. The French flagship *Languedoc*—with eighty cannon, the most powerful vessel in the fray—was dismasted, crippled in the tossing sea. The French had seemingly fared worse than their foe, and their earlier eagerness for battle was extinguished. While the French tried to avoid action, the British fleet held a different opinion; a sporadic and very disorganized battle began as the dispersed fleets encountered each other.

Nisbet Balfour—who had been promoted to lieutenant colonel eight months earlier—was present at the naval battle, along with his 23rd regiment. The British navy had recruited soldiers to serve as marines on their ships because of the desperate shortage of manpower in America. Balfour's musket-wielding fusiliers were obliged to learn to climb rigging and man the "tops," large platforms on the upper masts where they could act as snipers. When it became obvious on that day that the enemy had had enough and was heading out to sea, the British soldiers set up a war whoop in imitation of the Indian victory cries they had heard in America.[24]

Although naval maneuvers between the two opposing fleets continued along the coast over the next week, the French threat to Newport had been driven off. Without D'Estaing's ships as backup, the Americans were soon obliged to abandon their siege of Newport—to their disgust, for they had expected much from the French. The new allies, however, had not yet learned to work together effectively.[25] Richard, ever skillful and competent, had averted a damaging and embarrassing defeat.

With the enemy still near, Richard continued his diligent defensive

operations off the American coast throughout August. Meanwhile, Britain
waited impatiently for news; there was hope that Admiral Howe would
destroy the French fleet. But the British people would have to wait until
October for reports of the storm-tossed battle off Newport. As usual, Caroline sent Lady Spencer the details. Her brother had not been on his flagship during the action, she told her friend. He had supervised from a
frigate, which was almost crippled in the encounter: "[I]n the Storm that
parted the two fleets when they were only 3 miles asunder & preparing to
engage, my brother was on board a frigate reconnoitre-ing & giving orders,
she lost all her masts, we understand he is now at Rhode Island, & D'Estaing refitting at Boston."[26]

On September 26, Richard transferred his command to Vice Admiral
Byron and headed for England, making landfall on October 25. "We are
all half wild," wrote Caroline to her friend, "& you I am sure will sincerely
rejoice with us." Lady Howe had left home immediately to be reunited with
Lord Howe at Portsmouth. "[W]hat a difference has a few weeks made in
her feelings!"[27]

Richard remained in Portsmouth for five days, awaiting permission to
strike his flag. Once ashore, his first destination was Heckfield Park in
Hampshire, the Pitts residence. It was a family gathering; in addition to his
wife and his sister Mary and her husband, William and Julie were there.
His three daughters, Charlotte, Mary, and Louisa, were to be ferried by
their Aunt Caroline to Porter's Lodge, where they would see their father
again after a separation of more than two years. The youngest, Louisa, who
was only eleven, indulged her Aunt Caroline with a flight of fancy. "Little
Louisa t'other day talking of her father, said to me I know what he will say
with my mamma, 'what' says I. That he is very much grieved she has not
got a little boy ready for him, & that he shall only find the 3 girls he left. I
thought I shd. have fallen off my chair with laughing."[28]

Richard had defied etiquette by failing to proceed directly to London
to be received by the king, but Caroline was instructed to deflect curiosity by giving out that "Ld Howe was *not very well & a little fatigued with his
voyage.*"[29] Just a week later, Richard was graciously received at a royal levee,
and Caroline was soon back in Grafton Street, still rejoicing in her brother's safe return. "He is thinner but vastly well," she wrote, "his reception
at court has been of course gracious, but I believe nothing talked over." In
fact, the Howes were dissatisfied with William's treatment. "How it will

all end I cannot guess," Caroline continued. Both her brothers remained out of town until the opening of Parliament. "I fancy it will be a thorough bustling Sessions."[30]

"Thorough bustling Sessions" was an understatement. Much had changed since Richard had last trod upon English soil. Britain now feared a French invasion and, as ever, all eyes were on the Channel Fleet as the first line of defense. Military camps were being set up to protect England's principal naval bases and block any attempted enemy advance on London. Secret plans were made for a scorched-earth policy in the event of a French landing.[31]

Meanwhile, the British public was extracting some fun from the situation. The new military camps were an attraction. Crowds of visitors arrived to watch the troops review in a fairground atmosphere. Stalls and refreshments catered to the throng, musical comedies offered light-hearted takes on life in the camps, sham fights were put on, and the whole business helped to stoke a robust British war fever.[32] The people of Britain had found a cause they could sink their teeth into. The notion that the American rebels were fighting for liberty now seemed hollow as they allied themselves with the despotic regime of Louis XVI. The newspapers had found a new target:

Say, Yankees, don't you feel compunction,
At your unnatural, rash conjunction?
Can love for you in him take root,
Whose Catholic, and absolute?[33]

Those who earlier had voiced opposition to the war now joined the cause in defense of old England, and friends of the Howes were among them. The Duke of Richmond took up with zeal his formerly honorary office as lord lieutenant and colonel of the Sussex militia.[34] Lady Spencer's son, Lord Althorp, who had turned twenty in September, became a captain in the Northamptonshire militia. He was posted at Warley Camp in Essex, where he slept in a tent. Sanitation was rudimentary, and sickness spread as winter approached.[35] William Howe met the youth while making his professional round of visits to military camps, and he found time to send word to Lady Spencer via Caroline that he looked in perfect health. A month later, Althorp visited his virtual aunt in Grafton Street, on a prosaic quest for woolen nightcaps. "[H]e looks as well as possible," reassured

Caroline, who had probably plied him with tea and cakes. "[H]e went back to Warley the same day."[36]

Even Lord Althorp's sister, Georgiana, Duchess of Devonshire, spent time in a military camp during the dangerous year of 1778. Her husband, as Lord Lieutenant of Derbyshire, was training regiments of volunteers in Kent, and the duchess insisted on sharing in the duke's privations by living in the field in his tent. The ducal encampment was actually a vast network of marquees that included reception rooms, private sleeping areas, kitchens, and quarters for the servants. The duchess, unexpectedly, found herself drawn into a very different sort of predicament during that summer, as her husband began an affair with Lady Jersey. When Lady Spencer heard about it, she angrily confronted Lady Jersey on her daughter's behalf. Georgiana, meanwhile, rode on a surge of popularity as she designed and outfitted herself and the other aristocratic wives in riding habits inspired by the military uniforms of their men. The Whig party of the Devonshires had been under a cloud for its support of the American rebellion. Now the duchess charmed the public with her colorful demonstration of Whiggish war fever.

Georgiana was celebrated for her use of dress to make political statements. She was already notorious for donning the blue-and-buff colors of the American rebel Continental Army—colors that had been adopted by the male members of the Whig party in 1777 to demonstrate their opposition to the war.[37] Perhaps this taxed the indulgent good humor of her adoptive Aunt Caroline, whom she visited regularly and whose redcoat brother was now home from the war, but Caroline's letters were silent on the issue. Years later, however, Lady Spencer was advising on a new coat for Caroline's great-nephew that was to have buff trimmings. "I like anything with Buff," Lady Spencer let drop, "but Blue."[38]

In Parliament, the opposition group led by Lord Rockingham, which had opposed the war in America from its beginning, reacted to the news that France was entering the conflict by moving toward advocating recognition of American independence. Britain was perilously exposed, it was argued. There were cries against Lord Sandwich, the First Lord of the Admiralty, because the navy was not in a state of readiness for the emergency. The depredations of American sea captain John Paul Jones and his USS *Ranger* along the coast of Britain brought home Britain's vulnerability, even though the material damage inflicted was not serious.[39]

Richard's elderly patron the Earl of Chatham was horrified to hear the Rockinghams declare that they were ready to concede American independence. On April 7, he dragged himself on crutches into the House of Lords to declare that America, "the great source of all our wealth and power," must never be allowed to separate from Britain. His collapse on the floor of the House was high drama, and he died five weeks later.[40]

UPON HIS RETURN HOME, Richard would discover that the nation was in no mood to accept anything less than complete victory from its naval commanders, and that some viewed his success in Newport as a disappointment. Biting commentary from Horace Walpole reflected the opinion that Richard ought to have captured or blockaded D'Estaing and his ships in Boston. Instead, rather than taking the French fleet, sneered Walpole, "Lord Howe himself arrived on Monday, having taken nothing but his leave."[41]

Richard's most vociferous political critic was George Johnstone, one of the peace commissioners who went to America with Lord Carlisle. Johnstone was a naval officer and a member of Parliament who had served as governor of the new British colony of West Florida during the 1760s. He was a man of bold actions and strong opinions who was willing to resort to pistol or cudgel to enforce his views. Independent in his loyalties, he was nevertheless friendly with opposition leaders. In the early years of the war, he had opposed the coercion of America. But he returned from service on the Carlisle Commission with very different feelings, disgusted with the American Congress and highly motivated to join the war against the French.[42] Johnstone was now convinced that American loyalists had been right all along, that the upstart Continental Congress did not represent the opinions of most Americans, and that the Continental Army was breaking up. He was not slow to blame the Howes for the fiasco in America, and he was convinced that increased military pressure could still win the war for Britain.[43]

Thus began a tiresome tug-of-war, which would last for the remainder of the conflict, between those who thought three years of fighting had proven it to be a futile waste, and those who believed just one more big campaign would win the colonies back. The controversy over why the Howes had failed to achieve victory became politically loaded as it became entangled with the extremes of opinion over the war itself.

Opposition leaders contended that the conflict in America was unwinnable. The Americans should be conciliated—which effectively meant offering them independence—and the nation's firepower should be turned on the French. The danger to national security was great, and the imminent threat that Spain might soon declare war against Britain made it greater still.

The king and his government, on the other hand, remained adamantly opposed to recognizing American independence. The extent of popular loyalty in America was a key component in the government's argument for prolonging the war. Lord George Germain, clashing with the Rockinghams over the lessons to be drawn from the battle at Saratoga, pointed to testimonies of American loyalists in London. They corroborated the views of men like MP George Johnstone, arguing that loyal Americans were an oppressed majority in the colonies, and the rebellion's success did not reflect popular support for the war.[44] That meant, of course, that the blame had to lie elsewhere, and the Howes became the center of the growing storm. They had to be "guilty of something," whether it be treason or incompetence. If they were not, the war in America risked losing all credibility.

In December 1778, the Howe brothers took aim at Lord George Germain in the House of Commons. William declared bluntly that the war could not succeed under the direction of Germain. The brothers were openly gunning for the American secretary alone, rather than the North administration. Members of both houses scrambled to take sides. Lord North defended his fellow minister, declaring that the measures pursued were those agreed upon by the collective cabinet. Opposition leader Lord Shelburne, calling for a parliamentary inquiry into the conduct of the war, charged that nothing but "national ruin" could be expected as long as the present administration was in power.[45]

Shelburne was a natural ally of the Howes, having known the family for years, and he, like them, was a follower of Chatham. Upon the death of William Pitt in May, he assumed leadership of the Chatham group in Parliament. Thereafter, Shelburne was drawn into Caroline's social set, becoming another caller at 12 Grafton Street.[46] Like William Pitt, he opposed recognition of American independence, arguing that, with the loss of the colonies, "we shall no longer be a powerful or respectable people." But he also launched vigorous attacks on the policies of the North administration. He and Governor Johnstone clashed in debates that played out the spectrum of opinion on the war. Shelburne asserted that General

Burgoyne's catastrophic actions in the backwoods of New York had been an ill-conceived mistake from the start, and he laid the blame squarely on Germain. The Canadian army, he asserted, should have simply joined Howe's forces by sea.[47] Governor Johnstone thundered that it was General Howe's expedition to Pennsylvania that had led directly to "the ruin of General Burgoyne's army." Taking his cue, William Howe rose in the House and retorted that he trusted that Governor Johnstone would give his vote for a full parliamentary inquiry.[48]

The Howe brothers now sought a public inquiry into the war as a means of vindicating their record. In particular, they wanted a full disclosure of the correspondence between themselves and Germain. The prospect sent Germain scurrying to put his papers in order. He couldn't find some of his letters, he complained to his undersecretary; he had never imagined they would be wanted for a parliamentary inspection. He and his assistants trawled through letters from loyalists that found fault with the Howe command, seeking narratives that affirmed Germain's version of events.[49] As he constructed his defense, Germain received an unsettling letter from an army associate who warned him that either he or the Howe brothers would be forever cast in the role of "criminals with your country & with posterity."[50]

CHRISTMAS 1778 WAS a season of tension for all parties. Caroline was at Althorp, surrounded by opposition friends of the Spencers, who were preparing for an attack on the government in the new year.[51] Richard was at Porter's Lodge with his family, fretting that he could no longer obtain reliable news of the war in America.[52] Nisbet Balfour joined him there on New Year's Day, having resolved to assist with the Howe case in Parliament. In early January, the Scotsman visited William at Heckfield and then accompanied him to a royal levee, determined to remain by the side of "my old Master," as he called his former commander in chief.[53] It was William whose service in America was under question in official circles. Despite his reception at court, overt praise of the former commander in chief was withheld; behind the scenes, the king spoke to his ministers of General Howe's lack of zeal in pursuing the war.[54]

Richard, by contrast, still enjoyed royal favor, as was made clear early in 1779, when he saw his protégé, Captain Andrew Snape Hamond, knighted for his services in America.[55] Richard's navy had done a good job, and, despite criticism in some quarters, he enjoyed celebrity for the repulsion of D'Estaing's fleet off Newport. Perhaps, then, the elder Howe brother was not surprised to find himself wooed by cabinet ministers who sought to bring him into the government. The North administration wanted a cabinet reshuffle that would strengthen its position with critics of the war. Longtime followers of Chatham, who were conciliatory toward the Americans but could be relied on to oppose American independence, were under consideration, and friends of the Howes were involved in the behind-the-scenes maneuvers: their cousin, Thomas Thynne, 3rd Viscount Weymouth, as well as the Duke of Grafton.[56] Richard was offered the post of First Lord of the Admiralty, replacing Lord Sandwich.

Lord North, of course, would find that he could not divide the brothers. Richard set out four conditions for accepting the honor, one of which was that some mark of approval should be bestowed upon William. North and the king briefly considered what might be given to Sir William—a military promotion or a lieutenant governorship in Minorca? It might not be "right to do so," fretted North, but the House of Commons was "very indisposed" to the North administration, and something had to be done to strengthen support.[57] In the end, the negotiations came to nothing. The whole episode brought Richard as close as he ever would come to incurring royal displeasure. The king concluded, with some reason, that Richard wished to avoid service.[58]

Nevertheless, one final effort would be made to bring Richard into the government. In late February 1779, Admiral Augustus Keppel, who commanded the Channel Fleet, was threatening to resign unless Lord Sandwich were removed as First Lord of the Admiralty. Keppel and Sandwich had been embroiled in a high-profile controversy over the Battle of Ushant, which occurred on July 27, 1778. Fought against a French fleet at the mouth of the English Channel, it had ended inconclusively, and Keppel and his second-in-command, Sir Hugh Palliser, had descended into mutual recriminations.

The feud made waves far beyond the navy. Palliser was the protégé of Lord Sandwich, and Keppel was a supporter of Lord Rockingham. The political world quickly took sides. Caroline and her brothers were allies of Admiral Keppel. In terms reminiscent of the attacks on the Howes, Keppel was accused in the press of having done less than his duty against the enemy at Ushant, influenced, it was hinted, by his American sympathies. Caroline wrote with approval to Lady Spencer that the London mob was out making a show of support for Keppel, "[keeping] up my poor Servants" with its noise as it attacked windows and buildings. A court-martial in February 1779 cleared Keppel, but then he wanted Sandwich out. In exasperation, Lord North turned once again to Lord Howe. Would he accept command of the Channel Fleet in Keppel's place? But once again, Richard's loyalty to his brother proved an obstacle, and the Channel Fleet command went to Sir Charles Hardy.[59]

Richard's maneuvers to get the government to exonerate his brother had come to nothing. It was now inevitable that the Howes would join the opposition. On March 8, the foremost opposition speaker, Charles James Fox, stated in the House of Commons that the navy had been shamefully unprepared at the outbreak of war with France, pointing the finger at Lord Sandwich as the most responsible. He was seconded by Richard Howe, who declaimed in his supporting speech that he "was deceived into his command; that he was deceived while he retained it," stating emphatically that he would not serve again under the present ministers.[60] The usually silent admiral had made himself clear enough. "Lord Howe may now be ranked in Opposition, and therefore I shall not say more on that head," wrote the king the very next day.[61]

The position of the Howes had decisively shifted in the political world; as their dynasty lost influence, the effect was felt in their households as well. When Caroline received an appeal from a woman who sought a minor government post for her husband, she wrote back, explaining "how very much it was out of my power to be of any service to [you]."[62] No longer would she be courted as a woman who had the ear of government ministers.

But William was finally going to have a chance to defend himself. Before the 1779 Easter recess, a motion was agreed in Parliament that the correspondence of General Howe and Lord George Germain between August 1775 and May 1778 should be laid before the house, and a day was appointed to consider the papers and examine witnesses.[63] William spent the Easter recess working on his speech with Henry Strachey and Nisbet Balfour.[64]

On April 22, William Howe went to the House of Commons to give what was surely the longest speech of his life. He went over all his controversial actions in America as commander in chief: the halt of his troops in their charge on Long Island; the failure to attack the rebel position in White Plains; the fiasco at Trenton, when the Hessian troops were overwhelmed; the complex exchanges between himself and Germain as the campaign for 1777 took shape; the decision to land his forces at the Chesapeake Bay instead of the Delaware River; the wearisome campaigning around Philadelphia; his protestations that the role of peace commissioner had not conflicted with his performance as commander in chief.

The original manuscript of this speech has survived in Strachey's papers. Fascinatingly, it reveals what William did *not* say. Deleted sections give the king himself a share of the blame for the damagingly slow response to William's campaign suggestions in January 1777; other sections that were removed include the point that General Burgoyne might simply have joined General Howe by sea instead of struggling through the dense New England forests. These were omitted because William wanted to focus the blame directly upon Germain and his subordinates.[65]

The speech was well received in the newspapers. Sir William had defended his conduct of the war "in a firm and spirited manner," said one.[66] Caroline was happy. A friend called upon her in Grafton Street and found her pleased with her brother's speech, which she said had "fully justified his conduct of the war."[67] Caroline believed—or professed to believe—that the matter was settled.

The government had much to lose from prolonged public scrutiny into its conduct of the war. A few days after William's speech, Lord North attempted to give the Howes the exoneration they sought by declaring in the House of Commons that General Howe had done his duty in America and there was no need to look further into his conduct. There was no charge, he stressed, to be made against the brothers.[68] Balfour, who was present, wrote, "Every civility and every compliment passed to Sir Wm. Howe from Lord North." Germain, he noted, remained silent, despite William's attacks on his management of the war. North's motion to drop the inquiry passed by a narrow margin.[69]

But with the inquiry now safely out of the picture, Lord George Germain could not resist taking a stab at the Howes. On May 3, he rose in Parliament and cast aspersions upon the brothers' conduct of the Philadelphia campaign. The response from the House was strong and immediate; members were disgusted that Germain was attacking the Howes now, after a formal inquiry had been ruled out.[70] Germain had been indiscreet "beyond description," lamented a ministerial observer, and had created an opening for the opposition to once again demand a formal inquiry.[71]

Now John Burgoyne seized his opportunity to defend publicly his own conduct in America. On May 20, 1779, General Burgoyne stood before the House of Commons and delivered his own account of his wilderness expedition. Historians often compare it favorably to William's speech. Burgoyne, a writer and an amateur actor, was quicker on his feet than William Howe.[72] Nevertheless, his professional career would be forever tarnished by the debacle in America.

Nor would William Howe ever receive the full public exoneration he sought. Unlike Burgoyne and Keppel, the Howes were not disputing a single campaign or battle; rather, they were contesting two and a half years of warfare, with claims, counterclaims, and convoluted transatlantic messages. The testimony that was heard in Parliament during May and June only complicated the picture. Captain Andrew Hamond, who appeared as one of William's witnesses, concluded privately that the inquiry ". . . turned out the same as things of that sort generally do, where People have made up their Minds upon the Subject." The nation was more interested in the war with France, he noted; no one was in the mood to sift through the details of the quagmire surrounding the previous two years of war in America.[73] And further diverting attention away from the Howes was the threat from Spain, which was about to enter the fight as an ally of France.

The second wave of the inquiry eventually petered out at the end of June 1779. In a final session, the Howe brothers demanded that if ministers had any reason to think them unfit to serve their country, it had to be declared. The government front bench replied that no charges had been brought against the Howes, and no confidence was withdrawn from them in terms of future service. This time, Germain remained silent. "[A]nd thus the Enquiry was put an end to, without coming to a single Resolution upon any part of the business," concluded a report on the debate.[74]

WITH THE CLOSE of the inquiry, Caroline declared, with a distinct note of relief, "The American arguing is to be over for this year."[75] It was indeed over in Parliament, but the pamphlet war against the brothers that had begun in 1778 now escalated and continued until the close of the war. It became part of the media-based canon that established the narrative of how

Sir William Howe had lost the war in America. Chief among the pamphleteers were Israel Mauduit, whom the Howes had always believed to be in
the pay of Germain, and American loyalist Joseph Galloway. Once a patriot
and a friend of Benjamin Franklin, Galloway had defected to the British
cause after the Declaration of Independence. He had gone to New York, and
then to Philadelphia with the Howes and the British army in 1777, where
he held municipal offices. He was convinced that Britain could still win the
war, and, like many loyalists, he blamed the Howes. Galloway was in London by the end of 1778, closeted with Germain and eager to testify against
William and in favor of continuing the war.[76]

The pamphlet war waged by Galloway, Mauduit, and other loyalists in
London made the usual claims: Most Americans were loyal subjects of King
George; the war could still be won. Previous campaigns had failed because
of poor leadership, professional incompetence, personal greed, sympathy
for the rebellion that bordered on treason, or loyalty to the opposition party
in England.[77]

The Howes remained largely silent in the face of this verbal offensive.
Aside from a single laugh at Galloway's expense, Caroline made no mention of him or Mauduit in her letters. In 1780—possibly because it was an
election year—William published one pamphlet in response to his detractors, a reprint of his April 1779 speech before Parliament, to which he
added some personal commentary and testimonies.[78] Richard went so far
as to prepare a reply to a Galloway pamphlet of 1779 that had called him
"a secret Friend to the Rebellion." "To attempt a serious refutation of such
Absurdities, would be ridiculous," he pronounced.[79] In the end, he took his
own advice, and the manuscript remained unpublished until 1958.

But Galloway did force the Howes out in the open when he pointed
the finger at Caroline as a facilitator of the secret negotiations with Benjamin Franklin before the war. In late 1780, a newspaper column, signed
"Cicero," announced that it would reveal the origins of the supposedly trea-
sonous Howe intrigue in the War of Independence. Cicero knew "the whole
secret of the invitation to a game of chess, given to the Doctor [Franklin]
through a third person [Matthew Raper], by a Lady, an utter stranger to the
Doctor, and his consequent introduction to her noble brother the Admiral."

The Howes, charged Cicero, had conspired with the arch-rebel Franklin, under cover of the chess matches, and had subsequently procured their
appointments to command in America. "Cicero" was Galloway, who did

indeed know about the secret meetings in Grafton Street, because Benjamin Franklin had shared his journal with his erstwhile friend and ally in 1775.[80] Now, four years later, Galloway did not scruple to reveal what he had been told in private. It was a vindication of Richard's assertion in Parliament that Galloway was not "a man of honour" because he divulged things that were told to him in confidence. By repeating confidential information in order to point the finger at Lord Howe's sister as a conspirator, Galloway was proving Richard's point with a vengeance.

This could not pass in silence. Richard declared to the House that "A person, who had assumed the character of Cicero," had accused him of engaging in treason with Dr. Franklin under the cover of a game of chess. Richard now made a clean breast of it. "The matter did occur, and the game of chess was played," he confessed. "[I]f it was treason, however," he continued, "it was right the public should know all the traitors."[81] His fellow traitor, he pronounced, was none other than the prime minister. Lord North said nothing; how could he, when it was true? Although historians have disagreed over whether the prime minister was privy to the secret talks in Grafton Street in 1774–75, Lord North's silent consent during the scene that occurred on February 1, 1781, reveals that he was.[82]

Lord North would not have blamed Richard for making use of him in order to shield his sister from Galloway's shabby behavior. He liked Caroline and thought her very clever. Caroline recalled the good humor of the prime minister on an occasion when, partnering him at a game of whist, she was obliged to rescue him from his own maladroit play. After someone pointed out that he and his partner had achieved a great score from the previous deal, he replied, "Mrs. Howe has; your saying we have, puts me in mind of the Cobbler who lived next door to the Lord Mayor & was bragging, that he & his neighbour should lend the King 100 thousand pounds that year."[83] Whatever their politics, there was a general consensus within British high society that Lord North was genial and likable.

CAROLINE HERSELF WAS at last beginning to move on from her brothers' American travails. She wrote to Lady Spencer in July, summing up the Howe inquiry in positive terms: "[U]pon the whole, I fancy all who judge fairly are thoroughly satisfied with their conduct." William and Richard were home and safe, their ordeal was over. Her usual August stay at

Battlesden was almost a full family reunion, with William and Fanny, Mary and General Pitt, Charlotte Fettiplace and Julie all converging on their Aunt Juliana.[84]

Caroline, at fifty-seven, was entering a new phase of her life. Sometime in 1779, she began a relationship with Richard Rigby. The two were of the same age, and they had probably known each other all of their lives. The Rigbys were established members of the landed gentry with a seat at Mistley in Essex. Many years earlier, the young Richard Rigby had crossed metaphorical swords with George Lord Howe over cricket.[85] Like the Howes, Rigby had a hot temper, and he could be intimidating.

Horace Walpole wrote that Rigby had rugged good looks and good breeding, "though sometimes roughened into brutality." Walpole did not exaggerate; Rigby had a history of physical assaults and even a duel. On one occasion, after boldly rescuing the Duke of Bedford from a mob at the races, he acquired a lifelong friend who ensured him a seat in Parliament that he retained until his death. In the House of Commons, he became chief political manager of the duke's group, the Bedfordites. The duke arranged Rigby's appointment as Paymaster General of the Forces, with the authority to handle vast sums of public money. Rigby lent generously to friends and threw legendary parties at his office after the House of Commons had adjourned for the night.[86] In the process, he also made enemies, critics who saw him as corrupt and self-serving.

Richard Rigby never married, but during his lifetime he took two mistresses, both of them local women to whom he bequeathed small legacies.[87] Like many aristocratic figures of his day, he was open about his lifestyle. His daughter by one of his mistresses, Sarah Lucas, lived at Mistley Hall. He had close ties to the royal family, albeit not blood ties, and a contemporary belief that Rigby was close to royalty gave him additional sway in the House of Commons.[88]

Caroline saw Rigby regularly during her summer stays at Battlesden, for the Duke of Bedford's seat at Woburn Abbey was only ten miles away.[89] In May 1779, when Lord George Germain attacked William Howe in the House of Commons, there was astonishment when government supporter Mr. Rigby leapt to the defense of the general.[90] This was perhaps the first outward sign of a stirring of interest in the Howes, and one Howe in particular. Two months later, the friendship deepened when Caroline went to Rigby's country retreat with a number of other guests. Rigby had been at great pains to improve his estate, redecorating the interiors of Mistley Hall in luxury wall coverings and elegant furnishings. On the grounds, he cultivated exotic plants and trees, shady bowers, and garden beds, offset by distant views of woodlands.[91] "I never passed eleven days pleasanter than those I spent at Mistley," Caroline enthused to Lady Spencer.[92]

By the autumn of 1779, Mr. Rigby was a regular caller in Grafton Street, and he began to use Caroline's nickname, "Howey," a sure sign of intimacy in this era of prescribed formality.[93] A casual relationship grew between the two. They indulged in late-night confidential chats; she was a frequent guest at his dinners in town, sometimes the only lady present; and she came to be someone who knew his whereabouts, which he had made a practice of keeping to himself.[94]

What ensued for Caroline was a season of being teased about her admirer. Over a game of cards, Lady Mary Coke listened to Princess Amelia rib Caroline on the subject of matrimony. Caroline's discomfiture was obvious. Mrs. Howe, said Lady Mary, "appears displeased perhaps because there is no truth in it for I think she wou'd marry [Mr. Rigby] if he wou'd have her."[95] Lady Mary was trying to stick the knife in, as the saying goes, but Princess Amelia was simply high-spirited and tactless. For months to come, Caroline would have to endure the "old sisterly jokes," as she put it, from the princess. Even Lord and Lady Spencer good-humoredly quizzed their friend on the subject, especially after her second stay at Mistley Hall, where she wrote effusively about listening to nightingales with Mr. Rigby in his garden. Caroline's patience with the continuous banter finally wore thin, and anger boiled over. "I think at my age I may live with men as well as with women without scandal," she was provoked to write.[96] The teasing stopped, but the friendship between Caroline and Richard Rigby lasted until Rigby's death eight years later.

The holiday season of 1779 was in sharp contrast to the previous Christmas, when the Howes had been anxiously awaiting the parliamentary inquiry. Instead of going to Althorp, Caroline stayed in Grafton Street, enjoying the London festivities. Devonshire House hosted a pre-Christmas dinner, and after the duke and duchess had departed for Althorp, Caroline turned to Gloucester House, where the Duke of Gloucester held lively evening card parties.[97] Visiting Gloucester House risked incurring royal displeasure, as the Duke of Gloucester was the estranged brother of George III. He was excluded from court for his secret marriage in 1766 to Maria

Waldegrave, the illegitimate daughter of one of the Walpoles and a milliner's apprentice. Caroline Howe had barely missed becoming stepmother
to Maria back in 1741, when she had almost married her father, the eccentric Edward Walpole.[98] Princess Amelia disliked the Gloucesters intensely,
but Caroline deftly continued to play cards with both parties that holiday season without arousing hostility in either quarter.[99] Yet the war still
intruded. On a visit to a friend, Caroline sat down to dinner with the five-
year-old son of Lord Cornwallis, who was serving in America. The little
boy was obviously enjoying the gathering, and he burst out with, "[M]y
mama is dead, & my papa is as good as dead; it is well we meet with some
other good friends"—a "most melancholy observation" from a child, wrote
Caroline sadly.[100]

Lady Spencer was having a difficult time at Althorp. Her daughter the
duchess was ill, as she so often was. During her Christmas visit, she was
afflicted with vomiting and headaches. Alas, these proved not to be symptoms of pregnancy, a condition that still eluded her after five and a half
years of marriage. And Lady Spencer was seriously worried about her own
inability to resist gambling, which she attributed to her weak character.[101]

To Lady Spencer's dismay, the duchess had brought opposition leader
Charles James Fox with her to Althorp. "Mr Fox is still here," she wrote
significantly in early January. Her daughter thought Mr. Fox fascinating,
but neither Lady Spencer nor Caroline agreed. Lady Spencer confessed that
he made her feel uncomfortable.[102] Despite being a champion of British
liberty, Charles James Fox was hardly her type. A rake, a drinker, and a wit,
Fox was short, stout, unkempt, and generally unshaven. He also gambled
recklessly, frequently losing large sums of money.[103]

At Althorp, there was also talk of the war. A visiting British officer held
the attention of the guests as he sketched a map of the Siege of Savannah.[104]
The port city of Savannah, in the subtropical colony of Georgia to the north
of Florida, had been captured by the British in February 1779, marking a
successful beginning to a new British strategy for the war in America. The
plan was to shift the fighting to the supposedly more loyal southern colonies of Georgia, the Carolinas, and Virginia—"rolling up" the South, as it
came to be expressed. Other victories followed, although true pacification
of the South was never completely achieved. The British army in the southern colonies swelled its ranks with loyalist fighting men, part of a policy
of "Americanizing" the war, but it also gave rise to bitter, guerrilla-style

partisan fighting that impeded the establishment of law and order. And a dangerous new factor in the war was the threat from the sea posed by the French navy. In September and October, British-held Savannah was under attack by a joint Franco-American force, as D'Estaing's fleet and an American army besieged the port. On October 9, 1779, the allies gave up after a failed direct assault on the town. But the vulnerability of British stations in America was clear.

The danger the French posed from the sea had indeed been a game-changer for Britain, and the previous summer its effect had been felt much closer to home. That summer of 1779 saw a combined French and Spanish fleet menace the south coast of Britain, the most serious invasion threat since the Spanish Armada two centuries earlier. Enemy warships were plainly visible riding off Plymouth.[105] The Channel Fleet was not up to strength, and regular soldiers were in short supply in the event of an enemy landing. The nation resorted to desperate measures: Local counties were instructed that when they heard church bells signaling an invasion, all able-bodied men should be roused to dig defensive trenches. Only in late September did the combined fleet sail away. Meanwhile, the conflict was spanning the globe. The Dutch joined the war against Britain in 1780, and fighting spread to Spanish Central America, West Africa, and India.

DESPITE THE GLOBAL CONFLICTS, however, General Henry Clinton saw things take a turn for the better in America. He started off his campaign in May 1780 with the capture of Charleston, South Carolina, a significant victory for the British. For a time, things looked promising overall. In September 1780, American General Benedict Arnold was discovered to be a traitor, just before he could realize a scheme to hand over the fort of West Point to the British. Arnold escaped to British lines, but his coconspirator, Major John André, who had organized the Mischianza two years earlier, was captured. André's subsequent hanging did little to mollify public feeling in America, where there was widespread dismay at the sight of a senior American officer defecting to the British.[106]

If news from America was encouraging for the government in London that year, the Gordon Riots of June 1780 reversed its newfound peace of mind. Named for the leader of the anti-Catholic commotion in Parliament, Lord George Gordon, these disturbances began as a protest against

new laws that reduced discrimination against Roman Catholics. The protest rapidly turned into an anti-Catholic riot that raged in London streets
for six days, with troops deployed to restore order, prisons stormed, and
houses of the wealthy attacked. The crowds were large enough to draw
Richard from his house in Grafton Street to reconnoiter.[107] On June 7, in
the midst of the chaos, writing from her vantage point in the home of Lord
Gower, Caroline said, "Never was anything equal to the confusion of last
night." She was with Lord and Lady Gower until 2 a.m., and the noise of
troops passing back and forth never ceased. The inmates of Newgate and
Fleet Prisons were set free. The houses of prominent men were fortified,
and Lord Rockingham, who had been warned that he was a target of the
mob, stationed soldiers on his property. "I do not know whose house is
safe hardly," Caroline wrote.

The city was in an uproar, yet in Caroline's letters the whole thing
assumed something of the atmosphere of an open-air party. She spent her
evenings at the home of Lady Gower, where she could better observe the
commotion. She reassured Lady Spencer that the duke and her daughter
were "chearful & good humoured" at Devonshire House. For once it was
Caroline, and not her brothers, who was at the center of the action, and she
was determined to do her part. She took it upon herself to write lengthy
reports to friends and family. A couple of days of dashing off letters had
given her a headache, she complained. "I have just finished a 5th long one
that is to William who is at Highfield. I think I am upon as hard duty as
the poor soldiers."[108] Two days later, the riots had subsided, hundreds were
dead, and Lord George Gordon was a prisoner in the Tower of London. Ultimately, he was acquitted of responsibility for the riots.

A few weeks after the Gordon Riots, on July 2, Aunt Juliana Page died.[109]
Battlesden and Aunt Page had been a fixture in the Howe children's lives
since the death of their father forty-five years earlier. At seventy-eight,
Juliana was active to the end, visiting in Grafton Street and at Gloucester
House just months before she died, and hosting her nieces and nephews
over dinner in her London home. To Caroline and William fell the lot of
breaking the news to their mother Charlotte, who had been close to her
sister-in-law since they had both been very young. William proposed telling
her the news by letter, "to let her have some hours first by herself," and then
joining her at Richmond the next day. Caroline was left with a "very unclear

headache" after making these doleful arrangements, she reported to Lady Spencer unhappily, and she hoped to see her friend soon.[110]

Aunt Juliana's death was the beginning of another unpleasant summer for William. A general election had been called for the autumn, and William would have to stand again for Nottingham, a town where his service in America had been seen as a betrayal of his 1774 election promises. Since then, he had not returned home victorious, the sole circumstance that might have redeemed him in the eyes of Nottingham's citizens. One MP wrote of the Howe brothers, "[H]alf the Town abhor them for going to America, & the other half detest them for doing so little there."[111] It was an unenviable situation, and the results of the poll in September should have been no surprise. William was out of Parliament for the first time since George's death more than twenty years earlier. Richard, however, was duly returned as MP for Dartmouth. The pattern held: The elder brother was the lesser culprit in the minds of the public.

Charlotte Howe could not have been pleased to see her son William pushed out of the seat she had won for him through her bold move in 1758. But she was now too ill for such heroics. She had remained active in her old age, even traveling at the age of sixty-nine on a final tour of the Continent with the Dowager Princess Augusta. On her return a year later, in 1771, she had developed symptoms of a heart problem. Her doctor had advised that if she lived quietly, she might survive another year or two. Charlotte defied the doctor, lived on to grace drawing rooms and card tables, went to court to be congratulated on William's victory in New York, and confronted Lord George Germain in his own home for his abuse of her sons. She was still a presence to be reckoned with in 1780, when she caused Caroline some embarrassment in Grafton Street by snubbing a friend of William's whom she accused of having left her son to the mercies of an election mob at Nottingham.[112] A year later, she had another attack, but she still lived long enough to see her family's fortunes improve, ironically as a result of a new disaster for British arms in America: Yorktown.

In October 1781, the British surrendered to Franco-American troops at Yorktown, Virginia. When the news reached London on November 25, Lord North threw open his arms and said, "Oh God! It is all over!" But the North administration would drag on for a few months yet. George III was determined to retain at least a part of his dominions in the colonies, and he steadily opposed North's resignation. This was not entirely an instance of royalty in denial, for Britain could have fought on after Yorktown. There was still a British army in New York, and bases in Charleston and Savannah. By 1782, the French fleet was overextended, while the Royal Navy was in a fighting mood. Prior to Yorktown, behind-the-scenes negotiations with the French had occurred, proposing among other things that the British might retain the Carolinas in the event of recognizing America's independence.[113] The exact extent of the future United States of America was not a foregone conclusion.

But the nation was war-weary, and George III could not ignore Parliament. On February 27, 1782, Caroline's friend General Conway moved that offensive war in America should cease, and the motion passed. The next month, Lord North finally quit his office, probably with relief, in the face of a vote of no confidence.[114] Lord Rockingham was now prime minister of a new government that brought together the two main opposition groups: the Rockinghamites with their leading spokesman, Charles James Fox, and Lord Shelburne and his followers.

Now the fortunes of the Howe brothers changed for the better. On April 2, Richard took command of the Channel Fleet, to the joy of Lady Spencer, who had wished for it more than once, declaring, "[W]hen I have the disposal of the great affairs, he shall have the Admiralty," as well as the Channel Fleet.[115]

Richard hoisted his flag on HMS *Victory*, Keppel's old command and Lord Nelson's future one, on April 20, 1782. That same day, he was created Viscount Howe of the Kingdom of England, a title of nobility that moved him from the House of Commons to the House of Lords. Richard was still concerned about his brother, and William was appointed lieutenant general of the Ordnance, a government department that oversaw storage and supplies for the armed forces. Fortunately, Charlotte Howe lived long enough to hear of her sons' rehabilitation and restoration to honorable service. She must have been gratified indeed to see her eldest son raised to the ranks of full aristocracy. But he was unable to be at her bedside when his mother passed away on June 13, 1782, "perfectly quiet and free from pain," after having been critically ill for several days.[116]

Richard had a hard summer ahead of him, defending the western approaches of the English Channel against the French and Spanish navies, and the North Sea against the Dutch.[117] Yet it was Gibraltar, guarding the narrow sea passage separating the Atlantic Ocean and the Mediterranean

Sea, that would give him his major challenge. Spain had been trying to recapture Gibraltar from the British since 1713, and the fortress had been besieged since 1779, the garrison surviving with the aid of British relief convoys. In a war of few triumphs, Gibraltar's resistance was a matter of national pride for Britain.

By the time Richard took command of the Channel Fleet, it had been almost a year since the Gibraltar garrison had last been relieved; in August, he was ordered to resupply the fortress and escort merchant ships bound for the East and West Indies and Portugal. Richard had thirty-five ships of the line under his command, against a combined Franco-Spanish fleet of at least fifty that awaited him near Gibraltar. Richard has been lauded as one of those rare admirals with a special skill for fleet maneuvering, and he showed it here, bringing his convoy safely into the Bay of Gibraltar and resupplying the garrison, "despite a combined French and Spanish fleet snapping at his heels."[118] The British fleet turned back through the Strait of Gibraltar into the Atlantic, followed by the enemy fleet, for neither had room to form a line of battle until they had reached the open ocean. A sunset engagement ensued, and Richard succeeded in fighting off a far superior enemy fleet before heading homeward, arriving at St. Helens on the Isle of Wight on November 14.[119]

Ten days after the battle, Caroline was at Richard's home of Porter's Lodge with Lady Mary Howe and the children, waiting for news. She hoped to have certain intelligence by the end of the week or the beginning of the next, she told the impatient Lady Spencer, who was at the spa of Hotwells, near Bristol, with her husband. News did not come, and Lady Spencer was unsympathetic. She wrote crossly, "I hate you my D[ea]r Howey for not telling me what the reports were from Calais & Paris & I go, perfectly convinc'd they are bad." Caroline was always expected to be in the know. Two days later, back in London, she quoted verbatim a secret source with news from Paris: "Lord Howe passed thro' the Gut from the Eastward the 16th of October, he seems to have baffled the combined Fleets in the Mediterranean by a variety of masterly manoeuvres."[120]

As always, Caroline was wild with joy. She was in London, staying at the Spencers' residence in St. James's Place during Lady Spencer's absence, while her Grafton Street home was being redecorated. Callers sought her out to convey their congratulations; Lord Frederick Cavendish was there when Captain Adam Duncan made his appearance. The future hero of the

Battle of Camperdown in 1797, Duncan had commanded a ship of the line at the relief of Gibraltar and had been dispatched by Richard to carry the news home to England. He personally recounted details of the action to Richard's ecstatic sister. After scribbling the details to her friend, Caroline signed off: "I have so many to write to that I cannot add a word more." Other visitors soon followed: Lady Jersey, Richard Rigby, and brother William. In the evening, Caroline went to dine at the home of Lord Shelburne, "who seemed in great spirits, embraced and kissed me both sides my face."[121]

By the time he kissed Caroline, Lord Shelburne was prime minister. Rockingham had died on July 1, 1782. Shelburne now presided over the close of the war and the making of peace. In a century when the prevailing theory was mercantilism, and nation-states excluded one another from their trading systems, Shelburne promoted ideas of the advantages of free trade and desired a mutually beneficial trading relationship with the new United States of America. Adam Smith's *Wealth of Nations* had been published in 1776, with its forceful advocacy of free international markets, but it was still ahead of its time. Shelburne's views on the peace with America also reflected the influence of his mentor, Lord Chatham. Shelburne believed that Britain and the new United States had everything to gain from maintaining close ties in defense and trade. He hoped for a treaty that would leave Americans on the same footing as British citizens in many respects, with a shared trading system and a shared foreign policy.[122]

Shelburne's notions, however, did not prevail. In March 1783, his ministry was replaced by the Fox–North coalition. The final peace with the new United States of America rejected Shelburne's visions and dictated that the Americans now be treated as foreigners. In July 1783, they were excluded from trade with the British West Indies, a move designed to promote Britain's own merchants and shipbuilding industry. John Adams, in Paris on diplomatic service at the time, predicted that the British measure would backfire, causing the United States to draw closer to France. This, however, did not occur. The British knew that the Americans were dependent on British manufactured goods, and independence would not alter their habits of consumption—established channels of commerce are not easily diverted or changed. The United States would remain closely tied to her former mother country, locked in an unfavorable balance of trade for several decades. Many of the old markets of the thirteen colonies were closed, and it has been estimated that the performance of the American economy fell by 46 percent between 1775 and 1790.[123]

What the Howes thought of the absolute separation they had worked so hard to prevent is not known, but John Adams recalled years later that while he was in London as American ambassador, between 1785 and 1788, he encountered Lord Howe at a court ball. Finding nowhere to sit, he appealed to Richard to indicate "the Ambassadors Seats. His Lordship with his usual politeness, and an unusual Smile of good humour, pointed to the Seats, and manifestly alluding to the Conversation on Staten Island, said, 'Aye!, Now, We must turn you away among the foreigners.' "[124] Ever the pragmatists, the Howes accepted the new status quo and moved on.

Britain had lost her thirteen colonies, but she could still hold her head up at the close of the conflict. She had a string of successes at sea in 1782, including checks to the French in India, Rodney's notable victory over the French in the West Indies, and the relief of Gibraltar. Keen to drive a wedge between the new United States and its French allies, Lord Shelburne while still prime minister had agreed to allow the Americans generous boundaries, granting them the territory east of the Mississippi and rights to the Newfoundland fisheries. The prewar status quo in the all-important Caribbean remained much as it had been. With the world's sea-lanes open to it, Britain could look forward to an era of economic expansion. "Far from being fatal to Britain," it has been asserted, "the loss of America marked the beginning of her period of greatest power."[125]

What of Britain's European foes? Spain did not regain Gibraltar, but it did gain Minorca and Florida, only to lose the latter to the emerging United States less than forty years later. France gained very little from the war— nothing in India, and only the small island of Tobago in the West Indies. France had hoped that the new American republic would divert its commerce to its Gallic ally, but this did not transpire. Instead, France emerged from the war mired in crippling debt, a fact that contributed substantially to its own revolution only six years later.

For the Howes, the American War of Independence had been punctuated throughout by difficulties and aggravations, and the final months of the conflict were no exception. The signing of the preliminary peace treaty in January 1783 meant that French travelers once again ventured across the

English Channel to Britain. One of these was the Duke of Chartres, who arrived in London in early May. The duke and his companions were greeted by the highest ranks of English society in a flurry of social engagements, including at Devonshire House, where he was entertained with a "grand supper and ball." Caroline declined being one of the attendees, roundly stating her intention of "shirking the nasty foreigners."[126]

Caroline found a kindred spirit in Hugo Meynell, MP and Leicestershire landowner, who was the leader of the famous Quorn Hunt and known as England's foremost foxhunter.[127] Caroline declared approvingly of Mr. Meynell—the very stereotype of a John Bull—that he "hates all foreign company, says we shall never have peace, till we have another war." Caroline of course was glad to see the end of the war, but her instinctive animosity toward the old enemy was unabated. "I shall be sorry if we are to make peace with France without giving them first one good bang," she had written shortly after her brother's return from Gibraltar.[128]

Richard Howe's final engagement during the War of Independence was fought on English soil against an English foe. In October 1783, Captain John Hervey, Lord Hervey, a young naval officer, claimed in the newspapers that the relief of Gibraltar had been mismanaged, and an opportunity to strike a decisive blow at the enemy had been missed. Contemporary notions of honor required Richard to challenge him to a duel. Lady Spencer was beside herself with outrage, calling Hervey "a strange conceited pert Coxcomb." It was horrid, she went on, that "such a Man" should be in a position to put Lord Howe's life at risk.

The confrontation ended without violence, for Captain Hervey relented and begged Richard's pardon. Caroline, hearing it all from William, recounted the episode in detail to Lady Spencer: "[W]hen they came upon the Field my brother gave him a paper which he insisted upon his signing, [Captain Hervey] refused and the seconds were desired by Ld. Howe to retire," indicating that the duel would commence. At this point, Hervey seemed to lose his nerve:

> Ld. Hervey then said he would sign if one word was left out, this was consented to, & he did sign the second letter you read in the papers. I should mention that when he was compelled to sign, he said to Lord Howe I think I have a right to find fault with your publick conduct;

yes certainly, was the answer, and I never can desire to prevent any-one speaking their opinion upon any publick transaction of mine, it would look as if I was guilty if I did; it is the insult upon my private character that has brought me here, and I must add one thing more, that when you say any thing reflecting upon my publick one, take care of the truth of your facts.[129]

Richard's words carried an unmistakable threat; his raw Howe courage and deep sense of personal honor still burned strongly.

Fourteen

The Glorious Return

By the close of the American War of Independence in 1783, it had been almost fifty years since Scrope Lord Howe had died in Barbados, leaving the Howe dynasty with an uncertain future. The childhood world that centered on the village of Langar had all but disappeared; all the Howe children had left the neighborhood, and a steward now looked after crumbling, antique Langar Hall.[1] Caroline, casting a retrospective eye over the family adventures since the death of her aunt, Lady Pembroke, in 1749, might have wondered whether she and her siblings had lived up to the ambitious plans that lady had formed on their behalf.

The old Nottingham connections still survived within Caroline's London circle. Caroline's cousin Mary, who in 1747 had been married into the Smith banking family as part of Aunt Pembroke's scheme to get George Lord Howe into Parliament, had by now been resting in a Nottinghamshire graveyard for twenty years. Caroline encountered Mary's son Sir George Bromley and his wife in metropolitan drawing rooms.[2] Aunt Anne Mordaunt's sons Charles and Osbert, childhood companions of the Howe children, remained in touch with their Howe cousins, calling from time to time at Grafton Street. Both had careers in the army, and Charles would eventually become an aide-de-camp to George III.[3]

Though not a single Howe now sat in the House of Commons, Richard's elevation to the House of Lords would have greatly gratified Aunt Pembroke. Yet she would have been dismayed to see the problems with fertility endured by herself and her sister Juliana Page replicated in her brother's children. In 1783, six of Scrope Howe's children were still living, and five were married, yet only one, Admiral Richard Howe, had children, all of them girls who could not inherit their father's title.

At sixty-one, Caroline was on the threshold of old age. As with everything else, she had an opinion about getting old. After a visit to a woman who was nearing eighty, she wrote to Lady Spencer to express her sadness at seeing how altered one must become with advancing years, "& of how little use or entertainment one can be to any body." But, characteristically, she had a remedy: "Whilst a person can read & entertain themselves alone it is a different story."[4] Caroline, however, was in no danger of such isolation. Life in Grafton Street would continue to hold variety, and the Howe dynastic fortunes were still set to change.

Ironically, it was her younger friend Lady Spencer whose horizons would shrink. On October 31, 1783, after a prolonged illness, Lord Spencer died. He was only forty-eight. The new Dowager Lady Spencer could no longer be mistress at Althorp, Wimbledon, or Spencer House; she had to give way to her son George and his wife, Lady Lavinia Bingham, whom he had married in March 1782. An attractive and intelligent young woman, Lavinia would become a notable society hostess. On the surface of things, she also had much in common with Lady Spencer. Religious and charitable, she eschewed the gambling and high living of the two Spencer girls. Yet Lady Spencer's relationship with her daughter-in-law remained cool.[5]

Within days of her husband's death, Lady Spencer moved to Holywell House in St. Albans, Hertfordshire, near Lord Howe's seat of Porter's Lodge. Holywell was beautiful and secluded but decidedly run-down, with smoking chimneys and collapsing walls. Lady Spencer would be obliged to retreat from one section of the house to another to make way for renovations, but she preferred the inconvenience of the dilapidated old house to the sense of loss that overwhelmed her in the residences where she and Lord Spencer had spent their married life.[6]

Widowed now at forty-six, Lady Spencer had no intention of marrying again. She set forth her views on the subject in a letter to Caroline. If a woman had been unhappily married, she reasoned, how could she bring herself to risk wedlock a second time? If, on the other hand, she had truly loved her deceased husband, "Gracious God is it possible she can ever think of replacing what is lost[?]" Engrossed in her moralizing strain, Lady Spencer seemed to have forgotten that just three years earlier, Caroline had endured extensive teasing on the subject of matrimony and Mr. Rigby. Caroline retorted that if Lady Spencer would consider "a little more of human nature," and the wide variation in individual personalities, "perhaps your surprise & wonderment would not be so great, at the possibility of now & then a Lady thinking in a different manner than you do on the subject."

Not for the first time, Caroline put her rather smug friend in her place with what Lady Spencer called one of her "hard raps."[7]

As the war in America drew to its close, a new young royal made his entry into London society, and into Caroline's drawing room as well. George, Prince of Wales—destined to become George IV in 1820—is best remembered as the dissipated prince regent who occupied the throne of Britain during the final years of the reign of George III, when his father was notoriously stricken with mental illness. Born in 1762 and brought up under the strict regime of the royal household, the Prince of Wales early on evinced a proclivity for self-indulgence and loose living that would characterize his adult life. When he was just fifteen, a prescient tutor prophesied, "He will either be the most polished gentleman or the most accomplished blackguard in Europe, possibly an admixture of both."[8] His relationship with his straitlaced parent replicated the animosity between monarch and crown prince that had dogged each generation of Hanoverians since they had ascended the British throne in 1714.

By the time the prince reached sixteen, there were already rumors of affairs; a year later, his involvement with an actress was public knowledge.[9] This was followed by an infatuation with Elizabeth Armitstead, a fashionable courtesan who moved in the circle of Charles James Fox and his Whig friends. Mrs. Armitstead included among her clients Lord George Cavendish, who was part of Caroline's circle. Happening to visit Mrs. Armitstead late one evening, Cavendish found the prince cowering behind a door, hoping not to be discovered. Lord George's sense of humor came to his aid; he burst out laughing while managing a bow and made his departure, leaving the embarrassed prince alone with his favorite.[10]

Caroline doubtless heard all about it, for her source was impeccable. She would have heard, too, of the raucous party the prince attended at the home of Lord Chesterfield. The carousing reached such heights that a drunken guest seized an aggressive dog by the tongue and was mauled by the outraged beast. The rake who assaulted the dog was George Pitt, nephew of Caroline's sister Mary and her husband, General Pitt. The prince was too overcome with liquor by the end of the evening to drive home; his health was impaired for weeks afterward, causing alarm in the royal household.[11]

While Caroline was fully aware of such juvenile carryings-on, she encountered the prince in more decorous settings. He was infatuated with the Duchess of Devonshire, and Caroline met him on casual visits to Devonshire House and at fashionable parties, where they played cards together.[12] The prince also became part of Mr. Rigby's set, occasionally staying at Mistley Hall.[13]

In fact, the wild young prince seemed to appreciate the company of older people, provided they were good-humored and nonjudgmental. He was fond of Princess Amelia, his great-aunt, and he sometimes made an appearance at Gunnersbury, where he joined her elderly guests, including Caroline Howe, for cards.[14] George was aware of the kindredness between himself and the Howes. Years later, the prince's younger brother William, who would become King William IV, recalled that the Howes were "a sort of connexion of the family."[15] This was the last echo of the old blood relationship between the Howe children's German grandmother, Sophia von Kielmansegg, and the Hanoverian kings of Britain.

Caroline did seem to relate to George on the familiar footing of an aunt rather than as a courtier, just as her relationship with Princess Amelia was "sisterly." "[A] parcel of idiots" was what she bluntly labeled the Prince of Wales and his companions on an occasion when they dined with John Crawfurd, who lived two doors away in Grafton Street. Caroline had gifted Crawfurd a live pig, following the country practice of sending the animal to the butcher's to be slaughtered and roasted on the same day. But Crawfurd's West End kitchen staff proved to be too refined to understand such rural methods. Instead, they locked up the animal, and when the Prince of Wales arrived, he insisted on having the pig brought into the drawing room, "& Grunting, in it come," wrote Caroline in disgust. She added: "I am tired & can tell you no more of this history only that Mr Rigby insisted it could now never be put to death as being admitted into a royal presence was always a certain pardon, & hallowing & hooping at poor me, his life is spared." The illustrious guests presumably made do with cold meat. The fortunate pig was dispatched to an estate in the countryside to be kept for breeding purposes.[16]

Now that her brothers were no longer away at war, Caroline made room in her correspondence for more everyday topics. She was determined to keep fit, walking a great deal, just as her Aunt Pembroke had done years earlier. To push herself when she was in town, she would sometimes alight from her carriage ahead of her destination and proceed the rest of the way on foot.[17] At age fifty-seven, while on a visit to a riverside manor house, she spotted a barge drifting down the Thames and ran down to the waterfront, following it alongshore for as long as she was able. She returned "breath-less and sweaty," noted the ever-critical Lady Mary Coke.[18] Caroline never entirely lost her country manners, or the relative fitness they conferred.

Caroline, like all the Howes, loved dogs. In early 1782, when her dog Bella died, her personal maid Renshaw tried to console her with a puppy named Beau. "Renshaw has brought me a little black terrier from the dog man, I say I won't have it & I cd. cry every time it jumps up," she told Lady Spencer. A puppy, however, was not to be resisted. Soon it was play-ing around Caroline while she wrote at her desk, and she made excuses to Lady Spencer, telling her of "my little Beau with his ball every instant, which is this days excuse for blots & blurs" in her penmanship. His pedi-gree was dubious, probably a mix of terrier and spaniel. Caroline referred tactfully to his "elegant combined beauty," his "curled hair & a noble large Tail," telling Lady Spencer, "I assure you his father was a span[ie]l his mother French."[19]

Dogs repeatedly appeared in Howe family portraits and stories. Lady Charlotte Howe had her spaniel beside her in her 1719 wedding portrait. Her mother, Sophia von Kielmansegg, chose to have her likeness painted with her little black pug by her side. Famously, William's dog, by tradition a fox terrier, was found behind the American lines after the Battle of Ger-mantown in 1777, its collar revealing its redcoat master's name. The name of the dog has not been preserved, but its fate was well documented. Wash-ington ordered it to be returned to General Howe with a polite note. When it arrived in the British camp, an officer noted that Sir William was so grat-ified to see his pet again that he took the little dog up onto his lap, oblivious to its muddy coat and paws.[20]

Caroline's love of dogs preserved for us the story of another war dog, a Newfoundland, who also was a veteran of the War of Independence. The dog had belonged to the American General Richard Montgomery, who was slain in the unsuccessful American attack on Quebec in December 1775. At first, the faithful animal refused to leave his master's body, but eventually he was adopted by a British officer, who christened him Rebel.

It doubtless seemed a good jest to call Rebel to heel in the British camp, but in 1777, the situation was reversed, and the dog's new master was himself a prisoner at Saratoga. London newspapers reported good-humoredly that the redcoat officer found himself shouting "Rebel" in the midst of his captors, and then clumsily converted the call into a whistle.

By all accounts, the Americans thought it funny, and the dog was "held in great estimation."[21]

Caroline covered several sheets of paper chronicling the fate of Rebel and his progeny for Lady Spencer. The pet was brought to England and went on to sire a second generation. His son, also called Rebel, was adopted by another veteran of Saratoga, Lieutenant Colonel John Lind. Young Rebel lived in Plymouth and became as distinguished as his sire for loyalty. He was so "sensible," said the delighted Caroline, that when Colonel Lind went fishing, Rebel carried the day's catch home alone so that his master could remain out of doors. On one occasion, when Rebel stopped to fight another dog and left the catch forgotten by the roadside, he went back and retrieved it after being admonished by Lind.[22] Rebel's clever antics were a welcome diversion at the end of a wearisome and disappointing war, one of the longest of the century.

William showed signs of the immense strain he had endured in the wake of the parliamentary inquiry, and Caroline was concerned. Six months after its conclusion, she wrote to Lady Spencer that he had lost weight. But after April 1782, when business brought him once again into town as lieutenant general of the Ordnance, she was pleased to see an improvement. Fanny did not always accompany her husband, instead remaining at her mother's residence, Copt Hall, in nearby Twickenham. So brother and sister were often together, an arrangement that no doubt was mutually satisfactory, as they had always had a close relationship. They attended dinners, card parties, and the theater. At the end of 1783, Caroline wrote happily, "I think I never saw William look better."[23]

William wished to live near his family again. In 1782, he had been offered the post of commander in chief of the British forces in Ireland, but he declined; it went to Burgoyne.[24] He preferred a desk job. It is hard not to conclude that he had become disenchanted with the military career that fortune had obliged him to take up as a young man. He had joined the service not out of personal inclination but because it was what his family and his position in life required. Like all the Howe boys, he was gifted in the military arts, but that did not mean he would have chosen that path in life if he had been left to decide on his own. He had served with zeal in the wars against the French, he had shown himself keen to avenge the death of his brother George, and he had fought to the greatest of his ability in the War of Independence. Now, in his early fifties, he was disgusted and disillusioned with the disastrous fallout from his American command. Accusations of mistreatment of American civilians and prisoners that had dogged his command in that war particularly rankled; in his sole pamphlet, he gave a rare glimpse into his feelings on the matter: "I am contented that strictures should be made upon my professional conduct; but I feel myself hurt as a man, when I am accused of inhumanity."[25]

He now wanted the quiet life. When the London season was over, William and Fanny could remove to their country seat, Park House in Cholderton, Wiltshire.[26] William took up angling again, one of his favorite pastimes ever since his youth. He had acquired a fishing "cottage" in Ringwood, Hampshire, on the banks of the Avon River. A cottage it was in name, but it was sufficiently spacious and modernized to accommodate his wife and the occasional guest.[27]

Richard's future would unfold very differently from that of his brother William. On December 26, 1783, as another too-short period of peace dawned for the nation, Richard was appointed First Lord of the Admiralty by new Prime Minister William Pitt. Pitt the Younger, as he is best known to posterity, the second son of Lord Chatham, was only twenty-four when he became prime minister. Destined to become one of Britain's most famous political figures, he would oversee war against revolutionary France, agitation over the slave trade and Ireland, the crisis of royal insanity, and more.

Although the younger Pitt and Richard Howe were somewhat alike in their social personas, they did not get along. Both had famously remote manners, preferred work to play, and were unsocial to a degree that fitted poorly with their positions as leaders.[28] But there was one crucial difference between the two: Pitt was a political animal, Richard was not. For five years, Richard served at the Admiralty. He disliked the work and clashed with Pitt, who preferred to bypass Lord Howe and deal with the Controller of the Navy, Sir Charles Middleton, in carrying out his program of peacetime naval buildup.

Richard also locked horns with the Duke of Richmond over a fortifications bill, leading to what one historian has called "almost open warfare between the Admiralty and the Ordnance offices."[29] This may have been awkward for William, as he was directly answerable to the duke, who was master-general of the Ordnance, as well as a friend. But if it caused the younger and more genial of the Howe brothers any discomfort, he gave no sign. Like Caroline, he was skilled at getting along with people; while the

duke developed a lasting antipathy for Richard Howe that was wholly recip-
rocated, his friendship with William endured.

Richard would resign in July 1788, only to climb still higher. By this
time the good relationship between Richard and his sovereign had been
fully reestablished, the ripple of royal displeasure surrounding the 1779
parliamentary inquiry wholly forgotten. Caroline wrote to Lady Spencer "to
tell you a secret which will be known to all the Town next week," that her
brother was about to leave the Admiralty. He had informed the king of his
intention several months earlier, she went on, but was asked by His Majesty
to remain in the post until the end of the parliamentary session. George III
was now honoring Richard by making him an earl, "as a token of his entire
approbation, & yesterday he said that he hoped he would not change the
title of *Howe*." Richard became Earl Howe, and, in a striking mark of the
king's favor, he was also granted the title of Baron Howe of Langar, with
the unusual condition that should he have no sons, the baronetcy could go
to his eldest daughter.[30]

Richard's daughter Sophia Charlotte, called Charlotte in the family,
would thus become Baroness Howe upon the death of her father. In July
1787, Charlotte had married Penn Assheton Curzon, a member of Parliament with a seat at Gopsall Hall, Leicestershire. The old Nottingham connection came into play in this alliance, as Penn's sister Esther had married
Caroline's cousin Sir George Bromley.[31] There were two weddings at Porter's Lodge that summer. Charlotte's ceremony followed hard on the heels
of that of her youngest sister, Louisa, who was barely twenty when she married John Denis Browne, 3rd Earl of Altamont, in late May 1787. Louisa,
who counted the royal princesses among her friends, was known to possess
"ethereal" beauty. "[P]rettier than ever," the Princess Elizabeth, daughter of
George III, said of her two months before her wedding.[32]

Marriage, a rite of passage that heralds the rise of a new generation,
would have had special poignancy in the case of Louisa. Caroline's sister
Charlotte Fettiplace died very suddenly at the end of May. Taken ill with
what seemed a minor complaint, she was gone within hours. "I had not
the least warning nor even knew she was ill till ½ hour before the express
arrived," wrote Caroline unhappily to Lady Spencer. Caught unaware, the
family proceeded with the wedding celebrations and put on the mourning
immediately afterward.[33]

Portrait of Louisa Howe Brown, Lady Altamont, youngest daughter of Admiral Howe. Painted in 1788, the year after her marriage.

Two weddings were not enough to shake off the sense of the passage of time in the summer of 1787. Not since Thomas's death in 1771 had one of Caroline's siblings passed on. The previous autumn, on All Hallows' Eve 1786, Princess Amelia had died in her London home.[34] Amelia had been born in Hanover in 1711, a date almost equidistant between the birth years of Caroline and her mother. She had been a virtual sister to both Howe women.

The memories of long ago, when the cares and anxieties of the Howe dynasty had centered on the great house at Langar, were stirred for Caroline, who was now in her mid-sixties. In her correspondence, she almost never mentioned those who had gone before, but she made a rare reference to her father when she heard the news of the death of an old parliamentarian, Thomas Noel. "Old Tom Noel," as she dubbed him when she told the news to Lady Spencer, had been "a great friend of my fathers, & I remember him ever since I had a memory," a touch of nostalgia evident in her words.[35]

Shortly after Charlotte Howe's marriage, Lady Spencer made a visit in the neighborhood of Battlesden and took a detour to see the old grounds. The house had passed on to a distant family member, and the property was not being maintained as it had been in Aunt Juliana Page's day. "I went to visit Mrs. Pages Tomb," wrote Lady Spencer. "I was vexed at seeing it so ill taken care of, being over grown entirely with weeds & nettles." The woodland trails had become impassable; the roads were all "sadly neglected & in some places quite bad & the bridge that goes to the wood is broken down." These were the paths Richard had so often traversed alone when on shore leave from the Seven Years' War.

"Sad! The account you give of poor old Battlesden!" lamented Caroline. "Some of these things make me fancy myself seeing how matters go on after ones death & seems as if one had been dead, & returned again to give a peep."[36] The health of her friend Richard Rigby was failing; he would pass away in Bath less than eight months later.[37]

But the Howe dynasty was destined for a revival. Just a few months before he became an earl, Richard became a grandfather. His eldest daughter, Charlotte, gave birth to George Augustus William on May 14, 1788, at their London home. It was an easy delivery. Charlotte had been out paying visits in the afternoon, wrote her proud Aunt Caroline, and five hours later had given birth to a fine baby boy. "Mr Curzon is quite wild with joy, he says she was not more than 2 hours & ½ in strong Labor, wonderful for a first Child." Lady Howe sat up all night with her daughter and grandson.

Just days later, more joyous news followed. Louisa, now Lady Altamont, was expecting any day, and she was so heavily pregnant that it was thought she was carrying twins. "Lady Altamont my dear Lady Spencer was brought to bed at 4 this morning of *only one* fine fat great boy & both mother & Child as well as possible." The next day, Caroline had a glimpse of the new family member, "a trot up two pair of stairs to see the Babe," who was so big he looked like a month-old infant.[38] The "fat great boy" was named Howe Peter; Charlotte's boy, George Augustus, was named in memory of the heroic uncle Charlotte had never met but had heard of all her life.

There was of course a great christening for George Augustus Curzon, destined to become the new dynastic head. Caroline described the occasion: "All was as handsome & I may say elegant as possible, a vast heap of relations of the Curzon family came after the [christen]ing was over." There had been a struggle over who should stand godfather to little George

Augustus. Mr. Curzon, the paternal grandfather, wanted to defer to Lord Howe; Lord Howe politely returned the compliment. After a "great battle," it went to Mr. Curzon; Lady Howe was godmother. When Caroline left at half past nine, the young guests were dancing to the music of a harp.[39]

"Fine doings indeed with all your boys my Dr. Howey," wrote Lady Spencer, happy for her friend. Lady Spencer insisted on calling them Caroline's grandchildren. "I was right," she pronounced, "in calling little Curzon your Grand Child for nothing but looking upon him as such could have posted you up two pair of Stairs to see a new born infant."[40]

By now, Lady Spencer was a grandmother herself. Her youngest, Harriet, had married in 1780 to Frederick Ponsonby Viscount Duncannon, the future 3rd Earl of Bessborough. The fertility problems of her sister the duchess had not been replicated in her. Her son John Ponsonby was born the following year, on August 31, 1781, and Harriet continued to give birth with regularity every other year; by 1787, she had four children.[41]

George Spencer's marriage to Lavinia was equally fruitful. The couple produced the all-important son within a year of their wedding, and, by the time of the arrival of little George Augustus Curzon, they had a daughter as well. Even the Duchess of Devonshire finally gave birth in 1783, almost ten years after becoming a wife, although it would not be until 1790 that her only son, Hartington, was born.

Caroline had shown great interest in the children of Harriet, Lady Duncannon, her favorite of the Spencer brood. When Harriet arrived at 12 Grafton Street with her little boy, Caroline reported to her friend, "[H]e is quite charming, found out instantly I was a stranger & examined me in a wonderful manner with his great Eyes." He soon stopped exploring and was hungry. "[Lady Duncannon] gave him a little dinner here behind my screen."[42] Both of Lady Spencer's daughters were determined to breast-feed, a choice that was almost an "act of defiance" in an era when aristocratic women usually employed wet nurses.[43]

Soon after the arrival of the Howe grandchildren, momentous changes began to stir both at home and abroad. They were foreshadowed in a seemingly routine letter from Caroline to Lady Spencer that gave no inkling of what was to come. On October 23, 1788, Caroline passed on some court gossip: "The King has been exceedingly ill with Spasms in his stomach." She understood that his physician, Sir George Baker, opined that His Majesty would be well enough to attend the royal levee scheduled for the following day. In the next sentence, Caroline moved on to the international scene. It was predicted that there would be "great bustles" in France with the impending summoning of the Estates-General. The ruling powers of France would be confronted with a violent struggle for liberty, she predicted, and perhaps changes in their constitution. Trouble had come home to roost, pronounced Caroline, and deservedly so: "[T]he [French] King & his advisers will find, the mischief they did us in the American disputes coming home pretty handsomely to themselves."[44]

Now King George III was about to descend into the profound mental illness that would trouble him more or less for the rest of his life. He had suffered a bout of ill health in the summer of 1788, but, to all appearances, he had recovered by August. Very early on the morning after a royal drawing room, on October 17, he was seized with acute pains in his stomach, spasms in his limbs, and other symptoms. Three days later, he was hardly able to stand, and his mind kept wandering. After two more days, he appeared to be irrational, raging for three hours at Sir George Baker. This was the day when Sir George had claimed with dubious sincerity that the king was "much better" and would probably appear at court. The pronouncement was clearly meant for public consumption. The king was not better, and his appearance at the levee at St. James's Palace on October 24, disordered in dress and speech, caused dismay. On November 3, George III wrote what would be his last letter to his prime minister for many months.[45]

Caroline was soon in the know. Six days after the levee, she wrote that His Majesty was deranged: "[T]he delirium at times has been so strong that four men were obliged to hold him after he had knocked down two."[46] The malady, she feared, was in his brain.

Thus began the Regency Crisis, a three-month period when George III was too mentally unsound to govern. The royal disability was quickly entangled with party politics. Pitt and his government hoped that the king would recover; the Prince of Wales and his opposition friends, including Charles James Fox and Edmund Burke, hoped that he would not. A fierce political battle ensued over the terms by which a regent might be appointed, for the fates of Pitt and Fox were tied to the fates of their royal patrons.

Caroline heard it all, as she had friends on both sides. She wrote to Lady Spencer of a dinner party with the Devonshires where Edmund Burke, spokesman for the opposition, was in great spirits on the subject of the royal illness: "He talked of a recovery as quite impossible; not so the other side, they look upon it as certain, at least most probably so." Those who believed the king would recover cited for their authority Dr. Francis Willis, a Lincolnshire physician who had advanced ideas about the treatment of mental health.[47] Dr. Willis had been called in a month after the onset of the king's illness. Under his care, the king recovered early in 1789, at least for the time being.

Hard on the heels of George III's return to sanity came the other disorder presaged in Caroline's letter. In France, King Louis XVI had summoned his Estates-General in a desperate bid to save the nation from bankruptcy. Caroline had gloated at this development in October 1788. The famous events of 1789 ensued when the Estates-General met in May and the assembled delegates proved impossible to control. The Bastille fortress prison was stormed on July 14, and the National Assembly, now directing events, swept aside aristocratic privilege and determined to impose a constitutional monarchy.

Some in Britain, including opposition leader Charles James Fox, hailed these events as a step forward for humankind, as the French appeared to be embracing British notions of liberty.[48] Thomas Paine, the propagandist for the American rebellion, responded enthusiastically to the upheavals in France with his radical work *The Rights of Man*. Others were not so sure; the extreme ideas and actions of its powerful neighbor could pose a threat to England's peace and stability. By autumn 1789, Edmund Burke, once the champion of liberty in America, had become disgusted with developments in France, asserting that it was "a Country where the people, along with their political servitude, have thrown off the Yoke of Laws and morals." Burke would break with his Whig friends, writing his famous *Reflections on the Revolution in France*, published in November 1790.[49]

Popular opinion in Britain became polarized over the developments across the English Channel, but the Howes, as usual, were pragmatic and moderate. Richard believed that threats to peace and order would persist until "some regulated Monarchical Government is established in France."[50] For him, as for many Britons, the American War of Independence had not shaken their belief in the perfections of a constitutional monarchy. Little attention was paid in Britain to the constitutional experiments taking place in the new United States, despite their roots in British political thought. The prevailing view was that republics were doomed to remain minor powers on the world stage. There was a commonly held belief that the new American union would fall apart in the not-too-distant future.[51]

Richard had already resumed command of the Channel Fleet in 1790 when a minor territorial conflict between Britain and Spain in the remote Pacific (now part of British Columbia) threatened to break into armed confrontation. The Nootka Sound Crisis in some ways was a foretaste of nineteenth-century controversies. It was an imperial clash between European powers in what was for Europe an almost-unknown part of the globe.[52]

Distant as Nootka Sound was, it worried Britain, since conflict with Spain raised the specter of conflict with France. France and Spain were united by an alliance known as the Family Compact, which was founded on family ties between their respective monarchs, and in 1790, Louis XVI still reigned in Paris, at least in name. The crisis petered out within the year, for the new French National Assembly was unenthusiastic about helping Spain and denounced the royalist Family Compact. British supporters of the French Revolution hailed this as evidence of the beginning of a more enlightened French foreign policy.[53] Nevertheless, Richard had been obliged to undertake "the thousand little preparations necessary," as he put it, to ready the fleet for service that summer. His American butler Leveridge—probably a loyalist whose employment in the admiral's household was a legacy of the War of Independence—was obliged to assist him extensively, as the admiral's gout was becoming more severe with age.[54] Declining health, however, would not excuse Richard from serving his country for years to come.

Things changed rapidly in France after Nootka Sound. When the French royal family tried unsuccessfully to escape from their virtual house arrest in their flight to Varennes in June 1791, Richard commented, "To my dull apprehension, [events] promise a quick progress to a state of greater disorder, before [the French] acquire any systematic regularity in their proposed Constitution."[55] He was right. By 1792, France was at war with Austria and Prussia. The extremist Jacobins had assumed control. A republic was declared and the king was deposed. Violence escalated. The royal family was attacked at the Tuileries Palace on August 10, 1792, followed by the infamous September massacres, during which thousands were slaughtered in Parisian jails.

Many of the Englishmen who had looked with some favor on the revolution in France now began to change their minds. Even Charles James

Fox was horrified, writing, "There is not in my opinion a shadow of an excuse for this horrid massacre, not even a possibility of extenuating it in the smallest degree." Ominously, the new regime in France appeared to be exporting insurrection and revolutionary ideas.[56]

GEORGE III HAD ENJOYED a surge of popularity after his recovery from illness in 1788, and it did not abate with the commotion in France and the worrying rise of seditious groups in Britain. "God save the King was sung 5 times when the King was at Covent Garden last time," reported Caroline to Lady Spencer in November 1792. But there was a bustle at the Haymarket Theatre when the same patriotic song was called for, with someone in the audience shouting, "No, no, God save [Thomas] Paine." "[I]t put the whole House in a roar," wrote Caroline, and the man was turned out of his theater box.[57]

The Howes remained great supporters of the royal family. Since the death of Princess Amelia, Caroline had become a regular visitor to Queen Charlotte at Buckingham House. When a second son named Leicester was born to Charlotte Curzon in 1792 ("my additional *Grandchild*," Caroline called him), George Augustus Curzon, just four years of age, stood on the table at the christening and sang "God Save the King." Britain was not yet at war with France, but Caroline, as always, was well informed about what was going forward. "Our preparations both land & sea go on vigorously," she reassured Lady Spencer rather inaccurately, "so that we are ready both to quell home commotions or to go to war, in whatever mode fate may call upon us."[58]

Louis XVI went to the guillotine on January 21, 1793. A week later, Caroline described the atmosphere at the Court of St. James's. George III canceled his engagements, his royal drawing room, and his levee, "nor did he hunt on Saturday, yesterday the mourning was put on." The French ambassador, the Marquis de Chauvelin, was asked to leave, on the pretext that since his sovereign was now dead, his diplomatic accreditation as representative of the unrecognized new republic was not valid. Caroline recalled how Chauvelin was obliged to creep out of town, using the ruse that he was merely "going out a visiting," in order to avoid the hostile London crowds. The expulsion of Chauvelin was used by the French revolutionaries as provocation for an immediate declaration of war against Britain on February 1, 1793.[59]

As the French ambassador was slinking out of London, the Howe men were preparing once again for military service. In the same letter, Caroline reported that Lord Amherst was to be appointed commander in chief of the army: "The Lieutenants Genls. are to be five, Genl. [James] Johns[t]on, Sr W. Pitt, Sr W. Howe, Ld. George Lennox, & [Prince Frederick] the Duke of York, it is expected they will receive their Letters of service perhaps this day." "Sr W. Pitt" was Mary's husband, General William Augustus Pitt, who had been knighted in 1792. Sir William Pitt had not served in foreign lands since being a wounded prisoner during the Seven Years' War. Mary was afraid he would be sent to serve on the Continent. "Ly P[itt] is very happy," wrote Caroline, when, after all, he was not.[60] Both William Pitt and William Howe became full generals in 1793. For the next two years, General Howe would play an important role in supervising the training of troops and the defense of Britain.[61]

As Britain's new war with France began, Lady Spencer was on the Continent touring with her daughters and son-in-law. The escalation of fighting along France's borders had already prompted the little party to retreat from Switzerland to Italy, and they encountered French émigrés everywhere. On her homeward journey in 1794, Lady Spencer described the French refugees she saw as she passed through Bonn, Cologne, and Dusseldorf, "many of whom could not get lodgings or horses to go forwards & were sleeping & eating in their Carriages which crowd the Streets__many whom I am personally acquainted with are in actual & great distress. . . ."[62]

When Georgiana Duchess of Devonshire started for home in the summer of 1793, Lady Spencer remained in Rome because her younger daughter, Harriet, was too ill to travel.[63] By the time the duchess reached the port of Ostend in Flanders in early September, the French army was not far away, forcing the Duke of York and his troops into retreat near Dunkirk. English refugees were stranded and desperate at Ostend, looking for berths on any vessel to cross the Channel. A friend managed to squeeze the lovely duchess into his pleasure boat, and she was obliged to watch as her fellow countrymen faded into the distance, standing forlorn on the quayside. She was back in London by the time news arrived of the execution of Marie Antoinette in October.[64] The duchess had been a personal friend of the doomed queen.

Mainland Europe had become a dangerous place; some of the victims of the guillotine were known to both Caroline and Lady Spencer.[65] It is no wonder that Lord Howe berated his son-in-law, Lord Altamont, for traveling with Louisa and their little son by sea from Lisbon, where they had gone for Altamont's health, to their home in Cork, Ireland, in the summer of 1794. The Lisbon packet had already been taken by the enemy on one occasion, in the act making a prisoner of Lady Anne FitzRoy, sister to Arthur Welles-ley, the future Duke of Wellington. Richard noted, "[A]nd I had heard by an American ship come the same morning from Brest, that there was no indignity a Woman could receive, which she had escaped from that savage people." Richard bluntly insisted that the same crude treatment would not be meted out to any daughter of his: "I trust therefore, that it will be totally unnecessary for me to urge you not to hazard a similar disaster by her pass-ing back to Lisbon again, pending the War."[66]

Lady Anne FitzRoy was in her twenties when she was captured by the French. She remained a prisoner for several months. In keeping with the egalitarian ideology of the revolutionaries, her rank was ignored at first and she was incarcerated in a squalid common prison in Quimper, Brittany. Eventually she was allowed to take rooms in a local house and engage a ser-vant, but she remained closely guarded.[67] These facts became known to the British public within a year or so of her ordeal, but Lord Howe's letter hints at something worse than squalor.

At sixty-seven, when he assumed command of the Channel Fleet in 1793, Richard felt he was too old to go to sea again. But once in post, he showed his characteristic diligence. One aspect of his work that he resumed with zeal was his long-standing professional interest in rationalizing and improving the system of signaling used in the Royal Navy. In the eigh-teenth century, communications between ships used a system of flags that could signal only vague instructions. Richard was not the only naval officer trying to improve signaling, but he was one of the foremost.

Since the Seven Years' War, Richard had clarified, enlarged, rearranged, and improved the existing signaling system, producing the first printed reference book in 1758. His objective was to bring the operations of battle-ships during an engagement more directly under the control of the fleet commander. Signals from their commander during the action—rather than the written fighting instructions dispatched from the Admiralty prior to the battle—were what the fleet captains needed to heed first. This was a lifelong project for Richard, and in 1794 he finally arranged for the print-ing of all signal books and standing orders and their distribution to the fleet. One historian has written that Richard's interest in signals was an "enduring paradox," because he had a "crippling inability" to express himself, not only in speech but in writing. Horatio Nelson once received a letter from Howe that he described as a "jumble of nonsense."[68] In fact, Richard's speech and language issues, whatever the exact diagnosis may have been, probably sharpened his appreciation of the need for clear and rapid communication in a battle situation.

By the spring of 1794, a confrontation with the enemy was inevitable. The French navy had overcome a period of disorientation under the new revolutionary regime to reemerge as a credible fighting force. Richard knew that the French now had a considerable force of warships based at Brest, Brittany's largest port. In April 1794, he was ordered to intercept a large convoy of French merchant vessels loaded with provisions from the Caribbean and escorted by French ships of the line. On May 2, Richard departed from Portsmouth; on May 28, the enemy convoy was sighted.

For four days, the two fleets maneuvered on the high seas, both sides inflicting and taking damage, as Richard sought to bring the enemy to a full engagement.[69] At 5 a.m. on June 1, Admiral Howe finally placed himself in position upwind of the French and was able to force them to battle. Richard's intention was to sail downwind into the French line, break it, and fight the battle as an unstructured melee. The British were superior in discipline, sailing, and gunnery, and Howe wanted to make use of these advantages. At 7:15 a.m., Richard signaled his fleet to head directly for the French line; his flagship, the HMS *Queen Charlotte*, would attack the center of the line. Each of the British ships was directed to "break through the enemy line and engage the French ships from leeward." A second signal at 8:30 a.m. directed "each British ship to steer independently for and engage her opposite number in the enemy line." This last signal confused some captains, who interpreted it to mean they did not need to pass through the French line; as a result, only six British ships broke through.

Nevertheless, the battle descended into the free-for-all Richard had sought, as individual British and French ships took each other on. Within minutes of the start of the engagement, dense smoke everywhere obscured visibility. The *Queen Charlotte* bore down on the French flagship the *Montagne*, in the process taking fire from the ships *Vengeur* and *Achille*. Richard, cool as usual at the cannon's mouth, ignored the *Vengeur*, fired on the *Achille* with guns from his upper deck, and then blasted the stern of the *Montagne* with guns from the lower tiers of the *Queen Charlotte*. The

Montagne was obliged to withdraw from the battle. The British flagship then moved forward to engage the *Juste*. Thinking the enemy sought to break off the engagement, Howe gave the signal for a general chase.

The battle began at 9:30 a.m. and firing ceased by 1 p.m. The French admiral now managed to draw his remaining ships into a line of battle. In his one mistake, Richard, consulting with his staff, decided not to pursue, on the assumption that the enemy was determined to fight on. In fact, the French formation was wholly defensive, and much of the French fleet was in tatters. Richard returned to Portsmouth as a hero, with six enemy prizes in tow, a seventh French ship sunk, and the holds of the British warships packed with enemy prisoners.[70]

The Glorious First of June, as it became known, was Britain's first major naval victory of the Revolutionary and Napoleonic Wars, and the greatest in living memory at the time. Lord Nelson's later victories would be even greater, but for now the British public was elated. Actually, Richard had not achieved his objective of intercepting the French food convoy, and the French even claimed the battle as a victory for themselves. But the British public was far more interested in seeing a fighting victory over the hated French than in intercepting food supplies. The *St. James's Chronicle* crowed, "[T]he extacy of joy displayed by the public on receiving the news of Lord Howe's glorious victory, proves how much more Britons are delighted by success at sea than on land."[71]

Richard was exhausted. He had been awake for almost eight days, only occasionally resting in an armchair. The homeward journey, however, gave him an opportunity to relax, for the *Queen Charlotte* reached Spithead, Portsmouth, on June 13. Half of his fleet had been sent on to Plymouth for repairs.

Richard had sent Sir Roger Curtis ahead of his battered fleet to carry news of the victory to Britain; Curtis reached Plymouth on June 9, and Caroline knew of her brother's triumph by the following morning.[72] Two days later, she found time to write to Lady Spencer, her letter redolent not only of her own joy at witnessing the pinnacle of her brother's career, but also the ungrudging admiration of all of London:

> Half out of my senses, & wild with Joy ever since ½ past nine last
> Tuesday my dear Lady Spencer, you must not expect more than a
> few lines, & were I sober I could not send many, having hardly had a

moment to myself since Wednesday morn, all my friends & acquaintances, some even who have never visited me before, have come to
give me joy, & except a quarter of an hour that I was obliged to shut
my doors whilst I answered a Letter I had from the King, wrote
before he left Windsor to come to his Levee on Wednesday, I have
never been able to resist seeing every one who have chose to come
in. I have millions of notes very few I have had time to answer, this
morn at intervals Julie sitting by me I have contrived to do a little; the
King wrote a most excellent Letter too to Lady Howe & we had each
one later in the day from the Queen.[73]

Caroline had suffered from "a headache of agitation" for three days, but
she did not want to miss anything. She was out on Wednesday evening,
enjoying the sight of London illuminated in celebration of her brother's
great victory, and did not return until 2 a.m. Her only message to Richard,
she told Lady Spencer happily, was that she was glad she did not die of her
recent bout of scarlet fever and miss the whole thing.

Wednesday, June 11, saw London engulfed in what was effectively an
open-air party. Drury Lane Theatre lit up its cupola, then set off a display of
fireworks for the appreciative crowds below. Patriotic groups patrolled the
streets, compelling those in unlit dwellings to light their windows—"even
the stingy, the reluctant, and the disaffected [were made] to join in the general joy." The famous wedding-cake steeple atop St. Bride's Church dazzled
Fleet Street, and the Royal Opera House and St. James's Street were brilliant with lanterns. The newspapers reported, "We never recollect to have
witnessed more general joy, than was manifested on every countenance
throughout Wednesday, in consequence of the *glorious victory.* . . ."[74] Even
into the next morning, the bells were ringing, and "every FLAG, excepting
those bearing the THIRTEEN STRIPES [of the United States] were hoisted
in compliment to Lord Howe."[75]

The Howes had been spurned by an unappreciative British public in the
previous war; now they were welcomed back with open arms. "The scene at
the Opera & play houses was the most delightful glorious thing," scribbled
joyous Caroline in her letter of June 13, "& hardly to be bore." But she did
bear it, of course.

Lady Mary Howe had received word of her husband's victory a few hours
earlier than Caroline. At 2 a.m. on June 10, horses were heard outside of

Porter's Lodge. Mary, still in bed, heard the messenger's arrival, along with his cry, "Glorious news, my lady." Lady Elizabeth Foster, the intimate friend of the Duchess of Devonshire, recounted the humorous scene that ensued when Lady Howe called to the servant to enter her room: " 'I can't, my lady, I am naked.' 'Well,' says Lady Howe, 'I will get into bed again. Don't stay to dress but lay the letter on the table and get away.' " Caroline herself, who probably told this anecdote to Lady Elizabeth, "was quite nervous with the happiness," noted Lady Elizabeth.[76]

Lady Mary Howe reached London from Porter's Lodge on Wednesday morning, and on Thursday she set out for Portsmouth with her daughter Mary to greet her victorious husband. William and Fanny followed on Friday, the day that Lord Howe arrived in port. It was almost a complete Howe family gathering, with the Pitts there as well. Only Caroline and Julie, who was "as proud & happy as I am," Caroline assured Lady Spencer in her letter of June 13, remained in London. She added, "Sr Roger Curtis assures us Ld Howe is in perfect health, but that we shall find him thin, as well he may be, he & many officers not having taken off their cloaths for four nights."

The world now descended on Portsmouth, as word got out that the royal family would be honoring the victory with a fleet review. The House of Commons was adjourned for ten days to allow its members to join the throng.[77] Mary, Richard's middle daughter, who had been a Lady of the Bedchamber to the royal princesses since 1791, sent a description of the celebrations to her sister.[78] The royal family boarded the *Queen Charlotte*, where Mary and her mother were waiting to receive Queen Charlotte and the princesses. As they were with the royal ladies, the Howe women did not see the meeting between Lord Howe and the king, but it was described to them. "My father's knees trembled with emotion when he kissed the King's hand, who presented him with a most magnificent sword set with diamonds, and afterwards with a gold chain, to which is to be hung a gold medal struck for the occasion."[79] It is no wonder that Richard trembled, for this was the crowning moment of his life; he had vindicated his name, his family, and his claim to partake of national glory.

Once again, as in the Seven Years' War, the newspapers told of the daring of Black Dick Howe, the dynamic hero of old. The slurs and slanders of the American War of Independence now were entirely forgotten. The maneuvers of his flagship on June first were reported in detail to an appreciative public. "Never since England had a navy," concluded the report, not

King George III presenting Admiral Lord Howe with a diamond-hilted sword aboard the *Queen Charlotte*.

action better contested on both sides, or which terminated with so much honor to the British flag."[80]

Richard's new sword was valued at three thousand guineas, and the crew of HMS *Queen Charlotte* lined up after the presentation to touch it.[81] The royal family dined in the admiral's cabin and then walked the line of the ship's company, the king loudly praising the courage of the crew. The royals remained in Portsmouth until Monday, June 30; the town was the scene of pleasure cruises, dinners, fireworks, and balls. Young Mary had the thrill of being the leading lady at a Grand Ball.[82]

Caroline, in London with the delicate Julie, was not forgotten. As the eldest sister of the Howe dynasty, she was recognized by all as being entitled to bask in the reflected glory of her brothers' martial deeds. The king praised her "becoming ardour for the glory of her family." One of the "millions of notes" she received after the battle spoke of "the Joy, the Pride you must feel both as an Englishwoman and a Sister in your Glorious Brothers well acquitted Fortune."[83]

Five days after the close of the festivities in Portsmouth, Caroline wrote
to Lady Spencer that Richard would finally have a few days' rest at Porter's
Lodge. In fact, he would remain there for the summer. His "fine things"
would be gratefully put aside in exchange for some much-needed recuperation. But his sword, she could not help enthusing, "is the most mag[nifi-
cent]: & the most beautiful they say that ever was seen."[84]

A few weeks later, many of London's *"fashionable belles"* were sporting
an expensive new accessory, a memento of Lord Howe's victory. It was a
chain made of gold, "twisted into the form of a *cable*, and worn loosely
round the neck, to which is suspended a golden *anchor.*"[85] For high society's young ladies, national triumphs were an opportunity for conspicuous
consumption. But who should deserve to wear the necklace more than Lord
Howe's sister, now in her early seventies but still his most ardent admirer?
Young Lord Spencer presented his virtual aunt Caroline with one of the
nautical baubles—an "honor," she termed it happily, and a conversation
piece for someone who, throughout her life, had never really needed an
excuse for bringing up the accomplishments of her remarkable brothers.[86]

Epilogue

Legacy

Richard embarked on his final cruise less than a year after the Glorious First, in February 1795, when the fleet left Torbay, in Devon, to escort outward-bound convoys. The Glorious First of June was the pinnacle of his career, but it was not the last time he would be called into the service of his country. He would command the Channel Fleet for another three years. If waning health meant that he was unable to perform his duty to the full, he was nevertheless given a central role in the resolution of the Spithead Mutiny of 1797, a major protest by British sailors during wartime against pay and conditions. Once more, in a lifetime of service, Richard would use his personal popularity and leadership qualities with the seamen at Spithead in a negotiation to restore the fleet to active service in a time of national crisis.

Richard's gout became so severe that, by the end of his final cruise, he was confined to his bed. When he returned to Portsmouth, he asked to be relieved of his command. In Bath taking the waters by April, he confided to a friend that he was unable to stand without crutches. The next month, although still nominally commander in chief of the Channel Fleet, he was allowed to remain ashore. Admiral Alexander Hood was deputized to execute his orders, a situation that chafed, unsurprisingly, with that veteran sea officer. Richard did not improve, and in January 1797, he was still writing that he could only "walk across the room three or four times on my Crutches at Intervals."[1]

Richard's middle daughter, Mary, now stayed at home to support her father. Family tradition held that Mary was the favorite child of Lord and Lady Howe. In 1791, at the age of twenty-six, she had been appointed as a lady-in-waiting to the royal princesses, the daughters of George III, but her duties took her to court for alternate months only, leaving her time with her parents.[2] Mary was intelligent and educated, with a wide range of interests, and was much approved of by Lady Spencer, who wrote of her after a visit at Porter's Lodge: "I could not help telling her I was sorry she was too old for any of my Grandsons.__she is a dear thing."[3] Yet Mary, beneath her sweetness, was a typical Howe woman. Queen Charlotte wrote to Lady Howe that, while in service at court, the "mild and civil little Mary" beat the king at backgammon every night. When Queen Charlotte humorously chided her for disloyalty, she replied that she did the same to her father. "[U]pon that," concluded Her Majesty, "we settled that what was respectful and dutiful to Papa, must prove towards the King."[4]

Mary had resigned her post at court and was at Grafton Street in April 1797 when Lord Spencer, now First Lord of the Admiralty, called on Richard to accept his resignation. She described the gloom that reigned in the household as Richard confronted the reality of "shutting up forever the Prospect on what has been his Pursuit for above 63 years."[5] It was not easy for a man of his temperament to bring his naval career to a close.

Yet no sooner had Richard resigned when he was summoned back into service. There had been rumblings of mutiny within the Channel Fleet at Spithead since early March. The sailors' fundamental grievance was easy to understand, as sailors in the Royal Navy had not had a pay increase since 1652. Their protests were ignored at first, and when the fleet was ordered out in mid-April 1797, the men refused to set sail. Determined to show, however, that they were not traitors, the sailors stipulated that if a French fleet should appear, they would return to their duties.

The government acceded to most of the mutineers' demands and offered a royal pardon, for Britain was in grave danger. The alliances formed in 1793 against revolutionary France were collapsing. In 1795, the Dutch government of the United Provinces allied itself with France, and both Prussia and Spain concluded peace treaties with the revolutionary republic. A year later, Britain again was at war with Spain, and heavily outgunned in the Mediterranean. Admiral Sir John Jervis and a new naval hero, Captain Horatio Nelson, won the second great naval battle of the French Revolutionary Wars at Cape St. Vincent in February 1797.

The Battle of Cape St. Vincent had prevented Spanish reinforcements from joining with a French fleet to invade Ireland. It is no wonder that a few short months later, desperate to get the Channel Fleet to sea, the government offered a royal pardon for the Spithead mutineers. The seamen returned to their duty, only to go on strike again on May 7. The issue was trust. In an age when naval discipline was severe, they feared that government promises might not be honored, or, still worse, they feared reprisals.[6] The government needed someone beyond suspicion to talk with the mutineers, and Admiral Howe was their choice, as he was both popular and admired within the Channel Fleet, whose men well remembered the Glorious First of June.

This time, Richard's duty called him to a place where Lady Howe could also venture. They set out for Portsmouth together, arriving on May 11. Richard immediately visited several ships, including his old flagship, the *Queen Charlotte*. The Admiralty had shied away from recognizing the delegates appointed by the mutineers, but Richard accepted their petitions. He repeatedly read aloud the royal pardon for their past actions, and patiently reassured them over and over that the government intended to grant their demands. Finally, in order to allay their suspicions, he obtained printed copies of the royal pardon from the Admiralty.

The mutineers had another, highly irregular demand: that more than a hundred unpopular officers, notorious for their poor treatment of the men, were not to be returned to their ships. Richard sided with the sailors and requested the Admiralty to concede. For several days, Richard went unwearyingly from ship to ship at Spithead and St. Helens, addressing the malcontents. Gradually, by the force of his personality, he persuaded the men that they could trust the government. By May 14, the mutiny was over.[7]

Admiral Howe was heavily criticized for making the concession regarding unpopular officers, and he even acknowledged that it was not desirable for sailors to have "the assumed right of rejecting their officers." But he recognized this sticking point in the negotiations and solved it by stipulating that the officers should remain on full pay.[8] Britain had her fleet back, and the sailors' grievances were assuaged. Richard had sized up the situation correctly and used his leadership skills and the ability to win the trust of men in the ranks.

With the mutiny now over, Lord and Lady Howe were enveloped in another joyous celebration on May 15 in Portsmouth. Richard was hoisted onto the shoulders of exuberant seamen and carried to the Governor's House, a gratifying but perhaps painful experience for a gouty seventy-one-year-old.[9] General Sir William Pitt and Lady Mary Pitt arrived to participate in the celebration, and Lady Howe and Lady Pitt shook the work-roughened hands of the delegates for the mutineers, now lauded as "brave tars" by the press. Lord Howe was "the only man," declared the admiring delegates, who could have ended the dispute.[10]

May 1797 was a very busy month for Richard's family. Just days after the celebrations in Portsmouth, Lady Howe saw her daughter Mary act as a bridesmaid at the wedding of Princess Charlotte, the Princess Royal, to Frederick, Prince of Württemberg, at St. James's Palace in London. This was a dynastic marriage, but it suited the princess, who had long chafed at her confined life, referring to her home as "the nunnery." Princess Charlotte was thirty and unromantically plump; the bridegroom was even older and fatter. Nevertheless, this was a royal wedding with appropriate splendor. Bridesmaid Mary Howe was arrayed in finery that was second only to that of the princess, white silk trimmed in silver, diamonds and an ostrich feather on her headdress. The heat was so intense that she nearly fainted; it must have been worse for Princess Charlotte, who trailed a robe of crimson velvet trimmed in fur.[11]

Less than a week after the wedding, on May 23, a fête was put on at the royal retreat of Frogmore House. Nominally in honor of the royal newlyweds, it became virtually a tribute to Admiral Howe.[12] "[T]here was absolutely more Fuss made about [Lord Howe] than about the Würtembergs," recalled his daughter Mary, who was present. Her father was "the Courted Object of every body," she enthused. "Saviour of his Country was his common Appellation." The queen ordered her own carriage and pony to transport the infirm Richard around the walks, saying, "Nothing can be too much for the conqueror of the first of June and May," for the date of the fête fell between the date of Richard's recent triumph at Spithead and the anniversary of the Glorious First three years earlier.

In what would be Richard's final public accolade, King George III personally led him down the steps of Frogmore House to the lawn, where the royal princes and princesses were waiting, and pushed him among them. The royal family formed a circle around the old admiral and sang James Hook's popular song "The Glorious First of June." George, Prince of Wales, was in the middle of the royal grouping, with his siblings and Queen Charlotte gathered around. Mary was delighted:

> I never saw such a Scene, or any thing so thoroughly pleasing as the Wish of pleasing him shown upon every Countenance. He looking remarkably well, so much so that all the People in the Gardens (half

[of] Windsor) were running after him and calling him "that Dear old Man, that D[ea]r Lord Howe."

The company all walked together through the grounds, as Mary recalled, "[M]y Dear Father with a Stick and Mama's Arm (how happy did she look)."[13] On such a high note, Richard's career finally came to a close.

Richard was now fully retired and could rest as much as he pleased, but he never recovered his health. Two years after the fête at Frogmore, and growing characteristically impatient with his invalid status, he tried an experimental new treatment for gout, which involved the administration of electric shocks.[14] Surprisingly, his mobility began to improve under this crude procedure, and he was walking around at Porter's Lodge with just a cane when he suddenly fell ill late in the evening of Sunday, August 4, 1799. By midmorning the next day, he was gone.[15]

Richard Howe's final resting place was in the family vault in St. Andrew's Church, Langar, whose country fields and lanes he had not visited for many years. Lady Howe, together with her daughters Mary and Louisa, remained at home in London. As the funeral procession set out, crowds gathered in front of 3 Grafton Street, shedding tears. The procession was scheduled to reach Langar on August 18, and Lady Howe wept copiously as she imagined the hearse arriving at the village, where the tenants of the Howe estate were to carry the coffin to the church.

Aunt Caroline Howe of course assisted her nieces in supporting their mother, visiting every evening for several hours, "& during that time I never open my Lips being worn [out]," wrote the grateful Louisa.[16] The king waited until a fortnight after the funeral to send his condolences to Caroline, knowing her to be "fully employed in acts of attentive kindness to her relations." Like everyone, he saw her as the natural mainstay in the midst of a Howe family crisis.[17]

Lady Mary Howe was sixty-seven when she became a widow. With a weak heart, she moved to Porter's Lodge to recuperate over the winter, her three daughters at her side. There she learned that Parliament had voted for a monument of Admiral Lord Howe to be raised in London's iconic St. Paul's Cathedral. Some of her old spirit reasserted itself when she wrote waspishly to a friend that the MPs would have done better to have shown their appreciation during the lifetime of her husband, rather than "to cover their ill-conduct to him by this outward show of respect to his memory."[18]

Lady Howe had not forgotten the political attacks on Richard by his own countrymen during the American War of Independence.

In an age when sudden death could strike the young as well as the old, Richard and Mary's daughter Mary, after an illness of just a few weeks, died on March 9, 1800. She had just become engaged to George Douglas, Earl of Morton. Within the extended Howe family, the shock of Mary's death was devastating. Caroline predicted that it would prove fatal to Lady Howe, and so it was. "On the 9th of August 1800," wrote Caroline sadly, her sister-in-law and old friend, the companionable "Dickess" of her younger years, "was released from a year of sad sorrow, but her death was an easy one. Her two affectionate and dutiful daughters never left her side till the last scene was closed."[19]

Less than three years later, Caroline's younger sister Julie died. At seventy-one, she had lived a full life by the standards of the day. By nature retiring, she had spent much of her time since her mother's death staying in the homes of her various siblings, especially Caroline and the Pitts. For reasons that Caroline's letters do not disclose, at times Julie took laudanum— that universal remedy of the day for physical and mental suffering. Julie appears as an unassuming presence throughout Caroline's family chronicles: rather childlike in her interests, ill at ease in fashionable company, yet passionate in her private affections, notably her adoration for Lady Spencer.

It is a testimony to the close, affectionate nature of the Howe family that Julie remained central to her busy siblings' lives, though she shared none of their social or political ambitions. Caroline left a charming account of Julie at her home in Richmond, where she conscientiously fed the wild birds in her garden throughout September, the season when many birds migrate south and sparrows leave town for the countryside to take advantage of the harvest. "Julie has vast numbers flocking about," wrote Caroline, "which she used to feed with breadcrumbs when breakfasting in her tent, but they were many days before she could get them to eat at the little house before it's door."[20]

Old age was overtaking many of her generation, but Caroline Howe was destined to live many years longer. Decades prior to Julie's death, Caroline had commented on the sadness of aging. But it was not like Caroline to give in to circumstances. She surely had herself in mind when she added the caveat, "[W]hilst a person can read & entertain themselves alone it is a different story." She was certainly in this favored category. All her life,

Caroline had been an avid reader, sometimes reading in tandem with Lady Spencer. In her sixties, she was mastering ancient Greek; in her eighties, she was learning Spanish.

With advancing age, Caroline continued to make efforts to remain physically active as well. She still walked and went visiting into her final years. In her sixties, she confessed to feeling like an outsider in gatherings of young people, but she was still attending parties twenty years later, despite experiencing diminished mobility. She explained how she managed the crowded spaces: "I sit without moving in a corner, and can, by coming away a short time before they are over, avoid difficulty." Yet, just a few weeks after writing this, on the occasion of a ball to celebrate the Queen's Birthday, Caroline did not bother to make an early escape. She had just turned eighty-one, but she stayed out till 5 a.m., not "too much tired, but of course not up by Cockcrow."[21] She remained close to the royal family, boasting to Lady Spencer that the king had arranged for modifications to a colonnade adjoining Buckingham House in order to shelter her from the elements as she entered, walling it up and adding windows. "I have done it for *you*," said the king, "& I call it the Howe Gallery."[22]

Caroline once wrote to her friend Lady Spencer, "[W]hat unfortunate beings are all those, born with a bad temper, for a persons own private happiness I look upon as one of the best Gifts bestowed upon mortals, do you not feel it so?" She was indeed endowed with a resilient nature, one that saw her through the many vicissitudes of life. When she was almost ninety years old, she was still talked about in fashionable society; her sharp mind, her unremitting quest for knowledge, and her youthful enthusiasm for cards were remarkable enough to be the topic of discussion around a London dinner table.[23]

This was in May 1811, a few months after the Prince of Wales had been declared regent. George III had recently descended into his final, tragic period of mental illness that only ended with his death in 1820. Caroline would live long enough to have the satisfaction of seeing Napoleon Bonaparte imprisoned on the island of Elba in May 1814, vanquished after twelve years of bloody warfare. For more than a third of her life, Britain had been at war. Her brother William would in effect die in harness at age eighty-four, still undertaking limited military duties as governor of Plymouth.

The only surviving portrait of Caroline Howe was painted by the artist Henry Howard when she was around ninety years of age. She is seated

at a desk, a copy of *The Times* before her, pen in hand.[24] What looks to
be an Egyptian artifact of the god Horus is upon her newspaper, and
her chess pieces are visible under a glass dome. Behind her is a glazed
bookcase protecting her extensive library. Perhaps the neat bundle of
documents tucked into the wooden organizer to the left of *The Times* are
the results of the days she spent cataloging her book collection with the
assistance of her maid.[25] Seated in her Grafton Street drawing room, she
is portrayed here as her many callers would typically have found her, at
her writing desk busy with the thousands of letters she wrote over a lifetime. "I literally have not been above ½ an hour since I came down[stairs]
without a Pen in my hand," was a typical self-description. Close friends
looked forward to her literary productions; next-door-but-one neighbor
John Crawfurd, stopping in to invite her to dinner, "tore away my letter
& would read as far as I had got," a charming picture of how she united
her dedicated letter-writing with an atmosphere of informal sociability
in her drawing room.[26]

Caroline died in her Grafton Street home on June 29, 1814. She lies buried at St. Botolph's Church, Shenleybury, in Hertfordshire.[27] Lady Spencer
had died three months earlier, and William only survived his elder sister by
two weeks. Both William and his wife, Fanny, who outlived him by three
years, are buried near their home in Twickenham.[28] The Irish peerage that
William inherited from Richard became extinct upon his death. And the
title of Baroness Howe, now held by Richard's eldest daughter, Charlotte
Curzon, was in a precarious situation, for, of her four children, only two
were still living at the time of her Uncle William's death. Tragically, her
promising eldest son, George Augustus Curzon, had died in 1805 at the age
of sixteen, and her title ultimately passed to her youngest, Richard Penn
Curzon.[29] He and Louisa Lady Altamont's son, Howe Peter Browne, were
ultimately the sole survivors to carry on the line.

Of ten live infants born to Scrope Lord Howe and Charlotte von Kielmansegg almost a century earlier, just two great-grandchildren remained.
Yet they were sufficient. Mary, Countess Pembroke, Caroline's beloved aunt
and mentor, would rejoice to see Howe Peter Browne become the 2nd Marquess of Sligo and the founder of a large family.

Richard Penn Curzon took the name of Curzon-Howe after his marriage
in 1820; his mother Charlotte persuaded King George IV to grant him the
title of 1st Earl Howe, in effect re-creating the earldom of his grandfather,

Richard, despite that naval hero's lack of sons.[30] The title survives to this day in the Curzon family.

Admiral Lord Howe's personal legacy also has lived on. He would remain a celebrated figure throughout the nineteenth century, notably on the strength of his victory on the Glorious First of June. In 1894, on the centennial of that triumph, the newspapers compared the Glorious First to Waterloo and classed it among the compulsory British battles studied by schoolboys everywhere.[31] Today the Glorious First is no longer found in British school histories, but the name of Howe is still remembered in the United Kingdom through its association with Richard's great victory.

William's legacy turned out very differently. In Britain, he is still occasionally glimpsed in histories of the Seven Years' War as a heroic young officer, giving a triumphant hurrah as he and a handful of his comrades surprise the sentries at the clifftops in Quebec. In the United States, he is seen as the aristocratic British commander in chief who lost his nerve at Bunker Hill, failed the test against Washington's young Continental Army, and was mysteriously soft on the American enemy. In his own lifetime, the vitriolic critiques of the war years were distilled into historical accounts. The American War of Independence did not end William's career, but it did irretrievably mar it.

When the Howe women assumed direction of the family after the death of Scrope Lord Howe in 1735, their dynasty had aspirations to greatness. In an era when the nation's fortunes were closely linked to success in warfare, the brothers climbed high. While they were still young, they had served in the Seven Years' War, a conflict that would see Britain emerge as a major world power and the Howe brothers as household names.

But the dynasty's rise was disrupted by their association with a war that today has been called "Britain's Vietnam," a war the British nation could not recall with pride. With powerful friends and determined, skillful management, the Howe men and women always remained at the center of Britain's aristocratic world. Yet widespread suspicion of the brothers, their actions, and their motives during the war has never entirely gone away.

It is apt that their sister's correspondence has helped to restore to the brothers their true identities. George, Richard, and William would no doubt have agreed that there is much more to be revealed about them through their whole-family histories than through military dispatches and official correspondence. Caroline, in fact, possessed the same talents that

carried her brothers to the tops of their professions. Lady Spencer paid tribute to the distinctive persona of her lifelong friend when she unconsciously
slipped into language normally used in her day to dignify a public—and
masculine—figure:

> I often wonder how it happens that you & I see things as we fre-
> quently do, in the same light for nothing can be more diametrically
> opposite than our Characters in most things___You have a great deal
> of personal Courage, I am the veriest Coward that ever breath'd, Your
> Idea's are Lofty & Magnificent mine are all Low & Simple—You love
> the Towering Mountain, the foaming Torrent & the raging Ocean—
> I the Shady Wood the green Meadow & the Winding Stream.

"[I]n short," she rhapsodized, "you have a Soul that could govern a Nation &
I as I have often told you should have been the Curate's Wife—but all this is
Nonsensical my Dearest Howey we were both born for Noble ends to make
ourselves & others happy—let us follow our calling & not grow tir'd of the
delightful office."[32]

Caroline never tired of her "delightful office." Through triumph and
failure, victory and disaster, her belief in herself and the purpose of her
own life, the lives and destinies of her brothers, and the many great and
little doings all around her shine through in her written words.

ACKNOWLEDGMENTS

When I began working on *The Howe Dynasty* in 2014, I did not foresee what an enormously complex project it would be, one that would involve uncovering the backstory of a once-famous family now largely forgotten. It was a painstaking process that frequently took me outside of my historical expertise in eighteenth-century Atlantic history. Its successful completion drew upon the assistance and support of many people and institutions.

First and foremost is my husband, Andy, who encouraged the project from the start. His lifelong interest in British naval history meant that, despite being a biochemist, he was immediately supportive of the concept of the first-ever history of the family of Richard Admiral Lord Howe, the hero of the Glorious First of June of 1794. Andy was a constant source of reassurance and encouragement, but he also contributed in more substantial ways. His professional skill of adhering to rigid word totals while maintaining clarity, honed during a career writing scientific-grant applications, was brought to bear on the first complete draft of the book, greatly reducing its length and enhancing its readability. He drew the maps—a talent I didn't realize he had—and created mock-ups of the book cover that contributed to its final design. He provided IT skills and exercised editorial judgment when I was so close to the material that I needed a fresh eye.

I wish to thank the William L. Clements Library, University of Michigan, for funding a highly productive month in the Clements research room in 2015 through the generous award of an Upton Foundation Fellowship in American History. The dedicated research room staff assisted my project in numerous ways. The contributions of Brian Leigh Dunnigan, Cheney J. Schopieray, and Jayne Ptolemy ranged from identifying invaluable new sources to figuring out how to mute the screenshot sound on my Nikon camera. The month I spent at the Clements enriched my project in ways that I had not anticipated, and it broadened my treatment of the Howe family's experience during the War of Independence. Cheney Schopieray directed my attention to the Jane Strachey correspondence in the Somerset Archives, which yielded a trove of new material on the Howe women on the home front in 1776–77.

I am grateful to the Robert H. Smith International Center for Jefferson Studies for a fellowship to consult the resources at the Jefferson Library and the University of Virginia's Albert and Shirley Small Special Collections Library in October 2017. During our one-month stay in Charlottesville, Andy and I were welcomed and supported by Andrew O'Shaughnessy, Whitney Pippen, and all the staff at ICJS. Andrew O'Shaughnessy was enthusiastic about a biography of the Howe family from its earliest planning stages. He, Gaye Wilson, Marie Frank, and others contributed their enthusiasm and insight to many aspects of my work. Our friend Liz Poarch greatly contributed to the comfort of our visit by lending us the use of her home in Charlottesville while she was on holiday.

A number of individuals read and commented on the manuscript in various stages. I would like to acknowledge my special appreciation for the contributions of the late Professor Peter D. G. Thomas, whose enthusiasm for the project from its inception, willingness to read and reread every draft, and generous contribution of his preeminent expertise in eighteenth-century British politics enriched the book and encouraged me during the six years I labored on it. Sadly, his passing in July 2020 meant that he never saw the completed volume.

Stephen Brumwell generously agreed to give the manuscript the benefit of his critical eye as a military historian, rescuing me from errors and directing me to specialized scholarship that enhanced my accounts of the early army careers of George and William Howe. Steven Sarson, H. T. Dickinson, and Andrew O'Shaughnessy were all enthusiastic readers of the whole manuscript at various stages. Steve Sarson obligingly bandied about ideas over the telephone regarding various aspects of the book as it developed.

I am grateful to Professor John McCusker for the encouragement, support, and advice he offered in various stages of the project. Professor Ira Gruber generously shared with me his notes of the Dowager Countess Howe's correspondence with Count Kielmansegg in the von Kielmansegg family papers at Heinde, Lower Saxony. Martin Price, who shares my enthusiasm for the letters of Caroline Howe, contributed a number of little-known facts regarding her life, the results of his private research.

Thanks to my mother, Susan Zorn, who communicated her enthusiasm for the book, back when it was still just an idea, to friend and publisher Curtis Vouwie. Through him, my project was brought to the attention of Ike Williams and Katherine Flynn at Kneerim & Williams Literary Agency. Katherine Flynn has been my dedicated literary agent throughout the project, mentoring me through the proposal process and troubleshooting problems both small and large throughout the years of research and writing.

I wish to thank my editor, Bob Weil at Liveright, for his detailed and demanding line editing and for his insistence at every stage that there were always possibilities for improving this book. The result was a manuscript that achieved the very highest standard. Gina Iaquinta at Liveright worked closely with me to polish the final version, contributing not only her skill and experience as an editor but also her tremendous enthusiasm, an essential ingredient at a late and tiring stage of the project. Kathleen Brandes was a meticulous and thorough copyeditor. Thanks also to designer Yang Kim, and Steve Attardo and the Art Department, for the stunning book jacket.

Dave Flavell and Mel Clements put me up at their flat in London so many times I've lost count. Without their generous hospitality, I would not have been able to explore the letters of Caroline Howe as effectively and complete this project. A stay at the home of Nigel Carter and Jill Meisenhelder near San Diego, California, in 2014 enabled me to visit the Huntington Library in San Marino. Transport was generously provided by Nigel, whose patience while I was in the library allowed me to consult the Howe papers and other collections. I would also like to acknowledge the support of my children, Eve and Paul—now adults—throughout the gestation of the book, which has been with our family for many years.

I am grateful to Lord and Lady Howe for welcoming me to Penn House in Buckinghamshire to view their private collection of portraits of the eighteenth-century Howe family, as well as a collection of letters written by members of the royal family to Caroline Howe and others. Lord Howe kindly allowed me to arrange for the portraits to be photographed and reproduced in my book.

My research took me to numerous archives, where staff members helped in many ways. In addition to the staff at the British Library's Manuscripts

Reading Room who assisted me in exploring Caroline Howe's letters, Dr. Margaret Makepeace helped me retrieve information regarding the career of Thomas Howe from the British Library's voluminous East India Company Records. The National Register of Archives for Scotland arranged for me to consult the manuscript diary of Lady Mary Coke at General Register House in Edinburgh. Extracts from the diary of Lady Mary Coke are reproduced in this work by kind permission of the Douglas-Home family, Earls of Home. For permission to use the Strachey Collection in the Somerset Archives and Local Studies, I acknowledge the South West Heritage Trust. Extracts from the Westport Estate Papers and the Thomas Conolly Papers are reproduced courtesy of the National Library of Ireland. I am also grateful to the Sheffield Archives, Sheffield City Council, Libraries Archives and Information, for permission to cite from the 2nd Marquis of Rockingham series of papers within the Wentworth Woodhouse Muniments Collection. For anyone I have forgotten in a project that spanned six years, please accept my apologies and my sincere thanks.

Finally, I would like to thank my father, Bruce Richardson, and my brother, Joel Richardson, for their unfailing faith in my abilities as a writer and a historian as well as their admiration that lifted me up at some bad moments. They both passed away while the project was underway. I miss you guys, and I wish you could have stayed to see *The Howe Dynasty*.

NOTES

Abbreviations Used in the Notes

People

CH   Caroline Howe
LS   Lady Spencer

Repositories

BL   British Library
DRO   Derbyshire Record Office
NA   National Archives, Kew
NLI   National Library of Ireland
Notts. Archives   Nottinghamshire Archives
NRAS   National Register of Archives for Scotland
NRS   National Records of Scotland
WCL   William L. Clements Library, University of Michigan

Digital Resources

BC   17th–18th Century Burney Collection Newspapers [Farmington Hills, MI]: Gale Cengage Learning
BNA   British Newspaper Archive (www.britishnewspaperarchive.co.uk)
ODNB Online   Oxford Dictionary of National Biography Online, Oxford University Press, 2004

Frequently Cited Works and Collections

Anderson   Troyer Steele Anderson, *The Command of the Howe Brothers during the American Revolution* (New York and London, 1936)
Barrow   Sir John Barrow, *The Life of Richard Earl Howe, K.G.* (London, 1838; this edition Elibron Classics Replica Edition, 2005)
BL-AP   British Library, Althorp Papers
BL-NP   British Library, Newcastle Papers, Correspondence: 32686-32992

CPE	Sir Egerton Brydges, *Collins's Peerage of England: Genealogical, Biographical, and Historical* (9 vols., London, 1812)
Davies	K. G. Davies, ed., *Documents of the American Revolution, 1770-1783* (21 vols., Kill-o'-the-Grange, 1972–1981)
Gruber	Ira D. Gruber, *The Howe Brothers and the American Revolution* (New York, 1972)
HMC	Historical Manuscripts Commission
HWC	*The Yale Edition of Horace Walpole's Correspondence*, ed. W. S. Lewis (48 vols., London, 1937–1983)
LEC	Montagu Pennington, ed., *Letters from Mrs Elizabeth Carter, to Mrs Montagu, between the years 1755 and 1800 chiefly upon literary and moral subjects* (3 vols., London, 1817)
LLMC	*The Letters and Journals of Lady Mary Coke* (4 vols., first published 1889–96; Facsimile Edition published in Bath, 1970)
NRAS-DH/LMC	National Register of Archives for Scotland, Papers of the Douglas-Home Family, diary of Lady Mary Coke
PBF	William B. Willcox et al., eds., *The Papers of Benjamin Franklin* (42 vols., New Haven and London, 1959–2017)
PCC	The National Archives, Kew: Prerogative Court of Canterbury
SALS-DD/SH	Somerset Archives and Local Studies, South West Heritage Trust, Strachey Collection
Smith	David Smith, *William Howe and the American War of Independence* (London, New Delhi, New York, and Sydney, 2015)
Syrett	David Syrett, *Admiral Lord Howe: A Biography* (Stroud, Gloucestershire, 2006)
WCL-GSG	William L. Clements Library, George Sackville Germain Papers 1683–1785
WCL-HC	William L. Clements Library, Richard and William Howe Collection, 1758–1812
WCL-HCP	William L. Clements Library, Sir Henry Clinton Papers
WCL-KP	William L. Clements Library, William Knox Papers
WCL-SP	William L. Clements Library, Henry Strachey Papers, 1768–1802

Prelude: Dynastic Secrets

1 BL-AP, 75612, CH/LS, Dec. 2, 1774.
2 PBF, vol. 21, p. 566.
3 Horace Walpole, *Memoirs of the Reign of King George II* (3 vols., London, 1847), vol. 3, p. 50.
4 Anderson, p. 6; Gruber, p. 351.
5 Syrett, p. 156; Sam Willis, *The Glorious First of June: Fleet Battle in the Reign of Terror* (London, 2011), p. 43.
6 Smith, p. 1.

7 Amanda Vickery, "Home Truths: Amanda Vickery on Why David Starkey Is Wrong," *The Independent*, November 7, 2010.

8 Mary Beard, "The Public Voice of Women," *London Review of Books* 36, no. 6, 20 (2014), pp. 11–14.

9 Joseph J. Ellis, *First Family: Abigail and John Adams* (New York and Toronto, 2010), p. x.

One: The Howe Women

1 BL-AP, 75628, CH/LS, Sat., April 8, 1786. I am grateful to Martin Price for drawing this quote to my attention.

2 Matthew Kilburn, "Howe, (Mary Sophia) Charlotte [née Sophia Charlotte Mary von Kielmansegg], Viscountess Howe (1703–1782)," ODNB Online [accessed Nov. 1, 2019]. About names: Charlotte von Kielmansegg was born Sophia Charlotte Mary von Kielmansegg, but she changed the baptismal order of her name, placing Charlotte first, sometime after her marriage. See the Kilburn article, above. Scrope Howe is often called Emanuel Scrope Howe in biographical references, but he was baptized simply Scrope, so he is called Scrope in this work. See reference in Register of Baptisms for St. Andrew's Church, Langar, below. Emanuel Scrope Howe was the name of his uncle.

3 Claudia Gold, *The King's Mistress: The True and Scandalous Story of the Woman Who Stole the Heart of George I* (London, 2012), pp. 171, 174. For Alexander Pope cite, see p. 174.

4 Ragnhild Marie Hatton, *George I, Elector and King* (London, 1978), p. 152. Hatton locates the house in Great George Street. Gold, *The King's Mistress*, pp. 129–31, 171, cite from Gold, p. 128.

5 A. T. Thomson, *Memoirs of Viscountess Sundon: Mistress of the Robes to Queen Caroline* (2 vols., London, 1848), vol. I, pp. 16–17.

6 Eduard Georg Ludwig Kielmansegg, *Familien-Chronik Der Herren, Freiherren Und Grafen Von Kielmansegg* (Leipzig und Wien, 1872; this edition: Nabu Public Domain Reprint facsimile), pp. 127–52.

7 G. N. B. Huskinson, "The Howe Family and Langar Hall 1650 to 1800," *Transactions of the Thoroton Society*, 1952 (vol. 56), p. 54; DRO: Okeover Papers, D231M/E 5178: Survey book of part of the Nottinghamshire and Leicestershire estate of the Rt. Hon. Scrope Lord Viscount Howe, Baron of Cleonelly in Langar, Barnstone, Granby and Hose (1706).

8 CPE, vol. 8, pp. 133–38; http://www.historyofparliamentonline.org/volume/1660 -1690/member/howe-john-i-grobham-1625-79 [accessed Nov. 1, 2019].

9 http://www.historyofparliamentonline.org/volume/1690-1715/member/howe-sir -scrope-1648-1713 [accessed Nov. 1, 2019]; CPE, vol. 8, p. 142.

10 Huskinson, "The Howe Family and Langar Hall," p. 54; Robert Thoroton, "Parishes: Langar & Barneston and St. Aubrey's," in *Thoroton's History of Nottinghamshire: Volume 1, Republished With Large Additions By John Throsby*, ed. John Throsby (Not-

tingham, 1790), pp. 201–9. *British History Online:* http://www.british-history.ac.uk /thoroton-notts/vol1/pp. 201–9 [accessed Sept. 1, 2020].

11 Hatton, *George I*, p. 98.

12 DRO: Okeover Papers, D231M/E 5178: Survey book of part of the Nottinghamshire and Leicestershire estate of [Scrope Lord Howe]; Bodleian Library: MS. Eng. Misc. e. 452, 45865, "Volume containing accounts of personal expenditure of Scrope, 1st Viscount Howe, and memoranda and accounts of his wife Juliana, 1736-40," Fols. 87 r-v.

13 See A. A. Hanham, "Howe, John Grobham (1657–1722)" and Stuart Handley, "Howe, Emanuel Scrope (c. 1663–1709)," ODNB Online [both accessed Nov. 1, 2019].

14 B. H. Blacker, "Howe, Charles (1661–1742)," rev. by Adam Jacob Levin, ODNB Online [accessed Nov. 1, 2019]; Huskinson, "The Howe Family and Langar Hall," p. 55.

15 Scrope was baptized on July 18, 1699. His sisters Mary, Juliana, and Anne were baptized, respectively, on October 8, 1700, October 24, 1701, and May 7, 1704. A brother Richard, baptized March 14, 1703, died in childhood: Notts. Archives, Register of baptisms for St. Andrew's Church, Langar, PR/6822.

16 Amanda Vickery, *The Gentleman's Daughter: Women's Lives in Georgian England* (New Haven and London: 1998), pp. 72–86.

17 NLI, Westport Estate Papers [MS 40,909/7 (14)], Letter of Scrope Howe to [Juliana] Howe, Nov. 20, 1716.

18 BNA: *Stamford Mercury*, Sept. 22, 1720; *Ipswich Journal*, Nov. 19, 1720.

19 Caroline was born May 17, 1722. City of Westminster Archives Centre, St. Martin-in-the-Fields Baptisms, m/f 11.

20 Charlotte—baptized Sophia Charlotte—was born August 27, 1723. George Augustus was born on November 29, 1724. City of Westminster Archives Centre, St. Martin-in-the-Fields Baptisms, m/f 11, m/f 12; http://www.historyofparliamentonline.org /volume/1754-1790/member/howe-richard-1726-99 [accessed Nov. 1, 2019].

21 John is listed as the fourth son, who died in infancy, CPE, vol. 8, p. 144. His birth date is not given. He was buried at Langar on May 26, 1731: Notts. Archives, Register of burials for St. Andrew's Church, Langar, PR/6828.

22 William was born on August 10, 1729, http://www.historyofparliamentonline.org /volume/1754-1790/member/howe-hon-william-1729-1814 [accessed Nov. 1, 2019].

23 Thomas was baptized on March 12, 1730/31 (old style). Juliana was baptized at Langar on September 13, 1732: Notts. Archives, Register of baptisms for St. Andrew's Church, Langar, PR/6823. Mary was born in Barbados.

24 Scrope died on October 26, 1728. BC: *The Daily Post*, Jan. 2, 1729.

25 Lawrence Stone, *The Family, Sex and Marriage in England 1500-1800* (1st ed., London, 1977; abridged and rev. ed., London, 1979), p. 257.

26 BL-AP, 75633, CH/LS, Sept. 30, 1788; on the adoption of riding habits by women during the century, see Paul Langford, *A Polite and Commercial People: England 1727-1783* (Oxford and New York, 1989), p. 602.

27 See map, "Plan of the Lordships of Langar and Barnstone dated 1818," in the possession of John Wallwin of Newlands Farm, Langar, and reproduced with his per-

mission in "Langar in 1818," by Nigel Wood, http://www.langarbarnstone.com/local /local-history/langar-in-1818/.

28 My description of the village is based on a historical tour of Langar conducted by Nigel Wood, March 19, 2015.

29 Thomson, *Memoirs of Viscountess Sundon*, vol. I, pp. 247–48.

30 BC: *London Evening Post*, July 14–16, 1730.

31 T. F. Dale, *The History of the Belvoir Hunt* (1899), pp. 5–6, 27, 32–33.

32 Vickery, *The Gentleman's Daughter*, pp. 273–74.

33 Andrew Thompson, *George II: King and Elector* (London and New Haven, 2011), p. 21.

34 See Ellen T. Harris, *George Frideric Handel: A Life with Friends* (W. W. Norton, 2014), pp. 32, 65–66.

35 NRS, Papers of Major William Howe: Accounts Incurred in Paris, 1716-1718, RH15/17/12.

36 George C. Brauer, *The Education of a Gentleman: Theories of Gentlemanly Education in England, 1660-1775* (New York, 1959), pp. 74–76.

37 William was sent to Nottingham School on May 5, 1736. Bodleian Library: MS. Eng. Misc. e. 452, 45865, "Volume containing accounts of personal expenditure of Scrope, 1st Viscount Howe," fol. 7v. Richard began at Westminster School in 1732, http://www.historyofparliamentonline.org/volume/1754-1790/member/howe -richard-1726-99 [accessed Nov. 1, 2019]. On Richard at Eton, see Richard Arthur Austin-Leigh, *The Eton College Register 1698-1752* (Eton, 1927), p. 184.

38 Adam Thomas, *History of Nottingham High School* (1958), p. 95. I am grateful to Yvette Gunther, Head Librarian and Archivist at Nottingham High School, for drawing this book to my attention. See also John Knifton, *Lauda Finem: The History of Nottingham High School* [Kindle book], 2012.

39 Cited in Maldwyn A. Jones, "Sir William Howe: Conventional Strategist," George Athan Billias, ed., *George Washington's Generals and Opponents: Their Exploits and Leadership* (1st ed., New York, 1964, 1969; this ed., Da Capo Press, 1994), p. 64.

40 Gruber, pp. 47–48; Barrow, p. 119.

41 BL-AP, 75611, CH/LS, March 12, 1767; 75613, CH/LS, Aug. 3, 1775; 75614, CH/LS, Jan. 2, 1780; Jan. 5, 1780; 75615, CH/LS, Sat., April 15, 1780.

42 Rosemary Baird, *Mistress of the House: Great Ladies and Grand Houses 1670-1830* (London, 2003), p. 20.

43 Baird, *Mistress of the House*, pp. 17–18, 20, Montagu cite from p. 19; Flora Fraser, *The English Gentlewoman* (London, 1987), pp. 117–20.

44 "Memoir of the Honourable Mrs. Howe," *The Lady's Magazine* (July 1818). I am indebted to Martin Price for drawing my attention to this article.

45 Earl Spencer and Christopher Dobson, eds., *Letters of David Garrick and Georgiana Countess Spencer 1759-1779* (Cambridge, 1960), p. 22.

46 They married on May 27, 1725. CPE, vol. 8, p. 143. Cites from *The Autobiography and Correspondence of Mary Granville, Mrs Delany*, ed. Lady Llanover (3 vols.; London, 1861), vol. I, pp. 153–54.

47 http://www.historyofparliamentonline.org/volume/1715-1754/member/page-sir

-gregory-1668-1720; Charles Sebag-Montefiore, "Page, Sir Gregory, second baronet (1689–1775)," ODNB Online [both accessed Nov. 1, 2019].

48 Mary married Thomas Herbert, the 8th Earl of Pembroke, on June 14, 1725. CPE, vol. 8, p. 143.

49 George Sherburn, ed., *Correspondence of Alexander Pope* (5 vols., Oxford, 1956), vol. 2, pp. 201–2.

50 John Wilson Croker, ed., *Letters to and From Henrietta, Countess of Suffolk, and her second husband, the Hon. George Berkeley* (2 vols., London, 1824), vol. 1, pp. xxxi, 35–36, 38, 40–41, 49.

51 Lucy Moore, *Amphibious Thing: The Life of Lord Hervey* (London, New York, and Ringwood [Hants.], 2000), p. 14.

52 NRS, GD40/9/144 Letters of Sophia Howe et al.: GD40/9/144/5: S[ophia] Howe to Mrs Howard, nd; GD40/9/144/8: [Sophia Howe] to Mrs Howard, nd.

53 See Institute of Historical Research, Office-Holders in Modern Britain: Royal Households, Caroline Princess of Wales, 1714-1727, http://www.history.ac.uk/publications /office/caroline [accessed October 19, 2015].

54 Croker, ed., *Letters to and From Henrietta, Countess of Suffolk*, vol. 1, p. 36. See also advertisement for a new novel based on the story of Lowther and Howe, *The Reclaimed Libertine*, in BC: *Morning Chronicle and London Advertiser*, May 21, 1773.

55 Stone, *The Family, Sex and Marriage in England*, pp. 188–89.

56 R. O. Bucholz, "Herbert, Thomas, eighth earl of Pembroke and fifth earl of Montgomery (1656/7–1733), ODNB Online [accessed Nov. 1, 2019]; Coker, ed. *Letters to and From Henrietta, Countess of Suffolk*, vol. 1, pp. 191–92; James Wharncliffe and W. Moy Thomas, eds., *Letters and Works of Lady Mary Wortley Montagu* (2 vols., 3rd ed., London, 1861), vol. 2, p. 12fn.

57 John, Lord Hervey, *Memoirs of the Reign of George II from his accession to the death of Queen Caroline* (2 vols., London, 1848), vol. II, p. 157.

58 On Juliana Page's loss of a baby in 1727 or 1728, see *The Autobiography and Correspondence of Mary Granville, Mrs Delany*, vol. 1, p. 153.

59 Valerie Rumbold, "Madan, Judith (1702–1781)," ODNB Online [accessed Nov. 1, 2019]; Pat Rogers, *The Alexander Pope Encyclopedia* (Westport, CT, 2004), pp. 73, 161.

60 Thomson, *Memoirs of Viscountess Sundon*, vol. 1, pp. 229–31, 236, 240; *The London Magazine, Or, Gentleman's Monthly Intelligencer*, vol. 46, pp. 656–57.

61 BNA: *Caledonian Mercury*, Aug. 16, 1725.

62 R. O. Bucholz, "Seymour, Charles, sixth duke of Somerset (1662–1748)," ODNB Online [accessed Nov. 1, 2019].

63 *The Autobiography and Correspondence of Mary Granville, Mrs Delany*, vol. 1, p. 173. They were married on May 8, 1728: CPE, vol. 8, p. 143.

64 Hugh Stokes, *The Devonshire House Circle* (London, 1967), p. 172.

65 John B. Hattendorf, "Mordaunt, Charles, third earl of Peterborough and first earl of Monmouth (1658?–1735)," ODNB Online [accessed Nov. 1, 2019].

66 Lawrence Stone, *Uncertain Unions: Marriage in England, 1660-1753* (Oxford, 1992), pp. 230–31.

Two: Diaspora

1 Reed Browning, "Holles, Thomas Pelham, duke of Newcastle upon Tyne and first duke of Newcastle under Lyme (1693–1768)," ODNB Online [accessed Nov. 14, 2019]; Reed Browning, *The Duke of Newcastle* (New Haven and London, 1975), pp. 28, 30–31.

2 Brian Hill, *The Early Parties and Politics in Britain, 1688-1832* (Houndmills, Basingstoke, Hampshire and London, 1996), p. 25; H. T. Dickinson, *Liberty and Property: Political Ideology in Eighteenth-Century Britain* (London, 1977), pp. 93, 126–28.

3 Frank O'Gorman, *Voters, Patrons, and Parties: The Unreformed Electoral System of Hanoverian England 1734-1832* (Oxford, 1989), pp. 178–79.

4 Sir Lewis Namier and John Brooke, *The History of Parliament: The House of Commons 1754-1790* (3 vols., London, 1964), vol. I, pp. 47, 355; O'Gorman, *Voters, Patrons, and Parties*, pp. 21, 141–43.

5 Browning, *The Duke of Newcastle*, pp. 29, 34; Namier and Brooke, *The History of Parliament*, vol. I, p. 51.

6 Browning, *The Duke of Newcastle*, pp. 30–31; O'Gorman, *Voters, Patrons, and Parties*, p. 143.

7 The pleasure gardens at Langar Hall were extended. See DRO: Okeover Papers, D231M/E 5178: Survey book of part of the Nottinghamshire and Leicestershire estate of [Scrope Lord Howe]; see also K. Tweedale Meaby, *Nottinghamshire: Extracts from the County Records of the Eighteenth Century* (Nottingham, 1947), p. 197.

8 Cannon, *Aristocratic Century*, p. 139.

9 http://www.historyofparliamentonline.org/volume/1715-1754/member/howe-emanuel-scrope-1699-1735 [accessed Nov. 14, 2019].

10 Richard S. Dunn, "Servants and Slaves: The Recruitment and Employment of Labor," in Jack P. Greene and J. R. Pole, eds., *Colonial British America: Essays in the New History of the Early Modern Era* (Baltimore and London, 1984), pp. 165–66, 172.

11 Ian K. Steele, *The English Atlantic 1675-1740: An Exploration of Communication and Community* (Oxford, 1986), p. 283.

12 http://www.historyofparliamentonline.org/volume/1715-1754/member/howe-george-augustus-1724-58 and http://www.historyofparliamentonline.org/volume/1754-1790/member/howe-richard-1726-99 [accessed Nov. 14, 2019]. See also BC: *Daily Post*, Dec. 21, 1732.

13 Thomson, *Memoirs of Viscountess Sundon*, vol. I, p. 241–42. See also BC: *Read's Weekly Journal or British Gazetteer*, Jan. 6, 1733, and *General Evening Post*, June 14, 1735.

14 BC: *Daily Journal*, Oct. 3, 1732.

15 BC: *London Evening Post*, Nov. 16, 1732.

16 BC: *Country Journal or The Craftsman*, Nov. 4, 1732; *London Evening Post*, Feb. 20, 1733.

17 BC: *London Evening Post*, Feb. 20–22, 1733; *St. James's Evening Post*, March 6–8, 1733; BNA: *Derby Mercury*, March 15, 1733.

18 Thomson, *Memoirs of Viscountess Sundon*, vol. I, pp. 241–42.

19 BNA: *Derby Mercury*, June 21, 1733.

20 Richard S. Dunn, "The English Sugar Islands and the Founding of South Carolina," in *Shaping Southern Society: The Colonial Experience*, ed. T. H. Breen (New York, 1976), p. 56.

21 Andrew Jackson O'Shaughnessy, *An Empire Divided: The American Revolution and the British Caribbean* (Philadelphia, 2000), pp. 51–55.

22 BL-AP, 75614, CH/LS, Jan. 29, 1780.

23 Dunn, "The English Sugar Islands and the Founding of South Carolina," p. 53.

24 BC: *General Evening Post*, June 14–17, 17–19, 1735; *London Evening Post*, May 31–June 3, 1735.

25 BC: *General Evening Post*, June 14–17, 17–19, 1735; *London Evening Post*, May 31–June 3, 1735; PCC, PROB 11/682/273, "Will of the Right Honourable Scroop Lord Viscount Howe of Ireland," April 6, 1737.

26 BC: *Daily Courant*, June 28, 1735.

27 BC: *General Evening Post*, Sept. 30–Oct. 2, 1735; *London Evening Post*, October 4–7, 1735.

28 BC: *Daily Gazetteer*, June 30, July 3, 1735.

29 Matthew Kilburn, "Howe, (Mary Sophia) Charlotte, Viscountess Howe (1703–1782)," ODNB Online [accessed Nov. 14, 2019]; BC: *General Evening Post*, June 28–July 1, 1735; *Read's Weekly Journal or British Gazetteer*, June 21, 1735; BNA: *Derby Mercury*, June 26, 1735.

30 Cannon, *Aristocratic Century*, pp. 11–12fn, 129–30.

31 Public days were held at Langar Hall prior to Lord Howe's death. BC: *Read's Weekly Journal or British Gazetteer*, Dec. 8, 1733; *Daily Courant*, Oct. 19, 1734.

32 Bodleian Library: MS. Eng. Misc. e. 452, 45865, "Volume containing accounts of personal expenditure of Scrope, 1st Viscount Howe," fols. 7v, 8r, 122v; PCC, PROB 11/758/482, "Will of the Right Honourable Juliana Lady, Dowager, Widow of Epperstone," Sept. 23, 1747.

33 PCC, PROB 11/682/273, "Will of the Right Honourable Scroop Lord Viscount Howe of Ireland," April 6, 1737.

34 Friedrich Kielmansegge, *Diary of a Journey to England in the Years 1761-1762* (1st ed., London, 1902; Elibron Classics Replica Edition, 2005), pp. 83, 229–30.

35 Sebag-Montefiore, "Page, Sir Gregory, second baronet (1689–1775)," ODNB Online [accessed Nov. 14, 2019].

36 Lady Pembroke resided in a mansion house at Parsons Green, Fulham, which she held during her lifetime. See London Metropolitan Archives: City of London, Ref. Q/SHR/101, "Articles of Agreement, on intended marriage of 2 [Hon. John Mordaunt] and 3 [Lady Mary, Countess Dowager of Pembroke]," Sept. 4, 1735.

37 "Gerrard Street Area: The Military Ground, Gerrard Street," in *Survey of London: vols. 33 and 34, St. Anne Soho*, ed. F. H. W. Sheppard (London, 1966), pp. 384–411. *British History Online*, http://www.british-history.ac.uk/survey-london/vols33-4/pp384-411 [accessed Nov. 14, 2019]. On the names of the Mordaunt children, see CPE, vol. 3, p. 329.

38 "Townships: Halsall," in *A History of the County of Lancaster: Volume 3*, ed. William Farrer and J. Brownbill (London, 1907), pp. 191–97. *British History Online*,

http://www.british-history.ac.uk/vch/lancs/vol3/pp191-197 [accessed Nov. 14, 2019]. Lady Howe's visits to Langar and Halsall are mentioned in Bodleian Library: MS. Eng. Misc. e. 452, 45865, "Volume containing accounts of personal expenditure of Scrope, 1st Viscount Howe," fols. 7v, 8r. See also [Howe, Maria Sophia] Ch[arlotte Kielmansegge, Viscountess] Howe to [the Countess of Huntingdon], Parsons Green, April 1, 1740, Folder HA 6930-6934, Hastings Family Papers, ca 1100–1892, The Huntington Library, San Marino, California.

39 Syrett, pp. 1–3.

40 N. A. M. Rodgers, *The Wooden World: An Anatomy of the Georgian Navy* (Glasgow, 1986; this impression, 1990), pp. 254, 270–71.

41 Rodgers, ibid., pp. 253, 259, 264, 269.

42 On the voyage of the *Severn*, see Syrett, p. 2. Cite from Howe (Richard, Earl Howe, Admiral of the Fleet) to his mother, Rio de Janeiro, July 6–10 [1741], reprinted in part in *Catalogue of Important Historical Manuscripts & Autograph Letters and Some Printed Books: The Properties of the Most Honourable The Marquess of Sligo and Jasper More, Esq.* (London: Christie, Manson & Woods, 1958), p. 14. I am indebted to Cheney Schopieray of the William L. Clements Library for drawing this letter to my attention.

43 Syrett, pp. 3, 4; Barrow, p. 15. Barrow, Richard's Victorian biographer, suggested that it was the occasion of an interview with the Duke of Bedford, "then first lord of the Admiralty," at Woburn Abbey that led to Richard's first command [ibid., p. 11]. This is given added weight because the Page family at Battlesden knew the duke; the Pages had political "interest" in Bedfordshire. See, for example, BL-AP, 75610, CH/LS, 16 July 1763; CH/LS, 75611, 12 March 1767.

44 Syrett, pp. 2–8; *Oxford Journal*, Sat., November 22, 1760.

45 R. O. Bucholz, "Herbert, Thomas, eighth earl of Pembroke and fifth earl of Montgomery (1656/7–1733)," ODNB Online [accessed June 26, 2020].

46 See Institute of Historical Research, Office-holders in Modern Britain: Royal Households, Queen Caroline 1727-37, http://www.history.ac.uk/publications/office/queencaroline [accessed October 20, 2015]. She was "commonly called Countess Dowager of Pembroke." See her will, below.

47 http://www.historyofparliamentonline.org/volume/1715-1754/member/mordaunt-hon-john-1709-67 [accessed Nov. 24, 2019].

48 Announcing the death of Major William Howe, see BC: *Daily Courant*, Aug. 8, 1733; University of Nottingham Manuscripts and Special Collections: Sm 1112, "Case for Miss Howe," describes Mary as the ward of Lady Pembroke and states that Mary is about fifteen years of age at date of document, which is November 30, 1741.

49 Caroline's marriage certificate gives her parish as Fulham. She no doubt spent much of her time at Lady Pembroke's home as well as at nearby Battlesden. Lambeth Palace Library and Archives, FM I/80, FM II/87, marriage license of Caroline Howe and John Howe, dated April 19, 1742. I am grateful to Martin Price for providing me with a transcript of Caroline Howe's marriage license.

50 Hervey, *Memoirs of the Reign of George II*, vol. 2, p. 480; see also Institute of Historical Research, Office-holders in Modern Britain: Royal Households, Princess

Augusta 1736-72, http://www.history.ac.uk/publications/office/augusta [accessed Oct. 20, 2015].

51 Janice Hadlow, *The Strangest Family: The Private Lives of George III, Queen Charlotte and the Hanoverians* (London, 2014), pp. 42–43, 90–91.

52 Wharncliffe and Thomas, eds., *Letters and Works of Lady Mary Wortley Montagu*, vol. I, p. 482fn.

53 Stephen Brumwell, "Band of Brothers," *History Today*, vol. 58 (no. 6), June 2008, p. 27; http://www.historyofparliamentonline.org/volume/1754-1790/member/howe -george-augustus-1724-58 [accessed Nov. 14, 2019].

54 Austin-Leigh, *The Eton College Register*, pp. 184, 241.

55 *The Database of Court Officers 1660-1837*, comp. by R. O. Bucholz, J. C. Sainty, et al., http://courtofficers.ctsdh.luc.edu/ (2005; rev. 2019).

56 J. M. Beattie, *The English Court in the Reign of George I* (Cambridge, 1967), p. 103.

57 http://www.historyofparliamentonline.org/volume/1754-1790/member/howe-hon -william-1729-1814 [accessed Nov. 14, 2019]; Ira D. Gruber, "Howe, William, fifth Viscount Howe (1729–1814)," ODNB Online [accessed Nov. 14, 2019].

58 http://www.historyofparliamentonline.org/volume/1715-1754/member/mordaunt -hon-john-1709-67 [accessed Nov. 14, 2019].

59 http://www.historyofparliamentonline.org/volume/1715-1754/member/plumptre-john -1679-1751; http://www.historyofparliamentonline.org/volume/1715-1754/member/howe -george-augustus-1724-58 [both accessed Nov. 14, 2019].

60 Namier and Brooke, *The History of Parliament*, vol. I, p. 355.

61 http://www.historyofparliamentonline.org/volume/1715-1754/member/howe -george-augustus-1724-58 [accessed Nov. 14, 2019]; William Betham, *The Barone- tage of England, or the History of the English Baronets* (5 vols., 1801–1805), vol. 4, p. 9; Ian Roy, "Rupert, prince and count palatine of the Rhine and duke of Cumberland (1619–1682)," ODNB Online [accessed Nov. 14, 2019].

62 Cite from BNA: *Derby Mercury*, June 26, 1747; Browning, *The Duke of Newcastle*, p. 143.

63 Quoted in http://www.historyofparliamentonline.org/volume/1715-1754/member /plumptre-john-1679-1751 [accessed Nov. 14, 2019].

64 Romney R. Sedgwick, "Nottingham," http://www.historyofparliamentonline.org /volume/1715-1754/constituencies/Nottingham [accessed Oct. 21, 2015].

65 http://www.historyofparliamentonline.org/volume/1715-1754/member/howe-george -augustus-1724-58 [accessed Nov. 14, 2019].

66 BL-NP, 32711, fols. 395–96, [John] Plumptre to Newcastle, Nottingham, June 17, 1747.

67 O'Gorman, *Voters, Patrons, and Parties*, p. 255.

68 BL-NP, 32711, fol. 264, Mr John Sherwin to Newcastle, Nottingham, June 8, 1747; fol. 393, Mr John Sherwin to Newcastle, Nottingham, June 17, 1747.

69 BL-NP, 32712, fol. 95, J. S. Charlton to Newcastle, Staunton, July 11, 1747; 32711, fol. 130, J. S. Charlton to Newcastle, Staunton, May 25, 1747.

70 Namier and Brooke, *The History of Parliament*, vol. I, p. 355; Harry Tucker Easton, *The History of a Banking House (Smith, Payne and Smiths)* (London, 1903), p. 12; BL-NP, 32712, fol. 372: [John] Plumptre to Newcastle, Nottingham, August 12, 1747.

The townhouse is Bromley House, erected 1752, now the Nottingham Subscription Library. Elain Harwood, *Nottingham* (New Haven and London, 2008), p. 59. Many of its interiors are well preserved.

71 BL-NP, 32874, fol. 187: Lady Howe to the Duke of Newcastle, September 20, 1757.

72 Horace Walpole to Sir Horace Mann, November 23, 1741, HWC, vol. 17, p. 209.

73 Norma Clarke, *Queen of the Wits: A Life of Laetitia Pilkington* (London, 2008), pp. 74, 123, 149.

74 http://www.historyofparliamentonline.org/volume/1715-1754/member/walpole-hon-edward-1706-84 [accessed Nov. 14, 2019].

75 Bartle Grant, ed., *The Receipt Book of Elizabeth Raper* (Soho, London, 1924), pp. 6–7.

76 David P. Field, "Howe, John (1630–1705)," ODNB Online [accessed Nov. 14, 2019]; Henry Rogers, *The Life and Character of John Howe, M.A.* (London, 1863), pp. 438–39.

77 "Parishes: Hanslope with Castle Thorpe," in *A History of the County of Buckingham: Vol. 4*, ed. William Page (London, 1927), pp. 348–62. *British History Online* http://www.british-history.ac.uk/vch/bucks/vol4/pp348-362 [accessed Nov. 14, 2019].

78 John Howe is included in a portrait attributed to Charles Philips, "The 'Henry the Fifth' Club, or 'the Gang,' c. 1730–1735" [Oil on canvas | 72.4 x 90.5 cm (support, canvas/panel/str external) | RCIN 405737]. The club was started by Prince Frederick. See The Royal Collection Trust.

79 PCC, PROB11/773/272, "Will of Mary Mordaunt commonly called the Right Honorable Mary Countess of Pembroke, Wife, Dowager of Parsons Green, Middlesex," September 19, 1749.

80 BL-AP, 75610, CH/LS, Tuesday 1760; 75613, CH/LS, Nov. 30, 1776; Sept. 18, 1777.

Three: The Brothers

1 Syrett, pp. 11–12.

2 Derek Mackay and H. M. Scott, *The Rise of the Great Powers 1648-1815* (London and New York, 1983), pp. 177, 179–80; Fred Anderson, *The War That Made America: A Short History of the French and Indian War* (New York and London, 2005), pp. 43, 46–50.

3 Syrett, p. 12; Barrow, pp. 23, 25.

4 BNA: *Caledonian Mercury,* July 21, 1755; *Derby Mercury,* July 18, 1755; *Oxford Journal,* July 26, 1755.

5 BNA: *Leeds Intelligencer,* Aug. 5, 1755.

6 Roger Knight, "Howe, Richard, Earl Howe (1726–1799)," ODNB Online [accessed July 4, 2020].

7 Kathleen Wilson, *The Sense of the People: Politics, Culture and Imperialism in England, 1715-1785* (Cambridge, 1998), pp. 178–79.

8 Syrett, p. 12; cite from Browning, *The Duke of Newcastle*, p. 221.

9 Thompson, *George II*, p. 238.

10 Browning, *The Duke of Newcastle*, pp. 221–22.

11 J. C. D. Clark, *The Dynamics of Change: The Crisis of the 1750s and English Party Sys-*

tems (Cambridge, 1982), p. 224, 510fn. Cites from Walpole, *Memoirs of the Reign of King George II*, vol. 2, pp. 49, 56, 58.

12 Samuel Kirk, Grocer, Nottingham to General Howe, Feb. 10, 1775; on the town of Nottingham's opposition to the subsidy treaties, see BC: *London Evening Post*, Nov. 16, 1756.

13 BL-NP, 32732 Part I, fols. 336–37, Newcastle to Charlton, Claremont, July 21, 1753; 32732 Part II, fol. 393, Charlton to Newcastle, Wollaton, Aug. 1, 1753; fol. 437, Newcastle to Plumptre, Newcastle House, Aug. 9, 1753.

14 BL-NP, 32733, fol. 122, Mr. Clay to Newcastle, Nottingham, Oct. 24, 1753; fols. 234–35, Mr. Clay to Newcastle, Nottingham, Nov. 10, 1753; fol. 24, J. Bristowe to? [opens "Dear Sir"], Clumber, Nov. 12, 1753; fol. 619, Mr. Clay to Newcastle, Nottingham, Dec. 31, 1753.

15 Lewis Namier, *The Structure of Politics at the Accession of George III* (London and Basingstoke, 1929; 2nd ed., 1957), p. 92fn; BC: *London Evening Post*, May 4–7, 1754; J. D. Chambers, *Nottinghamshire in the Eighteenth Century: A Study of Life and Labour under the Squirearchy* (London, 1966), p. 33.

16 Harwood, *Nottingham*, pp. 8, 12, 68.

17 I am indebted to Dr. Stephen Brumwell for the suggestion that George served as an aide-de-camp, and for other insights regarding George Lord Howe's involvement at Bassignano.

18 BNA: *Derby Mercury*, Oct. 11, 1745.

19 BL, Hardwicke Papers, 35431, fols. 208, 209, George Augustus, 3rd Viscount Howe—Letter to his mother [1745—misdated in catalog as 1747].

20 BNA: *Caledonian Mercury*, Jan. 28, 1747; http://www.historyofparliamentonline.org /volume/1715-1754/member/howe-george-augustus-1724-58 [accessed July 8, 2020].

21 Basil Williams, *The Life of William Pitt, Earl of Chatham* (2 vols., London, 1915), vol. 1, p. 366.

22 James Dreaper, *Pitt's "Gallant Conqueror": The Turbulent Life of Lieutenant-General Sir William Draper K.B.* (New York, 2006), pp. 23–24.

23 T. A. B. Corley, "Chudleigh, Elizabeth [*married names* Elizabeth Hervey, Countess of Bristol; Elizabeth Pierrepont, Duchess of Kingston upon Hull] (c. 1720–1788)," ODNB Online [accessed July 7, 2020]; Claire Gervat, *Elizabeth: The Scandalous Life of the Duchess of Kingston* (London, 2003), pp. 40–45.

24 Charles E. Pearce, *The Amazing Duchess: Being the Romantic History of Elizabeth Chudleigh* (2 vols., London, 1911), vol. 1, p. 134.

25 BNA: *Caledonian Mercury*, April 27, 1776.

26 Gervat, *Elizabeth*, p. 55.

27 Lord John Russell, ed., *Correspondence of John, Fourth Duke of Bedford* (3 vols., London, 1842–1846), vol. 2, p. 103.

28 BC: *Whitehall Evening Post or London Intelligencer*, Aug. 17–20, 1751; *London Daily Advertiser and Literary Gazette*, Aug. 27, 1751.

29 On the Eton match, see Dreaper, *Pitt's "Gallant Conqueror,"* p. 22; for examples of subsequent matches, see BC: *Whitehall Evening Post or London Intelligencer*, July 2–4, 6–9, 1751; *Old England or the National Gazette*, July 20, 1751; *London Morning Penny Post*, July 15–17, 1751; *General Advertiser*, Aug. 5, 1751.

30 BC: *General Advertiser*, Dec. 12, 1751.

31 Weinreb and Hibbert, eds., *The London Encyclopedia*, p. 464.

32 Hadlow, *The Strangest Family*, pp. 97–98.

33 Chalus, *Elite Women in English Political Life*, pp. 223–24fn.

34 Matthew Kilburn, "Wallmoden, Amalie Sophie Marianne von, suo jure countess of Yarmouth (1704–1765)," ODNB Online [accessed July 4, 2020]; Andrew C. Thompson, *George II*, pp. 127–28.

35 Kielmansegge, *Diary of a Journey to England*, pp. 21, 54, 80, 83, 144, 148, 173, 176, 210, 212, 226, 238, 244, 277; on Lady Yarmouth's purchase of the house in Albemarle Street, see BC: *St James's Chronicle, or the British Evening Post*, June 6–9, 1761.

36 Kilburn, "Wallmoden, Amalie . . . countess of Yarmouth (1704–1765)"; Jeremy Black, *Pitt the Elder: The Great Commoner* (first published Cambridge, 1992; rev. ed. Stroud, Gloucestershire, 1999), pp. 133, 169.

37 Thompson, *George II*, pp. 180, 225–26, 232, 240, 251.

38 *The Diary of the Late George Bubb Dodington, baron of Melcombe Regis* (London: 3rd ed., 1785), pp. 12, 19, 28, 87, 161; Kielmansegge, *Diary of a Journey to England*, p. 83.

39 Beattie, *The English Court in the Reign of George I*, pp. 53–55; E. J. Burford, *Royal St James's: Being a Story of Kings, Clubmen and Courtesans* (London, 1988; paperback ed., 2001), p. 30.

40 Moore, *Amphibious Thing*, p. 189.

41 Hannah Greig, *The Beau Monde: Fashionable Society in Georgian London* (Oxford, 2013), p. 115–20.

42 *Diary of the Late George Bubb Dodington*, p. 74.

43 Beattie, *The English Court in the Reign of George I*, p. 54.

44 See *Diary of the Late George Bubb Dodington*, pp. 30, 161, and elsewhere.

45 Hadlow, *Strangest Family*, pp. 106–11.

46 Lord Fitzmaurice, *Life of William Earl of Shelburne* (2 vols., London, 1912), vol. I, p. 51.

47 Grace Countess of Middlesex. See Sidney Colvin, *History of the Society of Dilettanti* (London, 1914), p. 10; for the rumors about her, see Jason M. Kelly, *The Society of Dilettanti: Archaeology and Identity in the British Enlightenment* (New Haven and London, 2009), p. 76.

48 Clark, *The Dynamics of Change*, p. 202; John L. Bullion, "The Origins and Significance of Gossip about Princess Augusta and Lord Bute, 1755–1756," *Studies in Eighteenth Century Culture*, vol. 21 (1991), pp. 249–51.

49 Bullion, "Origins and Significance of Gossip," pp. 247–48; quote from John L. Bullion, "Augusta, princess of Wales (1719–1772)," ODNB Online [accessed July 9, 2020].

50 Hadlow, *Strangest Family*, pp. 106–7, 112.

51 PCC, PROB 11/682/273, "Will of the Right Honourable Scroop Lord Viscount Howe of Ireland," April 6, 1737; Randolph Trumbach, *The Rise of the Egalitarian Family: Aristocratic Kinship and Domestic Relations in Eighteenth-Century England* (New York, San Francisco, London, 1978), pp. 51–52.

52 Kielmansegge, *Diary of a Journey to England*, pp. 54, 57.

53 Chalus, *Elite Women in English Political Life*, pp. 77–78, 80, 84; Judith S. Lewis, *Sacred to Female Patriotism: Gender, Class, and Politics in Late Georgian Britain* (New York and London, 2003), pp. 94–99.

54　"Parishes: Hanslope with Castle Thorpe," in *A History of the County of Buckingham*: *Vol. 4*, ed. William Page (London, 1927), pp. 348–62. *British History Online*, http://www.british-history.ac.uk/vch/bucks/vol4/pp348-362 [accessed Sept. 10, 2015].

55　BL-AP, 75610, CH/LS, April 10, 1764.

56　*The Receipt Book of Elizabeth Raper*, pp. 5–6, 10.

57　BL-AP, 75610, CH/LS, July 7, 1763.

58　Cite from James Greig, ed., *The Farington Diary* by Joseph Farington (6 vols., London, 1922–1928), vol. 6, p. 271; Dale, *The History of the Belvoir Hunt*, p. 48.

59　Walpole cite from Jeremy Black, *The British Abroad: The Grand Tour in the Eighteenth Century* (Stroud and New York, 1992), p. 208; Colvin, *History of the Society of Dilettanti*, pp. 4–5; Kelly, *The Society of Dilettanti*, p. xiii.

60　Kelly, *Society of Dilettanti*, pp. 35–36, 74, 76, 77–78; N. A. M. Rodger, "Montagu, John, fourth earl of Sandwich (1718–1792)," ODNB Online [accessed July 8, 2020].

61　For a list of members, see Colvin, *History of the Society of Dilettanti*, Appendix.

62　A joint memorial to John Howe and Matthew Raper, F.R.S., testifying to their life-long friendship, is in the Church of St. James the Great, Thorley.

63　"Parishes: Thorley," in *A History of the County of Hertford: Vol. 3*, ed. William Page (London, 1912), pp. 373–77, *British History Online*, http://www.british-history.ac.uk/vch/herts/vol3/pp373-377 [accessed September 9, 2015]; *The Receipt Book of Elizabeth Raper*, p. 3.

64　Syrett, pp. 13–14.

65　*The Receipt Book of Elizabeth Raper*, pp. 5–9, 15, 23, 24.

66　I am grateful to Professor H. V. Bowen for providing me with information from Anthony Farrington's *Biographical Index of East India Company Maritime Service Officers 1600-1834* (1999), p. 396, revealing that Thomas Howe was 3rd mate on *Griffin* 1752/3, 2nd mate on *Rhoda* 1753/4; Commander of *Winchelsea* 1757/8 and 1761/2; and Commander of *Nottingham* 1765/6.

67　Stephen Brumwell, *Paths of Glory: The Life and Death of James Wolfe* (London and New York, 2006; paperback ed., 2007), pp. 92, 109–14. BL-AP, 75614, CH/LS, Feb. 3, 1780.

68　Brumwell, "Band of Brothers," p. 27.

69　Beckles Willson, *The Life and Letters of James Wolfe* (London, 1909), p. 251.

70　Ibid., pp. 338, 392–93.

71　Brumwell, *Paths of Glory*, p. 61; Clive Towse, "Mordaunt, Sir John (1696/7–1780)," ODNB Online [accessed July 7, 2020]. Anne Mordaunt's death was announced in BC: *London Evening Post*, August 21–23, 1753. On Caroline Howe's connection with Sir John Mordaunt, see, for example, BL-AP, 75611, CH/LS, Sept. 13, 1772; 75614, CH/LS, Jan. 30, 1780.

72　Brumwell, *Paths of Glory*, pp. 78–79.

73　Timothy J. Todish, ed., *The Annotated and Illustrated Journals of Major Robert Rogers* (New York, 2002), pp. 53–57; Browning, *The Duke of Newcastle*, p. 209.

74　Wallace Brown, "The British Press and the American Colonies," *History Today*, vol. 24 (1974), pp. 326, 329.

75　See, for example, BNA: *Pue's Occurrences*, Nov. 13, 1756; *Leeds Intelligencer*, Feb. 24, 1756.

76　Brumwell, *Paths of Glory*, p. 114; Browning, *The Duke of Newcastle*, pp. 232–35, quote on p. 234; Anderson, *The War That Made America*, p. 102; Daniel A. Baugh, "Byng, John (*bap.* 1704, *d.* 1757)," ODNB Online [accessed July 7, 2020].

77 Gerald Newman, *The Rise of English Nationalism: A Cultural History, 1720-1830* (London, 1987), p. 170.

78 Mackay and Scott, *The Rise of the Great Powers*, pp. 181, 187–89, 190–91, 191–92.

79 BNA: *Derby Mercury*, Feb. 25, 1757; Brumwell, "Howe, George Augustus, third Viscount Howe (1724?–1758)."

80 H. C. B. Rogers, *The British Army of the Eighteenth Century* (London, 1977), p. 71.

81 Cumberland to Loudoun, St James's, March 21, 1757, in Stanley Pargellis, ed., *Military Affairs in North America, 1748-1765: Selected Documents from the Cumberland Papers in Windsor Castle* (New York and London, 1936), p. 326.

Four: World War

1 Robin May and Gerry Embleton, *Wolfe's Army* (London, Auckland, and Melbourne, 1997), p. 22.

2 Fred Anderson writes, "[F]rom 1756 onward, the Anglo-American armies became arenas of intercultural contact." See Anderson, *Crucible of War: The Seven Years' War and the Fate of Empire in British North America, 1754–1766* (New York, 2000), pp. 288ff.

3 Rogers, *The British Army of the Eighteenth Century*, p. 26.

4 Peter E. Russell, "Redcoats in the Wilderness: British Officers and Irregular Warfare in Europe and America, 1740 to 1760," *William and Mary Quarterly*, 3rd series, vol. 25 (1978), pp. 630–37; I am indebted to Dr. Stephen Brumwell for drawing my attention to the irregular Miquelet light troops mentioned in the account of Bassignano in BNA: *Derby Mercury*, October 11, 1745.

5 Ian M. McCulloch and Tim J. Todish, *British Light Infantryman of the Seven Years' War* (Botley, Oxford, and New York, 2004), pp. 4–5, 14; Stephen Brumwell, *Redcoats: The British Soldier and War in the Americas, 1755-1763* (Cambridge, 2002), pp. 15, 138, 142, 143, 145–47; Anderson, *The War That Made America*, p. 126.

6 Loudoun to Cumberland, Albany, November 22, 1756; Pargellis, ed., *Military Affairs in North America, 1748-1765*, p. 269.

7 Anderson, *The War That Made America*, p. 119; BNA: *Derby Mercury*, September 23, 1757; Brumwell, "Howe, George Augustus, third Viscount Howe (1724?–1758)," ODNB Online [accessed July 10, 2020].

8 McCulloch and Todish, *British Light Infantryman*, p. 20; Timothy J. Todish, ed., *The Annotated and Illustrated Journals of Major Robert Rogers* (New York, 2002), pp. 65, 70, 76, cite from p. 70.

9 Ibid., p. 110; McCulloch and Todish, *British Light Infantryman*, pp. 11–14, 20; Anderson, *The War That Made America*, p. 130.

10 Todish, ed., *Journals of Major Robert Rogers*, p. 110.

11 WCL-HC, March 26, [1758]. [George Augustus Howe, 3rd Viscount] Howe ALS to [Mrs. Juliana Page], Albany, [NY].

12 Todish, ed., *Journals of Major Robert Rogers*, p. 85.

13 BNA: *Derby Mercury*. March 31 and July 14, 1758.

14 Pierre Pouchot, *Memoirs on the Late War in North America between France and England*, Rev. Ed. Trans. by Michael Cardy, ed. and ann. by Brian Leigh Dunnigan (Youngstown, NY, 2004), p. 147.

15 BNA: *Derby Mercury*, July 14, 1758.

16 Anderson, *Crucible of War*, pp. 228–29.

17 Van der Kiste, *King George II and Queen Caroline*, p. 208.

18 Anderson, *The War That Made America*, pp. 126–28, cite from p. 127.

19 Mary Cone, *Life of Rufus Putnam, with extracts from his journal and an account of the first settlement in Ohio* (Cleveland, OH, 1886), p. 32.

20 Rene Chartrand, *Ticonderoga 1758: Montcalm's Victory Against All Odds* (Botley, Oxford, 2000), pp. 26–28.

21 Fred Anderson, *A People's Army: Massachusetts Soldiers and Society in the Seven Years' War* (New York and London, 1984), p. 161.

22 Anne MacVicar Grant, *Memoirs of an American Lady: With Sketches of Manners and Scenes in America, as They Existed Previous to the Revolution*, ed. James Grant Wilson (Cambridge, 2011), pp. 221–26.

23 Chartrand, *Ticonderoga 1758*, p. 32; *Reminiscences of the French War: Robert Rogers' Journal and a Memoir of General Stark* (Freedom, New Hampshire, 1988), p. 201.

24 Chartrand, *Ticonderoga 1758*, pp. 32–37.

25 Ibid., pp. 37, 41.

26 Cited in William R. Nester, *The Epic Battles for Ticonderoga, 1758* (Albany, NY, 2008), p. 132.

27 WCL, Henry Foster Diary, 1757–1782.

28 Anderson, *The War That Made America*, pp. 135–38; Brumwell, *Redcoats*, pp. 27–28.

29 Nester, *The Epic Battles for Ticonderoga, 1758*, p. 129; "Another Account of the Operations at Ticonderoga," Camp at Lake George, July 14, 1758, E. B. O'Callaghan, ed., *Documents Relative to the Colonial History of the State of New York* (15 vols., Albany, 1853–1887), vol. 10, p. 735.

30 William Cutter, *Life of General Putnam, Major-General in the Army of the American Revolution* (New York, 1850), p. 89.

31 Dorothy Marshall, *Eighteenth Century England* (Harlow, Essex, and New York, 1962; this impression, 1985), p. 288.

32 See, for example, BNA: *The Scots Magazine*, Aug. 7, 1758.

33 On rumors of Richard's death, see BNA: *Derby Mercury*, July 11, 18, 1755.

34 Holden, "New Historical Light on the Real Burial Place of George Augustus Lord Viscount Howe, 1758," pp. 270–75. The British press reported that "The Body of the Right Hon. Lord Viscount Howe was brought to Albany last Monday." BNA: *Pue's Occurrences*, Sept. 12, 1758.

35 Mr. Pitt to Mr. Grenville, Aug. 22, 1758, *The Grenville Papers: being the correspondence of Richard Grenville, earl Temple, K.G., and the Right Hon. George Grenville* (4 vols., London, 1852–1853), vol. 1, p. 262.

36 Syrett, pp. 19, 23.

37 BL-NP, 32883, fols. 58–59, Newcastle to Richard Howe (now Lord Viscount Howe), Aug. 23, 1758.

38 Syrett, p. 15; Namier and Brooke, *The History of Parliament*, vol. I, p. 252.

39 BL-NP, 32883, fol. 141, Newcastle to Mr Charlton, Aug. 28, 1758.

40 Ibid.; fol. 308, Charlotte Howe to the Duke of Newcastle, Battlesden, Sept. 5, 1758; fol. 452, Charlotte Howe to the Duke of Newcastle, Albemarle Street, Sept. 14, 1758.

41 "To the Gentlemen, Clergy, Freeholders, and Burgesses of the town and county of the town of Nottingham," BNA: *The Scots Magazine*, Sept. 4, 1758.

42 HWC, vol. 37, p. 571fn.

43 BNA: *The Scots Magazine*, Sept. 4, 1758, "On reading Lady Howe's address."

44 BNA: *The Scots Magazine*, Sept. 4, 1758, "On the death of Lord Howe."

45 Wilson, *The Sense of the People*, pp. 51, 187–89. See also Hannah Barker and Elaine Chalus, eds., *Gender in Eighteenth-Century England: Roles, Representations and Responsibilities* (London and New York, 1997), "Introduction" by Barker and Chalus; Linda Colley, *Britons: Forging the Nation, 1707-1837* (London, 1992), pp. 252–63.

46 *Annual Register*, vol. 1, December 1758, p. 70fn. I am grateful to Sarah Deas of the Database of Court Officers Project (directed by Professor Robert Bucholz, Loyola University of Chicago) for drawing this source to my attention.

47 BNA: *The Scots Magazine*, Oct. 1, 1758, "On the death of Lord Howe."

48 NA, PRO 30/8. William Pitt, 1st Earl of Chatham Papers, Lady Howe to William Pitt, Albemarle Street, September 15, 1758.

49 Willson, *The Life and Letters of James Wolfe*, pp. 384, 392–93.

50 James Thacher, *American Medical Biography: Or, Memoirs of Eminent Physicians Who Have Flourished in America* (2 vols., Boston, 1828), vol. 1, p. 363.

51 WCL-HC, William Howe to Richard Howe, Halifax, Nov. 23, 1758.

52 Barrow, pp. 31–32, 34–35; Willis, *The Glorious First of June*, p. 47.

53 Knight, "Howe, Richard, Earl Howe (1726–1799)"; Barrow, p. 35; Brumwell, *Paths of Glory*, p. 131.

54 Syrett, p. 16; Richard Middleton, *The Bells of Victory: The Pitt-Newcastle Ministry and the Conduct of the Seven Years' War 1757-1762* (Cambridge, 1985), pp. 26, 40–42.

55 Towse, "Mordaunt, Sir John (1696/7–1780)."

56 Brumwell, *Paths of Glory*, p. 136.

57 Syrett, p. 17; Syrett gives March 10 as the wedding date, but Knight, op. cit., cites the date as February 16, 1758. Knight's date is corroborated by Miss Raper's diary: Grant, ed., *The Receipt Book of Elizabeth Raper*, p. 9.

58 BL-NP, 32733, fols. 144–45, Newcastle to Clay, Claremont, Oct. 27, 1753; fol. 122, Clay to Newcastle, Nottingham, Oct. 24, 1753; Anne French, ed., *The Earl and Countess Howe by Gainsborough: A Bicentenary Exhibition* (London, 1988), p. 11.

59 Grant, ed., *The Receipt Book of Elizabeth Raper*, p. 9.

60 BL-AP, 75610, CH/LS, Sunday 1759; Bristol, Aug [Wed] 1759.

61 Black, *Pitt the Elder*, pp. 146, 152–54.

62 Middleton, *The Bells of Victory*, pp. 69, 74, 84.

63 Syrett, p. 18.

64 Black, *Pitt the Elder*, pp. 169–79; Middleton, *The Bells of Victory*, pp. 74–75, 84.

65 Syrett, pp. 19–20; Knight, "Howe, Richard, Earl Howe (1726–1799)."

66 Alan Valentine, *Lord George Germain* (Oxford, 1962), p. 37.

67　Syrett, p. 21; Middleton, *The Bells of Victory*, p. 71; Valentine, *Lord George Germain*, pp. 29–30.

68　Walpole, *Memoirs of the Reign of George II*, vol. 3, p. 125.

69　Piers Mackesy, "Germain, George Sackville, first Viscount Sackville (1716–1785)," ODNB Online [accessed July 11, 2020]; Middleton, *The Bells of Victory*, p. 75; Matthew Kilburn, "Edward Augustus, Prince, duke of York and Albany (1739–1767)," ODNB Online [accessed July 11, 2020].

70　Syrett, p. 22; Romney Sedgwick, "Letters from William Pitt to Lord Bute: 1755-1758," in Richard Pares and A. J. P. Taylor, eds. *Essays Presented to Sir Lewis Namier* (London and New York, 1956), pp. 156–59.

71　Barrow, pp. 49, 57–59.

72　Syrett, pp. 22–23; Romney Sedgwick, "William Pitt and Lord Bute: An Intrigue of 1755-1758," *History Today*, vol. 6, issue 10 (Oct. 1956).

73　Barrow, pp. 51–52; Syrett, p. 24.

74　Ibid., p. 53.

75　http://www.historyofparliamentonline.org/volume/1754-1790/member/armytage -sir-john-1732-58 [accessed July 11, 2020]; Barrow, p. 38.

76　"Copy of a paragraph which appeared in a London Paper." West Yorkshire Archive Service, Calderdale: Armytage Family of Kirklees Hall, Clifton-cum-Hartshead, Records (Addnl), Ref. KMA: 1981, Miscellaneous Papers, (e) "Papers concerning Sir John Armytage who died at St Cas in 1758."

77　HWC, vol. 9, p. 264.

78　Middleton, *The Bells of Victory*, pp. 83–84.

79　Syrett, p. 25; Middleton, *The Bells of Victory*, pp. 144–45.

80　Syrett, pp. 26–27; F. D. Cartwright, ed., *The Life and Correspondence of Major Cartwright* (2 vols., London, 1826), vol. I, p. 15.

81　Anderson, *Crucible of War*, p. 382.

82　Cartwright, ed., *The Life and Correspondence of Major Cartwright*, vol. I, p. 17.

83　Syrett, p. 27.

84　BL-AP, 75610, CH/LS, Jan. 11, 1760.

85　Syrett, p. 27; BL-AP, 75610, CH/LS, Tuesday 1760.

86　BL-AP, 75610, CH/LS, Sunday 1759. Internal contents date this letter to December.

87　Dan Snow, *Death or Victory: The Battle for Quebec and the Birth of Empire* (London, 2009), pp. 318, 326, 327, 335–38; Brumwell, *Paths of Glory*, p. 274.

88　Anstruther's began as the 60th Regiment in 1755 and became the 58th two years later. Stephen Brumwell, "Rank and File: A Profile of One of Wolfe's Regiments," *Journal of the Society for Army Historical Research*, vol. 79 (2001), pp. 4–5, 10; Ira D. Gruber, "Howe, William, fifth Viscount Howe (1729–1814)," ODNB Online [accessed July 12, 2020]; Kielmansegge, *Diary of a Journey to England*, p. 234.

89　Cite from Brumwell, *Paths of Glory*, p. 158.

90　Ibid., pp. 144–46, 149–57.

91　Anderson, *Crucible of War*, p. 254.

92　Willson, *The Life and Letters of James Wolfe*, pp. 404–5.

93　Brumwell, *Paths of Glory*, pp. 166–68.

94 Brumwell, "Rank and File: A Profile of One of Wolfe's Regiments," pp. 9, 13.

95 Snow, *Death or Victory*, pp. 412–17.

96 Gruber, "Howe, William, fifth Viscount Howe (1729–1814)"; BNA: *Derby Mercury*, Oct. 17, 1760.

97 BNA: *Caledonian Mercury*, Sept. 29, 1760.

98 BNA: *Oxford Journal*, Sat., Nov. 22, 1760.

99 Middleton, *The Bells of Victory*, pp. 166, 181; Anderson, *Crucible of War*, p. 419; Black, *Pitt the Elder*, pp. 180, 205.

100 Christopher Hibbert, *George III: A Personal History* (London, New York, Victoria, Toronto, 1998), pp. 33–34.

101 Middleton, *The Bells of Victory*, p. 186; BNA: *Bath Chronicle and Weekly Gazette*, June 18, 1761, "List of the Officers Killed, Wounded, and Prisoners, at Belleisle, to June 4, 1761."

102 BL-AP, 75610, CH/LS, July 9, Aug. 16, 1761.

103 Kielmansegge, *Diary of a Journey to England*, pp. 234–35.

104 Langford, *A Polite and Commercial People: England*, pp. 348–49; Black, *Pitt the Elder*, p. 186.

105 Elena A. Schneider, *The Occupation of Havana: War, Trade and Slavery in the Atlantic World* (Williamsburg, VA, and Chapel Hill, NC, 2018), pp. 21, 73, 75, 77, 89.

106 David Syrett, *The Siege and Capture of Havana 1762* (London and Colchester, 1970), p. xiv; Black, *Pitt the Elder*, p. 205; Schneider, *The Occupation of Havana*, pp. 126–28.

107 Syrett, *The Siege and Capture of Havana*, pp. xiv, xvi, xx, xxv, xxix, xxxiv, xxxv; Brumwell, "Rank and File: A Profile of One of Wolfe's Regiments," p. 20.

108 Syrett, *Siege and Capture of Havana*, pp. xxiv-xxv, xxix, 170, 180, 182, 194, 225, 245, 253, 290, map facing p. 316, 317, 321.

109 WCL, Richard and Francis Browne Papers 1756–1765, F[rancis] Browne to [Jeremiah Browne], Havana [Cuba], October 26, 1762. I am indebted to Stephen Brumwell for drawing my attention to the Browne Papers.

110 Marshall, *Eighteenth Century England*, pp. 332–35; Wilson, *The Sense of the People*, p. 198.

111 Stephen Brumwell, "Home from the Wars," *History Today*, vol. 52 (no. 3), March 2002, http://www.historytoday.com.

112 "Parishes: Childrey," in *A History of the County of Berkshire: Volume 4*, ed. William Page and P. H. Ditchfield (London, 1924), pp. 272–79. *British History Online*, http://www.british-history.ac.uk/vch/berks/vol4/pp272-279 [accessed Sept. 10, 2015].

113 BNA: *Oxford Journal*, April 26, 1760.

114 Kelly, *The Society of Dilettanti*, p. 173.

115 Wilson, *The Sense of the People*, pp. 194–96, 198, 201.

116 BNA: *Leeds Intelligencer*, July 20, 1762.

117 BL-AP, 75612, CH/LS, March 13, 1773.

118 HWC, vol. 21, p. 245.

119 John Doran, ed., *The Last Journals of Horace Walpole During the Reign of George III from 1771-1783* (2 vols., London and New York, 1910), vol. I, p. 433; HWC, vol. 21, pp. 4, 347, vol. 28, p. 274, vol. 32, p. 370, vol. 37, p. 569; Walpole, *Memoirs of the Reign of King George II*, vol. 3, p. 50.

120 BL-AP, 75610, CH/LS, Sept. 3, 1763; LS/CH, Sept. 30, 1763; cite from T. Fry, *Alexander Dalrymple and the Expansion of British Trade*, p. 88.

121 HWC, vol. 12, p. 90.

122 Barrow, pp. 61, 405.

123 Cite from Brian Fitzgerald, ed., *Correspondence of Emily, Duchess of Leinster* (3 vols., Dublin 1949, 1953, 1957), vol. 2, p. 256; see also BL-AP, 75694, Rachel Lloyd, Housekeeper of Kensington Palace: Letters to Lady Spencer, Rachel Lloyd to LS, April 1, 1777.

124 BL-AP, 75661, CH/LS, Thurs., May 9, 1805.

125 Lord Howe was renting a house near Whitehall Stairs at the end of the war. BC: *London Chronicle*, May 17–19, 1763. BL-AP, 75610, CH/LS, May 1 [1763], manuscript marked "1762."

Five: The Peaceful Years

1 Peter Thorold, *The London Rich: The Creation of a Great City, from 1666 to the Present* (London, New York, Victoria, Toronto, 1999), p. 133; Black, *The British Abroad*, p. 9.

2 Heinde, Kielmansegg Family Papers, Charlotte Howe, Dowager Countess Howe to Frederich Count Kielmansegg, Richmond, June the 7th 1762. I am grateful to Professor Ira Gruber for providing me with his notes of the Kielmansegg manuscripts, referred to here and elsewhere in the text.

3 BL-AP, 75610, CH/LS, July 7, 1763.

4 French, ed., *The Earl and Countess Howe*, p. 11.

5 Hugh Belsey, "Gainsborough, Thomas (1727–1788)," ODNB Online [accessed April 6, 2020].

6 French, op. cit., pp. 19, 36; BNA: *Bath Chronicle and Weekly Gazette*, July 14, 1763.

7 French, ed., *The Earl and Countess Howe*, pp. 19–20, 32–33, 37–38, 45.

8 Ibid., pp. 19, 29, 39.

9 Trumbach, *The Rise of the Egalitarian Family*, p. 78.

10 BNA: *Newcastle Courant*, Sunday, March 8, 1755.

11 BL-AP, 75610, CH/LS, May 1 [1763]; manuscript marked "1762."

12 BNA: *Caledonian Mercury*, Nov. 8, 1760; *Derby Mercury*, Dec. 12, 1760.

13 http://www.historyofparliamentonline.org/volume/1754-1790/member/pitt-william-augustus-1728-1809 [accessed 6/7/20].

14 BL-AP, 75610, CH/LS, Nov. 28, 1763.

15 Heinde, Kielmansegg Family Papers, Juliana Howe to Fritz Count Kielmansegg, London, Nov. 22, 1763.

16 "Parishes: Childrey," in *A History of the County of Berkshire*: vol. 4, ed. William Page and P. H. Ditchfield (London, 1924), pp. 272–79. *British History Online*, http://www.british-history.ac.uk/vch/berks/vol4/pp272-279 [accessed Sept. 10, 2015].

17 HWC, vol 9, p. 140.

18 BL, Blenheim Papers, vol. DLXVII, fols. 159–63, Lady Susan Keck to the Duke of Marlborough, Great Tew, Jan. 29, 1753 [marked in pencil "1754?"].

19 Heinde, Kielmansegg Family Papers, Charlotte Howe, Dowager Countess Howe to Frederich Count Kielmansegg, London, May 11, 1762; cite from Charlotte Howe, Dowager Countess Howe to Fritz Count Kielmansegg, Richmond, June the 30th 1764.

20 BNA: *Manchester Mercury*, Aug. 19, Oct. 7, 1766; *Oxford Journal*, Aug. 3, 1765.

21 Black, *The British Abroad*, p. 9; BNA: *Newcastle Courant*, April 23, 1763.

22 Norman Davies, *Europe: A History* (Oxford, 1996; this ed. London, 1997), pp. 610, 648–49.

23 BL-AP, 75610, CH/LS, July 7, 1763.

24 Browning, *The Duke of Newcastle*, pp. 279, 285.

25 BL-AP, 75610, CH/LS, July 16, 1763; Black, *The British Abroad*, pp. 7, 181, 183.

26 Stokes, *The Devonshire House Circle*, pp. 45–47.

27 BL-AP, 75610, CH/LS, Nov. 28, 1763.

28 Epperstone Manor (formerly a residence of Lady Juliana Howe, see chapter 1) was torn down and rebuilt in the nineteenth century. It is now a Police Training School. http://henryhuskinson.weebly.com/ For William's residence there as MP, see BNA: *Caledonian Mercury*, April 4, 1768.

29 BL-AP, 75610, CH/LS, May 1 [1763], manuscript marked "1762"; July 7 and Aug. 18, 1763; July 28, 1765.

30 James Thomas Flexner, *America's Old Masters* (New York, 1939; this ed., New York, 1967), p. 54; LLMC, vol. 2, p. 321.

31 BL-AP, 75610, CH/LS, Friday 1762.

32 Gruber, p. 57fn.

33 David Hackett Fischer, *Washington's Crossing* (Oxford, 2004), p. 69.

34 Alan McNairn, *Behold the Hero: General Wolfe and the Arts in the Eighteenth Century* (Kingston and Montreal, 1997), p. 137; Marquess of Sligo, "Some Notes on the Death of Wolfe," *Canadian Historical Review*, vol. 3 (Sept. 1922), p. 278.

35 Daniel K. Richter, "Johnson, Sir William, first baronet (1715?–1774)," ODNB Online [accessed March 3, 2016]; McNairn, *Behold the Hero*, pp. 137–38.

36 Nicholas B. Wainwright, *George Croghan: Wilderness Diplomat* (Chapel Hill, NC, 1959), pp. 136–37.

37 See, for example, Fintan O'Toole, *White Savage: William Johnson and the Invention of America* (London, 2005), pp. 114–15, 124, 173, 188, and elsewhere.

38 James Austin Holden, "New Historical Light on the Real Burial Place of George Augustus Lord Viscount Howe, 1758," *Proceedings of the New York State Historical Association*, vol. 10 (1911), pp. 270–75.

39 BNA: *Derby Mercury*, Nov. 23, 1764.

40 For William's movements to and from his regiments in Ireland during this period, see BNA: *Bath Chronicle and Weekly Gazette*, Feb. 9, 1764; *Derby Mercury*, Aug. 3, Nov. 2 and 23, 1764.

41 Cite from M. E. A. Dawson and G. S. H. Fox-Strangways, eds., *The Life and Letters of Lady Sarah Lennox, 1745-1826* (2 vols., London, 1902), vol. I, p. 238.

42 Brian Fitzgerald, *Lady Louisa Conolly, 1743-1821: An Anglo-Irish Biography* (London and New York, 1950), p. 38.

43 BL-AP, 75610, CH/LS, May 9, 1765.

44 A. P. W. Malcomson, "The Fall of the House of Conolly, 1758-1803," in Allan Black-
    stock and Eoin Magennis, eds., *Politics and Political Culture in Britain and Ireland,
    1750-1850: Essays in Tribute to Peter Jupp* (Belfast, 2007), p. 111.

45 Malcomson, "The Fall of the House of Conolly," pp. 108, 109, 110, 112, cite from p.
    108; H. M. Stephens, "Conolly, Thomas (1738–1803)," rev. by A. T. Q. Stewart, ODNB
    Online [accessed July 6, 2020].

46 Fitzgerald, *Lady Louisa Conolly*, pp. 43–44, 56.

47 Stella Tillyard, *Aristocrats: Caroline, Emily, Louisa and Sarah Lennox 1740-1832* (Lon-
    don, 1994; paperback ed. London, 1995), p. 109; Fitzgerald, *Lady Louisa Conolly*, pp.
    33, 34.

48 Alison Gilbert Olson, *The Radical Duke: Career and Correspondence of Charles Len-
    nox, third Duke of Richmond* (Oxford, 1961), p. 2.

49 BL-AP, 75610, CH/LS, Oct. 11, 1764; University of Southampton, Special Collec-
    tions, Broadlands Archives, Papers of Henry Temple, second Viscount Palmerston,
    BR 11/3/7, Caroline Howe to Lord Palmerston, Hanslope Oct. 18 [1764].

50 https://www.historyofparliamentonline.org/volume/1754-1790/member/howe-hon
    -thomas-1728-71 [accessed Nov. 29, 2019].

51 *A Register of Ships Employed in the Service of the Hon. the United East India Com-
    pany, from the Union of the two Companies in 1707, to the Year 1760* (London, 1800),
    p. 21.

52 Anderson, *Crucible of War*, p. 417; Dreaper, *Pitt's "Gallant Conqueror,"* pp. 45–47, 52,
    55, 57.

53 Howard T. Fry, *Alexander Dalrymple and the Expansion of British Trade* (Routledge,
    1970), p. 88.

54 LEC, vol. II, p. 123.

55 BL-AP, 75610, CH/LS, Sept. 3, 1763.

56 Fry, *Alexander Dalrymple and the Expansion of British Trade*, pp. 24–25, 29–30, 226;
    James Dreaper, "Draper, Sir William (1721–1787)," ODNB Online [accessed July 6,
    2020].

57 BNA: *Caledonian Mercury*, March 12, 1766.

58 H. V. Bowen, "Privilege and Profit: Commanders of East Indiamen as Private Trad-
    ers, Entrepreneurs and Smugglers, 1760-1813," *International Journal of Maritime
    History*, vol. 19 (2007), pp. 65, 84–85. I am grateful to Dr. Margaret Makepeace,
    Lead Curator of the East India Company Records in the British Library, for the
    information regarding the seriousness of Thomas Howe's offenses, and his rein-
    statement in 1770. [BL, India Office Records/E/4/619, pp. 73–75, and IOR/E/4/620,
    pp. 2–3].

59 Cite from LLMC, vol. 2, p. 227.

60 Namier and Brooke, *The History of Parliament*, vol. 1, pp. 344–45; "The borough
    of Northampton: Introduction," in *A History of the County of Northampton: Volume
    3*, ed. William Page (London, 1930), pp. 1–26. *British History Online*, http://www
    .british-history.ac.uk/vch/northants/vol3/pp1-26 [accessed Sept. 1, 2020].

61 BL, The Cavendish Diary, Egerton MSS 215-63, 3711, MS No. 229, pp. 17–19. I am

grateful to Professor P. D. G. Thomas for providing me with his notes of references to the Howes in the Cavendish diary.

62 Huw Bowen, "The East India Company and Military Recruitment in Britain, 1763-71," *Bulletin of the Institute of Historical Research*, vol. 59 (1986), pp. 85, 87fn; cite from W. S. Taylor and J. H. Pringle, eds., *Correspondence of William Pitt, Earl of Chatham* (4 vols., London, 1838–40), vol. 4, p. 104.

63 BNA: *The Scots Magazine*, Dec. 1, 1760. Richard Howe is also listed as Lord of the Bedchamber to the Duke of York in *The Court and City Register* of 1762, p. 105. I am indebted to Robert Bucholz and Sarah Deas of the Database of Court Officers Project (Loyola University of Chicago) for providing this second reference to Lord Howe's appointment.

64 WCL-KP, Box 9, Vol. 9:19: George III to Richard Lord Viscount Howe and Sir William Howe, "Orders and Instructions May 6, 1776."

65 Stella Tillyard, *A Royal Affair: George III and his Troublesome Siblings* (London, 2006), pp. 41, 44, 47–49, 61, 63, 70.

66 BL-AP, 75616, CH/LS, May 20, 1780.

67 Cited in E. H. Chalus, "Amelia, Princess (1711–1786)," ODNB Online [accessed July 7, 2020].

68 Thomson, *Memoirs of Viscountess Sundon*, vol. I, p. 146.

69 Horace Walpole, "Reminiscences, written in 1788," in *The Works of Horace Walpole, Earl of Orford* (5 vols., London, 1798), vol. 4, p. 284.

70 Browning, *The Duke of Newcastle*, p. 62; John Van der Kiste, *The Georgian Princesses* (Stroud, Gloucestershire, 2000; paperback ed., 2002), p. 72.

71 Constance Russell, *Three Generations of Fascinating Women* (2nd ed., London, New York and Bombay, 1905), p. 40fn.

72 Kenneth J. Panton, *Historical Dictionary of the British Monarchy* (Lanham (MD), Toronto, Plymouth, UK, 2011), p. 45.

73 BL-AP, 75610, Caroline Howe to Lady Spencer, Jan. 20 and Aug. 16, 1764.

74 BL-AP, 75610, CH/LS, [Wed.] Aug. 1759; Aug. 31, 1759. On Harleyford Manor, see Mark Girouard, *Life in the English Country House: A Social and Architectural History* (New Haven and London, 1978), pp. 199, 211; on West Wycombe House, see Simon Jenkins, *England's Thousand Best Houses* (London, 2003), pp. 41–42.

75 BL-AP, 75610, CH/LS, Thurs, Sept. 1759; Oct. 1759; Sunday 1759. Internal contents date the final letter to December. Dale, *History of the Belvoir Hunt*, p. 47.

76 Baird, *Mistress of the House*, pp. 30, 31; Amanda Foreman, *Georgiana, Duchess of Devonshire* (New York, 1998), p. 24; Bernard Bailyn, *The Ordeal of Thomas Hutchinson* (Cambridge, MA, 1974), p. 372; Girouard, *Life in the English Country House*, p. 204; cite from Foreman, p. 203.

77 BL-AP, 75610, CH/LS, Nov. 11, 1762; Nov. 28, 1763; 75611, CH/LS, 4 Tues. [1767?].

78 Trumbach, *The Rise of the Egalitarian Family*, pp. 154, 167.

79 LLMC, vol. 4, p. 428.

80 BL-AP, 75610, CH/LS, April 24 [1763]; Dec. 31, 1763.

81 Trumbach, *The Rise of the Egalitarian Family*, pp. 167–68, 169.

82 BL-AP, 75613, CH/LS, Oct. 29, 1778; 75611, CH/LS, Sept. 22, 1772.

83 Foreman, *Georgiana, Duchess of Devonshire*, pp. 70, 180.

84 BL-AP, 75610, CH/LS, Oct. 24 [1763] (manuscript marked "1762").

85 Colvin, *History of the Society of Dilettanti*, pp. 16, 83, 217; A. F. Pollard, "Villiers, Thomas, first earl of Clarendon (1709–1786)," rev. R. D. E. Eagles, ODNB Online [accessed July 7, 2020].

86 CPE, vol. 5, pp. 130–31.

Six: Caroline and Company

1 Donna T. Andrew, "Spencer, (Margaret) Georgiana, Countess Spencer (1737–1814)," ODNB Online [accessed July 13, 2020].

2 See, for example, Amanda Foreman, *Georgiana, Duchess of Devonshire*; Janet Gleeson, *Privilege and Scandal: The Remarkable Life of Harriet Spencer, Sister of Georgiana* (New York, 2006); Earl of Bessborough, ed., *Georgiana: Extracts from the Correspondence of Georgiana, Duchess of Devonshire* (London, 1955).

3 BL-AP, 75610, CH/LS, Dec. 31, 1763; 75611, CH/LS, Sept. 1 [1771], dated 1770 on ms; Sept. 16 [1771]; Friday AM Oct. 1771.

4 BL-AP, 75611, CH/LS, Friday AM [1767?]; LS/CH, Southampton [Oct. 1771].

5 Institute of Historical Research, Office-Holders in Modern Britain: Royal Households, Princess Caroline 1714-27, http://www.history.ac.uk/publications/office/caroline [accessed Feb. 24, 2016]; Philip Woodfine, "Poyntz, Stephen (*bap.* 1685, *d.* 1750)," ODNB Online [accessed Feb. 24, 2016].

6 Arthur Collins, *A Supplement to the Four Volumes of the Peerage of England: Containing a Succession of the Peers from 1740* (2 vols., London, 1750), vol. 2, p. 5.

7 Stokes, *The Devonshire House Circle*, p. 38; Carola Hicks, *Improper Pursuits: The Scandalous Life of Lady Di Beauclerk* (London, Basingstoke, and Oxford, 2001), p. 60, cite from *Improper Pursuits*, p. 60.

8 Stokes, *The Devonshire House Circle*, p. 43; Foreman, *Georgiana, Duchess of Devonshire*, pp. 4–5.

9 Ibid., pp. 7–8; Stokes, *The Devonshire House Circle*, pp. 42, 43; Gleeson, *Privilege and Scandal*, p. 7.

10 Betty Rizzo, *Companions Without Vows: Relationships Among Eighteenth-Century British Women* (Athens (GA) and London, 1994), p. 240.

11 Ibid., p. 8.

12 Cite from Gleeson, *Privilege and Scandal*, p. 7.

13 BL-AP, 75617, CH/LS, June 1, 1780.

14 Foreman, *Georgiana, Duchess of Devonshire*, p. 4.

15 Cite from Foreman, *Georgiana, Duchess of Devonshire*, p. 11; BL-AP, 75610, CH/LS, Dec. 5, 1761.

16 BL-AP, 75614, CH/LS, Jan. 16, 1780.

17 BL-AP, 75610, CH/LS, Hanslope, October 1759; Sept. 26, 1760; April 24 [1763] (manuscript marked "1762"); Nov. 28, 1763; Oct. 11, 1764; 75611, CH/LS, Friday Morning Oct. 1771.

18 BL-AP, 75612, CH/LS, Dec. 20, 1774.

19   Liza Picard, *Dr. Johnson's London: Life in London 1740-1770* (London, 2000; paperback ed. London, 2001), pp. 131, 207; Phyllis Deutsch, "Moral Trespass in Georgian London: Gaming, Gender, and Electoral Politics in the Age of George III," *The Historical Journal*, vol. 39 (1996), p. 638.

20   Georgina Battiscombe, *The Spencers of Althorp* (London, 1984), p. 79.

21   BL-AP, 75617, CH/LS, Dec. 29, 1781; LS/CH, Bath, June 6, 1780.

22   Deutsch, "Moral Trespass in Georgian London," pp. 647–49, 650.

23   Chalus, *Elite Women in English Political Life*, pp. 19, 23, 78; Anna Clark, *Scandal: The Sexual Politics of the British Constitution* (Princeton (NJ) and Oxford, 2004), pp. 10, 12, 217.

24   Chalus, *Elite Women in English Political Life*, pp. 4, 7, 8, 13, 73, 77, 84.

25   Battiscombe, *The Spencers of Althorp*, p. 75.

26   Rizzo, *Companions Without Vows*, p. 256.

27   For example, see BC: *Middlesex Journal or Chronicle of Liberty*, August 24–26, 1769; *Whitehall Evening Post or London Intelligencer*, Aug. 31–Sept. 2, 1769.

28   Ian R. Christie, "William Pitt and American Taxation, 1766: A Problem of Parliamentary Reporting," in *Studies in Burke and His Time*, vol. 17 (1976), pp. 167–79.

29   Cite from Peter D. G. Thomas, *Revolution in America: Britain and the Colonies, 1763-1776* (Cardiff, 1992), p. 21.

30   Peter D. G. Thomas, *George III: King and Politicians* (Manchester and New York, 2002), pp. 24–25; Browning, *The Duke of Newcastle*, pp. 317, 320.

31   Dickinson, *Liberty and Property*, p. 207.

32   Hill, *The Early Parties and Politics in Britain*, pp. 105–6; cite from Browning, *The Duke of Newcastle*, p. 318.

33   http://www.historyofparliamentonline.org/volume/1754-1790/member/howe-hon -william-1729-1814 [accessed July 14, 2020]. John Brooke asserts that no record exists, but William presented a petition from his Nottingham constituents in February 1775. See chapter 7, below.

34   Syrett, p. 36.

35   Gruber, pp. 49, 50, cite on p. 49; see also Syrett, pp. 33, 35; Knight, "Howe, Richard, Earl Howe (1726–1799)."

36   BL-AP, 75610, CH/LS, April 24 [1763], manuscript marked "1762."

37   Paul Langford, *The First Rockingham Administration 1765-1766* (Oxford, 1973), pp. 10–13; Thomas, *George III*, p. 76.

38   BL-AP, 75610, CH/LS, Oct. 24 [1763], manuscript marked "1762."

39   Cited in Peter Durrant, "FitzRoy, Augustus Henry, third duke of Grafton (1735–1811)," ODNB Online [accessed Dec. 18, 2019].

40   Trumbach, *The Rise of the Egalitarian Family*, p. 157; Susan C. Law, *Through the Keyhole: Sex, Scandal and the Secret Life of the Country House* (Stroud, Gloucestershire, 2015), pp. 129–35.

41   William C. Lowe, "Liddell, Henry, first Baron Ravensworth (*bap.* 1708, *d.* 1784)," ODNB Online [accessed July 14, 2020].

42   Trumbach, *The Rise of the Egalitarian Family*, p. 157.

43   Law, *Through the Keyhole*, pp. 67, 68.

44 BL-AP, 75610, CH/LS, July 16, 1763; July 31, 1763; Dec. 31, 1763; LS/CH, Jan. 1764; Aug. 9 [1763], manuscript marked "1764."

45 Law, *Through the Keyhole*, p. 68; A. A. Hanham, "Parsons, Anne [Nancy] [*married name* Anne Maynard, Viscountess Maynard] (c. 1735–1814/15]," ODNB Online [accessed July 14, 2020].

46 SRO(B), FitzRoy Papers, HA513/4/72, Duchess to Duke, St James's Square, Dec. 20, 1764; Durrant, "FitzRoy, Augustus Henry, third duke of Grafton."

47 Law, *Through the Keyhole*, p. 68.

48 BL-AP, 75610, CH/LS, Sept. 10, 1764.

49 Kilburn, "Fitzpatrick, Anne, countess of Upper Ossory [*other married name* Anne FitzRoy, duchess of Grafton] (1737/8–1804)," ODNB Online [accessed July 14, 2020].

50 BL-AP, 75610, CH/LS, Nov. 8, 1764.

51 Lawrence Stone, *Road to Divorce: England 1530-1987* (Oxford, 1990), pp. 336–37, 341; Durrant, "FitzRoy, Augustus Henry, third duke of Grafton"; Kilburn, "Fitzpatrick, Anne, countess of Upper Ossory."

52 Hanham, "Parsons, Anne [Nancy] [*married name* Anne Maynard, Viscountess Maynard]."

53 BNA: *Salisbury and Winchester Journal*, June 26, 1780.

54 BL-AP, 75610, CH/LS, Aug. 2, 1764; 75611, CH/LS, Aug. 18, 1772; Oct. 22, 1772; Dec. 2, 1772.

55 BL-AP, 75610, CH/LS, Nov. 9, 1766.

56 BL-AP, 75743, List of the original members of the Ladies' Club, with notes of those who have attended, [1770?]. On Juliana Page's agreement to use her influence on behalf of Lord Ossory, see 75611, CH/LS, March 12, 1767.

57 I am indebted to Martin Price for the information on Hannah Read and her niece, also Hannah Read, and nephew William Thornton. Mr. Price has provided me with the following results of his private research: "Mrs. Howe was a witness at the signing of the Will of Hannah Read on 15 June 1776 and also a Codicil on 31 May 1777 (TNA: Prerogative Court of Canterbury, PROB 10/2890). Her Will shows that she held 3% Annuities in the East India Company, with the relevant Ledgers (British Library L/AG/14/5/267) and Stock Transfer Books (BL L/AG/14/5/294) of the East India Company giving the nominal value of this holding to be £900, and showing that the deceased Hannah Read was a servant of Mrs. Howe. The stock was bequeathed in equal portions to her niece, Hannah Read, shown in the Transfer Books in January 1783 as a servant of Lady Ossory's, and to her nephew William Thornton, shown similarly as a servant of Lord Howe."

58 BL-AP, 75610, CH/LS, July 7, 1763; July 16, 1763; Sept. 3, 1763; June 21, 1764.

59 BL-AP, 75610, CH/LS, Sept. 3, 1763.

60 Langford, *The First Rockingham Administration*, p. 9; Durrant, "FitzRoy, Augustus Henry, third duke of Grafton."

61 Williams, *Life of William Pitt, Earl of Chatham*, vol. II, p. 169.

62 Syrett, pp. 27, 34–35; cite on p. 35.

63 *Correspondence of William Pitt, Earl of Chatham*, vol. 4, pp. 56, 249; BL-AP, 75612, CH/LS, Feb. 12, 1772.

64 BC: *Middlesex Journal or Chronicle of Liberty*, Aug. 24–26, 1769; *Whitehall Evening Post or London Intelligencer*, Aug. 31–Sept. 2, 1769.

65 BL-AP, 75611, LS/CH, Aug. 31, 1769; Sept. 5, 1769.

66 Lady Spencer's letters to Caroline Howe are in BL-AP, 75620; her diary is in BL-AP, vol. 309. Miscellaneous family papers of Lady Spencer, 1654–1814.

67 LEC, vol. II, p. 44.

68 BL-AP, 75610, CH/LS, Aug. 16, 1761; April 11, 1762.

69 BL-AP, 75612, CH/LS, Dec. 16, 1774; "Parishes: Hanslope with Castle Thorpe," in *A History of the County of Buckingham: Volume 4*, ed. William Page (London, 1927), pp. 348–62. *British History Online*, http://www.british-history.ac.uk/vch/bucks/vol4/pp348-362 [accessed Sept. 1, 2020].

70 Richard Garnier, "Grafton Street, Mayfair," in *The Georgian Group Journal*, vol. XIII (2003), pp. 201, 215, 219, 223, 230, 231, 233, 253, 256; Ben Weinreb and Christopher Hibbert, eds., *The London Encyclopedia* (London, 1983; rev. ed. 1995), p. 329; HMC: *The Manuscripts of the Earl of Dartmouth* (3 vols., London, 1887, 1895, 1896), vol. II, p. 238. I am indebted to Martin Price for drawing my attention to the article by Richard Garnier.

71 Lewis, *Sacred to Female Patriotism*, pp. 98–99.

72 BL-AP, 75614, CH/LS, Jan. 22, 1780.

73 Spencer and Dobson, eds., *Letters of David Garrick and Georgiana Countess Spencer 1759-1779*, p. 134.

74 Stokes, *The Devonshire House Circle*, pp. 49, 72, 84fn, 258, 259.

75 BL-AP, 75615, CH/LS, April 19, 1780.

76 Theresa Lewis, ed., *Extracts of the Journal and Correspondence of Miss Berry, from the year 1783 to 1852* (3 vols., London, 1865), vol. I, p. 210.

77 Sources for citations in order of appearance: BL-AP, 75615, CH/LS, April 18, 1780; April 17, 1780; 75610, CH/LS, Tues. a.m., 1762; 75631, CH/LS, April 2, 1787.

78 Lewis Melville, ed., *The Berry Papers: Being the Correspondence Hitherto Unpublished of Mary and Agnes Berry (1763–1852)*, (London and New York, 1914), p. 209.

79 BL/AP, 75617, CH/LS, April 17, 1781.

80 Matthew Montagu, ed., *The Letters of Mrs Elizabeth Montagu* (3 vols., Boston, 1825), vol. 3, pp. 168–69.

81 Gerald Newman, ed., *Britain in the Hanoverian Age, 1714-1837: An Encyclopedia* (New York and London, 1997), pp. 516–17; John Brewer, *The Pleasures of the Imagination: English Culture in the Eighteenth Century* (London, 1997), pp. 364–65, 396–98.

82 Jennifer Hall-Witt, *Fashionable Acts: Opera and Elite Culture in London, 1780-1880* (Lebanon, NH, 2007), p. 195.

83 Gillian Russell, *Women, Sociability and Theatre in Georgian London* (Cambridge, 2010), pp. 12, 72.

84 BL-AP, 75611, CH/LS, Nov. 19, 1772; Dec. 11, 1772; 75612, CH/LS, Nov. 1, 1774.

85 BL-AP, 75743, List of the original members of the Ladies' Club.

86 Russell, *Women, Sociability and Theatre in Georgian London*, pp. 72–75.

87 BNA: *Bath Chronicle and Weekly Gazette*, Aug. 29, 1771.

88 BL-AP, 75611, CH/LS, Nov. 24, 1772.

89 BL-AP, 75612, CH/LS, March 9, 1773; 75616, CH/LS, May 9, 1780.

90 LLMC, vol. 4, p. 448, and see pp. 429, 449.

91 Gruber, "Howe, William, fifth Viscount Howe (1729–1814)."

92 George Mason, *The Life of Richard Earl Howe* (London, 1803), p. 34.

93 "Parishes: Heckfield," in *A History of the County of Hampshire: Volume 4*, ed. William Page (London, 1911), pp. 44–51. *British History Online*, http://www.british-history.ac.uk/vch/hants/vol4/pp44-51 [accessed Sept. 1, 2020].

94 BL-AP, 75611, Juliana Howe to LS, Aug. 12 [1771].

95 BL-AP, 75611, Juliana Howe to LS, Aug. 12 [1771]; Aug. 31 [1771]; CH/LS, Aug. 15 [1771]; Sept. 8 [1771].

96 BL-AP, 75611, CH/LS, Sept. 1 [1771], manuscript marked "1770"; Sept. 16 [1771]; Friday AM October 1771.

97 BL-AP, 75611, CH/LS, Sept. 22, 1772; 75612, CH/LS, Feb. 22, 1773; March 9, 1773.

Seven: A Game of Chess

1 Cited in Bernard Donoughue, *British Politics and the American Revolution: The Path to War, 1773-1775* (London and New York, 1964), p. 132.

2 H. W. Brands, *The First American: The Life and Times of Benjamin Franklin* (New York, 2000; paperback ed. New York, 2002), pp. 470–74.

3 David T. Morgan, *The Devious Dr. Franklin, Colonial Agent* (Macon, GA, 1996), pp. 225–26; Julie Flavell, *When London Was Capital of America* (New Haven, CT: Yale University Press, 2010), p. 228.

4 Peter D. G. Thomas, *Tea Party to Independence: The Third Phase of the American Revolution 1773-1776* (Oxford, 1991), pp. 43, 38; Thomas, *Revolution in America*, pp. 38–39.

5 Thomas, ibid., pp. 39, 41, 44.

6 Julie M. Flavell, "American Patriots in London and the Quest for Talks, 1774-1775," in *The Journal of Imperial and Commonwealth History*, vol. 20 (1992), pp. 339–40.

7 Thomas, *Tea Party to Independence*, p. 157.

8 WCL-KP, Box 2:15, John Pownall to William Knox, Whitehall, August 31, 1774.

9 PBF, vol. 21, p. 396.

10 G. M. Ditchfield, "Shipley, Jonathan 1713-1788, bishop of St Asaph," ODNB Online [accessed July 16, 2020]; Donoughue, *British Politics and the American Revolution*, p. 294.

11 Margaret DeLacy, "Fothergill, John (1712–1780)," ODNB Online [accessed July 16, 2020]; Flavell, *When London Was Capital of America*, p. 205; John Fothergill, *Chain of Friendship: Selected Letters of Dr. John Fothergill of London, 1735-1780*, eds. Betsy C. Corner and Christopher C. Booth (Cambridge, MA, 1971), pp. 15, 421.

12 PBF, vol. 21, pp. 550–51, 553.

13 Ibid., vol. 21, pp. 562–63; R. Hingston Fox, *Dr John Fothergill and His Friends* (London, 1919), p. 327.

14 PBF, vol. 21, p. 550.

15 BL-AP, 75612, CH/LS, May 12, 1774; Donoughue, *British Politics and the American*

Revolution, p. 294, presumes Lord Spencer voted against the Massachusetts Government Act on May 11; Caroline's letter of May 12 confirms this.

16 "*Noblesse oblige*: Female charity in an age of sentiment," by Donna T. Andrew in John Brewer and Susan Staves, eds. *Early Modern Conceptions of Property* (London and New York: 1996), pp. 292–93.

17 Langford, *A Polite and Commercial People*, pp. 481–86; Donna T. Andrew, *Philanthropy and Police: London Charity in the Eighteenth Century* (Princeton, 1989), pp. 3–4.

18 Ibid., pp. 57, 69, 70–71; Langford, *A Polite and Commercial People*, p. 486.

19 Andrew, *Philanthropy and Police*, pp. 60–61, 72, 110; cite on p. 110.

20 Andrew, "*Noblesse oblige*: Female charity in an age of sentiment," pp. 276, 278, 292–93, 294fn, 296; Andrew, "Spencer, (Margaret) Georgiana, Countess Spencer (1737–1814)."

21 BC: *London Evening Post*, March 22–24, 1774.

22 Foreman, *Georgiana Duchess of Devonshire*, pp. 18–20; *Georgiana: Extracts from the Correspondence of Georgiana, Duchess of Devonshire*, pp. 11–12, cite from p. 11.

23 Andrew, "Spencer, (Margaret) Georgiana, Countess Spencer (1737–1814)"; Foreman, *Georgiana Duchess of Devonshire*, pp. 10–13.

24 BL-AP, 75613, LS/CH, Dec. 3, 1776; see also CH/LS, Nov. 5, 1776.

25 BC: *Morning Post and Daily Advertiser*, Jan. 19, 1774; BL-AP, 75612, LS/CH, April 19, 1774; CH/LS, April 1774.

26 BL-AP, 75612, LS/CH, Aug. 18, 1774; Aug. 27, 1774; CH/LS, Aug. 19, 1774; Sept. 14, 1774.

27 Andrew, "*Noblesse oblige*: Female charity in an age of sentiment," pp. 292–93; BL-AP, 75612, CH/LS, Oct. 14, 1774; Nov. 4, 1774; Nov. 22, 1774; Nov. 26, 1774; Dec. 5, 1775; Dec. 13, 1774; Dec. 24, 1774; LS/CH, Dec. 16, 1774; Tuesday, N/D; Monday [1774?].

28 BL-AP, 75612, LS/CH, Nov. 25, 1774; CH/LS, Nov. 26, 1774.

29 BL-AP, 75612, CH/LS, Dec. 5, 1775; Dec. 24, 1774.

30 Andrew, "*Noblesse oblige*: Female charity in an age of sentiment," p. 278; Andrew, *Philanthropy and Police*, p. 83; BL-AP, 75612, CH/LS, Nov. 26, 1774; Dec. 5, 1775.

31 Montagu Pennington, ed., *A Series of Letters between Mrs. Elizabeth Carter and Miss Catherine Talbot, from the year 1741 to 1770* (1809), p. 99.

32 Flora Fraser, *Princesses: The Six Daughters of George III* (London, 2004), pp. 10–11, 14, 34–35; BL-AP, 75612, CH/LS, Dec. 5, 1775; Dec. 21, 1774.

33 B. D. Bargar, *Lord Dartmouth and the American Revolution* (Columbia, SC, 1965), pp. 6–7.

34 See, for example, BL-AP, 75612, CH/LS, Dec. 2, 1774; Nov. 22, 1774; Nov. 26, 1774.

35 LLMC, vol. 4, p. 420; CPE, vol. 4, pp. 122–23.

36 Syrett, p. 37.

37 Cited from PBF, vol. 21, p. 409. Other conjectures are found in Gruber, *The Howe Brothers and the American Revolution*, p. 53; Bargar, *Lord Dartmouth and the American Revolution*, p. 134; Donoughue, *British Politics and the American Revolution*, p. 221.

38 BL-AP, 75612, CH/LS, Nov. 1, 1774.

39 BC: *Public Advertiser*, Oct. 28, 1774; *Middlesex Journal and Evening Advertiser*, Nov. 8–10, 1774; LLMC, vol. 4, pp. 417, 420. I am indebted to Professor P. D. G. Thomas

for the suggestion that "St. Anthony's fire" most likely indicated scarlet fever in the case of the Dartmouth baby.

40 Thomas, *Tea Party to Independence*, pp. 158–59, cite from p. 159.

41 Ibid., p. 61.

42 Bargar, *Lord Dartmouth and the American Revolution*, p. 116.

43 Thomas, *Tea Party to Independence*, pp. 130, 132–38, quote from Thomas, pp. 137–38; David Ammerman, *In the Common Cause: American Response to the Coercive Acts of 1774* (Charlottesville, VA, 1974), pp. 23–33.

44 Josiah Quincy, *Memoir of the Life of Josiah Quincy, Jr. of Massachusetts, 1744-1775* (Boston, 1874), p. 206; BC: *St James's Chronicle, or the British Evening Post*, Nov. 19–22, 1774; *General Evening Post*, November 19–22, 1774; *London Chronicle or Universal Evening Post*, Nov. 19–22, 1774; Clifford K. Shipton, *Biographical Sketches of Those Who Attended Harvard College*, vols. 4–17 of Sibley's Harvard Graduates (Cambridge, MA, 1933–75), vol. 15, p. 489.

45 PBF, vol. 21, p. 562.

46 BL-AP, 75613, CH/LS, March 2, 1778.

47 BC: *Middlesex Journal and Evening Advertiser*, Nov. 8–10, 1774; *Memoir of the Life of Josiah Quincy, Jr.*, p. 204.

48 PBF, vol. 21, p. 550.

49 BL-AP, 75743, List of the original members of the Ladies' Club, with notes of those who have attended [1770?].

50 Lewis, *Sacred to Female Patriotism*, p. 90. On the Howe connection, the Shipleys were related through the Mordaunts. Spencer et al., eds., *Letters of David Garrick and Georgiana Countess Spencer*, p. 12.

51 Gruber, p. 58.

52 Samuel Kirk, Grocer, Nottingham to General Howe, Feb. 10, 1775, reproduced in Bellamy Partridge, *Sir Billy Howe* (London and New York, 1932), pp. 6–7.

53 Gruber, p. 58. For a recent example, see Rick Atkinson, *The British Are Coming: The War for America 1775-1777* (London, 2019), p. 134.

54 BL-AP, 75612, CH/LS, Oct. 14, 1774.

55 WCL-KP, Box 10:21, William Knox, "Secret proceedings respecting America in the new Parliament 1774 & 1775"; Thomas, *Tea Party to Independence*, p. 161; Donoughue, *British Politics and the American Revolution*, p. 211.

56 PBF, vol. 21, p. 572.

57 BC: *Public Advertiser*, Nov. 28 and Dec. 6, 1774; *Morning Chronicle and London Advertiser*, Dec. 22, 1774.

58 PBF, vol. 21, pp. 436–37, 550, 552, 566, 567.

59 See, for example, BL-AP, 75612, CH/LS, May 2, 1774; 75610, CH/LS, Nov. [8?] 1764; CH/LS, Oct. 24 [1762 or 1763].

60 "The Morals of Chess" [before June 28, 1779], PBF, vol. 29, p. 750.

61 BL-AP, 75615, CH/LS, April 21, 1780; 75612, CH/LS, May 2, 1774.

62 Kerry S. Walters, *Benjamin Franklin and His Gods* (University of Illinois Press, 1998), p. 195fn.

63 BL-AP, 75612, CH/LS, Dec. 2, 1774; BC: *Middlesex Journal and Evening Advertiser*, Dec. 1–3, 1774; *Morning Chronicle and London Advertiser*, Dec. 2, 1774.

64 BL-AP, 75612, CH/LS, Dec. 5, 1775.

65 PBF, vol. 21, p. 552.

66 Ibid., vol. 21, pp. 565–68.

67 Ibid., p. 571.

68 Donoughue, *British Politics and the American Revolution*, pp. 284–85.

69 *Chain of Friendship*, pp. 248–49; Eliga H. Gould, "Pownall, Thomas (1722–1805)," ODNB Online [accessed July 27, 2020].

70 Richard Koebner, *Empire* (Cambridge, 1961), p. 185; B. D. Bargar, "Lord Dartmouth's Patronage, 1772-1775," *William and Mary Quarterly*, 3rd series, vol. 15 (1958), p. 196. Franklin discovered that Pownall still hoped to be appointed a peace commissioner in January 1775. BPF, vol. 21, p. 568.

71 Donoughue, *British Politics and the American Revolution*, pp. 170–71, 206; Bargar, *Lord Dartmouth and the American Revolution*, pp. 109, 116–17.

72 PBF, vol. 21, pp. 553–63, 366–68, 583–88.

73 Dickinson, *Liberty and Property*, p. 155; Thomas, *Tea Party to Independence*, pp. 269–70.

74 Sheffield City Council, Libraries Archives and Information: Sheffield Archives: Wentworth Woodhouse Muniments, Rockingham Papers, R1-1244, Charles Watson-Wentworth, 2nd Marquess of Rockingham to William Legge, 2nd Earl of Dartmouth, November 1769.

75 Donoughue, *British Politics and the American Revolution*, p. 169.

76 WCL-KP, Box 2:17, John Pownall to William Knox, London, Sept. 13, 1774.

77 Ian R. Christie, *Crisis of Empire: Great Britain and the American Colonies, 1754-1783* (London, 1966), pp. 66–67.

78 "A Provisional Act for settling the Troubles in America, and for asserting the supreme legislative Authority and superintending Power of Great Britain over the Colonies," *Correspondence of William Pitt, Earl of Chatham*, vol. 4, pp. 533–36.

79 Arthur Lee, "A SECOND Appeal, published in a single volume with *An Appeal to the Justice and Interests of the People of Great Britain in the Present Disputes with America. By an Old Member of Parliament*" (London: 4th ed., 1776), p. 40.

80 WCL-KP, 10:21, William Knox, "Secret proceedings respecting America in the new Parliament 1774 & 1775."

81 Ian R. Christie and Benjamin Labaree, *Empire or Independence 1760-1776* (New York, 1976), pp. 228–29.

82 Donoughue, *British Politics and the American Revolution*, pp. 229, 254–55.

83 PBF, vol. 21, pp. 436, 573, 574, 587.

84 Ibid., vol. 21, p. 566.

85 PBF, vol. 21, pp. 586–90. On Barclay's proposal that both sides should back off from the conflict in a sequence of staged retreats, involving Boston's payment for the tea, followed by the appointment of a commissioner who could suspend the Boston Port Act and enter into negotiations, see "Barclay's Plan of Reconciliation," on or before February 16, 1775, Ibid., vol. 21, pp. 491–94.

86 Syrett, pp. 7, 27.

87 PBF, vol. 21, p. 573.

88 BL-AP, 75612, CH/LS, Dec. 5, 1774.

89 BC: *Middlesex Journal and Evening Advertiser*, Feb. 7–9, 23–24, 1775; *London Evening Post*, Feb. 21–23, 1775. On Nottingham's petitions against coercing America and loyal addresses in favor, see James E. Bradley, *Popular Politics and the American Revolution in England: Petitions, the Crown, and Public Opinion* (Macon, GA, 1986), pp. 21, 28–29, 198–200; see also letters of Burke to Mark Huish on the presentation of the petitions, George H. Guttridge, ed., *The Correspondence of Edmund Burke*, vol. III (July 1774–June 1778) (Chicago, 1961), pp. 121, 130.

90 Max M. Mintz, "Burgoyne, John (1723-1792)," ODNB Online [accessed Jan. 15, 2020].

91 James Lunt, *John Burgoyne of Saratoga* (London, 1976), pp. 74–75, 76, 78; Edward Barrington de Fonblanque, *Political and Military Episodes in the Latter Half of the Eighteenth Century. Derived from the Life and Correspondence of the Right Hon. John Burgoyne* (London, 1876), pp. 129–30.

92 In his final instructions to General Gage on April 15, 1775, Dartmouth allowed Gage some latitude in appointing either Howe or Burgoyne to New York. Four regiments were to be sent there from Ireland. By the time of this letter, the idea of a commissioner had been entirely given up. The military presence in New York was intended solely to prevent help from reaching New England from the southern provinces. Thomas, *Tea Party to Independence*, p. 229.

93 Donoughue, *British Politics and the American Revolution*, pp. 214–16, cite on page 216.

94 Bargar, *Lord Dartmouth and the American Revolution*, p. 147; Thomas, *Tea Party to Independence*, p. 189; BL-AP, 75612, CH/LS, Dec. 21, 1774.

95 PBF, vol. 21, pp. 589, 591–92, 595.

96 Thomas, *Revolution in Britain and America*, pp. 49–50.

97 Julie M. Flavell, "Lord North's Conciliatory Proposal and the Patriots in London," in *English Historical Review*, vol. 107 (1992), pp. 307–8.

98 PBF, vol. 21, p. 597.

99 BC: *Middlesex Journal and Evening Advertiser*, Feb. 9–11, 1775. Generals Howe, Burgoyne, and Clinton had all accepted appointments to go to America by February third. Thomas, *Tea Party to Independence*, p. 181.

100 Gruber, p. 59; Andrew Jackson O'Shaughnessy, *The Men Who Lost America: British Leadership, the American Revolution, and the Fate of the Empire* (New Haven (CT) and London, 2013), p. 89.

101 *The Last Journals of Horace Walpole during the Reign of George III*, vol. I, p. 420; Troy Bickham, *Making Headlines: The American Revolution as Seen through the British Press* (DeKalb, IL, 2009), p. 64.

102 *The Last Journals of Horace Walpole during the Reign of George III*, vol. I, p. 433.

103 Cited in Lunt, *John Burgoyne of Saratoga*, p. 69.

104 BC: *St. James's Chronicle, or the British Evening Post*, March 4–7, 1775; Thomas, *Tea Party to Independence*, p. 207.

105 LEC, vol. 2, p. 310.

106 Elizabeth Harris to [James Harris], February 6, 1775, J. H. H. Malmesbury, ed., *A Series of Letters of the First Earl of Malmesbury, His Family and Friends from 1745 to 1820* (2 vols., London, 1870), vol. I, p. 290.

107 Thomas, *Tea Party to Independence*, p. 229; Fitzgerald, *Lady Louisa Conolly*, pp. 39, 91–92; *Correspondence of Emily, Duchess of Leinster*, vol. 3, pp. 140, 144.

Eight: American Destiny

1 O'Shaughnessy, *The Men Who Lost America*, p. 86.

2 Anderson, p. 71.

3 Henry Lee, *Memoirs of the War in the Southern Department of the United States* (2 vols., Philadelphia, 1812), vol. I, p. 55.

4 An excellent account of the battle is Mark Urban, *Fusiliers: Eight Years with the Redcoats in America* (London, 2007), pp. 34–43. See also Sir John Fortescue, *The War of Independence: The British Army in North America, 1775-1783* (London, 1911; this ed. London and Mechanicsburg, PA, 2001), pp. 9–12; Thomas J. Fleming, *Now We Are Enemies: The Story of Bunker Hill* (New York, 1960), pp. 241–42, 250; Nathaniel Philbrick, *Bunker Hill: A City, A Siege, A Revolution* (New York, 2013), pp. 208–30; O'Shaughnessy, *The Men Who Lost America*, pp. 85–86.

5 Philbrick, *Bunker Hill*, pp. 224, 230, cite from p. 230; Fleming, *Now We Are Enemies*, pp. 267–68. According to Fleming, General Howe found himself standing entirely alone before the enemy on three separate occasions during the battle.

6 Gruber sums up William's career on pp. 56–57; his article in the ODNB, "Howe, William, fifth Viscount Howe (1729–1814)," is fuller but necessarily brief. Anderson gives a very sketchy account of William's background on p. 44; Smith, pp. 18–19, restricts his account of William Howe's experience in the Seven Years' War to the siege of Quebec in 1759 and the 1762 Havana campaign. He also considers William's interest in light infantry training after the Seven Years' War on pp. 20–23. Partridge, *Sir Billy*, the only dedicated biography of Sir William Howe, gives an overview of his career prior to the American War of Independence on pp. 9–11.

7 Among many examples, see Fleming, *Now We Are Enemies*, pp. 268, 270, and, more recently, Philbrick, *Bunker Hill*, who cites the phrase out of context and calls it evidence of a "life-altering sensation" (p. 225). See also note 15, below, for source of Howe quote.

8 WCL-HCP, Series 1, 10:5 [Sir Henry Clinton] [June 17, 1775] "Account of the battle of Bunker Hill. Part in cipher, with decipher for all but a few words." Not all historians treat William's "moment" out of context. See, for example, Mark Urban, *Fusiliers*, chapter 4, "Bunker Hill," discussing William's assessments of the battle in letters home on pp. 39 and 43, and O'Shaughnessy, *The Men Who Lost America*, p. 85.

9 William B. Willcox, *Portrait of a General: Sir Henry Clinton in the War of Independence* (New York, 1964), p. 48.

10 Fleming, *Now We Are Enemies*, p. 182. Fleming does not provide references, but the letters are: Staffordshire Record Office, Dartmouth MSS. Major General William Howe to Lord Howe, Boston, June 12, 1775, D(W)178-II-1315; "A Letter of Intelligence," Boston, June 12, 1775, *The Correspondence of King George the Third from 1760*

to December 1783, ed. Sir John Fortescue (6 vols., London 1927), vol. 3, pp. 215–18; General Howe to Lord Howe, June 22, 1775 (Copy), HMC, *Report on the Manuscripts of Mrs. Stopford-Sackville of Drayton House, Northamptonshire* (2 vols., London and Hereford, 1904, 1910), vol. 2, pp. 3–5.

11 Lieut.-General Thomas Gage to the Earl of Dartmouth, June 12, 1775. Davies, vol. 9, p. 170; in Peter Orlando Hutchinson, *The Diary and Letters of His Excellency Thomas Hutchinson* (2 vols., Boston, 1884–86), vol. 1, p. 539, Governor Hutchinson records that in September 1775, the flat-bottomed boats Howe requested were finally on their way.

12 Fleming, *Now We Are Enemies*, pp. 182, 204–5.

13 Willcox, *Portrait of a General*, p. 48; Ira D. Gruber, "Clinton, Sir Henry (1730–1795)," ODNB Online [accessed July 30, 2020].

14 William B. Willcox, ed., *The American Rebellion: Sir Henry Clinton's Narrative of His Campaigns, 1775-1782* (New Haven, 1954), pp. ix–x.

15 General Sir William Howe to [?the Adjutant-General], June 22 and 24, 1775, *The Correspondence of King George the Third*, vol. 3, p. 222–23.

16 BL-AP, 75613, CH/LS, Aug. 27, 1775.

17 *The Life and Letters of Lady Sarah Lennox*, vol. 1, pp. 235, 243.

18 *Correspondence of Emily Duchess of Leinster*, vol. III, pp. 144–45.

19 LEC, vol. II, p. 123.

20 BL-AP, 75611, CH/LS, Oct. 29, Dec. 29, 1772; 75612, CH/LS, Jan. 12, 1773.

21 BL-AP, 75611, CH/LS, March 17, 1767; 75612, CH/LS, Aug. 19, 1774; 75613, CH/LS, Aug. 27, 1775; 75614, CH/LS, Jan. 5, 1780.

22 *Private Papers of James Boswell from Malahide Castle*; In the Collection of Lt-Colonel Ralph Heywood Isham, ed. Geoffrey Scott and Frederick A. Pottle (1931), pp. 67–68.

23 BL-AP, 75613, CH/LS, July 20, 1775.

24 BC: *London Gazette*, July 22–25, 1775.

25 BL-AP, 75613, CH/LS, July 27, 1775.

26 Urban, *Fusiliers*, p. 45; Richard sent a copy of William's letter to Lord George Germain. *Report on the Manuscripts of Mrs. Stopford-Sackville*, vol. 2, pp. 3–5.

27 BL-AP, 75613, CH/LS, Aug. 3, 1775.

28 BL-AP, 75613, CH/LS, Aug. 11, 1775; for an example of a newspaper report on William Howe's danger at Bunker Hill, see BNA: *Derby Mercury*, July 28, 1775.

29 *Correspondence of Emily, Duchess of Leinster*, vol. 3, p. 145; BL-AP, 75613, CH/LS, Aug. 27, 1775.

30 *The Life and Letters of Lady Sarah Lennox*, vol. 1, p. 244.

31 Philbrick, *Bunker Hill*, pp. 57, 220, 226.

32 *The Life and Letters of Lady Sarah Lennox*, vol. 1, pp. 234–35, 243, 244.

33 BL-AP, 75613, CH/LS, Aug. 27, 1775.

34 Bradley, *Popular Politics and the American Revolution in England*, pp. 4, 7, 10, 12, 210–16.

35 Bickham, *Making Headlines*, pp. 72–73, 82–83; Stephen Conway, "From Fellow-Nationals to Foreigners: British Perceptions of the Americans, Circa 1739-1783," in *William and Mary Quarterly*, 3rd series, vol. 59 (2002), pp. 85–87.

36 R. C. Simmons and P. D. G. Thomas, eds., *Proceedings and Debates of the British Parliament Respecting North America, 1754-1783* (6 vols., Millwood, White Plains, NY, 1982–1987), vol. 6, p. 62.

37 Flavell, *When London Was Capital of America*, pp. 105–9; Bickham, *Making Headlines*, pp. 40–41.

38 Clive Towse, "Conway, Henry Seymour (1719–1795)," ODNB Online [accessed Aug. 1, 2020]; *Proceedings and Debates of the British Parliament Respecting North America*, vol. 6, p. 113.

39 Dickinson, *Liberty and Property*, pp. 206–9; citation from http://www.historyof parliamentonline.org/volume/1754-1790/member/cavendish-george-augustus -1727-94 [accessed Aug. 1, 2020].

40 Flavell, "American Patriots in London and the Quest for Talks, 1774-1775," pp. 355–56.

41 BL-AP, 75612, CH/LS, Saturday Oct. 1, 1774; 75613, CH/LS, Aug. 27, 1775.

42 Leslie Mitchell, *The Whig World, 1760-1837* (1st ed., London and New York, 2005; paperback ed., 2007), p. 18.

43 Foreman, *Georgiana Duchess of Devonshire*, pp. 30–34, 38, 39.

44 NRAS-DH/LMC: NRAS859/vol. 485, Box 4, Friday, Oct. 13, 1775.

45 Jill Rubenstein, "Coke, Lady Mary (1727–1811)," ODNB Online [accessed Aug. 3, 2020].

46 LLMC, vol. I, pp. 166, 190.

47 Rubenstein, op. cit.; LLMC, vol. I, pp. lix–lxxii, cite from p. lxvi.

48 NRAS-DH/LMC: NRAS859/vol. 485, Box 4, Monday, Oct. 23, 1775; Wednesday, Nov. 15, 1775; Sunday, Dec. 17, 1775.

49 HWC, vol. 24, pp. 157–58.

50 *Diary and Letters of Thomas Hutchinson*, vol. I, p. 475.

51 Staffordshire Record Office, Dartmouth MSS: Hyde to Dartmouth, July 4, 1775, [D(W)1778-II-1351; BC: *London Chronicle*, July 27–29, 1775; Flavell, "American Patriots in London and the Quest for Talks, 1774-1775," pp. 354–56.

52 Julie M. Flavell, "Americans of Patriot Sympathies in London and the Colonial Strategy for Opposition, 1774-1775" (PhD, University College London, 1988), pp. 251–52; Flavell, "American Patriots in London and the Quest for Talks," pp. 350–57.

53 Citation from Flavell, "Americans of Patriot Sympathies in London and the Colonial Strategy for Opposition, 1774-1775," p. 249.

54 PBF, vol. 22, pp. 112–14.

55 Flavell, "Americans of Patriot Sympathies in London and the Colonial Strategy for Opposition, 1774-1775," pp. 249–50, cite from p. 250.

56 Ibid., p. 250; William R. Anson, ed. *Autobiography and Political Correspondence of Augustus Henry, third Duke of Grafton* (London, 1898), p. 270.

57 Thomas, *Tea Party to Independence*, p. 263; Flavell, "Americans of Patriot Sympathies in London and the Colonial Strategy for Opposition," pp. 251–52.

58 Brumwell, *Paths of Glory*, p. 67.

59 These included William Pitt, as well as the set surrounding John Manners, Marquess of Granby. Valentine, *Lord George Germain*, pp. 46, 77, 84–85. In addition, the Duke of Richmond actively disliked Germain. Olson, *The Radical Duke*, p. 73.

60 Valentine, *Lord George Germain*, pp. 68–72, 97–98; Piers Mackesy, "Germain, George Sackville, first Viscount Sackville (1716–1785)," ODNB Online [accessed Aug. 3, 2020].

61 Cite from Valentine, *Lord George Germain*, p. 89.

62 Thomas, *Tea Party to Independence*, pp. 189, 214; Peter D. G. Thomas, *Lord North* (London, 1976), p. 89.

63 WCL-GSG, vol. 3: 1765–Oct. 1775: Lord Howe to Lord Germain, Porter's Lodge, July 22, 1775.

64 *Report on the Manuscripts of Mrs. Stopford-Sackville*, vol. 2, pp. 3–5, 6.

65 WCL-GSG, vol. 3: 1765–Oct. 1775, Richard Howe to Lord Germain, September 25, 1775.

66 Valentine, *Lord George Germain*, p. 146.

67 Cited in Piers Mackesy, *The War for America, 1775-1783* (Cambridge, MA, 1964; this ed. Lincoln and London, 1993), p. 74.

68 Ibid., p. 74; WCL-KP, 10:23 William Knox, "Account of the first peace commission of 1776."

69 University of Southampton, Special Collections, Broadlands Archives, Papers of Henry Temple, second Viscount Palmerston [BR11/1/1], Copy of a letter to the second Viscount Palmerston, docketed "Mrs Howe, 1761."

70 BL-AP, 75613, CH/LS, Sept. 12, 1775.

71 Gruber, p. 62fn. Gruber writes that, in late June 1775, Lord Hyde had put forward the idea of a naval commander in chief with powers to negotiate, but without mentioning Lord Howe. Sometime before September 29, Hyde was specifically recommending Richard for this dual commission to Lord Dartmouth. Bodleian Library, MS Clarendon dep. c. 347 (Letter-book 1770-1786 of 1st earl of Clarendon), Lord Hyde to Lord North, January 10, 1776; WCL-KP, 10:23 William Knox, "Account of the first peace commission of 1776."

72 BL-AP, 75612, CH/LS, Aug. 10, 1773; 75613, CH/LS, Sept. 29, 1777.

73 Valentine, *Lord George Germain*, pp. 19–20, 72, 87.

74 Citations from Thomas, *Tea Party to Independence*, p. 255.

75 Thomas, *Lord North*, pp. 87–88.

76 Thomas, *Tea Party to Independence*, pp. 269, 281; cite from Flavell, "American Patriots in London and the Quest for Talks, 1774-1775," p. 355.

77 See Flavell, ibid.; pp. 352–59, cite in Thomas, *Lord North*, p. 90.

78 *Report on the Manuscripts of Mrs. Stopford-Sackville*, vol. 2, p. 12.

79 WCL-KP, 10:23 William Knox, "Account of the first peace commission of 1776."

80 BL-AP, 75675, Lord Jersey to Lady Spencer, Blenheim, Monday, Oct. 16, 1775; see also Anson, ed., *Autobiography and Political Correspondence of Augustus Henry, third duke of Grafton*, p. 276.

81 NRAS-DH/LMC: NRAS859/Vol. 485, Box 4, Wednesday, Nov. 15, 1775.

82 BL-AP, 75694, Rachel Lloyd to Lady Spencer, Dec. 2, 1775.

83 BL-AP, 75613, CH/LS, Dec. 2, 1775.

84 WCL-HCP, 11:9 W[illiam] P[hillips] to [Sir Henry] Clinton, London, Sept. 14 and Oct. 4, 1775; 13:27 [William Phillips] to [Sir Henry] Clinton, Bath, Jan. 1776; 13:37 Francis Hastings 10th earl of Huntingdon to Sir Henry Clinton, Feb. 7, 1776.

85 Davies, vol. 10, p. 156, vol. 11, pp. 213–14; Philbrick, *Bunker Hill*, p. 258.

86 Ibid., p. 266.

87 Willcox, *Portrait of a General*, pp. 58-59; WCL, Thomas Gage Papers 1754-1807, American Series, vol. 133, Aug. 1–15, 1775: William Howe to General Gage, Charleston Camp, Aug. 1, 1775; American Series Vol. 134, Aug. 16–31, 1775: Howe to Gage, Aug. 29, 1775.

88 Philbrick, *Bunker Hill*, p. 257; Atkinson, *The British Are Coming*, pp. 138–39.

89 WCL-HCP, 12:32 Sir Henry Clinton, "Conversations with Sir W. H[owe]. relative to the Southern Expedition." In Drummond's hand.

90 WCL-HCP, 13:27 [William Phillips], 1731?–1781 to [Sir Henry] Clinton, Bath, Jan. 1776.

91 BNA: *Ipswich Journal*, Feb. 10, 1776; Syrett, pp. 42–43; *The Last Journals of Horace Walpole during the Reign of George III*, vol. I, pp. 521–23.

92 J. K. Laughton, "Shuldham, Molyneux, Baron Shuldham (1717/18?–1798)," rev. by Ruddock Mackay, ODNB Online [accessed Aug. 3, 2020].

93 O'Shaughnessy, *The Men Who Lost America*, pp. 322–23; James Sambrook, "Franciscans (*act. c.* 1750–*c.* 1776)," ODNB Online [accessed Aug. 3, 2020].

94 WCL-KP, 10:23 William Knox, "Account of the first peace commission of 1776"; Gruber, pp. 64–70, cite by Sandwich, Gruber, p. 86.

95 WCL-KP, 10:23, "Account of the first peace commission of 1776"; Valentine, *Lord George Germain*, p. 307; Gruber, p. 68.

96 WCL-KP, 10:23, Knox, "Account of the first peace commission of 1776."

97 Bargar, *Lord Dartmouth and the American Revolution*, p. 185.

98 WCL-KP, 10:23, Knox, "Account of the first peace commission of 1776."

99 Gruber, pp. 72–77.

100 A. M. W. Stirling, *The Hothams: Being the Chronicles of the Hothams of Scorborough and South Dalton* (2 vols., London, 1918), vol. 2, p. 131.

101 WCL-KP, Box 9, "Miscellaneous Manuscripts, 1757-1809," vol. 9:19: George III to Richard Lord Viscount Howe and Sir William Howe, "Orders and Instructions May 6, 1776."

102 Weldon A. Brown, *Empire or Independence: A Study in the Failure of Reconciliation, 1774-1783* (Baton Rouge, LA, 1941), pp. 82–83, 86. Brown notes that if the colonies did not accept the British view of parliamentary supremacy after they were pardoned, they could not be restored to peace until the commissioners had received further instructions.

103 WCL-KP, 10:23, "Account of the first peace commission of 1776."

104 Cite from Flavell, "Lord North's Conciliatory Proposal and the Patriots in London," p. 318; Anne Izard Deas, ed., *Correspondence of Mr. Ralph Izard* (first ed., New York, 1844; this ed. New York, 1976), pp. 139, 140–41.

105 *Report on the Manuscripts of Mrs. Stopford-Sackville*, vol. 2, p. 29.

106 *Proceedings and Debates of the British Parliament Respecting North America*, vol. VI, p. 593.

107 NRAS-DH/LMC: NRAS859/Volume 485, Box 4, Wed., Nov. 15, 1775.

108 Matthew Kilburn, "Fitzpatrick, Anne, countess of Upper Ossory [*other married*

name Anne FitzRoy, Duchess of Grafton] (1737/8–1804)," ODNB Online [accessed Aug. 3, 2020].

109　*The Last Journals of Horace Walpole during the Reign of George III*, vol. I, p. 435.

110　E. H. Chalus, "Gower, Susanna Leveson-, marchioness of Stafford (1742/3–1805)," ODNB Online [accessed Aug. 3, 2020]. The correspondence between Lady Gower and Caroline Howe can be found in PRO 30/29 Leveson-Gower. 1st Earl Granville and predecessors and successors: Papers, 30/29/4/8 Letters of Caroline Howe to Lady Gower.

111　*Proceedings and Debates of the British Parliament Respecting North America*, vol. VI, p. 447.

112　BL-AP, 75613, CH/LS, Sept. 23, 1776.

113　BL-AP, 75613, CH/LS, Nov. 20, 1776. John Collett's correspondence from Genoa, including mention of his wartime correspondence with Caroline Howe, is in the Huntington Library, San Marino, California (Correspondence of John Collett, 1776-1779).

114　BL-AP, 75613, CH/LS, Aug. 11, 1775.

115　Chalus, *Elite Women in English Political Life*, pp. 126–27.

116　Ruddock Mackay, "Hervey, Augustus John, third earl of Bristol (1724–1779)," ODNB Online [accessed Aug. 3, 2020].

117　BNA: *Caledonian Mercury*, April 27, 1776.

118　WCL-HCP, 13:37 Francis Hastings 10th earl of Huntingdon to Sir Henry Clinton Feb. 7, 1776.

119　T. A. B. Corley, "Chudleigh, Elizabeth [*married names* Elizabeth Hervey, Countess of Bristol; Elizabeth Pierrepont, Duchess of Kingston upon Hull] (*c.* 1720–1788)," ODNB Online [accessed Aug. 3, 2020].

120　Gruber, pp. 62–63, 70–71, 360–63. Syrett follows Gruber's thesis, stating that Richard "gained a vision of himself as the one man who was capable of negotiating with the Americans to reach a political settlement and end the civil war within the British empire." *Admiral Lord Howe*, pp. 40, 43.

121　Bodleian Library, MS Clarendon dep. c. 347, Lord Hyde to Lord North, January 10, 1776.

122　Guttridge, ed., *The Correspondence of Edmund Burke*, vol. III, pp. 298–99.

123　Brown, *Empire or Independence*, p. 88.

Nine: Home Front

1　BNA: *Ipswich Journal*, March 2, 1776.

2　Mackesy, *The War for America*, pp. 73, 102.

3　Julie M. Flavell, "Government Interception of Letters from America and the Quest for Colonial Opinion in 1775," in *William and Mary Quarterly*, 3rd series, vol. 58 (2001), p. 421; Bickham, *Making Headlines*, pp. 52–53.

4　BL-AP, 75613, CH/LS, June 9, 1776.

5　HWC, vol. 32, p. 308fn; NRAS-DH/LMC: NRAS859/Vol. 486, Box 1, Sunday, June 30, 1776, and Wednesday, July 10–July 15, 1776.

6 *Correspondence of Emily Duchess of Leinster*, vol. III, p. 226.

7 BL-AP, 75613, CH/LS, Sept. 6, 1776; Sept. 23, 1776; Nov. 20, 1776; 75628, CH/LS, Feb. 14, 1786.

8 BL-AP, 75613, CH/LS, Dec. 19, 1776.

9 John Van Der Kiste, *George III's Children* (Stroud, Gloucestershire, 1992; this ed. 2004), p. 14; Barrow, p. vii.

10 Hannah Greig, *The Beau Monde: Fashionable Society in Georgian London* (Oxford, 2013), pp. 108–9, 112, 113, 198, cite on p. 113; E. S Turner, *The Court of St James's* (London, 1959), p. 342.

11 http://www.historyofparliamentonline.org/volume/17541790/member/brett -charles-1715-99 [accessed Aug. 6, 2020].

12 http://www.historyofparliamentonline.org/volume/1754-1790/member/doyly -christopher-1717-95 [accessed Aug. 6, 2020]; Arthur Collins, *A Supplement to the Four Volumes of the Peerage of England: Containing a Succession of the Peers from 1740* (1750), p. 5.

13 BL-AP, 75611, CH/LS, Friday AM [1767?].

14 SALS-DD/SH 34, Jane Strachey to Henry Strachey, May 14, 1776 (Cheney Transcript); WCL-SP, Box 1:6, Jane Strachey to Henry Strachey, Greenwich, July 5, 1777.

15 SALS-DD/SH 34, Jane Strachey to Henry Strachey, Monday, Nov. 27, 1776.

16 John Rule, *Albion's People: English Society, 1714-1815* (London and New York, 1992), p. 61; http://www.historyofparliamentonline.org/volume/1754-1790/member/strachey -henry-1737-1810 [accessed Aug. 6, 2020].

17 H. V. Bowen, "Clive, Robert, first Baron Clive of Plassey (1725–1774)," ODNB Online [accessed Aug. 6, 2020].

18 BL-AP, 75612, CH/LS, Nov. 26, 1774.

19 The Florida plantation, Beauclerc Bluff, is documented in the Henry Strachey papers in the William L. Clements Library. It is not mentioned in the History of Parliament biography or the ODNB. It ultimately failed.

20 Most of the Jane Strachey letters are in Somerset Archives and Local Studies (SALS), South West Heritage Trust, Strachey Collection, DD/SH 34. I am indebted to Cheney Schopieray at the William L. Clements Library for drawing my attention to this collection, and for generously sharing his transcripts of the first twenty-three letters in the collection.

21 SALS-DD/SH 34, Jane Strachey to Henry Strachey, May 14, 1776 (Cheney Transcript).

22 SALS-DD/SH 34, Jane Strachey to Henry Strachey, March 17, 1777; April 20–24, 1777; Jan. 21, 1777; Dec. 21, 1776.

23 WCL-SP, Box 2:16, Henry Strachey to Jane Strachey, Dec. 28, 1776.

24 SALS-DD/SH 34, Jane Strachey to Henry Strachey, April 26, 1777; Jan. 30, 1777.

25 SALS-DD/SH 34, Jane Strachey to Henry Strachey, May 14, 1776 (Cheney Transcript).

26 SALS-DD/SH 34, Jane Strachey to Henry Strachey, Porter's Lodge, April 9, 1777.

27 SALS-DD/SH 34, Jane Strachey to Henry Strachey, Nov. 8, 1776; May 9, 1777; March 14, 1777.

28 SALS-DD/SH 34, Jane Strachey to Henry Strachey, Monday, Nov. 27, 1776.

29 SALS-DD/SH 34, Jane Strachey to Henry Strachey, Jan. 17, 1777.

30 H. M. Stephens, "Balfour, Nisbet (1743–1823)," rev. by Stephen Conway, ODNB Online [accessed Aug. 6, 2020].

31 PCC, PROB11/1678/109, "Will of Nisbet Balfour, General," December 3, 1823.

32 WCL-SP, Box 1, Folder 3, Henry Strachey to Jane Strachey, Eagle off New York, Sept. 26, 1776; SALS-DD/SH 34, Jane Strachey to Henry Strachey, Oct. 29, 30, 1776.

33 BL-AP, 75613, CH/LS, Nov. 2, 1776; BC: *London Chronicle*, Nov. 2–5, 1776.

34 SALS-DD/SH 34, Jane Strachey to Henry Strachey, Nov. 6, 1776; Nov. 8, 1776; Nov. 9, 13, 1776.

35 SALS-DD/SH 34, Jane Strachey to Henry Strachey, Oct. 29, 30, 1776; Jan. 17, 1777; Feb. 5, 1777; Feb. 10, 1777.

36 SALS-DD/SH 34, Jane Strachey to Henry Strachey, Feb. 25, 1777; July 17, 1777; March 24, 1777; WCL-SP, Box 1:5, Henry Strachey to Jane Strachey, New York, May 20, 1777.

37 Davies, vol. 13, p. 15.

38 SALS-DD/SH 34, Jane Strachey to Henry Strachey, Feb. 25, 1777.

39 SALS-DD/SH 34, Jane Strachey to Henry Strachey, Porter's Lodge, April 9, 1777.

40 SALS-DD/SH 34, Jane Strachey to Henry Strachey, Feb. 8, 1777.

41 Stephen Conway, *The British Isles and the American War of Independence* (Oxford, 2000), pp. 86–87; Mary Beth Norton, *Liberty's Daughters: The Revolutionary Experience of American Women, 1750-1800* (Boston, 1980); Linda K. Kerber, *Women of the Republic: Intellect and Ideology in Revolutionary America* (Chapel Hill, NC, 1980).

42 See, for example, SALS-DD/SH 34, Jane Strachey to Henry Strachey, May 15 and May 18, 1776 (Cheney Transcripts); May 9 [1777]; "Expenses in April 1777."

43 SALS-DD/SH 34, Jane Strachey to Henry Strachey, Porter's Lodge, April 9, 1777.

44 Mackesy, *The War for America*, pp. 123, 150.

45 SALS-DD/SH 34, Jane Strachey to Henry Strachey, June 14, 1776 (Cheney Transcript).

46 WCL-SP, Box 1, Folder 4, Henry Strachey to Jane Strachey [December 1776?], and see Box 1, Folder 5, same to same, New York, May 20, 1777.

47 BNA: *Derby Mercury*, December 29, 1776.

48 BL-AP, 75613, CH/LS, Aug. 14, 1776; Sept. 23, 1776; Sept. 30, 1776; Dec. 19, 1776.

49 BL-AP, 75613, CH/LS, Sept. 23, 1776; Nov. 20, 1776; Oct. 11, 1777.

50 Willcox, *Portrait of a General*, pp. 91, 92fn.

51 WCL-HCP, 18:8 Richard Reeve, d. 1789, to [Sir Henry] Clinton, Aug. 27, 1776.

52 Davies, vol. 10, pp. 329, 334; Gruber, pp. 91–92.

53 Bickham, *Making Headlines*, pp. 86–87; Conway, "From Fellow-Nationals to Foreigners," pp. 86–88.

54 WCL-GSG, vol. 5: July 1776–March 1777, Lord George Germain to Admiral Arbuthnot, Pall Mall, July 21, 1776.

55 NRAS-DH/LMC: NRAS859/Vol. 486, Box 1, Friday, July 19–July 23, 1776; Wednesday, September 11–September 16, 1776.

56 *Diary and Letters of Thomas Hutchinson*, vol. II, p. 97.

57 *Correspondence of Emily Duchess of Leinster,* vol. III, pp. 224, 226.

58 *The Life and Letters of Lady Sarah Lennox,* vol. 1, p. 252.

59 NRAS-DH/LMC: NRAS859/Vol. 486, Box 1, Tuesday, September 17–September 23, 1776.

60 BL-AP, 75613, CH/LS, Sept. 23, 1776; NRAS-DH/LMC: NRAS859/Vol. 486, Box 1, Saturday Oct. 5–Oct. 10, 1776.

61 BL-AP, 75613, CH/LS, Sept. 6, 1776; Sept. 23, 1776; Sept. 30, 1776.

62 BL-AP, 75613, CH/LS, Aug. 14, 1776.

Ten: New York, 1776

1 John J. Gallagher, *The Battle of Brooklyn 1776* (New York, 1995), pp. 33, 102–3; David Smith, *New York 1776: The Continentals' First Battle* (Oxford and New York, 2008), p. 39.

2 Cited in Gallagher, *The Battle of Brooklyn 1776,* p. 105.

3 WCL-GSG, vol. 3, Lord Howe to Lord Germain, Grafton Street, Sept. 25, 1775.

4 Stephen Brumwell, *George Washington: Gentleman Warrior* (London 2012), p. 223; Mackesy, *The War for America,* pp. 80, 82; Urban, *Fusiliers,* p. 67.

5 *Report on the Manuscripts of Mrs. Stopford-Sackville,* vol. 2, p. 31.

6 Howe–Germain, April 25, 1776, cited in Anderson, p. 121. This letter, from the Colonial Office Papers in the Public Record Office at Kew, is only paraphrased in the source normally consulted by historians (Davies, vol. 10, p. 275), and it does not reflect William's thinking and his sense of urgency in getting to New York.

7 Brumwell, *George Washington,* pp. 5, 228, 251. Cites on pp. 5, 228.

8 "A Letter of Intelligence," Boston, June 12, 1775, *The Correspondence of King George the Third,* vol. 3, p. 217.

9 "A Letter of Intelligence," vol. 3, pp. 215.

10 Julie Flavell, "British Perceptions of New England and the Decision for a Coercive Colonial Policy, 1774-1775," in Julie Flavell and Stephen Conway, eds., *Britain and America Go to War: The Impact of War and Warfare in Anglo-America, 1754-1815* (Gainesville, 2004), pp. 100–4.

11 Cites in Flavell, *When London Was Capital of America,* p. 106.

12 Davies, vol. 12, *Transcripts 1776,* p. 44.

13 Mackesy, *The War for America,* pp. 82–83; Gruber, p. 92.

14 Brumwell, *George Washington,* p. 223; Gruber, p. 100.

15 The fullest exposition of this long-standing idea is found in Gruber, pp. 116, 355, 360, 361, 363; Ira D. Gruber, "Howe, William, fifth Viscount Howe (1729–1814)," ODNB Online [accessed Aug. 7, 2020].

16 Gruber, pp. 62, 94–95, 99–100, 126; see also Syrett, pp. 39, 40, 43, 51–53.

17 WCL-HC: Richard Howe, 1st Earl Howe to George Washington, HMS *Eagle,* off Staten Island, (copy), July 13, 1776.

18 Gruber, pp. 94, 95; Henry P. Johnston, *The Campaign of 1776 around New York and Brooklyn* (Brooklyn, 1878), p. 98.

19 Joseph J. Ellis, *His Excellency George Washington* (New York, 2004), pp. 77–78.

20 WCL-SP, Box 2:7, "July-August 1776 Diary of events in America."

21 Gruber, p. 99.

22 Gruber, pp. 97, 99; Brown, *Empire or Independence*, pp. 90–92, 98, 103, 109, 111fn.

23 *Report on the Manuscripts of Mrs. Stopford-Sackville*, vol. 2, p. 37.

24 Brumwell, *Paths of Glory*, pp. 144–46; Anderson, *Crucible of War*, p. 499.

25 Davies, vol. 10, p. 352.

26 Smith, *New York 1776*, p. 33; Gruber, pp. 100-101.

27 Anderson, *The Command of the Howe Brothers*, and Brown, *Empire or Independence*, do not reference Strachey's letter of August 11, 1776. Ira Gruber cites it twice (pp. 99–100, 103), but he only makes limited use of what he believes are the opinions of Strachey himself.

28 WCL-SP, Box 2:7, "July-August 1776 Diary of events in America."

29 WCL-SP, Box 1:3, Henry Strachey to Christopher D'Oyly, *Eagle* off Staten Island, August 11, 1776.

30 WCL, Thomas Gage Papers, American Series, vol. 132, William Howe to General Gage, Charleston Camp, July 20, 1775.

31 WCL-HCP, 13:36 [Sir Henry Clinton] "Report of Conversations with L[ord] D[rummond] and Tryon," New York, Feb. 7 [1776]; 14:15, [Sir Henry Clinton] to [William Phillips], [Feb. 1776]; 14:25 [Sir Henry Clinton] to [Sir William Howe] [1776] after March 12.

32 BL-AP, 75613, CH/LS, Sept. 23, 1776; Sept. 30, 1776.

33 BNA: *Kentish Gazette*, October 12, 1776.

34 Bickham, *Making Headlines*, p. 90.

35 NRAS-DH/LMC: NRAS859/Vol. 485, Box 4, Oct. 3, 1776.

36 *Correspondence of Emily Duchess of Leinster*, vol. III, cite on p. 229, and see pp. 217, 264.

37 Bickham, *Making Headlines*, p. 91.

38 Andrew Oliver, ed., *The Journal of Samuel Curwen, Loyalist* (2 vols., Cambridge, MA, 1972), vol. 1, p. 200.

39 Stephen Conway, *The American War of Independence 1775-1783* (London, New York, Melbourne, and Auckland, 1995), pp. 83–84; Smith, *New York 1776*, pp. 26, 39–40, 42, 46.

40 O'Shaughnessy, *The Men Who Lost America*, p. 95; Urban, *Fusiliers*, p. 86.

41 General William Howe to Lord George Germain, Long Island, September 3, 1776, Davies, vol. 12, p. 217.

42 Mackesy, *The War for America*, p. 88.

43 An excellent review of the opinions of various historians is provided in Smith, pp. 67–81.

44 For example, Jones, "Sir William Howe: Conventional Strategist," pp. 52–54, argues that Howe was simply conventional and husbanded his army. Hugh Bicheno, *Rebels and Redcoats: The American Revolutionary War* (London, 2003), p. 46, Anderson, pp. 134–42, 147–48, and Urban, *Fusiliers*, p. 86, all think Howe was cautious but reasonable to act as he did. O'Shaughnessy, *The Men Who Lost America*, argues (p. 100) that Howe's caution was motivated by concern about British casualty rates.

45 WCL-SP, Box 2:51, "1779. Sir William Howe's Defence (before a Select Committee of the House of Commons) of his Conduct as Commander-in-Chief of the British Forces in the War of Independence." The draft of Howe's speech in the Strachey Papers has been in the possession of the William L. Clements Library since 2010. Before then, it was in private hands and not easily accessible.

46 Jones, "Sir William Howe: Conventional Strategist," p. 52; Bickham, *Making Headlines*, p. 91.

47 Smith, pp. 77, 82–83. Mark Urban has also noted William Howe's concern over discipline after Bunker Hill: *Fusiliers*, pp. 63–64, 67–69.

48 Smith, *New York 1776*, p. 55.

49 Smith, Ibid., pp. 55–58; Bicheno, *Rebels and Redcoats*, p. 46.

50 Cited in David Syrett, *The Royal Navy in American Waters, 1775-1783* (Aldershot, Hants., 1989), p. 51.

51 Smith, pp. 6–11, provides an excellent overview of the spectrum of scholarly opinions on Howe's performance, including historians who have argued that Howe's command decisions were influenced by a desire to broker a peace, or by other unacknowledged motives, or that he was simply unimaginative or a conventional tactician. See also C. Stedman, *The History of the Origin, Progress and Termination of the American War* (2 vols., London, 1794), vol. I, pp. 196–97, 198–99; Sydney George Fisher, *The True History of the American Revolution* (Philadelphia and London, 1902), pp. 312–13, 315–17, 323, 329; Fortescue, *The War of Independence*, p. 39.

52 Smith, pp. 84, 93, 95.

53 Cite from Gruber, p. 121.

54 For example, see Mackesy, *The War for America*, pp. 89–90, Bicheno, *Rebels and Redcoats*, p. 48, O'Shaughnessy, *The Men Who Lost America*, p. 95.

55 Syrett, *The Royal Navy in American Waters*, pp. 50, 52; Smith, *New York 1776*, p. 61; University of Nottingham, Manuscripts and Special Collections, Ne C 2738, Richard Rigby to H. F. C. Pelham-Clinton, 2nd Duke of Newcastle, October 10, 1776.

56 Anderson, p. 180; Davies, vol. 12, p. 227.

57 O'Shaughnessy, *The Men Who Lost America*, pp. 95, 100.

58 Thomas B. Allen, *Tories: Fighting for the King in America's First Civil War* (New York, 2010), pp. 170–71.

59 O'Shaughnessy, *The Men Who Lost America*, p. 101.

60 Smith, pp. 85–96; Smith, *New York 1776*, pp. 67–74; Gruber, p. 132.

61 Smith, pp. 96, 98–101; cite from Smith, *New York 1776*, p. 85.

62 Anderson, cite on page 337, and see also p. 343; see also Maldwyn Jones, "Sir William Howe: Conventional Strategist," p. 65.

63 Gruber, pp. 158–59; W. A. Speck, "William Augustus, Prince, duke of Cumberland (1721–1765)," ODNB Online [accessed Aug. 11, 2020].

64 Brown, *Empire or Independence*, p. 126.

65 Edward H. Tatum Jr., ed., *The American Journal of Ambrose Serle, Secretary to Lord Howe, 1776-1778* (San Marino, CA, 1940), pp. 80–81; Anderson, pp. 157–58; Charles P. Whittemore, "John Sullivan: Luckless Irishman," in Billias, ed., *George Washington's Generals and Opponents*, pp. 145–46.

66 Brown, *Empire or Independence*, pp. 116–17.

67 Anderson, p. 158; cite from Davies, vol. 12, p. 226.

68 It is now a museum: The Conference House, 7455 Hylan Boulevard, Staten Island, NY: http://conferencehouse.org/.

69 Walter Isaacson, *Benjamin Franklin: An American Life* (New York, 2003), p. 318; Thomas J. McGuire, *Stop the Revolution: America in the Summer of Independence and the Conference for Peace* (Mechanicsburg, PA, 2011), pp. 61, 65, 160.

70 Isaacson, *Benjamin Franklin*, p. 319; Charles Francis Adams, ed., *The Works of John Adams* (10 vols., Boston, 1856), vol. 3, pp. 77, 78.

71 Henry Strachey's account of the Staten Island conference is reproduced in full in Paul Leicester Ford, ed., "Lord Howe's Commission to Pacify the Colonies," *The Atlantic Monthly*, vol. 77 (1896), pp. 758–62. Cite on p. 759.

72 John Adams wrote to his wife that the delegates had "about three Hours Conversation" with Lord Howe [Letter from John Adams to Abigail Adams, September 14, 1776 (electronic ed.), *Adams Family Papers: An Electronic Archive*. (Massachusetts Historical Society, http://www.masshist.org/digitaladams/, March 21, 2018)]. A Hessian officer who was present, however, recorded that Lord Howe was shut up privately with the delegates for one hour after the meal [McGuire, *Stop the Revolution*, pp. 160–61].

73 John Ferling, *Independence: The Struggle to Set America Free* (New York, Berlin, London, Sydney, 2011), pp. 155, 166; cite from Adams, ed. *The Works of John Adams*, vol. 3, p. 80,

74 Letter from John Adams to Abigail Adams, September 14, 1776 (electronic ed.), *Adams Family Papers: An Electronic Archive* (Massachusetts Historical Society, http://www.masshist.org/digitaladams/, August 11, 2020).

75 Flavell, *When London Was Capital of America*, p. 113; Ferling, *Independence*, pp. 290, 296–97, 325.

76 Tatum, ed., *The American Journal of Ambrose Serle*, p. 167.

77 Isaacson, *Benjamin Franklin*, pp. 294–98, cite on p. 296.

78 WCL-SP, Box 1:3, Henry Strachey to Christopher D'Oyly, *Eagle* off Staten Island, August 11, 1776

79 Ford, ed., "Lord Howe's Commission to Pacify the Colonies," pp. 760, 762,

80 Cecil B. Currey, *Code Number 72: Ben Franklin, Patriot or Spy?* (Englewood Cliffs, NJ, 1972), pp. 73, 75–76.

81 Adams, ed. *The Works of John Adams*, vol. 3, p. 79.

82 Isaacson, *Benjamin Franklin*, p. 322.

83 Tatum, ed., *The American Journal of Ambrose Serle*, p. 132.

84 Ford, ed., "Lord Howe's Commission to Pacify the Colonies," p. 761; Isaacson, *Benjamin Franklin*, p. 319.

85 Davies, vol. 12, pp. 226–27.

86 WCL-GSG, vol. 5: July 1776–March 1777 ["Remarks upon the Petition & Declaration of the Congress," dated in pencil "1776"].

87 University of Nottingham, Manuscripts and Special Collections, Ne C 2719/1-2, Richard Rigby to HFC Pelham-Clinton, 2nd Duke of Newcastle, Nov. 4, 1776.

88 BNA: *Oxford Journal*, Oct. 19 and 26, 1776.

89 Troy O. Bickham, "Sympathizing with Sedition? George Washington, the British Press, and British Attitudes During the American War of Independence," in *William and Mary Quarterly*, 3rd series, vol. 59 (2002), p. 115.

90 BNA: *Northampton Mercury*, Nov. 4, 1776; BL-AP, 75613, CH/LS, Nov. 1, 1776.

91 NRAS-DH/LMC: NRAS859/Vol. 485, Box 4, Oct. 10, 1776; Oct. 17–21, 1776.

92 BL-AP, 75613, CH/LS, Oct. 12 and 16, 1776.

93 BNA: *Oxford Journal*, Oct. 19, 1776; Bickham, *Making Headlines*, pp. 89–91, cite on p. 90.

94 BNA: *Oxford Journal*, Oct. 26, 1776; Bickham, *Making Headlines*, p. 93.

95 Heinde, Kielmansegg Family Papers, Lady Howe to [ ] Kielmansegg, London, Nov. 1, 1776. (Transcript provided by Professor Ira Gruber.)

96 Mackesy, *The War for America*, p. 85; University of Nottingham, Manuscripts and Special Collections, Ne c 2758, General E. Harvey to HFC Pelham-Clinton, 2nd Duke of Newcastle, Nov. 4, 1776.

97 Brown, *Empire or Independence*, pp. 130–32; Flavell, "American Patriots in London and the Quest for Talks, 1774-1775," pp. 356–57; BL-AP, 75613, CH/LS, Nov. 2, 1776; Nov. 5, 1776.

98 Gruber, pp. 143, 146–47, 149, 152.

99 WCL-SP, Box 2:16, December 28, 1776, Autograph Letter from Strachey [to his wife] from New York.

100 Bickham, *Making Headlines*, p. 95; Mackesy, *War for America*, p. 93.

101 BL-AP, 75613, CH/LS, Dec. 19, 1776; Dec. 30, 1776.

Eleven: The Tide Turns in America

1 E. J. Climenson, ed., *Passages from the Diaries of Mrs. Philip Lybbe Powys of Hardwick House* (London, 1899), pp. 178–79, 183.

2 Jane Moody and Daniel O'Quinn, eds., *The Cambridge Companion to British Theatre, 1730-1830* (Cambridge, 2007), p. 199.

3 *Letters of David Garrick and Georgiana Countess Spencer*, pp. 55–57, 81.

4 *Passages from the Diary of Mrs. Philip Lybbe Powys*, pp. 179, 181–83, 186–87; BL-AP, 75613, CH/LS, Dec. 30, 1776.

5 BL-AP, 75613, CH/LS, Dec. 6, 1776.

6 *Letters of David Garrick and Georgiana Countess Spencer*, p. 81.

7 BC: *London Evening Post*, January 23–25, 1777.

8 Lunt, *John Burgoyne of Saratoga*, p. 136.

9 For example, a letter of Admiral Lord Howe to a friend was read aloud in Garraway's Coffee Shop, and subsequently reported in BC: *St. James's Chronicle, or British Evening Post*, Jan. 6–8, 1778. Major Balfour's conversation was reported in the *Boston Gazette* on March 3, 1777 [Readex, Early American Newspapers: Series 1, 1690–1876].

10 Conway, *The American War of Independence 1775-1783*, p. 84; Urban, *Fusiliers*, p. 94; Margaret Stead, "Contemporary Responses in Print to the American Campaigns of

the Howe Brothers," in Julie Flavell and Stephen Conway, eds., *Britain and America Go to War: The Impact of War and Warfare in Anglo-America, 1754-1815* (Gainesville, FL, 2004), pp. 120–22.

11 BL, Fox Papers, 47579, fols. 43–44, Richard Fitzpatrick to his brother Lord Upper Ossory, Dec. 1776.

12 Davies, vol. 10, p. 414; Bedfordshire Archives, Lucas Manuscripts, L29/214, "Conversation with Nisbet Balfour, Jan. 13, 1777"; Fortescue, *The War of Independence*, pp. 44–46.

13 WCL-KP, 2:73 Lord George Germain to William Knox, Dec. 31, 1776.

14 Davies, vol. 14, p. 30.

15 WCL-GSG, vol. 5: July 1776–March 1777, Lord Howe to Lord Germain, New York, March 23, 1777; Davies, vol. 14, p. 30.

16 Gruber, p. 193.

17 Anderson, pp. 314–16; Brumwell, *George Washington, Gentleman Warrior*, p. 299; Allen, *Tories*, p. 190.

18 Jacqueline Jones, "Race, Sex, and Self-Evident Truths: The Status of Slave Women During the Era of the American Revolution," in Ronald Hoffman and Peter J. Albert, eds., *Women in the Age of the American Revolution* (Charlottesville, VA, 1989), pp. 326–30; Simon Schama, "Dirty Little Secret," *Smithsonian Magazine* (May 2006).

19 Philip D. Morgan and Andrew Jackson O'Shaughnessy, "Arming Slaves in the American Revolution," in Christopher Leslie Brown and Philip D. Morgan, eds., *Arming Slaves: From Classical Times to the Modern Age* (New Haven and London, 2006), pp. 182, 187, 190.

20 See, for example, Vincent Caretta, "Richmond, Bill (1763-1829)," ODNB Online [accessed March 14, 2020]; Stephen Brumwell, "Revisiting B. E. Griffiths: Former Slave, Queen's Ranger, and 'Son of Africa,'" *Journal of the American Revolution*, vol. 5 (April 23, 2019).

21 Woody Holton, *Forced Founders: Indians, Debtors, Slaves and the Making of the American Revolution in Virginia* (Chapel Hill and London, 1999), pp. 156–58, 160; Robert M. Calhoon, "Loyalism and Neutrality," in Jack P. Greene and J. R. Pole, eds., *The Blackwell Encyclopedia of the American Revolution* (Cambridge, MA, and Oxford, 1994), p. 247; Allen, *Tories*, p. 171; Morgan and O'Shaughnessy, "Arming Slaves," p. 190.

22 Mary Beth Norton, *The British-Americans: The Loyalist Exiles in England 1774-1789* (Boston and Toronto, 1972), pp. 78, 219.

23 Gruber, p. 173; Anderson, p. 232.

24 *Letters of David Garrick and Georgiana Countess Spencer*, p. 81; Bedfordshire Archives, L29/214, "Conversation with Nisbet Balfour, Jan. 13, 1777."

25 *Diary and Letters of Thomas Hutchinson*, vol. II, p. 184.

26 Valentine, *Lord George Germain*, p. 15.

27 BL, Fox Papers, 47579, fols. 43–44, Richard Fitzpatrick to his brother, Lord Upper Ossory, Dec. 1776.

28 NRAS-DH/LMC: NRAS859/Vol. 486, Box 1, Dec. 8, 1776.

29 Anderson, pp. 109–10, 112–13, 214–15; see also Flavell, "British Perceptions of New England and the Decision for a Coercive Colonial Policy, 1774-1775."

30 Anderson, pp. 118–19, 215; cite on p. 215.

31 Davies, vol. 12, p. 268.

32 Fortescue, *The War of Independence*, p. 52; O'Shaughnessy, *The Men Who Lost America*, p. 102.

33 Davies, vol. 14, p. 33; *Report on the Manuscripts of Mrs. Stopford-Sackville*, vol. 2, p. 54.

34 Davies, vol. 14, p. 33; Stephen Conway, *A Short History of the American Revolutionary War* (London and New York, 2013), p. 75.

35 Cite from Willcox, *Portrait of a General*, p. 148.

36 Fortescue, *The War of Independence*, p. 20; cite from Jeremy Black, *War for America: The Fight for Independence 1775-1783* (Stroud, 1991; paperback ed. 2001), p. 129.

37 Anderson, p. 118; Fortescue, *The War of Independence*, pp. 17–18, 26–27; Davies, vol. 12, p. 46. See also Flavell, "British Perceptions of New England and the Decision for a Coercive Colonial Policy, 1774-1775," pp. 98–99.

38 WCL-SP, Box 2:51, "1779. Sir William Howe's Defence."

39 O'Shaughnessy, *The Men Who Lost America*, pp. 142–43, 144.

40 Lunt, *John Burgoyne of Saratoga*, p. 125.

41 Stokes, *The Devonshire House Circle*, pp. 87fn, 107.

42 O'Shaughnessy, *The Men Who Lost America*, p. 135; Lunt, *John Burgoyne of Saratoga*, pp. 48–51, 83, 106, 109.

43 Davies, vol. 14, pp. 4, 44–46.

44 Lunt, *John Burgoyne of Saratoga*, pp. 149–50.

45 WCL-SP, Box 1:7, Jane Strachey to Henry Strachey, Greenwich, Aug. 5 and 13, 1777; HWC, vol. 32, pp. 369–70; vol. 28, p. 337.

46 Willcox, *Portrait of a General*, pp. 133–35, 137.

47 Willcox, ibid, pp. 138, 141.

48 *Report on the Manuscripts of Mrs. Stopford-Sackville*, vol. 2, p. 55, and see Davies, vol. 10, p. 429, indicating letter would have been received by Feb. 23/24.

49 Bedfordshire Archives, L29/214, "Conversation with Nisbet Balfour, Jan. 13, 1777."

50 WCL-HCP 28:22 Sir H[enry] Clinton to [William] Phillips, New York, Dec. 11 [1777].

51 *The Last Journals of Horace Walpole During the Reign of George III*, vol. 2, p. 19.

52 Lunt, *John Burgoyne of Saratoga*, p. 129.

53 *Correspondence of Emily Duchess of Leinster*, vol. III, p. 231.

54 Willcox, *Portrait of a General*, pp. 25, 29, 32.

55 WCL-HCP, Series VIII, vol. 290: Harriot Clinton and Elizabeth Carter diaries, 1771–1795.

56 The best account of the correspondence between Sir William Howe and Lord George Germain during the months Burgoyne was in London is in Davies, vol. 14, pp. 2–7, 10. One of the important letters William wrote during this period, dated December 20, 1776, is not in Davies but is found in *Report on the Manuscripts of Mrs. Stopford-Sackville*, vol. 2, pp. 52–53. See also Anderson, p. 227, on the point that William's plans reached London in time for Burgoyne to be made aware of them.

57　Conway, *A Short History of the American Revolutionary War*, p. 155; Mackesy, *The War for America*, p. 65.

58　Middleton, *The Bells of Victory*, pp. 53–57, 79–80, 99–100.

59　Anderson, pp. 264–67; Smith, p. 129; Davies, vol. 14, p. 10.

60　Davies, vol. 12, p. 268; WCL-SP, Box 2:51, "1779. Sir William Howe's Defence."

61　"The Narrative of Lieut. Gen. Sir William Howe, &c.," in Partridge, *Sir Billy Howe*, p. 268; Davies, vol. 14, pp. 15–16.

62　Davies, vol. 14, pp. 6, 31; Smith, pp. 116–17, 119; O'Shaughnessy, *The Men Who Lost America*, p. 106.

63　*The American Journal of Ambrose Serle*, pp. 176–79, 186; *The Journal of Nicholas Creswell, 1774-1777* (London and New York, 1924), p. 222.

64　Gruber, pp. 190–91; *Journal of Nicholas Creswell*, pp. 216, 217, 219, 222, 223.

65　Allen, *Tories*, p. 171.

66　WCL-SP, Box 2:21, Feb. 17, 1777. An autograph letter by Henry Strachey to an unnamed recipient. Dated from "Hanover Square" [New York?].

67　*A View of the Evidence relative to the Conduct of the American War under Sir William Howe, Lord Viscount Howe and General Burgoyne; as given before a committee of the House of Commons Last Session of Parliament. To which is added A Collection of the Celebrated Fugitive Pieces that are said to have given rise to that Important Enquiry* (London, 1779), pp. 75, 95, 101, 110.

68　Conway, *A Short History of the American Revolutionary War*, p. 75; *A View of the Evidence. . . . To which is added A Collection of the Celebrated Fugitive Pieces*, p. 77; NRAS, Leven and Melville Muniments, GD26/9/513/1-24, Letter No. 9, A[lexander?] Leslie to the Earl of Leven, Brunswick, March 18, 1777.

69　Davies, vol. 14, pp. 4, 5, 64, 102.

70　Ian R. Christie, *Wars and Revolutions: Britain 1760-1815* (London, 1982), pp. 115–16; Bicheno, *Rebels and Redcoats*, p. 71.

71　See, for example, WCL-GSG, vol. 4: November 1775–June 1776, "Dr Shuttleworth's Plan for the reduction of Maryland," marked in pencil "late in 1775." See also Jonathan Boucher to Germain, Nov. 27, 1775, which advocates cutting off New England via the Hudson River only, so as to keep supply lines intact, and outlines the advantages of operating in the relatively less militarized colonies to the south.

72　Davies, vol. 14, p. 84; Valentine, *Lord George Germain*, p. 285.

73　Davies, vol. 14, p. 7.

74　Davies, vol. 15, pp. 267–68.

75　BNA: *Bath Chronicle and Weekly Gazette*, July 10, 1777; *Newcastle Courant*, July 12, 1777; *Manchester Mercury*, July 15, 1777; *Caledonian Mercury*, July 12, 1777.

76　"The Narrative of Lieut. Gen. Sir William Howe, &c.," in Partridge, *Sir Billy Howe*, p. 273; Mackesy, *The War for America*, pp. 117–18.

77　O'Shaughnessy, *The Men Who Lost America*, p. 112.

78　On Balfour, see Urban, *Fusiliers*, p. 136. The notion that Balfour carried significant separate instructions from Germain, transmitted by word of mouth, has persisted. See Gruber, pp. 207, 211, 214–15, and Valentine, *Lord George Germain*, pp. 179–80.

79 WCL-KP, 3:11 Lord George Germain to William Knox, June 11, 1777.

80 Davies, vol. 14, pp. 31, 48, 65.

81 Ibid., vol 14, p. 5.

82 *The Last Journals of Horace Walpole During the Reign of George III*, vol. 2, pp. 9, 15–16, 28–29.

83 NRAS-DH/LMC: NRAS859/Vol. 487, Box 1, May 30, 1777.

84 Black, *Pitt the Elder*, p. 256; HWC, vol. 24, p. 282.

85 BC: *Morning Post and Daily Advertiser*, June 11 and June 16, 1777, cite from June 16; HWC, vol. 24, p. 309.

86 Ibid., vol. 32, p. 354; Gruber, pp. 212–13.

87 SALS-DD/SH 34, Jane Strachey to Henry Strachey, June 9, 1777.

88 BL-AP, 75613, CH/LS, June 13, 1777.

89 *The Last Journals of Horace Walpole During the Reign of George III*, vol. 2, p. 39; Fortescue, *The War of Independence*, p. 63.

90 Bedfordshire Archives, Lucas Manuscripts, L30/12/3/2, Major Nisbet Balfour to Lord Polwarth, July 13, 1777.

91 Bickham, "Sympathizing with Sedition?" pp. 105–7.

92 Margaret Stead, "Contemporary Responses in Print to the American Campaigns of the Howe Brothers," in Flavell and Conway, eds., *Britain and America Go to War*, pp. 118–19.

93 BNA: *Stamford Mercury*, July 31, 1777; BC: *London Evening Post*, Aug. 7–9, 1777, Aug. 9–12, 1777.

94 BC: *London Evening Post*, July 8–10, 1777, Aug. 9–12, 1777.

95 John Sainsbury, *John Wilkes: The Lives of a Libertine* (Farnham, 2006), pp. 51–52; Wilson, *The Sense of the People*, pp. 188–89; Sarah Kinkel, "Comment: 'Byng's execution played a key role in turning the war around,'" *BBC History Magazine*, March 2018, p. 9; Daniel A. Baugh, "Byng, John (*bap.* 1704, *d.* 1757)," ODNB Online [accessed March 24, 2020].

96 M. John Cardwell, *Arts and Arms: Literature, Politics and Patriotism during the Seven Years War* (Manchester, 2004), pp. 210–11, 213; Marie Peters, *Pitt and Popularity: The Patriot Minister and London Opinion during the Seven Years' War* (Oxford, 1980), pp. 94–98; R. D. Spector, *English Literary Periodicals and the Climate of Opinion during the Seven Years' War* (The Hague, Paris, 1966), p. 50; Middleton, *The Bells of Victory*, pp. 41–42.

97 Bickham, "Sympathizing with Sedition?" pp. 103–4, 113, 121, cite from p. 113; Ellis, *His Excellency George Washington*, p. 74.

98 NRAS-DH/LMC: NRAS859/Vol. 492, Box 3, Dec. 21–23, 1782.

99 Bickham, "Sympathizing with Sedition?" pp. 102, 109, 117, cite from p. 102; Paul K. Longmore, *The Invention of George Washington* (Charlottesville and London, 1999), pp. 176, 177.

100 Stead, "Contemporary Responses in Print to the American Campaigns of the Howe Brothers," p. 129.

101 BC: *Morning Post and Daily Advertiser*, July 30, 1777.

102 Letter from John Adams to Abigail Adams, March 7, 1777, and same to same, April

13, 1777 [electronic ed.]. *Adams Family Papers*, http://www.masshist.org/digital adams/ [accessed March 21, 2018].

103   McNairn, *Behold the Hero*, pp. 215–16, 218–22.

104   Brumwell, *George Washington: Gentleman Warrior*, p. 226.

105   Thomas Paine, "The American Crisis," No. 2, Jan. 13, 1777.

106   Paine, "The American Crisis," No. 5, March 21, 1778.

107   NRAS-DH/LMC: NRAS859/Vol. 487, Box 1, July 17–23, 1777.

108   NRAS-DH/LMC: NRAS859/Vol. 487, Box 1, July 30–Aug. 4, 1777.

109   WCL-KP, 3:35 Henry Ellis to William Knox, Spa, Sept. 4, 1777.

110   NRAS-DH/LMC: NRAS859/Vol. 487, Box 1, Aug. 24, 1777.

111   PRO, Leveson-Gower Papers, 30/29/4/8 Caroline Howe to Lady Gower, Battlesden, Aug. 13 [1777] [Letter 2, fols. 1144–1145].

112   BL-AP, 75613, CH/LS, Aug. 6, 1777; Aug. 19, 1777.

113   NRAS-DH/LMC: NRAS859/Vol. 487, Box 1, Aug. 16–18, 18–22, 1777.

114   BL-AP, 75613, LS/CH, Aug. 29, 1777.

115   Syrett, pp. 62–65; Solomon Lutnick, *The American Revolution and the British Press, 1775-1783* (Columbia, MO, 1967), p. 150.

116   BL-AP, 75675, Lord Jersey to Lady Spencer, Tunbridge Wells, July 31, 1777; Aug. 27, 1777.

117   NRAS-DH/LMC: NRAS859/Vol. 487, Box 1, Dec. 17–21, 1777.

118   *Diary and Letters of Thomas Hutchinson*, vol. II, p. 336.

119   BL-AP, 75613, CH/LS, Sept. 29, 1777.

120   BC: *London Evening Post*, July 29–31, 1777; Jan. 8–10, 1778.

121   Wilson, *The Sense of the People*, p. 241. See Lutnick, *The American Revolution and the British Press*, pp. 15–21, and pp. 58–73 on the press and the establishment of war guilt during the American War of Independence.

122   Karl Wolfgang Schweizer, "Mauduit, Israel (1708–1787)," ODNB Online [accessed Aug. 17, 2020]; Valentine, *Lord George Germain*, p. 345; Anderson, p. 322; Worthington C. Ford, "Parliament and the Howes," *Proceedings* of the Massachusetts Historical Society, 3rd. Ser., 44 (1910), pp. 129–30, 135.

123   Stead, "Contemporary Responses in Print to the American Campaigns of the Howe Brothers," pp. 124, 137.

124   Urban, *Fusiliers*, p. 112.

125   Anderson, pp. 259–60, 267; O'Shaughnessy, *The Men Who Lost America*, p. 113.

126   BL-AP, 75613, CH/LS, Aug. 19, 1777; Urban, *Fusiliers*, p. 112.

127   O'Shaughnessy, *The Men Who Lost America*, pp. 107, 113; *Cobbett's Parliamentary History of England*, vol. 20, p. 745; W. H. Moomaw, "The Denouement of General Howe's Campaign of 1777," *English Historical Review*, vol. 79 (1964), p. 503; Anderson, p. 258.

128   Urban, *Fusiliers*, p. 115.

129   Brumwell, *George Washington*, pp. 299–300; Urban, *Fusiliers*, p. 117, cite from Urban.

130   Brumwell, *George Washington*, pp. 300–302.

131   Allen, *Tories*, pp. 240–41.

132 *The Correspondence of King George the Third,* vol. 4, p. 10.

133 O'Shaughnessy, *The Men Who Lost America,* p. 110; WCL-SP, Box 2:47, Jan. 28, 1778. Postscript to a letter to his wife from Strachey.

134 John W. Jackson, *With the British Army in Philadelphia 1777-1778* (San Rafael and London, 1979), pp. 209, 211, 213, 232–33, cites from pp. 232–33.

135 Conway, *A Short History of the American Revolutionary War,* p. 78; O'Shaughnessy, *The Men Who Lost America,* p. 110, cite from O'Shaughnessy.

136 O'Shaughnessy, pp. 150–52; Conway, *A Short History of the American Revolutionary War,* pp. 80–81.

137 Christie, *Wars and Revolutions,* p. 117; Conway, *A Short History of the American Revolutionary War,* p. 84; Mackesy, *The War for America,* p. 113.

138 WCL-SP, Box 2:8, Aug. 14, 1776. Extract of a letter in the handwriting of Henry Strachey in which he inquires whether he would be permitted to resign his post without the king's consent.

139 O'Shaughnessy, *The Men Who Lost America,* pp. 146–47.

140 James H. Merrell, "Indians and the New Republic," in Greene and Pole, eds., *The Blackwell Encyclopedia of the American Revolution,* pp. 392–93.

141 O'Shaughnessy, *The Men Who Lost America,* pp. 155–57.

142 Ibid., pp. 153–54, 158.

143 Bickham, *Making Headlines,* p. 105.

144 NRAS-DH/LMC: NRAS859/Vol. 487, Box 1, Dec. 3–4, 1777.

145 Bickham, *Making Headlines,* pp. 105–6; NRAS-DH/LMC: NRAS859/Vol. 487, Box 1, Dec. 5–11, 1777.

146 Bickham, *Making Headlines,* pp. 106–7; Lutnick, *The American Revolution and the British Press,* pp. 107, 109.

147 University of Virginia, Albert and Shirley Small Special Collections, Hamond Naval Papers, Box 4390.a: twenty-three letters between Hans Stanley and Andrew Snape Hamond, dated between 1766 and 1778. Jan. 12, 1778, Hans Stanley to A. S. Hamond.

148 *Diary and Letters of Thomas Hutchinson,* vol. II, p. 69; WCL-SP, Box 2:16, Dec. 28, 1776: Autograph Letter from Strachey [to his wife] from New York.

149 NRAS-DH/LMC: NRAS859/Vol. 488, Box 1, Jan. 7, 1778.

150 HWC, vol. 12, p. 90.

151 BL-AP, 75613, CH/LS, Jan. 8, 1778.

152 BL-AP, 75613, CH/LS, Jan. 2, 1778; Jan. 8, 1778; Jan. 15, 1778.

153 BC: *London Evening Post,* Jan. 8–10, 1778. Caroline had thought Lady Germain was recovering when she and Lady Howe visited a few days before January 8. See her letter to Lady Spencer of that date, above.

154 Anderson, pp. 294–95, and see Davies, vol. 14, pp. 237–38, for a letter from General Howe to Lord George Germain, dated October 21, 1777, updating the American secretary on the campaign in Pennsylvania and rumors regarding Burgoyne.

155 Davies inserted "not found" in brackets beside General Howe's reference to Germain's letter of August 4 in his letter dated October 22. See Davies, vol. 14, p. 241. Howe's full letter of October 22 is on pp. 241–43.

156 On the rumors about Burgoyne, see Howe's letters to Germain of October 21 and October 22, cited above, ibid, vol. 14, pp. 238, 242.

157 WCL-GSG, vol. 6: April–December 1777, Lord George Germain to Sir William Howe, Kew Lane, August 4, 1777. This letter is not reproduced in Davies, *Documents of the American Revolution*, or in *Report on the Manuscripts of Mrs. Stopford-Sackville*, vol. 2.

158 Stead, "Contemporary Responses in Print to the American Campaigns of the Howe Brothers," p. 118; Bickham, *Making Headlines*, p. 195, and see Richard's remarks in the House of Commons, *Cobbett's Parliamentary History of England*, vol. 20, p. 719.

159 Winthrop Sargent, *The Life and Career of Major John André* (Boston, 1861), pp. 160, 164–65, 167, 177fn, 177–81; O'Shaughnessy, *The Men Who Lost America*, p. 208.

160 Eliza Tamarkin, *Anglophilia: Deference, Devotion, and Antebellum America* (Chicago and London, 2008), pp. 127–33; Christopher Mulvey, *Transatlantic Manners: Social Patterns in Nineteenth-Century Anglo-American Travel Literature* (Cambridge and New York, 1990), pp. 123–31.

161 Captain Andrew Snape Hamond organized a ball and supper for General Howe on board the *Roebuck*, attended by 200 "Ladies & Officers" before the Mischianza. University of Virginia, Small Special Collections, Hamond Naval Papers, item 53, "Heads of the Life of Sir Andrew Snape Hamond, bart., written merely for the Private Information of his own Family; as the Narrative will shew; being of little Interest to the world at large."

162 Sargent, *The Life and Career of Major John André*, pp. 177–80.

163 For example, see BNA: *The Scots Magazine*, July 5, 1779, vol. 40, p. 369.

164 BNA: *The Scots Magazine*, Dec. 7, 1779, vol. 41, p. 722.

165 NRAS-DH/LMC: NRAS859/Vol. 488, Box 1, June 1, 1778; June 15, 1778.

Twelve: About Mrs. Loring

1 Kenneth Roberts, *Oliver Wiswell* (New York, 1940; this ed. Camden, ME, 1999), p. 134; Philip Young, *Revolutionary Ladies* (New York, 1977), p. 80.

2 Roberts, *Oliver Wiswell*, p. 86; Thomas Jones, *History of New York During the Revolutionary War*, ed. Edward Floyd De Lancey (New York, 1879), p. 351.

3 Young, *Revolutionary Ladies*, pp. 75–77; Jennifer Schuessler, "Confronting Slavery at Long Island's Oldest Estates," *New York Times*, August 12, 2015. See also *Papers of the Lloyd Family of the Manor of Queens Village, Lloyd's Neck, Long Island, New York, 1754-1826* (2 vols., New York, 1828), vol. 2, quote on p. 591.

4 John Alden, *A History of the American Revolution: Britain and the Loss of the Thirteen Colonies* (London, 1969), pp. 503–4; Young, *Revolutionary Ladies*, pp. 68–69, 76–77, 86; Eva Phillips Boyd, "Jamaica Plain by Way of London," *Old-Time New England*, vol. 49 (April–June 1959).

5 J. K. Laughton, rev. by Andrew Lambert, "Loring, Sir John Wentworth (1775-1852), naval officer," ODNB Online [accessed April 14, 2020].

6 Young, *Revolutionary Ladies*, pp. 68, 69, 74; Alden, *A History of the American Revolution*, pp. 503–4.

7   Laughton, rev. Lambert, "Loring, Sir John Wentworth."

8   Young, *Revolutionary Ladies*, pp. 69, 78, 84–86; Laughton, rev. Lambert, "Loring, Sir John Wentworth."

9   "Letter from New York," March 9, 1777, in *A View of the Evidence. . . . To which is added A Collection of the Celebrated Fugitive Pieces*, p. 77.

10 *Pennsylvania Evening Post*, May 22, 1777 [Readex, Early American Newspapers: Series 1, 1690–1876].

11 SALS-DD/SH 34, Jane Strachey to Henry Strachey, May 5, 1777.

12 Cited in Alden, *A History of the American Revolution*, p. 304.

13 Alden, ibid., pp. 304–5; Young, *Revolutionary Ladies*, p. 60, 69fn. Cite from Young, p. 60.

14 For historians who doubt the affair, see Young, "Mrs. Loring, and Howe," in *Revolutionary Ladies*, pp. 57–86; Alden, *A History of the American Revolution*, pp. 307, 504; Boyd, "Jamaica Plain by Way of London," *Old-Time New England* (April–June 1959); Derek W. Beck, *The War Before Independence, 1775-1776* (Naperville, IL, 2016), p. 432fn.

15 Thacher, *American Medical Biography*, vol. 1, pp. 361–64; Alden, *A History of the American Revolution*, p. 504.

16 Willcox, *Portrait of a General*, pp. 60, 69, 174, 199.

17 Edward E. Curtis, *The Organization of the British Army in the American Revolution* (New Haven, 1926; this ed. Gansevoort, NY, 1998), p. 31; Lunt, *John Burgoyne of Saratoga*, pp. 143, 255–56.

18 WCL-SP, Box 2:21, February 17, 1777. An autograph letter by Henry Strachey to an unnamed recipient. Dated from "Hanover Square" [New York?].

19 Young, *Revolutionary Ladies*, pp. 70, 78–79, 83–84.

20 James Sturgis, "Wentworth, Sir John, first baronet (1737-1820)," ODNB Online [accessed Aug. 19, 2020]; Paul W. Wilderson, *Governor John Wentworth & the American Revolution* (Hanover, NH, 1994), pp. 122, 136–37, 264; SCC:LAI: Sheffield Archives: Wentworth Woodhouse Muniments, Rockingham Papers, R1-1662, Frances Howe to Lady Wentworth [wife of Sir John Wentworth], dated May 3, 1776.

21 Alden, *A History of the American Revolution*, p. 504; Young, *Revolutionary Ladies*, p. 84; Laughton, rev. Lambert, "Loring, Sir John Wentworth." On Mrs. Loring's application for a pension, see Boyd, "Jamaica Plain by Way of London."

22 Aileen Sutherland Collins, ed., *Travels in Britain, 1794-1795: The Diary of John Aspinwall, Great-grandfather of Franklin Delano Roosevelt With a Brief History of His Aspinwall Forebears* (Virginia Beach, VA, 1994), p. 90; Young, *Revolutionary Ladies*, p. 84.

23 BC: *Public Advertiser*, Jan. 12, 1778.

24 Letter dated New York, January 25, 1778, in *Historical Anecdotes, Civil and Military: In a Series of Letters, Written from America, in the years 1777 and 1778, to different Persons in England; Containing Observations on the General Management of the War, and on the Conduct of our Principal Commanders, in the Revolted Colonies, During that Period* (London, 1779), pp. 40, 43, 48.

25 WCL-SP, Box 1:7, Jane Strachey to Henry Strachey, Sunday night August 17, 1777;

Box 2:42, December 2, 1777. Henry Strachey to Jane Strachey; Box 2:49. March 18, 1778, same to same.

26 Jones, *History of New York During the Revolutionary War*, pp. xi–xii.

27 *Private Papers of James Boswell from Malahide Castle*, p. 229.

28 Joseph Downs, "The Verplanck Room," *Metropolitan Museum of Art Bulletin*, vol. 36, no. 11 (Nov., 1941), pp. 218, 221; Marshall B. Davidson and Elizabeth Stillinger, *The American Wing at the Metropolitan Museum of Art* (New York, 1985), p. 56.

29 Janice Murphy Lorenz, "The Verplancks and their Historic Mount Gulian Home, Both with Historic and Huguenot Connections," in *The Cross of Languedoc: A Publication of the National Huguenot Society*, Fall 2014, pp. 2–3; Michael Diaz, " 'Can you on such principles think of quitting a Country?': Family, Faith, Law, Property, and the Loyalists of the Hudson Valley During the American Revolution," in *The Hudson River Valley Review*, vol. 28, no. 1, Autumn 2011, p. 16.

30 Davidson and Stillinger, *The American Wing at the Metropolitan Museum of Art*, pp. 56–59. On Gulian Crommelin Verplanck's memories of his grandmother, Judith Verplanck, see William Cullen Bryant, *A Discourse on the Life, Character and Writings of Gulian Crommelin Verplanck* (New York, 1870).

31 The full media-constructed version of General Howe's tainted career in America is neatly summarized in BC: *Morning Post and Daily Advertiser*, Jan. 20, 1778.

32 See, for example, Ellis, *Revolutionary Summer*, p. 37.

33 Longmore, *The Invention of George Washington*, pp. 168, 180–82, 214, 226.

34 John F. Watson, *Annals of Philadelphia and Pennsylvania, in the Olden Time* (2 vols., Philadelphia, 1857), vol. 2, p. 289.

Thirteen: Survival

1 NRAS-DH/LMC: NRAS859/Vol. 488, Box 1, July 2, 1778.

2 Bedfordshire Archives, Lucas Manuscripts, L30/12/3/9, Major Nisbet Balfour to Lord Polwarth, March 1779.

3 Davies, vol. 13, p. 254.

4 Donne, ed., *The Correspondence of King George the Third with Lord North*, vol. 2, p. 202.

5 O'Shaughnessy, *The Men Who Lost America*, p. 194.

6 WCL-KP, 10:25 William Knox, "Curious Political Anecdotes," 1779.

7 Gruber, p. 326.

8 BC: *Lloyd's Evening Post*, Aug. 10–12, 1778; BNA: *Bath Chronicle and Weekly Gazette*, Aug. 6, 1778; *Saunders's News-Letter*, July 16, 1778; *Manchester Mercury*, July 21, 1778.

9 NLI, Thomas Conolly Papers, MS 41, 341/5, William Howe to Thomas Conolly, July 12, 1778.

10 *Correspondence of Emily Duchess of Leinster*, vol. III, p. 307.

11 BL-AP, 75613, CH/LS, Aug. 16, 1778; Aug. 18, 1778.

12 BL-AP, 75613, CH/LS, Aug. 19, 1778; Aug. 23, 1778; Fanny Howe to LS, Aug. 17, 1778; Aug. 18, 1778; Aug. 20, 1778.

13 *Correspondence of Emily Duchess of Leinster,* vol. III, p. 311; NRAS-DH/LMC: NRAS859/Vol. 488, Box 1, Sunday Sept. 6–Sept. 9, 1778.

14 BNA: *Hibernian Journal; or, Chronicle of Liberty,* Sept. 28, 1778.

15 Thomas, *Lord North,* pp. 109, 118; Brown, *Empire or Independence,* pp. 216–17, 250.

16 Brown, *Empire or Independence,* pp. 219, 221; cites on p. 219.

17 Lutnick, *The American Revolution and the British Press,* pp. 136–39; NRAS-DH/LMC: NRAS859/Vol. 488, Box 1, June 24, 1778.

18 Brown, *Empire or Independence,* pp. 245, 260, 261, 263, 268.

19 Davies, vol. 13, p. 276; Syrett, pp. 74–75.

20 O'Shaughnessy, *The Men Who Lost America,* pp. 221–22; NLI, Thomas Conolly papers, MS 41, 341/5, Edmund Burke to Thomas Conolly, Beaconsfield, August 27, 1778.

21 Syrett, pp. 76–77.

22 Syrett, pp. 79–81.

23 BL-AP, 75613, CH/LS, Sept. 14, 1778. Surviving letters of Caroline Howe to her friend Lady Susanna Leveson-Gower during this period are good examples of the dedicated and extensive letter-writing she undertook in order to convey military news to fashionable society. The letters contain naval intelligence relating to Admiral Howe and were certainly intended to be passed around by the recipient. PRO, Leveson-Gower Papers, 30/29/4/8, Caroline Howe to Lady Gower, Grafton Street, Sept. 14 [1778] [Letter 4, fols. 1149–50]; same to same, Oct. 13 [1778] [Letter 5, fols. 1151–52]; same to same, Oct. 13, 1778 [Letter 6, fols. 1153–54].

24 Syrett, pp. 79, 83; Urban, *Fusiliers,* pp. 160–61, 163.

25 Stephen Brumwell, *Turncoat: Benedict Arnold and the Crisis of American Liberty* (New Haven and London, 2018), pp. 133–34.

26 BL-AP, 75613, CH/LS, Oct. 16, 1778.

27 BL-AP, 75613, CH/LS, Oct. 26, 1778.

28 Syrett, p. 87; BL-AP, 75613, CH/LS, Oct. 29, 1778.

29 BL-AP, 75613, CH/LS, Oct. 29, 1778.

30 *Diary and Letters of Thomas Hutchinson,* vol. II, p. 222; BL-AP, 75613, CH/LS, Nov. 14, 1778.

31 Mackesy, *The War for America,* p. 209.

32 Conway, *The British Isles and the War of American Independence,* pp. 118–20, 291.

33 *General Evening Post,* August 11, 1778, cited in Lutnick, *The American Revolution and the British Press,* p. 138.

34 Stanley Weintraub, *Iron Tears: Rebellion in America, 1775-1783* (London, New York, Toronto, Sydney, Dublin, 2005), pp. 148–49, 169.

35 Conway, *The British Isles and the War of American Independence,* pp. 290–91, 294.

36 BL-AP, 75613, CH/LS, Sept. 14, 1778; Oct. 16, 1778.

37 Amanda Foreman, "A politician's politician: Georgiana, Duchess of Devonshire and the Whig party," in Barker and Chalus, eds., *Gender in Eighteenth-Century England,* pp. 182–83; Foreman, *Georgiana, Duchess of Devonshire,* pp. 62–66, 75; Martyn J. Powell, "Rockingham Whigs (act. 1765-1782)," ODNB Online [accessed Aug. 31, 2020].

38 BL-AP, 75644, LS/CH, June 13, 1794.

39 Keith Perry, *British Politics and the American Revolution* (Basingstoke and London, 1990), p. 104; Weintraub, *Iron Tears*, pp. 149–50.

40 Marie Peters, "Pitt, William, first earl of Chatham [*known* as Pitt the Elder]," ODNB Online [accessed Aug. 30, 2020].

41 HWC, vol. 24, pp. 418–19.

42 Robin F. A. Fabel, "Johnstone, George (1730-1787)," ODNB Online [accessed Aug. 30, 2020].

43 BL, Fox Papers, 47579, fols. 57–58, Richard Fitzpatrick to Lord Ossory, Nov. 1778; Gruber, p. 329; Weintraub, *Iron Tears*, pp. 172–73.

44 O'Shaughnessy, *The Men Who Lost America*, pp. 34–35, 187–88; Norton, *The British-Americans*, pp. 159–68.

45 *Cobbett's Parliamentary History of England*, vol. 20, pp. 31, 78–79, 89.

46 For example, see BL-AP, 75614, CH/LS, June 28, 1779; 75615, April 14, 1780; Sunday Morning, April 17, 1780.

47 John Cannon, "Petty [*formerly* Fitzmaurice], William, second earl of Shelburne and first marquess of Landsdowne," ODNB Online [accessed Aug. 30, 2020], cite from this article; Lunt, *John Burgoyne of Saratoga*, p. 277.

48 *Cobbett's Parliamentary History*, vol. 20, pp. 77, 79–80.

49 WCL-KP, 4:23 Henry White to William Knox, New York, Aug. 17, 1778; 4:39 William Knox to Lord Germain, Oct. 31, 1778; 4:57 Lord George Germain to William Knox, Pall Mall, March 14, 1779.

50 WCL-GSG, Series I, Vol. 8: Aug.–Dec. 1778, Sir J. Dalrymple to Germain, Dec. 25, 1778.

51 BL-AP, 75614, CH/LS, Nov. 4, 1778.

52 Richard Howe to Sir Roger Curtis, Dec. 24, 1778, Porter's Lodge, HO 7, Richard Howe Correspondence, Huntington Library, San Marino, CA.

53 Bedfordshire Archives, Lucas Manuscripts, L30/12/3/5, Major Nisbet Balfour to Lord Polwarth, December 31, 1778; L30/12/3/6, same to same, January 6, 1779 [cite from Balfour]; Urban, *Fusiliers*, pp. 168–69, 180.

54 See, for example, Fortescue, ed., *The Correspondence of King George the Third*, vol. 4, pp. 266–67, 268–69, 334; and Willcox, *Portrait of a General*, p. 472.

55 University of Virginia, Small Special Collections, Hamond Naval Papers, Item 53, "Heads of the Life of Sir Andrew Snape Hamond, Bart."

56 Fortescue, ed., *The Correspondence of King George the Third*, vol. 4, pp. 264, 266–67, 344–46.

57 Fortescue, ibid., vol. 4, pp. 262–63, 267–68, 268–69, 276.

58 Gruber, pp. 332–34.

59 Weintraub, *Iron Tears*, pp. 167–68; Fortescue, ed., *The Correspondence of King George the Third*, vol. 4, p. 293; BL-AP, 75614, CH/LS, Feb. 14, 1779.

60 *Cobbett's Parliamentary History*, vol. 20, pp. 217–18.

61 Fortescue, ed., *The Correspondence of King George the Third*, vol. 4, p. 302.

62 BL-AP, 75614, CH/LS, June 28, 1779.

63 Ford, "Parliament and the Howes," p. 130fn; Gerald Saxon Brown, ed., *Reflections on*

a Pamphlet Intitled "a Letter to the Right Honble. Lord Vict. H—e" by Admiral Lord Howe. (Ann Arbor, 1959), pp. 9, 11.

64 Bedfordshire Archives, Lucas Manuscripts, L30/12/3/9, Major Nisbet Balfour to Lord Polwarth, March 1779. The contents of the letter date it as the end of March.

65 WCL-SP, Box 2, "1779. Sir William Howe's Defence."

66 BC: *Public Advertiser,* April 23, 1779; *General Advertiser and Morning Intelligencer,* April 24, 1779.

67 LEC, vol. 3, p. 102.

68 Brown, ed., *Reflections on a Pamphlet,* p. 12.

69 Bedfordshire Archives, Lucas Manuscripts, L30/12/3/10, Major Nisbet Balfour to Lord Polwarth, May 2, 1779.

70 Brown, ed., *Reflections on a Pamphlet,* pp. 12–13.

71 Fortescue, ed., *The Correspondence of King George the Third,* vol. 4, pp. 334–35.

72 Lunt, *John Burgoyne of Saratoga,* pp. 292–94, 297, 298, 301.

73 University of Virginia, Small Special Collections, Hamond Naval Papers, Item 53, "Heads of the Life of Sir Andrew Snape Hamond, Bart."

74 Brown, ed., *Reflections on a Pamphlet,* pp. 14–15; *Cobbett's Parliamentary History,* vol. 20, p. 817, cite from Cobbett.

75 BL-AP, 75614, CH/LS, June 28, 1779.

76 Fortescue, ed., *The Correspondence of King George the Third,* vol. 4, p. xxi.

77 For a summary of the attitudes of loyalists in London toward the Howes, see Norton, *The British-Americans,* pp. 158–65. Galloway's chief pamphlets against the brothers are listed in Oliver C. Kuntzleman, *Joseph Galloway, Loyalist* (Philadelphia, 1941), pp. 184–91. Anderson, pp. 355–57, gives an overview of pamphlet material directed against the Howes. See also Ford, "Parliament and the Howes."

78 *The Narrative of Lieut. Gen. Sir William Howe in a committee of the House of Commons, on the 29th of April, 1779* (London, 1780).

79 Brown, ed., *Reflections on a Pamphlet,* pp. 2, 36–37.

80 *Diary and Letters of Thomas Hutchinson,* vol. II, 237. Galloway's inside knowledge was no doubt what had triggered the rumors circulating among angry loyalists in New York that Franklin had manipulated Lord Howe in London, supposedly instilling in the brothers a false expectation that they could patch up the war. See *A View of the Evidence relative to the Conduct of the American War under Sir William Howe. . . . To which is added A Collection of the Celebrated Fugitive Pieces,* p. 94.

81 *Cobbett's Parliamentary History,* vol. 20, p. 808; vol. 21, pp. 1125–26.

82 The editors of the Franklin papers have asserted that no evidence can be found proving that Lord North was involved in the secret talks in Grafton Street. *Papers of Benjamin Franklin,* vol. 21, p. 409fn.

83 BL-AP, 75614, CH/LS, Jan. 4, 1780.

84 BL-AP, 75614, CH/LS, July 22, 1779; Aug. 1, 1779.

85 *Correspondence of John, Fourth Duke of Bedford,* vol. 2, p. 103.

86 Roland Thorne, "Rigby, Richard (1722–1788)," ODNB Online [accessed Aug. 30, 2020]; https://www.historyofparliamentonline.org/volume/1754-1790/member/rigby

-richard-1722-88, cite from History of Parliament; Ivan Garwood, *Mistley in the Days of the Rigbys* (Lucas Books, 2003), pp. 57–58.

87 Thorne, "Rigby, Richard (1722–1788)," ODNB Online.

88 Garwood, *Mistley in the Days of the Rigbys*, pp. 52–54, 59, 74–75.

89 BL-AP, 75610, CH/LS, July 16, 1763; 75611, CH/LS, March 12, 1767; 75613, CH/LS, Aug. 6, 1775; Sept. 6, 1776; Aug. 10, 1777.

90 Fortescue, ed., *The Correspondence of King George the Third*, vol. 4, p. 334.

91 Garwood, *Mistley in the Days of the Rigbys*, p. 47.

92 BL-AP, 75614, CH/LS, July 18, 1779.

93 BL-AP, 75614, CH/LS, Nov. 23, 1779; 75689, Richard Rigby to LS, "Saturday evening past nine," May 18, 1782.

94 BL-AP, 75614, CH/LS, Jan. 18, 1780; 75616, CH/LS, May 20, 1780; 75618, CH/LS, Jan. 19, 1782; 75619, CH/LS, Oct. 9, 1783.

95 NRAS-DH/LMC: NRAS859/Vol. 489, Box 1, Dec. 16, 1779.

96 BL-AP, 75614, LS/CH, Jan. 6, 1780; 75616, LS/CH, May 7, 1780; May 18, 1780; CH/LS, May 20, 1780.

97 BL-AP, 75614, CH/LS, Dec. 21, 1779; Dec. 22, 1779.

98 Matthew Kilburn, "William Henry, Prince, first duke of Gloucester and Edinburgh (1743–1805)," ODNB Online [accessed Aug. 30, 2020]; Tillyard, *A Royal Affair*, pp. 299, 300, 308.

99 BL-AP, 75614, CH/LS, Dec. 30, 1779; Friday Morning, Dec. 31, 1779; Jan. 6, 1780; Jan. 27, 1780.

100 BL-AP, 75614, CH/LS, Jan. 8, 1780.

101 BL-AP, 75614, LS/CH, Dec. 24, 1779; Jan. 3, 1780.

102 BL-AP, 75614, CH/LS, Jan. 5, 1780; LS/CH, Jan. 6, 1780.

103 Foreman, *Georgiana, Duchess of Devonshire*, pp. 54, 56.

104 BL-AP, 75614, LS/CH, Jan. 3, 1780.

105 Mackesy, *The War for America*, p. 291; Conway, *A Short History of the American Revolutionary War*, pp. 100–101.

106 Brumwell, *Turncoat*, pp. 298–300.

107 BL-AP, 75617, CH/LS, June 2, 1780.

108 BL-AP, 75617, CH/LS, June 7, 1780; June 8, 1780.

109 BNA: *Northampton Mercury*, July 10, 1780.

110 BL-AP, 75616, CH/LS, May 9, 1780; 75617, CH/LS, July 3, 1780.

111 University of Nottingham, Manuscripts and Special Collections, Portland (Welbeck) Collection, Pw F 6904, F. Montagu to [W. H. C. Cavendish-Bentinck] 3rd Duke of Portland, n.d. [Aug. 22, 1780].

112 Kilburn, "Howe, (Mary Sophia) Charlotte, Viscountess Howe," ODNB Online; BL-AP, 75611, CH/LS, Oct. 22, 1770; Sept. 16 [1771?]; 75615, CH/LS, April 6, 1780.

113 Jonathan R. Dull, *A Diplomatic History of the American Revolution* (New Haven and London, 1985), pp. 120, 123–24, 153.

114 Thomas, *Lord North*, pp. 111, 128, 130, 132.

115 BL-AP, 75615, LS/CH, April 12, 1780.

116 BC: *Parker's General Advertiser and Morning Intelligencer,* June 10, 1782; cite from NRAS-DH/LMC: NRAS859/Vol. 492, Box 3, June 13–[15?], 1782.

117 Syrett, pp. 100–101.

118 Conway, *A Short History of the American Revolutionary War,* p. 166; Willis, *The Glorious First of June,* p. 48, citation from Willis.

119 Syrett, p. 105.

120 BL-AP, 75618, CH/LS, Oct. 22, 1782; Sunday Morning, Nov. 3, 1782; LS/CH, Nov. 1, 1782.

121 BL-AP, 75618, CH/LS, Nov. 7, 1782; Nov. 8, 1782.

122 Richard B. Morris, *The Forging of the Union, 1781-1789* (New York, 1987), pp. 137–39.

123 John J. McCusker and Russell R. Menard, *The Economy of British America, 1607-1789* (Chapel Hill and London, 1985), pp. 367, 373, 371, 374.

124 Cited in McGuire, *Stop the Revolution,* p. 200, endnote 18.

125 Conway, *The American War of Independence 1775-1783,* pp. 230, 232; Dull, *A Diplomatic History of the American Revolution,* pp. 161, 162, cite on p. 161.

126 BL-AP, 75619, LS/CH, May 15, 1783 (1); CH/LS, May 8, 1783; "Monday 8 o'clock in the afternoon," May 19, 1783; BNA: *Derby Mercury,* May 22, 1783.

127 Adrian N. Harvey, "Meynell, Hugo (1735–1808)," ODNB Online [accessed Aug. 30, 2020].

128 BL-AP, 75619, CH/LS, Nov. 22, 1782; June 3, 1783.

129 BL-AP, 75620, CH/LS, Oct. 11, 1783; LS/CH, Oct. 13, 1783; BNA: *Kentish Gazette,* Oct. 15, 1783.

Fourteen: The Glorious Return

1 For the announcement of the death of Mr. Hall, the steward of Lord Howe at Langar, see BNA: *Derby Mercury,* March 1, 1798.

2 Edward Kimber and Richard Johnson, *The Baronetage of England: Containing a Genealogical and Historical Account of all the English Baronets now Existing* (London, 3 vols., 1771), vol. 3, pp. 149–50; BL-AP, 75615, CH/LS, Sunday Morning, April 17, 1780. Sir George Smith took on the name of Bromley in 1778 (Leonard Jacks, *The Great Houses of Nottinghamshire and the County Families* [Nottingham, 1881], p. 132).

3 BL-AP, 75611, CH/LS, [Oct. 1770], 75612, CH/LS, June 4, 1773; 75614, CH/LS, Nov. 14, 1778.

4 BL-AP, 75619, CH/LS, Nov. 29, 1782, "almost 3."

5 Malcolm Lester, "Spencer, George John, second Earl Spencer (1758–1834)" ODNB Online (accessed Aug. 24, 2020); Andrew, "Spencer, (Margaret) Georgiana, Countess Spencer (1737–1814)," ODNB Online [accessed Aug. 24, 2020].

6 Francis Harris, "Holywell House: A Gothic Villa at St Albans," *British Library Journal,* vol. 12, no. 2 (1986), pp. 176–77.

7 BL-AP, 75619, LS/CH, Nov. 22, 1782; Nov. 30, 1782; CH/LS, Nov. 26, 1782.

8 Saul David, *Prince of Pleasure: The Prince of Wales and the Making of the Regency* (London, 1998), pp. 12, 18.

9 Christopher Hibbert, "George IV (1762–1830)," ODNB Online [accessed Aug. 24, 2020].

10 Martin J. Levy, "Armitstead [née Crane; married name Fox], Elizabeth Bridget (1750–1842]," ODNB Online [accessed Aug. 24, 2020]; Foreman, *Georgiana, Duchess of Devonshire*, p. 78.

11 David, *Prince of Pleasure*, pp. 27–28.

12 Foreman, *Georgiana, Duchess of Devonshire*, pp. 83–84; BL-AP, 75619, CH/LS, June 6, 1783; May 15, 1783.

13 NRAS-DH/LMC: NRAS859/Vol. 492, Box 3, October 16, 1782.

14 NRAS-DH/LMC: NRAS859/Vol. 493, Box 3, July 23–29, 1783, Sept. 25-29, 1783.

15 Barrow, p. vii.

16 BL-AP, 75627, CH/LS, Dec. 17, 1785.

17 BL-AP, 75614, CH/LS, Jan. 27, 1780.

18 NRAS-DH/LMC: NRAS859/Vol. 489, Box 1, Tuesday, July 13, 1779.

19 BL-AP, 75618, CH/LS, Jan. 17, 1782; 75619, CH/LS, Nov. 19, 1782; Nov. 26, 1782; Nov. 28, 1782.

20 Caroline Tiger, *General Howe's Dog: George Washington, the Battle of Germantown, and the Dog Who Crossed Enemy Lines* (New York and London, 2005), pp. 93–97.

21 BC: *Public Advertiser*, Jan. 19, 1778.

22 BL-AP, 75620, CH/LS, "Friday evening," Oct. 24, 1783.

23 BL-AP, 75614, CH/LS, Jan. 30, 1780; 75619, CH/LS, Oct. 9, 1783; 75620, CH/LS, "Monday Morning," Oct. 13, 1783; Richard Stuteley Cobbett, *Memorials of Twickenham: Parochial and Topographical* (London, 1872), pp. 356–58.

24 BL-AP, 75614, CH/LS, April 1, 1782.

25 William Howe, *The Narrative of Lieut. Gen. Sir William Howe, in a committee of the House of Commons, on the 29th of April, 1779, relative to his conduct, during his late command of the King's Troops in North America* (London, 1780), pp. 39–40.

26 Daniel Paterson, *A New and Accurate Description of All the Direct and Principal Cross Roads in England and Wales* (1808), pp. 57, 59.

27 George Lipscomb, *A Journey into Cornwall: Through the Counties of Southampton, Wilts, Dorset, Somerset & Devon: Interspersed with Remarks, Moral, Historical, Literary, and Political* (Warwick, 1799), p. 88. The first mention of Avon Cottage is in BL-AP, 75619, CH/LS, May 16, 1783.

28 J. P. W. Ehrman and Anthony Smith, "Pitt, William [known as Pitt the younger] (1759–1806)," ODNB Online [accessed Aug. 24, 2020].

29 Syrett, pp. 110–11; cite from Knight, "Howe, Richard, Earl Howe," ODNB Online.

30 BL-AP, 75633, CH/LS, June 26, 1788; Syrett, *Admiral Lord Howe*, p. 113.

31 George Lipscombe, *The History and Antiquities of the County of Buckingham* (4 vols., London, 1847), vol. 3, p. 290.

32 Anne Chambers, *The Great Leviathan: The Life of Howe Peter Browne, 2nd Marquess of Sligo 1788-1845* (Stillorgan, County Dublin, 2017), pp. 16–19; BNA: *Caledonian Mercury*, June 2, 1787.

33 BL-AP, 75631, CH/LS, May 29, 1787; CH/LS, May 31, 1787.

34 Chalus, "Amelia, Princess (1711–1786)," ODNB Online.

35 BL-AP, 75633, CH/LS, June 20, 1788.

36 BL-AP, 75631, LS/CH, July 23, 1787; CH/LS, July 27, 1787.

37 Thorne, "Rigby, Richard (1722–1788)," ODNB Online [accessed Aug. 24, 2020].

38 BL-AP, 75633, CH/LS, May 15, 1788; [Sunday] May 18, 1788.

39 BL-AP, 75633, CH/LS, June 17, 1788.

40 BL-AP, 75633, LS/CH, May 21, 1788; May 20, 1788.

41 Amanda Foreman, "Ponsonby [née Spencer], Henrietta Frances [Harriet], countess of Bessborough (1761–1821)," ODNB Online [accessed Aug. 24, 2020].

42 BL-AP, 75618, CH/LS, Jan. 18, 1782.

43 Foreman, *Georgiana, Duchess of Devonshire*, p. 119.

44 BL-AP, 75633, CH/LS, Oct. 23, 1788.

45 David, *Prince of Pleasure*, pp. 93–94, 95–96.

46 BL-AP, 75634, CH/LS, Nov. 9, 1788.

47 BL-AP, 75634, CH/LS, Dec. 8, 1788.

48 John Derry, "The Opposition Whigs and the French Revolution, 1789-1815," in H. T. Dickinson, ed., *Britain and the French Revolution 1789-1815* (Houndmills, Basingstoke, Hampshire and London, 1989), pp. 40–41.

49 Cite from Paul Langford, "Burke, Edmund (1729/30–1797)," ODNB Online [accessed 24/8/20].

50 Richard Howe to Sir Roger Curtis, Grafton Street, 1793, April 9, HO 140, Richard Howe correspondence, The Huntington Library, San Marino, CA .

51 P. J. Marshall, *Remaking the British Atlantic: The United States and the British Empire after American Independence* (Oxford, 2012), pp. 63–75; Flavell, *When London Was Capital of America*, p. 248.

52 Jeremy Black, *British Foreign Policy in an Age of Revolutions, 1783-1793* (Cambridge, 1994), p. 227.

53 Derry, "The Opposition Whigs and the French Revolution," p. 45.

54 Richard Howe to Sir Roger Curtis, Grafton Street, 1790, July 5, HO 93; Richard Howe to Sir Roger Curtis, Grafton Street, 1790, June 14, HO 89, Richard Howe correspondence, Huntington Library, San Marino, CA.

55 Richard Howe to Sir Roger Curtis, Porter's Lodge, 1791, July 15, HO 111, Richard Howe correspondence, Huntington Library, San Marino, CA.

56 L. G. Mitchell, *Charles James Fox* (Oxford, 1992), pp. 119, 124, cite from p. 124.

57 BL-AP, 75642, CH/LS, Nov. 26, 1792; Dickinson, ed., *Britain and the French Revolution 1789-1815*, pp. 112–13.

58 BL-AP, 75642, CH/LS, Dec. 10, 1792; Jan. 1, 1793.

59 BL-AP, 75642, CH/LS, Jan. 28, 1793; Michael Duffy, *The Younger Pitt* (Harlow, Essex, 2000), p. 180.

60 BL-AP, 75642, CH/LS, Jan. 28, 1793; April 16, 1793; April 30, 1793. On William Augustus Pitt, see his brief biography, "Sir William Augustus Pitt (c. 1728–1809)," in G. F. R. Barker, rev. by R. D. E. Eagles, "Pitt, George, first Baron Rivers (1721–1803)," ODNB Online [accessed Aug. 24, 2020].

61 O'Shaughnessy, *The Men Who Lost America*, p. 121.

62 BL-AP, 75644, LS/CH, July 26, 1794.

63 Gleeson, *Privilege and Scandal*, p. 155.

64 Foreman, *Georgiana, Duchess of Devonshire*, pp. 267–75.

65 For example, see BL-AP, 75644, CH/LS, May 3, 1794; LS/CH, April 12, 1794.

66 Kent Archives Service, Knatchbull Manuscripts, Letters and Papers of Admiral Earl Howe, U951/C267/28, Admiral Howe to Lord Altamont, Porter's Lodge, July 13, 1794.

67 John K. Severn, "Wesley [Wellesley], Garrett, first earl of Mornington (1735–1781)," ODNB Online [accessed Aug. 24, 2020]; BNA: *Bury and Norwich Post*, May 28, 1794; Watkin Tench, *Letters written in France, to a friend in London, between the month of November 1794, and the month of May 1795* (London, 1796), pp. 157–59.

68 Willis, *The Glorious First of June*, pp. 50, 51; Syrett, pp. 115–17, 128.

69 Syrett, pp. 128–29, 131–33.

70 Willis, *The Glorious First of June*, pp. 198, 229; Syrett, pp. 133–35.

71 Willis, *The Glorious First of June*, pp. 233–35, 243.

72 Willis, ibid., pp. 213, 230–31.

73 BL-AP, 75644, CH/LS, June 13, 1794. The letter of George III to Caroline on the occasion of her brother's victory, together with her reply, is reprinted in Barrow, pp. 263–64.

74 BNA: *Kentish Gazette*, June 13, 1794.

75 Cite from Willis, *The Glorious First of June*, p. 232.

76 Dorothy Margaret Stuart, *Dearest Bess: The Life and Times of Lady Elizabeth Foster, Afterwards Duchess of Devonshire, from Her Unpublished Journals and Correspondence* (London, 1955), p. 72.

77 Willis, pp. 237–38.

78 French, ed., *The Earl and Countess Howe by Gainsborough*, p. 14.

79 Barrow, pp. 280–81.

80 BNA: *Kentish Weekly Post or Canterbury Journal*, June 13, 1794.

81 Syrett, p. 139; Barrow, p. 285. The sword is still in the possession of the present Earl Howe, Frederick Curzon, 7th Earl Howe, who has explained that the diamonds were removed in the nineteenth century "at the behest of the wife of the third Earl Howe who instructed that they be incorporated into two newly made bracelets for her personal use."

82 Willis, pp. 237–39; Barrow, pp. 282–84.

83 Barrow, p. 263; BL-AP, 75644, Lady Camelford to CH, Aug. 4, 1794.

84 BL-AP, 75644, CH/LS, July 5, 1794.

85 BNA: *Stamford Mercury*, July 11, 1794.

86 BL-AP, 75644, CH/LS, July 15, 1794.

Epilogue: Legacy

1 Syrett, pp. 142–43, 145–49. After 1789, Lord and Lady Howe stayed at 71 Great Pulteney Street when in Bath. French, ed., *The Earl and Countess Howe by Gainsborough*, p. 15.

2 Ruth Hayward, *Phippy: A Biography of Jonathan Wathen Phipps/Waller, Eye-surgeon to*

King George III (Studley, Warwickshire, 2014), p. 36; French, ed., *The Earl and Countess Howe by Gainsborough*, p. 14; Richard Howe to Sir Roger Curtis, 1791, May 12, HO 108, Richard Howe correspondence, The Huntington Library, San Marino, CA.

3 BL-AP, 75644, LS/CH, Sept. 8, 1794.

4 Cites from Chambers, *The Great Leviathan*, p. 16.

5 WCL-HC, [April 10, 1797]. Mary Juliana Howe to Louisa Catherine Howe Browne, countess of Altamont and marchioness of Sligo; Grafton Street.

6 Syrett, pp. 149, 150–51; Christie, *Wars and Revolutions*, pp. 233–35, 239.

7 Syrett, p. 151; Barrow, p. 342.

8 Barrow, pp. 338–39, 342, 344, cite on p. 344.

9 BNA: *Dublin Evening Post*, May 20, 1797.

10 BNA: *Gloucester Journal*, May 22, 1797.

11 Van Der Kiste, *George III's Children*, pp. 69–71; BNA: *Reading Mercury*, May 29, 1797.

12 BNA: *Reading Mercury*, May 29, 1797.

13 WCL-HC, [1798?] Mary Juliana Howe to Louisa Catherine Howe Browne, countess of Altamont and marchioness of Sligo; Grafton Street. The manuscript is incorrectly dated. The contents of the letter make clear that it was written on Wednesday, May 24, 1797. On Hook's song, "The Glorious First of June; or, Lord Howe's Victory," see Paul F. Rice, *British Music and the French Revolution* (Newcastle upon Tyne, 2010), pp. 361–62, 394.

14 Syrett, p. 152.

15 Royal Archives, Additional Papers relating to George III and Queen Charlotte, GEO/ADD/2/51, Louisa Countess of Altamont to the 3rd Earl of Altamont, Aug. 18, 1799.

16 GEO/ADD/2/51, Louisa Countess of Altamont to the 3rd Earl of Altamont, Aug. 18, 1799.

17 Cites from Barrow, pp. 387, 394.

18 Barrow, p. 391.

19 Chambers, *The Great Leviathan*, pp. 41–42; Barrow, pp. 392–95, cite from pp. 393–94.

20 BL-AP, 75644, CH/LS, Sept. 22, 1794.

21 PRO, Leveson-Gower Papers, 30/29/4/8 Caroline Howe to Lady Gower, Nov. 21 [1781] [Letter 15, fols. 1177–1181]; Melville, ed., *The Berry Papers*, pp. 268, 273.

22 BL-AP, 75642, CH/LS, April 16, 1793.

23 BL-AP, 75642, CH/LS, Feb. 13, 1793; Greig, ed., *The Farington Diary*, vol. 6, p. 271. Caroline's image as a conspicuously lively old lady held up to the end. At the time of her death, a literary magazine published a notice of the Hon. Caroline Howe, ". . . still living in Grafton-Street, who, though deaf, still talks, reads, writes, and plays at cards, at 93, with all the spirit and life of a girl, dresses in powdered hair, triple ruffles, furbelowed gowns, and is a fine model of the costume of the old Court. She died while this sheet was preparing for press." John Nichols, Samuel Bentley, *Literary Anecdotes of the Eighteenth Century: Comprizing Biographical Memoirs of William Bowyer, Printer, F.S.A. and many of his Learned Friends* (Volume IX, London, 1815), vol. 9, p. 527.

24 The portrait is entitled "The Honourable Mrs Caroline Howe, aged 90," but the edition of *The Times* is dated August 28, 1813, which would make her ninety-one.

25 BL-AP, 75619, CH/LS, "Monday 8 o'clock in the afternoon," May 19, 1783.

26 BL-AP, 75620, CH/LS, "Monday Morning," Oct. 13, 1783; BL-AP, 75633, CH/LS, May 24, 1788.

27 https://shenleymiscellany.wordpress.com/monumental-inscriptions/. I am grateful to Martin Price for identifying for me Caroline's burial place.

28 BNA: *Caledonian Mercury*, July 4, 1814; *London Courier and Evening Gazette*, July 14, 1814; Cobbett, *Memorials of Twickenham*, p. 76.

29 Hayward, *Phippy*, pp. 36–37, 56–57.

30 Ibid., p. 57.

31 BNA: *The Western Daily Press*, June 1, 1894.

32 BL-AP, 75614, LS/CH, Dec. 27, 1779.

BIBLIOGRAPHY

Archival Sources

Bedfordshire Archives and Records Service, Bedford

Wrest Park (Lucas) Manuscripts

Bodleian Library, University of Oxford

Correspondence and papers of Thomas Villiers, 1st Earl of Clarendon of the second creation, 1738–86

MS. Eng. Misc. e. 452, 45865, "Volume containing accounts of personal expenditure of Scrope, 1st Viscount Howe, and memoranda and accounts of his wife Juliana, 1736–40"

British Library, London

Althorp Papers, especially:

Add. Mss. 75610-75667: Correspondence of Lady Spencer with Caroline Howe, 1759–1814

Add. Mss. 75669-82: Letters to Lady Spencer from George Bussy Villiers, 4th Earl of Jersey

Add. Mss. 75689: Letters to Lady Spencer concerning politics, from Richard Rigby, MP, and others, 1777–88

Add. Mss. 75694-95: Rachel Lloyd, Housekeeper of Kensington Palace: Letters to Lady Spencer, 1773–1803

Add. Mss. 75743, List of the original members of the Ladies' Club, with notes of those who have attended, [1770?]

Blenheim Papers

Fox Papers

Hardwicke Papers

Newcastle Papers, Correspondence: 32686-32992

City of Westminster Archives Centre, London

St. Martin-in-the-Fields Baptisms

Derbyshire Record Office, Matlock

Okeover Family of Okeover: title deeds, estate and family papers

The Huntington Library, San Marino, California

Hastings Family Papers, ca 1100–1892
Howe Collection
Correspondence of John Collett, 1776–1779

Kent Archives Service, Maidstone

Knatchbull Manuscripts, Letters and Papers of Admiral Earl Howe

National Archives, Kew

Prerogative Court of Canterbury and related Probate Jurisdictions: Will Registers
William Pitt, 1st Earl of Chatham Papers
Leveson-Gower. 1st Earl Granville and Predecessors and Successors Papers: Letters of
Caroline Howe to Lady Gower

National Library of Ireland, Dublin

Westport Estate Papers
Thomas Conolly Papers

Nottinghamshire Archives, Nottingham

Register of baptisms for St. Andrew's Church, Langar, PR/6822, 6823
Register of burials for St. Andrew's Church, Langar, PR/6828

Royal Archives, Windsor Castle

Additional Papers relating to King George III and Queen Charlotte

Sheffield City Council, Libraries Archives and Information: Sheffield Archives

Wentworth Woodhouse Muniments, Rockingham Papers

Somerset Archives and Local Studies, South West Heritage Trust

Strachey Collection

Staffordshire Record Office, Stafford

Dartmouth Papers

Suffolk Record Office, Bury St. Edmunds

FitzRoy Papers

University of Nottingham, Manuscripts and Special Collections

Newcastle (Clumber) Collection
Papers of the Smith-Bromley Family of East Stoke Nottinghamshire, 1305–1876
Portland (Welbeck) Collection

University of Southampton, Special Collections, Broadlands Archives

Papers of Henry Temple, second Viscount Palmerston

West Yorkshire Archive Service, Calderdale

Armytage Family of Kirklees Hall, Clifton-cum-Hartshead, Records

National Records of Scotland, Edinburgh

Letters of Sophia Howe et al.
Leven and Melville Muniments
Papers of the Douglas-Home Family, diary of Lady Mary Coke. Extracts are reproduced in this work by kind permission of the Douglas-Home family, Earls of Home
Papers of Major William Howe 1705–1733

University of Virginia, Albert and Shirley Small Special Collections Library

Hamond Naval Papers

William L. Clements Library, University of Michigan

George Sackville Germain Papers 1683–1785
Henry Strachey Papers, 1768–1802
Richard and Francis Browne Papers 1756–1765
Richard and William Howe Collection, 1758–1812
Sir Henry Clinton Papers; Harriot Clinton and Elizabeth Carter Diaries, 1771–1795
Thomas Gage Papers, 1754–1807
William Knox Papers, 1757–1811

Pamphlets

A View of the Evidence relative to the Conduct of the American War under Sir William Howe, Lord Viscount Howe and General Burgoyne; as given before a committee of the House of Commons Last Session of Parliament. To which is added A Collection of the Celebrated Fugitive Pieces that are said to have given rise to that Important Enquiry (London, 1779).

Historical Anecdotes, Civil and Military: In a Series of Letters, Written from America, in the years 1777 and 1778, to different Persons in England; Containing Observations on the General Management of the War, and on the Conduct of our Principal Commanders, in the Revolted Colonies, During that Period (London, 1779).

[Howe, Admiral Lord (Richard)], *Reflections on a Pamphlet Intitled "a Letter to the Right Honble. Lord Vict. H—E,"* ed. Gerald Saxon Brown (Ann Arbor, 1959).

Howe, William, *The Narrative of Lieut. Gen. Sir William Howe, in a committee of the House of Commons, on the 29th of April, 1779, relative to his conduct, during his late command of the King's Troops in North America: To which are added, Some Observations upon a Pamphlet, entitled, Letters to a Nobleman* (London, 1780).

Digital Resources

Adams Family Papers: An Electronic Archive. Massachusetts Historical Society. http://www.masshist.org/digitaladams/.

America's Historical Newspapers, Including Early American Newspapers. Series 1–7, 1690–1922. New York and Chester, VT: Readex, 2006–.

British History Online. Version 5.0. www.british-history.ac.uk.

British Newspaper Archive. www.britishnewspaperarchive.co.uk. With thanks to the British Newspaper Archive.

Burney Collection. 17th and 18th Century Burney Newspapers Collection. Farmington Hills, MI: Gale Cengage Learning.

History of Parliament Online. historyofparliamentonline.org.

Office-holders in Modern Britain. Institute of Historical Research, London. http://www.history.ac.uk/publications/office/.

Oxford Dictionary of National Biography. Online ed. Oxford University Press, 2004. https://www.oxforddnb.com.

The Database of Court Officers 1660–1837. Comp. R. O. Bucholz, J. C. Sainty, et al., 2005; rev. 2019. http://courtofficers.ctsdh.luc.edu/.

Published Primaries

Adams, Charles Francis, ed. *The Works of John Adams.* 10 vols. (Boston, 1856).

Anson, William R., ed. *Autobiography and Political Correspondence of Augustus Henry, third Duke of Grafton* (London, 1898).

Bessborough, Earl, ed. *Georgiana: Extracts from the Correspondence of Georgiana, Duchess of Devonshire* (London, 1955).

Cartwright, F. D., ed. *The Life and Correspondence of Major Cartwright.* 2 vols. (London, 1826).

Climenson, E. J., ed. *Passages from the Diaries of Mrs. Philip Lybbe Powys of Hardwick House* (London, 1899).

Cobbett, William, ed. *Cobbett's Parliamentary History of England: From the Norman conquest, in 1066, to the year, 1803.* 36 vols. (London, 1806–1820).

Coke, Mary. *The Letters and Journals of Lady Mary Coke.* 4 vols. (1889–96; facsimile ed., Bath, 1970).

Collins, Aileen Sutherland, ed. *Travels in Britain, 1794–1795: The Diary of John Aspinwall, Great-grandfather of Franklin Delano Roosevelt With a Brief History of His Aspinwall Forebears* (Virginia Beach, VA, 1994).

Creswell, Nicholas. *The Journal of Nicholas Creswell, 1774–1777* (London and New York, 1924).

Croker, John Wilson, ed. *Letters to and From Henrietta, Countess of Suffolk, and her second husband, the Hon. George Berkeley.* 2 vols. (London, 1824).

Davies, K. G., ed. *Documents of the American Revolution, 1770–1783.* 21 vols. (Kill-o'-the-Grange, 1972–1981).

Deas, Anne Izard, ed. *Correspondence of Mr. Ralph Izard* (New York, 1844; this ed. New York, 1976).

Doddington, George Bubb. *The Diary of the Late George Bubb Dodington, baron of Melcombe Regis* (3rd ed., London, 1785).

Donne, W. Bodham, ed. *The Correspondence of King George the Third with Lord North from 1768 to 1783.* 2 vols. (London, 1867).

Doran, John, ed. *The Last Journals of Horace Walpole during the Reign of George III from 1771-1783.* 2 vols. (London and New York, 1910).

Fitzgerald, Brian, ed. *Correspondence of Emily, Duchess of Leinster.* 3 vols. (Dublin, 1949, 1953, 1957).

Fortescue, Sir John, ed. *The Correspondence of King George the Third from 1760 to December 1783.* 6 vols. (London, 1927).

Fothergill, John. *Chain of Friendship: Selected Letters of Dr. John Fothergill of London, 1735-1780,* ed. by Betsy C. Corner and Christopher C. Booth. (Cambridge, MA, 1971).

Greig, James, ed. *The Farington Diary by Joseph Farington.* 6 vols. (London, 1922–1928).

Grant, Anne MacVicar. *Memoirs of an American Lady: With Sketches of Manners and Scenes in America, as They Existed Previous to the Revolution,* ed. by James Grant Wilson (Cambridge, 2011).

Grant, Bartle, ed. *The Receipt Book of Elizabeth Raper* (Soho, London, 1924).

The Grenville Papers: Being the correspondence of Richard Grenville, earl Temple, K.G., and the Right Hon. George Grenville. 4 vols. (London, 1852–1853).

Guttridge, George H., ed. *The Correspondence of Edmund Burke,* vol. III (July 1774–June 1778) (Chicago, 1961).

Hervey, John. *Memoirs of the Reign of George II from his accession to the death of Queen Caroline.* 2 vols. (London, 1848).

Historical Manuscripts Commission. *The Manuscripts of the Earl of Dartmouth.* 3 vols. (London, 1887, 1895, 1896).

Historical Manuscripts Commission. *Report on the Manuscripts of Mrs. Stopford-Sackville of Drayton House, Northamptonshire.* 2 vols. (London and Hereford, 1904, 1910).

Hutchinson, Peter Orlando. *The Diary and Letters of His Excellency Thomas Hutchinson.* 2 vols. (Boston, 1884–1886).

Kielmansegge, Friedrich. *Diary of a Journey to England in the Years 1761-1762* (London, 1902; Elibron Classics Replica ed., 2005).

Lewis, Theresa, ed. *Extracts of the Journal and Correspondence of Miss Berry, from the year 1783 to 1852.* 3 vols. (London, 1865).

Lewis, W. S., ed. *The Yale Edition of Horace Walpole's Correspondence.* 48 vols. (London, 1937–1983).

Llanover, Lady, ed. *The Autobiography and Correspondence of Mary Granville, Mrs Delany.* 3 vols. (London, 1861).

Malmesbury, J. H. H., ed. *A Series of Letters of the First Earl of Malmesbury, His Family and Friends from 1745 to 1820.* 2 vols. (London, 1870).

Meaby, K. Tweedale. *Nottinghamshire: Extracts from the County Records of the Eighteenth Century* (Nottingham, 1947).

Melville, Lewis, ed. *The Berry Papers; Being the Correspondence hitherto unpublished of Mary and Agnes Berry (1763–1852)* (London and New York, 1914).

Montagu, Matthew, ed. *The Letters of Mrs Elizabeth Montagu.* 3 vols. (Boston, 1825).

Nichols, John, and Samuel Bentley. *Literary Anecdotes of the Eighteenth Century: Comprizing Biographical Memoirs of William Bowyer, Printer, F.S.A. and many of his Learned Friends.* Vol. IX (London, 1815).

O'Callaghan, E. B., ed. *Documents Relative to the Colonial History of the State of New York.* 15 vols. (Albany, 1853–1887).

Oliver, Andrew, ed. *The Journal of Samuel Curwen, Loyalist.* 2 vols. (Cambridge, MA, 1972).

Papers of the Lloyd Family of the Manor of Queens Village, Lloyd's Neck, Long Island, New York, 1754-1826. 2 vols. (New York, 1828).

Pargellis, Stanley, ed. *Military Affairs in North America, 1748-1765: Selected documents from the Cumberland papers in Windsor Castle.* (New York and London, 1936).

Pennington, Montagu, ed. *Letters from Mrs Elizabeth Carter, to Mrs Montagu, between the years 1755 and 1800 chiefly upon literary and moral subjects.* 3 vols. (London, 1817).

Pennington, Montagu, ed. *A Series of Letters between Mrs. Elizabeth Carter and Miss Catherine Talbot, from the year 1741 to 1770* (1809).

Pottle, Frederick A., and Geoffrey Scott, eds. *Private Papers of James Boswell from Malahide Castle* (Collection of Lt-Colonel Ralph Heywood Isham, 1931).

Pouchot, Pierre. *Memoirs on the Late War in North America between France and England,* rev. ed. Translated by Michael Cardy, edited and annotated by Brian Leigh Dunnigan (Youngstown, NY, 2004).

A Register of Ships Employed in the Service of the Hon. the United East India Company, from the Union of the Two Companies in 1707, to the Year 1760 (London, 1800).

Rogers, Robert. *Reminiscences of the French War: Robert Rogers' Journal and a Memoir of General Stark* (Freedom, NH, 1988).

Russell, John, ed. *Correspondence of John, Fourth Duke of Bedford.* 3 vols. (London, 1842–1846).

Sherburn, George, ed. *Correspondence of Alexander Pope.* 5 vols. (Oxford, 1956).

Simmons, R. C., and P. D. G. Thomas, eds. *Proceedings and Debates of the British Parliament Respecting North America, 1754–1783.* 6 vols. (Millwood, White Plains, NY, 1982–1987).

Spencer, Earl, and Christopher Dobson, eds. *Letters of David Garrick and Georgiana Countess Spencer 1759–1779* (Cambridge, 1960).

Tatum, Edward H., Jr., ed. *The American Journal of Ambrose Serle, Secretary to Lord Howe, 1776–1778* (San Marino, CA, 1940).

Taylor, W. S., and J. H. Pringle, eds. *Correspondence of William Pitt, earl of Chatham.* 4 vols. (London, 1838–40).

Tench, Watkin. *Letters written in France, to a friend in London, between the month of November 1794, and the month of May 1795* (London, 1796).

Thomson, A. T. *Memoirs of Viscountess Sundon: Mistress of the Robes to Queen Caroline.* 2 vols. (London, 1848).

Todish, Timothy J., ed. *The Annotated and Illustrated Journals of Major Robert Rogers* (New York, 2002).

Walpole, Horace. *Memoirs of the Reign of King George II.* 3 vols. (London, 1847).

Walpole, Horace. *The Works of Horace Walpole, Earl of Orford.* 5 vols. (London, 1798).

Wharncliffe, James, and W. Moy Thomas, eds. *Letters and Works of Lady Mary Wortley Montagu.* 2 vols. (3rd ed., London, 1861).

Willcox, William B., ed. *The American Rebellion: Sir Henry Clinton's Narrative of his Campaigns, 1775–1782* (New Haven, 1954).

Willcox, William B., et al., eds. *The Papers of Benjamin Franklin.* 42 vols. (New Haven and London, 1959–2017).

Secondaries

Alden, John. *A History of the American Revolution: Britain and the Loss of the Thirteen Colonies* (London, 1969).

Allen, Thomas B. *Tories: Fighting for the King in America's First Civil War* (New York, 2010).

Ammerman, David. *In the Common Cause: American Response to the Coercive Acts of 1774* (Charlottesville, VA, 1974).

Anderson, Fred. *A People's Army: Massachusetts Soldiers and Society in the Seven Years' War* (New York and London, 1984).

Anderson, Fred. *Crucible of War: The Seven Years' War and the Fate of Empire in British North America, 1754–1766* (New York, 2000).

Anderson, Fred. *The War That Made America: A Short History of the French and Indian War* (New York and London, 2005).

Anderson, Troyer Steele. *The Command of the Howe Brothers During the American Revolution* (New York and London, 1936).

Andrew, Donna T. *Philanthropy and Police: London Charity in the Eighteenth Century* (Princeton, NJ, 1989).

Atkinson, Rick. *The British Are Coming: The War for America 1775–1777* (London, 2019).

Austin-Leigh, Richard Arthur. *The Eton College Register 1698–1752* (Eton, 1927).

Bailyn, Bernard. *The Ordeal of Thomas Hutchinson* (Cambridge, MA, 1974).

Baird, Rosemary. *Mistress of the House: Great Ladies and Grand Houses 1670–1830* (London, 2003).

Bargar, B. D. *Lord Dartmouth and the American Revolution* (Columbia, SC, 1965).

Bargar, B. D. "Lord Dartmouth's Patronage, 1772–1775," *William and Mary Quarterly*, 3rd series, vol. 15 (1958).

Barker, Hannah, and Elaine Chalus, eds. *Gender in Eighteenth-Century England: Roles, Representations and Responsibilities* (London and New York, 1997).

Barrow, Sir John. *The Life of Richard Earl Howe, K.G.* (London, 1838; this ed., Elibron Classics Replica Edition, 2005).

Battiscombe, Georgina. *The Spencers of Althorp* (London, 1984).

Beard, Mary. "The Public Voice of Women," *London Review of Books*, vol. 36, no. 6, 20 (2014).

Beattie, J. M. *The English Court in the Reign of George I* (Cambridge, 1967).

Beck, Derek W. *The War Before Independence, 1775–1776* (Naperville, IL, 2016).

Betham, William. *The Baronetage of England, or the History of the English Baronets*. 5 vols. (1801–1805).

Bicheno, Hugh. *Rebels and Redcoats: The American Revolutionary War* (London, 2003).

Bickham, Troy. *Making Headlines: The American Revolution as Seen through the British Press* (DeKalb, IL, 2009).

Bickham, Troy O. "Sympathizing with Sedition? George Washington, the British Press, and British Attitudes During the American War of Independence," *William and Mary Quarterly*, 3rd series, vol. 59 (2002).

Billias, George Athan, ed. *George Washington's Generals and Opponents: Their Exploits and Leadership* (New York, 1964, 1969; this ed., Da Capo Press, 1994).

Black, Jeremy. *British Foreign Policy in an Age of Revolutions, 1783–1793* (Cambridge, 1994).

Black, Jeremy. *Pitt the Elder: The Great Commoner* (Cambridge, 1992; rev. ed. Stroud, Gloucestershire, 1999).

Black, Jeremy. *The British Abroad: The Grand Tour in the Eighteenth Century* (Stroud and New York, 1992).

Black, Jeremy. *War for America: The Fight for Independence 1775–1783* (Stroud, 1991; paperback ed., 2001).

Blackstock, Allan, and Eoin Magennis, eds. *Politics and Political Culture in Britain and Ireland, 1750–1850: Essays in Tribute to Peter Jupp* (Belfast, 2007).

Bowen, Huw. "Privilege and Profit: Commanders of East Indiamen as Private Traders, Entrepreneurs and Smugglers, 1760–1813," *International Journal of Maritime History*, vol. 19 (2007).

Bowen, Huw. "The East India Company and Military Recruitment in Britain, 1763-71," *Bulletin of the Institute of Historical Research*, vol. 59 (1986).

Boyd, Eva Phillips. "Jamaica Plain by Way of London," *Old-Time New England*, vol. 49 (April–June 1959).

Bradley, James E. *Popular Politics and the American Revolution in England: Petitions, the Crown, and Public Opinion* (Macon, GA, 1986).

Brands, H. W. *The First American: The Life and Times of Benjamin Franklin* (New York, 2000; paperback ed., New York, 2002).

Brauer, George C. *The Education of a Gentleman: Theories of Gentlemanly Education in England, 1660–1775* (New York, 1959).

Brewer, John. *The Pleasures of the Imagination: English Culture in the Eighteenth Century* (London, 1997).

Brewer, John, and Susan Staves, eds. *Early Modern Conceptions of Property* (London and New York, 1996).

Brown, Christopher Leslie, and Philip D. Morgan, eds. *Arming Slaves: From Classical Times to the Modern Age* (New Haven and London, 2006).

Brown, Wallace. "The British Press and the American Colonies," *History Today*, Vol. 24 (1974).

Brown, Weldon A. *Empire or Independence: A Study in the Failure of Reconciliation, 1774–1783* (Baton Rouge, LA, 1941).

Browning, Reed. *The Duke of Newcastle* (New Haven and London, 1975).

Brumwell, Stephen. "Band of Brothers," *History Today*, vol. 58 (6), June 2008.

Brumwell, Stephen. *George Washington: Gentleman Warrior* (London, 2012).

Brumwell, Stephen. "Home from the Wars," *History Today*, vol. 52 (3), March 2002.

Brumwell, Stephen. *Paths of Glory: The Life and Death of James Wolfe* (London and New York, 2006; this paperback ed., 2007)

Brumwell, Stephen. "Rank and File: A Profile of One of Wolfe's Regiments," *Journal of the Society for Army Historical Research*, vol. 79 (2001).

Brumwell, Stephen. *Redcoats: The British Soldier and War in the Americas, 1755–1763* (Cambridge, 2002).

Brumwell, Stephen. "Revisiting B. E. Griffiths: Former Slave, Queen's Ranger, and 'Son of Africa,'" *Journal of the American Revolution*, vol. 5 (April 23, 2019).

Brumwell, Stephen. *Turncoat: Benedict Arnold and the Crisis of American Liberty* (New Haven and London, 2018).

Bryant, William Cullen. *A Discourse on the Life, Character and Writings of Gulian Crommelin Verplanck* (New York, 1870).

Brydges, Sir Egerton. *Collins's Peerage of England: Genealogical, Biographical, and Historical.* 9 vols. (London, 1812).

Bullion, John L. "The Origins and Significance of Gossip about Princess Augusta and Lord Bute, 1755–1756," *Studies in Eighteenth Century Culture*, vol. 21 (1991).

Burford, E. J. *Royal St James's: Being a Story of Kings, Clubmen and Courtesans* (London, 1988; paperback ed., 2001).

Cannon, John. *Aristocratic Century: The Peerage of Eighteenth-Century England* (Cambridge, 1984).

Cardwell, M. John. *Arts and Arms: Literature, Politics and Patriotism during the Seven Years War* (Manchester, 2004).

Catalogue of Important Historical Manuscripts & Autograph Letters and Some Printed Books: The Properties of the Most Honourable The Marquess of Sligo and Jasper More, Esq. (London: Christie, Manson & Woods, 1958).

Chalus, Elaine. *Elite Women in English Political Life c .1754–1790* (Oxford, 2005).

Chambers, Anne. *The Great Leviathan: The Life of Howe Peter Browne, 2nd Marquess of Sligo 1788–1845* (Stillorgan, County Dublin, 2017).

Chambers, J. D. *Nottinghamshire in the Eighteenth Century: A Study of Life and Labour under the Squirearchy* (London, 1966).

Chartrand, René. *Ticonderoga 1758: Montcalm's Victory Against All Odds* (Botley, Oxford, 2000).

Christie, Ian R. *Crisis of Empire: Great Britain and the American Colonies, 1754–1783* (London, 1966)

Christie, Ian R., and Benjamin Labaree. *Empire or Independence 1760–1776* (New York, 1976).

Christie, Ian R. *Wars and Revolutions: Britain 1760–1815* (London, 1982).

Christie, Ian R. "William Pitt and American Taxation, 1766: A Problem of Parliamentary Reporting," *Studies in Burke and His Time*, vol. 17 (1976).

Clark, Anna. *Scandal: The Sexual Politics of the British Constitution* (Princeton and Oxford, 2004).

Clark, J. C. D. *The Dynamics of Change: The Crisis of the 1750s and English Party Systems* (Cambridge, 1982).

Clarke, Norma. *Queen of the Wits: A Life of Laetitia Pilkington* (London, 2008).

Cobbett, Richard Stuteley. *Memorials of Twickenham: Parochial and Topographical* (London, 1872).

Colley, Linda. *Britons: Forging the Nation, 1707–1837* (London, 1992).

Collins, Arthur. *A Supplement to the Four Volumes of the Peerage of England: Containing a Succession of the Peers from 1740*. 2 vols. (London, 1750).

Colvin, Sidney. *History of the Society of Dilettanti* (London, 1914).

Cone, Mary. *Life of Rufus Putnam, with Extracts from His Journal and an Account of the First Settlement in Ohio* (Cleveland, OH, 1886).

Conway, Stephen. *A Short History of the American Revolutionary War* (London and New York, 2013).

Conway, Stephen. "From Fellow-Nationals to Foreigners: British Perceptions of the Americans, Circa 1739–1783," *William and Mary Quarterly*, 3rd series, vol. 59 (2002).

Conway, Stephen. *The American War of Independence, 1775–1783* (London, New York, Melbourne, and Auckland, 1995).

Conway, Stephen. *The British Isles and the American War of Independence* (Oxford, 2000).

Cowie, Leonard W. "Leicester House," *History Today*, vol. 23, issue 1 (January 1973).

Currey, Cecil B. *Code Number 72: Ben Franklin, Patriot or Spy?* (Englewood Cliffs, NJ, 1972)

Curtis, Edward E. *The Organization of the British Army in the American Revolution* (New Haven, 1926; this ed., Gansevoort, NY, 1998).

Cutter, William. *Life of General Putnam, Major-general in the Army of the American Revolution* (New York, 1850).

Dale, T. F. *The History of the Belvoir Hunt* (1899).

David, Saul. *Prince of Pleasure: The Prince of Wales and the Making of the Regency* (London, 1998).

Davidson, Marshall B., and Elizabeth Stillinger. *The American Wing at the Metropolitan Museum of Art* (New York, 1985).

Davies, Norman. *Europe: A History* (Oxford, 1996; this ed., London, 1997).

Dawson, M. E. A., and G. S. H. Fox-Strangways, eds. *The Life and Letters of Lady Sarah Lennox, 1745–1826*, 2 vols. (London, 1902).

Deutsch, Phyllis. "Moral Trespass in Georgian London: Gaming, Gender, and Electoral Politics in the Age of George III," *The Historical Journal*, vol. 39 (1996).

Diaz, Michael. "'Can you on such principles think of quitting a Country?': Family, Faith, Law, Property, and the Loyalists of the Hudson Valley During the American Revolution," *The Hudson River Valley Review*, vol. 28, no. 1 (Autumn 2011).

Dickinson, H. T., ed. *Britain and the French Revolution 1789–1815* (Houndmills, Basingstoke, Hampshire, and London, 1989).

Dickinson, H. T. *Liberty and Property: Political Ideology in Eighteenth-Century Britain* (London, 1977).

Donoughue, Bernard. *British Politics and the American Revolution: The Path to War, 1773–1775* (London and New York, 1964).

Downs, Joseph. "The Verplanck Room," *The Metropolitan Museum of Art Bulletin*, vol. 36, no. 11 (Nov., 1941).

Dreaper, James. *Pitt's "Gallant Conqueror": The Turbulent Life of Lieutenant-General Sir William Draper K.B.* (New York, 2006).

Duffy, Michael. *The Younger Pitt* (Harlow, Essex, 2000).

Dull, Jonathan R. *A Diplomatic History of the American Revolution* (New Haven and London, 1985).

Dunn, Richard S. "Servants and Slaves: The Recruitment and Employment of Labor," in Jack P. Greene and J. R. Pole, eds., *Colonial British America: Essays in the New History of the Early Modern Era* (Baltimore and London, 1984).

Dunn, Richard S. "The English Sugar Islands and the Founding of South Carolina," in T. H. Breen, ed., *Shaping Southern Society: The Colonial Experience* (New York, 1976).

Easton, Harry Tucker. *The History of a Banking House (Smith, Payne and Smiths)* (London, 1903).

Ellis, Joseph J. *First Family: Abigail and John Adams* (New York and Toronto, 2010).

Ellis, Joseph J. *His Excellency George Washington* (New York, 2004).

Farrington, Anthony. *Biographical Index of East India Company Maritime Service Officers 1600–1834* (1999).

Ferling, John. *Independence: The Struggle to Set America Free* (New York, Berlin, London, Sydney, 2011).

Fischer, David Hackett. *Washington's Crossing* (Oxford, 2004).

Fisher, Sydney George. *The True History of the American Revolution* (Philadelphia and London, 1902).

Fitzgerald, Brian. *Lady Louisa Conolly, 1743–1821: An Anglo-Irish Biography* (London and New York, 1950).

Fitzmaurice, Lord. *Life of William Earl of Shelburne*. 2 vols. (London, 1912).

Flavell, Julie. "American Patriots in London and the Quest for Talks, 1774–1775," *The Journal of Imperial and Commonwealth History*, vol. 20 (1992).

Flavell, Julie. "Decadents Abroad: Reconstructing the Typical Colonial American in London in the Late Colonial Period," in Leonard J. Sadosky et al., eds., *Old World, New World: America and Europe in the Age of Jefferson* (Charlottesville and London, 2010).

Flavell, Julie. "Government Interception of Letters from America and the Quest for Colonial Opinion in 1775," *William and Mary Quarterly*, 3rd series, vol. 58 (2001).

Flavell, Julie. "Lord North's Conciliatory Proposal and the Patriots in London," *English Historical Review*, vol. 107 (1992).

Flavell, Julie. *When London Was Capital of America* (Yale, 2010).

Flavell, Julie, and Stephen Conway, eds. *Britain and America Go to War: The Impact of War and Warfare in Anglo-America, 1754–1815* (Gainesville, FL, 2004)

Fleming, Thomas J. *Now We Are Enemies: The Story of Bunker Hill* (New York, 1960).

Flexner, James Thomas. *America's Old Masters* (New York, 1939; this ed., New York, 1967).

Fonblanque, Edward Barrington de. *Political and Military Episodes in the Latter Half of the Eighteenth Century. Derived from the Life and Correspondence of the Right Hon. John Burgoyne* (London, 1876).

Ford, Paul Leicester, ed. "Lord Howe's Commission to Pacify the Colonies," *Atlantic Monthly*, vol. 77 (1896).

Ford, Worthington C. "Parliament and the Howes," *Proceedings of the Massachusetts Historical Society*, 3rd series, 44 (1910).

Foreman, Amanda. *Georgiana, Duchess of Devonshire* (New York, 1998).

Fortescue, Sir John. *The War of Independence: The British Army in North America, 1775–1783* (London, 1911; this ed., London and Mechanicsburg, PA, 2001).

Fox, R. Hingston. *Dr John Fothergill and His Friends* (London, 1919).

Fraser, Flora. *Princesses: The Six Daughters of George III* (London, 2004).

Fraser, Flora. *The English Gentlewoman* (London, 1987).

Fraser, Sir William. *The Elphinstone Family Book of the Lords Elphinstone, Balmarino and Coupar*, 2 vols. (Edinburgh, 1897).

French, Anne, ed. *The Earl and Countess Howe by Gainsborough: A Bicentenary Exhibition* (London, 1988).

Fry, Howard T. *Alexander Dalrymple and the Expansion of British Trade* (Routledge, 1970).

Gallagher, John J. *The Battle of Brooklyn 1776* (New York, 1995).

Garnier, Richard. "Grafton Street, Mayfair," *The Georgian Group Journal*, vol. 13 (2003).

Garwood, Ivan. *Mistley in the Days of the Rigbys* (Lucas Books, 2003).

Gervat, Claire. *Elizabeth: The Scandalous Life of the Duchess of Kingston* (London, 2003).

Girouard, Mark. *Life in the English Country House: A Social and Architectural History* (New Haven and London, 1978).

Gleeson, Janet. *Privilege and Scandal: The Remarkable Life of Harriet Spencer, Sister of Georgiana* (New York, 2006).

Gold, Claudia. *The King's Mistress: The True and Scandalous Story of the Woman Who Stole the Heart of George I* (London, 2012).

Greene, Jack P., and J. R. Pole, eds. *The Blackwell Encyclopedia of the American Revolution* (Cambridge, MA, and Oxford, 1994).

Greig, Hannah. *The Beau Monde: Fashionable Society in Georgian London* (Oxford, 2013).

Gruber, Ira D. *The Howe Brothers and the American Revolution* (New York, 1972).

Hadlow, Janice. *The Strangest Family: The Private Lives of George III, Queen Charlotte and the Hanoverians* (London, 2014).

Hall-Witt, Jennifer. *Fashionable Acts: Opera and Elite Culture in London, 1780–1880* (Lebanon, NH, 2007).

Harris, Ellen T. *George Frideric Handel: A Life with Friends* (W. W. Norton, 2014).

Harris, Francis. "Holywell House: A Gothic Villa at St Albans," *British Library Journal*, vol. 12, no. 2 (1986).

Harwood, Elain. *Nottingham* (New Haven and London, 2008).

Hatton, Ragnhild Marie. *George I, Elector and King* (London, 1978).

Hayward, Ruth. *Phippy: A Biography of Jonathan Wathen Phipps/Waller, Eye-surgeon to King George III* (Studley, Warwickshire, 2014).

Hibbert, Christopher. *George III: A Personal History* (London, New York, Victoria, Toronto, 1998).

Hicks, Carola. *Improper Pursuits: The Scandalous Life of Lady Di Beauclerk* (London, Basingstoke, and Oxford, 2001).

Hill, Brian. *The Early Parties and Politics in Britain, 1688–1832* (Houndmills, Basingstoke, Hampshire, and London, 1996).

Hoffman, Ronald, and Peter J. Albert, eds. *Women in the Age of the American Revolution* (Charlottesville, VA, 1989).

Holden, James Austin. "New Historical Light on the Real Burial Place of George Augustus Lord Viscount Howe, 1758," *Proceedings of the New York State Historical Association*, vol. 10 (1911).

Holton, Woody. *Forced Founders: Indians, Debtors, Slaves, and the Making of the American Revolution in Virginia* (Chapel Hill and London, 1999).

Huskinson, G. N. B. "The Howe Family and Langar Hall 1650 to 1800," *Transactions of the Thoroton Society*, vol. 56 (1952).

Isaacson, Walter. *Benjamin Franklin: An American Life* (New York, 2003).

Jacks, Leonard. *The Great Houses of Nottinghamshire and the County Families* (Nottingham, 1881).

Jackson, John W. *With the British Army in Philadelphia, 1777–1778* (San Rafael and London, 1979).

Jenkins, Simon. *England's Thousand Best Houses* (London, 2003).

Johnston, Henry P. *The Campaign of 1776 around New York and Brooklyn* (Brooklyn, NY, 1878).

Jones, Thomas. *History of New York During the Revolutionary War*, ed. Edward Floyd De Lancey (New York, 1879).

Kelly, Jason M. *The Society of Dilettanti: Archaeology and Identity in the British Enlightenment* (New Haven and London, 2009).

Kerber, Linda K. *Women of the Republic: Intellect and Ideology in Revolutionary America* (Chapel Hill, NC, 1980).

Kielmansegg, Eduard Georg Ludwig. *Familien-Chronik Der Herren, Freiherren Und Grafen Von Kielmansegg* (Leipzig und Wien, 1872; this ed., Nabu Public Domain Reprint facsimile).

Kimber, Edward, and Richard Johnson. *The Baronetage of England: Containing a Genealogical and Historical Account of all the English Baronets now Existing.* 3 vols. (London, 1771).

Kinkel, Sarah. "Comment: 'Byng's execution played a key role in turning the war around,'" *BBC History Magazine*, March 2018.

Knifton, John. *Lauda Finem: The History of Nottingham High School* [Kindle book] (2012).

Koebner, Richard. *Empire* (Cambridge, 1961).

Kuntzleman, Oliver C. *Joseph Galloway, Loyalist* (Philadelphia, 1941).

Langford, Paul. *A Polite and Commercial People: England 1727–1783* (Oxford and New York, 1989).

Langford, Paul. *The First Rockingham Administration, 1765–1766* (Oxford, 1973).

Law, Susan C. *Through the Keyhole: Sex, Scandal and the Secret Life of the Country House* (Stroud, Gloucestershire, 2015).

Lee, Henry. *Memoirs of the War in the Southern Department of the United States.* 2 vols. (Philadelphia, 1812).

Lewis, Judith S. *Sacred to Female Patriotism: Gender, Class, and Politics in Late Georgian Britain* (New York and London, 2003).

Lipscomb, George. *A Journey into Cornwall: Through the Counties of Southampton, Wilts, Dorset, Somerset & Devon: Interspersed with Remarks, Moral, Historical, Literary, and Political* (Warwick, 1799).

Lipscomb, George. *The History and Antiquities of the County of Buckingham.* 4 vols. (London, 1847).

Longmore, Paul K. *The Invention of George Washington* (Charlottesville and London, 1999).

Lorenz, Janice Murphy. "The Verplancks and their Historic Mount Gulian Home, Both with Historic and Huguenot Connections," in *The Cross of Languedoc: A Publication of the National Huguenot Society* (Fall 2014).

Lunt, James. *John Burgoyne of Saratoga* (London, 1976).

Lutnick, Solomon. *The American Revolution and the British Press, 1775–1783* (Columbia, MO, 1967).

Mackay, Derek, and H. M. Scott. *The Rise of the Great Powers, 1648–1815* (London and New York, 1983).

Mackesy, Piers. *The War for America, 1775–1783* (Cambridge, MA, 1964; this ed., Lincoln and London, 1993).

Marshall, Dorothy. *Eighteenth Century England* (Harlow, Essex, and New York, 1962; this impression, 1985).

Marshall, P. J. *Remaking the British Atlantic: The United States and the British Empire after American Independence* (Oxford, 2012).

Mason, George. *The Life of Richard Earl Howe* (London, 1803).

May, Robin, and Gerry Embleton. *Wolfe's Army* (London, Auckland, and Melbourne, 1997).

McCulloch, Ian M., and Tim J. Todish. *British Light Infantryman of the Seven Years' War* (Botley, Oxford, and New York, 2004).

McGuire, Thomas J. *Stop the Revolution: America in the Summer of Independence and the Conference for Peace* (Mechanicsburg, PA, 2011).

McNairn, Alan. *Behold the Hero: General Wolfe and the Arts in the Eighteenth Century* (Kingston and Montreal, 1997).

Middleton, Richard. *The Bells of Victory: The Pitt-Newcastle Ministry and the Conduct of the Seven Years' War 1757–1762* (Cambridge, 1985).

Mitchell, L. G. *Charles James Fox* (Oxford, 1992).

Mitchell, Leslie. *The Whig World, 1760–1837* (London and New York, 2005; paperback ed., 2007).

Moody, Jane, and Daniel O'Quinn, eds. *The Cambridge Companion to British Theatre, 1730–1830* (Cambridge, 2007).

Moomaw, W. H. "The Denouement of General Howe's Campaign of 1777," *English Historical Review*, Vol. 79 (1964).

Moore, Lucy. *Amphibious Thing: The Life of Lord Hervey* (New York, London, Ringwood, 2000).

Morgan, David T. *The Devious Dr. Franklin, Colonial Agent* (Macon, GA, 1996).

Morris, Richard B. *The Forging of the Union, 1781–1789* (New York, 1987).

Mulvey, Christopher. *Transatlantic Manners: Social Patterns in Nineteenth-Century Anglo-American Travel Literature* (Cambridge and New York, 1990).

Namier, Lewis. *The Structure of Politics at the Accession of George III* (London and Basingstoke, 1929; 2nd ed., 1957).

Namier, Lewis, and John Brooke. *The History of Parliament: The House of Commons, 1754–1790*. 3 vols. (London, 1964).

Newman, Gerald, ed. *Britain in the Hanoverian Age, 1714–1837: An Encyclopedia* (New York and London, 1997).

Newman, Gerald. *The Rise of English Nationalism: A Cultural History, 1720–1830* (London, 1987).

Nester, William R. *The Epic Battles for Ticonderoga, 1758* (Albany, NY, 2008).

Norton, Mary Beth. *Liberty's Daughters: The Revolutionary Experience of American Women, 1750–1800* (Boston, 1980).

Norton, Mary Beth. *The British-Americans: The Loyalist Exiles in England, 1774–1789* (Boston and Toronto, 1972).

Olson, Alison Gilbert. *The Radical Duke: Career and Correspondence of Charles Lennox, third Duke of Richmond* (Oxford, 1961).

O'Gorman, Frank. *Voters, Patrons, and Parties: The Unreformed Electoral System of Hanoverian England, 1734–1832* (Oxford, 1989).

O'Shaughnessy, Andrew Jackson. *An Empire Divided: The American Revolution and the British Caribbean* (Philadelphia, 2000).

O'Shaughnessy, Andrew Jackson. *The Men Who Lost America: British Leadership, the American Revolution, and the Fate of the Empire* (New Haven and London, 2013).

O'Toole, Fintan. *White Savage: William Johnson and the Invention of America* (London, 2005).

Panton, Kenneth J. *Historical Dictionary of the British Monarchy* (Lanham, Toronto, Plymouth, UK, 2011).

Pares, Richard, and A. J. P. Taylor, eds. *Essays Presented to Sir Lewis Namier* (London and New York, 1956).

Partridge, Bellamy. *Sir Billy Howe* (London and New York, 1932).

Paterson, Daniel. *A New and Accurate Description of All the Direct and Principal Cross Roads in England and Wales* (1808).

Pearce, Charles E. *The Amazing Duchess: Being the Romantic History of Elizabeth Chudleigh.* 2 vols. (London, 1911).

Perry, Keith. *British Politics and the American Revolution* (Basingstoke and London, 1990).

Peters, Marie. *Pitt and Popularity: The Patriot Minister and London Opinion during the Seven Years' War* (Oxford, 1980).

Philbrick, Nathaniel. *Bunker Hill: A City, A Siege, A Revolution* (New York, 2013).

Picard, Liza. *Dr. Johnson's London: Life in London, 1740–1770* (London, 2000; paperback ed., London, 2001).

Quincy, Josiah. *Memoir of the Life of Josiah Quincy, Junior of Massachusetts, 1744–1775* (Boston, 1874).

Rice, Paul F. *British Music and the French Revolution* (Newcastle upon Tyne, 2010).

Rizzo, Betty. *Companions Without Vows: Relationships Among Eighteenth-Century British Women* (Athens, GA, and London, 1994).

Rodgers, N. A. M. *The Wooden World: An Anatomy of the Georgian Navy* (Glasgow, 1986; this impression, 1990).

Rogers, H. C. B. *The British Army of the Eighteenth Century* (London, 1977).

Rogers, Henry. *The Life and Character of John Howe, M.A.* (London, 1863).

Rogers, Pat. *The Alexander Pope Encyclopedia* (Westport, CT, 2004).

Rule, John. *Albion's People: English Society, 1714–1815* (London and New York, 1992).

Russell, Constance. *Three Generations of Fascinating Women* (2nd ed.; London, New York, and Bombay, 1905).

Russell, Gillian. *Women, Sociability and Theatre in Georgian London* (Cambridge, 2010).

Russell, Peter E. "Redcoats in the Wilderness: British Officers and Irregular Warfare in Europe and America, 1740 to 1760," *William and Mary Quarterly*, 3rd series, vol. 25 (1978).

Sainsbury, John. *John Wilkes: The Lives of a Libertine* (Farnham, 2006).

Sargent, Winthrop. *The Life and Career of Major John André* (Boston, 1861).

Schama, Simon. "Dirty Little Secret," *Smithsonian Magazine* (May 2006).

Schneider, Elena A. *The Occupation of Havana: War, Trade and Slavery in the Atlantic World* (Williamsburg and Chapel Hill, 2018).

Schuessler, Jennifer. "Confronting Slavery at Long Island's Oldest Estates," *New York Times*, August 12, 2015.

Sedgwick, Romney. "William Pitt and Lord Bute: An Intrigue of 1755–1758," *History Today*, vol. 6, issue 10 (Oct. 1956).

Shipton, Clifford K. *Biographical Sketches of Those Who Attended Harvard College*, vols. 4–17 of Sibley's Harvard Graduates (Cambridge, MA, 1933–75).

Sligo, Marquess of. "Some Notes on the Death of Wolfe," *Canadian Historical Review*, vol. 3 (Sept. 1922).

Smith, David. *New York 1776: The Continentals' First Battle* (Oxford and New York, 2008).

Smith, David. *William Howe and the American War of Independence* (London, New Delhi, New York, Sydney, 2015).

Snow, Dan. *Death or Victory: The Battle for Quebec and the Birth of Empire* (London, 2009).

Spector, R. D. *English Literary Periodicals and the Climate of Opinion during the Seven Years' War* (The Hague, Paris, 1966).

Stedman, C. *The History of the Origin, Progress and Termination of the American War*. 2 vols. (London, 1794).

Steele, Ian K. *The English Atlantic 1675–1740: An Exploration of Communication and Community* (Oxford, 1986).

Stirling, A. M. W. *The Hothams: Being the Chronicles of the Hothams of Scorborough and South Dalton*. 2 vols. (London, 1918).

Stokes, Hugh. *The Devonshire House Circle* (London, 1967).

Stone, Lawrence. *Road to Divorce: England, 1530–1987* (Oxford, 1990).

Stone, Lawrence. *The Family, Sex and Marriage in England, 1500–1800* (London, 1977; abridged and rev. ed. published London, 1979).

Stone, Lawrence. *Uncertain Unions: Marriage in England, 1660–1753* (Oxford, 1992).

Stuart, Dorothy Margaret. *Dearest Bess: The Life and Times of Lady Elizabeth Foster, Afterwards Duchess of Devonshire, from Her Unpublished Journals and Correspondence* (London, 1955).

Syrett, David. *Admiral Lord Howe: A Biography* (Stroud, Gloucestershire, 2006).

Syrett, David. *The Royal Navy in American Waters, 1775–1783* (Aldershot, Hants., 1989).

Syrett, David. *The Siege and Capture of Havana, 1762* (London and Colchester, 1970).

Tamarkin, Eliza. *Anglophilia: Deference, Devotion, and Antebellum America* (Chicago and London, 2008).

Thacher, James. *American Medical Biography: Or, Memoirs of Eminent Physicians Who Have Flourished in America*. 2 vols. (Boston, 1828).

Thomas, Adam. *History of Nottingham High School* (1958).

Thomas, Peter D. G. *George III: King and Politicians, 1760–1770* (Manchester and New York, 2002).

Thomas, Peter D. G. *Lord North* (London, 1976).

Thomas, Peter D. G. *Revolution in America: Britain and the Colonies, 1763–1776* (Cardiff, 1992).

Thomas, Peter D. G. *Tea Party to Independence: The Third Phase of the American Revolution, 1773–1776* (Oxford, 1991).

Thompson, Andrew C. *George II King and Elector* (London and New Haven, 2011).

Thorold, Peter. *The London Rich: The Creation of a Great City, from 1666 to the Present* (London, New York, Victoria, Toronto, 1999).

Tiger, Caroline. *General Howe's Dog: George Washington, the Battle of Germantown, and the Dog Who Crossed Enemy Lines* (New York and London, 2005).

Tillyard, Stella. *A Royal Affair: George III and His Troublesome Siblings* (London, 2006).

Tillyard, Stella. *Aristocrats: Caroline, Emily, Louisa and Sarah Lennox, 1740–1832* (London, 1994; paperback ed., London, 1995).

Trumbach, Randolph. *The Rise of the Egalitarian Family: Aristocratic Kinship and Domestic Relations in Eighteenth-Century England* (New York, San Francisco, London, 1978).

Turner, E. S. *The Court of St. James's* (London, 1959).

Urban, Mark. *Fusiliers: Eight Years with the Redcoats in America* (London, 2007).

Valentine, Alan. *Lord George Germain* (Oxford, 1962).

Van Der Kiste, John. *George III's Children* (Stroud, Gloucestershire, 1992; this ed., 2004).

Van Der Kiste, John. *King George II and Queen Caroline* (Stroud, Gloucestershire, 1997).

Van der Kiste, John. *The Georgian Princesses* (Stroud, Gloucestershire, 2000; paperback ed., 2002).

Vickery, Amanda. "Home Truths: Amanda Vickery on Why David Starkey Is Wrong," *The Independent*, Nov. 7, 2010.

Vickery, Amanda. *The Gentleman's Daughter: Women's Lives in Georgian England* (New Haven and London, 1998).

Wainwright, Nicholas B. *George Croghan: Wilderness Diplomat* (Chapel Hill, 1959).

Walters, Kerry S. *Benjamin Franklin and His Gods* (University of Illinois Press, 1998).

Watson, John F. *Annals of Philadelphia and Pennsylvania, in the Olden Time.* 2 vols. (Philadelphia, 1857).

Weinreb, Ben, and Christopher Hibbert, eds. *The London Encyclopedia* (London, 1983; rev. ed., 1993).

Weintraub, Stanley. *Iron Tears: Rebellion in America, 1775–1783* (London, New York, Toronto, Sydney, Dublin, 2005).

Wilderson, Paul W. *Governor John Wentworth & the American Revolution* (Hanover, NH, 1994).

Willcox, William B. *Portrait of a General: Sir Henry Clinton in the War of Independence* (New York, 1964).

Williams, Basil. *The Life of William Pitt, Earl of Chatham.* 2 vols. (London, 1915).

Willis, Sam. *The Glorious First of June: Fleet Battle in the Reign of Terror* (London, 2011).

Willson, Beckles. *The Life and Letters of James Wolfe* (London, 1909).

Wilson, Kathleen. *The Sense of the People: Politics, Culture & Imperialism in England, 1715–1785* (Cambridge, 1998).

Young, Philip. *Revolutionary Ladies* (New York, 1977).

Unpublished Theses

Julie M. Flavell, "Americans of Patriot Sympathies in London and the Colonial Strategy for Opposition, 1774-1775" (PhD, University College London, 1988).

Matthew Charles Kilburn, "Royalty and Public in Britain: 1714-1789" (thesis submitted for the degree of Doctor of Philosophy in the University of Oxford, 1997).

INDEX

Italicized pages refer to photos or illustrations.